Macroeconomics

Oakham School

If there really is a complete unified theory, it would also presumably determine our actions. And so the theory itself would determine the outcome of our search for it! And why should it determine that we come to the right conclusion from the evidence? Might it not equally well determine that we draw the wrong conclusion? Or no conclusion at all?

STEPHEN W. HAWKING

Macroeconomics

Theory and Policy in the UK

Third Edition

**G. K. Shaw, Mike McCrostie
and David Greenaway**

Copyright © G. K. Shaw, Mike McCrostie and David Greenaway 1983, 1988, 1997

The right of G. K. Shaw, Mike McCrostie and David Greenaway to be identified as authors of this work has been asserted in accordance with the Copyright, Designs and Patents Act 1988.

First edition published 1983 by Martin Robertson & Co Ltd
© David Greenaway and G. K. Shaw.
Reprinted in 1984 by Blackwell Publishers Ltd
Second edition published by Blackwell Publishers Ltd 1988
Third edition published 1997
Reprinted 1998, 2000, 2001, 2002

Blackwell Publishers Ltd
108 Cowley Road
Oxford OX4 1JF
UK

Blackwell Publishers Inc.
350 Main Street
Malden, Massachusetts 02148
USA

British Library Cataloguing in Publication Data
A CIP catalogue record for this book is available from the British Library.

Library of Congress Cataloging-in-Publication Data
Shaw, G. K. (Graham Keith), 1938–
    Macroeconomics: theory and policy in the UK / G. K. Shaw, Mike
McCrostie, and David Greenaway. – 3rd ed.
        p.   cm.
    Rev. ed. of: Macroeconomics / David Greenaway and G. K. Shaw, 2nd ed. 1987.
    Includes bibliographical references and index.
    ISBN 0–631–20019–3 (pbk.: alk. paper)
    1.   Macroeconomics. 2. Great Britain – Economic policy – 1945–
I. McCrostie, Michael J. II. Greenaway, David. III. Greenaway,
David. Macroeconomics. IV. Title.
HB172.5.G75   1997
339'0941–dc20   96–23268   CIP

Typeset in 10 on 12pt Times
by Pure Tech India Ltd, Pondicherry

This book is printed on acid-free paper.

PMOS189 06113

Contents

List of Figures

List of Tables

Preface to the Second Edition

The response to the first edition of *Macroeconomics* exceeded our expectations. Whilst there were, of course, critical comments and valid objections raised by colleagues and reviewers in the field, none the less, the overall reaction was most pleasing and hopefully justified the decision to update the volume. In the present edition we have tried to take account of the criticisms made and to eliminate major sources of error as well as updating both data and references. In this regard the detailed comments of Jim Taylor (Lancaster University) and Alan Marin (London School of Economics) were particularly helpful. In addition, however, we have also extended the exposition in a number of areas. The initial introductory chapter has been extended in essentially a non-technical manner in an attempt to illustrate recent policy controversies in the UK. Also, extra material has been introduced to expand the importance attached to expectations formation in macroeconomic policy and contract theory in the analysis of employment. Elements of growth theory have been introduced into the final chapter to provide a more relevant framework against which growth policy might be evaluated. More weight has also been given to the open economy and the constraints upon policy generated by external influences. The policy sections have been updated to take account of developments since the first edition was written. We have kept faith with the original structure of the first edition as we believe this to fit well with the way intermediate macroeconomics is taught in universities and polytechnics in the UK.

We are indebted to former students who served as guinea pigs as the original volume developed; many of them diligently discovered typographical errors in the first edition. As always we are grateful to Mrs Linda Waterman for her outstanding secretarial assistance and we appreciate the efforts of Mr Ivan Araya-Gomez, who helped in the task of updating the data and checking data sources. Finally, our thanks to Basil Blackwell for their continued encouragement and confidence.

DAVID GREENAWAY
G. K. SHAW

Preface to the Third Edition

Once again, we are indebted to Blackwell Publishers for their encouragement and support in promoting the new edition of *Macroeconomics*. This edition has been substantially enlarged and updated to take account of recent developments in theory and policy and their implications for the UK economy.

In this endeavour, the original authors have been joined and substantially aided and abetted by the contribution of Mike McCrostie, who has taken on much of the responsibility for the UK orientation of the volume. We are, of course, grateful to former students and colleagues for their constructive critiques and, as always, we are indebted to Mrs Linda Waterman, not only for the excellence of her secretarial service but also for substantial improvements in style and exposition.

G. K. Shaw
Mike McCrostie
David Greenaway

Preface to the First Edition

There are many intermediate macroeconomic texts, a number of which are to be highly recommended for the serious student of economics wishing to obtain a more specialized insight into the controversies, theoretical and otherwise, deriving from modern macroeconomics. However, the vast bulk of this literature is distinctly American oriented, and the policy issues as well as the supporting empirical evidence and findings reflect the American scene. Not only is the American perspective on economic issues understandably different from that in the UK but also the institutional constraints upon policy formulation differ, and differ substantially, in a country with a federal system of government and where the party constituting the executive may have a minority voice in the legislature. Constraints upon policy formulation exercise subtle but persuasive influences upon areas of current interest and research. Comparisons of British and American academic journals offers an interesting commentary in this respect.

This book evolved as an attempt to produce an up-to-date macroeconomic text at the intermediate level which would take full account of the policy issues and controversies in the UK economy. It attempts full coverage of recent developments in macroeconomic theory and deals with the newer schools of economic thought but attempts to relate them specifically to the UK context. Thus particular emphasis is given to monetarist, new Cambridge and neo-classical supply side macroeconomics. At the same time, considerable attention is devoted to the changing status of fiscal policy in the UK, reflected in the importance attached to monetary targets, the public sector borrowing requirement and medium-term financial strategies. Finally, the theoretical exposition contained in this book attempts to assess the importance of the revolution in rational expectations as it impinges upon macroeconomic policy formation in the UK.

Although the book deals with these topics and their implications for economic policy, it is none the less the case that the traditional methods of analysis have been retained. In particular the authors have retained the well-known *IS/LM* framework, partly because they are convinced that this conventional analysis can be developed and extended to illustrate many of the topics just described. The importance attached to the budget constraint and the debate over the crowding out controversy provide a striking example of how the traditional apparatus can be manipulated to yield richer insights into the functioning of the economy than previously imagined. Whilst it is no doubt true that the *IS/LM* framework has been unjustly utilized to provide caricatures of extremist Keynesian, classical or monetarist positions, which inevitably distort the true stance of the protagonists in the debate, it is none the less of great pedagogical value when used sensibly – that is, when it is recognized as being but a tool of analysis derived from a number of mechanistic simultaneous equations, with all the qualifications that this implies.

The book itself falls naturally into three parts. Thus, following upon a general introduction indicating the nature and purpose of macroeconomic modelling, part I examines the individual macroeconomic sectors which collectively comprise the macroeconomy. The principal sectors here are the commodity market, comprising both consumption and investment goods, the money market, the labour market and the government sector. Each sector is examined in turn in relation to specific theories which attempt to account for its behaviour. Part II then examines how these various economic sectors can be analysed together under alternative economic systems of general theories. Thus, part II deals with classical, Keynesian and neoclassical/monetarist interpretations of the economic system as a whole with particular attention being given to the analysis of the open economy. This ordering – the examining of individual sectors in detail before proceeding to the analysis of economic theories dealing with the functioning of the economic system as a whole – is the one which appeals as the most logical to the authors. However, one can readily understand that there may be readers and instructors who would prefer the alternative approach – an analysis of broad economic systems followed by the analysis of the individual sectors. For those preferring this methodology there is no reason why the material of part II cannot precede that of part I. Regardless of which approach is preferred, part III then applies the analysis to the current policy problems confronting the UK economy, with particular attention being devoted to employment, inflation, balance of payments and economic growth. Each chapter is supplemented with suggestions for further reading which offer a guide to the more advanced literature.

It must be emphasized that this book is an intermediate text aimed at second-and third-year students. Accordingly, it assumes that the reader has already become familiar with macroeconomics at a more elementary level and that he is fully conversant with the standard 45° Keynesian model and with elementary concepts of measurement, national income accounting and so forth. These topics will not be examined in the present work.[1] It is also assumed that the reader will have acquired the necessary technical competence to be able to follow the elementary algebraic manipulations and simple differential calculus which accompany the formal analysis. The mathematics has been kept to a minimum and is used principally to fill out what is primarily a diagrammatic presentation. Nevertheless, it adds a certain rigour to topics which are often treated only intuitively (and which are therefore never fully appreciated) and fortunately the mathematics employed here is now commonplace in any university economics course which proceeds beyond the first year.

Any venture of this kind must inevitably be eclectic. Whilst we believe that there is some original material in these pages, such is the nature of a textbook that it must draw upon several sources. Hopefully, these sources are fully acknowledged in the text and in the references for further reading. The authors have also drawn upon their own previous publications in certain parts of the presentation. We are also indebted for constructive comments from a number of our colleagues in the field, including in particular Rod Cross of the University of St Andrews, Bob Elliott from the University of Aberdeen, Chris Milner from the University of Loughborough and Mike McCrostie from the University of Buckingham.

---

[1] For a relatively detailed discussion of measurement problems and national income acounting in the UK context, see Parkin and Bade (1982).

Several generations of former students have left their own mark upon the volume and have certainly been responsible for improving the exposition. No acknowledgement would be complete which did not mention the cheerful and painstaking secretarial contribution of Linda Waterman, of the University of Buckingham. Finally, we would like to acknowledge the constructive support of Michael Hay of Martin Robertson and his patience and understanding as the book developed both in content and in size. One is reminded of Pascal's famous dictum:

La dernière chose qu'on trouve en faisant un ouvrage, est de savoir celle qu'il faut mettre la première.

DAVID GREENAWAY
G. K. SHAW

1

The Nature of Macroeconomics

There is today a strong consensus that
there is no macroeconomic consensus.
Alan S. Blinder

The subject matter of macroeconomics is the performance of the economy in the aggregate and the underlying relationships between broad *economic aggregates*, and how those relationships alter over time. It is to be contrasted with *microeconomics*, which focuses primarily upon the rational decision-making processes of the individual unit, whether it be the consumer, the unemployed, the producer, the firm, the industry or even the market. An alternative way of making this distinction is to say that micro-economics looks at individual decision-making situations – how, for example, a representative firm might react to the imposition of a value added tax (VAT) – whereas macroeconomics would examine the same issues from the highly aggregative stance of all firms throughout the economy. At the risk of oversimplification, macro-economics deals with three broad market aggregates and their interrelationships; these aggregates are the labour market, the market for goods and services, and the financial market, where the last is understood to encompass the money market as well as the market in alternative assets.

In one sense, of course, the micro/macro distinction is inappropriate, since the whole is of necessity the sum of its parts, and hence any microeconomic decision must exert a macroeconomic impact no matter how negligible. Indeed, when the individual decision-making unit is, let us say, the British Steel Corporation, the impact upon crucial macroeconomic variables such as the price level or the balance of payments may be by no means insignificant. Moreover, it is rapidly becoming accepted that many of the deficiencies of modern macroeconomic theorizing stem from inadequate attention to the microeconomic underpinnings of macrotheory. This has been shown to be especially true with regard to theories involving expectations, search theories of unemployment and so forth. Equally, some very important macroeconomic concepts, such as the 'natural' rate of unemployment, are fundamentally determined by microeconomic forces and constraints.

Moreover, recent supply side economics in both the USA and the UK attaches considerable importance to the free play of competition in individual markets, and in particular to the power of relative price changes to generate efficient resource utilization and also to eliminate the obstacles to, and provide the incentives for, the full utilization of resources. In this view, dismantling the barriers to competition and permitting the flexible functioning of free markets is essential to the overall co-ordination of economic activity and to the attainment of macroeconomic objectives.

None the less, the traditional distinction between macro- and microeconomics is conceptually appealing and useful partly for historical reasons. Microeconomics, developed largely during a period when Utilitarian philosophy was very much in the ascendancy, tended to emphasize almost self-evident postulates of maximizing behaviour even though such theories did not lend themselves to empirical testing and in some cases were incapable of refutation.[1] In contrast, modern macroeconomics was a much later development and focused not so much upon premises of rational utility maximization but rather upon the formulation of aggregate hypotheses which would lend themselves to empirical testing. The Keynesian consumption function was undoubtedly a prime example of the latter approach and provided tremendous stimulus to empirical research and developments in applied econometrics.

Perhaps the most important reason for maintaining the traditional distinction between micro- and macroeconomics, however, is that assumptions which appear valid in a microeconomic setting may not be tenable when transferred to the sphere of macroeconomics. Thus, variables which are correctly judged to be exogenous from the microeconomic standpoint of a single firm – as, for example, the general price level – would be very much endogenous variables to be explained from the macroeconomic vantage point. In a similar vein, the individual firm under perfect competition, adjusting its output by moving along its upward sloping marginal cost curve, could very sensibly look upon existing factor prices as a datum. For the economy as a whole, however, attempts to adjust aggregate output are hardly likely to leave factor prices unchanged.

For these reasons, this book accepts the prevailing micro/macro dichotomy and considers its primary objective to be to provide an exposition of the functional relationships of aggregate economic behaviour and their implications for policy formulation and control. Conventionally, macroeconomics has been concerned with the determination of national income or output, its rate of change over time (economic growth), the associated level of employment and the causes of lapses from full employment, the determination of the general price level and its rate of change over time (inflation), and the overall balance of payments. In contrast, the province of microeconomics has concerned itself with the determination of comparative prices and their role in resource allocation, efficiency considerations and welfare optimization.

Broadly, this traditional dichotomy is the one adhered to in the present text as evidenced in part III. It is thus perhaps well to point out that it would not command universal acceptance and, indeed, in the wake of the supply side revolution in economics which dominated policy pronouncements in the 1980s, the attempt was made to assert the primacy of *microeconomics* in the pursuit of goals previously deemed macroeconomic. Thus, for example, the importance of demand management was downgraded to that of reducing or eliminating inflation, in the belief that the elimination of

---

1 The theory of consumer behaviour provides a case in point. The consumer is assumed to act so as to maximize his total welfare. If his income increases and he increases his consumption of a certain good, it is assumed that he is acting in accordance with the theory. However, if he decreases his consumption, it is still assumed that he is maximizing his satisfaction, and now the good is deemed to be 'inferior'. In short, whatever the observed outcome, it remains consistent with the underlying hypothesis which accordingly cannot be refuted.

inflation would create the conditions whereby microeconomic policies would exert maximum impact in promoting employment and economic growth. This *volte face* was emphatically stated by the then Chancellor of the Exchequer, Nigel Lawson, in his 1984 Mais Lecture, which warrants direct quotation:

> It is the conquest of inflation, and not the pursuit of growth and employment, which is or should be the objective of macro economic policy. And it is the creation of conditions conducive to growth and employment, and not the suppression of price rises which is or should be the objective of microeconomic policy. (Lawson 1984)

In the concluding part of this chapter we will attempt to explain the reasons leading to this reversal of the accepted conventional wisdom.

An alternative way to delineate the essence of macroeconomics is to distinguish between short-term and long-run considerations. From the long-term perspective, the only important issue is the long-term trend path of potential output – economic growth. Arguably, this is the most fundamental issue of all, in that it is essential to continued increases in economic welfare. Only if the growth rate of income is in excess of the growth rate of population expansion does a sustained increase in the level of income per capita become possible. The latter is a *necessary*, if *insufficient*, condition for permanent increases in economic welfare. Moreover, because of the compounding nature of the growth process, alternative measures, such as improved resource allocation or tax and transfer programmes, pale into insignificance as a means of raising welfare when compared to the phenomenon of economic growth.

If economic growth is the fundamental economic issue, it is none the less the short-term consideration of deviations around the long-term trend – which we may identify with the business cycle – which appears to be of major concern to most people. The concern with the short run reflects the fact that people are possessed of finite lives, that inflation and unemployment impose costs upon society and also the belief that the long-term growth rate is, to all intents and purposes, exogenously imposed as far as most individual economic agents are concerned.

These dual concerns are illustrated with the aid of figure 1.1. Y_g denotes the long-term growth rate of output, whilst Y_a represents the actual path of output around its long-run trend. When $Y_a > Y_g$, actual income, and therefore demand, is tending to run ahead of the trend growth of output, thus putting upward pressure upon prices. When $Y_a < Y_g$, the opposite situation prevails. Actual income is growing at a slower rate than potential, thus implying some unemployment of resources. In general, therefore, we associate peaks in Y_a with inflationary boom periods and, correspondingly, troughs in Y_a with unemployment characteristic of recessionary conditions.

Ideally, from the vantage point of policy, we would like to achieve a raising of the growth rate Y_g whilst simultaneously decreasing or eliminating the extent of fluctuations of Y_a around Y_g (as indicated by the dotted lines). This, however, may not be a policy option available to the authorities. The long-term growth rate may not be independent of the business cycle. Alternatively, increased instability may be the price one has to pay for enhanced economic growth. This is but one of the challenging issues generated by the advent of the real business cycle school in macroeconomics.

In making the distinction between the long-term consideration of economic growth and the short-run issue of the business cycle, it is necessary to note a subtle but important difference in the underlying assumptions. Most economists today would approach

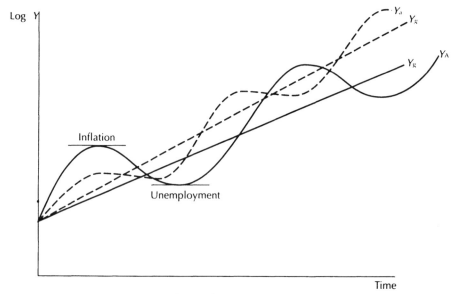

Figure 1.1 The dual nature of macroeconomics

the long-term question of economic growth in terms of a model in which all prices, including wages, are deemed ultimately flexible. In contrast, when discussing the business cycle, many commentators would posit a model in which prices, and especially wages, would reveal inflexibility or at least stickiness, particularly in a downward direction. Indeed, many explanations of the business cycle explicitly depend upon short-run wage and price inflexibility.

Methodology

Having indicated, along fairly broad lines, the major concerns of the book, it is perhaps appropriate to add a word about methodology. In this respect it is important to perceive the distinction between macroeconomic *theory*, which seeks to explain the structure and functioning of the economy – what *is* – and macroeconomic *policy*, which is concerned with normative issues – what *ought to be*. The latter cannot be derived from the former, for even if a complete consensus prevails on how the economy behaves, differences will still emerge about the competing priorities of alternative goals. Thus, for example, two economists with broadly the same view of how the economy actually behaves may differ substantially over the extent to which employment goals should be sacrificed to the objective of price stability; such disagreements reflect different value judgements as to the relative costs associated with inflation and unemployment, and differences which cannot be reconciled by objective enquiry. Whilst differences in political and moral judgements will make for disagreements between economists concerning the appropriate policy action, in many cases what appear to be normative differences turn out on closer examination to spring from differences concerning the structure of the economy.

If it is indeed the case that fundamental differences between economists reflect different views of how the economy behaves, then the obvious question which arises is, how does one correctly appraise competing theories? If monetarists take a distinctly different view of the functioning of the macroeconomy from that advanced by Keynesians, for example, then surely there should exist some rational basis for choosing between them and determining which is the more relevant to the UK economy? In principle, the answer to this question is in the affirmative and rests upon the proposition that useful theories should be capable of generating predictions which can be compared with the observable evidence. In this way, theories which perform well – generate predictions borne out by events – are to be preferred to theories generating predictions which are denied by the evidence. Whilst no theory can ever be established as being absolutely true (since it may be denied at a subsequent date) theories which have withstood severe tests are said to be corroborated. On these grounds, a useful theory must be formulated in such a way as to lend itself to possible refutation in principle. Theories which are refuted or falsified are then to be discarded. This is the *falsificationist principle* associated with Karl Popper's approach to the appraisal of science.

Unfortunately, whilst the falsification criterion may be acceptable in principle, there are considerable difficulties about it in practice. One problem stems from the measurement difficulties relating to the evidence which is used to test the theory. The measurement problem is especially acute for the social sciences; witness, for example, the various possible definitions of the money supply. This objection has been compounded by the increasing awareness of the limitations of econometrics and possibly by the misuse of econometrics in manipulating time lags, lead times and so forth until the resulting equation serves to more or less confirm the hypothesis under consideration. On this and related points, see especially the critical articles by Hendry (1980) and Leamer (1983).

A further difficulty arises from the fact that in certain cases economic theories are capable of generating multiple equilibrium outcomes. This is especially applicable to models involving expectations formation and the way economic agents anticipate the behaviour of others. Certain beliefs about the way the economy operates will, *if widely acted upon*, generate outcomes consistent with those beliefs. If all economic agents believe in a simple quantity theory view of price determination, for example, they will, upon observing a rise in the money supply, revise their expectations of the subsequent price level and modify their behaviour accordingly, thus virtually guaranteeing the predicted quantity theory outcome. In effect, the outcome is conditioned by the prevailing conventional wisdom.

Finally, an intriguing problem arises over whether it is meaningful or sensible to test single hypotheses. In general, economic theories are a complex combination of varied assumptions, laws, restrictions and so forth. Consequently, what is being appraised is not just a single simple universal statement (all swans are white, for example). Accordingly, refutation or falsification may merely imply that *one* of the underlying assumptions is false. Modification of the assumption may be sufficient to salvage the theory. For example, suppose a theory predicts that a 10 per cent growth in the money supply will imply 10 per cent inflation. Suppose the evidence subsequently falsifies the theory. It may still be possible to discover some additional auxiliary hypothesis linking monetary growth with output growth which then renders the original thesis fully consistent with the observed evidence. This is but one version of the *Duhem-Quine* thesis which argues that it may always be possible for sufficient auxiliary theses to exist such as to render the original hypothesis irrefutable. (For an elementary introduction to the Duhem-Quine thesis, see Cross, 1982a.) Arguments along these lines have led naturally to the attempt to appraise distinct competing schools of thought, as opposed to single hypotheses. Although the analysis is conducted issue by issue in this text, it is nevertheless useful to briefly consider the salient and distinguishing features of the principal macroeconomic schools in the UK.

Principal Macroeconomic Schools in the UK

Traditional Keynesianism

The traditional Keynesian school derives from the *IS/LM* portrayal of Keynes which will be examined in considerable detail later in the book. The essential belief is that output and employment are determined by expenditure flows and that the government, by operating upon monetary and fiscal policy, can effectively so regulate these demand flows as to generate the required degree of income and employment. Hence this school of thought is identified with politics of *demand management*, a belief in the ability to *fine tune* the economy and a general interventionist philosophy. In the main, the traditional Keynesian school, at least in the UK, has emphasized the supremacy of fiscal over monetary policy – often discounting the latter almost entirely. This emphasis has been accompanied by a general tendency to dispute any causal link between the money stock and inflation and to argue that the latter is caused essentially by sociological influences, trade union militancy and so forth and can be controlled by appropriate prices and incomes policies.

Traditional Keynesian analysis posited a demand determined model of the economy with scant attention given to the conditions of supply and with little or no regard paid to the determination of the price level. It was for this reason that the concept of the Phillips curve was eagerly seized upon by Keynesian economists. It appeared to provide the 'missing link' to account for prices and it did so in the context of aggregate demand. Demand pressures in the labour market as the economy moved closer to full employment would intensify the pressure upon the price level. The Phillips curve also suggested a menu of policy choice in that it implied that higher levels of employment could be purchased at the cost of accepting higher inflation. Moreover, this trade-off between the two was assumed to be a permanent one which the government could exploit in its conduct of macroeconomic policy. In this context, policies of price and income controls were viewed as a possible means of promoting a desirable inward shift of the Phillips curve.

There can be little doubt that the traditional Keynesian view dominated macroeconomics in the post-war period and, indeed, a broad consensus prevailed on both sides of the Atlantic as to the wisdom of Keynesian policies almost until the 1970s. It was true that controversy prevailed over the relative merits of monetary versus fiscal policy and some concern was expressed about the inflationary consequences of deficit finance sanctioned by the Keynesian ascendancy, but in general the phrase 'we are all Keynesians now' went unchallenged.

It is perhaps paradoxical that the collapse of the Keynesian consensus should turn so decisively upon the concept of the Phillips curve which Keynesians had been so eager to endorse. The collapse was compounded of both empirical and theoretical considerations. As Mankiw (1990) has persuasively argued, both were necessary to the reappraisal of macroeconomics. Upon the empirical level, the era of the 1970s ushered in a period of stagflation – a situation of rising unemployment and rising inflation – implying that the Phillips curve relationship had broken down or at least was subject to a progressive outward shift. Increasingly, economic forecasts of inflation and un-employment were shown to be widely off target.

To this empirical failure, which might otherwise have been explained away in terms of OPEC-induced supply shocks, was added the *theoretical* denial stemming from Friedman (1968a) and Phelps (1968). Stated simply, Friedman and Phelps demonstrated that the notion of a permanent trade-off between inflation and unemployment being available to the monetary authorities was inconsistent with basic microeconomic principles founded in maximizing utility behaviour. The critique of Friedman and Phelps turned upon the inclusion of *adaptive* expectations formation in labour market behaviour and served *inter alia* to draw attention to the inadequacy with which expectations formation had been treated in macroeconomics generally.[2] Henceforth, the subject of expectations formation would become a pivotal issue in macroeconomic research agendas culminating ultimately in the doctrine of rational expectations.

Friedman's critique of the presumed Phillips curve trade-off led to the concept of the *natural* level of employment to which the economy would inevitably return – a concept fundamentally at variance with traditional Keynesian doctrine. The demise of the conventional Keynesian paradigm was instrumental in bringing monetarism and, in particular, the monetarist critique of Keynesian economics into greater prominence and greater acceptance. From this time forward, Keynesians, forced increasingly upon the defensive, could no longer ignore the economics of the budget constraint and were increasingly compelled to accept the proposition that 'money matters'.

The emergence of monetarism (a comparatively recent term first coined in 1968) was essentially a restatement of the much older ideas embodied in the classical *quantity theory of money* but now reformulated into a theory of the demand for money. Essentially, it held that money had a major impact upon the level of economic activity and the price level and the undisputed link between monetary growth and inflation in the 1970s helped its meteoric rise.

Monetarism

The reformulation of the quantity theory of money as a theory of the demand for money, primarily under the aegis of Milton Friedman of the University of Chicago, sought to demonstrate that the demand for money was a relatively stable function of a few key variables. The implication is that the velocity of circulation of money was relatively constant; if this is the case, then it follows that an increase in the money stock would imply an increase in nominal national income and would not be countered by velocity changes as many Keynesians had claimed. However, the monetarist doctrine goes beyond a simple assertion of a link between money and nominal income. Although allowing for monetary influences upon the volume of real output in the short

---

2 Adaptive expectations assume that individuals learn from their past experience and mistakes. Thus, if last year's expected inflation was 5 per cent and inflation turned out to be 10 per cent, then this year's expectation will be equal to 5 per cent plus a fraction of the error made last year, that is

$$EP = 5 + \alpha(10 - 5)$$

where *EP* is this year's expected inflation rate and $0 < \alpha < 1$. If the rate of inflation suddenly became 10 per cent and remained at that level indefinitely, then this approach would possess the merit that individuals' expectations would progressively approximate the true inflation rate. If inflation is escalating, however, this approach performs badly in that expectations become increasingly falsified.

run, it is part and parcel of the revised theory that in the long term, output and employment will attain their *natural* levels, determined essentially by microeconomic influences and constraints; consequently, the monetarist doctrine becomes one of claiming that the rate of monetary expansion determines the rate of inflation.

The doctrine also has important implications for the balance of payments. In particular, it is argued that maintaining a regime of *fixed exchange rates* implies loss of control over the domestic money supply and thus the rate of inflation, which will then be determined by world inflation rates. In contrast, *flexible exchange rates* allow control over domestic monetary expansion and hence control over domestic inflation, with insulation from world inflation. In either case, if inflation is essentially a monetary phenomenon then again, in contrast to Keynesian theories, prices and income policies are at best an irrelevancy and at worse may imply serious resource misallocation.

New Classical Macroeconomics

The monetarist counter-revolution spearheaded by Friedman paved the way for a more radical assault upon the Keynesian ascendancy. This was the school of thought which became known as New Classical Macroeconomics and was intimately linked with the name of Robert Lucas (1976). Essentially, this approach extended the Friedman critique concerning the lack of adequate microeconomic underpinnings for Keynesian macrotheory.

New Classical Macroeconomics was based upon a dual premise. First and foremost was the assertion that all markets, including labour markets, reveal a distinct tendency to clear. Secondly, there was the belief that all economic agents pursue rational behaviour in seeking maximum utility. Indeed, the belief in market clearing was a direct result of the maximizing utility premise. The failure of a market to clear would imply a failure to exploit mutually beneficial trades – a loss of both consumer and producer surplus. Keynesian unemployment equilibria was therefore dismissed as being inconsistent with rational utility maximizing behaviour upon the part of economic agents.

Underpinning the New Classical Macroeconomics was a commitment to the doctrine of *rational expectations*. This thesis maintains that individual economic agents use all available information, including policy announcements by government, in a manner as efficient as possible in forming their expectations about the future state of the economy. In this respect, the New Classical Macroeconomics differs from monetarism in that the latter, adopting the adaptive expectations framework, permits temporary disequilibrium situations to be maintained for relatively long periods of time depending upon the value of the expectations coefficient, α. In contrast, New Classical Macroeconomics, incorporating a rational expectations framework, explicitly assumes a very rapid if not instantaneous response to disequilibrium situations. For the New Classical Macroeconomist, failure to adopt a rational expectations framework would be tantamount to non-utility maximizing behaviour.

It should be emphasized, however, that whilst rational expectations formation is a necessary ingredient for the New Classical Macroeconomics, it is not sufficient. The distinctive feature of the latter remains its market-clearing properties. Rational expectations, of itself, does not guarantee market-clearing solutions if there exist impediments to the implied adjustment. Indeed, many New Keynesian models, concerned to deny the market-clearing postulate, now incorporate rational expectations in their formal analysis.

Granted the market-clearing assumption, however, a number of surprising and perhaps disturbing conclusions follow. Of these, perhaps the most frequently cited, if often frequently misunderstood, is *the policy ineffectiveness proposition*. Simply stated, this argues that any *anticipated* monetary policy action via aggregate demand measures will not affect real output or employment. Only random or unanticipated policy measures will generate real effects. A more complete denial of orthodox Keynesianism would be hard to find. The government thus becomes powerless to influence output and employment by the pursuit of rational business cycle policy operating upon the side of aggregate demand. However, it must be noted that this is not to deny that *any* government policy can generate real effects. Thus, for example, tax incentives or investment allowances, even if anticipated, can, by changing comparative prices and rates of return, influence real investment decisions. Moreover, in this scenario, real magnitudes are determined primarily by microeconomic forces operating in market-clearing conditions; consequently, any measure aiding competition and the free functioning of the market economy is conducive to improved macroeconomic performance.

Supply Side Macroeconomics

Conventional Keynesian economics holds that output and employment are *demand determined*. In stark contrast, and reminiscent of Say's famous Law of Markets, the supply side school of macroeconomics maintains exactly the opposite. Output and employment are determined by the conditions of *aggregate supply*. Once determined, aggregate supply is assumed to be perfectly inelastic and thus Keynesian-type fluctuations in aggregate demand have impacts only upon the general price level. Hence it is the supply side view that expansionary demand management policies are likely to be inflationary. Although aggregate supply is held to be completely inelastic with respect to demand stimulus, policies do exist which can promote a favourable outward shift of the aggregate supply curve and hence of output and employment. Essentially, these policies influence the microeconomic environment which determines the position of the aggregate supply curve. They would include tax cuts, especially of high marginal rates, to provide incentives, restrictions upon trade union powers and the relaxation of minimum wage laws, measures to promote privatization in the belief that the private sector in intrinsically more efficient, and efforts to promote competition and enterprise.

The supply side school of economics has links both with the New Classical Macroeconomics and their rational expectations adherents in discarding aggregate demand as a source of fluctuations in output and employment. Accordingly, the business cycle is to be explained in terms of shocks from the supply side. In addition, however, there are also links with monetarism in providing an explanation of the *natural* level of output and employment and in suggesting means whereby appropriate policies may seek to raise the natural level. Although it has served as a useful antidote to Keynesian-oriented demand management policies, its policy prescriptions require an act of faith on the part of its adherents in the absence of any firm convincing empirical evidence.

New Keynesian Economics

The Keynesian response to these assaults upon traditional Keynesian orthodoxy was to devise internally consistent equilibrium models, grounded upon utility maximizing microeconomic axioms, which – confronted by constraints or impediments of one kind or another – reconciled the concept of unemployment equilibria. Thus, whilst accepting the equilibrium framework conceptually, the New Keynesian economics is basically in keeping with the spirit of Keynes in believing that the automatic adjustment mechanism underlying the classical model is fundamentally flawed and in suggesting that there may be grounds for discretionary stabilization policy. Essentially, these models have invoked imperfect competition upon one or both sides of the labour market to account for prolonged periods of non-clearing behaviour. Principal contributions have focused upon contract theory, insider–outsider analysis and efficiency wage models.

Contract theory advances reasons why risk-averse workers enter into agreements (implicit or otherwise) with employers to smooth incomes over the course of the business cycle as opposed to linking remuneration directly with volatile marginal productivity. Stability of wage income provides a form of insurance to the worker for which he is prepared to pay a premium to the employer in the form of a lower wage than would otherwise be dictated by expected productivity. The resulting outcome generates a degree of wage inflexibility and unemployment in recessionary periods.

Insider–outsider analysis distinguishes the employed (insiders) from the unemployed (outsiders) and suggest reasons why outsiders have no real influence upon the actual wage bargain. Increasing unemployment, therefore, does not impinge upon the power of workers involved in wage negotiation. The factors conferring monopoly power upon insiders turn upon the costs of hiring, training and dismissing workers (Okun, 1981).

Efficiency wage models relate productivity directly with the wage paid – partly because it raises the cost of job loss and thus induces improved performance upon the part of the worker anxious to retain his employment. This might be particularly relevant in situations where the worker enjoys a degree of discretion over how well he performs and where monitoring or policing performance may be impractical or costly. Thus, firms pursuing profit-maximizing behaviour may find it advantageous to pay wages in excess of the market-clearing wage.

What these models possess in common is a willingness to depart from the competitive framework of New Classical Macroeconomics which is held to be of questionable relevance to the analysis of the labour market. In doing so, they appear to be able to account for the observed persistence of unemployment being maintained over considerable periods of time without departing from assumptions of *Homo economicus*.

The Evolution of Ideas

It is perhaps useful in this introductory chapter to indicate some aspects of how the leading schools of thought have evolved with regard to policy prescription within the United Kingdom. In what follows, we will proceed in a none-too-rigorous manner, the reader being assured that these issues are taken up in considerably more detail and at a more technical level later in the volume. In particular, we will invoke elementary diagrammatic expositions whose precise underpinnings are for the moment assumed. The attempt is merely to convey an outline of the leading ideas and how they have impinged upon policy debate.

Consider, for example, figure 1.2, which depicts the supply and demand curves for labour, drawn as a function of real wages, and which shows that at the prevailing real

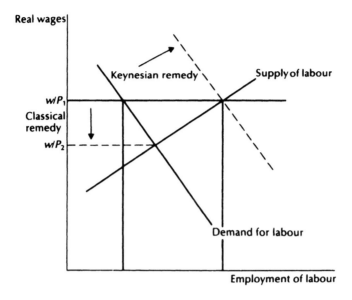

Figure 1.2 Classical and Keynesian remedies for employment creation

wage W/P_1, unemployment prevails. In other words, at the existing wage, there are more people seeking jobs than there are job vacancies – we have a situation of excess supply of labour. In such a situation, two possible remedies suggest themselves if the objective is the securing of full employment. Upon the one hand, we could resort to a *classical* remedy of reducing real wages which would extend the demand for labour whilst simultaneously inducing some people voluntarily to leave the workforce. If wages were to fall to W/P_2, unemployment would be eliminated. Alternatively, one could invoke a Keynesian solution and enlarge the level of demand possibly by increased government expenditure until full employment is secured at the prevailing wage.

Now of these two remedies – assuming they are both equally available – it is clear that the Keynesian alternative is to be logically preferred. This is because it is consistent not only with a higher level of real output and hence employment but also because it implies a higher real wage. In contrast, the classical remedy secures its objective partly by reducing wages sufficiently so that part of the workforce no longer wish to undertake remunerative employment. None the less, the classical solution is the preferred solution – and in many respects is the only solution – for those economists who are convinced that the Keynesian measure does not and cannot work. The classical rejection of the Keynesian policy proposal is summarized in the philosophy of the so-called Treasury View – which in current jargon is a version of crowding out. In this view, any attempt to raise public sector spending in the interests of promoting employment would involve a transfer of resources from the private to the public sector. Thus, any net gain in employment would be small, and would depend upon the possibility that public sector employment was intrinsically more labour intensive. In contrast, although very similar in spirit, and in many respects in substance, the Thatcher government's rejection of Keynesian demand management strategies was based upon a belief in a natural rate of employment to which the economy inherently gravitates together with a certain view as to the means of expectations formation. Implicit in this approach is the belief that Keynesian-type demand management strategies succeed only in generating

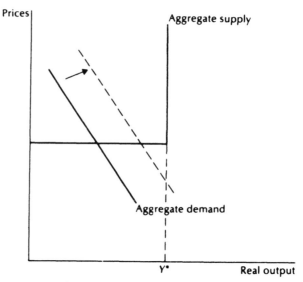

Figure 1.3 Aggregate demand measures to raise output and employment with zero price effects in the naïve Keynesian model

higher prices and are incapable of generating any long-term improvement in real output, and indeed, the strict version of this thesis would simultaneously deny the possibility of any short-term gains as well. In order to illustrate the essence of these ideas, we will invoke the concepts of aggregate supply and demand analysis whose precise construction is to be analysed in more detail later in the volume.

Consider, for example, figure 1.3 which we may think of as embodying the spirit of naïve Keynesianism. In this diagram the aggregate supply curve is drawn with perfect elasticity with respect to price until full employment output or capacity output is reached at Y^*. Before this point is attained, any increase in the level of aggregate demand as indicated by the hatched line exerts its entire impact upon output and

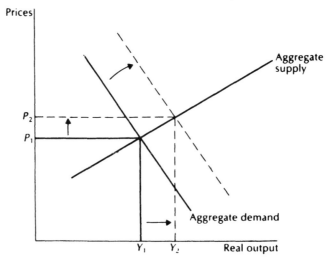

Figure 1.4 Aggregate demand measures to raise output and employment with positive price effects in the sophisticated Keynesian model

employment with no impact upon prices. In conditions of extreme unemployment both of labour and capital assets which characterized the conditions of the 1930s, this may not be a too unreasonable first approximation and certainly this assumption was a commonplace in simple Keynesian models which dealt in real terms and assumed away the question of price changes. The more sophisticated Keynesian model, however, which is the one to which Keynes himself ascribed, is shown in figure 1.4. Here, the aggregate supply curve is positively sloped, implying that any increase in the level of aggregate demand as indicated by the hatched line would generate not just output and employment effects but would also impinge upon prices. The aggregate supply curve is positively sloped because as you move closer to full employment income, less efficient and less well trained labour will be taken on, bottleneck shortages may appear, overtime rates may need to be paid and so forth. None the less, the implication is that demand management strategies can be effective in raising employment at the cost of a possibly higher price level; the essentially Keynesian notion of a trade-off between output and prices, epitomized in the concept of the Phillips curve, is implicit in this construct.

Consider now figure 1.5, which we may categorize as the monetarist approach and which owes much to the thinking of Milton Friedman and Edmund Phelps. In the short run, it is essentially similar to the sophisticated Keynesian model but the difference lies in the long-run adjustment of the positively sloped aggregate supply curve. To see this, let us assume the initial situation to be the price level P_1 and the income or output level Y_1 as determined by the intersection of the aggregate supply and demand curves. Let us now assume that an increase in government spending raises the level of aggregate demand, as indicated by the hatched line, so that output rises to Y_2 with prices rising to P_2. Essentially, this is precisely the adjustment underlying the sophisticated Keynesian model. However, for the monetarist, such an adjustment will be but short-lived. This is because the rise in prices curtails real wages – indeed it is the fall in real wages which is responsible in part for extending the demand for labour. As labour

Figure 1.5 Interdependence between aggregate supply and demand schedules, the monetarist approach and distinction between short-run and long-run effects

perceives a decline in real wages, it will commence to renegotiate its nominal wage contract so as to restore its former level of real wage consistent with the initial supply of effort reflected in the income level Y_1. Thus, the aggregate supply curve is shifted inwards over time, until the former output level is regained at the former real wage. The trade-off is short-term only, the movement being from A to B to C. The long-run aggregate supply curve is thus vertical above the income level Y_1, which is referred to as the natural level, and a corollary of the above is that the long-term Phillips curve (to be dealt with later in considerable detail) is also logically vertical above the natural rate of employment.

The rational expectations thesis takes this adjustment process one step further to reach what its proponents claim is the logical conclusion. Why should intelligent economic agents wait until their real wages actually decline? Will they not, in the light of their understanding of how the economy actually operates or upon the basis of past experience, anticipate that the increase in government spending will generate an increase in prices? As soon as the policy measure is announced or otherwise identified, labour should immediately renegotiate its nominal wage claim in order to defend the existing real wage. Indeed, one may take the argument one step further. If government policy is systematic in the sense of being countercyclical, then the policy measures may be anticipated even before they are announced or put into effect. If, for example, government spending always increases when unemployment passes a certain figure, or contracts when the balance of payments goes sufficiently into deficit, intelligent economic agents will recognize this recurrent process and will react accordingly, thus negating any macroeconomic impact. Predictable countercyclical policy becomes impotent. In other words, the monetarist distinction between the long term and the short disappears; there is no trade-off between output and inflation even in the short run. This situation is summarized with the aid of figure 1.6 displaying the vertical aggregate supply curve even in the short run. The contrast with the naïve Keynesian approach summarized in figure 1.3 could not be more stark.

An important feature of the rational expectations philosophy turns upon the conditioning of expectations. If the government announces substantially reduced money

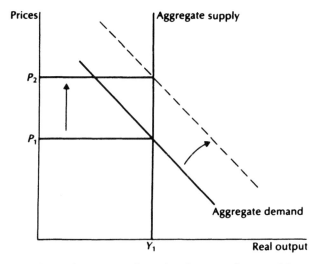

Figure 1.6 Aggregate demand impacts in the rational expectations model: zero output effects and positive price effects

supply targets, and if the policy announcement is credible to economic agents at large, then inflationary expectations will be swiftly adjusted downwards. These revised inflationary expectations will then form the basis of formal wage bargaining negotiations and output and employment will be speedily restored to natural levels at lower nominal wages than would otherwise have prevailed. In short, providing the policy is credible, chronic inflation can be substantially reduced or eliminated with fairly modest cost in terms of output and employment forgone. This apparently was what the government firmly believed in 1979; the fact that the reduction in inflation was substantially much more painful and long-drawn-out might be construed either as a critique of the rational expectations thesis or alternatively as evidence that the government policy was not credible. Certainly, there were those who believed in and even those who advocated (the 'wets') a 'U-turn' in policy as the number of the unemployed continued its persistent rise to record levels.

Finally, belief in the vertical aggregate supply curve signals not only the death knell of Keynesian-oriented demand management policies but also provides the a priori justification for the consideration of supply side policies. Policies to effect a favourable outward shift of the vertical aggregate supply curve, thus raising the natural rate of output and employment, are consistent with higher growth and greater economic welfare. Such policies are essentially microeconomic in nature and turn upon boosting incentives by tax cuts and arguably lower unemployment and associated benefits, by promoting competition through privatization programmes and trade union reform and similar measures designed to create initiative and a climate of enterprise. It is in this changed view of the aggregate supply curve that the remarks of Nigel Lawson, quoted above, are most fully understood.

The Neutrality Issue

In reviewing these various competing schools of macroeconomic thought, it is tempting to enquire as to whether the successive debates generate the establishment of a common ground and a common framework, acceptable to all parties concerned with broad agreement being reached upon the essential issues. For some economists, this question would ultimately be answered in the affirmative – in principle, at least. That is to say, the result of scientific debate will lead to the testing of hypotheses and the ultimate rejection of those hypotheses which fail to pass the required criteria. A convergence or consensus will prevail with respect to what remains, with disagreements being confined to differences in shades of emphasis or in new doctrinal disputes at the very frontiers of research.

The contrary view, stemming from the Duhem–Quine thesis sketched above, rejects the very premise that individual hypotheses can be tested and dispensed with in isolation so as to leave a body of accepted hypotheses for assembly into a coherent aggregate theory. It is only complete theoretical structures which can be subject to test and potential refutation. If Keynesian and non-Keynesian theories differ fundamentally in their implications, then a movement towards convergence is not a feasible possibility; one theory or the other must ultimately prove superior.

This is the position persuasively argued by Cross (1991), who argues that the fundamental point of dispute between Keynesian and non-Keynesian models turns upon the question of neutrality. Classical and non-Keynesian models maintain that temporary shocks of whatever origin do not have lasting real effects upon real variables such as output and employment. Different models differ in their speed of adjustment but ultimately all regain the initial equilibrium values. In contrast, Keynesian theory insists that temporary shocks do have real long-term consequences.

This Keynesian position has been illustrated in the concept of *hysteresis* – the notion that ultimate equilibrium solutions are path dependent or influenced by current values of the variable in question. If this is the case, equilibrium levels of unemployment are not independent of the recent history of actual unemployment and the level of aggregate demand. To illustrate, if deflationary policies generate long-term unemployment, and if, with the passage of time, some of those unemployed become unemployable, owing either to the atrophy of skills or the perception of potential employers, then the long-term *natural* rate of unemployment will be raised.

Concluding Comments

This taxonomy provides a useful framework of reference which can be invoked when appraising macroeconomic controversies. Although the methodological approach adopted here pursues the arguments on an issue-by-issue basis, the reader will readily identify the principal contributions of the leading schools of thought as the analysis of macroeconomic sectors, systems and policy is developed.

Further Reading

For a concise introduction to macroeconomic issues in the UK, see Curwen (1994). On methodological issues, the starting point for any discussion of the positivist approach must remain the classic paper by Friedman (1953a) and the subsequent critique by Nagel (1963), both reprinted in the volume of readings edited by Breit and Hochman (1968). The distinction between the is/ought dichotomy will be found in Blaug (1981) and Hudson (1979). On Popper and scientific appraisal, see the papers by Caldwell and Hands, both in Shaw (1991), as well as Redman (1994). On the Duhem–Quine thesis, see especially the important paper by Cross (1982b). On the various competing schools of macroeconomic thought, an excellent overview (including Austrian and Neo-Marxist approaches) is provided by Snowdon, Vane and Wynarczyk (1994). A detailed taxonomy of seven schools of macroeconomic thought is also presented by Phelps (1990).

Part I

Macroeconomic Sectors

It is difficult to see the picture
when you are inside the frame
R. S. Trapp

The first stage in constructing a macroeconomic model is to identify the relevant component parts of the system, and understand the behavioural relations involved. In the case of macroeconomic analysis this is especially important since much of the controversy about how the macroeconomy responds to various economic stimuli can be traced to disagreements about the nature and determinants of specific aggregates.

In this first part of the book the aim is to identify the component sectors of the macroeconomy and outline alternative views of the behavioural relations in each sector. Chapters 2, 3 and 4 will deal with the principal components of aggregate expenditure, namely consumption, investment and government expenditure respectively. Chapters 5 and 6 explore the demand and supply sides of the money market respectively. At the end of chapter 6, the three principal components of chapters 2, 3 and 4 will be combined to derive the aggregate demand curve. Chapter 7 analyses the labour market and derives the aggregate supply curve using different assumptions about the manner in which agents behave in that market.

The mode of analysis is essentially partial equilibrium in that each sector is analysed in isolation. Collectively, however, the chapters in this part form the essential background to part II, where complete systems are analysed.

2

Aggregate Consumption Expenditure

When asked what the major influence on consumption expenditure is likely to be, most lay commentators will undoubtedly reply that it is *income*. Indeed this may even be regarded as so self-evident as to obviate the need for thorough investigation. However, the purpose of this chapter is to consider more closely what precisely is meant by income, and how the concept of income is likely to affect aggregate consumption. There are a number of competing candidates to the title 'income'. Attention will be focused on concepts such as *absolute income, relative income, life cycle income, permanent income* and *endogenous income*. Having examined each of these, we will then briefly review existing empirical evidence on the consumption–income relationship.

Current Income Theories

The Absolute Income Hypothesis

Keynes viewed consumption expenditures in the aggregate as being primarily dependent on current net income.[1] He contended that, as net income increased, consumption expenditure would increase *but by less than the increase in income*. In other words, some savings will take place. If the *marginal propensity to consume* (MPC) is defined as the change in consumption which is associated with some small change in income, then this assumption imposes the restriction that the *marginal propensity to consume* will lie between zero and unity.[2]

As well as imposing this restriction, Keynes made two other behavioural assumptions. The first was that at 'low' (but unspecified) income levels, consumption will exceed income, expenditure being financed by dissaving. This amounts to saying that the MPC is less than the *average propensity to consume* (APC). The latter is defined as the ratio of consumption expenditure to income (C/Y). The second assumption was that the MPC or in the limit dC/dY will itself decline as income increases. If con-

---

1 Net income is here equated with consumption plus *net* investment. Thus, the provision considered necessary for depreciation needs ('financial prudence') is a factor influencing consumption expenditures. Keynes fully allowed for other influences on consumption, including windfall gains, interest rate changes, and fiscal policy. Modern Keynesians have emphasized the latter influence and in particular have considered consumption to be a function of *disposable* income.

2 As will be seen, the assertion that $0 < \text{MPC} < 1$ is not solely the result of armchair theorizing but is also a required condition for the stability properties of the elementary Keynesian model.

sumption is expressed as a function of *disposable* income, in keeping with modern practice, this consumption function can be formally represented as follows:

$$C = f(Y_d) \tag{2.1a}$$

$$Y_d = Y - T \tag{2.2}$$

$$T = tY \tag{2.3}$$

$$0 < \frac{dC}{dY_d} < 1 \tag{2.1b}$$

$$\frac{dC}{dY_d} < \frac{C}{Y_d} \tag{2.1c}$$

$$\frac{d^2C}{dY_d^2} < 0 \tag{2.1d}$$

where C is aggregate consumption, and disposable income (Y_d) is total income after deduction of direct taxes ($Y - T$). t is the average rate of income taxes. Expression 2.1b describes the MPC, expression 2.1c describes the relationship between the MPC and the APC, and expression 2.1d describes how the MPC will behave as income changes. The last inequality is particularly important since, if it holds, it will ensure that the APC (C/Y_d) declines as income rises, and that the APC is more than the MPC. These relations are summarized in figure 2.1 by the function C_1.

The implications of this relationship are worth emphasizing. First, it is clear that if information on the MPC exists, it is possible to predict how consumption expenditure will change in response to a change in disposable income (effected, for example, by a change in tax rates). Second, it implies that the percentage of income saved increases as society becomes richer. This in turn suggests that in a growing economy a greater proportion of investment will be required to maintain full employment income levels. Third, expression 2.1c suggests that a transfer of income from high-income to low-income consumers will raise the level of aggregate demand, since MPCs differ between the two groups. Thus, implicit in the Keynesian approach is a justification of progressive taxation as a basis of income redistribution in conditions of surplus capacity.[3]

Cross-Section and Time Series Consumption Functions   The Keynesian consumption function provided considerable impetus to empirical investigation. Early studies employing *cross-section budget data* appeared to support Keynes's intuition in almost every detail. Such cross-section data related the level of consumption to income levels for different income groups, and in so doing tended to generate consumption functions remarkably similar to C_1 in figure 2.1, or more accurately, given a linear functional form, similar to C_2 in figure 2.1.

Although the cross-section data lent some support to the Keynesian thesis, a number of early *time series* studies (that is, studies relating observations on consumption and income for specific groups through time) raised fundamental questions. Kuznets' (1946) classic study, for example, suggested that consumption was a linear function of disposable income with a *constant* MPC of approximately 0.9, which passed through the origin like C_3 in figure 2.1. This and other time series evidence implied that savings would be a constant rather than increasing proportion of national income, thus

---

3 Strictly speaking, the opposite conclusion follows in inflationary conditions.

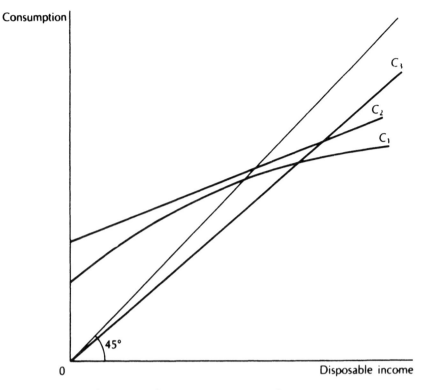

Figure 2.1 Alternative consumption functions

combatting the pessimistic leanings towards stagnation. Furthermore, it questioned whether redistribution from upper-to lower-income groups would have any impact upon the level of aggregate demand. This apparent conflict in empirical findings provided a challenge to the generality of the absolute income hypothesis and an impetus to further research directed at providing some plausible explanation of why cross-section and time series results should offer such conflicting views of the consumption function.

The Relative Income Hypothesis

One of the earliest influential treatises which sought to modify the Keynesian consumption function, and did so in such a way as to offer an explanation of the conflicting cross-section and time series findings, was advanced by Duesenberry (1952). He argued that Keynesian analysis focused on an inappropriate concept of income; he contended that, when explaining variations in consumption, the relevant concept of income was not absolute income but *relative* income. By relative income he had in mind the current disposable income of a consuming unit relative to previous peak income, *and* current disposable income of that same consuming unit relative to the current disposable income of other consuming units. The former of these two relativities is responsible for the so-called *ratchet effect* – that is, the idea that the consumption–income relationship may be asymmetrical in so far as there are downward rigidities to the reduction of consumption expenditure. The latter relativity has become known as the *demonstration effect* and refers to the possibility that consumption decisions may be *interdependent* rather than independent. If both of these effects are taken into consideration, it is possible to reconcile the findings of cross-section and time series evidence.

Duesenberry's Reconciliation of Cross-Section and Time Series Findings Formally the consumption function can be written as:

$$C_t = f(Y_t, \ Y_t/Y_0, \ \sigma Y) \tag{2.4}$$

where C_t is current consumption, Y_t current income, σY the distribution of income and Y_t/Y_0 the ratio of current income to previous peak income. Duesenberry's estimating equation took the form:

$$\frac{S_t}{Y_t} = a + b\frac{Y_t}{Y_0} \tag{2.5}$$

that is, current savings are a linear function of the relationship between current income and previous peak income. Since

$$\frac{C_t}{Y_t} = 1 - \frac{S_t}{Y_t} \tag{2.6}$$

then if equation 2.5 is substituted into equation 2.6, the following is obtained:

$$\frac{C_t}{Y_t} = 1 - a - b\frac{Y_t}{Y_0} \tag{2.7}$$

If income were to grow at a constant rate (of, say, g per cent) without declining, then clearly current income would always represent peak income and the previous year's income will *always* be previous peak income. If the trend growth of income is given as

$$Y_t = (1 + g)\,Y_{t-1} \tag{2.8}$$

then as income grows along trend

$$\frac{Y_t}{Y_0} = \frac{Y_t}{Y_{t-1}} = 1 + g \tag{2.9}$$

Substituting equation 2.9 into equation 2.7 yields

$$\frac{C_t}{Y_t} = 1 - a - b(1 + g) \tag{2.10}$$

In other words, if income grows along trend, the APC and the MPC are constant. The consumption function thus fits the time series 'facts'.

   Consider now the situation when income fluctuates around its trend rate of growth. In this situation, equation 2.9 no longer holds and the consumption ratio is no longer constant. This would still be given by equation 2.7. Given the negative coefficient on Y_t/Y_0, C_t/Y_t and Y_t/Y_0 will be inversely related. Furthermore, from equation 2.7

$$C_t = (1 - a)\,Y_t - b\frac{Y_t^2}{Y_0} \tag{2.11}$$

Differentiating gives an expression for the marginal propensity to consume

$$\frac{dC_t}{dY_t} = 1 - a - 2b\frac{Y_t}{Y_0} \tag{2.12}$$

Comparison of equations 2.12 and 2.7 reveals that the equality of the marginal and average propensity to consume no longer holds. In fact *the MPC is less than the APC*. This implies that when income is fluctuating around trend, the consumption function fits the short-run 'facts'.

An intuitive explanation of how these functions are related is given in figure 2.2. Assume that the typical consumer unit commences at point A. As income grows along trend, a roughly constant fraction of income will be consumed, with a relatively small proportion being saved. This pattern will continue as income rises through Y_1 to Y_2 to Y_3. The points are on the long-run time series consumption function. The ratio of savings to income will change very little because, typically, consumers strive to attain the standards of consumption set by consuming units in higher-income brackets. As long as the growth of income does not radically affect the distribution of income, once one set of aspirations are fulfilled a new target is set. Thus, as the consumer reaches income level Y_2 and consumption level C_2 (for example, one car and one overseas vacation per annum), consumers who were previously in income bracket Y_2 now occupy Y_3 (two cars and two overseas vacations per annum). The maintenance of such targets ensures that savings propensities remain constant and the consumer stays on his long-run consumption function.

Now suppose that at income level Y_2 the economy lurches into recession and average incomes fall. Typically, consumers will resist cuts in living standards as set by previous peak income. Thus, rather than moving back down the long-run consumption function, the APC from current income will rise, and current savings will fall in an effort to maintain living standards. If income falls far enough, a point such as E may be approached where current consumption exceeds current income – consumption levels

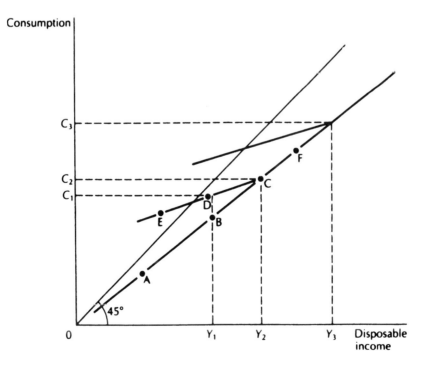

Figure 2.2 Consumption and the relative income hypothesis

are at least in part being maintained by running down past savings. Once the economy recovers and income begins to rise again, the consumer will move back along the short-run consumption function towards C. The APC falls initially as income rises and efforts are made to rebuild savings. Eventually, when the previous peak at C is reached and income increases beyond Y_2, the consumption-income relationship returns to its long-run trend.

This stylized description of the adjustment process serves to emphasize the role played by the ratchet and demonstration effects. The thesis has interesting policy implications. As was seen earlier, the simple Keynesian formulation suggested that government tax changes to alter the level of disposable income had a fairly predictable impact. The Duesenberry formulation suggests, however, that fiscal changes may have an asymmetrical effect. Tax reductions may well stimulate consumption spending. Tax increases, however, may have a limited impact in curbing demand in the short run, as consumers attempt to maintain consumption levels.

Duesenberry himself provided some empirical support for the relative income hypothesis, and a number of other studies have provided encouraging support. Subsequent developments in the analysis of aggregate consumption, however, suggested that one very important variable may have been omitted –namely, the role of wealth, and in particular the part which this may play in influencing expectations of future income. This is a variable which is given much greater prominence in the so-called *normal income theories*, the best known of which are the permanent income hypothesis and the life cycle hypothesis.

Normal Income Theories

Because both the Keynesian and Duesenberry explanations of consumption behaviour link current consumption closely to current income, they are found wanting when it comes to explaining consumption behaviour of groups whose income pattern is highly variable. The farmer (in the absence of income support schemes), the salesman or the professional gambler all tend to have fluctuating income. Nevertheless, one may still find that their consumption expenditure is relatively stable. The solution to the problem is simple. Individuals are not completely myopic. Thus, in the event of a good harvest the farmer does not increase consumption in line with his increased income. Nor when times are bad does he reduce consumption to some irreducible minimum. Over any given period, he is aware that his income will fluctuate. He is also aware, however, of what on average he can expect to earn. In other words, he has some idea of his *normal* income, and his consumption plans are based on this rather than current income. In years when current income is in excess of normal income, he will save, whilst in years when current income falls short of normal income, he will dissave.

Microeconomic Foundations

The normal income approach to the analysis of aggregate consumption has its roots more firmly embedded in microeconomic foundations than the current income approaches. A brief elaboration of these foundations is useful to identify certain characteristics of the normal income approach.

As was noted in the introductory points, the essence of the normal income approach is that the consumer aims to maximize utility by seeking the optimal pattern of con-

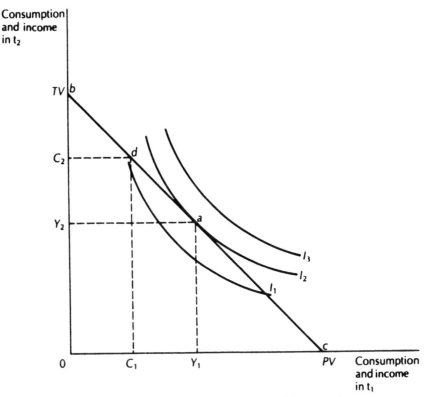

Figure 2.3 Consumption in a two-period framework

sumption expenditures through time. If for simplicity the choice is confined to two periods, the essential features of the analysis can easily be developed in a simple geometrical model.

In figure 2.3, consumption and income in period 1 and period 2 are measured along the horizontal and vertical axes respectively. It is assumed that the individual consumer receives an income of Y_1 in the first period and Y_2 in the second period, and furthermore for simplicity that $Y_1 = Y_2$. If current income were the principal determinant of current consumption, the individual might consume all of Y_1 in period 1 and all of Y_2 in period 2, ultimately reaching point a in consumption space. If, however, he can use the capital market to either deposit savings to finance future consumption $(C_2 > Y_2)$ or borrow against future income to support current consumption $(C_1 > Y_1)$, his options are rather wider. For instance, he could choose to consume C_1 in the first period and save $C_1 Y_1$ in order to consume C_2 in the second period, ultimately ending up at point d. There are in fact an infinity of possible combinations of consumption over the two periods which comprise the consumer's *budget constraint* (*bc*). The intercepts of the constraint are determined by the extremes of consuming all income in the first period, or all income in the second period. In the first case, the consumer would consume an amount equivalent to the *present value* (*PV*) of his income over the two periods, where

$$PV = Y_1 + \frac{Y_2}{(1+r)} \tag{2.13}$$

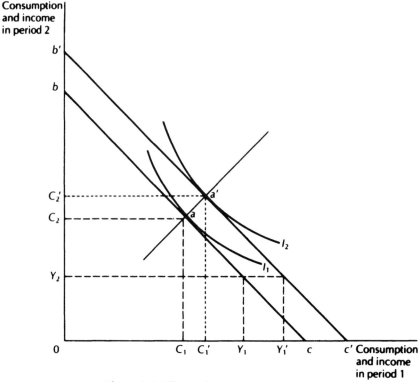

Figure 2.4 Effects of an increase in income

that is, his income in the first period and his income in the second period discounted at the current rate of interest (r). Alternatively, he could choose to consume none of his income, invest it at the current interest rate[4] and consume a *terminal value* of

$$TV = Y_2 + Y_1(1 + r) \tag{2.14}$$

Which of the infinity of possible consumption points is actually chosen depends on the consumer's tastes and preferences. These can be described by an *indifference set*.[5] Thus, in the event that the consumer had hedonistic tendencies, his indifference set would be mapped out close to the horizontal axis, whereas if he had distinct preferences for future consumption, his set would be mapped closer to the vertical axis. If preferences are described by the set $I_1 - I_3$ in figure 2.3, the consumer would clearly maximize utility by settling at point a and neither saving nor borrowing.

This simple framework is quite robust in terms of the range of problems it can analyse. For example, one could apply it to a situation where income received varies over the two periods. In figure 2.4, initially $Y_1 > Y_2$, which leads the consumer to settle at point a, saving from current income to support future consumption. If current

---

4 The assumption that borrowers and lenders face the same interest rate (which is tantamount to assuming a perfect capital market) is crucial to this model, and to the permanent income hypothesis. As Fleming (1973) has shown, if in fact borrowers and lenders face different rates the long-run consumption function which is derived from the permanent income hypothesis is no longer linear.

5 It is assumed that the indifference set accords with the usual axioms of consumer behaviour; that is they are non- intersecting, uniquely ranked from south-west to north-east, and are convex to the origin owing to a diminishing marginal rate of substitution between the objects of choice (in this case present and future consumption).

income increases, say from Y_1 to Y_1', this shifts the budget constraint from bc to $b'c'$ and the consumer maximizes utility at point d'. Note that the increment to current consumption $(C_1 - C_1')$ is less than the increment to current income $(Y_1 - Y_1')$. The increase in current income has caused the consumer to rearrange consumption over *both* periods.

One could also explore the implications of a change in the *relative price* of current and future consumption. Up to now, the slope of the budget constraint has not been commented upon. The observant reader may have noted that so far it has been drawn at 45° to both axes, i.e. with a slope of -1. This was deliberate, since the slope of the budget line is given by $-(1 + r)$; therefore imposing a 45° line amounts to assuming a zero rate of interest. Suppose, however, allowance were to be made for a positive interest rate. Clearly, *PV* as given by equation 2.13 would fall (discounting at a positive interest rate), whilst *TV* as given by equation 2.14 would rise (compounding at a positive interest rate). As a result, the budget constraint would rotate as in figure 2.5 with the old and new budget constraints intersecting at the initial values of income Y_1 and Y_2 (since their current values are unaffected by the interest rate change). If the consumer's income is held constant and it is assumed that no change in his preferences occurs, it can be seen that at the new equilibrium point e the consumer has reduced current consumption and increased future consumption. Note also that the increment in future

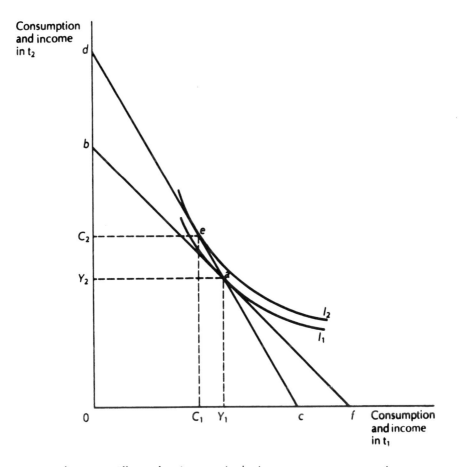

Figure 2.5 Effects of an increase in the interest rate on consumption

consumption $(Y_2 - C_2)$ exceeds the decrement in current consumption $(C_1 - Y_1)$ owing to the positive return on saving.

This introduction to the allocation of consumption through time has been brief, but nevertheless it serves to emphasize that there need not necessarily be any simple relationship between current income and current consumption. The pattern of consumption expenditure chosen depends in part on the individual's tastes and preferences. It depends also, however, on the pattern of the income stream through time (i.e. whether the individual expects to receive more in the future than he currently earns) and on the relative price of present and future consumption as given by the interest rate.

Two specific normal income theories will now be examined, namely the life cycle hypothesis and the permanent income hypothesis; it will be found that the postulates deduced in this simple framework are prominent features of these models.

The Life Cycle Hypothesis

The development of this hypothesis is associated with the names of Ando, Modigliani and Brumberg. At its simplest, the hypothesis argues that the individual will maximize his utility by maintaining a stable pattern of consumption throughout his lifetime – in figure 2.6 the trend line C_1. Over the life cycle, income from employment will behave in a fairly predictable way, being relatively low in the early parts of working life, zero in retirement, and relatively high in between. Thus, a stable consumption path will be maintained by redistributing resources from $t_1 t_2$ to $0 t_1$ and $t_2 \gamma$. This is accomplished by making use of the capital market, borrowing against expected future income perhaps to finance consumption over $0 t_1$, saving and generally accumulating assets to finance consumption over $t_2 \gamma$ – the period from retirement to death.

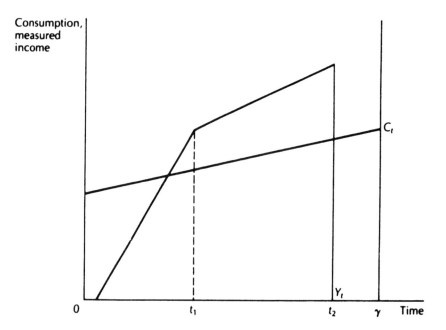

Figure 2.6 Life cycle hypothesis

Following Ando and Modigliani (1963):

$$C_t = \Omega_t V_t \tag{2.15}$$

$$V_t = a_{t-1} + Y_t + \sum_{t=1}^{n} \frac{Y_t^e}{(1 + r_t)^n} \tag{2.16}$$

Equation 2.15 tells us that current consumption is some fraction Ω of the present value of total resources (V_t) accruing to the individual over his lifetime. Equation 2.16 tells us that total resources comprises three components. The first is any net worth which is carried over from the previous period (a_{t-1}); this may take the form of inherited wealth or accumulated wealth. The second is current income (Y_t), and the third is the present value of expected future income from employment (Y^e) over the remainder of the individual's lifetime, n (where $n = \gamma - t$ and where γ is time of death).

Substituting 2.16 into 2.15 we can write,

$$C_t = \Omega_t a_{t-1} + \Omega_t Y_t + \Omega_t \sum_{t=1}^{n} \frac{Y_t^e}{(1 + r_t)^n} \tag{2.17}$$

The proportionality factor (Ω) *will depend on the specific form of the utility function, the rate of return on assets, and the present age of the person* (Ando and Modigliani, 1963). The last influence is particularly important since a basic tenet of the model is that the amount of total resources currently consumed varies systematically over the life cycle. Of course, in this form the consumption function is still concerned with the individual; as was emphasized at the outset, the interest here lies in explaining aggregate consumption. To convert equation 2.17 into an aggregate consumption function, one has to assume that for any given age group of consumers Ω is identical across consumers, and then simply aggregate age groups. This amounts to assuming that consumers in a given age group have similar tastes and preferences for present and future consumption.

This theory therefore argues that consumption patterns will exhibit much greater stability than those predicted by linking consumption to changes in disposable income. In so doing the theory also provides a plausible reconciliation of cross-section and time series empirical studies. Time series data capture the underlying relationship summarized in equation 2.15, where Ω can be viewed as the long-run MPC, although clearly this MPC refers to *total resources* rather than simply current income. Cross-section data, however, observes the relationship between consumption and current income for individuals at different stages of their life cycle; Ω differs across these age groups. Thus, the typical cross-section will include individuals in the early years of work and in retirement for whom the MPC appears to be greater than unity. Such individuals are dissaving. Those on higher levels of current income, who appear to have a much lower MPC, are in the middle stage of the life cycle and are saving a relatively large fraction of current income to pay off previous debts and make provision for the future.

Before proceeding to the permanent income hypothesis, two difficulties associated with the consumption function as specified in equation 2.17 should be acknowledged. The first is that it is clearly assumed that the factor of proportionality, Ω, is the same for all forms of resources. By implication, the individual is indifferent to the form in which resources accrue. A given increase in resources will have the same effect on current consumption whether that increase takes the form of an increase in current income, expected income, or net worth. This seems to imply that switching of assets is a relatively costless transaction (from the consumer's point of view).

The second and perhaps more fundamental problem arises from the difficulties associated with measuring expected income. In equation 2.17, a_{t-1} and Y_t are *relatively* uncontroversial to measure. (As anyone familiar with the literature is aware, they are not uncontroversial *per se.*) Expected income is more problematic; by definition it is not directly observable and its value has to be forecast. The latter is also a problem faced in the permanent income hypothesis; this will be returned to shortly.

To summarize briefly, the life cycle hypothesis directs attention away from current income derived from employment towards a broader concept of lifetime resources. Although this broader concept includes current income, it places much greater emphasis on expected income and wealth. There may be certain empirical difficulties associated with testing the hypothesis, but it is a plausible basis for analysing aggregate consumption, and certainly has more solid microeconomic underpinnings than the Keynesian or Duesenberry approaches.

The Permanent Income Hypothesis

Perhaps the best known critique of the Keynesian consumption function is that advanced by Milton Friedman (1957). This views current consumption as being geared not to current income (whether in an absolute or relative sense) but rather to long-term consumption possibilities, summed up in the concept of *permanent income.* Specifically,

$$C_p = k Y_p \qquad (0 < k < 1) \tag{2.18}$$

Permanent consumption is some fraction of permanent income. The precise value which the constant k takes is determined by wealth, age, tastes and interest rates. It can therefore differ between consumers, although it is independent of Y_p. Permanent income is defined as '*the amount a consumer unit could consume, or believes that it could whilst maintaining its wealth intact*'; permanent consumption is '*the value of services that it is planned to consume during the period in question*' (Friedman, 1957). Permanent income can therefore be looked upon as the *discounted value of expected income streams which, if expectations are justified, approximates long-term average income.* Like the life cycle model, this thesis possesses a strong intuitive appeal with regard to those people who experience highly unstable incomes. It differs from the life cycle model in a number of crucial respects, however. It can be seen from equation 2.18 that Y_p refers to *a flow* of resources which the individual consumer unit could consume *whilst maintaining its wealth intact.* In other words, wealth does not enter directly as an explanatory variable, as in the life cycle hypothesis. This is not to say that wealth is irrelevant. Both human and non-human wealth are relevant in so far as they yield a stream of income, which in turn may influence permanent income. Rather it is the actual *stock* of wealth which does not enter as a determinant of consumption. Thus, the life cycle hypothesis relies on a concept of total resources as the explanatory variable, whilst the permanent income hypothesis relies on a flow of income over a somewhat shorter time scale.

A further distinction which can be made is that in the life cycle hypothesis a specific explanation is offered to suggest that the factor of proportionality (Ω) will vary systematically over the life cycle. In the Friedman hypothesis, no such explanation is provided.

According to the Friedman thesis, permanent income and permanent consumption are related to *measured income* and *measured consumption* as follows:

$$Y_p = Y_m - Y_t \tag{2.19}$$

$$C_p = C_m - C_t \tag{2.20}$$

where the subscripts denote permanent, measured and transitory components. Permanent income can therefore differ from measured income, according to whether *transitory income* is positive or negative. Transitory income refers to windfall gains and losses. Thus an unexpected Christmas bonus would represent a transitory gain, whilst the loss of income arising from an unforeseen strike would represent a transitory loss. The distribution of such gains and losses through time and across consumers is essentially random.

Similarly, permanent (or planned) consumption may differ from recorded consumption owing to transitory gains and losses (e.g. the acquisition of a commodity at 'special offer' sale price in the case of the former, the incidence of unexpected medical expenses on holiday in the case of the latter).

Friedman argues that permanent and transitory elements are related in the following manner:

$$r Y_p Y_t = r C_p C_t = r Y_t C_t = 0 \tag{2.21}$$

where r is the correlation coefficient. The first two correlations assert in essence that transitory components of income and consumption are randomly distributed; this is relatively uncontroversial. The assertion that transitory income and transitory consumption have a zero correlation has been subjected to much closer scrutiny. After all, it seems to imply that if one were to win a substantial sum on the football pools one would be unlikely to buy a new car, or a larger house, or celebrate by taking a holiday in some exotic location. At first sight this appears counter-intuitive. Recall, however, the definition of permanent consumption –'the *value of services* that is planned to consume during the period in question'. This implies that the consumer will plan to consume a certain amount of non-durable and durable services over a given period. Purchase and consumption of the former will of course occur in the same accounting period. Where the latter is concerned, however, purchase occurs in one period and consumption takes place over a number of succeeding periods (depending on the length of life of the durable). Thus, the purchase of consumer durables is in fact a form of saving, and the increased purchase of consumer durables following an increase in Y_t is consistent with the proposition that variations in transitory income have an effect on the level of savings rather than on short-run consumption. Furthermore, a pools win may cause one to revise estimates of permanent income. When saved, it would yield a rate of return over future periods. In so far as this stream of expected income raises permanent income, it will raise permanent consumption. Note that this does not contradict either of the first two zero correlations in equation 2.21. It is not the transitory gain in income *per se* which has affected consumption; it is the conversion of this into wealth, and the subsequent impact of the return on the latter on estimates of permanent income, which affects consumption.

Friedman's Reconciliation of Cross-Section and Time Series Findings   Herein also lies Friedman's reconciliation of short-run and long-run findings. In figure 2.7, the true underlying relationship between consumption and income is traced out by the long-run function $C_p = k Y_p$. Cross-section data will typically capture individuals with positive or negative transitory income. For instance, individual B could estimate his permanent income at Y_p^b, which would result in a permanent consumption level of

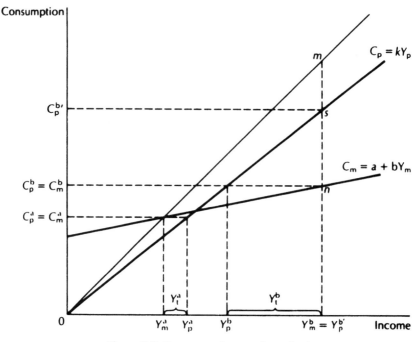

Figure 2.7 Permanent income hypothesis

C_p^b. The cross-section may be taken, however, when he enjoys a transitory gain of Y_t^b, giving the impression that measured income of Y_m^b results in measured consumption of C_m^b. In fact his savings ratio would be mn. This generates future income which may lead him to revise his estimate of permanent income. In the extreme case where the transitory component became permanent (for example, because the initially unexpected Christmas bonus becomes a permanent addition to income), Y_m^b would become $Y_p^{b'}$ and permanent consumption would be revised to $C_p^{b'}$, the savings ratio returning to its long-term trend ms. The same remarks apply *mutatis mutandis* to the case of individual A in the cross-section who is experiencing transitory negative income.[6]

Clearly, as with the life cycle hypothesis, if this model is to be made operational some proxy for permanent income must be found. Friedman suggested that it was reasonable to presume that individuals would estimate permanent income from past income. Specifically, he argued that

$$Y_{pt} = Y_{pt-1} + \lambda(Y_t - Y_{pt-1}) \qquad (0 < \lambda < 1) \tag{2.22}$$

that is, permanent income is equal to last year's estimate of permanent income, plus some fraction of the difference between current measured income and last year's permanent income. In the event that Y_t and Y_{pt-1} are identical, no alteration would be made to the estimate of Y_{pt-1}. If, however, $Y_t > Y_{pt-1}$ then the estimate of Y_{pt} would be revised upwards (and vice versa $Y_t < Y_{pt-1}$). This is a so-called *error learning process* and implies that the typical consumer unit forms his expectations of permanent income *adaptively*. Of course one might immediately question how an estimate of Y_{pt-1} was arrived at, since this is an integral component of equation 2.22. It too would

6 Similar conclusions are reached if one reasons from transitory consumption gains and losses.

have been estimated adaptively from Y_{pt-2}. Likewise, Y_{pt-2} would have been estimated from Y_{pt-3} and so on. Permanent income would therefore be estimated as a weighted average of past incomes with more distant observations being given less emphasis. With a geometrically declining series, observations beyond seventeen periods become insignificant and the equation becomes:

$$Y_{pt} = \lambda[Y_t + (1 - \lambda)Y_{t-1} + (1 - \lambda^2)Y_{t-2} + \ldots + (1 - \lambda)^{17}Y_{t-17}] \quad (0 < \lambda < 1)$$
(2.23)

which can be summarized by

$$Y_{pt} = \lambda \sum_{n=0}^{17}(1 - \lambda)^n Y_{t-n}$$
(2.24)

Since permanent consumption is some fraction of permanent income,

$$C_{pt} = k_{n=1}^{17}(1 - \lambda)Y_{t-n}$$
(2.25)

As was indicated at the outset, permanent consumption is dependent on permanent income, which is itself a function of past levels of income. As such it responds only modestly to changes in measured income.

Permanent Income and Rational Expectations

The permanent income hypothesis gears consumption demand to *expected* permanent income where the latter is derived *adaptively* by reference to former income levels with diminishing weight being given to the more distant income streams. What happens, however, if expectations of permanent income are derived in accordance with the rational expectations mode of behaviour?

This question was first addressed by Robert Hall (1978), who reached the conclusion that if the permanent income thesis of consumer behaviour was correct and if expectations were formed rationally, then changes in consumption demand become unpredictable. Essentially, they would follow a random walk.

The argument runs as follows. Under the permanent income hypothesis, consumers aim at a smooth and stable consumption pattern in accordance with their estimate of permanent income. Consumption demands will change if, and only if, some *new information* becomes available to alter the estimate of permanent income. But such 'new' information must be essentially unexpected; otherwise, under the rational expectations hypothesis it would already be incorporated into the determination of permanent income. Such new information, therefore, is akin to a 'surprise' not previously anticipated. An unexpected dismissal from employment, or a debilitating long-term illness, for example, might be viewed as an unforeseen surprise event which will have a major impact on revising expectations of permanent income downwards. But surprises of this type will be unpredictable and in the aggregate random. Consequently, changes in consumption demand will be equally random and unpredictable.

The policy implications of this insight are also significant. Combining the permanent income hypothesis with rational expectations formation implies that only *unexpected* policy changes can influence consumption demands. The introduction of a tax which has long been anticipated (say, to service and redeem a growing national debt, for example) will have minor impact upon consumer demand because expectations of such a change have already been incorporated into current estimates of permanent income.

By the same token, however, unanticipated policy announcements by the government –if believed –will condition expectations about future permanent income and will therefore exert an immediate effect upon demand even prior to the enactment of the policy measure. To this extent, attempts to influence the expectations of the private sector, may be viewed as an additional policy instrument.

Endogenous Income Theories

Perhaps the most significant contribution of the normal income theories is the way in which they highlight the intertemporal nature of consumption and savings decisions. It is this characteristic of consumption behaviour which serves to break any mechanistic link between current consumption and current income. Although this is an important development – and, within the context of the life cycle and permanent income hypotheses, provided a basis for reconciling the findings of cross-section and time series studies – the approach still leaves one fundamental issue open, namely the precise relationship between consumption and wealth. In the life cycle hypothesis, for example, wealth enters the model as an explanatory variable – that is, as a determinant of current consumption. If, however, one gives a moment's thought to the determinants of wealth, it is clear that this is ultimately a function of consumption. A decision to save now presumably increases future wealth, which in turn increases future consumption. The implications of saving for the accumulation of wealth were not in fact explored by the normal income theories. A number of models which were subsequently developed, however, recognized and explored this interdependence (for example, Spiro, 1962; Ball and Drake, 1963; Clower and Johnson, 1968).

Microeconomic Foundations

Like the normal income hypotheses, the *endogenous income hypothesis* is microeconomic in spirit. It commences from the observation that wealth is endogenous, and that it is a choice variable. When an individual consumer makes a choice between consuming and saving, he is effectively choosing between consumption and wealth, since saving is an addition to wealth. Over a given period, therefore, the individual consumer (or, more accurately, the household) will strive to maximize utility, where utility is a function of consumption and wealth.

In figure 2.8 the objects of choice, consumption and wealth are plotted on the vertical and horizontal axes respectively. For any given household, the constraints on choice can be shown as given by a budget constraint (bc), the location of which is determined by the household's total resources. As long as consumption and wealth can be measured in similar units, this budget constraint must have a slope of -1 on the assumption that total resources are used on consumption or wealth (via saving) or some combination thereof, such as $C_1 W_1$.

Suppose the budget constraint is shifted from bc to $b'c'$ by allowing for, say, a secular growth in income. With a budget constraint of bc, the household is in equilibrium at point e. The desired amount of consumption of C_1 is taking place, and the desired amount of wealth of W_1 is held. Since *actual* wealth is equal to *desired* wealth, zero savings take place and current consumption exactly equals current income. If the

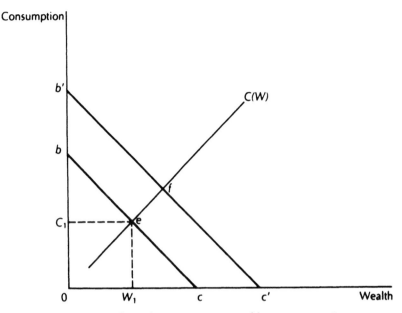

Figure 2.8 Effect of an increase in wealth on consumption

resources constraint were to shift to $b'c'$, when full adjustment has taken place such that actual wealth is equal to desired wealth, the household is settled at point f. When all such equilibrium points are joined up a *consumption-wealth locus* can be traced out. This gives the long-run relationship between consumption and wealth once full adjustments have taken place, and is analogous to the long-run consumption function. It has the characteristics of a zero intercept and a long-run savings ratio of zero. The configuration of the short-run consumption function can be explained by reference to disequilibrium situations.

Consider now figure 2.9. Suppose the initial position is that all households in a given wealth group are optimally adjusted at point e. Since this point is on the $C(W)$ locus, consumption is equal to income and the position is also on the $C = Y$ line in the right-hand segment. Suppose now that one household in the group experiences an increase in its income from bc to df. The resource constraint which it faces would shift as a consequence from bc to df and, once its optimal consumption and wealth combination were attained, equilibrium would be established at point k (and k' in the right-hand segment). In moving towards point k the household has to rearrange its consumption wealth portfolio. Initially, it would shift to point g with wealth of W_2 and income of Y_4. At the new level of income, however, actual wealth (W_2) is less than desired wealth (W_4) and savings would take place in an attempt to increase wealth holdings. Initially, savings would amount to eg. As wealth increases, consumption increases and the household moves out along the $C(W)$ locus towards equilibrium. An intermediate stage could be at point h where wealth has increased to W_3, consumption has increased to C_3 and savings amount to hj. If this is taken across to the right-hand segment, the income-consumption combination of Y_4C_3 is found. By connecting a series of such 'disequilibrium' points, a consumption function can be derived like C_1 in the right-hand segment which appears to fit the cross-section 'facts'. Thus the endogenous income approach views the estimated cross-section consumption function simply as a record of disequilibrium situations – in any given cross-section there will be house-

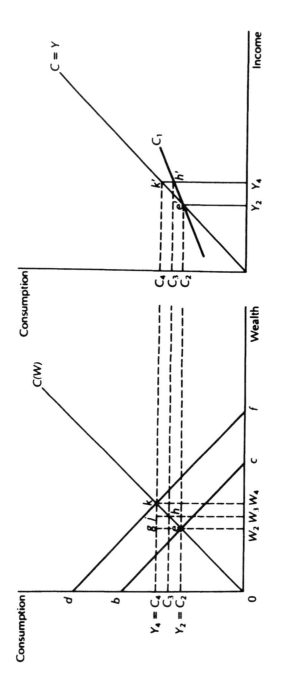

Figure 2.9 Endogenous income hypothesis

holds consuming less than current income as they save to accumulate wealth, whilst other households will be dissaving to decumulate their wealth holdings towards some equilibrium level. In the long run, once all adjustments have taken place consumption will equal income in each wealth/income class and the long-run consumption function will have a zero intercept.

Thus, like the normal income theories, the endogenous income approach down-grades the importance of current income as a determinant of current consumption. Also in line with the normal income theories, the approach has solid microfounda-tions. It diverges from the normal income theories, however, in focusing on the interre-lations between consumption, saving, wealth and income. In ascribing a central role to wealth as the principal determinant of consumption a variable is chosen which is *relatively* more precise than normal income.

Some Empirical Evidence

At an early point in this chapter we mentioned some empirical evidence on the con-sumption–income relationship, specifically the apparent contradiction between the short-run and long-run consumption functions. From the seminal work by Kuznets and others, a vast literature has now emerged. Comprehensive surveys of this evidence are provided by Mayer (1972) and Leighton Thomas (1984). In this section we shall sketch out the main features of the evidence.

One widely used approach to testing has been to examine the relationship between current consumption and current income. Friedman (1957), for example, followed this approach and estimated that the MPC out of current income was low (0.3), compared with an MPC out of permanent income which exceeded 0.8. Friedman's results have not gone unchallenged. For instance, Wright (1969) used a similar data set to Friedman and estimated a much smaller difference in the MPCs. On the other hand, as Darby (1974) has shown, also in the case of the USA, if consumption of durable goods is exclu-ded from consumers' expenditure, Friedman may even have underestimated the differ-ence between the two MPCs.

An alternative way of focusing on the relationship between current income and cur-rent consumption is to examine the impact of once-and-for-all changes in income, i.e. explore the impact on consumption of transitory income. This has been tested by refer-ence to a number of cases. Kreinin (1961), for example, assumed that reparation pay-ments from West Germany to Israel constituted a windfall. He then estimated the MPC out of this windfall and found it to be very low, much lower than the MPC out of permanent income. Modigliani and Steindel (1977), using a life cycle model, found that the short-run effect on consumption of an unexpected income tax rebate was also rel-atively small (though still positive). Blinder (1981) examined the same tax rebate (as well as others), and concluded that temporary tax changes have a much smaller effect on consumption than permanent tax changes (although, again they *do* have an impact). This evidence certainly seems to be consistent with the view that some notion of nor-mal income is more appropriate in explaining consumption behaviour than current income. As Mayer (1972) stated in an early survey of the empirical literature, 'While the more extreme ideas of the full permanent income and life cycle theory are invalidated, the tendency they describe . . . is . . . strongly confirmed' (p. 350).

One final point on empirical evidence is relevant. During the 1970s, savings propen-sities in many industrialized economies appeared to rise sharply. For instance, in the

UK the average propensity to save increased from about 8 per cent at the end of the 1960s to about 16 per cent at the end of the 1970s. Since, as we shall see in part III of this text, the 1970s were a period of accelerating inflation, many analysts suspected this may have had something to do with changes in the price level, and several studies addressed this issue. For example, one possible explanation is that consumers suffer from 'money illusion'. This is something we shall discuss in greater detail in part II. In the present context it could be used as follows: an increase in the price level is perceived by consumers, but they do not notice the commensurate increases in income and wealth. They erroneously believe real income to have fallen and reduce consumption accordingly. Although Branson and Klevorick (1969) provide evidence to support the money illusion hypothesis, it is not a satisfactory explanation. As we shall argue later, it is unappealing to contend that economic agents suffer from complete money illusion.

An alternative possibility was explored by Deaton (1978). He argued that it is the gap between actual and expected inflation which is relevant. In a period of accelerating inflation consumers may make errors in forecasting inflation and as a result they may confuse relative price changes and general price level changes. For example, when inflation turns out to be higher than expected, the consumer may interpret the increase in the price of some product currently being contemplated for purchase as a *relative* price change and as a result may refrain from purchasing. If this occurs across a wide range of consumers then an increase in the APS is recorded. Deaton (1978) offered some support for this hypothesis for the USA and UK, as did Townend (1976) for the UK.

Yet other possibilities have been explored, such as the possibility that increased inflation leads to increased uncertainty and this in turn raises savings. Whatever the precise mechanism, and this is still the subject of ongoing research, it seems that rising inflation does appear to reduce aggregate consumption.

Concluding Comments

The significance of having a clear idea of the determinants of aggregate consumption cannot be underestimated. Consumption expenditure is the largest component of aggregate expenditure. As such, variations in aggregate consumption exert a significant influence on aggregate expenditure. Clearly, if 'normal' income rather than 'current' income is the principal determinant of consumer expenditure, then aggregate expenditure is likely to be inherently more stable. Inevitably, much of the empirical evidence is conflicting. What does seem clear, however, is that some notion of normal income or wealth, apart from being intuitively more appealing than current income, performs quite well as the principal determinant of current consumption.

It has to be emphasized that this chapter has not made an exhaustive survey of possible explanatory factors. For example, only a little time has been spent examining the influence of price level changes and expectations of price level changes. Nor has much attention been devoted to interest rate changes. The way in which future consumption can become attractive relative to present consumption was discussed within the permanent income model. Basically, it was seen that savings increase following a rise in the interest rate because the return on wealth has increased. It should be noted, however, that the relationship need not be so simple, in part because of the diversity of assets which can be held as wealth, and in part because capital market imperfections may result in different interest rates applying to borrowers and lenders. Furthermore, interest rate expectations may also be important.

The acceleration of inflation in many developed market economies in recent years has resulted in considerable academic interest in the effect of changes in nominal variables like interest rates and the rate of inflation on aggregate consumption (see, for example, Pissarides, 1978 or Jackman and Sutton, 1982). The tools to explore fully these links have not yet been assembled here, and for the moment some poetic licence must be exercised in noting that evidence is growing that increases in the price level and increases in nominal interest rates do have a contractionary effect on aggregate consumption.

Further Reading

As with any other topic where the subject matter is controversial (which applies to most of the issues raised in this text), the best advice which can be given to students is look to the original sources. In this regard, chapters 6, 7, 8 and 9 of Keynes (1936) develop the principles of the absolute income hypothesis, whilst Duesenberry (1952) is the original statement of the relative income hypothesis. Friedman (1957) is the classic statement of the permanent income hypothesis, whilst the papers by Ando and Modigliani (1963), and Modigliani and Brumberg (1954) constitute the original sources of the life cycle hypothesis.

A useful introduction to the life cycle thesis is provided by Modigliani (1986). Clower and Johnson (1968) were responsible for initiating much work on the endogenous income approach. Edited extracts from Friedman (1957), Ando and Modigliani (1963) and Clower and Johnson (1968) are to be found in Surrey (1975).

An early survey on theories of aggregate consumption paying particular attention to the normal income theories is Farrell (1959). More recent survey articles are Mayer (1972) and Ferber (1973); the latter can be found in Korilas and Thorn (1979). Bruce Johnson (1971) provides a concise and clear review of the principal hypotheses (although since the book is now out of print it is not easy to obtain). A shorter review is offered by Leighton Thomas (1984).

A more recent survey of all the major issues, both micro and macro and including empirical evidence for the UK economy is to be found in Surrey (1989).

Good examples of some of the recent work on consumption behaviour and liquidity are Jackman and Sutton (1982) and Pissarides (1978).

The survey papers mentioned above give some details of empirical studies of consumption; for a couple of specific tests in the UK context see Bean (1978) and Davidson, Hendry, Srba and Yeo (1978). Life cycle models have been increasingly attacked in recent years on econometric grounds. See Hall (1978), Sargent (1978) and Eichenbaum, Hansen and Singleton (1984). A notable defence is provided by Miron (1986).

3

Aggregate Investment Expenditure

Investment outlays are among the less stable components in the national income identity, and fluctuations in investment are a major factor underlying fluctuations in the level of economic activity generally. A knowledge of the determinants of investment behaviour, therefore, is important not only to the understanding of national income determination but also to any satisfactory explanation of the business cycle. Moreover, there are many economists who attach considerable importance to the relationship between investment outlays (as a percentage of gross national product (GNP)) and the rate of economic growth of GNP, or who see investment as the vehicle for endogenous innovation and technical change. Unfortunately, despite the undisputed importance attached in investment generally, this is still one of the most unsettled areas in macroeconomics, and one where the available empirical findings are subject to substantial differences in interpretation.

One difficulty arises from the heterogeneous nature of investment spending – a heterogeneity which tends to be masked by the aggregative symbol I in the national income equation. Essentially, four components of the investment aggregate may be distinguished.

Business Investment in Plant and Equipment   This is undeniably the most important and most volatile element in the total of investment spending, and the one which most theories, implicitly or otherwise, attempt to explain. Normally such theories are stated in terms of constrained optimizing behaviour by rational investing agents. Moreover, they tend to assume the profit maximizing motive, and thus are couched in terms of investment being continued up to the point where additional financial returns are just adequate to compensate for the additional costs incurred. As will be appreciated from even a rudimentary knowledge of microtheory, firms may in fact pursue other goals which violate this general principle.

Investment Undertaken within the Public Sector   Investment by public bodies, nationalized industries and so forth, is in complete contrast to the first component. In public sector investment decisions, economic logic may take second place to political or social considerations. The desire to maintain employment, especially in depressed regions, or the attempt to minimize the adjustment problems associated with the secular decline of a traditional localized industry, may dictate an investment pattern at variance with that which would be undertaken by private enterprise. Since such investment is essentially political in nature it is unlikely to be explicable in terms of economic theory *per se.* However, it may either compete with investment undertaken within the private sector or be complementary to it; failure to take account of such interdependence may seriously flaw one's approach to private sector investment.

Residential Construction   The decision to purchase a house, and the type of house which one elects to buy, is influenced by a host of factors, amongst the most important of which are government tax and monetary policy. However, house purchase is not necessarily an act of investment from the viewpoint of the national economy; the latter is concerned only with the net addition to the total housing stock. This net addition, new houses minus houses scrapped and depreciation on existing houses, is such a comparatively small portion of total house buying that it is difficult to identify with precision the governing influences. Given the lag between construction and sale, however, it would seem that credit policy must exercise a major role. Also, since house building is predominantly a labour intensive activity, it is of interest to a government concerned with unemployment figures and trends.

Investment in Inventories   Economists have long since recognized the importance of investment in stocks and inventories – indeed, at one extreme, inventory cycles geared to fluctuations in short-term interest rates have been suggested as the major cause of the trade cycle. Rationally, the short-term rate of interest would appear to be an important determinant of the decision to carry stocks. However, other influences undoubtedly enter the picture. Thus, for example, the decision as to the optimum inventory size will depend upon estimates of future demand conditions which may ultimately be shown to be widely inaccurate. This inaccuracy is reflected in unintended investment or disinvestment in stocks and inventory which plays havoc with regression coefficients aimed at explaining *intended* inventory investment decisions.

Our primary concern in the present chapter is with the theory governing business investment in plant and equipment. Here the investment decision is often of a long-term nature, being dictated by the expectation of benefits accruing over an extended time horizon.

It is because of this time dimension that it becomes imperative to be able to evaluate future returns and compute their present value or worth in order to understand the rationale of an investment decision.

Approaches to Investment Theory

Broadly, there are two main approaches in considering the firm's investment decision. On the one hand, and along more traditional lines, it can be assumed that the firm estimates the future benefits obtainable from the possession of a capital asset and compares this with the asset's purchase price. If the comparison is favourable, it is then concluded that the firm will go ahead and *purchase* the asset outright. Whether the firm uses internal reserves or resorts to external sources of finance is really immaterial, although the relevant costs may differ. But the point to be emphasized here is that the decision taken by the firm involves outright ownership of the asset.

This indeed is the way that most firms undertake capital investment – by actually purchasing capital assets. And it is for this reason that it is the approach favoured in the present chapter. However, an alternative approach, which has found favour in the majority of intermediate textbook presentations, assumes that the firm, instead of purchasing a capital asset, decides to *rent* the services provided by the asset.

This approach, associated especially with the name of Dale Jorgenson (1963, 1967), has certain conceptual advantages. It makes the investment decision, for example, directly comparable with the decision to employ labour. A firm hires the services provided by labour; it does not – outside the context of a slave economy – actually own the labour inputs. Moreover, the decision as to how much capital services to rent then follows along standard microeconomic lines. Just as the profit maximizing firm will hire labour as long as the marginal revenue product exceeds the marginal wage cost, so too will the firm hire capital inputs as long as the marginal revenue product exceeds the marginal rental cost.

The beauty of this approach, however, lies in the fact that by adopting the same procedure in respect of the employment of capital and labour, we can examine the consequences of a change in comparative factor prices upon the investment decision. A firm's optimum capital stock will not be independent of the price paid to the cooperative input labour; an increase in the price of wage labour will, *ceteris paribus*, promote a substitution effect in favour of capital. Tacitly, we assume that the production function is continuous and that we can move along well-defined isoquants by infinitesimal amounts. It is this feature which identifies the Jorgenson approach as being in keeping with conventional neo-classical economics. Finally, of course, it must be admitted that there are some firms which do indeed choose to rent the services of capital assets – witness the popularity of car leasing agreements by business enterprise.

We will return to the Jorgenson approach in more detail later in this chapter. For the present, however, we will pursue the more traditional approach which accepts the dichotomy that firms purchase capital assets whilst they hire labour services. As we have already indicated, this is the way most firms actually behave in practice, which would appear justification enough. In addition, however, even if we were to accept that firms producing goods and services were to rent capital assets, this would merely postpone the ownership decision one stage back. Those firms in the business of leasing capital assets would still face the question of how many assets to acquire before they could commence to lease. Let us then approach the question of what is the optimum stock of capital assets to acquire.

The Cost of Capital and Investment

The Present Value of an Asset

Let a sum of money S_0 be invested at the market rate of interest i for a period of one year. At the end of the year the investment will be worth $S_0 + S_0 i$ or $S_0(1 + i)$. Let this amount be denoted as S_1, where the original *principal* was S_0 and the subscripts indicate the point in time. If the amount S_1 is now reinvested for a second year at the same rate of interest, it will subsequently be worth $S_1 + S_1 i = S_1(1 + i)$, written as S_2. But recall that S_1 is merely $S_0(1 + i)$; hence S_2 –the amount that the sum S_0 will be worth if invested for two years at the interest rate i – is simply equal to $S_0(1 + i)(1 + i) = S_0(1 + i)^2$. Proceeding in this way, a sum of money S_0 invested for t years will realize $S_t = S_0(1 + i)^t$.

Let the argument now be reversed and the following question posed. If one knew *with certainty* that one could receive a sum of money in, say, t years' time by making a given outlay today, what size of outlay would justify the future income receipt? Suppose, for example, that one could be sure of obtaining the amount S_3 in three years' time. Since $S_3 = S_0(1 + i)^3$, the amount S_0 invested at current interest rates would yield the sum S_3 after three years. S_0 is accordingly the *present value* of the amount S_3 to be received in three years' time, and it would be foolish to pay more than S_0 to obtain this future receipt. The present value of S_3 therefore is simply $S_3(1 + i)^3$; in general, the present value of a future receipt S_t to be received in t years' time is simply $S_t/(1 + i)^t$.

This is the essence of the investment decision –the determination of how much it is worthwhile to pay to obtain an asset which will yield a future income receipt. In practice of course the issues are more complex. To begin with, the future income receipt expected from the asset will not be known with certainty, and indeed its *expected value* may be highly speculative. This will be particularly the case if the income receipt is expected far into the future. Second, the above argument is implicitly stated in real terms with no allowance being made for future inflationary price movements. To the extent that inflation is anticipated, the present value of any future income receipt is accordingly reduced. Finally, the problem posed here is that of parting with a given sum of money today in order to receive a fixed sum at a finite date in the future. In practice, of course, the investment decision is more complex in that it involves the purchase of an asset which will yield successive income streams over the course of its expected useful life. Thus, in computing the present value V of any investment asset, it is required to estimate

$$V = \frac{Y_1}{(1 + i)} + \frac{Y_2}{(1 + i)^2} + \frac{Y_3}{(1 + i)^3} + \cdots \frac{Y_n}{(1 + i)^n} + \frac{J_n}{(1 + i)^n} \qquad (3.1)$$

where Y is the net income yield in the period of the subscript, n is the anticipated life of the asset and J is its scrap value. In this manner, it becomes possible to compute the present value of any investment asset, making allowance for conditions of uncertainty concerning net income yields, asset life and so on.

It should be clear from this formulation that distant income streams exercise a comparatively minor influence upon the present valuation of an asset and hence upon the ultimate investment decision. The following example may serve to illustrate this point. Consider an asset with a five-year life yielding a net income stream of £100 per annum and possessed of a scrap value of £50. With an interest rate of 10 per cent its computed present value will be given by

$$V = \frac{100}{(1 + 0.1)} + \frac{100}{(1 + 0.1)^2} + \frac{100}{(1 + 0.1)^3} + \frac{100}{(1 + 0.1)^4} + \frac{100}{(1 + 0.1)^5} + \frac{50}{(1 + 0.1)^5}$$
$$= 90.909 + 82.645 + 75.131 + 68.301 + 62.093 + 31.046$$
$$= 410.125 \qquad (3.2)$$

Thus the first year's income stream is worth approximately 50 per cent more than that of the fifth year; had the asset yielded an income of £100 in the tenth year its present value would have been £38.551 and in the twentieth year £14.863.

Now consider the same asset possessed of identical yields but assume the market rate of interest is but 5 per cent. Its computed present value is

$$V = \frac{100}{(1 + 0.05)} + \frac{100}{(1 + 0.05)^2} + \frac{100}{(1 + 0.05)^3} + \frac{100}{(1 + 0.05)^4} \frac{100}{(1 + 0.05)^5} + \frac{50}{(1 + 0.05)^5}$$
$$= 95.238 + 90.703 + 86.386 + 82.270 + 78.352 + 39.176$$
$$= 472.125 \qquad (3.3)$$

The halving of the rate of interest raises the present value of the asset – in this case by approximately 15 per cent. However, the point to be stressed here is that the augmentation of present values in both absolute and percentage terms is greater for the more distant income streams. The value of the fifth year's revenue yield, for example (as well as the potential scrap value) rises by more than 26 per cent compared with the augmentation in value of the first year's receipts of less than 5 per cent.

This analysis suggests that when interest rates are high there will be a marked preference for investment in short-lived assets; alternatively, policies to lower long-term interest rates may influence not only the volume but also the allocation of investable funds, with arguably beneficial impact upon long-term growth rates.

The foregoing has suggested that the present value of an asset is related to the expected net income yield to be derived from ownership of that asset. The question which remains is what determines the expected net income yield. Inevitably, a host of influences enter here, including psychological factors such as the state of business confidence, which may or may not be grounded on relevant economic criteria. Undoubtedly, however, one of the more objective influences will be the existing stock of the asset in question. If one is contemplating building a hotel upon the Aegean shore, one's expected return might well depend upon whether there existed other hotels in competition. Increasing the stock of an asset increases the potential supply of goods and services to be derived from that asset, and thus *ceteris paribus* reduces potential prices and anticipated revenue yields. Hence an inverse relationship might be postulated between the present value of an asset and the existing stock of such assets. Such a relationship is indicated in figure 3.1.

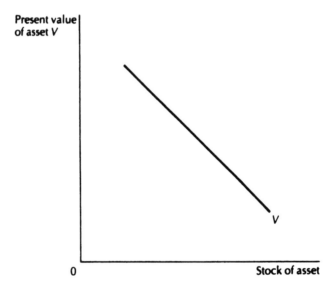

Figure 3.1 Present value of an asset in relation to the capital stock of the asset

The Decision to Invest

So far the concern has been with determining the present value of an investment asset – that is, what the asset is judged to be worth. Following Keynes (1936), this may be referred to as the *demand price*. But the decision to invest not only involves the demand price but also hinges upon the cost of acquiring the asset. Clearly, if the present value of an asset exceeds the cost of acquiring it, then it is rational to purchase the asset; equally, if the present value falls short of the purchase cost of the asset, then it would be foolish to acquire the asset. Thus, following marginalist principles and tacitly assuming profit maximizing behaviour, the proposition is approached that investment in any asset will be pushed to the point where the demand price or present value is just equated with its cost.

However, it is necessary to distinguish between an act of investment upon the part of an individual and investment from the point of view of society. As far as the individual is concerned, in deciding whether or not to 'invest' he weighs the demand price of an asset against its acquisition costs; in many cases the latter will refer to the sum needed to induce an existing investor to transfer ownership of the asset. The concern here, however, is with investment as it enters into the national income accounting identity, and consequently such transfers of existing second-hand assets are not relevant. By investment is meant the creation of newly produced assets by the capital goods industry, and thus the term 'cost of the asset' should be taken to refer to the price needed to induce the capital goods industry to produce an additional unit of the asset. Again, following Keynes, this cost may be termed the *supply price* of the asset.

A simple statement of investment behaviour may now be presented. If the demand price or present value of an asset, V, exceeds its supply price, X, it is rational to invest in the asset. On the other hand, if the demand price falls short of the supply price, investment is not warranted. If this argument is pursued to its logical conclusion, and avoiding complications arising from indivisibilities and so forth, it is evident that the optimal stock of any capital asset will be determined by the equation of its demand price with its supply price. This situation is portrayed in figure 3.2. The optimal situation is indicated by K^* where V equals X and net investment demand is zero. Before this level of the capital stock, V exceeds X, the actual capital stock falls short of the desired or optimal, and *net investment demand* is accordingly positive; beyond this level

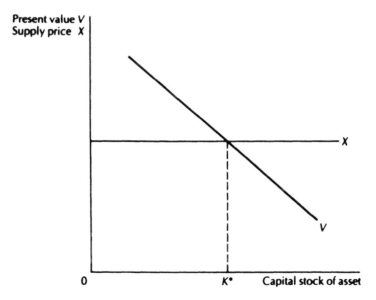

Figure 3.2 Determining the optimal stock of a capital asset

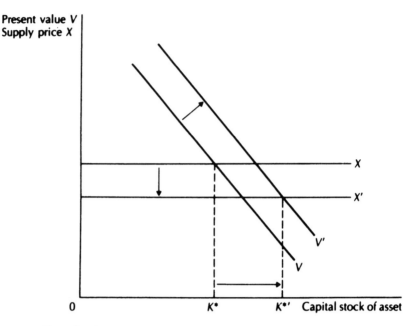

Figure 3.3 Effect of a decrease in interest rates on the optimal stock of a capital asset –
present value approach

of the capital stock, V is less than X, the actual capital stock is too large, and there will accordingly be incentives to disinvestment.[1]

It can now be understood why economists have long argued that investment spending will be inversely related to the rate of interest. Whilst the interest sensitivity of investment spending is a matter of some empirical dispute, there is no mistaking the underlying rationale of the assertion. A fall in the market rate of interest will, as has already been demonstrated arithmetically, raise the present value of the asset reflected in the upward shift of the demand price. Equally, however, a decrease in interest rates may reduce costs in the capital goods industries and generate a fall in the prevailing supply price. Both influences serve to generate a new optimal level of the capital stock in question, as illustrated by figure 3.3.

The Marginal Efficiency of Capital

An alternative but not identical way of approaching the investment decision was proposed by Keynes with his concept of the *marginal efficiency of capital* (MEC). Essentially, the marginal efficiency of capital, r, is that rate of discount which will equate the anticipated net income streams to be derived from the asset to the supply price of the asset. More formally, if X is again the supply price of the asset,

$$X = \frac{Y_1}{(1+r)} + \frac{Y_2}{(1+r)^2} + \frac{Y_2}{(1+r)^3} + \ldots + \frac{Y_n}{(1+r)^n} + \frac{J_n}{(1+r)^n} \tag{3.4}$$

---

1 The horizontal supply price of capital schedule derives from the assumption of perfect capital markets. A departure from this assumption – by assuming, for example, that greater risk is involved in supplying a large amount of capital to one firm as opposed to smaller amounts to many firms, or by invoking differences in physical or subjective supply costs – would be sufficient to generate an upward-sloping schedule.

Whatever the value of the income streams and whatever the cost of the asset, there is some rate of discount r which can be chosen so as to equate the two. This is what Keynes chose to call the marginal efficiency of capital.

It should be clear that the marginal efficiency of capital is in some sense a rate of return upon the asset in question. To illustrate, consider the simplest possible example, namely that of an asset which costs £1,000 and lasts for but one year whereupon it falls to pieces with no possible scrap value. If during the course of its short life it returns, say, £1,300 net of labour, materials, and similar 'user' costs, then its marginal efficiency of capital would be derived from

$$£1,000 = \frac{£1,300}{(1+r)}$$

and $r = 0.3$. Alternatively, its rate of return over cost may be said to be 30 per cent. As long as the computed marginal efficiency of capital is positive, it implies that net revenue yields are sufficient to cover the supply price of the asset. However, this is not sufficient to justify the act of investment, for the money allocated to the purchase of the asset could equally have been loaned out at the market rate of interest. Only if the marginal efficiency of capital is in excess of the going market rate of interest would investment be justified. The rational investment decision, therefore, requires a comparison of the marginal efficiency of capital with the current rate of interest, and the logic of this argument leads to the conclusion that

> the actual rate of current investment will be pushed to the point where there is no longer any class of capital asset of which the marginal efficiency exceeds the current rate of interest. (Keynes, 1936, p. 136)

Diagrammatically, this situation is portrayed in figure 3.4, where once again K^* is the indicated optimal capital stock.[2] The effect of a decrease in the rate of interest, i, may be examined. Clearly, the interest rate line is lowered suggesting a positive expansion of investment, but if reduced interest charges also lower the supply price of the asset, this movement is reinforced by an upward shift in the marginal efficiency schedule. The broken lines illustrate this combined influence and indicate a new equilibrium at K^*.

The marginal efficiency approach may be considered as an alternative to the direct comparison of present value and supply price, and the situation $V > X$ will often imply the condition $r > i$. However, it is important to note that the two approaches will not always give the same result, at least from the vantage-point of the individual investor choosing between two alternative investment decisions. This arises because, whilst an interest rate change will not affect the marginal efficiency of capital in any systematic way,[3] it will exert differing effects upon the present values of assets with differing time profiles, as has already been noted.[4]

---

2 The marginal efficiency of capital schedule is drawn with a negative slope with respect to the capital stock for precisely the same reasons as applied to the concept of present value. As the capital stock is increased so too is the potential supply of goods and services derived from the asset, with a consequent fall in their prices and hence in the expected net revenue yield.

3 Indeed, an interest rate change will leave the MEC schedule unchanged if it does not affect the supply price of capital assets.

4 Keynes was clearly not aware of this discrepancy and believed that his marginal efficiency of capital concept was simply a restatement of Irving Fisher's rate of return over cost. See Keynes, 1936, pp. 140–1. For comment on the distinctions see especially Alchian (1955).

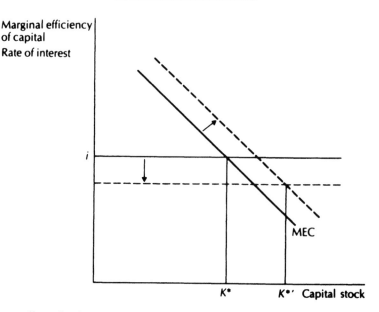

Figure 3.4 Effect of a decrease in interest rates on the optimal stock of a capital asset –
marginal efficiency of capital approach

The Rate of Investment

Thus far the concern has been with formulating a simple rule to determine the optimal
amount of any capital asset from the viewpoints of both the individual investor and the
macroeconomy as a whole. In equilibrium, no asset would have a demand price in
excess of its supply price or a marginal efficiency of capital in excess of the rate of interest. What has not been done, however, is to indicate how the economy makes the adjustment from one indicated equilibrium to another. Consider again figure 3.3, where the
initial demand and supply prices of a capital asset suggest the optimal amount of the
asset to be K^*. Suppose that this indicated optimum actually prevails, so that net
investment demand is zero. Now assume a fall in the market rate of interest. It may be
supposed that this raises the present value of the asset in question as well as reducing
the supply price, and the new indicated optimal stock of the asset is accordingly $K^{*\prime}$.
Thus the actual capital stock now lags behind the optimal or desired stock by the
amount $K^* - K^{*\prime}$.

Is there any satisfactory way in which this discrepancy in the desired *stock* of
capital can be translated into an investment *flow* demand? What is needed is a statement to explain the size of the investment flow demand by which the capital stock is
enlarged or contracted. Without such a statement there can be no acceptable theory of
investment as such but only a theory of optimum capital stocks. It is at this point that
certain conceptual and empirical difficulties are encountered that are not readily
resolved.

Until now it has been assumed, albeit tacitly, that the supply price of capital assets
was given as a datum existing independently of the actual speed of the capital stock
adjustment process. For any individual firm this is probably acceptable, as it can purchase from existing inventories and stocks, but for the economy as a whole it is probably false. More reasonably, the supply price of capital assets will be positively related

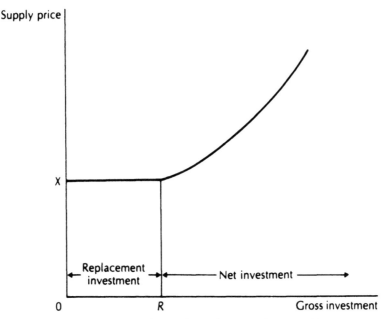

Figure 3.5 Supply price of capital in relation to the rate of investment

to the speed of adjustment.[5] This situation is illustrated in figure 3.5, where the capital goods industry is assumed to be geared to meeting normal replacement demands, OR, at a constant cost X. Beyond this point, however, positive net investment is assumed to encounter progressively rising marginal costs and hence a rising supply price positively related to the rate of investment.

The salient features of the analysis contained in figures 3.3 and 3.5 are now combined. In figure 3.6, where the actual capital stock is denoted by K^* whilst the optimal stock is $K^{*\prime}$, the demand price of an *incremental* unit of the asset is indicated by $v£$ whilst the supply price of the incremental unit is $x£$. This incremental unit will accordingly be produced within the current period. As the capital stock is adjusted, however, the demand price of successive incremental units will decline whilst, under present assumptions, the supply price will rise. Clearly the indicated equilibrium is at K^e where demand and supply prices are equated. Thus, the optimal amount of investment during the current period is $K^e - K^*$, and similar reasoning will imply a determinate optimal investment strategy in succeeding periods with the positive portion of the curve now emanating from K^e. In this manner the gap between the initial actual and desired capital stock will be progressively eliminated over succeeding investment periods, with investment demand in the current period always being less than in the immediately preceding period.[6]

It is now a simple step to generate the investment demand curve. In the initial equilibrium situation the desired and actual capital stock were equated and consequently the level of investment demand was zero. With the decline in the interest rate a first-period

---

5 Were it not, investors would seek to make indicated adjustments instantaneously, giving rise to infinite rates of investment and disinvestment demand. In such circumstances, actual investment spending would be determined by the capacity of the capital goods industry on the one hand and by the rate of depreciation and obsolescence on the other.

6 Strictly, under present assumptions, the gap between K^* and $K^{*\prime}$ will tend to but never actually attain zero.

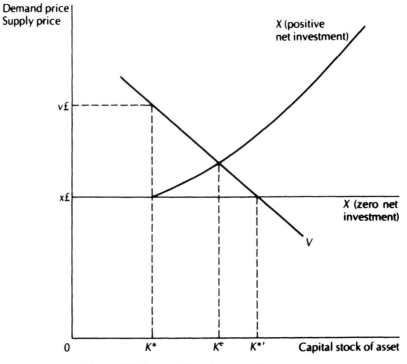

Figure 3.6 Determining the rate of investment

investment demand equal to $K^* - K^e$ was generated. Thus a normal investment demand curve is obtained, inversely related to the rate of interest. In successive periods, the level of investment progressively falls as the gap between actual and desired capital stocks is reduced. Ultimately, as a new equilibrium is regained the level of

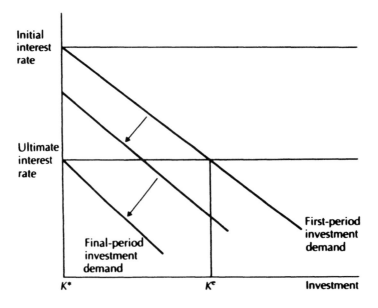

Figure 3.7 Investment demand function

investment demand falls to zero. Thus a fall in the rate of interest will generate a positive and determinate investment demand curve which over succeeding periods is progressively shifted inwards until it ultimately coincides with the vertical axis at existing interest rates. This process of adjustment from one equilibrium to another is shown in figure 3.7.

The foregoing analysis has indicated that investment involves two distinct issues: first, the need to determine the desired capital stock, and second, the need to determine the pace at which any indicated adjustment to the desired capital stock will occur. It follows, *inter alia*, that monetary policy must be evaluated in terms of this dual context. Thus, for example, a given interest rate change may have a profound impact upon the desired capital stock but exert a minor influence upon the level of current investment spending. It is the latter consideration which is paramount in short-term stabilization policy.

Dynamic Theories of Investment Behaviour

Admittedly, the previous analysis has been static and has dealt with interest rate changes under the assumption of *ceteris paribus*. This implies that once an equilibrium has been attained, net investment will return to zero and all investment spending will be replacement investment only.

However, if a growing economy is postulated, then the argument is modified substantially. Rising national income enhances sales, profits and, more importantly, expectations of future sales and profits. In the context of the former analysis this would imply a rising of discounted present values or the demand prices of capital assets and justify positive net investment. If the economy were growing in a steady state equilibrium this would generate a steady state growth of net investment spending. Although the existence of steady states cannot be assumed, it can none the less be asserted that investment will be positively related to movements in national income.

There are a number of theories which relate investment to income levels. By far the most well known, and certainly one of the oldest, is the so-called *accelerator theory* of investment.[7] This postulates a fixed technical relationship between capital and output. An increase in final demand justifies more output and hence calls forth more net investment. A simple example will illustrate the essence of the doctrine and also highlight its limiting assumptions. Assume that the capital stock consists of 10 units, each with a life of five years and each producing ten units of final output per year. Then in a steady state situation final demand would be equal to 100 units of output, net investment would be zero and replacement investment would equal 2 units per year. In such a situation, suppose final demand rises to 120 units. Given a fixed capital output ratio, this would require 12 units of capital, implying net investment equal to 2 units. A 20 per cent increase in final demand, therefore, is responsible for generating a 100 per cent increase in total investment spending. Moreover, assume that in the following period final demand remains unchanged at its new level; there is no further justification for net investment, and in this example gross investment spending would now be halved although final demand has not fallen. Thus the accelerator theory relates the level of investment spending to *changes* in the rate at which output is changing, and in large measure goes a long way to explain the unstable nature of investment outlays.

---

7 The first attempts to formulate a coherent accelerator theory of investment appear to have been by Bickerdike (1914) and Clark (1917).

The elementary model outlined above is altogether too mechanistic to furnish a precise insight into investment behaviour in the real world. It assumes away the existence of stocks and inventories and the possibility of excess capacity. It assumes that there are no constraints upon new investment activity, whether financial or otherwise, and further it postulates an automatic response to temporary fluctuations in consumer spending without any lags to establish the permanency of the demand change. None the less, it goes some way to explain the volatility of investment spending, and the acceleration principle is an indispensable element (in some form or another) in almost any modern explanation of the business cycle. Its dynamic nature derives from the fact that investment in the current period depends upon the state of demand in the immediately preceding period. Formally, the elementary model outlined may be specified as

$$I_t = \alpha(S_t - S_{t-1}) \tag{3.5}$$

where I is net investment, S is final sales demand and the subscript denotes the period involved. If it is assumed that final sales demand is proportional to national income, the more usual formulation of the acceleration principle is obtained:

$$I_t = \beta(Y_t - Y_{t-1}) \tag{3.6}$$

In this formulation the accelerator coefficient (α or β) is taken to be a constant, and the indicated investment spending is assumed to be completed within one period, permitting net investment to return to zero if there is no further change in demand.

Both of these are fundamental shortcomings of the naïve or simple accelerator model. A *constant accelerator coefficient* implicitly assumes that the firm is operating at full capacity and will respond to an increase in demand with new investment. It goes without saying that if a firm has spare capacity then this will be utilized prior to any new investment. In an economic climate with many firms operating at less than full capacity, one would imagine that as and when an upturn occurred it would be some time before investment responded as idle capacity was used up. Furthermore, even if the firm is operating at full capacity, there are bound to be lags involved in the reaction to any perceived change in demand. New capacity is unlikely to be planned, let alone investable funds committed, until such time as the firm is confident that the change in demand is permanent rather than transient. Even when a decision to commit funds has been taken, there are inevitably supply lags of the type mentioned in connection with the Keynesian marginal efficiency of capital approach.

These difficulties can be relatively easily accommodated. For example, one could allow for spare capacity by rewriting equation 3.6 as

$$I_t = \beta(Y_t - Y_{t-1}) - \delta K_t \tag{3.7}$$

where δK_t is the proportion of the capital stock which is currently idle. Likewise, lags can be accommodated by permitting adjustment to occur over a number of periods. This more realistic version of the acceleration principle is sometimes referred to as the *flexible accelerator model*.

According to this formulation, which enjoys a certain amount of empirical support, investment is geared to the difference between the actual and the optimal capital stock with the latter being linked to income growth. Thus,

$$I_t = \alpha(K^* - K_{t-1}) \tag{3.8}$$

and $K^* = \gamma Y$. Rising income generates an increase in the optimal capital stock and thus raises net investment outlays. It will be noted that the adjustment to the optimal

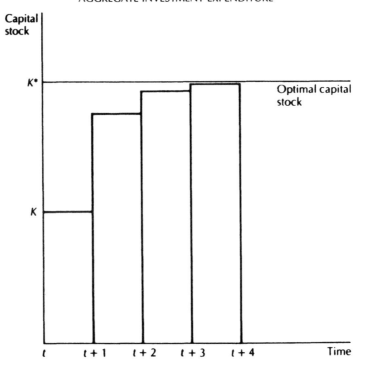

Figure 3.8 Investment with the flexible accelerator

capital stock occurs with progressively declining magnitudes of net investment, in keeping with the static analysis of the capital stock adjustment process. The process is shown in figure 3.8. At time t the optimal capital stock, K^*, is assumed to be double the actual capital stock, K. With an accelerator coefficient equal to 0.75, three-quarters of this deficiency will be made up over the succeeding period t_1, three-quarters of the remainder (that is, three-sixteenths) will be made up in period t_2, and so forth. As before, the actual capital stock asymptotically approaches but never actually attains the optimum.

Another conceptual problem with the fixed accelerator coefficient, which strictly speaking is not accommodated by the flexible accelerator in any systematic manner, is that it does not allow for changes in production techniques due to variations in relative factor prices. In microeconomic terms it assumes, in effect, that movement from one isoquant to another takes place along a linear expansion path. Intuitively, this is not an attractive or appealing proposition; it denies the possibility of adjustments towards the optimal capital stock being relatively labour saving or capital saving or, more accurately, it precludes switches from one to the other. It is the neglect of this aspect of investment behaviour which has encouraged the modern neo-classical approach.

The Neo-classical Analysis of Investment

As indicated, the neo-classical approached associated with the name of Jorgenson (1963, 1967) emphasizes the cost of capital relative to other factor inputs rather than the cost of capital *per se*. We can illustrate this approach in the following way.

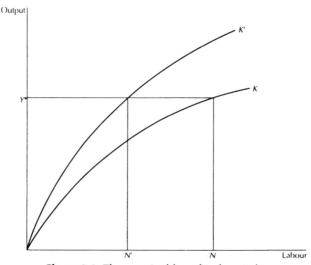

Figure 3.9 The marginal benefit of capital

We assume that the firm will rent capital as long as the marginal benefit of doing so exceeds the marginal cost of renting – the rental charge. The marginal benefit of renting capital can be identified with the financial savings obtained by the savings on alternative factor inputs. Consider figure 3.9. The production function associated with the existing capital stock, K, indicates that the amount of labour required to produce the desired output level Y^* is the amount N. Now, if the firm decides to rent more capital – say, K' – the production function will be shifted upwards as indicated and the amount of labour required to produce Y^* falls to N'. The marginal benefit of the additional unit of capital is simply $(N - N')W$, where W is the wage paid to labour. Again, the marginal benefit of capital is not independent of the wage paid to the cooperative input labour.

Diminishing returns to capital implies that the marginal benefit will decline as the firms hires a larger capital stock. This is shown in figure 3.10, which also illustrates that if the rental price of capital is constant at R, then the optimal capital stock for the firm to rent is K^*. An increase in the wage rate, *ceteris paribus*, will shift the position of the marginal benefit curve to the right and so increase the optimal amount of capital that the firm should rent.

The above is a perfectly consistent statement as to how the individual firm will behave in determining the amount of capital that it should ideally rent. However, it will be appreciated, that in itself, it says nothing about *investment* as such. A firm may rent capital assets given up by another firm in the economy without any change in the actual capital stock of the economy. In order to explain the investment decision, we need to determine the factors which govern the leasing firm's decision to purchase new capital assets. Not surprisingly, this decision will hinge upon the rental price of capital assets.

The rental price of capital assets, R, will be determined by the market within the context of competition. Broadly, we can identify four elements entering into its determination. First, there is the purchase price of producing a new capital asset – the supply price, P^k. Secondly, there is the expected rate of depreciation, d, upon the asset over the rental period, normally a year. Thirdly, there is the real rate of interest, i.

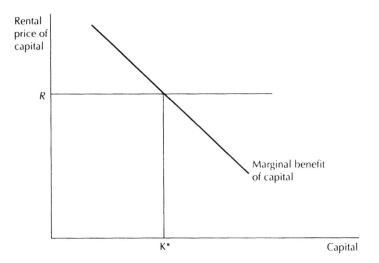

Figure 3.10 Marginal benefit and optimal capital stock

Finally, we need to take account of any expected change in the *relative* price of capital assets during this period, ΔP^k, since this will impinge upon the comparative value of the asset, or its scrap value when it is regained by the leasing company. Thus, we may write the rental charge as

$$R = P^k(i + d) - \Delta p^k \qquad (3.9)$$

The right-hand side of equation (3.9) merely sums up the costs borne by the leasing firm over the rental period. Thus, for example, if the purchase price of the asset were £1,000, the interest rate 10 per cent, the expected rate of depreciation 20 per cent, and if the relative price of the asset were expected to *fall* by £100 over the rental period, then the costs to the leasing firm would be £400. The assumption underlying equation 3.9 is that competition will force the market rental charge (R) into equality with these costs. If the market rental charge exceeded these costs, more leasing firms would be induced to enter the market and drive rental charges down. Conversely, if the rental charge fell short of normal costs, leasing firms would be induced to leave the industry and rental charges would rise.

Once determined, the rental price governs the decision to invest in capital assets. Any investment project earning more than the rental price is worth undertaking. Given diminishing returns to the capital stock, at the margin investment in new projects will be carried to the point where earnings are brought into line with the rental price. It is for this reason that it is immaterial whether firms choose to purchase or rent capital assets; both approaches will imply the same optimal stock of capital.[8] Likewise, once the optimal capital stock has been determined, both approaches imply a lagged adjustment to the new optimal level in accordance with maximizing principles. Regardless of whether firms rent or buy capital assets, the rental price of capital can be viewed as the crucial economic variable underpinning the investment decision.

---

8 A neat formal demonstration of this point is provided by Hall and Taylor (1993), pp. 431–2.

From Jorgenson's standpoint, the crucial variable in the determination of the optimal capital stock is the real user cost of capital relative to the real wage rate. Other things being equal, increases in the real wage rate relative to the real user cost of capital will result in a more capital intensive production technique, and therefore increases in the optimal capital stock. The approach is compelling in its simplicity and, at the very least, has helped redirect attention towards the role of relative factor prices. Moreover, changes in taxation may impinge upon comparative prices. Investment tax credits, investment allowances and so forth are all factors which serve to lower the rental value of capital and thus stimulate investment.

Investment and Tobin's q

The neo-classical theory of investment focuses upon the rental price of capital, R, in relation to the marginal benefit of capital MB_k. If the ratio $MB_k/R > 1$, the implication is that the firm will wish to increase its capital stock and its demand for capital assets will be positive. Conversely, a ratio of $MB_k/R < 1$ would imply the opposite, and firms would seek to reduce their capital stock. Either way, the adjustment process is a separate decision involving the choice of time period over which the adjustment is to be carried out.

An interesting variant of this approach, proposed by Tobin (1969), links investment directly to variations in the stock market. Tobin's thesis differs from the neo-classical in one important respect. Whereas the latter sees investment in two stages – namely, determination of the optimal capital stock followed by the adjustment process – Tobin's formula implies a single determination of the optimal amount of investment at any given point in time. In this approach, the crucial ratio is that between the value of a firm's capital assets as determined by the valuation of the stock market and the replacement cost of acquiring identical capital. More formally,

$$q = \frac{\text{Market value of existing capital}}{\text{Replacement cost of existing capital}}$$

If this q ratio is in excess of one it implies that the stock market is valuing existing capital at more than its replacement cost. *Ceteris paribus*, this should promote new investment, since the purchase of new capital assets will raise the capital value of the company. Conversely, a q ratio of less than one would imply that new investment should not be undertaken since this would diminish the capital value of the company. Indeed, in this situation it would not be sensible to replace existing assets as they wear out. If q were equal to one, a firm's investment would consist solely of replacement investment equal to the rate of depreciation of its capital assets.

Tobin's thesis thus suggests that the stock market may have a major influence upon the volume of investment spending and hence upon the macroeconomy. Moreover, the relationship does not depend upon lags. A sudden fall in the stock market evaluation of a company should imply an immediate fall in investment spending.

Although perhaps not immediately obvious at first glance, Tobin's q theory is closely related to the neo-classical model outlined above. This is because the stock market evaluation reflects the profitability of the firm's capital. Thus, ideally, the market value of a firm's shares would be such that the return to those shares – the ratio of the marginal benefit of the firm's capital to the market evaluation of the worth of that capital – would be equal to returns available elsewhere – say, to the market interest rate i. Accordingly, market value of a company's assets should be given by

$$MV = MB_k/i$$

In like manner, we would expect a relationship to exist between the price of capital and the rental rate of capital. More formally, the rental price of capital, R, should be equal to the price of capital, P_k. i. Hence, combining the above, we have

$$P_k \cdot i = R$$
$$MV = MB_k/i$$

Therefore,

$$i = R/P_k/i = MB_k/MV$$

and

$$MV/P_k = MB_k/R$$

But the left-hand side of this equation is simply Tobin's q, whereas the right-hand side is simply the neo-classical ratio of the marginal benefit to rental price of capital. Essentially, therefore, the two are identical in long-run equilibrium.

Unfortunately, the empirical evidence concerning the validity of Tobin's q is a subject of debate. One difficulty springs from the fact that a company's capital will be of different vintages and yet the stock market evaluation will refer to the total capital of the firm. That is to say, it will provide an *average* valuation of a firm's capital, which may understate the true value of new investment in more recent assets. An OPEC-induced oil price hike, for example, might diminish the overall stock market evaluation of the British motor car industry, whilst simultaneously raising the rate of return on new investment in smaller, more fuel-efficient economy cars.

The Importance of Profit and Retained Earnings

Implicit in the accelerator analysis is the notion that profits, or the expectation of profits, is an essential ingredient in the investment decision. Certain commentators have refined this notion to focus upon one element of profits – namely, *retained earnings* – as being a crucial determinant in the volume of investment spending. The reason is that firms will have a strong preference to finance investment out of retained earnings, as opposed to using debt finance or issuing new equity. The (imputed) cost of using retained earnings will be less, often substantially less, than the cost of borrowing in the capital market whilst the issue of new equity suggests a weakening of overall control by increasing the number of shareholder votes. Retained earnings are equal to net profits (after meeting provision for depreciation needs) less any tax payments to government or dividend payment to shareholders. One policy implication of the analysis is that any factor increasing the size of retained earnings, such as tax cuts or more generous depreciation allowances, may have a sizeable impact on investment outlays.

This situation is illustrated in figure 3.11, which reverts to the Keynesian marginal efficiency of capital approach. Although it has previously been indicated that this approach is logically inferior to the discounted present value approach, it does possess one expositional virtue in *explicitly* including the current cost of funds in the determination of the optimal capital stock. In figure 3.11, the cost of using internal funds is i_i and the cost of employing external funds is i_e. If internal funds are limited to ox, the optimal capital stock is shown to be K^*; with unlimited internal funds the optimal

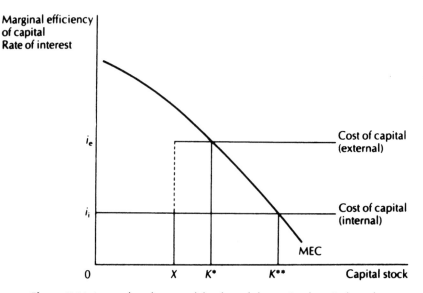

Figure 3.11 Internal and external funds and the optimal capital stock

capital stock would be K^{**}. The size of retained earnings, therefore, may be an important determinant of the desired capital stock but of itself it does not specifically indicate anything about the nature of investment demand –that is, the speed of adjustment to the desired capital stock. For this, some other hypothesis is needed, such as the flexible accelerator model briefly outlined earlier.

Some Policy Implications

Various possible determinants of investment behaviour have been indicated, and it is now possible to take stock and describe, if only briefly, the distinct policy stances arising from the analysis. For this purpose, the classification originally proposed by Jorgenson and Siebert (1968) is followed. Competing theories are denoted as

(1)   Neo-classical theories

(2)   Keynesian-oriented (accelerator/expected profit) theories

(3)   Liquidity (retained earnings) theories.

Neo-classical theories are predictably marginalist in approach and view the cost of capital, relative to other factor inputs, as crucial in the investment decision. Markets are assumed to clear, and profit maximizing behaviour requires that firms seek to maximize their present values. The fundamental conclusion of these models is that the demand for investment goods depends upon the cost of capital. The principal objection to neo-classical theory rests upon the premise that the demand for investment goods cannot be derived from the profit maximizing theory of the firm. Following the stock/flow distinction between capital and investment first noted by Lerner (1944), it is argued that finite variations in interest rates will *ceteris paribus* generate finite variations in the desired capital stock which in turn will imply either *infinite* rates of investment or disinvestment or zero investment demand in the condition of equilibrium.

There is accordingly only one rate of interest consistent with a finite investment demand and that demand is purely replacement demand. It is difficult to construct a worthwhile theory of investment upon such a premise. Even if it is possible to derive a meaningful investment demand function from the conventional theory of the firm, as Jorgenson (1967) insists, by adopting the thesis that the firm pursues a continuous optimal path of capital accumulation, significant policy conclusions do not necessarily follow. The importance of changes in relative prices, occasioned by monetary changes operating upon the rate of interest or fiscal changes upon the user cost of capital, will depend upon the elasticity of substitution of the aggregate production function.[9] It is generally conceded that the value of this coefficient will lie between zero and one. A value close to one will imply that an interest rate change, for example, will exert a significant impact upon investment demand, whereas an elasticity of substitution coefficient close to zero will imply that comparative factor prices changes exert but minimal effect.

Keynesian-oriented theories posit that interest rate changes and relative factor price changes have a minor effect in comparison with changing profit expectations associated with the uncertain level of future demand. This indeed appears to be Keynes's emphasis in his celebrated defence of the *General Theory* (Keynes, 1937a). To the extent that future profit expectations disproportionately reflect the current state of affairs, this contention would appear to lend support to the accelerator theory. The policy implication is that investment can be stimulated by suitable demand management policies.

The neo-classical thesis suggests that price flexibility, and especially comparative price flexibility, fulfils an important role in determining the investment decision. Policies which promote competition and allow free movement of labour and capital are thus important to the efficient allocation of investable funds. Keynesian-oriented policies, on the other hand, tend to question the significance of comparative factor price flexibility on grounds of empirically observed price rigidities.

A compromise position which straddles these two opposing schools of thought suggests that interest rates and relative prices are important in determining the desired equilibrium capital stock, whereas the level of aggregate demand together with profit expectations remains a powerful tool.

Concluding Comments

In this chapter a variety of approaches to the determination of investment has been considered: these approaches emphasize in particular either the role of output changes

---

9 The elasticity of substitution measures the responsiveness of the change in factor combinations in response to the change in comparative factor prices. It can be represented as

$$E_s = \frac{d(L/K)}{d(r/w)} \frac{(r/w)}{(L/K)}$$

where L and K are the labour and capital inputs and w and r are their respective prices per unit of time. In the mathematically convenient (and hence frequently invoked) Cobb–Douglas constant returns production function

$$Q = AL^{\alpha}K^{1-\alpha}$$

the elasticity value is equal to one, so that as relative factor prices alter, exactly compensatory changes occur in factor proportions leaving respective income shares constant.

(like the accelerator approach) or some aspect of the cost of capital. As was seen in the final section there is a certain amount of empirical support which can be advanced in support of both factors. This should not be read as evidence of inconclusiveness since both may have a role to play. Some notion of the cost of capital is clearly relevant to the determination of the optimal capital stock, with variations in output and profit being more relevant to the analysis of adjustments when there is some discrepancy between the actual and optimal capital stocks.

Further Reading

Keynes's (1936) analysis of the marginal efficiency of capital approach to investment remains one of the clearest outlines of the basic principles involved. Although the acceleration principle was first formally identified by Clark (1917), Eckaus (1953) is a neat statement of the theorem. Knox (1952) provided a lucid and thorough critique of the simple accelerator model. Flexible accelerator models have been developed and refined over the past fifteen years or so. Jorgenson (1967) is usually credited with the seminal contribution to the neo-classical approach to investment.

Surveys of empirical studies of investment behaviour are available in Jorgenson (1971) and Lund (1971). A concise (if inevitably terse) survey of theoretical and empirical studies of investment is given in Junankar (1972).

A useful collection of readings is provided by Helliwell (1976). More recent contributions include Clark (1979), Summers (1981) and Taylor (1982). The latter are of interest in invoking a rational expectations approach to the question of anticipated changes in investment incentives. An earlier influential article dealing with the influence of taxes upon investment behaviour is that of Hall and Jorgenson (1967). Tobin's q theory originates with Tobin (1969). Later discussion is provided by Tobin and Brainard (1977), Hayashi (1982), and Abel (1985). Empirical findings are summarized by Summers (1981).

4

The Government Sector

Of all the sectors making up the macroeconomy, the government sector ranks as both the most important and in many respects the least susceptible to economic analysis. The importance of government in influencing the aggregate economy cannot be underestimated and it stems from a combination of the following factors.

Size   The sheer size of the government sector means that virtually any government decision will impinge upon the economy at large. The government is a substantial employer of labour and hence the adoption of a given stance upon public sector pay will have repercussions upon private sector pay bargaining. The government will also exercise considerable discretion in matters of timing when meeting backdated pay settlements, for example, and thus will be able to time such payments so as to exert their most favourable macroeconomic impact. Finally, the government is the prime example of a monopsonistic buyer and is able to command substantial discounts in its buying policies which inevitably impinge upon contracts in the private sector.

Production and Consumption   The government sector plays a major role in both producing and consuming national output. It is therefore of considerable importance not only as a constituent of aggregate demand but also in supplying resources to the private sector. In particular, its pricing policy for public sector services and the output of nationalized undertakings will have major implications for private sector profitability. In this connection, it may be noted that the price index for public sector output and services often deviates substantially from general price indices invoked to measure overall inflation.

Regulatory Powers   Third, the government exercises considerable regulatory powers which often imply substantial compliance costs for the private sector. Stipulations about safety procedures, pollution control, product liability legislation and so forth may exercise considerable influence, especially upon exporters competing in international markets where such restrictions may not apply. Other legislation, such as employment protection legislation, termination agreements and legislation determining the rights and obligations of trade unions, carry obvious implications for private sector employment costs. Recently, this issue has taken on renewed significance in the United Kingdom where membership of the European Union and the harmonization proposals associated with the formation of the single market raised the prospect of rising costs for British industry. Alarmed by the already increasing unemployment levels, the British government refused to sign the so-called Social Chapter of the celebrated Maastricht conference – as well as avoiding any definite commitment to a single European currency which would curtail macroeconomic autonomy.

Policy Control Of principal importance is the fact that the government shapes and dictates the course of macroeconomic policy and is able to impose coercive penalties upon the other sectors in the form of tax and interest rate changes. Alternatively, of course, the government may choose to pursue a monetary and fiscal stance deemed favourable to the private sector. Of fundamental importance will be the government's strategy on regional policy, or upon the adoption of exchange controls, import controls and so forth. Above all, the government more than any other economic sector will exert a dominant influence upon the formation of expectations.

Debt Funding Although any economic sector is able to enter into debt obligations, the government sector, at least at the central government level, is unique in being able to fund its debt obligations by measures which are tantamount to an increase in the supply of high-powered money.

Political Influences Finally, the government sector may adopt a pattern of behaviour which departs from the strictly economic rationale which is assumed to underlie behaviour in other sectors. This is not to deny the premise of maximizing behaviour *per se* upon the part of the government sector, but merely to assert that political considerations may take precedence over purely economic ones.

The Composition of Government Expenditure and Revenue

With reference to the size of the government sector, central and local government combined are responsible for expenditures totalling approximately 40 per cent of GNP (see Curwen, 1994). This figure, however, should not be taken to indicate the actual command of the government sector over resources, since a substantial portion of government spending takes the form of *transfer payments* to the private sector. None the less, government transfer payments will influence the overall allocation of resources, even though control of such expenditure remains with the private sector. This will be the case, for example, with taxes imposed upon the relatively well-to-do to finance unemployment benefit and supplementary benefits to the poor and unemployed.

Government expenditures can be conveniently subdivided into three main groups. First of all, there is current spending upon goods and services such as health, education and defence. Second, there are transfer payments in the form of pensions, unemployment benefits, student grants and interest payments upon the national debt. Third, there is real capital expenditure upon social infrastructure such as roads, hospitals, schools and housing, together with grants and loans to nationalized undertakings. It is interesting to observe how these categories change in their relative importance over time. During the first decade of the Conservative government following its victory in 1979, for example, there was a marked increase in spending on social security, reflecting the growth in both unemployment and those of pensionable age. There were also significant percentage increases, in real terms, in outlays on health, defence and law and order, although the last was from a comparatively much lower base. Significant declines were recorded in industry, trade and energy, housing and transport – see Curwen (1994).

The recorded increase in real outlays upon health (of approximately 40 per cent in real terms under Conservative rule) is of interest in view of the political debate in the United Kingdom concerning the funding of the National Health Service. At first glance, the increase in real expenditure is impressive; however, if the cost of inputs employed within the Health Service are rising faster than the rate of inflation, as may be expected in a labour-intensive service, the actual increase in real resource inputs into the health service may be far less than the quoted 40 per cent figure. Again, population growth together with an increasing age distribution of the population generates increased demand for health services. Considerations along these lines have led Levitt and Joyce (1987) to conclude that the increased expenditure recorded between 1979 and 1986 has served to maintain health care per capita virtually constant.

Turning to government sector receipts, by far the most important source continues to be direct income taxes which, together with National Insurance contributions, account for some 40 per cent of the total. Value added tax accounts for a further 17 per cent; corporate income tax, 7 per cent; and tobacco, alcohol and petrol duties collectively make up approximately 10 per cent.

Under the Conservative government, which was first elected in 1979, there has been a marked decline in the relative importance of personal income taxes, where the standard rate has been reduced from 33 to 24 per cent and higher rates in excess of 40 per cent have been abolished. At the same time, Value Added Tax has increased in importance, with the standard rate more than doubled from 8 to 17.5 per cent. Although widely regarded as regressive in certain circles, the latter measure is broadly in keeping with the need to harmonize indirect taxes with those prevailing within the European union in the advent of the single market.

More significantly, it is perhaps of interest to note that the average tax burden – indicated as total taxes as a percentage of GNP – has actually *increased* since 1979. In part, this is to be explained by the phenomenon of fiscal drag – the tendency for tax revenues to increase at a faster rate than the increase in national income. In addition, however, it also reflects the difficulty in making significant reductions in expenditures in those sectors, particularly health, where real outlays have to be increased in order to maintain the same level of provision. Finally, any excess of expenditures over receipts will be met by government borrowing from the other sectors. The last item, which can loosely be identified with the *public sector borrowing requirement* (PSBR), grew sharply in the late 1970s and became prominent as the linchpin in the medium-term financial strategy announced by the Conservative administration returned in 1979. Detailed discussion of the PSBR and its importance to the money supply will be deferred until chapters 6 and 19.

The Changing Status of Fiscal Policy

The economic analysis which followed in the wake of the Keynesian revolution transformed the macroeconomic status of the government sector. Previously it had been assumed that the government sector was unable to appreciably influence the macroeconomy, since government outlays would have to be financed by drawing resources from the private sector.[1] The net impact upon the aggregate economy, therefore, was considered to be of minimal importance and from this chain of reasoning it was a relatively simple step to the proposition that 'good government is government which governs least'. The Keynesian revolution transformed this thesis and with it the entire nature of fiscal policy. Now it became understood that changes in government expenditures and taxes could become the primary determinants of the level of economic activity and the budgetary or financial implications could be conveniently ignored. Government tax and expenditure changes would directly contribute to or subtract from the level of aggregate demand, and moreover these initial impacts would be magnified in their influence upon the economy by virtue of the machinations of the Keynesian multiplier. It suggested, perhaps over-optimistically, that comparatively small changes in taxation or government expenditures would have a dramatic impact upon the economy. In the wake of these developments, considerable attention was accorded to a precise theoretical analysis of tax and expenditure changes. It was quickly concluded that changes in government expenditure were more high powered than equivalent costing changes in taxation, and from this developed the theorem of the balanced budget multiplier. Second, and along essentially similar lines, considerable attention was given to the comparative impact of direct and indirect tax changes from which it was concluded that indirect taxes were superior in their macroeconomic impact. Throughout these theoretical developments, which provided the analytical basis for the advocacy of fine tuning and demand management generally, comparatively scant attention was given to the monetary or financial implications of government fiscal measures. Monetary policy was relegated to a minor role and Keynesianism became equated with fiscalism – with or without Keynes's blessing. Accordingly, it is appropriate to examine the underlying reasons for this optimism in the use of fiscal instruments. In what follows, the theorem of the balanced budget multiplier and the composition of the tax mix will be examined in some detail. Consideration of the monetary and financial implications of government budgetary measures and their relation to the so-called crowding out controversy will be deferred until chapter 12.

The Balanced Budget Multiplier

An important theoretical implication of the Keynesian analysis which rapidly gained acceptance and influenced attitudes towards fiscal intervention lay in the formulation of the so-called *balanced budget multiplier theorem*. The essence of this theorem is relatively simple. It lies in the assertion that marginal propensities to consume will differ throughout the economy and accordingly that transfers of income to those possessing high marginal propensities to consume, financed by tax levies upon those with lower marginal propensities, will raise the overall level of aggregate demand within the economy. The theorem has been developed primarily within the context of public versus private sector, with the public or government sector possessed of the higher marginal propensity ($MPC = 1$). This leads to the conclusion that an increase in government outlays upon goods and services, financed by additional taxation upon the private sector (so that the overall budget balance remains unchanged), will not be neutral with respect to the level of income. More specifically, the theory was developed to show that

---

1 This version of the 'crowding out' controversy was aptly summarized as 'What was gained on the swings of public investment was, therefore, liable to be lost in part on the roundabout of private investment' (Middleton, 1982).

an increase in government outlays upon goods and services, financed by additional tax levies, would lead to a raising of the income level by an amount precisely equal to the increase in government spending. This precise formulation of the theorem was the consequence of the elementary economics involved and was illustrative only; it was not intended as a precise guideline for practical policy purposes. Indeed, to the extent that the precise formulation spelled out the restrictive assumptions under which its conclusions would hold, it emphasized that the actual outcome might be subject to a wide range of uncertainty. None the less, the concept was of importance to the development of fiscal policy and macroeconomic intervention generally, and paradoxically it carried implications which might appear anti-Keynesian.

First of all, the balanced budget theorem is of particular interest in the assessment of the efficacy of fiscal policy measures, for it is only here that resulting financial changes may legitimately be ignored. In the case of increased expenditures being financed by increases in the money stock or by the sale of bonds to the private sector, the total impact upon the economy is compounded by the monetary or interest rate/wealth changes. Accordingly, it becomes conceptually difficult to isolate the purely fiscal change from the other attendant influences, which creates problems in the assessment of the fiscal measure. With a balanced budget fiscal change, however, there is a 'pure' fiscal measure which in principle should permit its net impact to be adequately assessed. Although, as will be seen, some conceptual problems remain (with regard to the appropriate definition of a balanced budget change) when tax receipts are endogenous, none the less the underlying theory pointed to the conclusion that 'pure' fiscal policy could significantly affect income and employment levels. Indeed, the balanced budget multiplier theorem becomes a Keynesian justification for non-deficit finance. Budgetary deficits are not necessary for full employment to prevail, providing the authorities are willing to expand the public sector sufficiently. It is, of course, implicit in the theorem that £ for £ changes in government expenditure upon goods and services are more effective in their macroeconomic impact than equivalent changes in tax revenues; indeed, it is upon this premise that the theorem rests. However, it does not follow that changes in government expenditure are necessarily more efficient as a means of macroeconomic control. Tax changes may be easier to enact and administer. They may possess a shorter lag in effect and have a wider regional impact than expenditure changes, which by their nature tend to have a regional concentration.

Now that these initial points have been made, a more rigorous formulation of the balanced budget multiplier is presented before discussing some of the more important reservations and qualifications to the theorem.

The Multiplier with Exogenous Taxes

For ease of exposition it will be assumed that private investment outlays are autonomous, and complications arising from consideration of the monetary sector will be dispensed with. In order to bring out some of the implications more clearly, explicit distinction will be made between government expenditures upon goods and services and government transfer payments, as well as between endogenous taxes and taxes which may be considered independent of income. Then, within the context of a closed economy,

$$Y = C + I + G \qquad\qquad\qquad (4.1)$$

$$C = a + bY_d \tag{4.2}$$

$$Y_d = -n + Y(1 - t) + R \tag{4.3}$$

$$I = \bar{I} \tag{4.4}$$

$$G = \bar{G} \tag{4.5}$$

where Y, C, I and G are national income, consumption, investment and government expenditures upon goods and services respectively, and Y_d is disposable income or income net of tax. t is the income tax rate, and n denotes autonomous taxes such as lump sum levies, licence fees and the like. R refers to transfer receipts accruing to the private sector from the government. Solving for the equilibrium level of income,

$$Y = \frac{a - nb + bR + I + G}{1 - b + bt} \tag{4.6}$$

Total taxes, T, are simply equal to income taxes plus non-income taxes. Thus

$$T = tY + n \tag{4.7}$$

For the moment, assume that the income tax rate is zero ($t = 0$) and thus that all tax receipts stem from the autonomous element n. Accordingly, the government expenditures multiplier is given by

$$\frac{dY}{dG} = \frac{1}{1 - b} \tag{4.8}$$

whilst the tax multiplier is

$$\frac{dY}{dn} = \frac{-b}{1 - b} \tag{4.9}$$

and the total change in income arising from a balanced budget fiscal change is simply

$$dY = \frac{\partial Y}{\partial G}dG + \frac{\partial Y}{\partial n}dn \quad \text{where } dG = dn \tag{4.10}$$

$$= \left(\frac{1}{1 - b} + \frac{-b}{1 - b}\right)dG = dG \tag{4.11}$$

This result (that the increase in income is exactly equal to the increased government outlay upon goods and services) is the traditional conclusion of the balanced budget multiplier theorem. Although it rests upon a number of simplifying assumptions, and in particular ignores the monetary sector, it serves to emphasize a number of issues pertinent to the analysis.

First, *the income expansion so obtained is independent of the value taken by the marginal propensity to consume*. This follows because the increased expenditure is simply given by

$$\Delta G - \Delta T(MPC) = \Delta T - \Delta T(MPC) = \Delta T(1 - MPC) \tag{4.12}$$

The MPC refers here to the private sector since the MPC of the government is assumed to be unity. To this increase in expenditure, a normal multiplier must be applied in order to determine the total impact upon the level of national income. But in this simple model the multiplier is given by

$$\frac{1}{1 - b} = \frac{1}{1 - MPC} \tag{4.13}$$

Consequently, the total expansion of income arising from the balanced budget change is simply

$$\Delta T(1 - MPC)\frac{1}{1 - MPC} = \Delta T = \Delta G \qquad (4.14)$$

Second, and following on from the first point, the result of equation 4.11 implies that *extending the analysis to the open economy in no way modifies the analysis as long as the government expenditure falls solely upon domestic output which has no import content.* Allowing for imports by the private sector is simply akin to a decrease in the MPC.

What if the increased expenditure by government had not fallen upon goods and services but instead had taken the form of increased transfer payments? Then, as intuition would suggest, the income expansion is negated and the multiplier is zero. Transferring money from one sector of the economy to another via the tax transfer mechanism would leave the level of income unchanged provided marginal consumption propensities are equal in the two sectors. More formally,

$$dY = \frac{\partial Y}{\partial Y}R + \frac{\partial Y}{\partial n}dn \qquad \text{where} \quad dR = dn$$

$$= \left(\frac{b}{1 - b} + \frac{-b}{1 - b}\right)dR = 0 \qquad (4.15)$$

The Multiplier with Non-zero Income Taxes

The assumption that income tax rates are zero is now dropped. Income tax receipts (and thus total tax receipts) are now endogenous upon the level of income. Does this affect the argument in any systematic way? The first difficulty which arises concerns the appropriate definition of a balanced budget fiscal change. If the increase in government expenditure upon goods and services is financed by an equal increase in autonomous taxes then there will be a balanced budget fiscal change in the short run; however, with income taxes endogenous, the resulting income expansion will imply a movement towards fiscal surplus. The induced increase in fiscal receipts over and above the increased government expenditure will have repercussions upon money and bond markets and there will no longer be a 'pure' fiscal change in the long run. Alternatively, if a balanced budget change is defined to include the induced increase in direct taxes, then initially the tax proceeds will be insufficient to cover the increased government outlays. Monetary and/or bond market repercussions will thus arise in the short run and it will only be in the long run that fiscal receipts rise sufficiently to cover the increased expenditure. When taxes are endogenous upon income changes, therefore, the concept of a 'pure' fiscal change becomes exceedingly nebulous. Indeed, the ideal of a fiscal experiment which is not in some way contaminated by accompanying monetary, interest rate or wealth effect changes is shown to be an impossibility – a conclusion which carries implications for the assessment of the respective potencies of monetary and fiscal policy.

None the less, each of these situations is now pursued in turn when the income tax rate is positive. Consider first a balanced budget fiscal change defined with respect to the short run. In the case of increased government outlays on goods and services, $dG = dn$, and in the case of increased government transfers payments, $dR = dn$ as before. In the former case, the total change in income is given by

$$dY = \frac{\partial Y}{\partial G}dG + \frac{\partial Y}{\partial n}dn \qquad \text{where } dG = dn$$

$$= \left(\frac{1}{1-b+bt} + \frac{-b}{1-b+bt}\right)dG$$

$$= \left(\frac{1-b}{1-b+bt}\right)dG < dG \qquad (4.16)$$

The total multiplier is now *less than unity* in contrast to the conventional conclusion. Moreover, the value of the multiplier is no longer independent of the value taken by the marginal propensity to consume. Somewhat surprisingly, the multiplier as defined above is *less* the *greater* the marginal propensity to consume, and vice versa. That is to say,

$$\frac{d\left(\frac{1-b}{1-b+bt}\right)}{db} = \frac{-(1-b+nt)-(t-1)(1-b)}{(1-b+bt)^2}$$

$$= \frac{-t}{(1-b+bt)^2} < 0 \qquad (4.17)$$

The intuitive explanation for this result is that the ultimate multiplier incorporates the additional deflationary consequences of the induced fiscal receipts arising from the endogenous income tax. The greater the MPC, the greater will this additional deflationary impact be for any given rate of income tax. Similar reasoning suggests that the multiplier as defined above will be greater the smaller the rate of tax and vice versa; thus,

$$\frac{d\left(\frac{1-b}{1-b+bt}\right)}{dt} = \frac{-b(1-b)}{(1-b+bt)^2}$$

$$= \frac{-b+b^2}{(1-b+bt)^2} < 0 \qquad (4.18)$$

for all *b* less than one, the normal case.

This suggests that the conventional conclusions of the balanced budget multiplier theorem are modified once income taxes are considered endogenous and the balanced budget multiplier is defined with respect to the short run. However, no such modification is implied with respect to the increase in government outlays being directed towards increased transfer payments. Then

$$dY = \frac{\partial Y}{\partial R}dR + \frac{\partial Y}{\partial n}dn \qquad \text{where } dR = dn$$

$$= \left(\frac{b}{1-b+bt} + \frac{-b}{1-b+bt}\right)dR$$

$$= 0 \qquad (4.19)$$

Thus, whether or not taxes are endogenous, the zero outcome of the balanced budget multiplier with transfer payments remains the same – again, in accordance with intuitive reasoning.

A balanced budget fiscal change is now defined to refer to the long term. In this case the increased government spending upon goods and services, or alternatively upon transfer payments, is just matched by increased taxes, including any endogenous increase in taxes arising from income expansion. This implies that the condition for a balanced budget change is given by either

$$dT = dn + dYt = dG \qquad \text{where } dG = dT \tag{4.20}$$

or

$$dT = dn + dYt = dR \qquad \text{where } dR = dT \tag{4.21}$$

Consider the former. This can be written

$$dn = dG - dYt \tag{4.22}$$

Accordingly, the balanced budget fiscal change is derived from

$$
\begin{aligned}
dY &= \frac{\partial Y}{\partial G} dG + \frac{\partial Y}{\partial n} dn \qquad \text{where } dn = dG - dYt \\
&= \left(\frac{1}{1 - b + bt}\right) dG + \left(\frac{-b}{1 - b + bt}\right) (dG - dYt) \\
&= \frac{dG - bdG + bdYt}{1 - b + bt} \tag{4.23}
\end{aligned}
$$

Hence,

$$dY(1 - b + bt - bt) = dG(1 - b) \tag{4.24}$$

and

$$dY = \frac{dG(1 - b)}{1 - b} = dG \tag{4.25}$$

Thus, when the balanced budget multiplier is defined with respect to the long term, where the increased government outlays upon goods and services are covered by both autonomous and induced fiscal receipts, the traditional conclusion of the unity multiplier is restored. The long-term zero-transfers multiplier is also unaffected, as the reader will readily be able to verify for himself by similar reasoning. In the latter case the induced tax proceeds are, of course, also zero.

Figure 4.1 illustrates the logic of the unity balanced budget multiplier. In this figure, increased government expenditure raises aggregate demand by ΔG but the effect of taxation is to reduce it by $\Delta T (MPC)$. As long as the MPC is less than one, the net effect is to raise aggregate demand, and income rises from $0Y^1$ to $0Y^2$ equal to 0A to 0B.

Table 4.1 summarizes the analysis to date.

TABLE 4.1
The Balanced Budget Multiplier Theorem
Equation $Y = \frac{a - bn + bR + I + G}{1 - b + bt}$

Balanced budget change Pure fiscal measure $t = 0$	Short-run balanced budget change $t > 0$	Long-run balanced budget change $t > 0$
$dY = dG$ for $dn = dG$	$dY < dG$ for $dn = dG$	$dY = dG$ for $dn = dG - dYt$
$dY = 0$ for $dn = dR$	$dY = 0$ for $dn = dR$	$dY = 0$ for $dn = dR - dYt$

Transfer Payments in Kind

Thus far the balanced budget multiplier theorem has been analysed by invoking two polar cases, the one where the government raises expenditures upon goods and services and the other where it increases the existing level of transfer payments. There is, however,

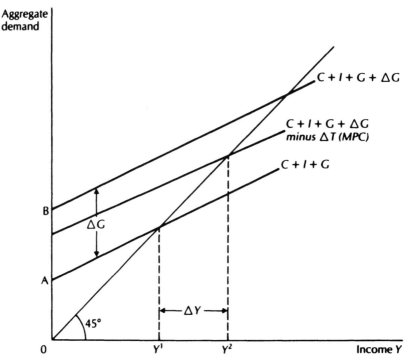

Figure 4.1 Logic of the balanced budget multiplier $\Delta G = \Delta T$

an intermediate situation, that of a combined policy whereby the government increases taxation to purchase additional goods and services which it then gives to recipients in the form of transfer payments in kind. This, of course, reflects the situation with respect to the provision of free dental care, certain maternity benefits and so forth. This form of benefit is often advocated upon the grounds that it enjoys the support of the taxpayer whereas untied cash payments might not. The issue of concern here, however, is the extent to which such provision influences the value of the balanced budget multiplier.

This question can perhaps most readily be approached in terms of conventional indifference analysis. Figure 4.2 shows savings on the vertical axis and the consumption of composite goods on the horizontal. Given the indifference curve, the optimal combination of consumption and savings for some hypothetical individual is revealed to be at point E with consumption of goods equal to 0A and savings 0Y. Now assume that in this situation the individual concerned suddenly finds himself the recipient of a composite bundle of goods bestowed upon him by government and equal to the amount 0X. How will the individual respond? His initial reaction is to experience an income gain which allows him to raise both his level of consumption and his level of saving. In terms of the diagram, his budget line MN is altered to MPT by the free provision of goods 0X and his optimal consumption/savings combination is now indicated by E'. His savings have increased from 0Y to 0Q. However, except in very trivial cases, it is not possible to save out of payments in kind; consequently, the increased savings takes the form of saving out of alternative monetary income and this saving serves to offset the multiplier impact of the increased government outlays on goods and services. In the extreme case, where the recipient values the income gain experienced as equal to its cost and where he has the same marginal propensity to consume as the taxpayer, the entire impact of the multiplier is negated. This is because he increases his

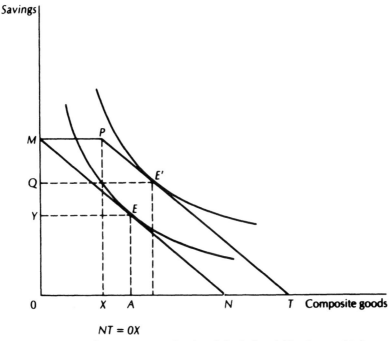

$$NT = OX$$

Figure 4.2 Transfer payments in kind and the balanced budget multiplier

saving by the amount of the income gain experienced, ΔY, multiplied by his marginal propensity to save, whilst the taxpayer will reduce his saving by the amount of the tax to finance the provision of goods ΔT, multiplied by his marginal propensity to save. If the goods or services are valued at cost, ΔY equals ΔT, and if marginal saving propensities are uniform, there is no net change in the level of aggregate demand.

The Composition of the Tax Mix

Virtually every elementary treatment of Keynesian economics includes reference to the theory of the balanced budget multiplier. It is therefore somewhat surprising that elementary expositions of macroeconomics fail to make a similar and arguably more important distinction between the aggregate demand impact of a change in direct taxation and that of an *equal yield* change in indirect taxation. Just as a change in the composition of government outlays between goods and services and transfer payments may have a net demand impact, so too may a change in the composition of the tax mix exert inflationary or deflationary consequences.

The reasons for this comparative reticence are not hard to find. Indirect taxes are notoriously difficult to incorporate into formal national income models because they imply price changes of unknown degree which cannot be readily accommodated by an analysis stated in real terms. Moreover, indirect taxes raise the possibility of *money illusion* on the part of consumers which further complicates the analysis.[2] In

___

2 A commonly accepted definition of money illusion would contend that money illusion is present when a consumer continues to make the same nominal money outlay in the face of a tax-induced price rise. In con-trast, if he takes the tax into account and raises his outlay in order to maintain, if only partially, his former real consumption standard, he is said to be free of money illusion.

consequence, many formal models of fiscal policy admit of the existence of lump sum taxes or primitive proportional income taxes whilst simultaneously denying the presence of sales or consumption taxes. A priori, such a procedure is difficult to justify when it is recalled that indirect taxes often account for 50 per cent or more of total tax proceeds. Arguably, such a departure from reality would be permissible if it could be shown that the nature of the tax source was of no consequence to the subsequent analysis and conclusions of the model. However, precisely the opposite situation prevails; it has long been argued, as part of the conventional wisdom of public finance, that indirect tax levies exert a greater deflationary impact upon the macroeconomy than do equal yielding direct taxes.

This argument may be traced back, at least implicitly, to Keynes, who proposed a consumption function which was non-linear and which exhibited a declining marginal propensity to consume with rising income. If this is the case, and if direct taxes (income taxes) fall primarily upon the rich whilst exempting the poor, whereas sales taxes are more regressive and impinge upon the total population, it follows that £ for £ the sales tax will exert a greater impact upon the level of demand. Alternatively, the income tax exerts a greater impact upon saving than does a comparable sales tax. When compared upon an equal yield basis, therefore, the sales tax will exert the stronger impact upon the level of aggregate demand. Even if the differential impact upon demand is slight, it will be magnified in its income and employment impacts by the operation of the Keynesian multiplier.

The Keynesian demonstration of the superiority of indirect taxes was never particularly convincing, partly because consumption taxes need not be especially regressive. Such taxes include specific excises which can be (and often are) imposed at decidedly high rates upon luxury products consumed by the comparatively wealthy. In addition, however, the empirical evidence culled from studies of consumer behaviour indicated little difference in marginal consumption patterns of different income groups over a broad range of incomes. A linear consumption function destroys the entire basis of the Keynesian claim, whether sales taxes are regressive or not.

It is precisely for this reason that the contribution by Cary Brown (1950) takes on renewed significance. Adopting a simple Keynesian model for a closed economy, Brown demonstrated that a sales tax would exert a greater macroeconomic impact than an equal yield income tax even under the assumption of a uniform marginal propensity to consume, and regardless of whether money illusion existed or not. This demonstration served to confirm the earlier Keynesian intuition in that the result derived from the greater propensity of the income tax to deplete savings.[3]

This analysis is subject to several qualifications, however. First, it rests upon the assumption that the sales tax is passed forward in its entirety in a tax-induced price rise. No further price changes are then permitted to occur.[4] Second, the comparative effectiveness of the two taxes is demonstrated solely with respect to comparative yields; the period of adjustment is not considered within the conventional comparative static framework. Finally, perhaps the most serious reservation noted by Peston (1971) stems

---

3 Strictly, the result is demonstrated only for an economy with positive savings and the demonstration relied upon a rather complicated algebraic manipulation not reproduced here. A full treatment is presented in Shaw (1972).

4 This is the basis of a critique by Peacock and Williamson (1967) which formulated a wage response to the increased price level implicit in the case of a sales tax and assumed absent in the case of the income tax. With prices related to wage increases, they then went on to develop a wage price spiral which showed that the sales tax could generate more inflationary consequences than the income tax.

from the unrealistic model analysis which posits the existence of an income tax, when sales taxes are absent, for purposes of comparison with a world characterized by sales taxes but possessed of no income taxes. In a real world situation, the two types of taxes would exist simultaneously and, moreover, their yields would be highly interdependent.

In attempting to deal with this additional complication Peston adopts the analytically convenient device of holding total tax proceeds constant whilst changing the ratio of direct to indirect taxes. In doing so, he is able to demonstrate unambiguously that an increase in the direct/indirect tax ratio with total tax proceeds held constant will be expansionary in its impact upon real output. Thus, Peston's model reaffirms the conventional wisdom of the superiority of indirect taxes but this time within the context of a multi-tax world. Again, this conclusion rests upon the assumption of the full shifting of indirect taxes, but none the less it represents a considerable advance upon the analysis of single-tax states.[5]

Quite apart from the conclusions of the formal model analysis, there are other reasons to suggest that indirect taxes will exert a greater deflationary impact. Thus, for example, indirect taxes will raise prices; to what degree will depend upon the actual patterns of incidence, but none the less it is reasonable to conclude that they will generate an increase in the aggregate price level. To this extent, they will imply an increased demand for transactions balances and, *ceteris paribus*, lead to an increase in interest rates. The latter may be expected to 'crowd out' a certain amount of private sector expenditure, both because of the presumed relationship between investment and interest rates and also because of negative wealth effects as the real value of bonds are reduced. To the extent that higher interest rates lead to a raising of the exchange rate, the demand for domestic output will fall as export demand contracts and imports become more price competitive. All things considered, therefore, there are convincing reasons for believing that indirect taxes have greater real effects. If this is the case then they should be fully allowed for in any reforms aimed at restructuring the overall tax burden. And the composition of the tax mix should be logically included in the armory of fiscal instruments.

A change in the composition of the tax mix leaves the budget surplus/deficit unchanged and hence involves no change in the money stock. How then are the expansionary real effects associated with a switch from indirect to direct taxation to be financed? Under the present assumptions of complete shifting, any change in the composition of tax receipts involves price effects. It is the change in the aggregate price index consequent upon the tax mix change which implies changes to the *real* money stock. Thus, in contrast to the theorem of the balanced budget multiplier, which abstracts from price changes, a change in the composition of the tax mix has dual consequences. It involves first of all an expenditure shift, along Brown–Pestonian lines, but equally it involves price changes which alter the real value of the money stock.

Concluding Comments

This chapter began by indicating the overriding importance of the government sector to the macroeconomy, and it has been demonstrated how government decision-

---

5 Peston's technique maintains tax proceeds constant in nominal terms. Thus, as the direct/indirect tax ratio is increased, the shifting assumption implies falling prices. Total tax proceeds rise in real terms and yet the net effect on real output is expansionary.

making will exercise a pervasive influence upon private sector behaviour even whilst maintaining or adopting a strictly non-interventionist stance. Not only is the government of dominant importance in its expenditure and employment policies, but its policy announcements – or the lack of them – will condition expectations throughout the private sector. Indeed, from the standpoint of the rational expectations school, the conditioning of appropriate expectations is a valid function of government in conducting the adjustment to a preferred state of affairs – a lower inflation rate, for example.

Two theoretical analyses of the government sector which evolved from the Keynesian model analysis were examined in some detail. The first of these, the well-known balanced budget multiplier theorem, was analysed in regard to both income and non-income taxes, to demonstrate the proposition that a change in the level of government outlays, with no change in the position of the budget surplus or deficit, will not normally be neutral in its impact upon the equilibrium level of national income.

A very similar but comparatively little-known issue, namely the question of the composition of the tax mix, was then examined. Again the consequence of Keynesian model analysis, this thesis demonstrates that indirect taxes are usually more high powered in their macroeconomic impact than equivalent direct taxes. Thus, as in the case of the balanced budget theorem, government can influence the macroeconomy without necessarily disturbing its overall budgetary deficit/surplus position – in this case by changing the composition of its tax receipts. It should be emphasized that the formal analysis of this chapter is decidedly Keynesian oriented and that alternative statements, such as the monetarist contention of the importance of the budget constraint, are deferred until chapter 12.

Further Reading

An elementary guide to the significance of the government sector can be culled from Black (1985) and (Curwen, 1994). For detailed analysis of government expenditure and receipts there is no substitute for the annual blue book on *National Income and Expenditure* (HMSO), together with the short guide published every ten years (HMSO, 1991). For an analysis of the elementary multiplier models stemming from government expenditures and taxation, see Peacock and Shaw (1976). Significant articles on the balanced budget multiplier include Salant (1957) and Peacock (1972). With regard to the analysis of the tax mix, the principal references are the ones already mentioned in the text, specifically Brown (1950) and Peston (1971). Other contributions include the Peacock and Williamson (1967) attempt (already mentioned) at extending the analysis to an inflationary setting, Forster and Shaw (1976) and subsequent critiques by McLean (1978) and Signer (1978).

5

The Demand for Money

Individuals demand goods and services because they yield utility. In the same way, they demand money because of the benefits yielded by the possession of money. In this respect, money may be deemed a 'good' on a par with any other commodity. It follows that the demand for money, like the demand for any other good, is a real demand; it is a demand for the actual services yielded by the possession of a *real* stock of money and not simply a demand for a nominal amount of cash denominated in sterling, dollars or any other currency unit.

Although money may be regarded as a good it is none the less the case that the services yielded by money are unique. It is owing to the unique role and functions performed by money that it takes on a dominant role in the functioning of the economy, and for this reason economists have given considerable time and effort to analysing the factors influencing the demand for money. The importance of this question cannot be overestimated. If the demand for money is stable – that is to say, if the demand for money responds in a clearly defined way with respect to a few key variables – then it follows that changes in the money supply will have a reasonably predictable impact upon prices and nominal income. If this is the case, then effective control of the money supply gives considerable influence and power to the monetary authorities. Indeed, the entire logic of money supply targets rests upon the assumption that the demand for money be relatively stable.

Whether the demand for money is reasonably stable and whether the authorities possess effective control over the money supply are of course empirical questions open to debate. In general, monetarists are inclined to argue both that the demand for money is reasonably stable (implying relatively stable if not constant velocity) *and* that the authorities have effective control over the money supply. Both serve to reinforce their belief in the efficacy of monetary policy.

In contrast, Keynesians are wont to argue that the demand for money is relatively unstable (implying great variability in velocity) and that the money supply is effectively endogenous beyond the control of the monetary authorities. They therefore tend to play down the importance of monetary policy *per se* and instead advocate the superiority of fiscal policy. In the present chapter we focus upon the first issue – the nature of the demand for money. The question of its controllability will be taken up in chapter 6.

In the main, there is broad agreement upon the factors which may influence the demand for money. These are income (however defined) and interest rates. Expected inflation is also a factor which may influence the demand for money but in large measure one would expect this to be reflected in nominal interest rate changes. As a first approximation, therefore, income (positively) and interest (negatively) might be expected to be the key determinants influencing the overall demand for money.

In general terms, the early research tended to conclude that the demand for money was indeed a relatively stable function of these key variables over quite long periods of time. However, this general consensus tended to break down in the 1970s as predictions derived from data estimated in the 1950s and 1960s seriously understated the extent of monetary growth. The 1970s witnessed a sustained period of deregulation and innovation in financial markets and suggested that the earlier confidence in single equation estimates may have been misplaced.

The Functions of Money

The essential functions performed by money can be enumerated as follows.

The Medium of Exchange Function   Money acts as a medium of exchange and hence permits an interval of time to separate the act of buying and selling commodities. In the context of a barter economy, the exchange of goods would imply the simultaneous occurrence of buying and selling commodities upon the part of each transactor to an exchange. Money eliminates this need for a 'double coincidence of wants'. It allows one to sell commodities or services without simultaneously purchasing. In this way it greatly facilitates exchange and thus widens the scope for profitable exchanges to take place. This medium of exchange function is undoubtedly the single most important function possessed by money and without it it is difficult to imagine how society could acquire the benefits stemming from specialization and the division of labour.

The Store of Value Function   A moment's reflection will indicate that money is able to perform its medium of exchange function primarily because it acts as a store of value. The reason why one is willing to sell commodities or services in exchange for money which will be used to make purchases at a later date is because of the fact that money retains its value over time. If this were not the case individuals would be unwilling to hold money and it would cease to perform its primary exchange function.

Money is not of course a perfect store of value, since its real value is eroded at a rate equal to the rate of inflation. The greater the rate of inflation, the less well will money perform its store of value function and the less readily will it serve as a medium of exchange. At the same time, other assets will serve as a store of value and some – antiques, old masters and so forth – may outperform money in this respect. Money, however, has one great advantage over such real assets, namely that in principle it is readily divisible.

The Standard of Deferred Payment Function   Closely related to the store of value function is the function of deferred payment performed by money. This means simply that loans and future payments are agreed and contracted in money terms, the monetary unit being accepted as the means of settling future accounts. Clearly, this function can only be adequately performed by money if it is sufficiently protected against inflation in being able to perform its store of value function.

The Unit of Account Function   It is convenient to adopt the monetary unit as the unit of account in which prices are quoted and accounting records kept, although it is by no means essential. Virtually any commodity with a reasonably stable value could serve as *numeraire*, although here too the potential divisibility of money is an additional asset.

The unit of account function performed by money illustrates graphically the gains in efficiency, in the form of reduced transactions costs, obtained by the existence of money. In a pure barter economy, for example, with n commodities there will be $n(n-1)$ exchange ratios since every commodity would have an exchange ratio with every other (whereas with itself, the exchange ratio is automatically unity). Of these exchange ratios, however, only half are required, since the rate of exchange between a table and a chair is precisely equal to the inverse of the rate of exchange between a chair and a table. Hence a total of $n(n-1)/2$ independent exchange ratios is obtained. With one commodity acting as a unit of account, however, only $n-1$ independent exchange ratios are needed, which implies a considerable reduction in the information needed for rational trading to take place.

The nature of the demand for money is of paramount importance to the entire question of the significance of the monetary variable and to the role of monetary control of the macroeconomy. Essentially the value of money, as indeed that of any other commodity, can be viewed as being determined by the forces of supply and demand. An explanation of the extent to which the authorities can in practice control the money stock is delayed until the next chapter; for present expositional purposes, the money supply will simply be assumed to be exogenously determined.

Classical Monetary Theory – the Traditional Quantity Theory

The Transactions Approach

Fisher's famous equation of exchange, $MV = PT$, where M is the total money stock, V its velocity of circulation or the average number of times that each monetary unit is utilized in a given accounting period, T the total number of all transactions and P the general price level, is justifiably one of the best-known tautologies in economics. It is a tautology in that it asserts merely that total monetary expenditure is equal to the monetary value of all goods traded. By invoking certain assumptions it is, however, possible to transform the identity into a theory. If velocity is determined by habit, institutional arrangements, banking practices and so forth, then it may be assumed constant in the short term, and if T is also rendered a constant, which is not so unreasonable if full employment output is posited, then the following well-known result is obtained:

$$M\bar{V} = P\bar{T} \quad or \quad P = \frac{M\bar{V}}{\bar{T}} \tag{5.1}$$

$$\therefore \Delta M \Rightarrow \Delta P$$

Here the increase in the money stock is the causal agent in initiating the rise in prices, and the transactions demand for money then responds passively to this price increase. *Ceteris paribus*, the demand for money would be unit elastic.

The Cambridge Cash Balance Approach

An alternative formulation of the traditional quantity theory of money was propounded by the Cambridge school of economists, led by Marshall, Pigou and Robertson. The general approach taken by the Cambridge cash balance equation is to express the demand for money as a percentage of the real income of society. Thus, the real demand for money may be expressed as kY, where Y is real income and k is the percentage of real income which people collectively wish to command in the form of cash holdings. If the nominal money stock is exogenously determined to be M, then the required equilibrium between supply and demand is brought about by the price mechanism. Then

$$M = pkY \tag{5.2}$$

where p is the price index of current output. Thus,

$$p = \frac{M}{kY} \tag{5.3}$$

which can be compared to Fisher's equation[1]

$$p = \frac{MV}{T} \tag{5.4}$$

Hence,

$$\frac{M}{kY} = \frac{MV}{T} \tag{5.5}$$

or

$$\frac{1}{V} = \frac{kY}{T} \tag{5.6}$$

Providing the ratio of income to transactions, Y/T, remains constant, the Cambridge k is simply proportional to the reciprocal of V. An increase in k implies a decrease in V and vice versa, and both indicate a decrease in the velocity of circulation. The demonstration of the strict quantity theory of money requires constancy in both k and V. This is hardly surprising; the Cambridge k was purely a transactions demand for money and as such was implicit in Fisher's formulation.

The Keynesian Analysis of the Demand for Money

The demise of the traditional quantity theory of money was closely associated with the evolution of Keynes's thinking on monetary matters and culminated in the publication of the *General Theory*, which claimed that the money stock was important only to the extent that it influenced the rate of interest and set up repercussions stemming from the interest rate change. Moreover, the thesis was propounded, later to be eagerly seized upon by Keynesians if not by Keynes himself, that situations could exist whereby an increase in the money stock would have zero impact upon interest rates and hence zero effect on the economy *in toto*. What was involved in this proposition was the assertion that an increase in the money stock could generate countervailing changes in velocity so as to completely cancel and negate the impact of a changed money supply. In short, this thesis implied the extreme variant of the view that the demand for money is interdependent with its supply – completely contrary to the traditional formulation of the

---

1 Strictly speaking, the comparison is invalid since the P in Fisher's equation refers to the price level of all transactions including those in second-hand goods, whereas the p in the Cambridge formulation refers to price index of current output.

quantity theory of money. Fundamental to this assertion was the distinctly Keynesian emphasis upon the importance of expectations in influencing the demand for money balances. The so-called *speculative* motive of the demand for money was added to the traditional transactions demand. This is the distinguishing characteristic of the Keynesian contribution and it is this feature, or rather the significance of this feature, which the revised monetarist doctrine has sought to deny or play down in its empirical importance.

Keynesian Motives for Money Holding

In the *General Theory*, Keynes divided the motivation for holding money balances into three component parts, namely

1 The Transactions Motive
2 The Precautionary Motive
3 The Speculative Motive.

The Transactions Motive for maintaining cash balances is essentially akin to the classical thesis. Given institutional lags between the receipt of factor incomes and expenditure outlays, a certain amount of money will be required to permit normal day-to-day transactions within the economy and the real value of this transactions demand will be closely related to the real income of society. The assumption here is that the real volume of transactions will be closely related to the real income of the economy and this in turn will imply a nominal demand for transactions cash related to the monetary value of national income. Thus the transactions demand for cash can be indicated as

$$L_1 = kPY \tag{5.7}$$

The Precautionary Motive is very closely related to the transactions motive in that it may be considered as the amount of cash that one carries in excess of one's expected transactions needs owing to the existence of uncertainty. Certain outlays, essentially of a transaction nature, may be unforeseen (as in the case of an unexpected medical bill, for example) and the rational individual will therefore demand a sum of money over and above his expected transactions needs to deal with such contingencies. This amount will be determined by the individual's subjective expectation or probability of finding himself in some unforeseen condition and will clearly differ between individuals, but in the aggregate it seems reasonable that it should be related to the level of real income and in nominal terms to the price level. Accordingly, there would appear to be very little justification for distinguishing between the transactions and precautionary motives.[2] Thus a generalized transactions demand for cash, L_1, can be considered which encompasses the precautionary element, and it can be posited that

$$\frac{\mathrm{d}L_1}{\mathrm{d}PY} > 0 \tag{5.8}$$

The Speculative Demand for money or, alternatively, the asset demand for money is the amount of money that the individual desires for speculative financial transactions when the conditions appear favourable. To simplify the analysis conceptually, Keynes assumed the existence of only two financial assets, non-interest-bearing cash and

---

2 For an opposite view, see Whalen (1966).

interest-bearing non-redeemable government bonds (consols). Now, although such bonds are never redeemed by the government, they are nevertheless exchanged in the capital market and their market value will fluctuate with changes in the market rate of interest.

To illustrate, suppose the government issues a non-redeemable bond for £100 which pays a yearly dividend of £5. The effective interest rate is accordingly 5 per cent. The fact that the government is able to sell such a bond at this price implies that the market rate of interest is in the order of 5 per cent. If some time later the market rate were to rise to 10 per cent, the holder of this bond would be able to obtain only £50 consequent upon its sale, since now £50 is all that is required to yield an interest income of £5. In a similar fashion, had the market rate of interest fallen to $2\frac{1}{2}$ per cent, the bondholder might reasonably expect its market value to approximate £200. The example here is extremely simplified but the point being laboured is that bond prices are inversely related to market rates of interest. The reader will appreciate that what is involved is determining the present value of an interest-yielding asset as was demonstrated in chapter 3.

In deciding whether to keep a certain portion of his wealth in the form of money or bonds, therefore, the rational investor will consider not simply the interest yield differential between the two assets but also his expectation of a possible change in the market value of government bonds. In short, a decision to purchase bonds involves not only the prospect of an interest income stream but also the prospect of a capital gain or loss.

It was Keynes's contention that the asset or speculative demand for money, L_2, would be inversely related to the rate of interest. Three arguments support this stance. First, the cost of keeping money idle in the form of speculative balances is of course the interest forgone. The cost is therefore higher when interest rates are high and on this ground alone one would be induced to economize on speculative cash holdings when interest rates are high.

Second and most important is the part played by the expectation of capital gains or losses. It is assumed that the rational individual entertains some expectation as to the

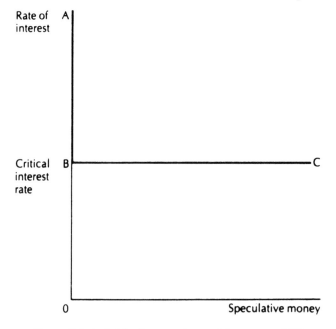

Figure 5.1 Individual's asset demand for money ABC

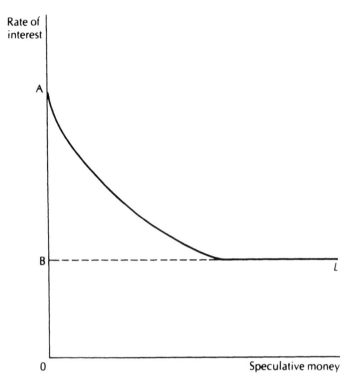

Figure 5.2 Aggregate demand for asset money A*L*

future course of interest rates. He has some expectation of a *normal* rate of interest with which he expects the existing market rate ultimately to coincide. If this expected or normal interest rate is above (below) the current market rate, he is expecting the market rates to rise (fall) and therefore bond prices to fall (rise). In such a situation he will move out of bonds (cash) and hold cash (bonds) in order to avoid any capital loss (make a capital gain). In the intermediate case where the potential investor expects the interest rate to be unchanged he will, of course, hold bonds and no cash in order to take advantage of the interest yield. This analysis suggests that the investor maintains *either* cash *or* bonds but not both simultaneously. His situation is akin to that depicted in figure 5.1 where B represents the critical expected interest rate.

However, different individuals will entertain different ideas as to the probable future rate of interest, and in the aggregate will in all probability be holding a combination of both cash and bonds. At higher rates of interest, however, more and more individuals will, *ceteris paribus*, entertain the belief that interest rates must fall in the future. The aggregate demand for speculative cash balances will accordingly decline. Ultimately, a rate of interest may be attained at which no one believes it can go higher and the expectation of a future fall in the market rate will become universal. At this point, the demand for idle cash balances will become zero, as everybody will try to move into bonds in the certain expectation of making a capital gain. This situation is depicted at point A in figure 5.2. Conversely, the lower the interest rates, the more general the belief that future rates must rise; the more general the belief that future bonds prices will decline, the greater will be the movement into cash. Ultimately, there will be some minimal rate of interest such that the universal expectation is for a future rise, and at this point there will be no call for bonds with the demand for idle balances becoming infinite up to total wealth. In figure 5.2 this situation is depicted at point B. This is, therefore, the rationale for the general conclusion that the demand for speculative cash holdings will be inversely related to the rate of interest for the aggregate economy.

A third and related argument reinforces this conclusion by comparing the extent of any capital loss against interest yields at different rates of interest. As might be expected, the extent of any given loss net of interest yield will be greater at lower rates of interest for any given increase in the prevailing market rate.[3] The force of this point stems from the fact that interest rate changes on the part of the monetary authorities are of finite amounts, a change of $\frac{1}{4}$ per cent being normally the smallest feasible.

Thus, whilst the transactions cum precautionary demand for money is related to income levels directly, the asset demand for money is inversely related to the rate of interest.

$$\frac{\mathrm{d}L_2}{\mathrm{d}i} < 0 \tag{5.9}$$

Since the total demand for money is simply L_1 plus L_2, equal to L, it follows that the total demand for money must also be inversely related to interest rates. To illustrate, consider the composite figure 5.3. In part (a) is depicted the transactions demand L_1 as invariant to the interest rate and in part (b) the asset demand L_2 as a negative function of the interest rate. In part (c) the total demand (or *liquidity preference* in Keynes's terminology) is shown as a combination of (a) and (b) and must also therefore reveal some interest elasticity. The issue which is crucial for policy purposes turns upon the extent of this interest elasticity.

Money Market Equilibrium

The implication of figure 5.3(c) is that the demand for money will increase as interest rates fall. The question remains, why do interest rates fall? The Keynesian answer is simplicity itself; the rate of interest is determined by the supply and demand for money and hence a fall in the rate of interest is associated with an increase in the money stock. But since the interest rate fall increases the demand for money, this implies that supply and demand are interdependent. The situation is therefore one in which an increase in the supply of money generates a complementary increase in the demand for money (akin to a decrease in velocity) so as to negate or minimize the impact of the monetary change. This situation is brought out with the aid of figure 5.4. The value of money, $1/P$, is shown to be determined by the demand for money and the money stock, M. If the money stock is doubled to $2M$ but the demand for money is also doubled, then the value of money is left unchanged. This is the essence of the Keynesian denial of the traditional quantity theory of money. Even if the demand does not double, any increase in demand will offset in part the predictions of the traditional statement.

The Keynesian doctrine of liquidity preference is thus fundamentally at odds with the traditional quantity theory. The latter had minimized the role of changes in the demand for money (velocity) and in particular had tended to exclude supply changes

---

3 To illustrate, consider an investment of £1000 in consols at 5 per cent. This will yield £50 per annum. If after three years the interest rate rises to 6 per cent, the value of the consol will fall to £833. The loss is £167 or, after consideration of the interest yield, £17. The same example, assuming an initial interest rate of 2 per cent rising to 3 per cent after three years, provides a capital loss of £333 less the yield gain of £60 – implying a net loss of £273. This example stems from Dillard (1948).

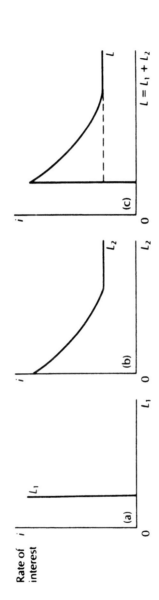

Figure 5.3 Interest sensitivity of the demand for money

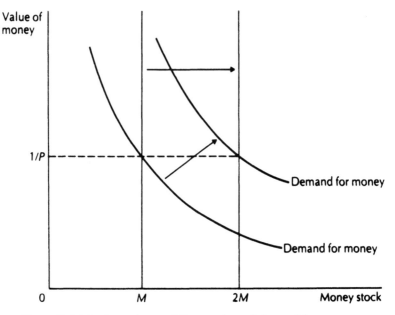

Figure 5.4 Interdependence of the supply and demand for money

as a possible cause of changes in demand. None the less, it should be emphasized that Keynes was not seeking to minimize the role of money, although this was the emphasis to be pursued by many of his later disciples. The emphasis that Keynes was insistent upon was that the impact of a money stock change would work through the associated change in the interest rate. In the normal course of events, an increased money supply would imply a fall in interest rates (see figure 5.5) which in turn would stimulate both investment and consumption outlays. These in turn would be magnified in their impact upon the economy by the normal operation of the multiplier and the result would be

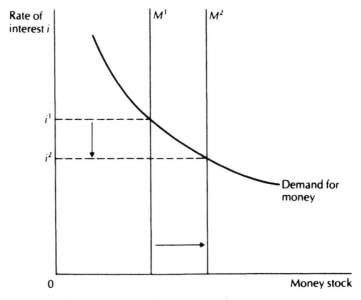

Figure 5.5 Impact of an increase in the money stock on interest rates in conventional Keynesian theory

an expansion of money national income. Whether this increase occurs upon the side of output changes or price changes would depend largely upon whether there existed unemployed resources. If resources were fully employed, then the impact of increased investment and consumption expenditure would necessarily be reflected in price increases and the quantity theory would be vindicated in principle – although with a distinctly different *transmission mechanism* than that employed in the traditional doctrine.

However, there remains one important theoretical exception to the sequence of events described, an exception that Keynesians tended to believe provided the *coup de grâce* to the quantity theory. This is the case where an increase in the money stock has no impact whatsoever upon interest rates and hence no impact at all upon the macroeconomy. Consider again point B in figure 5.2. At this point there exists the universal belief that interest rates must rise. Accordingly, no one is willing to buy more government bonds. In such a situation, if the government were to enlarge the money supply there would be no effect upon the interest rate. Since the money stock at any time must be held by somebody, the enlarged money supply would find its way into the hands of the public. But with no change in the income level there is no desire to add to transactions balances. With no desire to purchase government bonds on the understandable grounds that future bond prices must fall, the additional cash must be added to existing idle speculative money holdings. The asset demand for money is thus rendered infinite at this point, imposing a minimum constraint upon interest rates.

This is the situation which became referred to as the *liquidity trap* and implies the complete impotence of monetary policy. It will be illustrated by reference to figure 5.6. In such a situation any increase in the money stock is simply accumulated in the form of idle cash balances. Now clearly the velocity of an idle deposit is nil. Consequently, this process is accompanied by a general decrease in the average velocity of money. In terms of Fisher's equation, the increase in the money stock is exactly offset

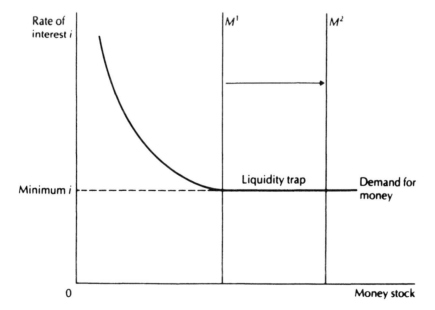

Figure 5.6 Liquidity trap – zero impact of an enlarged money supply upon the rate of interest

by a decrease in the average velocity of money so that no change takes place in total expenditures and no impact is transmitted to the remainder of the economy. The quantity theory is denied.

It should be emphasized that Keynes did not appear to attach much importance to this situation, except as an interesting theoretical possibility, and generally held that an increase in the money stock would be accompanied by a decline in interest rates. None the less, the analysis indicated that the decline in interest rates could be substantially limited and small variations in the rate of interest might not be expected to exert much impact upon investment or consumption spending. Any generalized statement about the effect of a change in the volume of money upon the aggregate economy could not longer be maintained. The traditional quantity theory appeared to have been eclipsed in the upheaval of the Keynesian revolution.

Post-Keynesian Modifications to the Demand for Money

Whilst in keeping with Keynes's original statement, and whilst generally sceptical of the claims of the quantity theory, a number of contributions have taken issue with Keynes's specification of the demand for money and have proffered alternatives. The most important of these contributions are summarized briefly in the following. In many respects, they question the usefulness of maintaining the distinction between the transactions demand and the asset demand for cash as separate components in the total demand for money holdings.

Baumol and the Interest Rate Sensitivity of Transactions Demands

The logic of Baumol's (1952) model leads to the assertion that the transactions demand for cash will respond inversely to changes in interest rates, thus reinforcing, *ceteris paribus*, the interest elasticity of the total demand for cash holdings. It is assumed that the rational individual will prefer to transfer his income receipt into an interest-yielding asset and then successively transfer portions of the asset back into cash to fulfil his transactions needs. The cost of holding idle transactions cash is the interest forgone; this explains the incentive to minimize cash holding by increasing the frequency with which one turns assets into cash. However, there are costs associated with liquidation of the asset – not least the cost of inconvenience. Hence the dilemma confronting the rational maximizing individual – how to allocate one's assets between cash and interest-yielding bonds, given that there are costs in holding cash and costs associated with turning bonds into cash. More formally, if Y is the income receipt, i the rate of interest, b the cost of turning bonds into cash and K the value of the bonds turned into cash to meet successive transactions needs, the question confronting the utility maximizer is how to determine the size of K, the cash holding per transactions period. Since the average cash holding will be $K/2$, the interest forgone by holding cash will be $(K/2)i$. The cost of turning assets (bonds) into cash will be determined by the number of occasions liquidation is resorted to; thus the liquidation cost is $b(Y/K)$. Total costs are, accordingly,

$$TC = b(Y/K) + (K/2)i \qquad (5.10)$$

which will be minimized when

$$\frac{d(TC)}{dK} = 0 \quad \text{or} \quad -bY/K^2 + i/2 = 0 \tag{5.11}$$

Solving for K yields

$$K = \sqrt{\frac{2bY}{i}} \tag{5.12}$$

and the transactions demand for cash, the average cash holding, is

$$\frac{K}{2} = \left(\frac{1}{2}\right)\sqrt{\frac{2bY}{i}} \tag{5.13}$$

The rational individual thus acts to minimize the total costs associated with meeting his transactions needs, and a raising of the rate of interest will decrease his demand for transactions cash and vice versa. It may also be noted that if the act of liquidation were costless there would be no demand for transactions balances – a conclusion intuitively appealing.[4]

Tobin and the Keynesian Asset Demand for Cash

The Keynesian asset demand for cash rests upon the assumption that individuals possess a concept of a normal or expected rate of interest. If the existing market rate of interest is in excess of the normal rate, then the expectation is that market rates will fall or, alternatively, that bond prices will rise. In such a situation, all asset cash would be turned into the purchase of bonds in the anticipation of making a capital gain and consequently the individual's asset demand for cash would be zero. Conversely, if existing market rates lie below that expected, the individual would possess a zero demand for bonds and his demand for asset cash would be infinite. The logic of the Keynesian position, therefore, is that the individual holds either asset cash or bonds but not both simultaneously; the conventional Keynesian aggregate demand curve for asset money holdings is accordingly derived from the assumption that different individuals possess different expectations about the normal rate. This dichotomy has been summarized with the aid of figures 5.1 and 5.2.

The difficulty with such a statement lies in the fact that it does not accord with the observation that individuals are inclined to hold both speculative balances and bonds simultaneously. To meet such an objection, Tobin (1958) proposed a reformulation of the Keynesian demand for asset money which asserts that potential bondholders are uncertain about future interest rates. If uncertainty prevails, then investment in long-dated bonds involves the risk of a capital gain or loss. The potential investor therefore must weigh the element of risk against the expected return his investment will yield. Optimal decision-making requires resort to conventional indifference analysis and suggests that normally the individual will hold both bonds and speculative balances.

The argument is summarized with the aid of figure 5.7. The lower portion of the figure depicts the allocation of total assets between idle cash holdings and bonds, whilst the upper portion illustrates the trade-off between risk, measured on the horizontal

---

4 It will be appreciated that Baumol's specification modifies the Keynesian transaction demand in one further respect. Whereas the Keynesian demand for transaction balances was strictly proportional to the income level, Baumol's model implies possible economies of scale in cash holding by positing a non-proportional relationship.

Figure 5.7 Risk and the simultaneous holding of cash and bonds

axis, and expected return,[5] measured on the vertical. Assume the initial interest rate i_1. Then, as revealed by the indifference curves, the optimal combination will be 0X of risk combined with an expected return 0Z, implying an investment of 0A in bonds and retention of YB in cash. Now consider the effect of an increase in the rate of interest. The interest line will be pivoted leftwards to i_2, raising the expected return associated with any degree of risk. How will the individual investor respond? A priori, it is not possible to provide a definitive answer to this question. The rise in interest rates will incorporate an *income effect*, permitting the investor the luxury of undertaking less risk, whilst also promoting a *substitution effect* in favour of more risk as the cost of maintaining idle balances is now increased. However, if, as depicted in the diagram, the substitution effect is the stronger, the investor will increase his risk-taking and deplete his holding of asset cash. In the figure, the degree of risk rises to 0R, the expected yield becomes 0E, investment in bonds is indicated as 0C and speculative money balances fall to YS. All that is needed to obtain the Keynesian result of an inverse relationship between the asset demand for money and the rate of interest is the assumption that the substitution effect outweighs the income effect in an analysis that reconciles the simultaneous holding of both cash and bonds.

Tobin's analysis must be considered an advance upon conventional Keynesian analysis primarily because it is consistent with the empirically observed fact that certain individuals do indeed hold both bonds and money for speculative purposes, which is implicitly denied in the Keynesian analysis. In so doing, it fully allows for differences

---

5 The expected return includes the expectation of a capital gain or loss possessing an expected mean value of zero.

in individual preferences and tastes towards risk and can, of course, be generalized to choices involving more than two assets. Together with Baumol's specification of an interest-sensitive transactions demand for money which is non-proportional to income, it serves to strengthen the case for the overall Keynesian approach to the demand for money.

The Revival of the Quantity Theory

The revival of the quantity theory of money is primary due to the work of Milton Friedman and a group of adherents who, rightly or wrongly, have been dubbed members of the 'Chicago school'. The association between the quantity theory and the University of Chicago is in part explained by Friedman's claim that this institution 'was one of the few academic centers at which the quantity theory continued to be a central and vigorous part of the oral tradition throughout the 1930s and 1940s, where students continued to study monetary theory and write theses on monetary problems' (Friedman, 1956a). It should perhaps be mentioned that this claim has been challenged, notably by Patinkin (1969). What cannot be denied, however, is that in 1956 there appeared under Friedman's editorship a most important volume entitled *Studies in the Quantity Theory of Money* (Friedman, 1956b), the product of the Workshop in Money and Banking at Chicago, and which more than any other event signalled the re-emergence of the quantity theory.

The statement which emerges from this volume is strikingly different from the orthodox version of the quantity theory. Whereas the latter had been concerned primarily to explain fluctuations in the price level, the modern quantity theory is a theory of the determination of *money national income*. A monetary change is looked upon as being the causal agent in generating a change in money GNP, whether on the side of output, prices or some combination of the two. In this respect, at least, it is similar to the conventional Keynesian theory which argues that a change in the money supply will normally generate a change in money GNP by working through interest rate changes. Indeed, one of the controversies between Keynesians and monetarists turns upon the most appropriate approach to national income determination. Keynesians emphasize income expenditure relationships and the stability of the multiplier (stable marginal propensity to consume), where monetarists point to the alleged stability of the velocity function.

If the quantity theory is a theory of the determination of money national income, it follows that the impact of a change in the money stock can be either upon physical output, or prices, or some combination of the two. In this respect, it is not unlike the modern Keynesian approach which argues that the impact of a change in the money stock will reveal itself either in output or in price changes, depending upon the extent of unemployed resources. However, in contrast to the Keynesian statement, the relationship between changes in the money stock and resulting changes in money national income is held to be much more predictable and the special case of the liquidity trap, whereby a change in the money stock exerts no effect, is explicitly denied. Further, the extent to which changes will occur upon the side of output or prices will depend in large measure upon the period employed. It is Friedman's assertion that whilst changes in the volume of money may influence short-term movements in output, employment and interest rates, in the long run these variables will approach their 'natural' levels which exist independently of the volume of money.

Of central importance to the revised quantity theory is the assertion that there exists a stable demand function for real money holdings. This of course is not to assert that the quantity of real money holdings remains unchanged but only that it varies in a reasonably predictable way in response to changes in a few key variables. For Friedman, the most important elements influencing the demand for money are the rates of return on money and other assets, both real and financial, the level of permanent income, and the ratio of non-human to total wealth. More specifically, the demand for real money holdings may be written as

$$\frac{M}{P} = f(r_m, \ r_b, \ r_e, \ P^e, \ Y, \ w, \ u) \tag{5.14}$$

r_m is the expected nominal rate of return on money; it will ordinarily be zero for money kept in the form of cash but may be either positive or negative with regard to money held in the form of bank deposits, according to whether such deposits yield net interest or are subject to net service charges. r_b is the expected nominal rate of return on bonds, including expected changes in their prices, and likewise r_e is the expected rate of return on equities, allowance again being made for expected price changes. P^e is the expected rate of change of prices, and hence the expected nominal rate of return on real assets if for simplicity their expected yield is ignored. Y is permanent income and hence an index of total wealth, and w that percentage of total wealth which is held in non-human form and thereby readily realizable – for example, as property holdings. Finally, the variable u takes account of all other influences which may determine preference patterns generally. Thus, for example, an increase in the expectation of inflation would normally produce a decline in the demand for money holdings – that is, a rise in velocity. Far from velocity being constant, as was tacitly implied in many of the more naïve versions of the traditional approach, it will respond to significant changes in the above variables in a *predictable* and rational manner. But – and this seems to be the essence of the modern approach – the variables described are normally subject to only slow change over time whereas the supply of money may experience abrupt change. If this is the case, and velocity is subject only to gradual change over time whilst the money stock may rise and fall rapidly, the clear implication is that the demand for money is independent of its supply.

If the demand for money does not show great variation by comparison with the supply, which may experience considerable and rapid fluctuation, then changes in the value of money – which as anything else are to be explained in terms of supply and demand – are almost always supply determined.

To quote Friedman (1968b):

It is clear from this discussion that changes in prices and nominal income can be produced either by changes in the real balances that people wish to hold or by changes in the nominal balances available for them to hold. Indeed, it is a tautology, summarized in the famous quantity equation. . . . The quantity theorem is not, however, this tautology. It is, rather, the empirical generalization that changes in desired real balances (in the demand) tend to proceed slowly and gradually or to be the result of events set in train by prior changes in supply, whereas, in contrast, substantial changes in the supply of nominal balances can and frequently do occur independently of any changes in demand. The conclusion is that substantial changes in prices or nominal income are almost invariably the result of changes in the nominal supply of money.

This passage also makes it clear why the interest rate sensitivity of the demand for money is such a vital issue. In the UK the attempt has been made to control the money supply by controlling interest rates. Accordingly, it follows that if the demand for money was highly interest elastic, supply and demand would be interdependent and no precise causal influence could be discerned.

The fundamental point of issue between the traditional quantity theory and the Keynesian onslaught turns upon the crucial question of what constitutes an effective substitute for money balances. The Keynesian position is to contend that the only close substitute for money is alternative financial assets. It follows that if the monetary authorities increase the volume of money excessively a purchase of financial assets will occur and interest rates will fall. The reduction in interest rates renders money holding more attractive and other assets less attractive until eventually a new equilibrium is restored between the actual money stock and desired holdings. The implication is that the demand for money would be unstable or – what is the same thing – the velocity of money would be subject to considerable variation as a consequence of changes in its supply. Irrespective of the extent of the interest rate effect, the conventional Keynesian position is to postulate that the induced consequences for investment and consumption spending would be limited. The limitation on investment spending derives from the assumption that investment demands are often interest inelastic whilst the limitation on induced consumption effects implies that the wealth effect of a fall in interest rates (applicable to the holders of government debt, for example) is a minor factor in the consumption function.

In contrast, the traditional quantity theory had maintained that the only possible substitute for excessive money balances was goods and services; the role of financial assets was virtually ignored. There followed the common conclusion that an enlargement of the total money stock would increase the monetary expenditure on commodities, thereby generating price increases. Implicit in this approach and essential to the validity of the doctrine was the assumption that the demand for money was comparatively stable – that is, the velocity was comparatively constant. This assumption was usually justified upon the grounds that the only demand for money was the normal transactions demand. Moreover, if the principal determinant of consumption expenditure is permanent income (as monetarists would contend) then it is likely that the demand for transactions balances will be stable and predictable.

The modern revival and reformulation of the quantity theory straddles both these viewpoints. Money is looked upon as a substitute for all assets whether real or financial. An increase in the quantity of money will accordingly generate a general increase in demand for commodities in addition to exerting an impact upon interest rates. Although the immediate impact may indeed be felt in financial markets, complete adjustment will involve the commodity markets as well.

Of fundamental importance to the modern quantity theory is the belief that the demand for money is generally insensitive to changes in the interest rate. If the demand for money were to reveal a substantial degree of interest elasticity it would imply that a change in the money stock should be accommodated by a comparatively small change in interest rates, inducing people to extend their demand for money to match the supply. Under these conditions little could follow from a change in the money stock; the impact upon commodity markets would be minimized and the enlarged money supply would simply be held at the lower interest rate, implying a significant decline in the average velocity of money. If, on the other hand, the demand for money were decidedly interest inelastic then the initial interest rate change would not satisfy those people holding excessive money balances; direct spending on goods and services would occur, influencing the level of money incomes within the economy. Implicit in this contention of interest rate insensitivity is the notion that the transactions motive dominates the asset motive in the total demand for money.

Some Empirical Evidence

The preceding theoretical arguments have suggested reasons why the demand for money might be expected to respond positively to real income changes on the one hand and negatively to interest rate changes upon the other. Before the empirical evidence is briefly reviewed, it may be noted that the extent of this responsiveness is crucial for policy purposes and for the relative efficacy of monetary versus fiscal policy. In addition, the stability of any alleged relationship is fundamental to the monetarist inflationary mechanism and also carries implications for monetary control upon the part of the monetary authorities. Thus, for example, if the demand for money is a relatively stable function of income and the rate of interest, then it suggests that the monetary authorities may be able to control the supply of money by operating upon the demand for money by changes in the rate of interest. It is indeed the case in the UK that the authorities have relied upon the interest rate as a principal means of controlling and regulating the demand for money by the private sector. Finally, knowledge of the income elasticity of the demand for money is needed to establish money supply targets consistent with given rates of inflation, real gross domestic product (GDP) growth and interest rates. To illustrate, suppose the authorities are aiming at a 5 per cent increase in nominal GDP composed of a 2 per cent increase in real GDP and 3 per cent inflation, and that the income elasticity of the demand for money is estimated at 0.5. Then an increase in the nominal money supply equal to 4 per cent will be required in order to leave interest rates unchanged, since this is the amount by which the demand for nominal money is expected to increase.[6] Empirical findings concerning the determinants of the demand for money, therefore, are of interest in terms not only of the validation of theoretical standpoints but also of the formulation of the appropriate policy stance.

Virtually all the available evidence confirms the expected positive relationship between the demand for money and income on the one hand and the negative relationship between the demand for money and interest rates upon the other. However, considerable variation emerges in the values of the regression coefficients obtained. A good deal of this variation may be accounted for by pointing to differences in the definition of income, money and interest rates employed.

Thus, for example, in the UK the demand for money exhibits greater interest elasticity when regressed against long-term rates of interest as opposed to short-term rates, and the interest elasticity is lower the broader the definition of money employed. It is also of interest to compare UK and USA data. In an important and influential early study, Laidler (1971a), whilst emphasizing the similarity of British and American findings, noted that the UK results were much more sensitive to the definitions of money, income and interest rates employed and also more sensitive to changes in the length of the lag structure assumed.

---

6 Since the demand for money is a real demand, a 3 per cent inflation rate will generate a 3 per cent increase in the demand for nominal money holdings, *ceteris paribus*. The additional 1 per cent then arises from the assumption of a 2 per cent growth in real income and the income elasticity of demand of 0.5.

Although there is now a general consensus that interest rates are important in the overall demand for money, there is little evidence to support the proposition that the interest elasticity of the demand for money increases as interest rates decline. This finding would appear to exclude both the vertical LM curve of classical monetary economics on the one hand as well as the Keynesian case of the liquidity trap on the other.

There also appears to be fairly general agreement that whilst the demand for money appeared to be a relatively stable function of a few key variables until the early 1970s, this stability appeared to break down in the wake of the institutional changes which characterized the 1970s and 1980s. In the case of the UK the date 1971 is significant, since this marked the introduction of competition and credit control which foreshadowed considerable aggressive competition between the banks and other financial institutions. This would suggest that the stability of the demand for money function would itself depend upon the nature of institutional changes.

The Friedman Findings

No discussion of the empirical evidence would be complete without mentioning the controversial and provocative attempts of Milton Friedman to establish an independent *causal* role for money and monetary policy. In an important early (1958) study, Friedman compared the turning points in the rate of change in the money supply with the turning points in the level of economic activity (income) for the US economy, using data going back to 1870. His findings – namely that the peaks in the change in the money supply preceded peaks in the level of economic activity, by some 16 months on average, whilst the troughs in the change in the money supply preceded troughs in economic activity by some 12 months on average – was taken by Friedman to provide persuasive evidence of a causal link running from money to income.

Not surprisingly, Friedman's thesis was quickly challenged along essentially '*Post hoc ergo propter hoc*' modes of attack. The timing evidence in itself cannot be taken as conclusive – as indeed Friedman had initially conceded. In figure 5.8, for example, it is not impossible that the peak in the rate of change in the money supply occurring at time t_2 is caused by the prior peak in the level of income at time t_1, as opposed to being the cause of the peak in the level of income occurring at time t_2. Alternatively, both money supply and income level peaks could be caused by some third external factor with the money supply peaks showing the quicker response.

The most damning charge against Friedman's claim, however, stemmed from Kareken and Solow (1963) on purely methodological grounds. Essentially, their critique turned upon the comparison being made between the peaks in the *rate of change* in the money supply and the peaks in the *level* of economic activity. If, instead, the comparison is made between the peaks in the *rate of change* in the money supply and the peaks in the *rate of change* in the level of economic activity, using the same data, the alleged lead of money over activity disappears.

The time series data presented by Friedman in 1958 was but a forerunner to the monumental Friedman and Schwartz (1963) volume *A Monetary History of the United States, 1867–1960*. This elegant and influential book presented time series data on the money supply (primarily M2), its components, and its perceived influence upon the economy. Essentially, the argument presented here suggested that the history of the money stock was able to provide a complete macroeconomic history of the US demonstrating long-run neutrality combined with short-run non-neutrality given short-run price rigidities. In particular, the Great Depression was explained in terms of

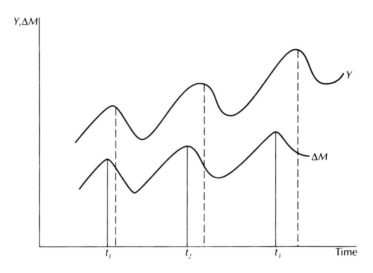

Figure 5.8 Money and income: lags or leads?

mistaken Federal Reserve policy failing to prevent an undue contraction of the money supply.

The framework is unmistakably that of the modern quantity theory with interest rates accorded a comparatively minor role. Whilst the importance of money is dominant the theoretical framework and the transmission mechanism by which money takes its effects are treated only minimally. In particular, the source of monetary change in held to be immaterial which was a point seized upon by the critics. For Tobin (1963), for example, the 'fountain pens of commercial bankers are essentially different from the printing presses of government'. None the less, *A Monetary History* remains a classic which greatly influenced the rise of the monetarist counter revolution. For a recent appraisal, thirty years on, see especially Lucas (1994).

Finally, mention may be made of Friedman and Meiselman's (1963) study for the Commission on Money and Credit which provoked an heated exchange with DePrano and Mayer (1965) and Ando and Modigliani (1965) and which was notable primarily for pointing to the limitations of simple regression analysis. Stated simply, Friedman and Meiselman regressed changes in income, firstly against money supply changes and secondly against changes in autonomous expenditure. In this manner, they hoped to compare the explanatory powers of quantity theory and Keynesian approaches to national income determination. Not surprisingly, Friedman and Meiselman concluded that the money supply equation provided the better fit.

Much of the subsequent debate turned upon the appropriate definition of autonomous expenditure and it was argued that alternative definitions could overturn the Friedman–Meiselman conclusion. However, regardless of definitions, it was unlikely that simple regression analysis could ever be conclusive. Indeed, it is perfectly possible for the empirical findings to suggest the wrong conclusion. Suppose, for example, that money is the driving force in determining national income. An increase in the money supply could be expected to lower interest rates and in so doing promote an increase in investment expenditure. It would then be possible for the empirical evidence to identify increased 'autonomous' investment expenditure as being the main determinant of income change. For more detailed critique along these lines, see especially Snowdon, Vane and Wynarczyk (1994).

In the ultimate analysis, simple regression equations can imply nothing about causation. Indeed, regardless of the equations, the economy may be driven neither by quantity theory nor Keynesian models but rather by some third force – sun spot activity, for example, to invoke the spirit of Jevons. The debate stemming from the Friedman–Meiselman findings was probably of value in highlighting this point.[7]

Finally, it should perhaps be emphasized that whilst Friedman sought to demonstrate the primacy of money supply changes in governing the progress of the macroeconomy, he did not seek to advocate *discretionary* monetary policy. Because of the uncertainty and variability of the time lags involved in the formulation and execution of monetary policy, and because of the lag in effect, discretionary monetary changes were perceived as potentially destabilizing. Instead of discretionary monetary intervention, Friedman was to advocate simple monetary rules such as expanding the money supply in line with the long-term growth path of the economy. Indeed, simple rules of this nature, by removing an element of uncertainty, would of themselves be conducive to enhanced macroeconomic stability.

Concluding Comments

This chapter has attempted to analyse the major influences governing the demand for money. This issue is of considerable importance owing to the unique role performed by money in the modern economy. Any significant change in the demand for money will have repercussions throughout the rest of the economy, with particular implications for interest rates and the price level. It has been seen that the evolution of ideas upon the demand for money has generated considerable controversy and has produced a conceptual revolution in the way economists view the macroeconomy. Today there is a general consensus to the effect that two of the major influences on the demand of money are the rate of interest and the level of income, but differences still exist about the significance of the statistical relationships so obtained and indeed about the manner in which these variables are to be defined. Considerable dispute still remains in the area of policy implications. For example, if the demand for money is sensitive to a change in the rate of interest, however defined, it suggests that interest rate policy may be one means of controlling the supply of money by governing the demand. These issues, *inter alia*, will be taken up in the next chapter.

Further Reading

One of the best all-round texts on the demand for money remains Laidler (1977, 4th edn 1993). This provides an overview of all the principal approaches as well as a concise and lucid review of empirical problems and empirical studies. An equally valuable presentation is that offered by Cuthbertson (1985). Principal research findings for the UK economy are ably surveyed in Artis and Lewis (1991). Many of the issues discussed in

---

7 Although this did not prevent similar exercises evaluating the comparative effectiveness of fiscal and monetary policy emanating, in particular, from the Federal Reserve Bank of St Louis. See, for example, Andersen and Jordan (1968).

the present chapter are examined in the New Palgrave volume *Money,* edited by Eatwell, Milgate and Newman (1989).

Chapters 13–15 of Keynes (1936) provide the original statement on the Keynesian transactions, precautionary and speculative motives for holding money. The seminal contributions on the post-Keynesian refinements of the transactions and speculative motives respectively are to be found in Baumol (1952) and Tobin (1956, 1958), and the seminal contribution on the modern monetarist approach in Friedman (1956a). Edited versions of the first two are to be found in Surrey (1975).

For a detailed analysis of the theoretical underpinnings of the demand for money, see especially Patinkin (1965) and Rousseas (1972).

6

The Supply of Money

In the analysis of the demand for money in chapter 5, it was assumed that the supply of money was exogenously determined and could be readily controlled by the monetary authorities. As we shall see later, control of the money supply is an important element in several strategies for economic management, in particular the several variants of 'monetarism'.

In this chapter we will examine the money supply process in somewhat greater detail. We will first of all attempt to establish whether in principle the money supply can be controlled, and the instruments which may be deployed in any attempts at monetary control. Following that, with particular reference to recent UK experience, we will consider whether in practice the money supply can be controlled. This issue has been the subject of heated debate in recent years and has exercised the minds of a great many academics, administrators and politicians.

The Money Supply Process

Before comment is made on the instruments which can be and have been employed to try and influence the money supply, the process by which the money supply expands or contracts in a modern developed market economy ought to be considered in more detail.

Money Multipliers

Most readers will be familiar with the proposition that if the central bank increases its liabilities and injects a volume of new notes and coins into the banking system, the commercial banks, in seeking profitable outlets for any addition to deposits, can expand the money stock by several times the original injection. The old adage 'every deposit creates a loan and every loan creates a deposit' concisely summarizes this process. Because the original increase in central bank liabilities results in a multiplied expansion of bank deposits, the original injection is referred to as *high-powered money*. The extent to which any change in high-powered money is multiplied into a greater change in the money supply is dependent on the value of the *money multiplier*.

One of the most celebrated and frequently cited money multiplier models is that due to Friedman and Schwartz (1963). The details of this model can be elaborated quite easily. Assume that all banks in the system maintain a certain fraction *r* of their deposit liabilities, D, in the form of liquid assets to meet the needs of day-to-day demands for cash balances. These will be referred to as *bank reserves R*. Therefore

$$R - rD \tag{6.1}$$

The *reserve ratio r* may be set by the authorities in a regulated system, or determined by prudential judgement in an unregulated system. *Deposit liabilities* are the assets of the general public. Not all of the public's financial assets will normally be deposited in the banking system, however. Ordinarily a certain fraction c of D will be held in the form of notes and coin, C, for day-to-day transactions and precautionary motives. Thus,

$$C = cD \tag{6.2}$$

Given equations 6.1 and 6.2, the stock of high-powered money can be defined as

$$H = C + R \tag{6.3}$$

Variations in H result in multiplied variations in the money stock, M, where this is defined as:

$$M = C + D \tag{6.4}$$

The relationship between H and M can be easily ascertained. First, divide equation 6.4 by equation 6.3:

$$\frac{M}{H} = \frac{C + D}{C + R} \tag{6.5}$$

Then divide the right-hand side of equation 6.5 through by D:

$$\frac{M}{H} = \frac{c + 1}{c + r} \tag{6.6}$$

which can be rearranged to

$$M = \left(\frac{c + 1}{c + r}\right) H \tag{6.7a}$$

According to equation 6.7a, the money stock and changes in the money supply are determined by the volume of high-powered money, the general public's currency/deposit ratio and the bank's reserve ratio. These factors are referred to as the *proximate determinants* of the money supply, and influence the money supply as follows:

$$\frac{\partial M}{\partial H} > 0 \tag{6.7b}$$

$$\frac{\partial M}{\partial c} < 0 \tag{6.7c}$$

$$\frac{\partial M}{\partial r} < 0 \tag{6.7d}$$

The Relationships between M, H, c *and* r

The interrelationships between M, H, c and r can be illustrated diagrammatically. In figure 6.1 it is assumed for simplicity that the only source of reserves to the banks is currency, and that the volume of currency made available is determined by the public's currency/deposit ratio. If the central bank issues 0A of currency and the general public

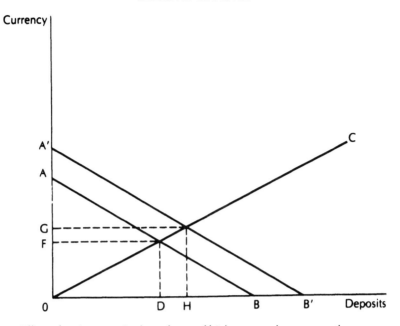

Figure 6.1 Effect of an increase in the volume of high-powered money on the money supply

holds 0F, the remainder FA will be held by the banks. The extent to which the banks can use these reserves to create loans and further deposits is determined by their reserve ratio. If this were set at unity, then every deposit would have to be backed by currency and the slope of the line AB would have an absolute value of one. When the reserve ratio is less than one, of course the banks need only hold a certain fraction of any deposit in currency and lend the remainder to deficit units, some of which will ultimately be redeposited. Thus, when the reserve ratio is less than unity, the slope of AB will have an absolute value of less than unity, reflecting the fact that the volume of bank deposits exceeds the volume of currency held by the banks. In figure 6.1, the position and slope of AB are determined by the stock of currency and the reserve ratio respectively, whilst the ray 0C is determined by the public's currency/deposit ratio. A higher value for this ratio would result in a steeper 0C, whilst a lower value would result in a shallower 0C.

This framework can be used to explore the impact of changes in H, c and r on M.

Assume initially that the stock of currency is given by 0A. Given an initial currency/deposit ratio of 0C, 0F is held by the public and FA deposited with the banks. Given a reserve ratio as reflected by the slope of AB, the banks use this currency to back loans, and the equilibrium volume of deposits which results from reserves of FA is 0D. The money supply initially amounts to 0F (currency held by the public) and 0D (bank deposits). Suppose now that the central bank increases the stock of currency from 0A to 0A'. With an unchanged c, the public's holdings of currency increase to 0G whilst the amount held by the banks increases to GA'. With a given reserve ratio, this increase in reserves facilitates a multiplied expansion of bank deposits from 0D to 0H. The ultimate effect of the increase in currency (high-powered money) is an increase in the money supply from 0F + 0D to 0G + 0H. It should be clear by inspection that DH > FG; in other words, the money supply process has resulted in a multiplied expansion of M such that $\Delta M > \Delta H$. This follows because the reserve ratio has been set at less than one, and because the public's currency/deposit ratio is also less than one.

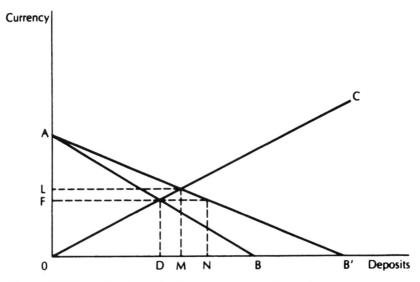

Figure 6.2 Effect of a change in the reserve asset ratio on the money supply

The latter ensures that part of the initial increase in currency is redeposited with the banks, whilst the former generates a loan deposit process.

Figure 6.2 outlines the effect of a fall in the reserve ratio, given a stock of currency of 0A and given a currency/deposit ratio of 0C. AB rotates to AB'. The reduction in the reserve ratio facilitates increased lending and multiplied deposit creation of up to 0N. Given, however, that a proportion of new loans is held in currency and not redeposited, bank deposits increase from 0D to 0M, whilst currency held by the public increases from 0F to 0L, the overall impact being a rise in the money supply from 0D + 0F to 0L + 0M. The same analysis would apply, *mutatis mutandis*, to a rise in the reserve ratio.

Finally, in figure 6.3 the implications of a fall in the currency/deposit ratio are explored. Assume that this falls; and results in 0C rotating to 0C'. With an unchanged

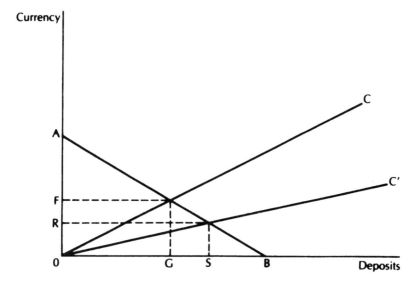

Figure 6.3 Effect of a change in the currency/deposit ratio on the money supply

reserve ratio, and a fixed stock of currency of 0A, the volume of currency held by the banks increases from FA to RA, which in turn facilitates a multiple expansion of deposits from 0G to 0S. Here one component of the money supply, currency held by the public, contracts whilst the other, bank deposits, expands. As long as the banks' reserve ratio is less than one, however, the expansion of deposits will exceed the contraction in currency holdings, and the overall impact will be an increase in the money supply. (It can readily be seen that this is the case in figure 6.3 where GS > FR.)

Thus, the money multiplier model, or *monetary base* model, as it is sometimes known, predicts that the money supply will be determined by *the volume of high-powered money* in the system, *the banks' reserve ratio*, and *the public's currency/deposit ratio*. From the point of view of monetary control, this implies that if r and c could be taken as given, the authorities can control variations in M by manipulating H. If, however, c and r are essentially unstable and unpredictable, it could be that efforts to control M by controlling H are frustrated.

Controllability of High-powered Money

In the simple model of figures 6.1–6.3 it was assumed that the only component of H was currency. In equation 6.3, however, H was defined as equal to $C + R$, where the latter constitute non-currency reserves. If both C and R were liabilities of the central bank, then it would be reasonable to conclude that the central bank is in a position to influence H. Certainly in most developed market economies, currency is unambiguously a liability of the central bank. (In the UK this stock is controlled by the Issue Department of the Bank of England.) In principle, therefore, C is under the direct control of the authorities. In practice, however, C is not used as a means of influencing M. The authorities tend to permit C to be determined by the needs of exchange. Thus attempts to control H are directed at R or *non-currency reserve assets*.

Since the central bank decides what constitutes *eligible reserve assets*, in principle this too should be under its control. In practice, however, this may not be so. In the UK, for example, largely for historical reasons, reserve assets have been defined in such a way that certain components are not subject to direct influence by the central bank. Although the system of monetary control was altered in 1981, it is worth dwelling on arrangements in the period immediately preceding this in order to elaborate on this point. Not only does it serve to highlight some of the fundamental difficulties of monetary control, but also it will help towards an understanding of the rationale behind recent changes.

Between 1971 and 1981, reserve assets of the clearing banks in the UK were defined to include: the banks' balances with the Bank of England; UK Treasury bills; money at call in the London discount market; British Government stocks with up to one year to maturity; local authority bills eligible for rediscount at the Bank of England; and commercial bills. Clearly there are certain components over which the central bank can exercise direct influence – namely, balances with the Bank of England, the total volume of Treasury bills and Government stocks – though not the accounts actually held by the banks. In addition, in principle the issue of local authority bills can be controlled if central government imposes limits on the amount which local authorities can borrow using this source. In so far as these volumes are controllable, the stock of high-powered money can be controlled. There are two components, however, over which complete control cannot be exercised – namely, commercial bills and money at call. It is worth noting, however, that this may still serve to complicate monetary control if the banking system were holding commercial bills at a very low level prior to a period of monetary restraint. Money at call is a substantial fraction of total reserve assets. In principle the central bank has some control over this volume in that money at call with the discount houses has largely been made available for the purchase of Treasury bills. Other things being equal, therefore, a reduction in the number of Treasury bills released to the discount houses should result in a reduction in their demand for money at call from the clearing banks. A complication for monetary control could, however, arise if the discount houses place with the clearing banks reserve assets (like commercial bills) which are not included in the banks' own portfolio.

It might be argued that such complications are marginal and that the central bank can in practice exercise control over the bulk of high-powered money. To assume that, because the central authorities are the source of most reserve assets, they can therefore actually control the flow of such assets, is to oversimplify the process of monetary control in the extreme. To see why, consider further the source of variations in the supply of reserve assets.

The change in the volume of high-powered money over any given period is determined by the amount which the authorities have to borrow over that time period, and the way in which this is borrowed. Specifically,

$$PSD + MAT = ECF + OMO_N + NMD + OMO_B + \Delta H \tag{6.8}$$

where PSD is the public sector deficit, MAT are funds required for debt maturities, ECF is the change in foreign exchange assets, OMO_N are open market operations with the non-bank private sector, NMD are transactions in non-marketable debt (e.g. National Savings), OMO_B are sales of non-reserve asset debt to the banking system, and ΔH is the change in high-powered money (that is, the issue of currency and sales of securities to the clearing banks).

If equation 6.8 is rearranged, then

$$\Delta H = PSD + MAT - ECF - OMO_N - NMD - OMO_B \tag{6.9}$$

The change in high-powered money is therefore determined by the extent to which the authorities can fund the *public sector deficit* without recourse to issuing notes and coin, and without recourse to selling government bonds to the clearing banks. Although the relationship between the public sector deficit and the volume of high-powered money will be examined in greater detail later, a number of observations should be made. First, the change in the volume of high-powered money is dependent on non-bank demand for short-term government securities, bank demand for non-reserve asset (long-term) debt, the sale of non-marketable debt to the general public, and the magnitude of any balance of payments imbalance. The sale of non-reserve asset debt clearly depends on the yields offered on such securities relative to competing assets. The demand for such assets may not be easily predicted. This may be further complicated by the fact that the size of the deficit may turn out to be different from what is 'planned'. If, for example, interest rates are raised to restrict credit and to increase the attractiveness of government securities to the non-bank public, one outcome may be that output and employment are reduced. If this follows, the public sector deficit will automatically increase as tax receipts fall and social security transfers increase. The borrowing requirement is correspondingly increased and, *ceteris paribus*, so too is the extent to which this has to be funded by high-powered money.

The second complication which must be noted is the role played by the balance of payments. It can be seen from equations 6.8 and 6.9 that balance of payments surpluses and deficits (which for present purposes will be equated with ECF) will affect the borrowing requirement. If, for example, the UK runs an unanticipated balance of payments surplus, there would be net purchases (sales) of foreign exchange (sterling). To acquire the excess supply of foreign exchange, the central bank would either have to issue more notes and coin, or have to sell some of its holdings of Treasury bills to obtain the necessary notes and coin. In the former case there would be a net increase in high-powered money. In the latter case there would also probably be an increase in high-powered money, since the existence of the surplus means that, other things being equal, more Treasury bills must be sold to the banks or the stock of notes and coin has to increase. The point is that the balance of payments is not an easily predictable magnitude, and in an open economy like that in the UK, it may have important implications for monetary control. (This is something which will be returned to in chapters 14 and 15.)

Stability of the Reserve and Currency/Deposit Ratios

Even if the caveats which have been noted with respect to the controllability of H are inapplicable, it should be clear from equation 6.8 that for a systematic relationship to hold between H and M, the money multiplier has to be stable. In other words, the ratios r and c have to be taken as parameters. If they are variable rather than constant, then variations in r and c could offset variations in H.

There have been many occasions when a minimum value for r has been set in the UK by the central bank. The rationale behind such a requirement is that the clearing banks are forced to maintain a certain fraction of their assets in relatively liquid form in keeping with the tenets of financial prudence. Furthermore, by setting a reserve asset ratio, the authorities are provided with a further control variable whereby they can influence the amount of credit creation which takes place. Clearly, however, even when a minimum reserve asset ratio is set, the clearing banks still have a certain amount of discretion over the actual reserve asset ratio maintained. When, for example, nominal and real interest rates are relatively high, they may be expected to run down the ratio to its minimum (that is, become fully *loaned up*) compared with a situation of low interest rates and recessionary pressure. In such circumstances, a higher probability of default on loans might encourage them to permit the ratio to rise. (Interestingly, the UK experienced both high interest rates and recessionary pressures in the late 1970s and early 1980s and again in the late 1980s and early 1990s. If anything, the influence of high interest rates appears to have predominated, with banks tending to become fully loaned up.)

Much of the debate over whether the money supply is controllable or not centres on the stability of c, the public's currency/deposit ratio (or the general public's demand for cash balances). As has been seen in the previous chapter, those who argue that the demand for money is essentially a demand for a transactions asset would contend that c is both stable and predictable (and therefore so too is velocity). They would argue that c changes only slowly in response to technological change in the banking system. Thus, for example, over the long run c has tended to fall with increased use of credit cards' and other substitutes for currency.

It was noted in the last chapter, however, that the demand for money can be viewed as an exercise in portfolio selection and may therefore vary systematically with (for instance) changes in the rate of interest. Furthermore, as Baumol's model demonstrated, this may be so not only in considering a demand for speculative balances, but also in the case of transactions balances. If this is the case then this would comprise another potential source of variation in the money stock. Variations in H could be offset by variations in c. For example, a restriction of H which resulted in a rise in interest rates could stimulate a fall in c (and therefore an increase in velocity), which would serve to offset the effects of the initial contraction in the monetary base.[1]

Following from the simple multiplier approach, then, there are a number of question marks which can be placed against the controllability of the money supply. On the one hand, those of a monetarist persuasion would tend to argue that r and c can both be regarded as stable, the former because it can be set by the authorities, the latter because the demand for money is stable, and therefore control of H is both necessary and sufficient for control of M. Those of a more Keynesian persuasion would question the stability of c and the controllability of H. Furthermore, they would in general be more sceptical of the presence of a clear break in the liquidity chain between money and near money which monetarists contend exists. This scepticism has tended to become more acute as the importance of non-bank financial intermediaries (NBFIs) has increased. Clearly, if it is the case that money is readily substitutable for other financial assets, then the supply of money will be endogenous and less easily controlled by the monetary authorities. Monetary control requires the existence of a distinct group of assets for which the demand is stable and which are not readily substitutable for other financial assets.

Delineating the Money Stock

As was seen in chapter 5, the distinguishing characteristic of money is that it is an asset which can be used in the final settlement of a debt. In most societies, however, there may be more than one such asset in circulation at any time. Clearly, therefore, if one wishes to attempt to 'control' the size of the money stock, then one must delineate one group of assets which might be regarded as money from another group of assets regarded as non-money. The problem is of course that money is used not only for transactions purposes but also as a store of value. There may be certain highly liquid assets that are clearly and closely identified with the *transactions function*, such as notes and coin in circulation. Similarly, at the other end of the spectrum there exist certain highly illiquid assets which are clearly and closely identified with the *store of value function* such as long-term bonds. In between these extremes, however, there exists a range of assets of varying shades of liquidity, and it is far from obvious where the line should be drawn between money and non-money. In other words, there is no obvious break in the *liquidity chain*.

The point is easily illustrated by reference to the liquidity spectrum or chain in the UK. As has been noted, notes and coin in circulation are unambiguously 'money' used for transactions purposes; so too are demand deposits at commercial banks. If the authorities decide that notes and coin in circulation plus demand deposits are the relevant control variable, however, and pursue a policy of monetary contraction, one response on the part of economic agents might be to transfer cash balances from time

---

1 Note that this depends on the definition of the money stock which we are working with. If this is a narrow definition (currency plus demand deposits), then the statement holds true. If, however, it is a broader definition (currency plus demand deposits plus interest bearing deposits), then it need not be true.

deposit accounts to demand deposit accounts. Although time deposits are (in principle) less liquid than demand deposits, in practice they are quickly realizable. One might therefore include deposit accounts in the definition of the money supply. If one does, however, are deposits in the home currency only included, or are domestic residents' deposits in other currencies also to be included? If there are no exchange controls, then clearly domestic residents' deposits in overseas currencies could have a marked influence on the domestic money stock. (One outstanding example of this is the 'repatriation' of Eurodollars which often accompanies monetary restraint in the USA.) Furthermore, if time deposits with commercial banks are included in the definition of the money stock, what about time deposits with non-bank financial intermediaries, such as building societies? After all, to many these are regarded as substitutes for commercial bank time deposits. If one is including time deposits because they can be realized relatively quickly, then what about other assets whose capital value can be realized almost as quickly – short-term securities like Treasury bills, for example? If short-term securities are included, what is the appropriate definition of the short term?

Clearly, as soon as a move is made away from assets whose capital value is immediately realizable (notes and coin) towards assets whose capital value it takes time to realize, the problem is faced of deciding where the line should be drawn. It could be argued that the issue is an empirical one, and the 'appropriate' definition of the money supply is dependent on the reason for control. Suppose, for example, one wishes to control the rate of growth in money supply because one is convinced that it is systematically related to the rate of change of prices. Careful perusal of time series data would perhaps reveal that one monetary aggregate bears a closer relationship to changes in the price level than others. If so, then this is the aggregate to be controlled. This view too has been challenged, most notably by Goodhart (1989), who has argued that *any* measure of the money supply which is officially controlled loses its meaning because agents search for ways around the control in a relatively short space of time. This possibility is well illustrated by the experience in the UK of monetary targeting. Introduced by the Labour government in 1976, it was carried forward and extended by the succeeding Conservative government in its Medium Term Financial Strategy. Between 1979 and 1986, no less than 20 targets for sterling M_3 ($£M_3$)[2] were announced and only three were achieved. This led to the abandonment of $£M_3$ as a monetary target in 1986.

Money Supply Definitions in the UK

The uncertainty and what precisely constitutes the money stock in the UK is illustrated by the number of measures that have been used in recent years. The main money measures current in 1995 were as follows.

M_0 (The monetary base)   This measure comprises all the currency in circulation outside the Bank of England plus bankers' operational deposits with the Bank of England.

M_2 This measure comprises currency in circulation with the public plus sterling retail deposits with UK banks and building societies.

---

2 This was the main definition of broad money used during the period and comprised currency in circulation plus sterling sight and time bank deposits held by UK residents.

M_4 This measure comprises M_2 plus all other private-sector sterling deposits at banks and building societies including certificates of deposit.[3]

Table 6.1 shows the size of the various measures of the money supply in March 1995.

TABLE 6.1 UK Money Supply, March 1995*

	£M
Notes and coin outside of England	21 943
Bankers' operational deposits at Bank of England	304
M_0	21 884
Notes and coin with the public	18 459
Bank/retail deposits	189 258
Building society retail deposits	211 089
M_2	418 806
Wholesale bank deposits and CDs	150 971
Wholesale building society deposits and CDS	17 320
M_4	587 097

*M_0 is not a subset of M_2 and M_4 since it includes notes and coin held by the banks which are excluded from the latter.

Source: *Bank of England Quarterly Bulletin*, May 1995

M_0 is the *narrow* definition of the money supply and is sometimes referred to as the monetary base being analogous to high-powered money in the money multiplier model developed earlier. This measure was first introduced in 1982 and is one of the easiest for the authorities to control through open market operations. It has been criticized as being of little use as a measure of spending power in the economy, as the number of 'cash' transactions has declined as alternative means of payment have been developed and expanded in recent years.

To account for some of these criticisms, M_2 was also introduced in 1982 (and then modified in 1992). By including retail deposits of banks and building societies, it is a *transactions* measure of the money supply. In contrast, M_4, by including wholesale deposits, is the main *broad* measure of the money supply.

The variety of measures means that talking about *the* money supply is not sufficient. This is especially true if different measures are indicating different rates of growth. For example, a switch from sight deposits to time deposits as a result of a change in the interest rate differential would cause M_2 to fall but the M_4 measure would remain unchanged.

A recent development by the Bank of England has been the construction of a divisia index of the money stock. The idea behind the index is that different components be given different weights according to their ability to provide various services. Traditional monetary aggregates simply give a weight of one to all included elements and a weight of zero to those excluded. In constructing a transactions divisia index, those elements most likely to be used for such purposes such as cash and low-interest-bearing deposits might have a weight of one, whilst those less liquid high-interest-bearing deposits a weight closer to zero.

The Bank of England has constructed such an index which is calculated back to 1977 and published in their *Quarterly Bulletin*. Elementary statistical analysis would indicate that such an index might have proved a better indicator of future

---

3 M_4 is effectively the former measure with the inclusion of the building society sector.

economic performance than other measures. Whether this will prove true in the future is uncertain as one should always bear in mind Goodhart's caveat mentioned earlier.

Monetary Control in the UK

Figure 6.4 presents a simple model of the complete money market, in which is assumed a stable money demand function, M_d, inversely related to the rate of interest, and an exogenously given money supply function insensitive to interest rate changes. Suppose initially the money supply is M_1. If the authorities desire a money supply of M_2, it can be seen from the diagram that this can be attained through either a change in the quantity of money from M_{s1} to M_{s2} (which will raise its price), or a change in the price of money – that is, an increase in the interest rate from r_1 to r_2 – which results in a contraction of the demand for money. This might suggest that the choice of technique is simply a case of selecting between quantity controls or price controls. At the simplest level this is certainly so. When it is recalled, however, that any change in the money supply is itself the outcome of changes in a number of aggregates, it can be seen that the choice of technique is rather more complicated. Thus, quality controls could apply to bank deposits, or bank lending or private lending to the public sector, or changes in the reserve ratio; price controls could apply to bank deposits, bank lending, public borrowing from the private sector and so on. In fact, Gowland (1982) identifies no less than 17 methods of controlling M.

Constraints on space prevent the examination of the effects of all of these techniques in detail. Besides which, only a few have been relied on to any significant extent in the UK over the post-war period. These will be focused on with a view to commenting on some of the practical problems faced in controlling the money supply. The instruments which have been most widely applied in the UK are:

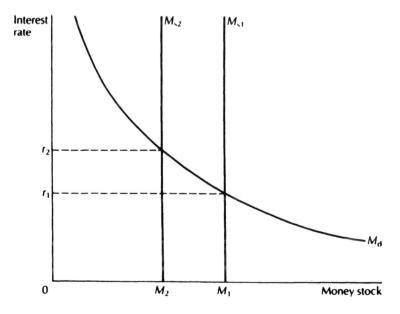

Figure 6.4 Money market equilibrium

1   *Quantity controls*
    (a) On bank lending to the non-bank private sector
    (b) On deposits through the supplementary special deposit scheme

2   *Price manipulations*
    (a) Sales of public sector debt to the non-bank private sector (open market operations)
    (b) Price effects on bank lending to the non-bank private sector

3   *Portfolio constraints*
    (a) Reliance on reserve asset ratios

4   *Monetary targets and the public sector borrowing requirement (PSBR)*

Before Competition and Credit Control

Prior to 1971, monetary control was largely attempted via *credit control* – that is, control of bank lending to the non-bank private sector. The central instruments deployed for this purpose were *credit ceilings*, imposed on the clearing banks, and *directives or moral suasion*. The former aimed to contain the total volume of credit creation, whilst the latter sought to influence the allocation of a given volume by, for example, directing the clearing banks to give priority to export-oriented firms or public corporations. It is not unusual to find that, when quantitative controls are imposed on any commodity or service, inefficiencies arise as individuals invest resources in seeking ways around the controls; attempts to control the growth of the money supply via quantitative restrictions generated similar avoidance activities.

For example, because Bank of England controls applied only to the clearing banks, there was a tremendous growth in *secondary banks* (merchant banks, savings banks, trade banks and so on), which were outside the London clearing system and were at the same time not subject to credit controls. Another by-product of using controls was the growth of so-called *disintermediation* – that is to say, borrowing-lending agreements which bypass the banks completely. In some cases the process actually became institutionalized, as, for example, in the *intercorporate money market* where companies borrow and lend to each other directly without a bank acting as financial intermediary.

This growth of secondary activities is entirely predictable in some respects. The Bank of England exercised some discretion over the structure of interest rates via its control of bank rate (that is, the rate at which it would lend money to the clearing banks). The fact that secondary banking and disintermediation became increasingly important in the 1960s is presumably indicative of an excess demand for credit at the administered price. Interest rate manipulations were on occasion used to try and influence credit demand through price; invariably, however, this instrument was only used when there was a balance of payments crisis. (As will be seen in chapter 21, since interest rate variations have a direct impact on the capital account of the balance of payments, they were frequently used in this period as an instrument for external balance.)

Note that although the potential usefulness of r (the reserve ratio) as a control variable was stressed earlier, it was simply not used over this period. Although a *cash ratio* (of 8 per cent of reserve assets) and a *liquidity ratio* (of 28 per cent of reserve assets) applied to the clearing banks, no systematic manipulation of these ratios for monetary control was practised. Monetary control via manipulation of r would amount to what is currently referred to as *monetary base control*; one feature of this is the market determination of interest rates, something which the UK authorities have been reluctant to accept.

One instrument which was used, however, and which has effects qualitatively similar to changes in r, was the use of *special deposits*. These were introduced in the UK in 1958. Their use entailed the placing of deposits by the clearing banks with the Bank of England, to be frozen at the latter's discretion, their objective being to reduce bank liquidity and reduce the ability of the banks to create credit. Special deposits were in fact employed quite frequently, and although Coghlan (1973) found some evidence to indicate that their use was effective, Crouch (1970) and Goodhart (1973) are sceptical of their impact.

Competition and Credit Control

In 1971 a new approach to monetary control was adopted with the introduction of *competition and credit control* (CCC), which seems to have been motivated by two objectives. On the one hand it was hoped that the new arrangements would stimulate greater competition between the clearing banks; on the other hand it was hoped that credit would be controlled more effectively than before 1971. The latter objective was born out of a dissatisfaction with the operation of direct controls, which not only were felt to have been ineffective but also made it difficult to measure changes in the volume of credit with any precision, since one could never be entirely clear on how much avoidance was actually taking place. Accordingly, reliance on quantitative controls was eschewed under CCC and instead greater emphasis placed on instruments which affected the money supply via price; in other words interest rate manipulations were thrust to the forefront. The target variable was seen as M_3 and it was planned to control the change in this variable by operating on the demand for credit. (It might also be noted that CCC replaced the cash and liquidity ratio with a $12\frac{1}{2}$ per cent reserve asset ratio, although there was no intention to move to a system of monetary base control as a consequence of this.)

The CCC arrangements lasted until the end of 1973. In 1972 M_3 grew by 22 per cent and in 1973 by 27 per cent. Since one of the principal objectives of the arrangements was to control credit in a more efficient way than previous arrangements, something clearly went badly wrong. The complete loss of control of the growth of the money supply can be traced to two factors. The first was the change in the reserve asset ratio. Gibson (1971) estimated that prior to the change, the clearing banks held around 20 per cent of reserve assets in the form of eligible liabilities. The reduction in the legal requirement to $12\frac{1}{2}$ per cent created considerable scope for a once and for all credit expansion. This could have been avoided if the cost of credit were permitted to rise sufficiently to choke off demand or if the authorities had used open market operations to counteract it.

The second factor was that, given the political sensitivity of interest rates, the authorities were apparently unwilling to permit nominal interest rates to rise to levels which would have allowed them to gain effective control over credit creation (see Gowland, 1982). As a result, real rates of interest were extremely low. In the end an attempt to regain monetary control was made via the reintroduction of quantitative controls in the form of the *supplementary special deposit* scheme often called the 'corset'. This effectively placed ceilings on the volume of deposits which banks could accept, and therefore the volume of lending in which they could engage. As was noted earlier, these controls (like credit controls in the 1960s) generated avoidance activity with the result that distortions were created. The corset was extensively used during the Labour governments of 1974–79. In addition, the PSBR was manipulated through a combination of increases in taxation and reductions in public expenditure.

Monetary Policy since 1979

Following the election in 1979 of the Conservative government under Margaret Thatcher, there was a reappraisal of monetary policy. The PSBR and debt management components continued but the corset was phased out and ceased in June 1980. There was also greater reliance placed upon the exchange rate and even more so on interest rates as the major weapon of monetary policy. There was also a suspension of MLR (minimum lending rate) and its substitution by an intervention rate that was unannounced in advance.

This brief review of UK experience with quantitative controls and price manipulations serves to give some flavour of the practical difficulties of monetary control. In the case of the former, one inevitably has to make some judgement about what constitutes 'money'; if one makes an erroneous judgement then avoidance activity is inevitable. In the latter case some judgement has to be made about the interest elasticity of the demand for credit; if an erroneous judgement is made here, or if the political will is lacking to raise nominal interest rates to a sufficient extent, the growth of the money supply exceeds any targets laid down.

Public Sector Borrowing Requirement and the Money Supply

These difficulties are in part responsible for another approach to monetary control which has been applied in the UK possibly since 1974, certainly since 1979 – namely, manipulation of the PSBR. As can be seen from equation 6.9, the magnitude of the public sector deficit (which for simplicity will be equated with the PSBR) affects the change in high-powered money. Although there is some controversy over the precise relationship between the PSBR and the money supply (see Peacock and Shaw, 1981), basically the contribution which the PSBR makes to the change in high-powered money is equivalent to the PSBR minus that part of it which can be financed by sales of government bonds to the non-bank private sector. This relationship has been recognized for a very long time, but an erroneous belief in the independence of fiscal policy, combined with a reluctance to use the PSBR as an instrument of monetary control, precluded the use of this as a target. Since 1979 the recognition of a budget constraint and the interdependence of fiscal and monetary policy resulted in the Conservative government using the PSBR as an instrument of monetary control, basically by setting targets for monetary growth then fixing targets for the growth of the PSBR as part of the original Medium Term Financial Strategy. As will be seen in chapter 19, however, the PSBR proved no more straightforward to control than a given money supply target. This was in part due to the presence of political constraints, which were (rightly or wrongly) frequently difficult to resist. Thus, cash limits set for particular public corporations were relaxed. A more important problem, however, has been that the PSBR is itself endogenous. In recession, *ceteris paribus*, government revenues automatically fall as unemployment rises, and expenditure automatically increases as transfer payments increase. This was something which the Conservative administration made insufficient allowance for in 1979–81 and was the principal element in the PSBR overshoot (see table 19.6).

Thus, in the UK most attempts at monetary control have revolved around attempting to control H in equation 6.4, by quantitative controls directed at bank credit and from there bank deposits; or by manipulating price, again primarily by influencing bank credit, and by controlling the government budget. Many of the problems which were alluded to in the discussion of monetary multipliers have been shown to have been experienced in the UK; there is another, the influence of the overseas sector, discussion of which will be deferred until the analysis of the balance of payments. These difficulties have led some commentators to advocate an entirely different system of monetary control, namely manipulation of r. From equation 6.4 it should be clear that, *ceteris paribus*, systematic manipulation of the banks' reserve asset ratio results in systematic variations in the money supply. This of course requires that the central bank or government is sole supplier of reserve assets and that it polices the system carefully, the result being a system which would operate in a fashion analogous to a commodity-based regime (that is, a currency issue backed by a precious metal). In principle, such monetary base control would give the authorities control of the money supply but at a cost, namely complete surrender over interest rates. Interest rates become endogenous under a system of monetary base control. In the UK this, more than any other argument, is likely to mean that manipulation of r is eschewed as the principal instrument of monetary policy. Instead, throughout the 1980s and 1990s the authorities have continued to use interest rates as the main weapon in attempting to control the money supply. The effectiveness of such a weapon is dependant upon the stability of the demand for money and the speed at which agents react to changes. For these and other reasons, critics of interest rates have often accused it of being a 'slow and blunt' instrument of economic policy.

Concluding Comments

In principle, a small number of proximate determinants of the money supply can be identified which may give the central authorities a 'handle' to influence the amount of money in circulation. In practice, however, monetary control may present intractable problems. These are in part related to the difficulty of isolating an asset which can be called 'money' and for which the demand is stable, and in part due to the way in which the volume of high-powered money is determined. The issue of controllability has been widely debated in recent years, and it will be returned to in the examination of the determinants of inflation in chapter 19.

Appendix: The Aggregate Demand Curve

In chapters 2–4 were analysed the determinants of the principal components of aggregate expenditure: consumption, investment and government expenditure. All of these functions were derived and discussed in real terms for analytical convenience. For certain policy discussions it is, however, important to have an idea of the money value of aggregate expenditure, or *aggregate demand*. The means for establishing this are now available, the money market having been discussed in chapters 5 and 6. Specifically, the aggregate demand (AD) for a given money supply can be ascertained. Strictly

speaking, however, some familiarity with the *interaction* of the goods and money market is required for a formal derivation of the *AD* schedule. Most texts derive *AD* from
the *IS/LM* model, and indeed this is done in this book in chapter 11. Since, however, the
aggregate supply curve will be derived in the next chapter, and since this will provide
the opportunity to consider some interactions between aggregate demand and aggregate supply, the *AD* schedule will be derived in this appendix. (Anyone already familiar
with the *IS/LM* framework may find the derivation of *AD* in chapter 11 more to their
liking.)

Consider first the aggregate expenditure function – that is, the sum of consumption,
investment and government expenditure. This is graphically represented in figure 6.5
by the vertical addition of an investment and government expenditure function to a
Keynesian consumption function, within a familiar Keynesian cross diagram. For
simplicity, it is assumed that both investment and government expenditures are
exogenously given. *AE* therefore represents intended or *ex ante* real expenditure. This
schedule is, however, derived against the backcloth of a given real money stock. The
nominal value of the intended expenditure will be referred to as aggregate demand.

Consider now figure 6.6. In the upper panel the intended (real) expenditure is E_1
which is consistent with a level of real income of Y_1. Given the nominal money supply,
this will also be consistent with a price level of P_1, giving a price income combination
of $P_1 Y_1$ in the lower panel. Suppose now that intended expenditure increases, perhaps
as a consequence of increased government expenditure, and that this shifts AE_1 to
AE_2 in the upper panel. If the nominal money supply is held constant, the only way in
which this increase in intended expenditure can be translated into monetary demand
is if the price level falls. A price level fall would increase the real value of money balances and support the increase in real expenditure. Hence the higher real expenditure
level E_2, and the higher level of real income, Y_2, are associated with a lower price level

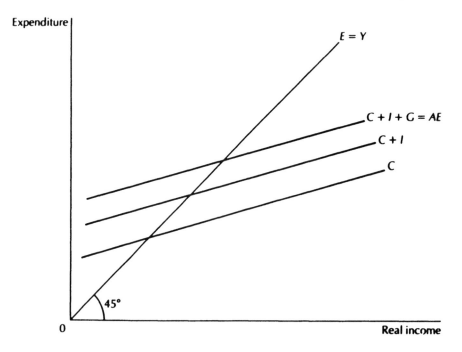

Figure 6.5 Aggregate expenditure function

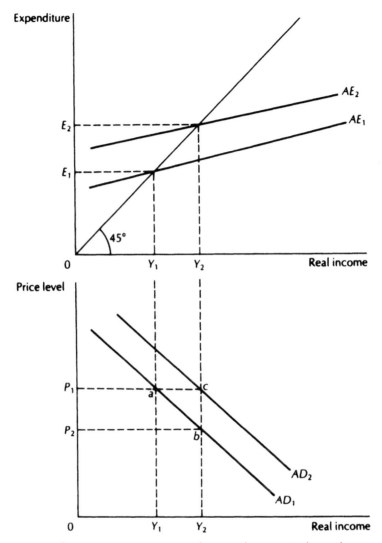

Figure 6.6 Aggregate expenditure and aggregate demand

P_2. Points a and b turn out to be two points on an aggregate demand curve AD_1. Further points could be generated by repeating this process, and it would be found that aggregate demand is an inverse function of the price level. (Note that for expositional convenience we have drawn this schedule as linear – it may in fact be non-linear.)

Of course, the intended increase in government expenditure could have been accompanied by monetary relaxation. In other words, the money supply could have been permitted to expand to accommodate the increased expenditure. In fact it is possible to conceive of a situation where the money supply is permitted to increase such that the price level is maintained at P_1. In such circumstances the real value of cash balances is maintained, but their supply is increased; hence the level of real income rises. In other words the AD schedule shifts to the right (to AD_2).

As will be seen, this device is analytically extremely useful since it permits, for example, a summary of the effects of monetary and fiscal policies via shifts in the schedules. For instance a shift from AD_1 to AD_2 is, as has been seen, consistent with expansionary demand management policies; on the other hand a shift from AD_2 to AD_1 would imply contractionary policies. Once the aggregate supply schedule is introduced, as in the next chapter, a framework is obtained for evaluating the effect of demand management policies on the price level and the level of real income.

To summarize, aggregate demand is a relationship between the quantity of goods demanded and the price level. A given AD schedule is constructed against the backcloth of a given monetary and fiscal stance and, if either monetary or fiscal policy is changed, AD will shift. Since it is a relationship between real spending and the price level it is downward sloping (like a market demand curve). The derivation of AD will be re- examined in chapter 11, after the interactions of the goods and money markets within the IS/LM framework have been discussed and have become familiar.

Further Reading

The discussion of the money multiplier process in the text was based on the Friedman and Schwartz (1963) work. There are a good number of monetary economics texts which give detailed accounts of the money supply process and take the discussion beyond that outlined in this chapter. Especially recommended are Bain (1976), Coghlan (1980) and Dennis (1981). As well as discussing the supply of money within the money multiplier model, all of these texts consider further the role of non-bank financial intermediaries.

Gowland (1982, 1990) offers a thorough review of monetary control, with particular reference to UK experience over the post-war period. This is well supplemented by Artis and Lewis (1981, 1991) and Dow and Saville (1990). Dennis (1980) focuses on UK monetary experience in the 1970s in particular. A comprehensive analysis of money and prices in the USA and the UK over the period 1867–1975 can be found in Friedman and Schwartz (1982).

A number of the Working Paper Series produced by the Bank of England address some of the more technical aspects of the Money supply.

The Medium Term Financial Strategy stimulated a great deal of interest in the precise relationship between the PSBR and the money supply; Peacock and Shaw (1981) focus on this relationship.

7

The Labour Market

The analyses of aggregate consumption, aggregate investment and government expenditure permitted an examination of the components of aggregate demand. As was seen at the end of chapter 6, these various functions can be aggregated in order to derive an aggregate demand function for the closed economy as a whole.

The analysis of aggregate demand has, however, been conducted without reference to aggregate supply. This is analytically useful, since it permits a focus on each sector or aggregate individually; however, in order to comment on how the system as a whole may function under alternative scenarios, something must be said about the determinants of aggregate supply. Clearly, the supply of goods and services in an economy, at a particular period in time, will depend upon the relationship between inputs and outputs. It will depend, in other words, on the economy's production function. The simplest representation of the production function we can take is:

$$Y = f(N, \bar{K}) \tag{7.1}$$

where N refers to the level of employment and K to the capital stock. If we assume the latter to be exogenously determined and fixed, then variations in the supply of real output can be attributed solely to variations in the level of employment. The benefit of holding the capital stock constant, and essentially focusing on the short-run production function, is that we can concentrate our analysis exclusively on the operation of the labour market. Later, in chapter 22, we shall evaluate how changes in the quality and quantity of the capital stock impact upon changes in the supply of real output through time. For the moment we will review the operation of the labour market as follows. First, we shall examine the determinants of the supply of labour and demand for labour. Having done this, we will identify the relationship between aggregate supply and the labour market, under alternative assumptions regarding the competitiveness of the labour market. Third, we will review the role of expectations in market clearing, and finally evaluate the impact of various institutional arrangements on market clearing. The reader might note that some of the major issues in this chapter are developed further in chapters 13 and 20.

The Supply of Labour

Microeconomic Foundations

Traditionally the analysis of the supply of labour is conducted within a choice-theoretic framework whereby the individual is presented with the choice between using his time

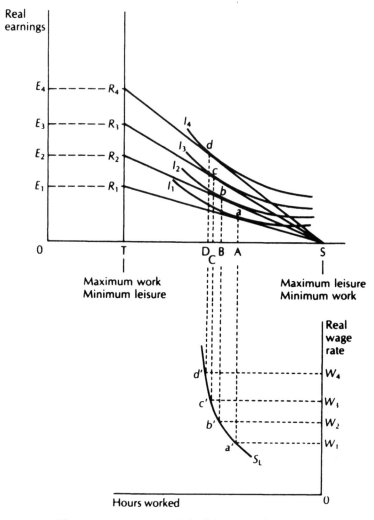

Figure 7.1 Derivation of the labour supply curve

for work or leisure. His allocation of time between work and leisure is then determined by his tastes and preferences for the two activities and by the opportunity cost of leisure.

Consider figure 7.1. In the upper panel, 0S denotes the maximum number of hours in a day whilst 0T indicates the minimum number of hours which will have to be reserved for 'leisure' purposes (that is, the minimum number of hours necessary for sleep, eating, and so on). The individual therefore has TS hours which he can allocate between leisure and work. The two activities are mutually exclusive; the former is unpaid, whilst the latter is rewarded by income. If the individual is free to choose the number of hours in a day which he will work, and he decides to use all of his time for leisure purposes, real earnings would clearly be zero.[1] If, on the other hand, all avail-

---

1. This is not the same as saying that his income will be zero. Given the existence of income support schemes, transfer payments like child benefit, family income supplement and social security benefits will ensure that a certain minimum income is guaranteed.

able time were spent working, real earnings would be maximized. If some intermediate position were chosen then real earnings would lie somewhere between their minimum and maximum.

If the real wage rate per hour is known, and it is assumed that this wage rate is invariant to number of hours worked (overtime payments are therefore ignored), an *earnings–leisure trade-off* can be traced out. Thus, with a real wage rate of W_1, working maximum hours would yield real earnings of $E_1(= R_1)$. For every hour less than the maximum which is used for leisure purposes, earnings are sacrificed, until with 0S hours allocated to leisure, real earnings are zero. The line R_1S is therefore the earnings–leisure trade-off (or budget constraint), the slope of which is determined by the wage rate.

The precise allocation of hours between work and leisure will be determined by the individual's tastes and preferences. These can be depicted by an indifference map. Indifference curves are ranked from south-west to north-east (indicating that both real earnings and leisure are 'goods' in the sense that more is preferred to less). Given the indifference map superimposed in figure 7.1, individual utility will clearly be maximized with TA hours devoted to leisure and AS hours worked. The real earnings associated with this choice are A*a* (less than the maximum $0E_1$).

If the hourly wage rate were to increase, the slope of the earnings–leisure trade-off would become *steeper*, indicating that the opportunity cost of leisure had increased. Given the configuration of his indifference map, this will cause the individual to substitute work for leisure. Leisure hours decrease to TB, hours worked increase to BS and real earnings increase to B*b*(> A*a*). Further increases in the real wage rate which generate budget constraints of R_3S and R_4S stimulate further increases in hours worked and further reductions in leisure time. If this information is transposed to the lower panel of figure 7.1, we see that the points generate a labour supply curve with points *a*, *b*, *c* and *d* being the analogues of points *a*, *b*, *c* and *d* in the upper segment. Over the range *d'* to *d'* the supply curve is positively sloped, indicating that increases in real wage rates result in an increase in the number of hours worked. It is conceivable that beyond a certain point further increases in the wage rate do not stimulate further increases in hours worked but may even result in a reduction in hours worked. This could occur at relatively high wage rates when the *income* effect of an increase in the wage rate (resulting in increased consumption of leisure) outweighs the *substitution* effect (resulting in decreased consumption of leisure). In this case the supply of labour curve S_1 would be backward bending. However, concentration here will be on the positively sloped labour supply curve.

Aggregate Labour Supply

This analysis then suggests that the supply of labour will be positively related to the real wage rate or, for brevity, real wages. It can be argued that if this is the case for individuals then the horizontal summation of individual labour supply curves will generate an aggregate labour supply curve. Clearly this analysis has some relevance to aggregate labour supply in that it emphasizes the role of the real wage rate in influencing the choice of whether to work more or less hours. In some respects, however, the analysis has certain shortcomings from the standpoint of commenting on the aggregate supply of labour. In many cases, individuals have limited scope for varying the length of the working day or week. In this sense the analysis is clearly more appropriate to the self-employed than to most wage earners. In the case of the latter, the work–leisure choice is very much one of deciding whether to work, say, 40 hours per week or not to work at all. In other words, the decision for many on whether or not to join the labour force is very much a non-marginal decision. (It might be noted, however, that with the increase in female participation and the growth of part-time employment, this is no longer as true as it once was.)

This does not invalidate the above framework of analysis entirely, since clearly the decision of whether or not to join the labour force will be influenced by the going real wage rate. In the case of such a 'lumpy' decision, however, the opportunity cost of leisure will be determined not by the real wage rate *per se* but by the real wage per period, less an allowance for the use to which one's time could otherwise be put. In this respect Sapsford (1981) emphasizes that the relevant unit for decision-taking about labour force participation ought to be the household rather than the individual. Where the two are not synonymous, the decision about which member(s) of the household joins the labour force will be influenced not only by 'expected market earnings' *per se* (which is clearly dependent on the going real wage rate), but also by the availability of income transfers like unemployment benefits and the comparative advantages of members of the household as between market and non-market activities. The latter will include not simply leisure, as figure 7.1 implies, but also domestic pursuits such as child-minding and home maintenance. The structure of real wages, the real value of unemployment benefit (and of course the demand for labour) will determine the opportunity cost of having one member of the household refrain from becoming part of the labour force, but the decision will also be affected by tastes and preferences. In other words, given the structure of real wages, some households may have one member refrain from becoming part of the labour force owing to an unwillingness to employ a child-minder, or an unwillingness to live off convenience foods. Other households may be happy to employ child-minders, consume convenience foods, employ a housemaid and so on. Thus, although it probably remains true to say that an increase in real wages will result in increased labour force participation (given the demand for labour), the extent of any response will depend on tastes and preferences.

The Demand for Labour

Microeconomic Foundations

The basic analysis of the demand for labour is also rooted in microeconomic analysis and, as with labour supply, it is possible to derive an aggregate curve from individual demand curves.

The short-run firm demand for labour can be easily derived. Take the case of a firm which sells its output and purchases inputs in perfectly competitive markets. As both buyer and seller, the firm is therefore a price taker. If it is assumed that capital costs are given and labour is the only variable input, the price of this input which the firm faces is the real wage rate. When faced with a given real wage rate – say, $(W/P)_1$ – how many labour inputs will be purchased? From the firm's viewpoint the relevant calculation is the value of output produced by an additional unit of labour, relative to the cost of employing that unit. The value of an additional unit produced can be referred to as the *value of marginal product* (VMP), where

$$VMP = MPP \times P \tag{7.2}$$

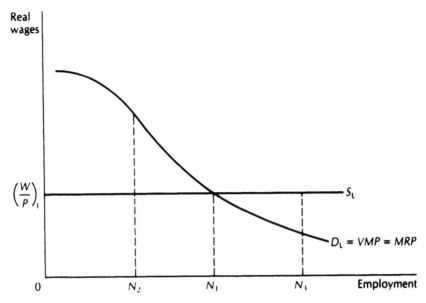

Figure 7.2 Derivation of the labour demand curve

That is, the value of marginal product is equal to the *marginal physical product* (the increment to total product) times the price at which the increment will sell. In the case of a perfectly competitive firm, price will be fixed. MPP will, however, vary as employment of labour varies in accordance with the principle of *diminishing marginal productivity.* Thus, with a fixed price of output and diminishing marginal productivity of labour, the VMP curve will take a negative slope as in figure 7.2. Furthermore, since in perfectly competitive product markets price is equal to marginal revenue, this curve can also be labelled as the *marginal revenue product* curve (MRP), where

$$MRP = MPP \times MR \tag{7.3}$$

This is the increment to total revenue associated with the employment of an additional unit of labour, and it is this which determines the firm's demand for labour.

To ascertain how much labour will actually be employed, the real wage rate is introduced. If the firm is a price taker, labour supply S_L will be perfectly elastic at the going real wage rate of $(W/P)_1$. Given $(W/P)_1$ the firm will employ N_1. Expansion (contraction) of employment from levels below (above) N_1 would always result in total profit increasing. For example, if the firm employed N_2 units, increases in employment would add more to total revenue than to total cost for all increments up to N_1. Further expansion of employment beyond N_1, however, say to N_3, would add more to total cost than total revenue (since $(W/P)_1 > MRP$) and total profit would decline. Clearly, with a given MRP schedule a rise (fall) in the real wage rate would result in a contraction (expansion) of labour demand.

Aggregate Labour Demand

Given a diminishing marginal product of labour, therefore, the demand for labour would be expected to be inversely related to the real wage rate. However, one cannot simply horizontally sum labour demand curves to derive an aggregate demand curve without acknowledging at least two complications.

1   The foregoing analysis assumes that the firm concerned is a perfect competitor in
    its product markets. This assumption ensured an equality between VMP and MRP.
    Were an allowance to be made for monopoly or imperfectly competitive conditions
    in product markets, then clearly an allowance would have to be made for the fact
    that the firm's average and marginal revenue curves will diverge. Although MRP
    will still be downward-sloping (as therefore will be demand for labour), it will lie
    below VMP, and therefore employment under monopoly or imperfect competition
    will be less than that associated with perfect competition (on *ceteris paribus*
    assumptions).

2   Short-run conditions have been explicitly assumed. In the long run, when the
    firm is free to vary its inputs of both factors, an allowance would have to be
    made for substitution between factor inputs as relative factor prices altered. In
    fact, the application of this analysis to a long-run perspective still results in the
    conclusion that the firm's demand for labour will be inversely related to the
    real wage rate, but the long-run labour demand curve will be more elastic (over
    the relevant range) than any given short-run curve. The reason for this is that
    variations in labour inputs will affect the marginal productivity of other
    factors. Thus, given a fall in the real wage rate, employment will increase. This will
    tend to raise the MRP of capital; more capital will be employed which will tend
    to shift the MRP of labour out to the right, which in turn will tend to increase
    employment further. Thus the long-run change in employment in response to a
    change in the real wage rate will be greater (other things being equal) than the
    short-run change.

Once the industry demand curve is identified, the aggregate labour demand curve can
be derived by horizontally summing industry demands. In the aggregate, the demand
for labour will therefore be inversely related to the real wage rate, but without very
detailed knowledge about industry demand curves, it is not possible to be more specific about its precise configuration.

Employment and Aggregate Supply

Now that labour supply and labour demand have been discussed, labour market equilibrium and its relationship to aggregate supply can be considered. To simplify matters,
the short-run situation given by the production function of equation 7.1 is taken where
labour is the only variable factor of production.

Labour market equilibrium occurs when a real wage rate is established which
equates aggregate labour demand with aggregate labour supply. In figure 7.3 this
occurs with a real wage rate of $(W/P)_e$ and N_e. In a competitive system where both
labour demand and labour supply are a function of the real wage, the equilibrium
established at e would be stable in the sense that any deviation away from $(W/P)_e$ will
set in motion forces which will push the real wage rate back to its equilibrium level. If,
for example, a real wage of $(W/P)_1$ were established, excess supply of ab would result.
Competition between labour for the relatively scarce jobs would tend to depress money
wages (and therefore real wages) and push the system back towards $(W/P)_e$. The same
would apply *mutatis mutandis* to the excess demand of cd which is associated with a real
wage of $(W/P)_2$.

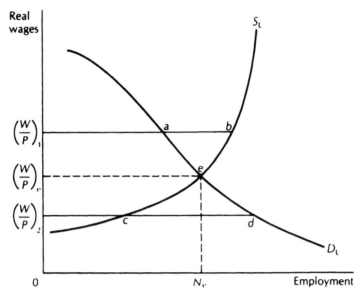

Figure 7.3 Labour market equilibrium

Aggregate Supply with a Perfectly Competitive Labour Market

The derivation of the aggregate supply function under competitive conditions can be demonstrated by reference to figure 7.4. In quadrant (a) labour market equilibrium is established with a market clearing real wage of $(W/P)_1$. It will be assumed that this is consistent with full employment (N_F).[2] Given the aggregate production function in quadrant (b), this is consistent with a level of national income of Y_F. Quadrant (c) traces out the *aggregate supply* curve – that is, the relationship between the level of income and the price level. With full employment income of Y_F, an aggregate supply curve, AS_F, is found which is completely inelastic with respect to the price level and is dependent only on real variables, namely the productivity of labour and the real wage rate. The only function of the price level in this model is to determine the nominal wage rate consistent with the equilibrium real wage rate of $(W/P)_1$. This can be demonstrated by reference to quadrant (d). W_1 denotes a given nominal wage, its inverse slope indicating that as the price level rises the real wage will fall. A rise in the price level from P_1 to P_2 would therefore tend to reduce the real wage towards $(W/P)_2$, stimulating an excess demand for labour. This excess demand would be eliminated by the bidding up of money wages to W_2 – that is, a level which re-establishes the real wage of $(W/P)_1$. If the price level were to fall from P_1 to P_0, inducing a rise in the real wage and an excess supply of labour, competition would depress the money wage to W_0 and re-establish equilibrium at $(W/P)_1$. Thus, the aggregate supply curve AS_F is consistent with *any* price level.

Note that in this model, any movements from equilibrium are little more than tendencies, and adjustment is assumed to be rapid. The implications of lags in the adjustment process will be examined shortly. The important point to note for the moment is the proposition that if money wages are flexible in both upward and downward direc-

---

2 For the moment, no precise definition will be given for full employment. This will be considered more fully in chapter 20. Here full employment is equated with an absence of all involuntary unemployment.

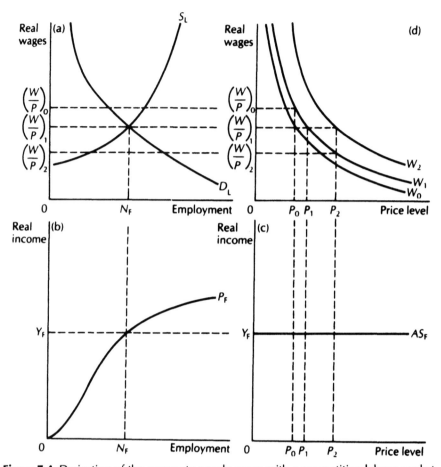

Figure 7.4 Derivation of the aggregate supply curve with a competitive labour market

tions, income and output will always tend to their full employment levels, and aggregate supply will be invariant to the price level. As will be seen in part II, this is a central proposition in the classical model of the economic system. Furthermore, if N_F is defined as the *natural rate of unemployment* – that is, that level of unemployment consistent with a stable rate of price inflation – it is also a central tenet of many neo-classical models.[3] If this AS curve is combined with the AD curve derived earlier, some extremely important policy implications can be deduced. In figure 7.5 the price level is plotted on the vertical axis and level of real income on the horizontal axis, and the perfectly inelastic AS curve is reproduced. If an expansionary demand management programme shifts AD from AD_1 to AD_2, it can be seen that the level of output is unaffected, whilst the price level increases from P_1 to P_2. *With a vertical aggregate supply curve, demand management policies have no impact whatsoever on the level of employment and real output.* Put another way, nominal policies only affect nominal variables. Because a frictionless labour market has been assumed, variations in prices quickly feed through to variations in money wages leaving real wages unaltered. Consequently, the labour market always clears. In a 'typical' classical model, the market clearing level of employment would coincide with full employment. In a 'typical' neo-classical

---

3 The concept of the natural rate of unemployment is discussed more fully below, and in chapter 13.

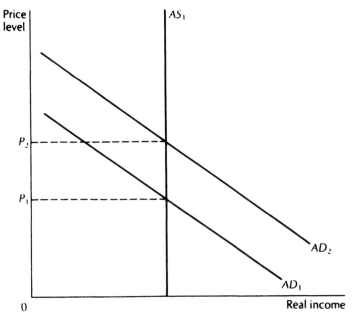

Figure 7.5 Effect of a shift in AD with a perfectly inelastic AS

model, it would coincide with the natural rate of unemployment. If the latter happens to be consistent with a socially undesirable level of unemployment, it cannot be altered by fiscal and monetary policies. In the same way as nominal instruments affect only nominal variables, real instruments must be used to influence real variables (like employment). Thus AS can only be shifted through policies designed to influence the way in which the labour market operates.

Aggregate Supply with Labour Market Imperfections

As will be seen in the next chapter, the proposition that the real economy would be unresponsive to changes in nominal demand (as reasoned via the vertical aggregate supply curve) was a central feature of the classical paradigm. The kind of institutional arrangements and market imperfections which might mitigate against a frictionless labour market and invalidate the classical paradigm formed part of the substance of the Keynesian revolution (although they were also explicitly recognized by leading classical theorists, most notably Pigou, 1944). Keynes focused on two factors in particular – imperfectly competitive labour supply as a result of the importance of labour unions, and the possibility of *money illusion* on the part of wage bargainers. The presence of labour unions could mean that there are adjustment asymmetries to shifts in AD. If AD shifts to the right such that the price level is raised and 'the' actual real wage lies below the market clearing wage, upward adjustment of the money wage could follow quite quickly. If, however, contractionary fiscal and monetary policies shift AD to the left, money wage cuts might be resisted, perhaps as a result of money illusion – that is, the proposition that labour supply is a function of the money wage rate rather than the real wage rate. In this case, money wage reductions would be resisted even when price level reductions are occurring concurrently. Consequently, the real wage is maintained at a level above the equilibrium real wage (such as $(W/P)_1$ in figure 7.3) and the labour market fails to clear. Excess supply (unemployment) of ab ensues.

In figure 7.6 is outlined the implications of downward inflexibility of money wages for aggregate supply. Commencing from a price level of P_1 and a market clearing real wage of $(W/P)_1$, which is consistent with full employment, assume that the price level falls from P_1 to P_2. To maintain the full employment level of output, money wages should fall to W_2. If money wage reductions are resisted such that nominal wages remain at W_1, real wages rise to $(W/P)_2$ and the level of employment becomes demand determined. It can be seen from quadrant (a) that with a real wage of $(W/P)_2$ employment would contract to N_2. Given the production function PF in quadrant (b), this results in a reduction in output to Y_2. If this is taken across to quadrant (c), it is clear that AS is positively sloped over the range $Y_2 Y_F$. If the assumption is made of a further fall in the price level to P_3 with the maintenance of money wages at W_1, the consequent increase in the real wage to $(W/P)_3$ further reduces employment to N_3 and output to Y_3, indicating that AS is also positively sloped in the range $Y_3 Y_2$.

Contrast this with the situation where, again commencing from equilibrium, the price level rises to P_4. In the strict case of money illusion, no change in labour supply would occur, and aggregate supply would remain unaffected. In the case where labour unions are active full compensation for the rise in the price level may be sought, the outcome being that the real wage is maintained at $(W/P)_1$ and aggregate supply is again unaffected.

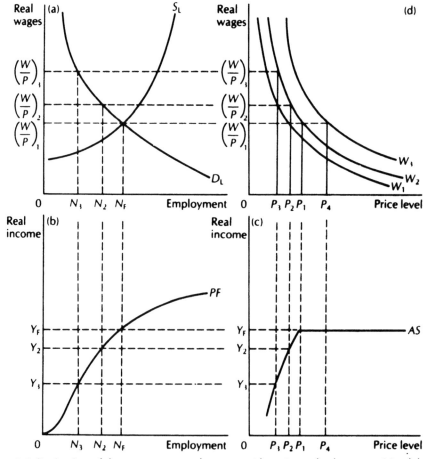

Figure 7.6 Derivation of the aggregate supply curve with an imperfectly competitive labour market

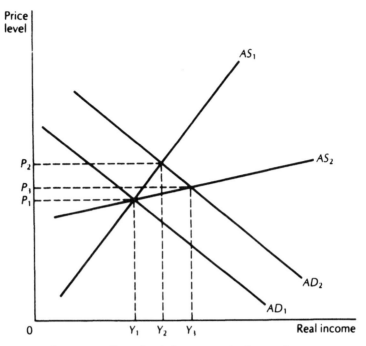

Figure 7.7 Effect of a shift in AD with elastic AS curves

The model of figure 7.6 therefore suggests that aggregate supply will be positively sloped below the full employment level of output. That is to say, there may exist a direct relationship between price level changes and changes in output up to full employment.[4]

It has already been seen in figure 7.5 that, when AS is inelastic, policy-induced shifts in aggregate demand can have no effect on the level of output but only alter the price level. By contrast, when AS is positively sloped, as in figure 7.7, the same policy-induced shift would result in both the price level and the level of output being affected with the relative impact on prices and output being determined by the slope of the AS schedule over the relevant range. As can be seen from figure 7.7, the shift in AD has a relatively greater impact on output relative to prices in the case of AS_2 compared with AS_1.

Clearly, therefore, if the policy-maker believes that labour market forces operate in such a way as to generate a vertical (or steeply sloped) AS curve, he is likely to see the role of demand management policies as being one of changing the price level. If, on the other hand, he is convinced that behavioural relations in the labour market generate an AS schedule which is relatively flat, he would take the view that active demand management policies can effect changes in output and employment. This is an issue which has received a great deal of academic attention recently, and, as will be seen, it is at the heart of much macroeconomic controversy of recent years.

---

4 It ought to be noted that given the assumptions of this analysis, there is likely to be a ratchet effect present. Thus, when the price level rises to P_4 and the money wage to W_3, the latter would be viewed as the minimum wage, reductions in which are unacceptable. The positively sloped section of AS would then emanate from point 2. Further increases in the full employment price level would shift the elastic section of the curve further up the vertical section.

Expectations Formation and Market Clearing

Adaptive Expectations and the Labour Market

In order to elaborate further, the assumption is retained that both labour supply and labour demand are a function of the real wage rate. In a situation where the price level is changing, however, it may not be a straightforward matter for agents in the labour market to evaluate how the real wage is changing. In order to evaluate a given money wage rate, agents need to make a forecast of how the price level will change over the period to which the given money wage applies. In other words, they need to form expectations of price level changes, and the manner in which those expectations are formed has a crucial bearing on market clearing in the labour market.

The way in which agents form their expectations depends on the quantity and quality of information which they have at their disposal. Other things being equal, the better informed agents are about the way in which economic processes operate, and the better the quality of their information, the less likely they are to make errors in forecasting. Initially, consider a situation where labour demand is a function of the money wage rate deflated by the *actual* price level, whilst labour supply is a function of the money wage deflated by the price level *expected* when a wage agreement is struck. One could rationalize this by arguing that since employers are involved in price setting, they have good-quality information on how prices are changing and forecast accurately. Employees, on the other hand, do not have such ready access to information on price changes and have to make a guess at how prices will change. Thus,

$$D_L = f(W/P^a) \tag{7.4}$$

$$S_L = f(W/P^e) \tag{7.5}$$

Clearly if any divergence between P^a and P^e occurs between one wage agreement and the next, there is scope for divergence between D_L and S_L and disequilibrium in the labour market which could be influenced by variations in fiscal and monetary policy. Such a divergence could occur if employees formed their expectations about changes in the price level *adaptively* – that is to say, they used past experience as a guide to forecasting changes in the price level. A simple adaptive process would be the one described by equation 13.12, namely

$$P_t^e = \lambda P_{t-1} + (1 - \lambda)P_{t-1}^e \tag{7.6}$$

This implies that agents *forecast* the price level on the basis of the price level in the previous period (P_{t-1}) and the extent to which their forecast of the price level in the previous period (P_{t-1}^e) was wrong. The adjustment coefficient λ lies between zero and one. This system of expectations formation will be discussed more fully in chapter 13. The important characteristic to note for the present is that if expectations are formed adaptively, they can lag behind reality, and P^e and P^a can diverge.

Take a specific example. Suppose a wage agreement is reached in time t on the basis of $P^e = \varepsilon$, where ε is some positive price level. Between t and $t + 1$ an unexpected price change occurs such that $P^a > \varepsilon$. Employers take as their reference point actual prices and would therefore correctly perceive any increase in the price level as being associated with a fall in the real wage and labour demand expands. Employees, on the other hand, whose expectations lag behind reality, fail to perceive that the real wage has changed, and employment and output increase. This describes a world with a positively

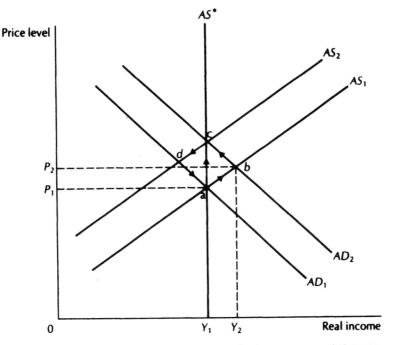

Figure 7.8 Short-run and long-run AS curves and adjustment to a shift in AD

sloped *AS* curve. Thus in figure 7.8 the shift in *AD* from AD_1 to AD_2 raises the price level from P_1 to P_2, and increases real output from Y_1 to Y_2.

The objection has been made that this type of mechanism relies on money illusion in some form on the part of employees. This may be a reasonable postulate in the short run. In the long run, however, the gap between actual and expected price level changes will be perceived and adjustments made accordingly. In other words, once it is realized that the real wage has fallen in the move from *a* to *b* in figure 7.8, employment (and output) will contract along AD_2. This contraction will cease when actual and expected price levels are equal – that is to say, when D_L and S_L are equated. This in fact occurs at the initial level of output . Note now, however, that the price level has been raised. The only *long-run* consequence of the expansionary demand management policy is to increase the price level but leave the level of employment and output at their 'natural' levels, that is, those levels consistent with a stable price level.

The process would be exactly reversed for a leftward shift in aggregate demand stimulated by contractionary fiscal and monetary policies. If AD_2 is shifted to AD_1, the actual price level falls and initially expected prices lag behind. Real wages are increasing as a consequence. The increase in real wages is, however, perceived first by employers (since $P^a < P^e$) and labour demand contracts. There is a movement from point *c* to point *d* on AS_2. Gradually, as expectations catch up with reality and the real wage returns to its equilibrium level, there is a shift from *d* to *a* and equilibrium is re-established at the natural level of output and employment.

These ideas were originally enunciated by Friedman (1968a) and Phelps (1968) and refined in the 1970s. This line of analysis suggests that in fact both positively sloped and vertical *AS* curves coexist. In the short run, the *AS* schedule is positively sloped because those agents supplying labour services adjust gradually to changes in nominal demand, rather than instantaneously as the competitive model requires. In the short run, then, shifts in *AD* can affect output and employment as well as prices. The process of adjustment is gradual rather than partial, and ultimately expectations catch up with reality and full adjustment takes place. This occurs when actual changes in the price level are the same as expected changes, that is, at the natural rate of output and employment. In the long run, therefore, output and employment are completely insensitive to changes in nominal demand, and this is described by the vertical aggregate supply curve AS^* in figure 7.8.

From the standpoint of demand management policy, this view of the way in which adjustments to disequilibrium in the labour market occur has two crucially important implications.

1   It unequivocally suggests that in the long run the government cannot systematically influence the level of output and employment through manipulations in monetary and fiscal policy.

2   It implies that deviations in the level of employment from its natural level are a consequence of mistaken expectations. In the event that unemployment rises in the adjustment $c \rightarrow d \rightarrow a$ in figure 7.8, it is as a consequence of individuals temporarily withdrawing from the labour market in the belief that the real wage has fallen.

Rational Expectations and the Labour Market

As a result of the importance of these propositions, this line of analysis has been exhaustively examined and re-examined over the last decade. One line of development has been to question the expectations mechanism in such a way as to conclude that changes in AD may not even influence output and employment in the short run. This is one of the central propositions of the *rational expectations* (RE) school of thought.

The RE school dates back to two papers by Muth (1960, 1961) but owes much to the work of Lucas (1973, 1975) and Sargent and Wallace (1975), among others. This line of analysis contends that the expectations mechanism implied by equation 7.6 is fundamentally unsound because it suggests that, when forecasting the rate of inflation for the purposes of concluding a wage agreement, employees take account only of past events and not of current and future possible events. To dramatize this, it implies that if OPEC raises the price of oil by x per cent on the day a wage deal is concluded, it will be ignored. Furthermore, as will be seen in chapter 13, the mechanism in equation 7.6 means that the rate of inflation may be *systematically* underpredicted from one period to the next. Both of these propositions, it is argued, are inconsistent with rational optimizing behaviour. If, instead, individuals formed their expectation of price level changes rationally rather than adaptively, the adjustment to a change in nominal demand is rather different.

If an agent forecasts the expected price level rationally, P^e would be

$$P_t^e = E(P_t | I_{t-1}) \tag{7.7}$$

In other words, the expected price level would be equal to a forecast which is made on the basis of *all* relevant information available at the time of the forecast. This relevant information would include current information on, for example, government intentions about fiscal and monetary policy. We are, in effect, assuming that employees are as well informed as employers. Thus, in the event that it was known that the government intended to shift AD_1 to AD_2 in figure 7.8, the effects of this expansionary demand management intervention would be anticipated. In other words, *expected prices would not lag behind actual prices but would move along with them* and adjustment would take place directly from *a* to *c*. (The same applies *mutatis mutandis* for a shift from AD_2 to AD_1). Therefore, agents in the labour market adjust quickly to changes in nominal demand and, consequently, nominal changes do not influence real magnitudes *even in the short run* – the short-run *AS* curve is also vertical. In fact, the only circumstances under which employment and output can deviate from their natural levels is if a mistake is made when forecasting price changes. This could occur if some completely unexpected event occurs (like an OPEC price hike) or if the authorities say they are going to shift AD_2 to AD_1 but instead shift AD_2 to AD_3, as in figure 7.9. Because agents are taken by surprise in both these circumstances, there may be some real effects in the short run. Thus, in figure 7.9 the announcement of an intention to shift AD_2 to AD_1 by contractionary fiscal and monetary policies would lead to adjustment from *a* to *b*. Instead, however, the authorities shift AD_2 to AD_3. Agents in the labour market are initially taken by surprise and output and employment temporarily rise above Y_1. However, once it is realized what the authorities have actually done, output and employment would return to their natural levels, the adjustment path being $b \rightarrow c \rightarrow d$. The locus *bc* would be referred to as the *surprise supply function*. If the policy intention of shifting AD_2 to AD_3 had been preannounced, adjustment would have taken place from *a* to *d*. The implications of the analysis are therefore that as long as policy intentions are preannounced and are stuck to, real output and employment will be unaffected by changes in demand management policies even in the short run.

The rational expectations paradigm has generated a great deal of controversy and it will be examined more critically in chapter 13. For the moment, the interest is simply in the implication that the labour market can clear in a reasonably frictionless manner, and in the implication that because the labour market is self-equilibrating, all unemployment is essentially voluntary. Thus a glance forward to figure 20.1 shows that a dramatic increase in unemployment has taken place in the UK in recent years.

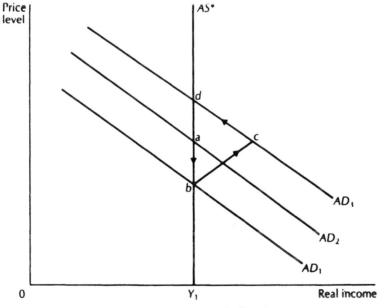

Figure 7.9 Surprise supply function

The labour market has manifestly failed to clear, despite preannouncement of policy intent on *AD.* This would be explained by the RE school as the outcome of a combination of unanticipated shocks (like the 1979 oil price hike), and an increase in voluntary unemployment as a result of rising real unemployment benefits and falling real wages. In terms of the analysis earlier in this chapter, it is claimed that households are taking a rational intertemporal decision to take leisure time now (for home maintenance and so on) and work later when real wages rise. For many commentators, the very idea that so many should 'choose' leisure is inherently implausible as is the entire notion of zero involuntary unemployment. The dissatisfaction has resulted in a re-evaluation of the way in which labour markets operate and a closer examination of the kind of institutional arrangements which exist and which may make the labour market less than perfectly frictionless.

Institutional Arrangements and Market Clearing

Both the classical and neo-classical (rational expectations) analyses treat the labour market as if it were like any given competitive commodity market (such as the market for carrots or potatoes). It is this which leads to the presumption of flexible prices and rapid adjustment to equilibrium. One important feature of labour markets in most developed market economies is that they are not freely competitive. This is partly for one very obvious reason – labour unions result in the supply of certain types of labour being monopolized. Microeconomic analysis predicts that, as would be expected, wages will be higher and employment lower with unionization than without; and furthermore, the presence of labour unions might result in a downward rigidity of money and/or real wages. This much has been recognized for a very long time by classical/ neo-classical and Keynesian/neo-Keynesian economists. In recognizing that labour unions might lead to frictions which frustrate adjustment, the RE solution is to remove the source of the friction – that is, reduce the ability of labour unions to generate inflexibilities through recourse to law. This might be regarded as a legitimate or illegitimate policy response depending on one's views of the role which labour unions play in a modern society. Even if one were to endorse such a policy, however, a further question is begged: would the labour market suddenly become frictionless and adjust quickly to changes in aggregate demand, or are there other imperfections which contribute to relatively slow adjustment?

Labour Market Segmentation

One important characteristic of the labour market which will limit flexibility by restricting mobility is that it is *segmented*, both geographically and occupationally. There are sociocultural ties which tend to restrict geographical mobility, and there are acquired skills which tend to restrict occupational mobility. As a result of this segmentation, one might find a mismatch of labour demand and supply by geographical region and/or occupational category. The excess supply which emerges as a consequence of the labour market failing to clear owing to this segmentation is frequently referred to as *structural unemployment* and, as will be seen in chapter 20, this is viewed by many as being at the heart of the UK regional problem.

One might object that labour market segmentation is a necessary but not sufficient condition for a non-clearing labour market since, if there were free and unfettered competition, there would still be a tendency to equilibrium as a result of wage flexibility within and between (geographical and occupational) segments. Thus, wage differentials between occupational groups would emerge, reflecting relative scarcities, and different prices for the same occupational group across regions would emerge, again reflecting relative scarcities. This may very well be true. It does not, however, invalidate the fact that attachment to a particular locality may generate inflexibility.

Search Costs

Many classical and neo-classical models implicitly assume that search costs are zero. In effect, every worker has full information on the structure of wages, and the distribution of wage offers available to employed workers who are thinking of quitting, or unemployed workers who have actually quit. In reality, of course, job search is not costless. An unemployed individual can be expected to have in mind a reservation wage – that is, a minimum wage which is required to induce him to sacrifice leisure for work. In order to establish whether to accept employment, the individual needs to search firms to obtain information on wage offers. This process clearly takes time, especially since empirical evidence suggests that unemployed individuals search for permanent rather than temporary jobs. Moreover, the reservation wage may itself change during search in a way that prolongs the period of unemployment. For example, other things being equal, an increase in the ratio of vacancies to unemployment should increase the probability of a job offer, which in turn will tend to increase the reservation wage. In addition, an increase in the distribution of wage offers raises the expected returns to search and in turn the reservation wage. In both cases the individual would be willing to search for longer.

Social Convention

Consider further the question of wage flexibility. It is often argued that wages are inflexible (especially in a downward direction), simply as a consequence of the activities of labour unions, and that free competition is frustrated only by such institutions. This *simpliste* view has been challenged recently. Akerlof (1979) has pointed to the role of such intangible forces as notions of 'fairness' and good behaviour, bolstered by social pressure, as being important forces mitigating against free competition. Thus, even in a situation where close to 2 million people are recorded as unemployed in the UK, one finds few (if any) examples of individuals offering their services to a given employer at a wage of less than he is paying existing employees. As Solow (1980) remarks:

> Obviously there are no Emily Post manuals to consult as regards the behaviour of laid off workers, but you would certainly not be astonished to learn that self-esteem and the folkways discourage laid off workers from undercutting the wages of their employed colleagues in an effort to displace them from jobs. (p. 8)

The neo-classical (rational expectations) paradigm suggests that as an unemployed worker spends a longer time unemployed, he will engage in search activity and ultimately realize that real wages are falling, which will cause him to reduce his reservation wage. In response to this, Solow continues,

Reservation wages presumably fall as the duration of unemployment lengthens but my casual reading suggests that this shows up more in a willingness to accept lower paid sorts of jobs than in thorough going competition for the standard job. (p. 8)

Unemployment Benefits

Solow goes on to note that this sort of behaviour is accommodated by the availability of unemployment benefit, and indeed this is another institutional feature of the labour market which may help slow down the adjustment process. In terms of the simple model discussed in figure 7.1, the provision of unemployment benefit would mean that the budget lines do not converge at point S but at some point vertically above S, indicating that real earnings (or, strictly speaking, income) are positive with maximum leisure time. Furthermore, since the provision of unemployment benefit reduces the relative price of leisure, the individual may substitute leisure for work, as in figure 7.10. In a situation where no benefits are provided, the budget line is Y^*RS, the relative price of leisure being given by the slope of RS. The utility maximizing individual settles at a on I_1 working L_1S hours and taking $0L_1$ for leisure, thereby earning income of Y_1. Once benefits are introduced, the individual can have an income of Y_B, with maximum leisure (and zero work). In effect the relative price of leisure is reduced as shown by the budget line Y^*RT. The individual could reach a higher indifference curve without working any hours at all. In simple terms, this is the analysis which underlies the disincentive argument about benefits.

Since, as was noted earlier in this chapter, the work–leisure decision is a 'lumpy' one – one either works or does not (for the majority of wage earners anyway) – the availability of unemployment benefits might lead some individuals voluntarily to leave the

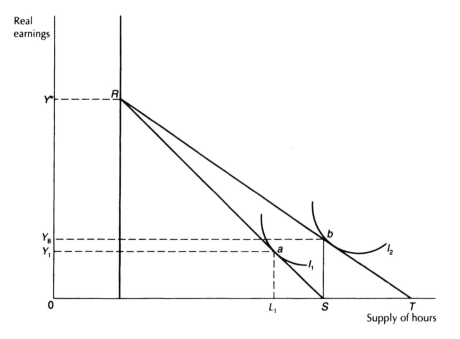

Figure 7.10 Disincentive effect of unemployment benefit

labour market to engage in non-market activities either of a legal (DIY) or illegal (working for cash in hand) variety.

Some argue that this is an increasingly important consideration. Indeed, Minford and Peel (1981) have argued that the real value of social security benefits should be cut in order to increase the attractiveness of work at the margin. The precise effects of unemployment and social security benefits are contentious, although two qualitative judgements can be made. First, the availability of unemployment benefit does permit more prolonged job search and therefore *ceteris paribus* will slow down adjustment to any disequilibrium. Second, unemployment provisions will influence the work–leisure choice at the margin. Note that these are comments on the efficiency of the market and do not entail any value judgement about the appropriate level of unemployment benefit *per se*. This is an issue of equity.

Explicit and Implicit Contracts

Another institutional feature which might be commented on and which can generate non-market clearing situations is the presence of contracts, whether of the legal variety (as is common in the USA) or of the informal, implicit variety (as is more common in the UK). In a flexible competitive market, prices would be changed regularly. In an ideal labour market, money wages would adjust quickly to productivity changes and changes in the price level. In most developed market economies however, one observes, the agreement of contracts between employer and employee which deliberately fixes the wage for a specified period of time. In the UK this is usually a year; in the USA it can be as much as three years. Once a contract is agreed, it is unusual to have it altered before its expiry date. Thus, the individual is committed to a given money wage for a specified period of time. This can certainly explain stickiness or inflexibility of money wages which frustrates market clearing. Furthermore, it may also provide a basis for justifying an upward-sloping *AS* curve even in a rational expectations model (albeit as a short-run phenomenon). If all contracts expire simultaneously (as in the Japanese system) there may be a fairly well defined short run *AS* curve. If, however, contracts are overlapping, the possibility of leapfrogging is introduced, reducing further the probability of a market clearing equilibrium. (Gordon, 1982a, invokes this feature of the Japanese wage bargaining system as being a contributory factor to macroeconomic stability in that country compared with the UK and the USA.)

The response of some neo-classical economists to the role of long-term contracts is similar to their response to labour unions or unemployment benefit, namely if the institutions impede market clearing, and if there is no foundation for the institutions in rational optimizing behaviour, then they should be removed or reformed. This is certainly the case where contracts are concerned which, it is argued, engender macroeconomic instability and are inefficient from the individual's viewpoint (see Barro, 1977). A good deal of recent research suggests, however, that although wage contracts may very well prevent a tendency to continuous market clearing, they may be rational from the point of view of employer and employee. Hahn (1980), for example, emphasizes the role of transactions costs. Changing wages is not a costless activity, especially since the probability of disagreement between employers and employees is high. Employers wish to avoid continuous conflict over wages (the cost of which may be high in lost output) whilst employees also have an incentive to avoid continuous conflict, again because it is costly (in terms of income forgone). A satisfactory way of minimizing conflict may be to negotiate contracts, even though there may be a trade-off with macroeconomic efficiency. (Gordon, 1982a, argues that the single most important factor in explaining the three-year contract system in the United States is conflict avoidance.)

Employers may have other incentives for negotiating contracts. If wages are changed on a continuous basis then so too must be prices. This may be appropriate in auction markets, but may be less practical in other commodity markets. The administered price controversy of the 1930s generated many insights into the transactions costs of changing prices, and Gordon (1981) has documented reasons why price adjustment may be gradual.

The work of Azariadis (1975) on *implicit contracts* documents how risk-averse workers may enter into a contract to ensure a stable rather than fluctuating wage over a given period. From the firm's standpoint, there is an additional incentive provided by the firm's investment in specific skill development. A longer-term contract ensures that the firm reaps some benefit from such investment. It may also provide employers with the incentive to hoard labour during the downswing of a business cycle to save on recruitment costs in the upswing. Given the easier access to funds on the capital market which firms enjoy, such arrangements may be more efficient than the alternative of fluctuating wages with consumers/households using the capital market to smooth earnings themselves.

Thus, all these institutional factors might result in the AS curve being positively sloped, at least in the short run. Furthermore, they may also help explain why the slope of the AS curve may appear to differ from country to country. For example, Gordon (1982a, p. 41) concludes a cross-country comparison of the role of institutional factors by contending that as a result of institutional differences 'of any given fluctuation in aggregate nominal demand, a larger fraction takes the form of a change in real output and employment in the United States than in the United Kingdom or Japan'. In other words, the UK and Japanese AS curve might be described by AS_1 in figure 7.7, whilst the USA curve is described by AS_2.

Trade Unions

Whilst trade union membership fell from a peak of 13.3 million in 1979 to an estimated 9 million in 1993, it is clear that they are still significant players in the UK labour market. However, the scope of their power has been curtailed by legislation in recent years. The main elements that impinge on their activities are the Employment Acts 1980, 1986, 1988, 1989 and 1990, the Trade Union Act 1984 and the Trade Union Reform and Employment Rights Act 1993.

When taken together, all these changes mean that the environment faced by trade unions in the 1990s is considerably more hostile than that of the 1970s. Despite these facts, unions have been cited as one of the elements to explain the sluggishness of the labour market to respond to changing economic conditions. This can be theoretically explained by the insider–outsider theory developed by Solow (1985) and Lindbeck and Snower (1988).

Insiders can best be defined as existing employees whose position is protected by the existence of significant costs involved in their replacement by outsiders, principally the unemployed. The framework suggests that wage rates are largely determined by unions acting on behalf of the insiders while ignoring the existence of outsiders. However, a study by Nickell, Vianiomanski and Wadhani (1992) that considered more than 800 UK manufacturing companies over the period 1972–86 failed to find significant insider–outsider effects. In attempting to explain *persistent* rather than *rising* unemployment, insider–outsider theory provides support for the *hysteresis* view of unemployment which will be considered in chapter 20.

Concluding Comments

Some time has been spent studying the labour market, and many of these issues will be returned to in chapter 13 and chapter 20. The way in which the labour market adjusts to changes in nominal demand is at the heart of most macroeconomic controversy. This follows because labour supply is integrally linked to the shape of the aggregate supply curve, and this in turn determines whether there is any scope for demand management policies to influence real output and employment. In a smoothly operating, frictionless labour market, money wages would adjust quickly to changes in prices in order to ensure continuous adjustment to the market clearing real wage. In such circumstances, policy-induced variations can have no effect on real output and employment. It has been seen, however, that there are many institutional features of labour markets which might result in a tendency to sticky rather than smooth adjustment, and perhaps also non-market clearing.

Further Reading

The traditional microeconomic analysis of labour demand and labour supply is outlined in most specialist texts on labour economics; a useful text to consult is Sapsford and Tzannatos (1990).

Macroeconomic controversies over the efficacy of stabilization policy has resulted in a blossoming of the literature on the microfoundations of the labour market and the way in which it responds to demand stimuli. Expectations formation will be examined in a great deal more detail in chapter 13. For the moment, however, two useful introductory overview articles are noted which will provide an extremely good foundation to chapter 13, namely Maddock and Carter (1982) and Mayes (1981). More advanced literature on expectations will be discussed at the end of chapter 13.

An excellent treatise on the role of labour market institutions is Okun (1981), whilst Hall (1980) provides a survey of recent work on contracts. A useful empirical assessment of the effects of labour market institutions on aggregate supply is Gordon (1982a). Pissarides (1985) provides a survey paper of recent work on search theory and several of the papers in Sapsford and Tzannatos (1988) relate to labour market institutions.

Nickell (1979) provides an analysis of the effect of a rising replacement ratio on unemployment levels in the UK, and Nickell (1980) an analysis of the pattern of unemployment in the UK. The volume edited by Sapsford and Tzannatos (1990) contains a useful number of essays. A comprehensive series of papers relating to the nature and causes of unemployment in a number of industralized economies is to be found in the August supplement of volume 53 of *Economica* (1986). The paper on the UK in this volume by Layard and Nickell is an excellent piece of applied economics.

Part II

Macroeconomic Systems

*The number of rational hypotheses that
can explain any given phenomenon is
infinite.*
Robert M. Pirsig

This part of the book will examine competing theories of the relationships underlying broad economic aggregates and of the behaviour of the macroeconomy. A largely historical or evolutionary approach will be adopted, even though this implies the examination of theories now defunct or which have been effectively refuted and falsified if only in part. The justification for adopting this procedure springs from a conviction that to understand fully the significance of intellectual endeavour, in whatever field of study, requires a knowledge of what has gone before. Is it really possible to comprehend the revolutionary nature of Einstein's theory of relativity, for example, without a knowledge of Newtonian mechanics? Such examples could be repeated endlessly and in whatever field of study one would care to select. And the same is no less true of economics. Such has been the remarkable development of economics over the past 30 years, reflected in an enormous growth of specialized academic journals on both sides of the Atlantic, that the amount of time formally devoted to the history of economic thought and economic history, once commonplace in undergraduate economic courses, has been placed at a premium. Now, even at a fairly early stage of one's economic training, specialized courses abound in quantitative techniques, statistics, linear programming, econometrics, operations research and mathematics for economists of differing degrees of sophistication. Such developments are obviously inevitable and doubtless desirable; after all, the changing composition of undergraduate degree courses merely reflects efficient resource allocation in response to the changing composition of demand. None the less, there is a cost, and the cost is a diminished awareness of past intellectual developments in one's chosen field of study. And, to repeat, an understanding of the past is imperative to a full appreciation of the present.

First, therefore, an examination is made of a stylized version of classical economics and of the reasons why the logic of the theory suggests that the system will attain a state of full employment as the normal state of affairs. Lapses from full employment could occur but they would be but temporary disturbances from the long-term equilibrium state. Next are discussed the possible grounds upon which Keynes attempted to challenge and deny the classical thesis, and then the various interpretations that have been made of the *General Theory* in an attempt to decipher its true message. Considerable attention is then devoted to the Hicksian *IS/LM* framework, since this structure, more than any other, has been employed to encapsulate the essence of 'Keynesian' economics and of the ensuing controversy of the 'Keynes versus the classics' debate and of the relative efficacy of monetary versus fiscal interventionist policies. For all its shortcomings, the *IS/LM* framework is capable of considerable modification and extension, and by introducing the concept of the budget constraint it is possible to explore a good many of the tenets of modern monetarism and of the debate over 'crowding out'.

With this broad theoretical framework as a background, specific theoretical issues such as conflicting theories of output and inflation can be examined. Once again, an evolutionary approach is adopted so that, for example, the modern theory of rational expectations is seen in part to be a reaction against the earlier ascendency of adaptive expectations. Once the leading schools of thought have been examined and compared, a major step forward is undertaken by extending the analysis to the open economy and by examining the implications of alternative economic theories operating under different exchange rate regimes. This permits account to be taken of the constraints generated by the existence of the external account in the formulation of macroeconomic policies.

8

The Classical Economic System

The body of macroeconomic thought existing prior to the publication of Keynes's *General Theory of Employment Interest and Money* in 1936 has become known as the *classical macroeconomics* and culminates in a particular view of employment creation, the so-called classical theory of employment. This classical period allegedly stems from the time of Adam Smith, Say and Ricardo through J. S. Mill, Marshall and ultimately to the work of A. C. Pigou. To suggest that there was a unified theory of employment spanning such an interval of time is to perpetrate a gross distortion; the suggestion is primarily Keynes's and must be included amongst his lesser achievements. Not only did the so-called classical economists exhibit substantial differences of opinion over many fundamental issues, but even when there appeared to be agreement there were often major differences in interpretation.[1] For the most part, Keynes equated classical employment theory with the work of A. C. Pigou, which he regarded as the most complete exposition of the classical viewpoint.[2] It is in fact the case that one can identify certain elements or strands of thought in the earlier classical writers, which when combined permit a certain caricature of an employment theory which would not be widely at variance with the underlying thesis propounded in Pigou's influential work (Pigou, 1933). It is in this sense that it becomes tenable to depict a certain 'classical' macrostructure. Whilst there would be no unanimity amongst the classical scholars with regard to the individual building blocks, and whilst different classical writers might choose to emphasize different aspects of the foundations, there would in all probability be a general consensus with regard to the desirability of the edifice as a whole.

The Essential Features of Classical Macroeconomic Systems

It is in this sense that reference may be made to the 'classical macroeconomics'. What are its essential features? First of all, and largely under the influence of Benthamite or utilitarian philosophy, the classical economists postulated an economic system which

---

1 This was particularly true with reference to the interpretation accorded to Say's Law of Markets (see Schumpeter, 1961, pp. 619–25). The belief that there was a unified body of mainstream macroeconomic thought was probably reinforced by Keynes's favourable references to Malthus, Gesell, Marx and other heretical dissenters to economic orthodoxy.

2 'I have criticized at length Professor Pigou's theory of unemployment not because he seems to me to be more open to criticism than other economists of the classical school; but because his is the only attempt with which I am acquainted to write down the classical theory of unemployment precisely' (Keynes, 1936, p. 279).

assumed rational maximizing behaviour upon the part of all classes and agents in society. Capitalists would seek maximum profits whilst wage earners would seek to maximize the difference between the utility of income earned and the disutility of work effort. Moreover, this maximizing behaviour would be played out against a background of competition and within a time horizon which, whilst generally unspecified, implied a term sufficiently long and flexible to permit any indicated adjustment. Expectations were generally stable, the role of uncertainty being minimized, and knowledge was a relatively inexpensive good. *False trading* – that is, trading at non-equilibrium prices – accordingly, did not arise.

The analysis was couched in flows rather than stocks and the governing influence upon relative flows was relative prices. Money, whilst important to the absolute price level à la quantity theory, was accorded very little influence upon the real forces and magnitudes of the economy. It facilitated exchange by acting as a medium of exchange and avoiding the need for a double coincidence of wants, but beyond this obvious gain in efficiency it was immaterial to the real welfare of the economy. Indeed, it is probably correct to say that the classical economists held a conceptual view of the economy which would correspond to the economics of barter: money, in Pigou's words, was a 'veil' beyond which it was necessary to trespass in order to understand the real forces governing the economy.[3] These comments provide a basic framework of the classical model; they suggest the following tenets, which will be identified with classical employment theory.

(1)   Unemployment, often on a sizeable scale, can and does occur and for a variety of reasons. The peace of 1815, and the too sudden substitution of machinery for labour-intensive activity, provide graphic examples.

(2)   In the event of such unemployment, there would be set in force automatic tendencies which ultimately would serve to restore full employment equilibrium, providing free competition were permitted.

(3)   Finally, there is little or nothing that the government can do to hasten the process of adjustment other than to ensure that the forces of competition are allowed to reign. In particular, government spending upon public works programmes would merely drain employment-creating resources from the private sector and would have no net impact upon the volume of employment *per se*. This thesis, which became known as the 'Treasury view', provided the cornerstone for the advocacy of non-interventionist policies, and also provides the classical precursor to the present-day 'crowding out' controversy, to which frequent reference will be made.

As has been indicated, to encapsulate the classical employment model in this way is altogether too *simpliste* and arguably does less than justice to the main protagonists in the evolution of macroeconomic thinking prior to Keynes. None the less, it is this framework which Keynes set himself to deny and under Keynes's persuasive influence it is this framework which has survived the Keynes versus the classics controversy and

---

3 This distinction was subsequently to become known as 'the classical dichotomy'. Again, numerous exceptions could be cited providing exceptions to the dichotomy. An increased money supply might lower interest rates and stimulate increased output – in a manner very similar to subsequent Keynesian analysis. Likewise, Ricardo acknowledged that changes in the money supply could raise prices with money wages responding with a lag – thus raising short-run profits and investment. See Sowell (1994).

the appraisal and reappraisal of Keynesian economics. Regardless of its historical accuracy, therefore, it behoves us to examine its theoretical underpinnings in more detail.

The Classical Model

Classical writers tended to divide the economy into its real and monetary sectors and generally assumed that the two were essentially independent of each other.

Fundamentally, the real sector of the economy is determined solely by two behavioural equations concerning the supply and demand for labour in the labour market and a technical relationship specifying the relationship between the volume of labour employed and the level of national output.

To consider the latter first, with the capital stock assumed constant in the short run, output Y is positively related to labour input N. Thus,

$$Y = Y(N) \tag{8.1}$$

and $dY/dN > 0$, which implies that the marginal product of labour is always positive, but $d^2Y/dN^2 < 0$, which reiterates the classical belief in the Law of Diminishing Returns.

The demand for labour is negatively related to the real wage, which in turn is equated with the marginal product of labour. Hence,

$$N_d = N_d\left(\frac{W}{P}\right) = \frac{dY}{dN} \tag{8.2}$$

where W is the money wage and P a representative price index.

The supply of labour is likewise treated as a function of the real wage, so that

$$N_s = N_s\left(\frac{W}{P}\right) \tag{8.3}$$

and it is assumed that $dN_s/d(W/P) > 0$. Thus, it is assumed that higher real wages will always call forth more labour effort – substitution effects always predominate over income effects in modern terminology – and problems arising from the possibilities of backward-bending supply curves are neatly side-stepped. Thus, both demand and supply curves of labour will be normally sloped and, given the existence of competition, a determinate market clearing solution is indicated, providing both the equilibrium real wage and the amount of labour actually employed. To this given volume of employment there will correspond, given the state of technology, a determinate amount of real output. This composite solution is depicted in figure 8.1. Conceptually, and in keeping with Ricardian tractability, one can think in terms of a one-commodity economy, corn, with wage labour being paid in kind. Labour receives the amount (W/P)EQ0 whilst the employing classes retain SE(W/P). Such an analysis neatly avoids any difficulties arising from the 'sale' of national output. Not only is money not a determinant of the system, it is not even necessary; in such an economy, money does not matter.

A number of comments appear pertinent to the analysis. First of all, the employment level so determined represents full employment and consequently the level of output is the full employment level of output. This is because at the going rate of real wages no labour is unemployed which wishes to work for that wage; in this sense, there is no *involuntary* unemployment. Providing competition is allowed free reign, whatever

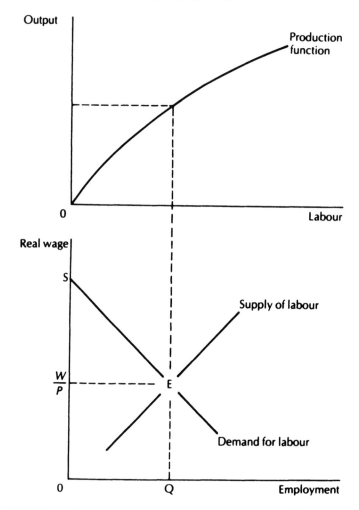

Figure 8.1 Classical determination of output, employment and the real wage

disturbance arises within the labour market (as, for example, a sudden increase in the desire for leisure reflected in an upward shift of the supply curve) there will always be some equilibrating adjustment to the real wage rate that is able to clear the market and maintain full employment. Second, *ceteris paribus*, any increase in the level of employ-ment is only accommodated by a decrease in the real wage; employment levels and real wages are inversely related in terms of this analysis.

Given the logic of the model, it follows that involuntary unemployment equilibrium is only possible in the long run if artificial restrictions are placed upon the equilibrat-ing role of real wages. These restrictions may arise on the supply side in the form of trade union intervention. Unemployment will occur if real wages are maintained above that level which equates supply and demand. Sustained unemployment, there-fore, is the consequence of monopoly trade union power overriding the forces of com-petition. The policy implication is clear; employment can be increased by decreasing the real wage and for the classical economist the real wage can be reduced by cutting the money wage. It is for this reason that any attempt to deny the classical *theoretical* tradition must analyze the effects of cutting money wages in some detail. It is not suffi-cient to sidestep the issue by asserting the downward inflexibility of money wages. Such inflexibility may indeed be empirically the case, thus rendering the classical policy prescription irrelevant, but it cannot deny the theoretical underpinnings. It is for this reason that it is both misleading and belittling to Keynes to suggest that his objection to classical employment theory rested upon the premise of wage inflexibility.

It is perhaps worth while pointing out that Keynes would not have objected to the classical solution depicted in figure 8.1 as a possible outcome. Indeed, for Keynes it was a possible outcome but one he would have regarded as a *special* case – the case where aggregate demand was just sufficient to absorb the full employment level of output.[4] His objection lay in the assertion that there was no guarantee that the requisite demand would always be forthcoming. The classicists were able to ignore this complication primarily because they found refuge in Say's Law of Markets – which will be examined in the next section – which was generally taken to imply that whatever level of output was forthcoming demand would always be sufficient to absorb it.[5] In a very fundamental sense, therefore, Keynes's real objection to classical employment theory was directed against Say's Law of Markets.

Say's Law and the Monetary Sector

Keynes's objection to the conclusion of the classical model just outlined is relatively straightforward and may be summed up in one simple but penetrating question: what guarantee is there that the requisite level of aggregate demand will be sufficient to absorb the output arising from the classical analysis? Diagrammatically, this question can be posed with the aid of figure 8.2, which simply appends the conventional Keynesian 45° line diagram to the previous figure. In part (a) of the figure the level of aggregate demand indicates the sustainable level of real output at Y_1. Part (b) of the figure translates this output level into the required number of labourers via the production function (employment function) and in part (c) of the figure the resulting degree of unemployment is indicated by the distance U. Keynes's elementary model, therefore, is a demand determined model with the direction of causation being clearly (a) to (c). Moreover, for Keynes there can be no assurance that cutting money wages – the classical prescription for unemployment – will provide the appropriate remedy, for in this case there may well be feedback effects upon the level of aggregate demand, especially if money wage cuts generate expectations of future price declines.

The essential issue raised here is, why did the classical economists believe that they could dispense with the demand element? The answer stated simply is that they took refuge in Say's Law of Markets which appeared to affirm that in the *aggregate* a deficiency of demand is a logical impossibility. Say's Law has been subject of considerable interpretation of varying degrees of sophistication. Say's initial assertion that 'goods always exchange for goods' merely reinforces the comparative unimportance of money, relegating it to a purely intermediary role. However, the later translation of Say's Law into the dictum that 'Supply Creates Its Own Demand' not only embraces the nature of exchange in a specialized economy but also generates macroeconomic implications.

---

4 Significantly, the title of Keynes's book is *The General Theory*. . . .

5 Say's Law of itself guarantees not full employment but merely that whatever level of output is forthcoming will be fully taken up. Thus Say's Law is equally applicable to the depressed levels of output which characterized the 1930s as it is to full employment. The classical argument for full employment is accordingly based upon other considerations, of which, as has been indicated, the assumption of competition is vital.

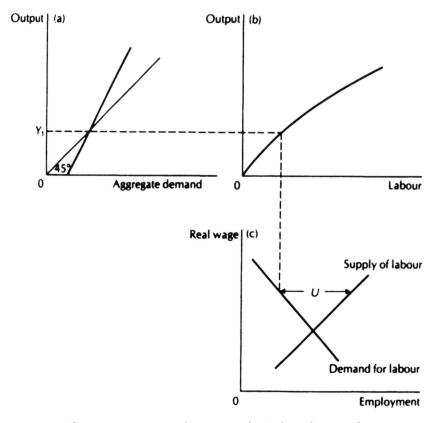

Figure 8.2 Keynesian objection to classical employment theory

With regard to the nature of exchange, where the division of labour exists, the only reason for producing goods in excess of one's own needs is in order to exchange them for other commodities. In this sense, an act of supply creates an equivalent demand *ex ante*. But there is no guarantee that the demand *ex ante* will be translated into an equivalent demand *ex post*. The act of supply may involve the production of commodities for which no one else possesses any demand, or may involve expectations of comparative prices which are overly optimistic.

In this event, demand will be deficient, gluts will occur and unemployment will be the consequence in the supplying industry. The constraint imposed upon income in the supplying industry will then transmit itself to the rest of the economy generating a general deficiency of demand. Say's Law in no sense constitutes a denial of unemployment. Keynes's interpretation that Say's Law implies no impediment to full employment income is difficult to reconcile with the writings of the classical economists. But, presumably, such unemployment will be short-lived. Comparative prices will change and the 'mistaken' act of supply will not be repeated. The unemployment stems from resource misallocation and the market economy will provide the necessary corrective. Accordingly, Say's Law may be taken as implying that demand deficiency will not be a *permanent* feature of the macroeconomy.

To summarize the argument so far: clearly the production of output will always generate purchasing power equal to the *realized* (*ex post*) value of that output. When this realized (*ex post*) value conforms with the expected (*ex ante*) value, the initial act of supply is justified and presumably will be repeated, maintaining employment in the

supplying industry. When *ex post* and *ex ante* values do not coincide, time will be needed for the market economy to adjust comparative prices to bring about the required
equation. During this time period unemployment can indeed occur.

But the question remains: even when *ex ante* and *ex post* values coincide, will the purchasing power so generated by the act of supply be transmitted into an *equal* effective
demand upon the rest of the economy? This is what is required for the proposition that
supply creates its own demand to be translated into the proposition that aggregate
demand will not, in the long term, be deficient and unable to absorb the output associated with equilibrium employment determined in the labour market.

In the context of a barter economy, and allowing for a time horizon long enough to
permit the required adjustment in barter exchange ratios, the law becomes almost tautological. But does the law hold for a monetary economy, where workers do not produce final goods for direct barter but instead sell their labour services for money
income?[6] In this case, the act of supply creates not an equivalent demand but rather an
associated monetary income. In order for the law to hold, the monetary income so created must generate a demand equal to the monetary value of the act of supply. Symboli-
cally it is required that

$$\varphi \Rightarrow Y \Rightarrow D = \varphi \tag{8.4}$$

where φ is the value of goods produced, Y is the monetary income and D is the aggregate level of monetary demand. It is reasonable to postulate an equality between φ and
Y since one acceptable method of estimating national income is simply to sum all the
attendant production costs. Thus, the condition for Say's Law to remain valid reduces
to the proposition that $Y = D$ – that is, that all monetary income is translated into
monetary demands. In the Keynesian formulation, the marginal propensity to consume is less than one. An increase in income generated by the act of supply, therefore,
will not generate an equivalent increase in *consumption* demand. What is required for
Say's Law to hold is the belief that additional investment demand will be forthcoming
to match the increase in savings. For the classical economist this proposition appeared
almost self-evident, and indeed had been explicitly stated by Adam Smith in his
famous assertion 'that what is annually saved is as regularly consumed as what is
annually spent, and nearly in the same time too: but it is consumed by a different set of
people'. Clearly, what is required is the condition that saving be equated with investment in the *ex ante* sense. Since monetary income is either consumed or saved, and
demand is for either investment goods or consumption goods,

$$Y = C + S \tag{8.5}$$

$$D = D_c + D_i \tag{8.6}$$

and since D_c is by definition equal to C, the condition $Y = D$ requires $S = D_i$.

For the classical economist this equality is a logical consequence of classical interest
rate theory. According to this doctrine, the fundamental determinants of the rate of
interest are the twin forces of productivity and thrift. The former provides a demand for
capital (supply of bonds) determined by the marginal productivity of capital, whilst the
latter provides a supply of saving. More formally, saving is related to the rate of interest,
so that,

---

6 This distinction is sometimes referred to in terms of Say's Identity and Say's Equality (see Becker and
Baumol, 1952).

$$S = S(i) \tag{8.7}$$

and $dS/di > 0$ where i denotes the interest rate. Investment demand is equally geared to the rate of interest, so that

$$I = I(i) \tag{8.8}$$

and $dI/di < 0$.

Thus, the supply and demand curves for capital are normally sloped, and appending the equilibrium market clearing condition that

$$S = I \tag{8.9}$$

permits the determination of saving, investment and the rate of interest.

The classical theory of interest determination is illustrated in figure 8.3. The rate of interest becomes the equilibrating force which maintains equality between saving and investment and thus maintains the level of aggregate demand. An increase in the desire to save, for example, implies an outward shift in the supply curve of capital, an immediate fall in the rate of interest and an extension of investment spending equal to the cutback in consumption demand. The classical theory of interest rate determination, and in particular the belief that interest rates revealed great flexibility in response to any change in underlying market conditions, thus becomes the cornerstone of classical macrotheory by underpinning the validity of Say's Law within the context of a monetary economy.

The rate of interest which equated savings and investment was to become known as the 'natural rate of interest', following Wicksell in his *Lectures on Political Economy* (Wicksell, 1934) and Keynes in his *Treatise on Money* (Keynes, 1930). The classical

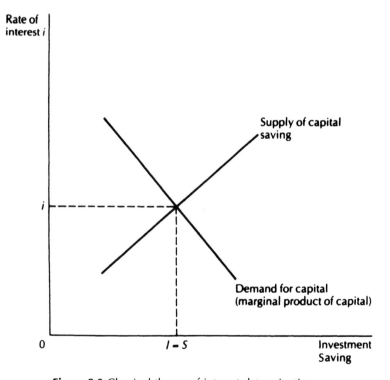

Figure 8.3 Classical theory of interest determination

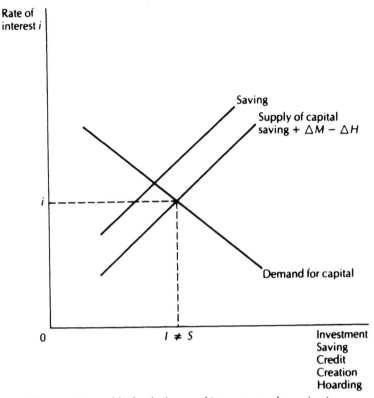

Figure 8.4 Loanable funds theory of interest rate determination

model implicitly assumed that the market rate of interest would always correspond to the so-called natural rate. But both Wicksell and Keynes were to explore conditions under which the market rate of interest might deviate from the natural rate and thus destroy the equality between saving and investment required for Say's Law.

Why should such a divergence occur? A number of possibilities present themselves. On the one hand, not all savings may be placed on the market in the form of demand for bonds. People may find themselves with a demand for cash and thus decide to hoard out of their savings. This is one consequence of permitting money to possess a store of value function in addition to the conventional transactions demand function assumed in classical economics. On the other hand, the supply of capital placed on the market may exceed the supply of savings if the banking sector is engaged in credit creation. This more sophisticated formulation of interest rate theory, which was to become known as the *loanable funds theory*, is illustrated by reference to figure 8.4. The demand for loanable funds is equated with the demand for productive capital assets (supply of bonds) as before, but now the supply of loanable funds is equal to saving plus the flow of new money originating from the banking sector (ΔM) less any hoarding element (ΔH). It follows that there is no longer any guarantee that savings and investment will be equated. The level of aggregate demand may thus exceed or fall short of that required to sustain current output with inflationary or deflationary consequences; Say's Law is invalidated. A more specifically Keynesian objection to classical interest rate theory turned upon the notion that there may be an institutionally determined minimal limit to interest rates below which the market rate could not fall. Much of Keynesian interest rate theory is concerned with establishing the conceptual

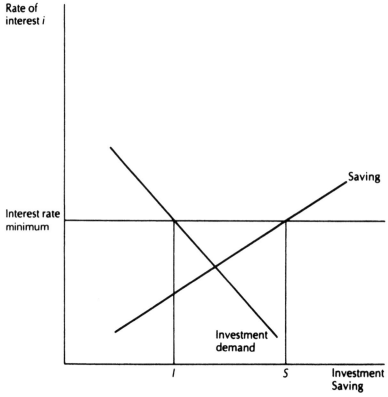

Figure 8.5 Keynesian denial of classical interest rate theory – an institutional floor to interest rates

justification for such a minimal market rate.[7] Now if the required equality between saving and investment demands an interest rate below this minimal possible level, Say's Law is immediately denied. Such a situation is depicted in figure 8.5, where at the institutionally determined minimal interest rate *ex ante* saving exceeds *ex ante* investment by the amount *IS* with predictable deflationary consequences.[8]

The following is a summary of the argument so far. The classical system had posited that full employment would be the normal outcome of the bargaining process in the labour market if the natural play of competition was allowed. Moreover, whatever the output level corresponding to this full employment equilibrium, the level of aggregate demand would be sufficient, ultimately, to absorb it. The latter assurance derived from Say's Law of Markets which in turn depended upon the classical formulation of interest rate determination. Thus, to a large extent, Keynes's attack upon the classical structure was an assault upon their formulation of the theory of interest. The alternative formulation proposed by Keynes does not guarantee the *ex ante* equation of savings and investment; nor does it guarantee that current output levels are sustainable. It can

---

7 Prior to Keynes, all excessive saving doctrines had foundered upon this very point. Malthus, for example, had been unable to explain why the excessive accumulation of capital did not lead to a zero rate of interest.

8 As will be seen (chapter 11), it was left to Pigou to salvage the classical system from the force of this attack. The celebrated Pigou Effect would show that in such an event automatic tendencies would arise to arrest the rate of saving. The saving schedule would be progressively shifted inwards until it intersected the investment demand curve at the minimal interest rate level.

hardly be considered surprising therefore that much of the immediate post-Keynesian controversy should focus so heavily upon the question of interest rate determination.

Say's Law was clearly important in buttressing the prevailing commitment to non-interventionist policies and the belief in the forces of automatic adjustment to autonomous disturbance. It did not guarantee full employment. Indeed, it specifically allowed for situations of demand deficiency and indeed for conditions of crisis when an excess demand for money would imply an excess demand for goods. However, it did provide a macroeconomic counterpart to Adam Smith's 'invisible hand' by suggesting that unemployment would be temporary and not permanent and that aggregate demand would ultimately be adequate. In doing so, it provided the justification for the dynamic view that there was no limit to economic growth. In turn, this led Ricardo to the view that there could be no limit to the extent of capital accumulation in an economy and thus to a denial of the Malthusian notion that saving propensities could be excessive. It was ideally suited to the prevailing philosophy of the time and widely endorsed and invoked. In one form or another, it became the unifying strand in classical macroeconomics despite the caveats and reservations which were to stem from J. S. Mill and even J. B. Say himself.[9]

The Role of Money

The classical model just outlined is a model stated in real terms, with the nominal money stock exercising no influence upon the real sector of the economy. In such a model, the role of money is significant solely for nominal values. With a given money stock and a constant velocity, money national income is given as

$$\bar{M}\bar{V} = Y_m \tag{8.10}$$

Since real income is already determined, the equation

$$Y_m = PY \tag{8.11}$$

permits the determination of the price level and hence the determination of the nominal wage

$$W_m = \frac{W}{P}P \tag{8.12}$$

It follows that a doubling of the money stock, from whatever cause, with a constant velocity will merely double prices, nominal income and nominal wages whilst leaving real variables unchanged. This is the nature of the *classical dichotomy* between the real and monetary sectors as well as an affirmation of the quantity theory of money. For the classical writers the quantity theory of money was an integral element in the dichotomy and in the alleged neutrality of money.

Implicit in this approach is the assumption that the demand for money is essentially a transactions demand and thus that the amount of nominal money balances demanded will be a function of nominal income. With real income determined by the forces of competition in the labour market, it follows that the demand for money will vary

---

9 Mill is explicit in denying Say's Law: 'Although he who sells, really sells only to buy, he need not buy at the same moment when he sells; and he does not therefore necessarily add to the *immediate* demand for one commodity when he adds to the supply of another'(Mill, 1844).

directly with the price level. With a constant velocity, a doubling of the price will lead to a doubling of the nominal demand for money to maintain real demand constant. Accordingly, the demand for money would reveal itself as being a unit elastic schedule when plotted against the value of money – the inverse of the price level – as previously indicated in chapter 5.

As we have seen, prolonged unemployment in the classical model can only be explained in terms of rigidities in the labour market which prevent the required downward adjustment in real wages. But the authorities, assuming they can control the money stock, possess the means to bring about the required adjustment. An increase in the money stock, *ceteris paribus*, will raise prices, reduce real wages and accordingly extend the demand for, and contract the supply of, labour. However, the classical economist would not have considered this as a reasonable policy alternative. Monetary expansion to deliberately generate inflation would have been deemed irresponsible. Advocates of monetary expansion were, like Gesell and his schemes of stamped money, relegated to the underworld of economics. Moreover, if the money stock is endogenously determined – as, for example, by committment to an international gold standard – then even this potentially discretionary power is called into question.

Aggregate Supply and Demand Analysis

It is instructive to consider the classical macro-model in terms of aggregate supply and demand analysis. Simply stated, the classical aggregate supply curve is vertical, since output determination is independent of the price level. This is a logical implication of the classical dichotomy. An increase in the price level would lower the real wage below its market clearing level and thus generate a situation of excess demand in the labour market. In turn, the excess demand would quickly raise nominal wages and thus restore the real wage back to its former equilibrium level. With the equilibrium real wage unchanged, so too is the equilibrium level of output. The full employment level of output is thus invarient to the price level and its determiant the money stock.

Of course, *the position* of the vertical aggregate supply curve may itself be subject to change over time. Technological progress which raised the marginal product of labour, for example (by increasing the tangent slope to the production function at any given employment level), would increase the demand for labour and generate a higher level of real wages. With a positively sloped labour supply curve, more labour would be employed and the full employment level of output increased. Conversely, the vertical aggregate supply curve could be shifted inwards if the size of the working population fell or if households were to alter their preference sets in favour of greater leisure. Presumably, however, there is very little the government can do to alter the position of the aggregate supply curve. In particular, its position is unaltered by changes in monetary aggregates.

With regard to the aggregate demand schedule, logic dictates that it take the shape of a rectangular hyperbola. With a given money stock and a constant velocity we have a constant level of monetary expenditure to be divided between output and prices. With a given velocity, the position of the aggregate demand curve will be determined by changes in the money stock; an increase in the money stock will shift the aggregate demand curve outwards and raise prices whilst a decrease will have the opposite effect. The classical aggregate supply and demand analysis is summarized with the aid of figure 8.6. The affinity with the New Classical Economics should be obvious.

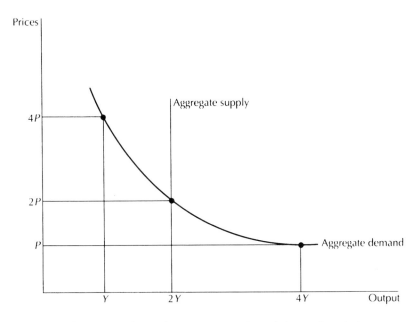

Figure 8.6 Classical aggregate supply and demand analysis

Concluding Comments

In this chapter an attempt has been made, albeit far too briefly, to outline the essential features of the classical system and the reasons for the classical belief that the natural long-run equilibrium condition for the macroeconomy implied a state of zero involuntary unemployment. It has been shown that the classical conclusion rested upon certain postulates and conditions including Say's Law of Markets, whose validity, in turn, is seen to depend crucially upon the classical theory of interest determination. If this interpretation is correct, it would suggest that Keynes's assault upon the classical model was in large part an attack upon classical interest theory. Finally, an outline was given of the nature of the classical dichotomy and the reasons for the belief that money stock changes would influence only nominal magnitudes – a conclusion, as will be seen, remarkably similar to certain modern-day monetarist contentions.

Further Reading

Any genuine understanding of classical economics and the classical theory of employment demands a reading of the original source material. Reliance upon secondary sources, no matter how perceptive or authoritative, always encounters the danger of caricaturing the classical writers. In particular, the writings of Smith (1904), Ricardo (1951–55), Mill (1966) and Say (1964), together with Ricardo's correspondence with Malthus, provide valuable insight into issues where the classical economists differed with regard to their views on the macroeconomy; such differences are invariably obscured by attempts to survey the content of classical economics.

With regard to the secondary sources, however, Schumpeter's monumental work (1954) is especially rewarding Sowell (1972, 1987, 1994) is particularly illuminating with respect to Say's Law whilst Leijonhufvud (1981) highlights the difficulties of coordination failure implicit in its application. A detailed analysis of Ricardo's macroeconomics is provided by Shoup (1960). A carefully researched study of the classical economists is that by O'Brien (1975), whilst Corry (1962) provides an analysis which emphasizes the homogeneity of classical thinking with respect to macroeconomic issues. On policy issues generally, Robbins (1952) and Samuels (1966) deserve particular mention whilst Presley (1979) provides a recent re-evaluation of the contribution of Robertson. Cochrane (1970) provides an exhaustive attempt to summarize pre-Keynesian macrotheory. Interesting shorter expositional pieces on classical macrotheory are to be found in Hagen (1966) and Ackley (1961, 1978). More recent contributions include Carlin and Soskice (1990) and Hillier (1991).

9

The Economics of Keynes

The previous chapter has sketched, albeit in a somewhat *simpliste* fashion, the essence of classical employment theory with which Keynes was to take issue. That Keynes was seeking to deny the classical thesis is beyond doubt; the question which remains, however, and which is still unresolved, is the precise nature of Keynes's attempted denial. That this question should remain in contention some sixty years after the publication of the *General Theory* is in itself remarkable, particularly in view of the detailed analysis to which the latter has been subject. None the less, this is in fact the case, and it is possible to identify three distinct and opposing interpretations of Keynes which command respect. These might be characterized as the unstable expectations thesis, the general equilibrium model and the Hicksian income–expenditure approach.

The Context and Scope of the General Theory

Before turning to these three opposing viewpoints of the message of the *General Theory*, it is perhaps necessary to point out what that volume was *not* concerned with. Keynes was not attempting to argue that unemployment was the consequence of a lack of flexibility in money wages. Indeed, had he done so he would have been postulating the classical theory of unemployment, as he fully recognized.

> For the Classical Theory has been accustomed to rest the supposedly self-adjusting character of the economic system on the assumed fluidity of money wages; and, when there is rigidity, to lay on this rigidity the blame of maladjustment. (Keynes, 1936, p. 257)

Keynes was not merely attempting to deny one of the assumptions underlying the classical model on the grounds of its being at variance with the real world. The *General Theory* occupied Keynes for fully five years:[1] had he merely been refuting the plausibility of downward wage flexibility, it would scarcely have taken half an hour. Keynes was not simply questioning the assumptions of classical theory but attempting to deny the theoretical model given its assumptions. He believed himself to be writing a major work in economic theory, and as he made clear in a letter to George Bernard Shaw he had no doubts that he was involved in his *magnum opus*.

---

1 See his letter to Florence Keynes (Moggridge, 1973, vol. XIII, p. 653).

I believe myself to be writing a book on economic theory which will largely re-
volutionise – not, I suppose, at once but in the course of the next ten years – the
way the world thinks about economic problems. . . .

I can't expect you, or anyone else, to believe this at the present stage. But for
myself I don't merely hope what I say, in my own mind I'm quite sure. (Moggridge, 1973, vol. XIII, p. 492)

Whether Keynes succeeded in denying the classical theory is a matter of dispute depending upon the interpretation to be accorded to Keynes. The conventional wisdom would
tend to the view that Keynes failed in his theoretical objective but none the less succeeded
in revolutionizing the policy climate in sanctioning a far greater degree of policy intervention.[2] This issue will be returned to later; first, however, the question why these difficulties of interpretation should arise, and persist for so long, must be confronted.

First and foremost, the *General Theory* is an extremely difficult book. It is difficult to
read and all the evidence suggests that Keynes found it difficult to write. At times the
syntax becomes extremely tortuous and unclear; at others the tone is almost flippant
and suspiciously tongue in cheek. It was written over a considerable time and doubtless
Keynes's own perception of the issues altered over the years. Inconsistencies arise and
accordingly it is possible by careful selection to derive opposing viewpoints. The difficulties are compounded by the introduction of new terminology for established economic concepts.[3] Moreover, it is arguable whether the definition of income adopted
or the emphasis upon user costs, supplementary costs, windfall losses, wage units and
so forth are appropriate to the methodology adopted; certainly, these terms have disap-
peared from elementary 'Keynesian' textbook expositions. More than one eminent
scholar has suggested that Keynes was not fully aware of what he was writing or where
it was to lead him.[4] Many of the difficulties might have been resolved had Keynes
revised the work in the light of subsequent criticism and commentary. But this was not
to be. The nearest that Keynes came to a restatement was in a defence to the critics[5] in
his famous *Quarterly Journal of Economics* article (Keynes, 1937a). Here Keynes
emphasized the importance of the state of long-term expectations, or rather the
unstable nature and uncertainty surrounding long-term expectations, as a pivotal
point of departure from classical theory.

One notable feature of the *General Theory,* which is in part responsible for a certain
lack of precision to the arguments proffered, is that Keynes avoided any attempt at a
formal mathematical model. Indeed, he specifically warned against the employment
of mathematics on the grounds that it would cloak interdependencies between variables. Thus,

---

2 Long before Keynes, other economists in both the UK and the USA had advocated public works programmes and similar measures to alleviate unemployment. Keynes, however, particularly with the multiplier
concept borrowed from Kahn, provided the required theoretical rationale.

3 Thus, for example, the marginal efficiency of capital replaced the Marshallian marginal productivity
concept, whilst the doctrine of liquidity preference substituted *inter alia* for the Cambridge *k* of earlier analysis.

4 'Thus, Keynes became "the greatest economist of our time" (meaning that his contribution was so indis-
putable that no one need concern himself over precisely what it was) and the *General Theory* an "acknowledged classic" (meaning that no active economist reads it, for fear of discovering that the master was himself
confused about the message he had to impart to posterity)' (Johnson, 1970) and, 'There were'moments when
we had some trouble in getting Maynard to see what the point of his revolution really was, but when he came
to sum it up after the book was published he got it into focus' (Robinson, 1973).

5 The critics were formidable, being Leontief, Robertson, Taussig and Viner and published in the November 1936 edition of the *Journal.*

It is a great fault of symbolic pseudo-mathematical methods of formalising a system of economic analysis... that they expressly assume strict independence between the factors involved and lose all their cogency and authority if this hypothesis is disallowed.... Too large a proportion of recent 'mathematical' economics are mere concoctions, as imprecise as the initial assumptions they rest on, which allow the author to lose sight of the complexities and interdependencies of the real world in a maze of pretentious and unhelpful symbols. (Keynes, 1936, pp. 297–8)

None the less, despite this stricture, Keynes was to endorse the simultaneous equation model presented by Hicks in his famous 'Mr Keynes and the Classics' (Hicks, 1937). Keynes 'found it very interesting and really had next to nothing to say by way of criticism' (Moggridge, 1973, vol. XIV, p. 79).

One fundamental difficulty in the interpretation to be accorded to the *General Theory* rests upon its presumed relationship with the *Treatise on Money*. That the former derived in part from the discussions and controversies surrounding the latter is beyond dispute. Whether the *General Theory* should be looked upon as replacing the *Treatise* or merely extending and building upon its foundations is altogether a more difficult issue to resolve. If the *General Theory* is regarded as a distinct break from its predecessor, presumably now discarded by its author, a more radical interpretation is suggested. In contrast, if the *General Theory* is looked upon as a continuation and evolution of the *Treatise* upon which Keynes sought to improve by adding a theory of output changes to the theory of prices changes already contained therein, then arguably the break with tradition is less sharp and revolutionary. This issue is of importance to the subsequent interpretation to be accorded to 'Keynesian' positions upon the relative potency of monetary versus fiscal actions.

In the *General Theory* Keynes makes frequent reference to the *Treatise* partly to clarify changes in terminology. More specifically, however, he writes:

The relation between this book and my *Treatise on Money*, which I published five years ago, is probably clearer to myself than it will be to others; and what in my own mind is a natural evolution in a line of thought which I have been pursuing for several years, may sometimes strike the reader as a confusing change of view. (Keynes, 1936, p. vi)

None the less, the evolutionary process is dramatic involving the transition from a static to a dynamic view of the economy. Thus,

my lack of emancipation from preconceived ideas showed itself in what now seems to be the outstanding fault of the theoretical parts of that work (namely, Books III and IV), that I failed to deal thoroughly with the effects of *changes* in the level of output.... The dynamic development as distinct from the instantaneous picture, was left incomplete and extremely confused. (Keynes, 1936, pp. vi–vii)

The foregoing discussion has suggested reasons why there may exist legitimate differences over the question of Keynes's fundamental message and his assault upon classical employment theory. One's perception of Keynes's views cannot be divorced from their period, and this is as true of Keynes's fellow disciples as it is of latter-day commentators. In the last resort, the question of what Keynes really meant (or arguably, what he should have meant) turns upon

> a view as to what is central and what is merely peripheral, what is essential and what is merely incidental, in his writings; in this way apparent inconsistencies and obscurities may readily be resolved, at least to the satisfaction of those adhering to that interpretation. (Coddington, 1976)

In what follows, three opposing interpretations of the *General Theory* are outlined.

The Unstable Expectations Thesis

Classical economics viewed the world as consisting of individual economic agents, motivated by the desire to maximize their own individual welfare, subconsciously promoting the aggregate good whilst simultaneously generating market clearing situations. Such was the power of the 'invisible hand' and the force of competition. Implicit in the classical approach is the belief in the existence and attainment of a market equilibrium and more importantly that individual maximizing behaviour will promote such an equilibrium. Such a solution requires certain constraining conditions, the presumption of reasonable knowledge about markets and market behaviour, and the existence of stable expectations about the future.

If these conditions are not satisfied, and in particular if expectations about the future are continually changing in the light of events, then there can be no guarantee that the indicated equilibrium will be attained. Moreover, if there exists interdependence between expectations so that one person's beliefs influence another's, divergent movements away from the indicated equilibrium may be experienced.

According to one influential interpretation of Keynes, this was precisely his belief with respect to investment demands. The state of long-term expectations, or the state of confidence, has a profound impact upon the marginal efficiency of capital schedule. But the state of long-term expectation would be an extremely unstable and precarious thing; it will be unduly influenced by the facts of the current situation which will be subject to sudden change. Ignorance is the dominant characteristic in estimates about future prospective yields of capital assets, and accordingly such estimates will be held in little confidence. Moreover, the valuation of future capital assets will be greatly influenced by current evaluation of existing assets upon the stock exchange. But the stock exchange evaluation may have little relevance to the true value of the asset. The increasing ownership of equity by persons having no involvement in day-to-day management of the business in question accentuates possible divergencies of stock market valuations from true valuations of the asset. Moreover, professional investors are not concerned with the true valuation of an asset as such; rather their concern is with what the market evaluation will be over the next few months no matter how irrational or divorced from true values that may be. In these circumstances there can be no guarantee that the volume of investment will conform to the needs of society, or that it will generate a situation whereby capital markets are cleared. Thus

> There is no clear evidence from experience that the investment policy which is socially advantageous coincides with that which is more profitable. (Keynes, 1936, p. 157)

and

> When the capital development of a country becomes a by-product of the activ-
> ities of a casino, the job is likely to be ill-done. (Keynes, 1936, p. 159)

In addition, however, there is another consequence of the existence of uncertainty and
ignorance surrounding future values of capital assets. Given the existence of a liquid
asset, namely money, in a world of uncertainty and erratic capital valuations, it
becomes open to the individual to opt out of investment in real assets altogether and
in so doing to opt out of any accompanying employment creation. Hoarding is a logical
counterpart to uncertainty and ignorance.

This interpretation of the essence of Keynes culls support principally from the 1937
Quarterly Journal of Economics article and chapter 12 of the *General Theory*. In essence,
it throws doubt upon the private enterprise system's ability to generate the required
amount of investment; moreover, it suggests that monetary policy directed merely
towards controlling the rate of interest may be inadequate to provide the corrective.
Keynes did not shrink from the obvious conclusion:

> I expect to see the State, which is in a position to calculate the marginal efficiency
> of capital goods on long views and on the basis of the general social advantage,
> taking an ever greater responsibility for directly organising investment; since it
> seems likely that the fluctuations in the market estimation of the marginal effi-
> ciency of different types of capital, calculated on the principles I have described
> above, will be too great to be offset by any practicable changes in the rate of inter-
> est. (Keynes, 1936, p. 164)

The revolutionary nature of this interpretation of Keynes should not be overlooked.
In this view, Keynes was not merely suggesting that the classical macroeconomic
model of the economy was at fault; rather he was stating that no such complete model
of the economy was possible if it were to do justice to the state of long-term expectations. In short, orthodox economics was adrift and there was nothing that could be put
in its place. As will be seen in chapter 13, it is ironic that recent work on generating theories of endogenous expectations formation has largely been formulated within a neo-
classical framework.

The General Equilibrium Model

The Marshallian theory of value is essentially partial equilibrium analysis; it studies
individual market situations under the assumption of *ceteris paribus*. That is to say, it
assumed that it is feasible to analyse changes in individual market supply and demand
curves in isolation from what is happening in other markets. This assumption is, of
course, strictly untenable, as Marshall was fully aware.[6] The real world is characterized

---

6 Marshall was extremely careful in his choice of market examples in an attempt to minimize the obvious
difficulties. Thus, for example, the *ceteris paribus* assumption encompasses real income despite the fact that
any price change occurring in the market in question must affect real income. Marshall thus chose commodities such as tea which occupied a minor fraction of consumers' budgets and thus minimized attendant income
effects (see Marshall, 1920, p. 92ff.)

by interdependence; changes in any one market will exert feedback influences upon markets elsewhere which in turn will rebound once more upon the market initiating the change.

General equilibrium theory expressly allows for such interdependence. It views the economy as a series of mutually interdependent markets for each and every good in the economy. It thus attempts to analyse the economy from a microeconomic viewpoint by focusing upon individual markets, but since it examines all markets simultaneously, allowing for interdependencies, it is equally macroeconomic in character. An alternative way of approaching this distinction is to say that whereas in partial equilibrium analysis the prices of all goods other than the one under observation are exogenous, in general equilibrium analysis all prices are endogenous.

Now whilst the Marshallian approach is obviously the pragmatic way to analyse any given market structure, and whilst it has great expositional value, its very incompleteness renders it conceptually unsatisfactory. In contrast, the Walrasian[7] general equilibrium model is intellectually appealing if at the same time mathematically demanding. It conceives the world in terms of a series of complex simultaneous equations, and the intriguing question which then arises for mathematicians is whether or not a solution will exist; that is to say, will there be a price vector which is able to equate supply and demand in all markets simultaneously? The answer to this question raises all sorts of difficult problems which have only recently produced satisfactory answers.[8]

The economist, however, is concerned not just with the possible existence of a solution to a set of simultaneous equations. He insists that the indicated solution possess possible economic significance; that is to say, negative values must not enter the price vector. Moreover, the question which intrigues him is whether the market system, assuming competitive maximizing behaviour, is capable of attaining any indicated solution. This is the question which is neatly sidestepped in Walrasian economics by the adoption of the mathematically convenient but artificial device known as *tâtonnement*. This takes the form of assuming the existence of an auctioneer (presumably possessed of a minicomputer) who calls out prices for each and every good. Prospective buyers and vendors then respond to these prices by tendering 'fictive tickets' indicating the quantities they wish to buy and sell. If the price vector so established does not clear all markets simultaneously, no exchange is permitted to take place. The auctioneer will revise his prices and the whole process will recommence. In this way, the market gropes towards the equilibrium price vector and no false trading – that is, trading at non-equilibrium prices – is allowed to interfere with the indicated adjustment process.

Now it is precisely this fiction of the auctioneer which renders general equilibrium theory largely irrelevant to the problems which concerned Keynes. For if false trading is ruled out so too is any analysis of disequilibrium sequences by which the economy might move from one equilibrium to another. Moreover, such an assumption elim-

---

7 Leon Walras is generally regarded as the founder of modern general equilibrium theory in that he first posited, if he did not entirely answer, the fundamental issues of whether in such a system there would exist a competitive equilibrium; would it be unique and would it be stable? For a penetrating insight into Walras's *Elements d'Economie Politique Pure ou Theorie de la Richesse Sociale*, see especially Schumpeter (1961, pp. 998–1026).

8 Walras's approach to this question was in terms of equating the number of equations with unknowns given certain restrictions upon the nature of permissible equations, but it was not until the development of fixed point theorems in mathematics in the 1950s that a general proof was finally possible. The major innovators in the development of the Walrasian tradition have included Hicks, Arrow, Hahn, Debreu and Malinvaud.

inates any uncertainty about the future – the future is always a market clearing one. Restricting oneself solely to equilibrium conditions permits the absence of time; the world is one of timeless truths. In contrast, Keynes was attempting to confront the problems of a modern capitalist economy in which production involved *time* and hence involved expectations about the future which might be held with differing degrees of confidence and certainty. The issues with which Keynes grappled have all been neatly put aside by the benevolent role of the omnipotent auctioneer. What then is the relevance of general equilibrium theory to the message of the *General Theory*?

It is at this point that a neo-Walrasian interpretation of Keynes is encountered which is intimately linked with the names of Clower and Leijonhufvud (see Clower and Leijonhufvud, 1975; Leijonhufvud, 1968). What is suggested here is that Keynes moved away from the partial equilibrium analysis of the Cambridge Marshallian world towards a general equilibrium approach along Walrasian lines but characterized by its extremely aggregative nature. Thus Keynes viewed the economy in terms of four all-inclusive and interdependent markets – the markets for commodities, money, bonds and labour. In addition, Keynes readily conceded that within this aggregative system a set of prices could exist so as to clear all markets simultaneously, including the market for labour. But in the absence of the calculating auctioneer the stability of such a price vector cannot be guaranteed. Prices may be established in the various aggregated markets which do not equate supply and demand and yet a certain amount of trading will take place. Moreover, the existence of such false trading may aggravate the disequilibrium situation.

If this interpretation is correct then Keynes made a fundamental break from the Marshallian tradition. For in the Marshallian theory, if prices do not equate supply and demand then a fairly immediate price change is indicated in the market period. In the market period, supply conditions are assumed perfectly inelastic, as Marshall's example of the fish catch makes perfectly clear. In the short run, quantities will adjust to the new price now prevailing; supply conditions will become more elastic as the fishing fleet can spend more time at sea. In the long run, defined as the time required for the combination of all factors to be changed, even more of the adjustment will be thrown upon the side of quantities. This is the case of the building of new trawlers. Indeed, if perfect competition prevails, the ultimate restoration of normal profits will throw the entire adjustment upon the side of quantity. Since Marshall predominantly emphasized the long term, quantity adjustment is the presumed response to disequilibrium situations.

In contrast, in the Walrasian framework there is no adjustment in terms of quantities. False trading – exchange at disequilibrium prices – is ruled out by the presence of the auctioneer who immediately adopts a new price vector. In contrast to the Marshallian world, adjustment to disequilibrium is entirely upon the side of prices.

But what if we dispense with the fiction of the auctioneer? This is the question essentially posed by the Clower–Leijonhufvud interpretation of Keynes. In the absence of information as to what the market clearing price should be, there is no reason to assume prices will change. In the market period – in stark contrast to Marshallian analysis – the market price will be maintained, false trading will occur and the entire adjustment will be thrown upon the side of quantity changes. Moreover, such quantity changes imply further income changes which may exert disequilibrating feedback impacts upon other markets. To illustrate the argument advanced here, consider figure 9.1. Two markets are illustrated – the market for commodities and the labour market. Assume initially that full employment prevails but that prices are too high to clear the

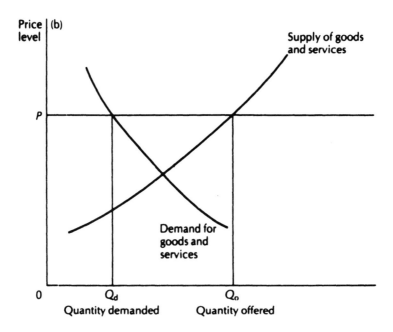

Figure 9.1 False trading and market interdependence in the (a) labour market and (b) commodity market

commodity market. If traders attempt to maintain existing prices then the adjustment process is thrown upon the side of quantity changes. A situation of excess supply develops with stocks and inventories increased as effective demand falls short of supply at existing prices. The decision to maintain existing prices, it may be noted, is perfectly rational, given uncertainty about the permanency of the shortfall in demand and changing expectations about possible future price levels. But the build-up of unsold stocks implies income changes for would-be suppliers and ultimately feeds back upon the demand for labour. As indicated by the line D_1 in figure 9.1(a), the demand for labour falls, suggesting the new equilibrium market clearing wage $(W/P)_1$. But once again, labour will resist the implied price adjustment. With real wages unchanged, changes in the volume of employment result. But unemployment does not bring about the equilibrating fall in wages – at least not initially – as the unemployed enter into search procedures to find work at the previously experienced wage. Moreover, this tendency may be reinforced by social conventions. On the one hand, the unemployed will regard it unethical to attempt to undercut the wages of fellow employed workers whilst, on the other, considerations of fairness and a concept of a 'conventional' wage (sometimes supported by social conventions and legislation) will deter employers from pursuing wage cuts (Solow, 1980). Comparative wage rigidity will again imply quantity and income changes with feedback effects upon demands in commodity markets. Thus, the disequilibrium situation generates further disequilibrium, in stark contrast to the Marshallian solution.

This sequence demonstrates two concepts which may be considered essential to Keynesian thought. The first is the notion that the *effective demand* for goods depends upon actual income received (the consumption function) and may fall short of *notional demand*, regarded as that level of demand that would have been forthcoming had labour been able to sell its desired quantity of labour time at existing wage levels. In effect, under conditions in which labour markets fail to clear, the worker has two decisions to make with regard to future consumption expenditure. One is unconstrained, based upon the premise that he can work as much as he wishes at the going wage, whereas the other is constrained by the fact that potential employers may only be willing to hire him for a shorter period. This is the dual decision hypothesis, first outlined by Clower (1965), in his suggested interpretation of Keynes attempting to grapple with an economy in the absence of market clearing behaviour. Secondly, the sequence of income constrained *divergence* from the indicated equilibria outlined above is very reminiscent of the pivotal position of the Keynesian multiplier in magnifying the initial disturbance to income and employment levels.

This interpretation of Keynes differs sharply from the conventional, which views the *General Theory* primarily in terms of comparative statics. In contrast, the attention is pivoted firmly upon disequilibrium situations and analyses the resulting adjustments in dynamic terms. Ultimately, even in the absence of the auctioneer, adjustments will occur upon the side of prices as both workers and entrepreneurs experience the painful learning process that their reservation prices are too high. A classical full employment solution is not inconsistent with the underlying model; none the less, in this interpretation, Keynes's achievement is very real. It lies in pointing out that the automatic adjustment of the classical analysis rests upon the highly artificial assumption of perfect price flexibility guaranteed by the auctioneer; in emphasizing that price rigidity is the consequence not of monopoly but of imperfect information, and that in the absence of such *tâtonnement* the disequilibrium adjustment process could be extremely long; and further in stressing that initial reactions to disequilibrium situations are more likely to widen the discrepancy between actual and equilibrium prices/quantity relationships. Keynes thus emerges as a major theorist of macroeconomic disequilibrium.

This interpretation of Keynes does not necessarily imply that Keynes believed himself to be working in a Walrasian framework or that he concerned himself unduly with the Walrasian issues of the existence of a competitive equilibrium. Indeed, as Joan Robinson (1969) has commented, Keynes started from a Marshallian short-period situation in which *money* prices are linked to the state of effective demand. In contrast, the Walrasian approach effectively dispenses with money to the extent that all transactions are conducted in kind. Indeed, according to Clower (1975),

> Keynes must rather have intended to offer the world an analytically manageable aggregative version of the kind of *general process analysis* that Marshall himself might have formulated had he ever felt the need explicitly to model the working of the economic system as a whole.

None the less, it does suggest that Keynes was indeed a major theoretical innovator whose main achievement lay in breaking away from equilibrium theorizing which had dominated economics for more than a century. It is not so much that Keynes provided the answers but rather that he groped towards a methodological procedure which in the last analysis represented a truly revolutionary break from established tradition.

The Hicksian Income–Expenditure Approach

The foregoing interpretations of the *General Theory* have viewed that work as a major and radical departure from prevailing classical orthodoxy and suggested that Keynes made a revolutionary breakthrough in theoretical economics. In contrast, the more modest and widely accepted view, which perhaps can be termed the conventional wisdom, springs from the interpretation of Hicks (1937) and suggests not so much a revolution in economic thinking but rather a far-ranging reformation of classical ideas. In this view, Keynes accepted much of classical thought with his major innovation being the emphasis upon a monetary theory of interest. Moreover, this interpretation of Keynes leads essentially to the judgement that Keynes failed to overthrow the theoretical framework of classical economics in that his demonstration of unemployment equilibria is shown to depend upon very restrictive assumptions such as wage rigidity. Keynesian unemployment theory is thus shown to be a special case of the classical system and one fully allowed for by the classical writers. In short, on a *theoretical level* the 'Keynes versus the classics' controversy is shown to be essentially bogus or else relatively trivial and concerned with minor issues such as the comparative influence of money and saving upon interest rates.

None the less, it is this interpretation that 'Keynesian disciples' have seized upon to proclaim their version of the Keynesian message. For they argue that the Keynesian special case is the only relevant one for modern-day economies. Money wage rigidities preclude dependence upon automatic adjustment mechanisms. Moreover, the beauty of the Keynesian formulation lies in the fact that it clearly indicates the manner in which the authorities can rectify the deficiency of the market system. The Hicksian income-expenditure model suggests that stable relationships exist between aggregate flows of income, expenditure and output and thus provide the basis for the claim that by controlling income flows the government can control the level of aggregate demand, output and employment. The Hicksian interpretation of the *General Theory* heralds the changed status of fiscal and budgetary control and the belief that the authorities can so 'fine tune' the economy that unemployment is eliminated as a major scourge of modern society. Thus, in these terms, Keynes's achievement lies not on the purely theoretical level but rather in the realm of economic policy. Keynes is credited with underpinning the rationale for interventionist policies at the aggregative level, whilst leaving individual decision-making largely unconstrained; he is responsible for the changed status of fiscal policy and indeed for exercising a humanizing influence upon the cold logic of the dismal science.

It is this interpretation which has dominated macroeconomic thinking in the post-war period and the policy discussions and controversies surrounding the relative potency of monetary versus fiscal action. Whether it is the economics of Keynes or not, it is none the less the content of modern macroeconomics, and it is this interpretation which will be explored in detail in this book. For present purposes, however, merely the essential characteristics of the so-called *IS/LM* model will be indicated. The model contains two fundamental and *independent* equations: one relating the level of real income and rate of interest consistent with equilibrium between the supply and demand for goods and services (the goods market equation), and the second relating the level of real income and rate of interest consistent with equilibrium between the supply and demand for money (the money market equation). These two simultaneous equations can then be combined to provide a solution for the level of real income, and hence output and employment and also the rate of interest. The original Keynesian assertion was that the employment level so obtained need not comply with the full employment level, and moreover that in such an event there need be no automatic adjustment towards full employment income. The resulting debate followed two distinct paths – a theoretically oriented argument which led to a general consensus denying the latter proposition or granting that it was tenable only if money wages revealed rigid downward inflexibility, and a policy-oriented argument focused upon the relative potency of monetary versus fiscal policy. Keynesian-oriented economists directed their attention primarily towards the policy implications, with a marked tendency to downgrade the efficacy of monetary changes upon the grounds that both investment and consumption expenditures were in practice relatively insensitive to interest rate changes. A feature of Keynesian policy-oriented economics, therefore, has been a tendency to place emphasis upon fiscal or budgetary means of controlling the level of aggregate demand with scant attention given to the financing implications of any resulting budgetary deficits.

In recent years, the Hicksian income-expenditure model has been subject to a two-sided assault. On the one hand, the monetarist/neo-classical revival has been accompanied by the assertion that the goods and money markets are not formally independent as represented in the elementary model but are intimately linked, so that any change in the money stock exerts fairly predictable impacts upon spending flows in commodity markets. This criticism has been reinforced by recent analysis of the government budget constraint and the monetary implications of fiscal deficits. This has called into question the efficacy of fiscal policy by suggesting that fiscal measures could be being offset or 'crowded out' by accompanying monetary or wealth changes.

On the other hand, the Hicksian *IS/LM* model has been portrayed as a complete distortion of the economics of Keynes, most particularly by Leijonhufvud who draws a distinction between Keynesian economics – meaning the *IS/LM* model interpretation of the *General Theory*, with its emphasis upon comparative static equilibria – and

Keynes's economics – by which Leijonhufvud means the disequilibrium economics derived from a neo-Walrasian view of the *General Theory* and the *Treatise on Money* combined.

Concluding Comments

This chapter has grappled with the thorny question of the real nature of Keynes's attempt to deny the classical thesis. That this issue should persist and still arouse major controversy sixty years later is in itself remarkable. As has been seen, the major interpretations can be reduced to the following:

1   That Keynes was emphasizing the unstable, erratic and unpredictable state of long-term expectations in contrast to classical assumptions of relative certainty and predictability.

2   That Keynes was presenting a highly aggregative general equilibrium approach to macroeconomic problems in place of the partial equilibrium analysis which dominated classical thinking.

3   That Keynes was attempting to integrate real and monetary forces in the determination of output and employment in contrast to the prevailing classical dichotomy between real and monetary sectors.

Whatever the truth, there is no doubt that, as far as the conventional wisdom is concerned, victory belonged to the third interpretation; Keynesian economics has largely been identified with the Hicksian framework, which has dominated macroeconomic theorizing. The subsequent analysis, therefore, will concentrate upon this framework and the later modifications to it.

Further Reading

Needless to say, in order to try and understand the true meaning of Keynes there can be no substitute for the original sources – although this does not constitute any guarantee of success! Certainly, both Keynes (1936) and Keynes (1937a) must be regarded as essential reading, and it is interesting to relate both to the content of at least volume one of Keynes (1930). Since Keynes directed his attack upon classical employment economics primarily at Pigou's (1933) interpretation, it is instructive to read the latter and obtain a 'feel' for the structure which Keynes sought to deny in addition to his critique of Pigou in (Keynes, 1937b). The magnificent edition of Keynes's collected writings, produced for the Royal Economic Society, permit one to glimpse the intellectual excitement created by the Keynesian revolution, and the correspondence between Keynes and both his disciples and critics makes for fascinating reading. In this respect volumes XIII and XIV edited by Moggridge (1973) are certainly worth perusing.

Such has been the overwhelming influence of Hicks's (1937) seminal paper reprinted in both Mueller (1966) and Lindauer (1968) that it is wise to include it amongst one's primary sources of reading. At the same time, however, it is instructive to relate it to

Hicks's changing view of Keynes and his increasing sense of dissatisfaction with the *IS/LM* framework. In this connection one should look to Hicks (1973, 1974, 1980).

In addition to Leijonhufvud's influential work referred to in the text, a much simpler introduction to the essence of his interpretation can be culled from Leijonhufvud (1969) or alternatively Hines (1971). Additional commentary is to be found in Brothwell (1975), Jackman (1974) and Shaw (1976), whilst Cross (1982a) provides an introduction to the policy implications. In addition to the other references mentioned in the text, Harcourt (1977) and Loasby (1976) are particularly useful. A highly readable and magnanimous retrospective view of Keynes is provided by Pigou (1952), and an interesting question is posed by Grossman (1972). Recent reinterpretations of the *General Theory* include Fender (1981), Chick (1983), Coddington (1983), Kohn (1986), Hutton (1986), Sardoni (1987), Amadeo (1989), Patinkin (1987, 1991), whilst a stimulating if one-sided reassessment is provided by Burton (1986).

The dual decision hypothesis is first given in Clower (1965), and reprinted in Shaw (1988c) together with other articles deemed compatible with the spirit of Keynes. Hillier (1991) provides an interpretation broadly sympathetic to the Clower–Leijonhufvud thesis. A very detailed, and comparatively technical analysis of the *IS/LM* model is provided in Carlin and Soskice (1990). The same authors also present a detailed analysis of Walras's Law as applied to the macroeconomy and Clower's dual decision hypothesis, as well as Leijonhufvud's defence of Keynes against the classical attack. Much of the material in the present chapter is surveyed in Shaw (1988b).

10

The Hicksian *IS/LM* Analysis

Regardless of the interpretation to be accorded to the economics of Keynes, there can be no doubt that within a very short space of time of the appearance of *The General Theory* there evolved a body of thought labelled Keynesian which was to be contrasted with the classical economics. This doctrine was essentially the economics of the simultaneous equation model derived by Hicks in his famous 'Mr Keynes and the Classics' (1937), and it is this model which has dominated the development of macroeconomic thinking to the present day.

Essential Features of the *IS/LM* Framework

The essence of this Keynesian framework can be summarized very simply. Full equilibrium requires equilibrium in the commodity market and equilibrium in the money market. Only then will the economy experience a stable volume of real output and employment.

Commodity market equilibrium is summarized in the *IS* equation or the *IS* curve, which expresses a relationship between real output and real interest rates such that the aggregate demand for goods and services is just equated with their supply in the *ex ante* sense. That is to say, it summarizes all possible combinations of income and interest rate consistent with the *ex ante* equality of supply and demand in the goods market.

With regard to money market equilibrium, stability requires that the total demand for money in the economy be equated with the money stock. The demand for money, as was seen in chapter 5, will depend upon the level of income and the rate of interest. The money stock, on the other hand, is assumed to be determined by the monetary authorities working through the banking system. The *LM* equation or *LM* curve summarizes such equilibrium positions. More specifically, it summarizes the relationship between real output and real interest rates such that the aggregate demand for money is just equated with the money stock.

Equilibrium in the goods market implies that there is no excess demand or excess supply of goods. Equilibrium in the money market implies that there is no excess demand or excess supply of money. If these conditions are met, it follows also that equilibrium obtains in the bond market. That is to say, there will be nobody attempting to trade bonds to acquire either goods or money. If, conceptually, we think in terms of a three-sector economy – goods, bonds and money – equilibrium in any two markets necessarily implies equilibrium in the third.

Derivation of the *IS* Curve

In the simplest Keynesian model, national income is given by consumption plus investment demand, and both the government sector and international trade are dispensed with.[1] The national income equation is then

$$Y = C + I \tag{10.1a}$$

Assume that consumption is a linear function of the level of income and that investment demand is a linear (negative) function of the rate of interest. Thus,

$$C = a + bY \tag{10.2}$$

where a is consumption at zero income and b is the marginal propensity to consume, and

$$I = d - fi \tag{10.3}$$

where d is the autonomous component in investment demand and f indicates the interest rate sensitivity of investment spending.

Combining equations 10.1a, 10.2 and 10.3,

$$Y = a + bY + d - fi \tag{10.4}$$

which yields

$$Y = \frac{a + d - fi}{1 - b} \tag{10.5}$$

Equation 10.5 is essentially a representation of the *IS* or goods market equation. It specifies, firstly, that the income level cannot be determined without reference to the rate of interest. Second, it highlights that for any given consumption function and any given investment demand curve there will be a rate of interest consistent with any predetermined income level. Alternatively, it may be said that the *IS* equation summarizes all possible combinations of interest rate and level of income which satisfy equality between savings and investment in the *ex ante* sense.

These relationships are perhaps made clearer if they are derived geometrically. In the composite figure 10.1, part (a) depicts the investment demand schedule as a negative linear function of the rate of interest. Again, it should be emphasized that this demand schedule, as any demand schedule, is an *ex ante* concept displaying a set of intentions indicating what the level of investment spending would be at any given interest rate. Since, in the context of the present model, savings and investment are equated *ex post*, part (b) of the figure invokes a 45° construct to depict this *ex post* equality. In part (c) the Keynesian consumption function shows the level of income necessary to generate any required degree of savings *ex ante*. Thus, for example, assume the interest rate i_1. Given the investment demand schedule, this implies the *ex ante* investment demand OX. If this investment demand is ultimately realized, it implies an equivalent amount of *ex post* saving, OS, as shown in part (b) of the composite figure. The generation of this amount of saving *ex ante* would require an income level OY. One combination of inter-

---

1 This is indeed the model used by Keynes and by Hicks in his famous article. Conceptually, it is perhaps worth while to note that the absence of a government sector or international trade raises no real problems. Government expenditures can be decomposed into consumption and investment outlays respectively, and for purposes of analysis the absence of international trade can be assumed away by tacitly adopting the vantage point of the world economy.

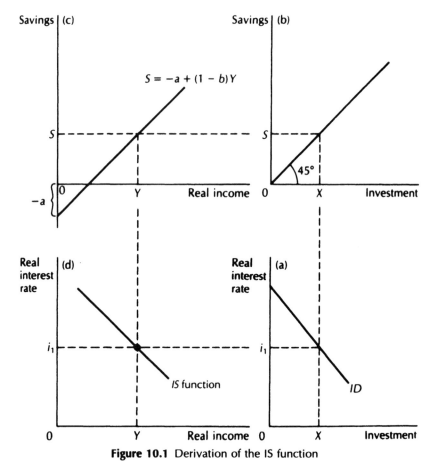

Figure 10.1 Derivation of the IS function

est rate and income level OY is thus obtained consistent with the *ex ante* equation of savings and investment, and this combination plotted in part (d) of the figure provides one point on the *IS* curve. Proceeding in this manner by selecting alternative initial interest rates, the *IS* curve is generated and depicts all feasible combinations of income and interest rate providing equilibrium in the goods market.

Derivation of the IS Curve with a Government Sector

It is now a simple matter to extend the analysis to take specific account of a government sector financed by a proportional income tax. Such a modification is useful because it allows consideration of fiscal policy specifically within the model analysis. The national income equation will now be represented by

$$Y = C + I + G \tag{10.1b}$$

Consumption will now be a linear function of disposable income so that

$$C = a + bY(1 - t) \tag{10.6}$$

where t is the proportional rate of income tax. As before, investment is given by equation 10.3 and it is assumed that government spending upon goods and services is autonomously determined, so that

$$G = \bar{G} \tag{10.7}$$

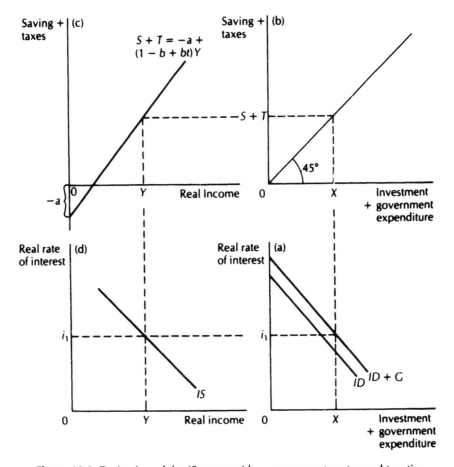

Figure 10.2 Derivation of the IS curve with a government sector and taxation

Solving for Y provides a new *IS* equation, namely,

$$Y = \frac{a + d - fi + \bar{G}}{1 - b + bt} \tag{10.8a}$$

Equation 10.8a conveys essentially the same information as equation 10.5, namely that the income level cannot be determined without reference to the rate of interest and that, for any given income level, there will be an interest rate consistent with the *ex ante* level of aggregate demand being equal to the supply of output.

As before, the *IS* relationship can be represented graphically. Essentially, the procedure adopted in the construction of figure 10.1 is repeated but part (a) of the composite figure is modified to allow for the element of government expenditure and part (c) to allow for the influence of the proportional income tax. Thus in figure 10.2 part (a) shows the level of investment demand, *ID*, pertaining to any given interest rate together with the autonomously determined volume of government expenditure. Hence the *ID + G* curve is obtained. Thus, for any given rate of interest, there will be a determinate volume of investment demand plus government expenditure, *OX*. Part (b) of the figure now invokes the 45° line to translate this into an equivalent amount of saving plus taxes, since *ex post* the two must be equal within the confines of the present model. With a determinate consumption function and known rate of taxation, part (c) then determines the income level needed to generate this amount of savings plus taxes *ex ante*.[2] As before, therefore, a given point on the *IS* curve is obtained corresponding to the initial interest rate , and proceeding in this manner, taking alternative initial rates of interest, the required *IS* curve incorporating a government sector is generated.

Derivation of the *LM* Curve

As long as investment demand (or indeed, consumption demand in more sophisticated models) is functionally related to the rate of interest, it is not possible to determine the equilibrium level of income without appealing to the money market. The *IS/LM* analysis possesses the great virtue of taking the money market into account and giving it equal weight in the joint determination of national income and the rate of interest. This emphasis is very much in keeping with Keynes's own views upon the importance of money, and marks a departure from the classical dichotomy between the real and the monetary sectors.[3]

For purposes of exposition, in the present chapter it will be assumed that the monetary authorities can effectively control the money supply, and hence this will be treated as an exogenously determined variable.[4] This permits a focus solely upon the demand for money, and in keeping with the analysis of chapter 5, the demand for money will be taken to be determined by the level of income and the rate of interest. More specifically, the demand for money is considered to be positively related to the income level and negatively related to the rate of interest, as depicted by the following linear equations:

$$L = \theta + vY - qi \tag{10.9}$$

where L is the total demand for money, and θ is the demand for money regardless of the income level or rate of interest and reflects a precautionary demand. Assuming the money stock, M, is exogenously determined, money market equilibrium requires $L = M$ or, alternatively,

$$M = \theta + vY - qi \tag{10.10}$$

which gives

$$i = \frac{vY - M + \theta}{q} \tag{10.11}$$

as the solution for the rate of interest. Equation 10.11 may be regarded as the *LM* equation, which argues that the level of income enters as a determinant of the rate of inter-

---

2 The $S + T$ schedule falls, of course, to the left of the original savings schedule. This is because the tax reduces saving by the amount $T(1 - b)$ where T is the tax yield, whilst adding to the savings plus taxes curve by the amount T. The net increase is thus $T - T(1 - b) = Tb = bY_t$. The intercept of the two curves is of course the same and equal to $-a$.

3 This is in stark contrast to the elementary 45° line portrayal of Keynesian economics which, by treating investment demand as either autonomous or functionally related to the income level via the accelerator, effectively dismisses the role of the money market entirely. Paradoxically, it was the 45° line model which captured the spirit of Keynesianism in later controversies and which highlighted the claims of fiscal policy intervention and minimized the importance of monetary variables.

4 As was seen in chapter 6, this issue of effective control over the money supply is one which often divides monetarists from Keynesians even when there is broad general agreement concerning the importance of money. Monetarists tend to favour exogenous relationships (subject to policy control) whilst Keynesians lean more to endogenous relationships.

est. In addition, the *LM* equation specifies that for any given demand for money function and exogenously determined money stock, there will be a combination of interest rate and income level consistent with equality between the supply and demand for money.

In order to derive the *LM* function graphically, it is necessary to break down the demand for money into its two component parts, the income component and the interest rate component. Thus,

$$L = L_t + L_a \tag{10.12}$$

$$L_t = \theta_1 + vY \tag{10.13}$$

$$L_a = \theta_2 - qi \tag{10.14}$$

where L_t is the transactions demand for money, L_a the asset demand for money and θ_1 and θ_2 sum to θ. Figure 10.3 part (a) depicts the asset demand for money as a negative function of the rate of interest. In part (b) of the figure, the exogenously determined money stock may be divided between transactions needs, M_1, and asset needs, M_2.

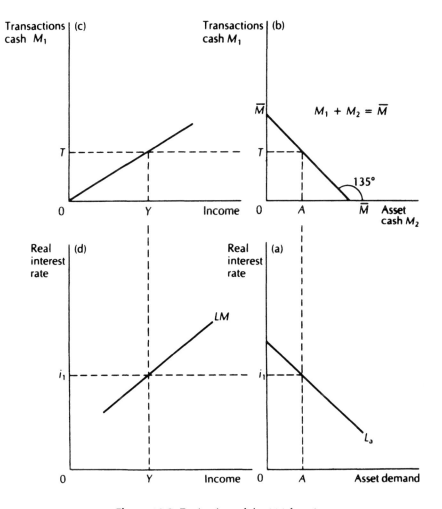

Figure 10.3 Derivation of the LM function

Thus, with the interest rate i_1, the asset demand will be $0A$. Given the exogenously determined money stock, $\bar{M}$, this implies that the amount remaining to fulfil transactions purposes will be $0T$, since the distance $\bar{M}T$ on the vertical axis is equal to the distance $0A$ upon the horizontal axis. This follows from the fact that the money stock can be used to meet either asset demands or transactions needs, the relationship between the two being given by the invariant 135° line.

With a given amount of money $0T$ allocated to transactions purposes, and with a given transactions velocity of circulation, indicated by the slope of the ray in part (c) of the composite figure, the determinate income level $0Y$ will be obtained. Thus, given the asset demand for money, the exogenously determined money stock and the velocity of circulation, the income level $0Y$ which in conjunction with the interest rate i_1 equates the total supply and demand for money. Proceeding in this way, by selecting alternative initial rates of interest, the LM curve is derived in part (d), and shows all feasible combinations of income level and interest rate consistent with equilibrium in the money market.

Equilibrium

The IS function summarizes all combinations of interest rate and income level consistent with equilibrium in the goods market; the LM function provides identical information consistent with equilibrium in the money market. By combining the two, a unique combination of interest rate and income level can be achieved which reconciles equilibrium in both markets simultaneously. This is the situation portrayed in figure 10.4, where Y^* and i^* denote the equilibrium values of income and interest respectively.

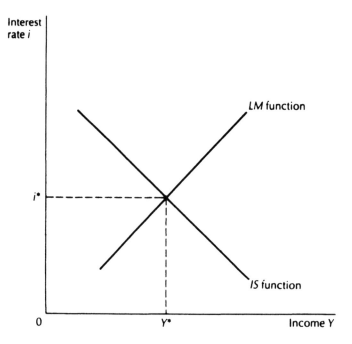

Figure 10.4 Determination of equilibrium income level and rate of interest

Mathematically, what is implied by the equilibrium condition is simply the solution of two simultaneous equations. Taking the elementary non-government *IS* equation 10.5 in conjunction with the *LM* equation 10.11,

$$Y = \frac{a + d - f\left(\frac{vY - M + \theta}{q}\right)}{1 - b} \tag{10.15}$$

and

$$i = \frac{v\left(\frac{a + d - fi}{1 - b}\right) + \theta - M}{q} \tag{10.16}$$

from which the equilibrium values of Y and i can be derived:

$$Y = \frac{a + d + f\left(\frac{M - \theta}{q}\right)}{1 - b + \frac{fv}{q}} \tag{10.17}$$

and

$$i = \frac{\theta + v\left(\frac{a + d}{1 - b}\right) - M}{q + \frac{vf}{1 - b}} \tag{10.18}$$

Alternatively, taking the government sector *IS* equation 10.8a in conjunction with the *LM* equation 10.11,

$$Y = \frac{a + d + \bar{G} - f\left(\frac{vY - M - \theta}{q}\right)}{1 - b + bt} \tag{10.19}$$

and

$$i = \frac{\theta - M + v\left(\frac{a + d - fi + \bar{G}}{1 - b + bt}\right)}{q} \tag{10.20}$$

from which the equilibrium levels of income and rates of interest can be derived:

$$Y = \frac{a + d + \bar{G} + f\left(\frac{M - \theta}{q}\right)}{1 - b + bt + \frac{fv}{q}} \tag{10.21}$$

and

$$i = \frac{\theta - M + \left(\frac{va + vd + v\bar{G}}{1 - b + bt}\right)}{q + \frac{vf}{1 - b + bt}} \tag{10.22}$$

The foregoing analysis is essentially the Hicksian interpretation of the *General Theory* which sees the equilibrium level of income being determined by both classical and 'Keynesian' influences. The equilibrium so determined may be considered a stable one in that with supply and demand being equated in both commodity and money markets simultaneously and in the *ex ante* sense, there is no tendency for any change. Moreover, there is no guarantee that the equilibrium so obtained will correspond to full employment. In the Hicksian interpretation, this is what Keynes was attempting to demonstrate, against the logic of the classical model. Subsequent analysis was to question the permanency of the Hicksian unemployment equilibria in the absence of extremely

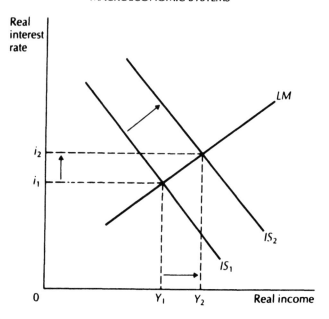

Figure 10.5 Effect of an increase in autonomous expenditure in the Hicksian IS/LM model

restrictive and unrealistic assumptions; none the less, this was the framework which was eagerly accepted by fiscally oriented 'Keynesians' and endorsed by Keynes himself.

Characteristics of the *IS/LM* Analysis

In order to bring out some of the implications of the analysis, it is useful to examine the characteristics of the model in more detail. In particular, it is crucial to an understanding of the subsequent 'Keynes versus the classics' controversy to know how the position and slopes of the respective *IS* and *LM* curves are determined.

The IS Curve

First consider the *IS* curve. Any increase in autonomous expenditure, whether investment, consumption or government expenditure, will have the effect of shifting the *IS* curve outwards to the right. *Ceteris paribus* therefore, and assuming the *LM* curve is positively sloped, the net effect would be to secure a raising of national income and the rate of interest – the latter arising from the increased transactions demand for cash consequent upon the higher level of national income. This situation is depicted with the aid of figure 10.5.

Returning to the quadrant diagram of figure 10.2, an autonomous increase in either investment expenditure or government expenditure would generate an outward shift of the combined *ID* + *G* curve in part (a) of the figure, whereas an autonomous increase in consumption spending is revealed as a downward shift of the combined *S* + *T* curve in quadrant (c).[5] Both serve to occasion an outward shift of the *IS* curve in part (d) of

---

5 As the consumption function $C = a + bY(1 - t)$ now becomes $C = a + \Delta a + bY(1 - t)$.

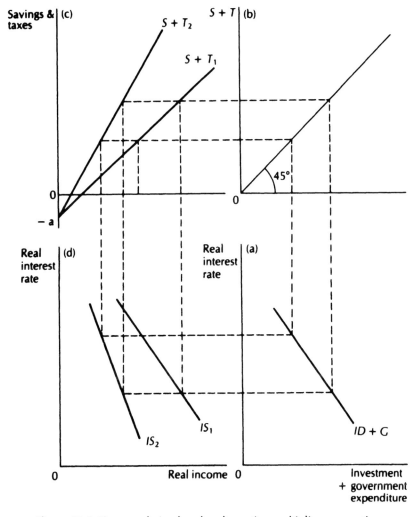

Figure 10.6 IS curve derived under alternative multiplier assumptions

the figure. It is perhaps of greater interest to enquire as to the extent of the outward shift of the *IS* curve arising from the autonomous expenditure increase. To pursue this point, from figure 10.6 will be derived two distinct *IS* curves corresponding to differing assumptions made with respect to the savings plus taxes curve of part (c) of the composite figure. In part (a) there is a given $ID + G$ curve from which the required *IS* curve can be derived by selecting appropriate initial interest rates. However, if the savings plus taxes curve $S + T_1$ is assumed, the *IS* curve IS_1 is obtained, whereas if the savings plus taxes curve $S + T_2$ is invoked, the *IS* curve IS_2 is obtained. Note that the *IS* curves differ not only with respect to position but also with respect to slope, the IS_1 being possessed of a flatter slope than IS_2. Note also that the autonomous spending components are identical in the two cases; investment, government expenditure and the autonomous consumption element *a* are the same in both derivations. The only difference, responsible for generating a new *IS* curve distinct in *both position and slope*, is the difference in *slope* of the $S + T$ curves. The slope of the $S + T$ curve is of course determined solely by the marginal propensity to consume upon the one hand and the rate of income taxation upon the other – precisely the variables entering into the multiplier equation for a change in autonomous expenditures. To see this, refer back to the *IS* equation 10.8a for a government sector and write *A* for the sum of autonomous components *a*, *d* and $\bar{G}$. Then

$$Y = \frac{A - fi}{1 - b + bt} \tag{10.8b}$$

and

$$\frac{dY}{dA} = \frac{1}{1 - b + bt} \tag{10.8c}$$

represents the autonomous expenditures multiplier.

The following is a summary of the argument thus far. For any given level of autonomous expenditure, the *IS* curve will fall farther to the right the flatter the slope of the combined savings plus taxes curve. Moreover, for any given increase in autonomous expenditure the outward shift of the *IS* curve will be greater the flatter the combined slope of the savings plus taxes curve. In turn, the savings plus taxes curve will be flatter the greater the marginal propensity to consume *b* and the lower the rate of income taxation, *t*. As inspection of equation 10.8c demonstrates, the greater the marginal propensity to consume and the lower the rate of income taxation, the greater will be the autonomous expenditures multiplier. The conclusions are, first, that for any given level of autonomous spending the position of the *IS* curve will lie further to the right the greater the value of the multiplier; and second, for any given increase in autonomous spending the induced outward shift of the *IS* curve will be greater the greater the value of the multiplier. Indeed, it may be demonstrated that the outward shift of the *IS* curve is equal to the increase in autonomous expenditure multiplied by the value of the multiplier.[6]

With regard to the slope of the *IS* schedule, it has been demonstrated in figure 10.6 that this slope will normally be flatter the greater the value of the multiplier. In addition, however, there is a second influence governing the slope of the *IS* function, namely the initial slope of the investment and government expenditures function in part (a) of the composite figure. The greater the interest rate sensitivity of investment demand, the flatter will be the slope of the combined investment and government expenditures schedule and the flatter the resultant *IS* curve. The less interest elastic is investment the steeper will be the resultant *IS* curve. In the extreme case, that of a perfectly inelastic investment demand function, the *ID* + *G* schedule will be vertical and so too will the resulting *IS* function. In this case, the value of the multiplier has no influence upon the shape of the *IS* curve.

From the above analysis, it should be clear that the effect of an increase in the rate of taxation is to shift the *IS* curve inwards,[7] with the extent of the inward shift being governed by the income tax multiplier, given by,

---

6 It will be noted that as long as the *LM* curve is positively sloped the outward shift of the *IS* curve will always be greater than the increase in national income. This is because the autonomous expenditures multiplier referred to here does not take into account the repercussion of higher income levels on the rate of interest – and hence upon the volume of private sector investment spending.

7 The qualification referred to in footnote 6 of this chapter is equally applicable here. The inward shift of the *IS* curve derived from the *IS* equation will be greater than the decline in income because now as income falls, so too will the transactions demand for cash and the rate of interest – giving some positive stimulus to private investment spending.

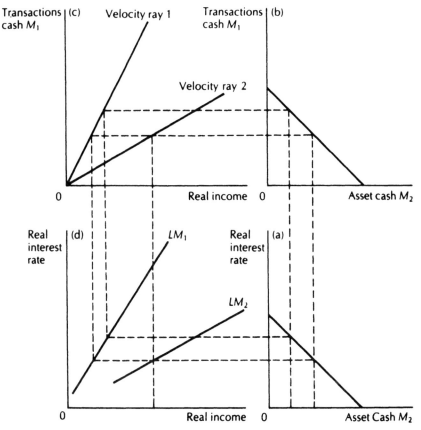

Figure 10.7 Importance of velocity to the position of the LM function

$$\frac{\mathrm{d}Y}{\mathrm{d}t} = \frac{-b(A - fi)}{(1 - b + bt)^2} < 0 \qquad (10.8\text{d})$$

It follows also, *ceteris paribus*, that the *IS* function will be more steeply sloped the greater the rate of taxation.

The LM Curve

The determinants of the position and slope of the *LM* curve are now considered. First of all, it is clear that with a given money stock and a given asset demand for cash, the initial position of the *LM* curve will be determined by the income velocity of money. This is demonstrated in figure 10.7, where two distinct *LM* curves are derived by invoking differing assumptions with regard to the velocity relationship. The greater the velocity of circulation of money, revealed by the lesser slope of the ray in part (c) of the figure, the more the *LM* curve will lie to the right. Increasing the velocity of circulation rotates the velocity relation in a clockwise direction, and as it rotates so too will the *LM* relation. Second, an increase in the money stock, *ceteris paribus*, will imply an outward shift of the *LM* curve. In the context of figure 10.3 the extent of the outward shift of the *LM* curve due to any given increase in the money stock, depicted in the outward movement of the 135° line of quadrant (b), will be determined by the velocity of circulation. Other things being equal, the outward shift of the *LM* curve will be greater the higher the degree of income velocity and *vice versa*. Essentially, therefore, an increase

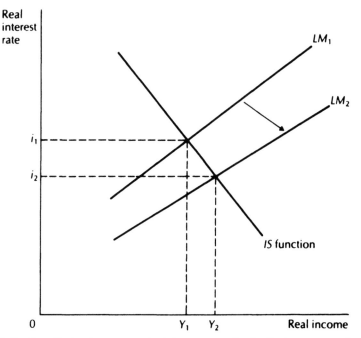

Figure 10.8 Similar effects of a money stock increase and velocity increase on income and the rate of interest

in the money stock and an increase in the velocity of circulation of the money stock have virtually identical effects in moving the *LM* relation outwards,[8] and normally, assuming a negatively sloped *IS* curve, will have the effect of raising income and lowering the equilibrium rate of interest. This situation is portrayed in figure 10.8.

Other influences may effect a shift of the *LM* function. A change in the expectations of the holders of speculative asset cash, for example, will change the position of the asset demand for money curve in quadrant (a) of figure 10.3. Thus, if asset cash holders become more convinced that lower interest rates are here to stay they will have less fear of investing in government bonds and therefore will reduce their demands for idle money. The net effect is to release more cash to meet transactions needs, with the result that the *LM* curve is again shifted outwards. Such a change in expectations as described here is essentially equivalent to an increase in the total money stock with regard to the position of the *LM* schedule. By very similar reasoning, account may be taken of the impact of a change in the general level of prices upon the position of the *LM* function. If prices fall, *ceteris paribus*, there will be a reduced demand for transactions balances permitting the given volume of transactions cash to support a higher level of transactions. Once again, the net effect is similar to an increase in the total money supply. Equally, a general increase in the price level is tantamount to a reduction in the money supply in terms of the position of the *LM* curve.

The all-important question of the slope of the *LM* function is now considered. In chapter 5 it was seen that the issue of the interest sensitivity of the asset demand for cash was of fundamental importance to the overall Keynesian demand for

---

8 Strictly speaking, a velocity increase and a money stock increase are not formally identical in terms of the *LM* construct, since the former pivots the *LM* function in a clockwise direction whilst the latter generates a positive outward shift of the curve. To all intents and purposes, however, the two are very similar in the expansionary effects they imply for income and employment.

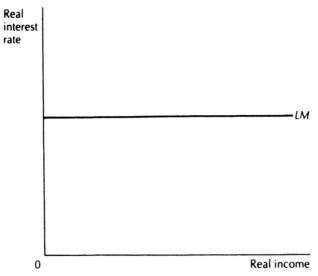

Figure 10.9 Horizontal LM curve stemming from the perfectly interest elastic asset demand for cash

money function and was one of the questions tending to divide Keynesians and monetarists. The relevance of this issue to the slope of the *LM* function is now examined. Clearly, the more interest elastic the asset demand for cash, the flatter will the *LM* function tend to be. Also, in chapter 5, was explored the rationale for the assertion that at suitably low interest rates the demand for cash would become perfectly elastic and that there would be no demand to invest in government bonds. This situation, that of a perfectly elastic demand for money, which has hitherto been described as the liquidity trap, generates a perfectly horizontal *LM* schedule as depicted in figure 10.9.

So far, in the elementary algebraic representation of the *IS/LM* analysis, simple linear relationships have been used to summarize the *IS* and *LM* equations. Clearly, however, there is no need for the relationships to be linear. Indeed, the arguments advanced in chapter 5 would suggest that the interest sensitivity of the asset demand for cash would increase progressively with the fall in interest rates until the region of the liquidity trap was reached. Invoking such a non-linear asset demand for cash in the quadrant diagrams would understandably generate an equally non-linear *LM*

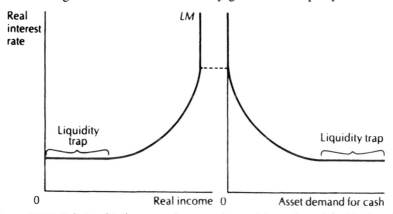

Figure 10.10 Relationship between the asset demand for cash and the LM function

schedule. Figure 10.10 shows the typical Keynesian asset demand for cash as described in chapter 5 together with the corresponding *LM* function. In the region of the liquidity trap when the asset demand for money becomes perfectly interest elastic, the *LM* function is horizontal. Conversely, at sufficiently high rates of interest the asset demand for cash is reduced to zero and the *LM* function is correspondingly vertical. In between these two regions the *LM* function is positively sloped with the degree of curvature increasing as interest rates rise and presenting a mirror image of the asset demand for money function.

The Meaning of Equilibrium

The meaning of the Hicksian *IS/LM* equilibrium can now be examined more closely. As has been seen, any position upon the *IS* curve implies that savings and investment are equated *ex ante* so that the demand for goods and services is precisely matched by the forthcoming supply. There is thus no tendency towards unintended investment or disinvestment in stocks and inventories; realized sales are equated with planned sales and expectations are fulfilled. The goods market displays no justification for any change. Similar reasoning applies to the money market. A position on the *LM* curve implies that the *ex ante* demand for cash is exactly matched by the available supply. There is no unintended accumulation of money or running down of money balances below that which is considered optimal. In short, the authorities are supplying just the amount of money – no more and no less – that the private sector wishes to hold. In such a situation there can be no reason for any change to occur *unless there are forces set in motion to alter the underlying IS/LM functions themselves.* The initial Keynesian postulate was to suggest that full equilibrium could prevail in a situation of less than full employment without any tendency for such equilibrium to be disturbed. In contrast, the classical rebuttal to this Keynesian model argued that if less than full employment equilibria prevailed then there would be forces set in motion which would feed back upon the basic *IS/LM* functions and disturb the initial equilibrium. The conditions under which such forces would or would not prevail became the crux of the theoretical

Figure 10.11 Complete disequilibrium in the Hicksian IS/LM model

dispute between Keynes and the classics, as will be examined in some detail in the next chapter. For present purposes, it is perhaps useful to fix the concept of equilibrium in mind by examining the situation where it does not prevail, in *either* the commodity market or the money market. Consider the situation depicted in figure 10.11 where initially, at X, equilibrium does not prevail in either market. At the existing income and interest level denoted by point X the rate of interest and/or income is too low to equate either the supply and demand for money or savings and investment. A possible dynamic adjustment to this is as follows. This rate of interest will imply *ex ante* investment spending in excess of *ex ante* savings, implying expansionary income movements. At the same time, such a rate of interest will mean that the demand for money is in excess of the available stock. The upward pressure upon interest rates, therefore, is in two parts – one stemming from the excess demand for cash, the other from positive income expansion raising the transactions demands for cash. Income expansion also implies an increase in the planned level of savings. Once again, full equilibrium is indicated by the intersection of the *IS* and *LM* curves, where supply and demand are again equated simultaneously in all markets. Whatever the initial situation, the existence of a negatively sloped *IS* curve in conjunction with a positively sloped *LM* curve implies negative feedback and strongly suggests that the indicated equilibrium will be attained.

It is for this reason that the Hicksian interpretation of Keynes focuses attention firmly upon conditions of equilibrium. It is the prime example of the comparative static methodology. Any autonomous disturbance, such as an increase in the money supply, can be superimposed on a given equilibrium and the resultant new equilibrium immediately identified. Time is eliminated from the adjustment process. Moreover, the adjustment process is always one of convergence to the new equilibrium. It is for these reasons that critics of the *IS/LM* apparatus, in particular Leijonhufvud, maintain that the *IS/LM* model involves a fundamental distortion of Keynes's position; on their reading. Keynes was primarily concerned with disequilibrium uncertainties arising from the time paths of adjustment and the possibility of false trading generating increasingly divergent movements from the indicated solution.

The Policy Framework

One reason for the undoubted success of the Hicksian *IS/LM* analysis was that it literally bristled with policy implications at a time when policy prescription was at a premium. Moreover, although the formal framework became identified with the 'Keynesian school' of economics there was nothing explicit in the underlying theory to suggest a predilection for fiscal as opposed to monetary policy. The 'Keynesian' orientation toward fiscal as opposed to monetary policy, therefore, does not derive from the basic model *per se* but rather from specific Keynesian assumptions that were to be incorporated into the model. Whether Keynes himself would have approved of these later 'Keynesian' mutations is perhaps open to dispute. Certainly the basic model gives equal weighting to monetary and to fiscal intervention in being able to enhance income and employment, as illustrated in figure 10.12. Part (a) of the figure illustrates fiscal intervention either in the form of increased government expenditures or reduced taxation (or indeed some combination of both), whereas part (b) illustrates the effect of an enlarged money stock. Indeed, a priori, one might expect a monetary change to exert a greater impact upon the economy than a fiscal oriented change, to the extent that in the former case the interest rate falls whilst in the latter it rises. With a given money

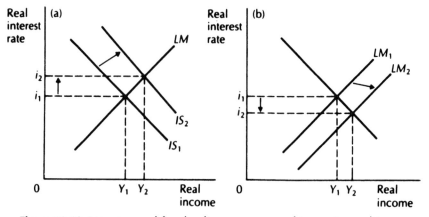

Figure 10.12 Monetary and fiscal policy as a means of increasing real income by (a) increased expenditure change, decreased tax change or a combination of both or by (b) increased money stock change

stock any attempt at expansionary fiscal policy whether by increasing government expenditure or reducing taxes must imply some increase in the rate of interest, which in turn will choke off a certain amount of investment spending in the private sector. This offset to expansionary fiscal policy provides an example of automatic stabilization; here the fixed money stock is acting as an automatic stabilizer which 'crowds out' a certain portion of the fiscal impact. The extent to which fiscal policy is *crowded out* will depend upon two influences; first, the impact of the fiscal change upon the rate of interest, and second the interest sensitivity of private sector investment demand to the interest rate change. Zero crowding out will occur if the fiscal change exerts no interest rate impact (the case of a horizontal *LM* curve) or if the investment demand function is perfectly inelastic with respect to interest rate changes (the case of a vertical *IS* curve). These cases are illustrated by figures 10.13 and 10.14. Complete crowding out occurs if the rise in the interest rate is sufficient to curtail private sector investment by

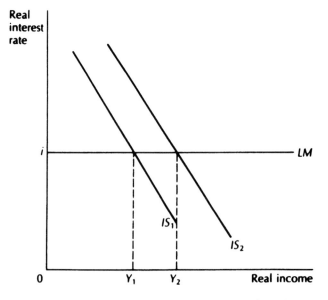

Figure 10.13 Zero crowding out with horizontal LM function

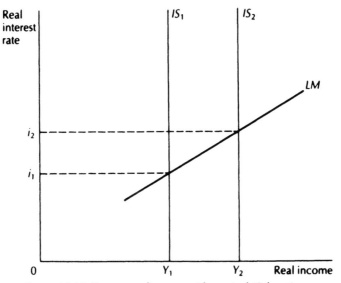

Figure 10.14 Zero crowding out with vertical IS function

the amount of the fiscal stimulus. This is the case of the vertical *LM* curve illustrated in figure 10.15. The 'normal' situation, presumably, would be that of partial crowding out where both *IS* and *LM* functions are normally sloped. This situation is described in figure 10.16. Here fiscal intervention raises the income level from Y_1 to Y_2. In the absence of crowding out, which arises in consequence of the interest rate rise and the negative slope of the *IS* curve, income would have risen to Y_3. The extent of crowding out is accordingly given by $Y_3 - Y_2$.

Concluding Comments

In this chapter the derivation of the *IS* and *LM* functions has been considered in detail, and the determinants of their positions and slopes have been examined. The meaning of equilibrium has been emphasized, and the obvious policy implications of

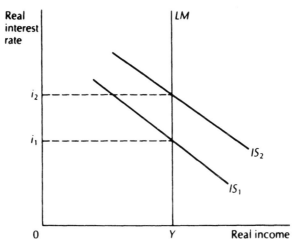

Figure 10.15 Complete crowding out with vertical LM function

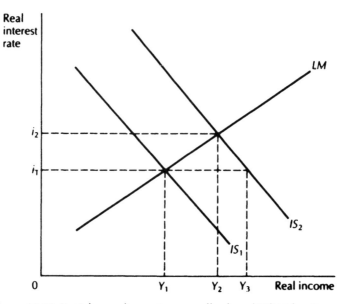

Figure 10.16 Partial crowding out – normally sloped IS/LM functions

the analysis have been indicated. As a pedagogical device, the *IS/LM* construct has no equal in the sphere of economics, unless it be the concept of supply and demand itself. The reader will, however, appreciate that it is a highly mechanistic construct, and the results deriving from it and the policy controversies to which it gives rise depend ultimately upon the underlying assumptions incorporated into the model analysis. Their relevance to reality will be crucial in determining the appropriateness and utility of the framework.

Further Reading

As mentioned in chapter 9, any introduction to *IS/LM* analysis must logically begin with Hicks's seminal paper (1937). An important elaboration of the Hicksian framework was made by Modigliani (1944). That Keynes appeared to be essentially in sympathy with Hicks's interpretation is fully brought out in Hicks (1973). Also, the fact that Hicks's attempt to *interpret* Keynes did not necessarily constitute his own view of the working of the macroeconomy is made clear in Hicks (1980) and in Brunner and Meltzer (1973). The latter make the point that the conventional treatment of *IS/LM* obscures the role of relative prices change which was an important part of the classical system, which Hicks was attempting to incorporate into a classical–Keynesian synthesis. Also of interest from a retrospective viewpoint are chapters 8 and 9 of Hicks (1967). The former of these, 'The classics again', appeared initially as a critical review of Patinkin (1955) in the *Economic Journal*. It brought forth a spirited reply (Patinkin, 1959) in which Patinkin argues the case for interdependence between a change in the money stock and the position of the *IS* function. There are, of course, numerous textbook expositions of the derivation of *IS* and *LM* curves and their attendant policy implications. Useful expositions include Dornbusch and Fischer (1994), Parkin and Bade (1982), Carlin and Soskice (1990), Hillier (1991) and Mankiw (1991).

11

Comparative Statics of Classical, Keynesian
and Monetarist Models

The Hicksian *IS/LM* framework was readily accepted as being the appropriate model for macroeconomic analysis by both Keynesians and classicists. Its ready adoption was partly to be explained by Keynes's own endorsement, but in addition it provided a firm and logical foundation to which the participants in macroeconomic controversies could refer. In brief, something concrete was provided in place of the rather implicit structure which had gone before. Moreover, the *IS/LM* analysis was appealing in its own right. It was consistent with orthodox maximizing behaviour and it took full account of the importance of monetary influences upon the rate of interest. Rooted in elementary simultaneous equations, it was easily and readily grasped and lent itself to mechanical manipulations with engaging simplicity whilst at the same time suggesting a pseudoscientific basis to economic enquiry. Whatever the reasons, the framework itself was never a major source of contention; rather it was the assumptions underlying the framework and the use to which it could be put which divided economists into their Keynesian, classical and monetarist camps.

The Policy Dispute

As was demonstrated in chapter 10, there is theoretical justification for believing that the *LM* curve will exhibit variations in slope going from horizontal to vertical. For purposes of exposition, three regions of the *LM* curve are distinguished in the stylized figure 11.1. (For expositional convenience we have drawn these as linear segments. It may be that the functions are curvilinear.)

If the *IS* curve intersects the *LM* curve in region 1, then monetary policy exerts no influence upon the level of income, only fiscal policy being able to raise income and employment. If the intersection occurs in region 2, then both monetary and fiscal policy are able to generate increased income and employment levels. Finally, if the intersection occurs in region 3 then monetary policy alone is effective in generating expansionary forces. Fiscal policy is revealed to be completely ineffective as the accompanying rise in interest rates chokes off an equivalent amount of spending from the private sector. These relationships, admittedly mechanical and *simpliste*, are illustrated in figure 11.2.

The Keynesian Scepticism

The viewpoint that became readily identified with Keynesian economics (though not necessarily with Keynes himself), namely that in conditions of severe unemployment monetary policy was likely to be largely ineffective, can now be analysed. Two distinct lines of thought leading to this position can be identified. On the one hand, there was the view buttressed by considerable empirical evidence (Wilson and Andrews, 1951; White, 1956) to the effect that the rate of interest was of but minor influence upon the volume of investment spending. In the extreme case of a completely interest inelastic investment schedule, the *IS* curve would be vertical and increases in the money stock would exert no impact whatsoever upon the level of income and employment. This extreme situation is depicted in figure 11.3. On the other hand, there was the Keynesian assertion which suggested that the supply and demand for money were interdependent. That is to say that an increase in the money stock would lower the rate of interest and the resulting fall in the interest rate would extend the speculative demand for money. The increase in the holdings of speculative idle balances, with a zero velocity, implies a decline in the average velocity of money generally. In terms of the simple quantity theory equation, $MV = Y_m$, the increase in M is being countered by the induced fall in V. In the limiting case, the entire increase in the money stock is being absorbed into idle balances so that the fall in the average velocity of money exactly offsets the increased monetary stock with no change in the level of money national income. This is the situation implicit in figure 11.2(a) but it is perhaps useful to spell out

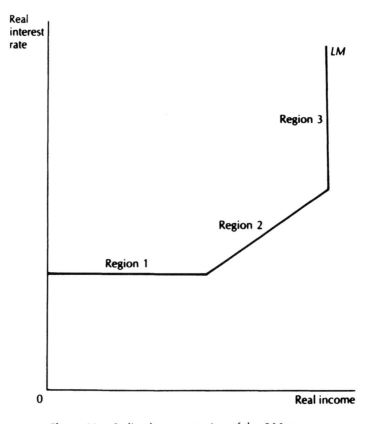

Figure 11.1 Stylized representation of the *LM* curve

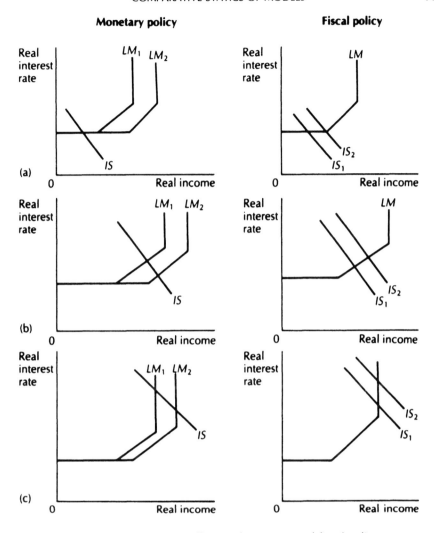

Figure 11.2 Comparative efficacy of monetary and fiscal policy

the argument in greater detail with reference to figure 11.4. In part (a) of the figure is shown the situation consistent with the general tenor of Keynes's argument whereby the rate of interest i_1 is the consequence of the demand for money L_{y1} and the initial money stock M_1. Now assume an increase in the money stock to M_2. The immediate consequence is a reduction in the rate of interest to i_2, which extends the total demand for money from $0L_1$ to $0L_2$. This extension in money demand implies a decline in velocity which offsets in part the monetary increase. However, this is not the end of the story, for the fall in interest rates under normal Keynesian conditions will stimulate investment spending. The increase in investment spending implies an increase in the level of income (equal to the increased expenditure multiplied by the multiplier) which in turn serves to raise the transactions demand for cash. The increase transactions demand raises the total demand for money to L_{y2} and the interest rate to i_3. Although monetary expansion has been countered in part by the induced velocity change, there is none the less a positive expansion of income. This is the normal Keynesian sequence

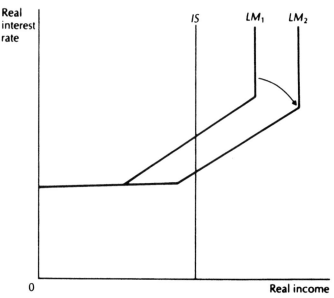

Figure 11.3 Interest inelastic investment demand and the ineffectiveness of monetary policy

which Keynes made explicit in the *General Theory* and which may be summarized notionally as

$$\Delta M \Rightarrow -\Delta i \Rightarrow \Delta I \Rightarrow \Delta Y \Rightarrow \Delta Ik$$

where k is the multiplier.[1]

In contrast to this normal sequence of events, however, there is the special case, eagerly seized upon by Keynesians, whereby the increased demand for cash negates the entire impact of monetary expansion and prevents any fall in the rate of interest. This situation, usually referred to as the liquidity trap, is depicted in figure 11.4(b), where the increased money stock M_2 leaves the interest rate unchanged; this is the case where the decline in velocity exactly offsets or crowds out the impact of monetary expansion. There is no doubt that Keynes considered this a distinct possibility although he gave it no more than passing mention in one paragraph of the *General Theory* (Keynes, 1936, p. 172). None the less, in 'Keynesian' hands not only was it the ultimate sanction of fiscal policy but equally it became the kingpin in the attempt to deny the classical theory of self-adjustment to full employment equilibrium. This topic is now discussed.

---

1 Although Keynes is explicit about this sequence it is perhaps of interest to note that he was guilty of the age-old confusion between a shift of the curve and a movement along it. Thus he assumes that the total demand for money schedule (liquidity preference) is negatively related to the rate of interest because of both the transactions motive and the asset motive. Thus,

As a rule, we can suppose that the schedule of liquidity-preference relating the quantity of money to the rate of interest is given by a smooth curve which shows the rate of interest falling as the quantity of money is increased. For there are several different causes all leading towards this result.

In the first place, as the rate of interest falls, it is likely, *ceteris paribus*, that more money will be absorbed by liquidity-preferences due to the transactions motive. For if the fall in the rate of interest increases the national income, the amount of money which it is convenient to keep for transactions will be increased more or less proportionately. ... In the second place, every fall in the rate of interest may, as we have just seen, increase the quantity of cash which certain individuals will wish to hold because their views as to the future of the rate of interest differ from the market views. (Keynes, 1936, pp. 171–2)

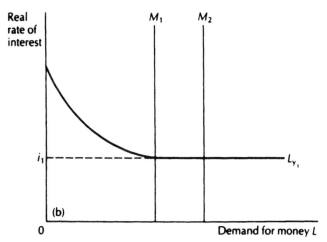

Figure 11.4 Monetary expansion under (a) 'normal Keynesian' and (b) liquidity trap conditions

The Theoretical Controversy

As has been seen, the classical economists assumed that unemployment would be self-eliminating given conditions of competition in the labour market which would ultimately lead to a decline in money wage rates. If Keynes was to deny the classical self-adjustment process to full employment equilibrium upon a theoretical level he obviously had to examine the consequence of declining money wages in some detail regardless of the practicality of pursuing such a policy. And indeed, Keynes paid considerable attention to this question.[2]

---

2 Apart from the somewhat meandering excursion into the history of economic thought in chapter 23, where Keynes deals with mercantilism, the usury laws, stamped money and theories of underconsumption, chapter 19 on changes in money-wages, with an appendix on Pigou's theory of unemployment, is the longest chapter of the *General Theory.*

In general, it would be fair to conclude that Keynes was generally agnostic with respect to the outcome of wage cuts upon employment. He conceded that there were circumstances in which the net effect would be beneficial. Thus, for example, he allowed that in the context of an open economy wage cuts leading to lower prices would be beneficial to employment in the export sector which would exert multiplier impacts elsewhere in the economy. The entire issue is bedevilled by expectations as to possible further cuts but in the main Keynes concluded that the principal beneficial impact would be upon the rate of interest. For if wage reductions generate falling prices there will be a reduction in the transactions demand for cash conducive to a fall in the rate of interest. The fall in the rate of interest would stimulate investment and thus raise income and employment. This effect, *the Keynes effect* of a decrease in money wages, is identical to an increase in the quantity of money, as Keynes fully recognized:

> We can, therefore, theoretically at least, produce precisely the same effects on the rate of interest by reducing wages, whilst leaving the quantity of money unchanged, that we can produce by increasing the quantity of money whilst leaving the level of wages unchanged. (Keynes, 1936, p. 268)

Two conclusions automatically follow. If money wage cuts and increasing the money stock are alternative policies then there is no question as to which is the preferred option. The government can readily influence the volume of money through open market operations. In contrast, attempts to cut money wages will be long drawn out, will be socially divisive and will involve distributional changes generally to the disadvantage of the weaker classes of society.[3] It is not so much that Keynes denied the efficacy of money wage cuts under certain conditions; rather, his opposition rests upon there being a much simpler, easier and fairer alternative.

The second conclusion, however, is the one that Keynesians depended upon to deny the automatic self-adjustment of the classical system. If money wage cuts are formally identical to increases in the money stock then it follows that in those circumstances where the money stock is impotent to influence income and employment, then policies of money wage cuts are equally impotent. Clearly, this is the situation of the liquidity trap already depicted in figure 11.2(a). Keynes is explicit upon this point:

> It follows that wage reductions, as a means of securing full employment, are also subject to the same limitations as the method of increasing the quantity of money.... Just as a moderate increase in the quantity of money may exert an inadequate influence over the long-term rate of interest, whilst an immoderate increase may offset its other advantages by its disturbing effect on confidence; so a moderate reduction in money-wages may prove inadequate, whilst an immoderate reduction might shatter confidence even if it were practicable.
>
> There is, therefore, no ground for the belief that a flexible wage policy is capable of maintaining a state of continuous full employment.... The economic system cannot be made self-adjusting along these lines. (Keynes, 1936, pp. 266–7)

---

3 Wage cuts also face the drawback of increasing the real burden of the national debt and hence taxation and through it the state of business confidence (see Keynes, 1936, p. 264).

The Vindication of Classical Employment Theory

Keynes had argued that the beneficial effect of a cut in money wages would be akin to an increase in the money stock and thus in the context of the *IS/LM* framework would be represented by an outward shift of the *LM* curve. Moreover, in the case of the liquidity trap, such a policy would be completely ineffectual in raising income and employment. Such was the denial of the automatic adjustment mechanism of classical employment theory. Clearly, in such a situation the classical theory could only be salvaged if it could be shown that there existed automatic tendencies to effect an outward shift of the *IS* function. It was this task which A. C. Pigou was to set himself when he came to compose his study *Employment and Equilibrium* (1941) to be published some five years following the *General Theory*. In a very real sense, therefore, the evolution of a consistent, coherent and logical classical theory of employment was a post-Keynesian phenomenon and one for which the credit must very largely belong to Keynes.

Pigou's thesis, stated simply, was that a cut in money wages would raise the level of aggregate demand quite independently of any interest rate effect. Assuming that prices fall proportionately to the fall in money wages, aggregate monetary demand will be reduced in line with the price level leaving real aggregate demand unaffected. But in addition, the decline in the price level will raise the real value of all money cash balances and other forms of private sector wealth which have a fixed monetary value – such as redeemable national debt. This increase in private sector wealth will stimulate consumption spending by reducing the need to save out of any given income level. The celebrated *Pigou effect* thus reveals itself in an outward shift of the *IS* curve. Providing both wages and prices exhibit unlimited downward flexibility the outward shift of the *IS* curve will be made continuous, generating an expansion of income

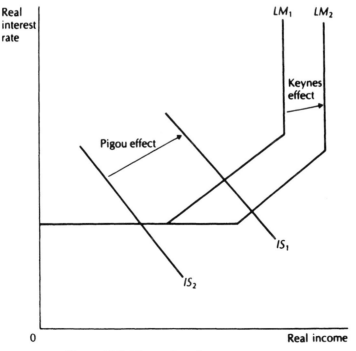

Figure 11.5 Effects of cutting money wages

and employment. Ultimately, even if the initial intersection of *LM* and *IS* occurs in the region of the liquidity trap, the outward shift of the *IS* curve will be such as to allow the Keynes effect to come into operation. This is the situation summarized in figure 11.5.

It should be strongly emphasized that Pigou was concerned only with a theoretical nicety to demonstate the impossibility of permanent unemployment equilibria given the assumption of unlimited wage and price flexibility. He was concerned to vindicate the classical belief that the economy would tend towards full employment equilibrium on purely theoretical grounds. He was not advocating that reliance be placed upon the automatic adjustment mechanism or that policies advocating wage cuts should be adopted on practical grounds. Indeed, Pigou endorsed many of the policy implications of the Keynesian model.

Reliance upon the Pigou effect as a practical policy measure must be ruled out on a number of grounds. All the evidence would indicate that the empirical significance of the Pigou effect is limited, thus requiring an inordinate degree of wage and price flexibility (Mayer, 1959). In turn, the required degree of flexibility would demand an extremely lengthy period in order to be effected. Meanwhile it would be socially divisive and involve income distribution changes determined solely by the respective bargaining strengths of the various classes involved and being difficult to reconcile with accepted notions of fairness and equity. Thus the conventional wisdom became one in which Keynes had lost the theoretical fight but had won the policy war and in particular had provided a theoretical framework to which positive fiscal and monetary policy could be related.

The mystery which remains is, why did Keynes ignore the Pigou effect? He was clearly aware of the importance of wealth in influencing spending patterns and included unforeseen changes in the money value of wealth as a major factor in causing short-run changes in the propensity to consume (Keynes, 1936, pp. 92–3). It is arguable that Keynes discounted the Pigou effect on the grounds of its minor empirical significance, but this would be inconsistent with his avowed *theoretical* aim. After all, he had paid great attention to the effect of wage cuts even though the practicality of such cuts was of necessity limited. Nor does it seem realistic to propose that Keynes was dealing with a model which admitted only inside money, for he was always, even as a theoretician, concerned with the relevance of economics to practical policy-making and the affairs of the real world. It is inconceivable that he would have formulated a model which did not treat of outside money.[4] The simplest answer to the riddle is that the Pigou effect was something that Keynes overlooked when developing the implications of his theory. Nor would such an oversight be exceptional; Pigou himself was to make no mention of it in his controversial attack dealing with wage cuts in the *Economic Journal* (Pigou, 1937).[5]

---

4 The distinction between inside and outside money is a simple one. Inside money refers to monetary creation by the private banking sector in the process of creating bank deposits. Outside money is the fiat money issued by the government authorities through the central bank. The Pigou effect does not arise in the case of a pure inside money economy because although price falls will increase the net worth of creditors this effect will be offset by the increased real indebtedness of debtors. The Pigou effect arises in the case of outside money because the issue of such money by the government ensures that the private sector is on balance a net creditor.

5 Keynes considered this 'the work of a sick man, which no one would print who was in his right mind'. Joan Robinson concurred, adding 'he is so far gone that you have to rationalise him to find a coherent error'. According to Kahn, 'Gerald Shove says that without exception this is the worst article he has ever read', a ver-

An alternative and extremely ingenious explanation has been put forward by Leijon-hufvud. In his view Keynes ignored the Pigou effect because it was irrelevant to the central issue of unemployment. In this interpretation unemployment is the consequence of relative prices being out of line and in particular the demand price of capital assets being too low relative to the price of labour. If this is the case then all-round deflation as implied by the Pigou effect becomes an irrelevancy since it leaves relative prices unchanged. In sharp contrast, the Keynes effect is relevant because it leads to a decrease in the rate of interest and hence to an increase in the demand price of capital assets relative to the wage cost of labour. Thus Keynes was being perfectly logical in pursuing the claims of wage cuts via the interest rate effect whilst simultaneously ignoring the Pigou effect. The *IS/LM* analysis only serves to cloud the argument since, encompassing solely a one-product economy, it is unable to deal with relative prices upon which employment ultimately depends. The Leijonhufvud interpretation, it should be noted, represents an attempt to re-establish Keynes's reputation as the major theoretical innovator as opposed to the conventional wisdom which sees his achievement to lie primarily in the policy field.

Extending the Hicksian Framework

Consumption and the Rate of Interest

Thus far, consumption demand has been assumed to be a linear function of the level of income. In addition, however, it has been argued that consumption will depend upon prevailing rates of interest. Indeed, this was part and parcel of classical interest rate theory, which assumed that a greater volume of saving would be forthcoming at higher rates of interest. As has been seen, the classical postulate of a positive association between the rate of interest and the flow of savings is open to dispute. Both income and substitution effects are involved. A rise in the rate of interest makes saving more attractive at the margin (the substitution effect) but equally it implies a real income gain which permits the greater consumption of goods (the income effect). A priori, therefore, it is not possible to provide a determinate conclusion to the issue of how an interest rate change will affect the choice between consumption and saving out of a given income *flow*.

There is, however, another reason to suggest that a decline in interest rates may stimulate consumption spending, and this refers to the relationship between the rate of interest and the net value of the *stock* of existing assets including government bonds and securities. Keynes did not attach much importance to the influence of the interest rate upon consumption out of a given income flow, but he clearly thought the influence of the interest rate upon capital values an important factor. Thus,

> There are not many people who will alter their way of living because the rate of interest has fallen from 5 to 4 per cent, if their aggregate income is the same as before.

but

> The consumption of the wealth-owning classes may be extremely susceptible to unforeseen changes in the money-value of its wealth. This should be classified

dict with which Piero Sraffa was to concur (see Moggridge, 1973, vol. XIV, p. 234f). Yet within a matter of a few years Pigou was to provide the theoretical foundation that classical employment theory had hitherto lacked.

amongst the major factors capable of causing short-period changes in the propensity to consume.

and

Perhaps the most important influence, operating through changes in the rate of interest, on the readiness to spend out of a given income, depends on the effect of these changes on the appreciation or depreciation in the price of securities and other assets. (Keynes, 1936, pp. 92–4)

There would thus appear some justification for making consumption not just a positive function of the level of income but also a negative function of the rate of interest. Such a modification is easily accommodated in the *IS/LM* framework and reveals itself in a decrease in slope of the *IS* curve.

Investment and the Level of Income

Hitherto, investment demand has been regarded solely as a function of the rate of interest. However, as suggested by the well-known accelerator concept of investment behaviour, examined in chapter 3, investment may also be related to the level of final sales demand and hence to the level of income. The inclusion of income as an argument in the investment decision carries far-reaching implications for the *IS/LM* framework which threatens the entire stability of the model's analysis.

The analysis of chapter 10 depicted investment spending as a simple function of the rate of interest. From equation 10.3,

$$I = d - fi$$

If this investment schedule is modified to allow for the influence of income changes,

$$I = d - fi + jY \tag{11.1}$$

where j is the marginal propensity to invest. This equation may be combined with the elementary framework developed in chapter 10, equations 10.1a and 10.2, to yield

$$Y = a + bY + d - fi + jY \tag{11.2}$$

This gives

$$Y = \frac{a + d - fi}{1 - b - j} \tag{11.3a}$$

as the solution for the *IS* equation. It will be noted that the *IS* equation can be rewritten as

$$Y = \frac{a + d}{1 - b - j} + \frac{-f}{1 - b - j} i \tag{11.3b}$$

where $(a + d)/(1 - b - j)$ is the intercept and $-f/(1 - b - j)$ the slope of the *IS* curve. It follows that it is possible for the *IS* curve to possess a positive slope if, and only if, the term in the denominator is negative. But such an outcome is perfectly plausible; the condition for a positively sloped *IS* curve is simply the condition that the marginal propensity to invest exceeds the marginal propensity to save.

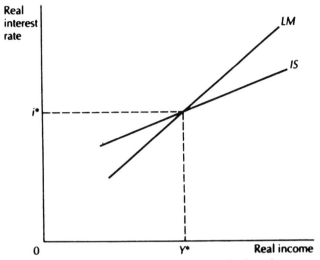

Figure 11.6 Stable equilibrium with a positively sloped IS curve

The possibility of an upward sloping *IS* curve, which characteristically was antici-pated by Hicks in his seminal article (Hicks, 1937), raises many intriguing issues and carries important implications for policy. First of all, a stable solution for the level of income now requires that the slope of the *IS* curve be less steep than the slope of the *LM* curve. This situation of stable equilibrium is illustrated by figure 11.6. Second, an increase in the quantity of money now implies an *increase* in the rate of interest. This is pertinent to much of the controversy between Keynesians and monetarists. The former tend to look upon movements in the rate of interest as being indicative of monetary stringency or monetary ease, whilst the latter tend to disregard interest rate movements *per se*, preferring to focus their attention upon the volume of money. The existence of an upward sloping *IS* curve would tend to substantiate the monetarists' position and suggest that the rate of interest is a poor indicator of expansionary or contractionary policies. Finally, if the *IS* curve is upward sloping, then the impact of an increase in the money stock upon the level of income will be greater the more *interest elastic* the demand for money. This runs counter to the Keynesian claim that monetary policy is likely to be ineffectual the more interest elastic the demand for money, since it implies greater scope for offsetting velocity changes. This counter-argument based upon the positive sloped *IS* curve is given in figure 11.7.

The Flex Price Model

The foregoing analysis has been implicitly stated in real terms with prices assumed constant. In terms of the depressed conditions of the 1930s from which the model evolved this seems a perfectly reasonable postulate. With both surplus supplies of labour and capital in abundance, there was no reason why an increase in aggregate demand should not be translated into an increase in output with prices holding con-stant. In essence, the Keynesian model is demand determined with supply conditions assumed perfectly elastic until full employment is approached. In terms of the aggre-gate demand and supply analysis advanced in chapter 7, the Keynesian model can be caricatured as in figure 11.8. Aggregate supply is assumed to be perfectly elastic until

Figure 11.7 Monetary expansion with (a) interest elastic money demand $\Delta Y = Y_3 - Y_1$ (solid LM lines) and (b) interest inelastic money demand $\Delta Y = Y_2 - Y_1$ (dashed LM lines)

Figure 11.8 Aggregate supply and demand and Keynesian price determination

capacity income, Y^*, is attained; until this point any increase in aggregate expenditure translates into output increases; beyond this point, any increase in aggregate demand implies increased prices.

It is a simple matter to link this aggregate demand and supply model with the Hicksian *IS/LM* model in a world of constant prices. This is done with the aid of figure 11.9. The upper part of the figure shows the *IS/LM* determination of income and interest at Y_1 where capacity income is assumed to be Y^*. The lower portion depicts the aggregate supply and demand equation giving price-income combination $P_1 Y_1$. If government policy now effects a shift of the *IS* curve to achieve the full employment income level (indicated by the IS_2 line) this will be matched by the outward shift of the aggregate demand curve in the lower part of the figure. Capacity income Y^* prevails in both cases, and there is no change in the price level although an increase in the real rate of interest occurs in consequence of the higher demand for transactions balances.

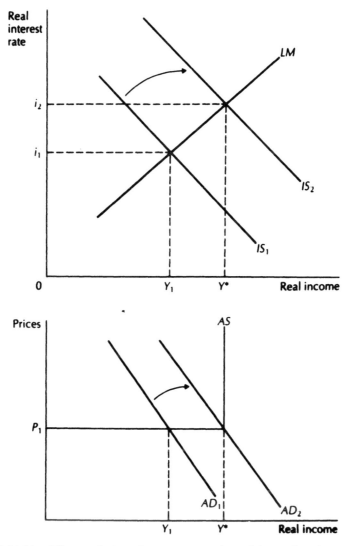

Figure 11.9 Linking IS/LM analysis and aggregate supply and demand analysis with constant prices

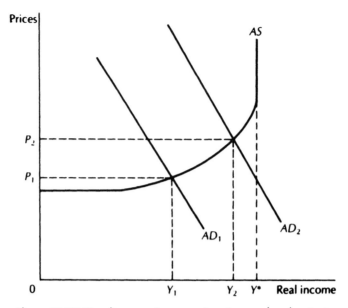

Figure 11.10 Simultaneous increases in prices and real output

However, once the assumption of a perfectly elastic aggregate supply curve at less than full capacity income is dropped, the analysis becomes considerably more complex.[6] Increases in aggregate demand will then have the effect of generating simultaneous increases in both prices and output as indicated in figure 11.10. Once it is attempted to incorporate a variable price level into the basic *IS/LM* framework, a conceptual difficulty is encountered. The *IS* curve, being a *real* expenditure demand, is drawn as a function of the *real* rate of interest and is invariant with respect to price changes.[7] The *LM* curve, however, as has previously been seen is not invariant with respect to price level changes. An increase in prices will shift the curve inwards as the real value of the stock of money is decreased and vice versa.

To consider the link between the Hicksian framework and aggregate supply and demand analysis, consider figure 11.11. In the upper portion of the figure the *IS* and *LM* schedules determine an initial interest–income combination given by $i_1 Y_1$. The *LM* schedule is drawn for a specific price level, P_1, and hence is indicated as LM_1. In

---

6 Keynes fully recognized that prices would in fact increase before full employment was reached. Thus,

The increase in effective demand will, generally speaking, spend itself partly in increasing the quantity of employment and partly in raising the level of prices. Thus instead of constant prices in conditions of unemployment, . . . we have in fact a condition of prices rising gradually as employment increases. (Keynes, 1936, p. 296)

and

As output increases, a series of 'bottle-necks' will be successively reached, where the supply of particular commodities ceases to be elastic and their prices have to rise to whatever level is necessary to divert demand into other directions. (Keynes, 1936, p. 300)

7 Strictly speaking, if we allow for wealth effects, this statement is untrue. When discussing the Pigou effect, for example, we expressly assumed that declining prices would generate an outward shift of the *IS* curve. However, for expositional clarity, we will avoid this complication here and justify our position upon the grounds that empirically the Pigou effect is likely to be extremely limited. This will allow us to concentrate attention upon the price induced shifts of the *LM* curve.

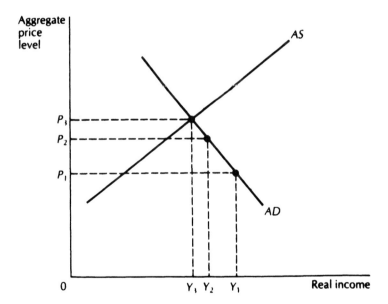

Figure 11.11 Linking IS/LM analysis and aggregate supply and demand analysis with variable prices

the lower portion of the figure is the aggregate supply and demand analysis. At the price level indicated by P_1, it is known that demand is equal to Y_1 (as determined above) and consequently the point $P_1 Y_1$ is one point on the aggregate demand schedule. Suppose, however, that this point does not fall upon the aggregate supply curve. With the aggregate supply curve as shown in the lower figure there is excess aggregate demand at the price P_1. *Ceteris paribus* the price level will rise, and as it increases it will generate an upward shift in the LM function in the upper figure. As the price level increases to P_2, the applicable LM curve becomes LM_2 and in conjunction with the invariant IS curve will imply the interest-income combination $i_2 Y_2$. Thus, at the price level P_2 aggregate demand is equivalent to Y_2, providing a second point upon the aggregate demand curve. Here again demand exceeds supply, generating further price increases, and this process will continue until generation of the equilibrium denoted by the combination $P_3 Y_3$ in the lower figure and the combination $i_3 Y_3$ given by IS/LM_3 in the upper figure.

Does such an equilibrium as indicated by the combined $P_3 Y_3$ and $i_3 Y_3$ situation imply full equilibrium for the macroeconomy? To return to the classical emphasis, the answer to this question depends upon whether full employment prevails within the labour market and whether, if full employment does not prevail, the force of competition will drive real wages down. If unemployment and flexible wages coexist, the decline in real wages will extend the volume of aggregate output; aggregate supply will now exceed demand and prices will fall, with feedback effects upon the Hicksian IS/LM framework. Ultimate equilibrium will require the simultaneous equation of IS/LM curves, aggregate supply and demand curves and labour supply and demand curves in the labour market. For the sake of completeness, these conditions are illustrated in the composite figure 11.12.

In part (c) equilibrium is assumed to prevail between aggregate supply and aggregate demand at the price level P_1 and income level Y_1. It is also assumed that this combination is consistent with equilibrium in both commodity and money markets as depicted in part (b) of the figure with the interest rate i_1. Part (a) of the figure merely invokes a 45° line to translate the income level Y_1 to the production function quadrant of part (d). From the production function can be derived the amount of labour N_1 needed to produce the output Y_1, and in turn this will imply a real wage equal to $(W/P)_1$ in part (e). However, at this real wage the amount of labour on offer is indicated as N_2. Unemployment prevails to the extent $N_1 - N_2$. In the classical world, competition will then cause money wages and real wages to fall; as wages fall, profit maximizing behaviour will extend the demand for labour and output will increase. The increase in output implies an outward shift of the aggregate supply function of quadrant (c), causing prices to fall, and as prices fall an outward shift of the LM function is generated in part (b) of the composite figure. Linking all these arguments together and following through with the underlying logic of the model will ultimately generate full equilibrium at the values denoted by Y^*, i^*, N^* and $(W/P)^*$. Assuming complete wage and price flexibility and ignoring the time horizon involved, there is a strong disposition in the present framework for a complete and full equilibrium to be attained. Nor is this conclusion inconsistent with the economics of Keynes. Indeed, what is being depicted in the composite figure 11.12 is nothing less than the normal workings of the Keynes effect. Declining money wages, leading to falling prices, lower interest rates, increased employment and lower real wages as marginal productivity falls, is the normal Keynesian sequence. Arguably, it would be easier and far more convenient to achieve the same outcome by increasing the money supply, but this is not to deny the theoretical

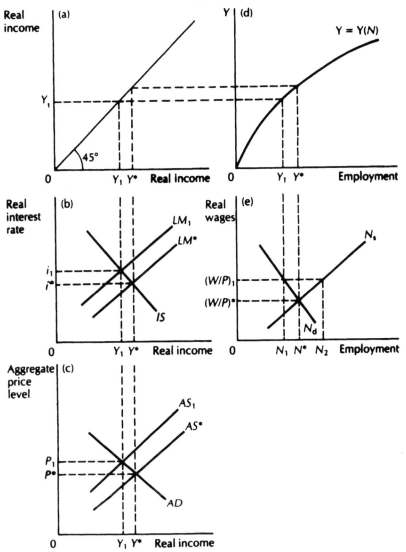

Figure 11.12 Linking IS/LM analysis, aggregate supply and demand analysis with the production function, employment and real wages

logic of the analysis. What could prevent the indicated adjustment would be the existence of an horizontal *LM* function preventing the fall in interest rates. This indeed, constitutes the Keynesian denial of classical employment theory. Then, as we have seen, other aids would have to be invoked to salvage the classical model, such as the inclusion of wealth effects in the consumption function. This is indeed the generalized conclusion of the so-called *neo-classical synthesis* which followed upon the Keynesian revolution giving particular emphasis to the equilibrating role performed by relative price changes.

The Monetarist Contention

As previously indicated, much of the early controversy between Keynes and the classics turned upon the question of the respective slopes of the *IS/LM* curves; Keynesians emphasized those situations where monetary policy was relatively ineffective, whilst classicists took the contrary view. The appropriateness of the *IS/LM* formulation was not itself a matter of contention, and in particular the assumed independence between the *IS* function and the *LM* function was not called into question.

It is precisely upon the latter question, that of independence between *IS* and *LM* equations, that the monetarists have taken issue with Keynesian interpretations. Both Keynesians and monetarists would concur in the belief that an increase in the money stock will exert expansionary influences upon the macroeconomy. Where they differ is over the *transmission mechanism* by which the monetary change exerts its influence. Keynesians emphasize that any change in expenditure flows, whether upon the side of consumption or investment, will stem from the accompanying change in the rate of interest. The direct impact of an increase in the money stock is seen to fall upon interest rates as the excess money is channelled into financial assets. The indirect impact then follows from the influence exerted by lower interest rates upon consumption and investment spending – an influence which may be weak and uncertain depending upon the circumstances of the particular case. The underlying assumption in this analysis is that the only meaningful substitute for money is alternative financial assets. In contrast, monetarists are disposed to argue that an increase in the money stock will impinge upon expenditure flows irrespective of any change in the rate of interest. The increase in the money stock disturbs the equilibrium between actual money balances and desired money balances and, in the attempt to eliminate the excess supply, increased expenditure is generated over a wide range of goods and services as well as financial assets. It may well be the case that some reduction in interest rates occurs, stimulating additional spending, but quite apart from any interest rate induced effect there will be increased demands for national output. If unemployed resources exist this increase in the money stock will generate additional output; if resources are fully employed the outcome will be inflation and a higher level of imports. The underlying assumption here is that there are far wider substitutes for money than merely financial assets.

Essentially, the monetarist argument suggests that *IS* and *LM* functions are interdependent; an increase in the money stock implies not only an outward shift of the *LM* curve but also an outward shift of the *IS* curve and not merely a movement along it as Keynesians are wont to believe. This issue of interdependent *IS/LM* functions has considerable relevance to the potency of monetary and fiscal policy and in particular to the controversy over the crowding out debate. Recognition of possible interdependence between *IS* and *LM* functions has increased, with the greater awareness now being given to the financial implications of budgetary policies and in particular of the need to take account of the government budget constraint.

As we have indicated, Keynesian economics tended to view the importance of money stock changes in terms of their impact upon interest rates, whereas monetarist doctrine contends that such changes are likely to be important regardless of any interest rate effect. This leads naturally into the question of whether it is better to pursue money supply targets – which effectively renders interest rates endogenous – or interest rate targets – leaving the money stock to be determined endogenously. Of course, it is to be understood that both money supply targets and interest rate targets are *intermediate* targets only, chosen for their relevance in securing the ultimate targets which we shall identify with the desired income level Y^*.

If one lived in a world of complete certainty, it would be immaterial which intermediate target one pursued. This can be demonstrated with the aid of figure 11.13. If the position of the IS schedule is known with certainty, then either a money supply target indicated by LM_m or the interest rate target indicted by LM_i would suffice to achieve the target income level Y^*. Suppose, however, that the *IS* curve is known only imperfectly to the monetary authorities and may fluctuate between IS_1, and IS_2. In such a situation, the money supply target is demonstrated to be superior to the interest rate target in that it serves to minimize the divergence from the desired income level Y^*. In the former case, the money supply target achieves income levels Y_1 or Y_2, whereas the interest rate target would imply income levels Y_3 or Y_4.

The reason for this result is obvious enough. With a money supply target, fluctuations in the position of the *IS* schedule imply fluctuations in interest rates. In turn, the interest rate changes act as an automatic stabilizer to constrain the movements in income. In contrast, if the government is committed to an interest rate target by buying or selling government bonds in the required quantities, no such automatic offset can occur. Hence, in the monetarist viewpoint the money supply target is preferable.

It can, however, be demonstrated that the opposite conclusion follows if uncertainty exists with respect to the *LM* schedule. If the authorities are uncertain with regard to the demand for money and therefore with respect to the position of the *LM* schedule, whereas the *IS* curve is known with reasonable confidence, then an interest rate target becomes the preferable policy. However, it is the monetarist contention that uncertainty applies primarily to the goods market, whereas the money market is characterized by reasonable stability and the demand for money is subject to but slow change over time. Accordingly, the money supply target is perceived as being the preferable alternative. This conclusion would appear to be broadly in line with the position of Keynes, who stressed the volatility of investment demands under uncertain and unstable expectations as well as the influence of 'animal spirits'.

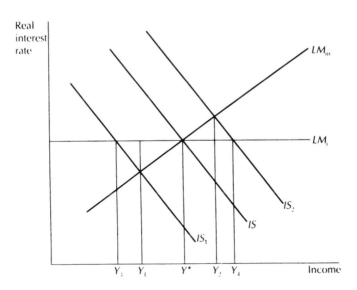

Figure 11.13 Money supply versus interest rate targets

Concluding Comments

This chapter has utilized the Hicksian *IS/LM* analysis to survey a considerable amount of ground. First, the conditions under which fiscal or monetary policy would exercise the greater potency were examined, and a possible source of dispute between Keynesians and the classics was indicated. Second, a framework was adopted to explore the possibility of stable unemployment equilibria given wage and price flexibility, and it was concluded that the combined workings of the Pigou effect and the Keynes effect would render this a logical impossibility in the long term. Several extensions of the *IS/LM* analysis were then explored, including the implications of a positively sloped *IS* function, and the link between the basic analysis, aggregate supply and demand and the labour market was examined. At each step the versatility of the analysis was extended without detracting from its relative simplicity and easy manipulation. The existence of possible interdependence between *IS* and *LM* functions was considered, leading into the subject matter of the next chapter. Finally, we examined the conditions under which money supply targets would be preferable to interest rate targets as an intermediate policy objective.

Further Reading

The classic article on the Pigou effect is by Patinkin and it appears in two distinct versions (Patinkin, 1948, 1951), the latter being reprinted in both Mueller (1966) and Lindauer (1968). A critical empirical study of the significance of the Pigou effect is provided by Mayer (1959). Additional useful comments are to be found in Stein (1949) and Tobin (1947), also reprinted in Mueller (1966). A detailed and controversial distinction between the Keynes effect and the Pigou effect is made by Leijonhufvud (1968, part VX).

The possibility of a positively sloped *IS* function with its implications for policy is analysed by Burrows (1974). The classic article upon the choice of money supply versus interest rate targets is by Poole (1970). Similar issues are raised by Brunner (1981) and Kaldor and Trevithick (1981).

12

The Government Sector, the Budget Constraint and the Crowding Out Controversy

Hitherto the manner in which government expenditure is to be financed has been played down. It is, however, necessary to examine this question in some detail. Much of the earlier Keynesian analysis had been negligent in dealing with this issue, and this neglect ultimately led to the monetarist charge of naïvety in the formulation of policy measures and in particular to the charge that Keynesian measures fail to take into account the inflationary implications of deficit finance.

Crucial to this entire question is the manner in which the private sector responds to the issue of government bonds. Indeed, the ability of Keynesian-oriented policies to stimulate the economy by the creation of budgetary deficits financed by the sale of bonds depends critically upon the private sector perceiving that bond finance differs in many important respects from the method of tax finance. If this is not the case, then Keynesian deficit spending will simply not work. Suppose, for example, that the private sector is ultra-rational and perceives that tax finance and bond finance are formally identical. That is to say, suppose the private sector perceives the future fiscal burden necessary to service and ultimately redeem the debt. Suppose also that, possessed of finite lives, the private sector wishes to bequeath inter-generational transfers which guarantee their descendants a real post-tax wealth status. Bailey (1962) has stated the crux of this argument in no uncertain terms:

> It is possible that households regard deficit financing as equivalent to taxation. The issue of a bond by the government to finance expenditures involves a liability for future interest payments and possible ultimate repayment of principal and thus implies future taxes. . . . If future tax liabilities implicit in deficit financing are accurately foreseen, the level at which total tax receipts are set is immaterial; the behaviour of the community will be exactly the same as if the budget were continuously balanced. (pp. 75–7)

As we shall see later in the present chapter, this is an issue which turns upon the perception of private sector wealth. In particular, it depends upon the extent to which the private sector identifies its holding of government bonds as part of its collective net worth. Initially, however, we will ignore this question and adopt a Keynesian perspective in tacitly assuming that tax finance and bond finance do differ in their aggregate

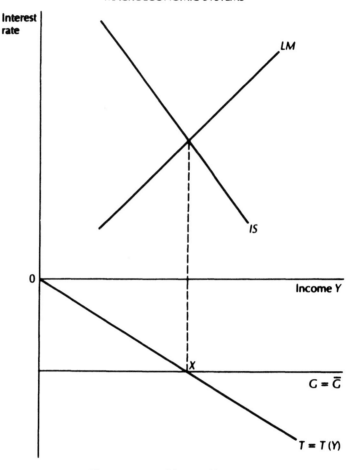

Figure 12.1 Stable equilibrium

impact. Finally, we will look at the policy implications of dispensing with this crucial assumption.

The Government Budget Constraint in the *IS/LM* Model

As has been seen in chapter 10, the *IS/LM* framework can be readily adapted to incorporate the government sector. In figure 12.1 the *IS/LM* construct is reproduced, but now the implications for the government budget constraint are considered. This is depicted in the lower portion of the composite figure, where it has been assumed that whilst government outlays are constant, tax revenues are endogenous upon income.[1] The significance of the intersection at point X is that here government outlays upon goods and services[2] are exactly offset by taxes, so that the government deficit is zero;

---

1 This is not to imply that all taxes are income taxes. Sales taxes, licence fees, and so on, will also normally display a positive relationship with income.

2 Perhaps it should be pointed out that government outlays in the form of transfer payments are included in the tax schedule, since conceptually these are negative taxes. The tax schedule drawn, therefore, is to be interpreted as taxes less transfer payments.

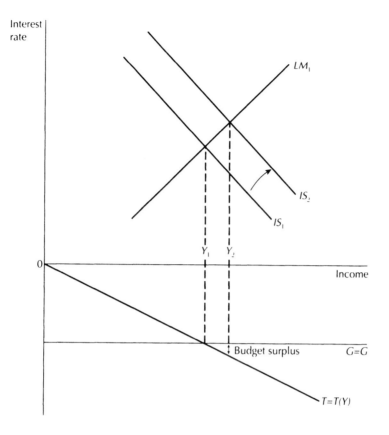

Figure 12.2 Budget constraint and the induced surplus

the government has no need to recourse to issue of national debt or to the creation of
new money. If this is not the case, then the government budget surplus or deficit will
exert feedback effects upon the *IS* and *LM* curves, thus generating a new equilibrium.

If government tax receipts fall short of government outlays then the deficit must be
financed either by additional bond sales, or by the creation of new money, or by some
combination of the two. Thus,

$$G - T = \Delta H + \Delta B \tag{12.1}$$

where G is government outlays upon goods and services, T is net fiscal revenue, transfer
payments having been treated as negative taxes, ΔH is the increase in the high-powered money stock and ΔB is the monetary value of new bonds issued to the private sector.[3] Notice that the condition for a stable equilibrium level of national income is that
at the point of intersection between the *IS* and *LM* schedules, the government budget
surplus or deficit must be equal to zero and *both* ΔM and ΔB are also equal to zero. It
is not sufficient, for example, for $\Delta M + \Delta B$ to equal zero.

---

3 Thus ΔB is the money obtained by the government upon the sale of additional bonds and not the par
value of the bonds themselves. If all bonds are consols then ΔB is equal to PV/i, where PV is the par value of
the bonds and i is the long-term rate of interest.

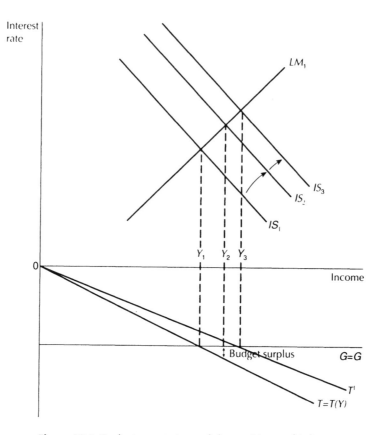

Figure 12.3 Budget constraint and the positive multiplier

By way of illustration, consider the analysis depicted with the aid of figure 12.2. Assume an initial equilibrium income level Y_1 with government outlays exactly offset by fiscal receipts allowing for no change in the money stock or in the holding of government bonds. Now assume, for purposes of exposition, an autonomous change in export demand. We consider the case of exports because it conveniently dispenses with the need to enquire into how such expenditures are to be financed. Such a change will be reflected in an outward shift of the *IS* curve generating the income level Y_2 in keeping with standard Keynesian analysis. The relationship between the change in income and the change in export demand provides us with a measure of the conventional Keynesian multiplier.

Now, however, this is no longer the end of the story, for at the income level Y_2 the government budget has moved into surplus. This is the direct consequence of tax receipts being endogenous upon income. Given the logic of the government budget constraint, the increase in fiscal receipts will be applied in one of the following ways. It may permit a decrease in tax rates. Secondly, it may be utilized to cut back the supply of high-powered money. Alternatively, it may be used to retire part of the national debt by the purchase of outstanding government bonds. Finally, of course, it may be used in some combination of the above, although this is not a case we need to analyse independently.

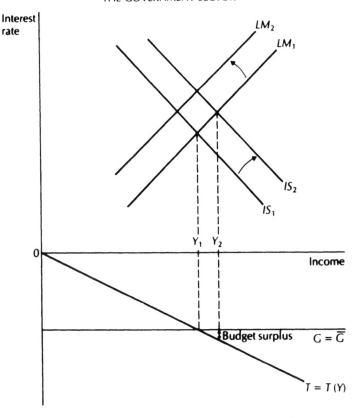

Figure 12.4 Budget constraint and the zero multiplier

Consider first a decrease in tax rates. This will raise disposable income and enhance the level of aggregate demand. The *IS* curve, therefore, will shift outwards still further; at the same time, the decrease in tax rates will pivot the tax schedule outwards. Equilibrium will ultimately be regained at the income level Y_3 as depicted in figure 12.3, when the budget surplus has again returned to zero. In this case, the ultimate multiplier is positive and exceeds that of the short-term conventional Keynesian model.

Let us now assume that the induced fiscal receipts are utilized to reduce the supply of high-powered money which shifts the *LM* schedule inwards. This is the situation analysed with the aid of figure 12.4. The relationship between the reduction in the high-powered money supply and the induced shift of the *LM* curve will be determined by the extent of credit creation by the banking sector.[4] Regardless of this relationship, the inward shift of the *LM* curve will be known precisely, and it will be made continuous until once again the original income level Y_1 is regained. Only at this level of income will government outlays be once again equated with fiscal receipts. Consideration of the government budget constraint not only implies interdependence between *IS* and *LM* functions, but also in this case completely negates the Keynesian multiplier. In the present example the autonomous increase in export spending generates a long-run multiplier equal to zero.

Suppose, however, that the induced tax receipts caused by income expansion are now utilized to retire part of the national debt. This is the situation examined in figure

---

4 With a 100 per cent required cash deposit ratio the two are rendered identical.

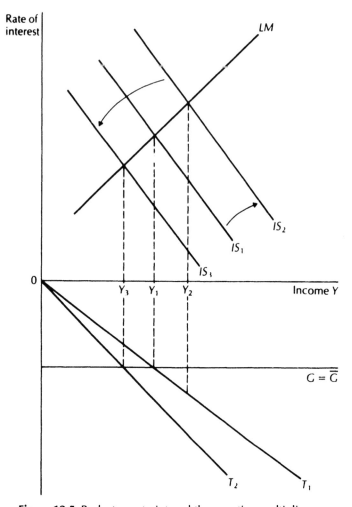

Figure 12.5 Budget constraint and the negative multiplier

12.5. As before, assume the initial increase in investment demand will raise the income level to Y_2 and generate a budget surplus. As the government now retires national debt, interest payments to the private sector will fall, reducing disposable incomes. In turn, this promotes an inward shift of the *IS* curve offsetting the previous expansionary income movement. However, in the present case, this offset influence will not come to an end when the original income level Y_1 is regained, because now, at this previous equilibrium point, the budget will still be in an overall surplus. This follows from the fact that retirement of the debt reduces government transfer payments (negative taxes), thus generating an increase in slope of the endogenous tax schedule. The ultimate equilibrium is accordingly indicated as being at Y_3, implying that the long-run Keynesian multiplier is actually *negative* in the present case.

What this analysis demonstrates is the importance of the government budget constraint in determining the ultimate outcome. We have three strikingly different outcomes to the same presumed increase in export demand depending upon how we assume the government deals with the induced fiscal proceeds. Moreover, all these results differ from that implicit in the conventional short-run Keynesian multiplier analysis. Clearly, conventional textbook Keynesianism must be judged incomplete in ignoring the financial implications of the budget constraint.

The difference in the tax reduction case and the debt retirement case is particularly striking: on the one hand, the normal Keynesian multiplier is reinforced; on the other, it is rendered negative. The reader will appreciate that whether this difference is real and significant, or whether it is totally artificial and false, turns again upon the issue of whether tax finance and bond finance are logically equivalent in their impacts.

The Nature of the Budget Constraint

In the preceding analysis it was seen that whatever the original position of *IS* and *LM* curves the ultimate equilibrium must coincide with the intersection of the government tax and outlay curves – the position of a balanced budget. It is now posited that such an equilibrium exists; consider then the consequences of expansionary fiscal policy occasioned by an increase in government expenditure. This is the situation summarized with the aid of figure 12.6. Y_1 represents the initial stable equilibrium level of

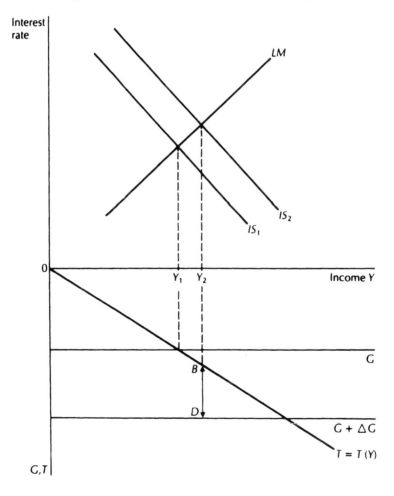

Figure 12.6 Budget constraint and fiscal policy

income consistent with a balanced budget. An increase in government expenditure will now alter this equilibrium, reflected in an outward shift of the *IS* curve and a downward shift of the government outlay curve. The short-run Keynesian equilibrium is denoted by the income level Y_2, and this outcome provides the justification for Keynesian-oriented fiscal policy in periods of recession and unemployment. However, at the income level Y_2 a budget deficit of *BD* is incurred. The logic of the budget constraint insists that this deficit must be financed, and financed at all points in time. The question which remains is the nature of this financing.

A budget deficit can be financed in one of three ways – first by an equivalent increase in tax revenues, second by an equivalent increase in the high-powered money supply, and third by an equivalent increase in proceeds obtained by bonds sales to the private sector.[5] Each situation is examined in turn. In the case of tax increases, the slope of the endogenous tax function is raised, the *IS* curve is shifted inward and an eventual stable equilibrium is indicated at Y_T in figure 12.7. The tax-financed increase in government expenditure raises the income level above the original level Y_1 but below the short-term Keynesian equilibrium Y_2. The tax increase partially offsets the expansionary impact of increased government expenditure.[6]

Figure 12.8 analyses the same situation, but this time assuming the increased government expenditure is financed by an increase in the high-powered money supply. This is reflected in an outward shift of the *LM* curve with no change in the slope of the endogenous tax function, so that the ultimate equilibrium is indicated at the income level Y_M. The monetary financed deficit thus reinforces the expansionary effects of increased government expenditure and leads to an income level in excess of the short-term Keynesian equilibrium level Y_2. It is partly this conclusion which forms the basis of the monetarists' claim that fiscally oriented policies will exert a minor impact unless they are accompanied by accommodating changes in the money supply.

Finally, figure 12.9 which analyses the case where the increase in government outlays is financed by the sale of additional bonds to the private sector – the case of debt finance. Here the increase in bond sales implies additional interest payments to service the enlarged debt. Such payments raise disposable income and hence consumption demands. Diagrammatically, this change implied an induced outward shift of the *IS* curve, reinforcing the previous outward shift occasioned by the increased government outlays. In addition, however, the increase in transfer payments to the private sector implies, in terms of the analysis which treats transfer payments as negative taxes, a decrease in the slope of the endogenous tax function. Full stable equilibrium is accordingly achieved at the income level Y_B, which not only exceeds the short-run Keynesian solution Y_2 but also is in excess of the monetary financed deficit Y_M. Figure 12.10 summarizes these various respective final solutions.

Clearly, the least expansionary type of policy is the tax-financed increase in government outlays – the so-called 'pure fiscal policy' which leaves the budget surplus or deficit unchanged. The monetary-financed increase in government expenditure has a much greater impact upon the level of income, partly because the increase in the

---

5 Or alternatively by some combination of these methods. For expositional purposes, they will be treated as being mutually exclusive, although the reader can readily analyse combined solutions should he/she so wish.

6 The increase in government expenditure adds directly to demand an amount equal to the government outlay. The increase in taxes depletes demand by an amount equal to the tax increase multiplied by the marginal propensity to consume. If the latter is less than one, some net expansionary impact will remain. The balanced budget multiplier theorem was analysed in detail in chapter 4.

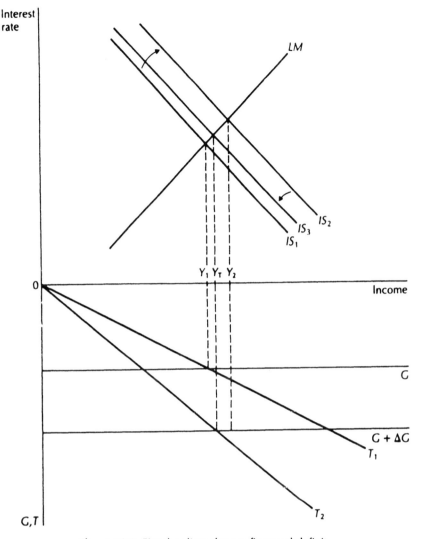

Figure 12.7 Fiscal policy: the tax financed deficit

money stock exerts downward pressure upon interest rates. Both Keynesians and monetarists would agree with these results. However, the most successful policy is shown to be the bond-financed expenditure measure, and implicitly, it is upon this case that Keynesians have rested their advocacy of the potency of fiscal policy. This position rests fundamentally upon two assumptions which are seldom explicitly specified – first that there is no limit to the extent to which the authorities can sell government bonds, and second that the resultant bond sales generate wealth effects. The first assumption clearly does not have universal application. In many of the less advanced economies, for example, the absence of confidence in the government of the day virtually prohibits this method of finance.[7] Whether bonds issued by the central government constitute net wealth from the viewpoint of the private sector is altogether a different issue and one which has generated considerable controversy.

---

7 Suggesting that the nature of the budget constraint may differ significantly for less advanced economies. On this point and some of the inflationary implications, see Shaw (1981).

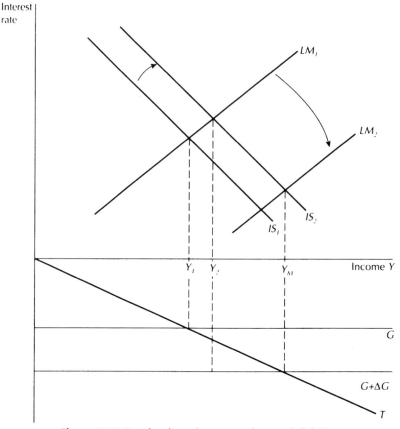

Figure 12.8 Fiscal policy: the money financed deficit

Deficit Financing and Private Sector Wealth

At any time, private sector wealth can be thought of as comprising the holding of real capital assets (including equity holdings) and the holding of debt, both monetary and non-monetary, issued by the government. The nominal value of the latter varies inversely with movements in the interest rate. If it is assumed, for simplicity, that all government bonds are consols, then private sector real wealth may be represented as

$$W = K + \frac{M}{P} + \frac{N/i}{P} \qquad (12.2)$$

where W is private sector real wealth, K the holding of real capital assets and claims to such assets, M the money stock in circulation, N the par or nominal value of government bonds, i the long-term rate of interest and P an aggregate price index. How is private sector wealth influenced by the issue of new bonds? Clearly, the short-run value of *real* capital assets is unaffected by the manner in which the authorities choose to finance new expenditures.[8] Equally, the total private holding of money balances will also remain unchanged when the government receives money balances from the public (in exchange for bonds) which it then puts back into circulation when it spends the proceeds. The total of privately held money balances is unaltered, in the aggregate, by the

---

8 Strictly speaking, this is incorrect, since relative capital values may be influenced by resulting interest rate movements, especially if the time profiles of future income streams differ.

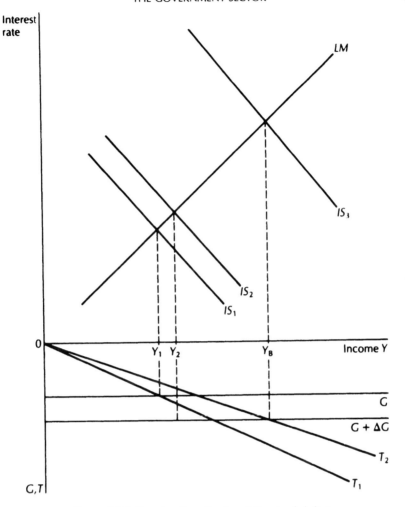

Figure 12.9 Fiscal policy: the bond financed deficit

transaction, as long as the price level remains unchanged. The only change, therefore, is the increase in privately held government bonds, and it is this increase which constitutes the perceived increase in private sector wealth.

Of course, any one individual giving up cash for bonds will not experience a wealth effect. He has merely altered the composition of his portfolio. But from the viewpoint of society *in toto*, aggregate bondholding has increased. And just as any individual would be justified in perceiving an increase in personal wealth if his bondholding in increased *ceteris paribus*, so too will this perception be applicable to the private sector in general.

Keynesian fiscal policy thus relied upon a dual premise, namely that debt financing gives rise to wealth effects as perceived by the private sector in its increased holding of government bonds, and that the resultant expansionary impetus is translated into output changes and not price changes – the latter implying compensatory falls in the real value of both cash and bond holdings.

The Keynesian analysis also implicitly assumes that there is no limit to the amount of bonds that the government can sell. However, this may not be the case; confidence in the ability of the government to be able to redeem and service a given debt may well

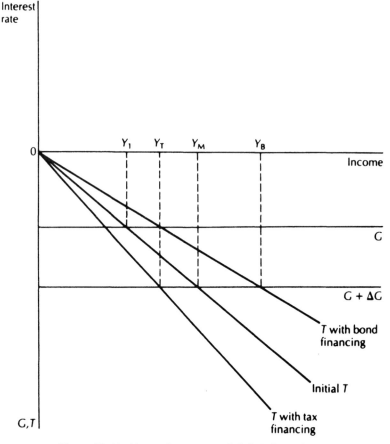

Figure 12.10 Alternative means of deficit financing

depend upon its extent in relation to GNP. Moreover, even if the government can sell bonds, the interest rate required to induce the necessary purchase may be politically unacceptable and may force abandonment of the policy in favour of tax or money finance. Also, of course, any rise in interest rates will imply a fall in the nominal value of existing bonds thus countering the wealth effect, if only partially.

Opponents of Keynesian economics tend to deny the wealth effect associated with enlarged bondholding. The more rational economic agents are, the more they will appreciate the implications of enlarged national debt in terms of future taxes to service and redeem the debt. This depletion of permanent income must reduce the expansionary potential of bond financed debt finance. Indeed, in this view, if taxpayers and bondholders apply the same rate of discount to future taxes as they do to future interest receipts, the wealth effect should be negated in its entirety. Bond financed deficits will then be formally equivalent to methods of tax finance.

To complicate the argument even further, it may be noted that a monetarist argument exists disputing the potency of Keynesian fiscal policy which depends upon the very existence of perceived wealth effects. So far we have assumed that if increased bondholding induces wealth effects, it will induce additional spending thus shifting the *IS* schedule outwards. This outward shift of the *IS* function serves to decrease the amount of bond sales needed to regain stable equilibrium. However, by the same token, increased wealth may permit an increased demand for money, allowing greater convenience and liquidity, thus promoting an inward shift of the *LM* schedule. The inward shift of the *LM* schedule serves both to raise interest rates and the amount of bond sales required to restore equilibrium. If the sensitivity of the demand for money to wealth is high (and here Friedman's findings on the income elasticity of the demand for money is suggestive), this offset to the outward shift of the *IS* curve may be considerable. This argument takes on renewed force if there is a limit, political or otherwise, to the interest rate or to the volume of additional bonds that the government can realistically float.

The Crowding Out Controversy

It is now possible to examine the claim, associated largely with the monetarist revival and in particular with the Federal Reserve Bank of St Louis (see Andersen and Jordan, 1968) that expansionary fiscal policy may be largely ineffective in that it may be offset or crowded out by compensatory action occuring within the private sector.

Four distinct types of crowding out can be identified. First, there is *direct crowding out*, whereby an increased government outlay in real terms generates a fall in private sector real outlays; this may be either because the government provision is regarded as a substitute for a service hitherto provided by the private sector, or alternatively, if full employment prevails, because the increased government share of GNP must claw resources away from the private sector. In the first case, the provision of the government service induces a rise in saving and the increase in the overall savings propensity will counter, if only partially, the effects of the increased government outlay. Thus, for example, provision of free medical services will reduce the demand for private sector health care. The net effect is akin to a transfer payment in kind which generates an income gain and permits additional saving out of alternative income (a case that was considered in connection with the balanced budget multiplier theorem in chapter 4). In the second case, which implicitly assumes a fixity of resources, the increased government outlays are obtained only at the expense of the private sector, the resources being induced to transfer from private to public employment by the prospect of higher nominal earnings. In general, therefore, the latter type of crowding out will be accompanied by inflationary tendencies.

Second, there is *indirect crowding out*, whereby the fiscal change exerts side-effects quite apart from any financing considerations which may run counter to the direction of the fiscal thrust. The obvious example, to which reference has already been made, is the automatic stabilizing influence exerted by the existence of a fixed money stock. The increase in government spending, for example, generates a rise in income which increases the transactions demand for cash and *ceteris paribus* raises the rate of interest. As long as private sector investment spending is sensitive to interest rate changes some offsetting decline in investment demand will occur. In addition, the induced rise in the rate of interest will decrease the value of existing bondholdings, implying a negative wealth effect which will impinge upon consumption spending. The sensitivity of both investment and consumption spending to interest rate changes is summarized in the slope of the *IS* curve. The flatter the slope of the *IS* function, the greater will be the interest-induced offset to expansionary fiscal policy. At the same time, however, the slope of the *LM* curve will impinge upon the extent of the interest rate change associated with any given increase in government expenditure. The flatter the slope of the *LM* curve, the less will be the interest rate change. This argument is summarized with

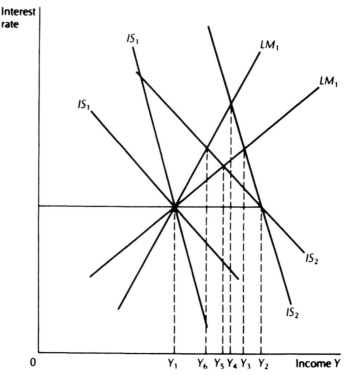

Figure 12.11 Interest elasticity of IS and LM functions and the degree of crowding out

the aid of figure 12.11. Here are displayed two *IS* functions, one relatively interest elastic and the other interest inelastic. Equally there are two *LM* schedules, again being relatively interest elastic and interest inelastic respectively. Assume the initial income level Y_1. An increase in government expenditure will raise the income level to Y_2 if no change in the interest rate is permitted to occur – that is, if monetary policy is accommodating. However, assuming the money supply remains fixed and acts out its permitted role as automatic stabilizer, the income level will fall below Y_2 and will be either Y_3, Y_4, Y_5, or Y_6 depending upon which of the *IS* and *LM* schedules is invoked. The least expansionary outcome will be the income level Y_6, obtained by the assumption of interest elastic *IS* schedules and interest inelastic *LM* schedules. In the extreme case, that of a vertical *LM* curve, the degree of crowding out is complete – irrespective of the shape of the *IS* schedule.

A second case of indirect crowding out arises from consideration of tax changes upon the demand for money. Keynes, in the *General Theory*, had related both consumption spending and the demand for money to the level of income. Later commentators were to specifically take account of the government sector, and in so doing they made consumption depend more correctly upon the level of *disposable* income. However, they failed to apply this modification to the demand for money, thus perpetuating an inconsistency; if consumption demand is related to disposable income then logically so too will the transactions demand for money. Once this modification is allowed the possibility of indirect crowding out is again raised.[9] This situation is illustrated with the aid of figure 12.12. Assume an initial equilibrium at the income level Y_1, determined by the intersection of the IS_1 and LM_1 schedules. Now assume an attempt to impart an

---

9 The first recognition of this possibility appears to have been by Holmes and Smyth (1972).

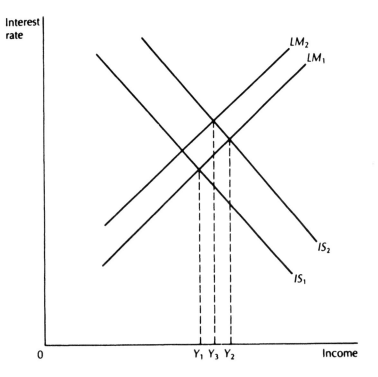

Figure 12.12 Tax multiplier with crowding out

expansionary fiscal stimulus by cutting taxes. The increase in disposable income will generate an increased consumption demand, thus effecting an outward shift of the *IS* curve. At the same time, however, the increase in disposable income will generate an increased demand for transactions cash and thus imply an offsetting inward shift of the *LM* curve. Theoretically, depending upon the sensitivity of the transactions demand for money, the tax multiplier could be positive. In the present case this extreme assumption has not been made. None the less, a considerable degree of crowding out is depicted; instead of the income level Y_2 implied by conventional Keynesian models, the income level Y_3 is obtained. This situation, it will be appreciated, does not arise from an assumed interdependence between *IS* and *LM*; rather it stems from the assumption that both *IS* and *LM* functions respond to the same fiscal stimuli – an assumption which is diametrically opposed to the conventional Keynesian wisdom.

Cases of direct and indirect crowding out are the ones which have figured relatively prominently in macroeconomic literature in one form or another. In contrast, the third classification of crowding out, *financial crowding out*, is relatively new and stems directly from consideration of the government budget constraint, which implied that a fiscal deficit could be financed in one of three ways. If the deficit is tax financed then there is substantial crowding out (figure 12.7). In contrast, if the deficit is financed by an increase in high-powered money no crowding out occurs, and indeed the expansionary impact of the fiscal measure is reinforced by the expansionary impact of the enlarged money stock (figure 12.8). It is also possible to finance accompanying deficits by bond finance. Here, the expansionary impact of fiscal policy becomes more controversial. Once again, crowding out is absent providing we assume the existence of private sector wealth effects and providing the government can market additional debt. In this case, the expansionary impact of fiscal policy exceeds even that associated with monetary financing (figure 12.9). In contrast, strict adherence to rational expectations philosophy would deny the logic of wealth effects and render the debt-financed case equivalent with the tax-financed outcome – and therefore, consistent with considerable crowding out. Finally, it should be noted that the logic of the budget constraint overrides all other forms of crowding out. In particular, indirect crowding out is of a temporary duration only, given that in the last resort full equilibrium requires that the budget be finally balanced.

The Budget Constraint and Inflation

Hitherto, the financial implications of the government budget constraint have been examined with respect to movements in real output and employment but under the tacit assumption that prices are held constant. However, much of the interest in the government budget constraint springs from the belief that a deficit and the manner of its financing will be of considerable importance for the rate of inflation, and indeed much of the monetarist critique of Keynesian oriented policy measures springs from a feeling that the inflationary consequences have been inadequately analysed.

From this perspective, ideally, government spending would be matched by taxes and the deficit would be zero. If a deficit does prevail, then it is preferable, given the overriding commitment to curb inflation, that it should be financed by the sale of bonds to the private sector rather than by increasing the high-powered money supply.[10] However, even if the budget deficit implies an increase in the money stock, the consequences may still be deflationary within an inflationary setting if the increase in the money stock falls short of the rate of inflation. To pursue this argument further, a simple numerical example is given. Suppose the total money supply is £100m, whilst government outlays total £10m and endogenous taxes equal £9m. The current budget deficit is accordingly £1m. If this deficit is financed by an increase in high-powered money it may lead to a total increase in the money supply by, say £5m. The net impact of financing the deficit, therefore, is an increase in the total money stock of 5 per cent per annum. Now if the rate of inflation were also equal to 5 per cent, this situation would tend to *continue indefinitely*. At least, this conclusion follows from invoking assumptions which do not stretch realism unduly. If government outlays are maintained in real terms and if endogenous taxes respond *pari passu* with nominal income levels so that the deficit is maintained at 10 per cent of government outlays, and if the relationship between the total money supply and the high-powered money supply remains a constant, then the increase in the money supply will be exactly equal to the inflation rate. In this situation there will be no increase in the *real* money supply arising from the financing of the deficit to disturb the existing situation. Thus, although the money supply will be increasing at an annual rate of 5 per cent this will be absorbed into monetary holdings since the demand for money, being a real demand, will also be increasing at a 5 per cent annual rate. That is to say, both the asset and transactions demand for cash will tend to rise in line with the increase in the nom-

---

10 It should not be assumed that deficit financing by bond sales has no impact upon inflation. If the money transferred into bonds had constituted 'idle' balances, its activization upon being spent by the government is in reality an increase in velocity, similar in its effects to an increase in the money supply.

inal money supply; there will be no change in the position of the *LM* curve and no change in the real level of income.

This example is now repeated but under the assumption that inflation is initially running at an annual figure of 10 per cent. In these conditions, the annual increase in the money supply will be insufficient to meet the annual increase in the nominal demand for money balances. In effect, the real money stock will decline and the *LM* function will gradually be shifted inwards with deflationary consequences for the real economy. Under existing assumptions (that government outlays are maintained in real terms whilst tax receipts are effectively indexed to nominal income movements), the budget deficit will increase in both absolute and percentage terms. Thus the situation occurs, contrary to the earlier analysis, of a budgetary deficit being financed by an increasing money supply with deflationary repercussions upon the real economy reinforced by a raising interest rate. This scenario is precisely that of the monetarist contention that unemployment and a loss of output is the price to be paid for the elimination of inflation. For with the rate of monetary increase well below that of inflation, the rate of price increases will ultimately fall; there will be insufficient means of finance to transact the turnover of GNP at the constantly rising price level.[11] The rising deficit in real terms will necessitate a further increase in the money supply in excess of its annual 5 per cent rate. At the same time, as the rate of inflation falls the two rates will eventually coincide. Stability will be regained when the annual increase in monetary growth is again equated with the rate of inflation, in the present case within the range 5–10 per cent.[12]

According to this analysis, the rate of inflation will continue to fall as long as the rate of monetary growth lies below the annual rate of inflation. It follows that the way to reduce and eventually eliminate inflation is to reduce progressively the growth of the money supply, despite the deflationary impacts this will exert upon the real sectors of the economy. In return, this necessitates reducing the fiscal deficit by reducing government expenditure and raising taxes upon the one hand and by financing any deficit that remains by bond sales to the private sector on the other hand, even though this may necessitate extremely high rates of interest.

Once inflation has been eliminated the logic of the budget constraint will again reassert itself, with the consequences of the deficit revealing itself in expansionary real movements in the economy, assuming perfectly elastic supply conditions. If supply constraints exist, part of the impetus will be dissipated into price rises and may once again initiate an inflationary spiral.

In conclusion, consideration of the budget constraint generates two opposing eventual outcomes. In the absence of inflation, full equilibrium necessitates equality between government outlays and government taxes with zero change in the money supply and the volume of bonds issued. Policy multipliers should reflect this eventual outcome. If inflation exists, then a stable solution to the model no longer requires equality between government outlays and government receipts to the extent that the financial implications of any deficit (surplus) are just sufficient to accommodate the ongoing rate of inflation (deflation).

---

11 This conclusion makes clear two underlying assumptions which are fundamental to the monetarists' belief in the efficacy of money supply control – first that velocity increases are limited, and second and more important that the relationship between the high-powered monetary base and the total money stock is relatively constant. On the latter point see Chick (1977).

12 The inflationary effects of monetary growth will be reinforced by the decline in real output.

Concluding Comments

The previous discussion of the government sector has not specifically dealt with methods of finance (other than when dealing with the balanced budget multiplier theorem, when it was assumed that all outlays were tax financed). Now, however, the method of finance has been made explicit, and as a result many important conclusions have been reached:

(1)   That *IS* and *LM* curves are interdependent and linked through the budget constraint.

(2)   That monetary-financed expenditure policy is inevitably more high powered than equivalent tax-financed expenditures.

(3)   That Keynesian belief in the long-term efficacy of fiscal policy rests upon the assumption of unlimited debt finance.

(4)   That various possibilities exist for the short-term crowding out of fiscal policy measures.

Finally, it can be observed that the stability conditions for the extended *IS/LM* framework with a government budget constraint differ under inflation, in that monetary creation will not be disequilibrating if it is just sufficient to match the inflation rate.

Further Reading

The literature on the government budget constraint and the crowding out controversy is now extensive. Useful surveys are to be found in Artis, Burrows and Taylor, all published in Cook and Jackson (1979) with extensive references. Likewise, Currie (1978, 1981) is recommended for providing a comprehensive summary of the leading issues. An elementary introduction to the crowding out controversy is presented in Shaw (1977) and Peacock and Shaw (1978). Amongst the seminal and influential papers, reference must be made to Blinder and Solow (1973) and Hansen (1973). A useful paper presented in terms of the *IS/LM* analysis is that of Silber (1970). Other interesting articles making specific reference to fiscal policy effectiveness include Buiter (1977), Scarth (1975) and Turnovsky (1977). Extensions to the basic analysis presented here include Alpine (1985) and Shaw (1987c), whilst a disturbing scenario outlining the possible consequences of runaway government debt is presented by Tobin (1986).

13

Output, Employment, Expectations and the Price Level

Chapters 8 to 12 contrasted the Keynesian and classical models within a conventional *IS/LM* framework. This framework has been used as an expository device for many years and is useful for bringing out the principal contrasts between the two systems. There are, however, certain fundamental shortcomings inherent in this methodology. First, it is basically a static framework which, although useful for comparative static analysis, is of rather limited value for analysing the dynamics of each system. In other words, the framework is helpful in comparing equilibria but has little to contribute to the analysis of movements from one equilibrium to another. Second, the methodology implicitly assumes that monetary and fiscal policy are independent instruments. Increasingly the interdependence of the two instruments is being appreciated, as has already been noted in the analysis of the government budget constraint and the crowding out controversy in chapter 12. Third, and related to the above, the analysis is essentially conducted against the backcloth of a stable price level. Thus it is assumed that as *IS* and *LM* shift around up to the full employment level of output, the price level remains stable. Although it is implicit that increases in output beyond the full employment level may be inflationary, it is also implicit that such increases are easily reversible.

It has become increasingly obvious over the past twenty-five years or so that such behavioural assumptions about what are essentially the dynamic characteristics of the system are not entirely plausible, and that the relationship between output and changes in the price level may be rather more complicated than that portrayed by the mechanics of the simple model.

This chapter will consider explicitly the causes of variations in the aggregate price level, and in particular the manner in which variations in the price level might be affected by variations in output. Such an analysis goes to the very heart of recent work in macroeconomic theory and policy, and serves to highlight the important role which expectations may play.

Inflation and its Causes

Inflation is a *sustained* upward rise in the *general* price level. By emphasizing 'sustained' this definition clearly excludes temporary jumps or falls in prices related perhaps to specific events such as a bad harvest. The 'general' price level refers to some representative price level which affects the majority of individuals. Thus the *retail price index*, which is the most frequently referred to indicator of inflation in the UK, is a weighted average of prices of a standard basket of goods and services. Variations in this index indicate how variations in prices are affecting economic agents 'on average'.

As will be seen in chapter 19 governments are concerned with inflation because it tends to generate certain distortions in the economic system; that is, it can redistribute income in a capricious manner, it can raise the average costs of transactions, and it can result in relative prices being distorted. These issues will be considered more fully later. For the moment it will be taken as given that the authorities have an interest in controlling inflation, and first the causes of inflation and its relationship to output variations will be explored.

From elementary microeconomics, it is clear that an increase in the price of a given commodity can result from a shift in demand and/or supply. An analogous distinction can be made with respect to the macroeconomy. Thus, from the aggregate demand and aggregate supply curves which were derived in chapters 6 and 7, it can be seen that it is possible for price level changes to occur as a consequence of shifts in AD and/or AS.

It will be recalled that a given AD curve is derived on the assumption of money market equilibrium. Therefore as the price level falls (increases) the real value of a given stock of money balances increases (falls), real expenditure increases (falls) and real income increases (falls). In other words the AD schedule has a negative slope. Given the implicit assumption of money market equilibrium which underpins AD, any increases (decreases) in the money supply would shift AD to the right (left).

In chapter 7 was introduced the AS schedule. The slope of this was determined by the manner in which agents in the labour market responded to changes in the price level. It was seen that if labour supply was a function of the real wage, and the labour market cleared quickly, AS would be vertical. In other words, employment and real income would be insensitive to variations in the price level (and perforce to policies which changed the price level). If, on the other hand, labour supply were a function of the money wage rate, then AS could be positively sloped, at least up to the full employment level of real income. The latter possibility really relied on some market imperfection being present, such as money illusion, or contracts which fixed the price of labour for a given period. This in turn introduced a third possibility, namely that positively sloped and vertical AS curves could coexist – the former being short-run functions, the latter the long-run AS when full adjustment has taken place.

Demand Pull Inflation

Figure 13.1 outlines in stylized terms the simple mechanics of demand pull inflation. Assume the initial output level is Y_1 and price level P_1 (point a), and this equilibrium is disturbed by an increase in the money supply. This increases aggregate expenditure and shifts AD to the right, from AD_1 to AD_2. If aggregate supply is depicted by AS_1 then real output increases to Y_2 and the price level rises to P_2 (point b). If the AS curve is vertical, the shift in AD results in an increase in the price level from P_1 to P_3 (point c). Further shifts might take the equilibrium to d or e.

The manner in which any increase in the nominal money supply affects prices and output, and the extent to which any increase is divided between increases in output and increases in prices, has been the subject of some controversy. The latter question has

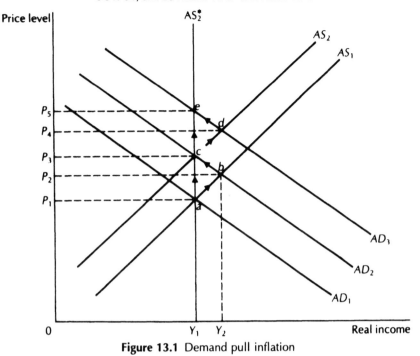

Figure 13.1 Demand pull inflation

been especially topical in recent years, and it will be examined in detail later in the chapter. For the moment concentration will be on the former.

Chapter 5 set out the simplest possible statement of the monetarist position on inflation in the form of the simple quantity theory equation

$$M\bar{V} = P\bar{Y} \tag{13.1}$$

This encapsulates two central propositions of the classical quantity theory position; first, the demand for money is a stable function of a small number of variables, and therefore the velocity of circulation V can be taken as stable; second, the factors which affect the supply of money M are separate from those which influence demand. If the classical assumption is invoked that real output Y will automatically tend to its full employment level, it follows that

$$\Delta M\bar{V} \rightarrow \Delta P\bar{Y} \tag{13.2}$$

that is, there is a deterministic link between the rate of change in the money supply and the price level, and furthermore changes in the supply of money will change the price level and leave real income unaffected. In figure 13.1 there would be a shift from a to c as a result of the shift in AD from AD_1 to AD_2.

As was also seen in chapter 5, the Keynesian analysis of the demand for money suggested that V could in fact be unstable and unpredictable, especially in conditions of underemployment equilibrium, the most graphic example of this being provided by the liquidity trap. Although most neo-Keynesian analysis views the liquidity trap as a purely pathological case, it was seen that the Keynesian demand for money was refined by, *inter alia*, Baumol (1952) and Tobin (1958), and it is this analysis which underpins the neo-Keynesian view of the *transmissions mechanism* that is, the way in which a change in the money supply affects money income (PY). According to this view an increase in M causes wealth holders to substitute money for bonds and other financial assets in their portfolios. The more closely substitutable a given asset for money, the bigger the change that occurs, and there is a 'ripple'effect throughout the liquidity spectrum. Changes in the money supply do not therefore affect final expenditure directly but rather indirectly through its influence on real investment.When the money supply is increased, this could be stimulated directly through a reduction in the interest rate (as in the simple Keynesian analysis of investment of chapter 3), and/or through increases in the price of equities stimulating further equity issues. In this schema, then, changes in M can affect Y and can affect P (through the subsequent pressure of demand). The precise relationships are, however, essentially unpredictable, and depend on the sensitivity of investment to monetary policy and the extent to which V changes if M changes.

Friedman's (1956a) reformulation and refinement of the simple quantity theory analysis accepted the basic principle that changes in the supply of nominal money balances would result in adjustments in individual portfolios, but contended that the links between monetary expansion and final expenditure were altogether more direct than those posited by the neo-Keynesian approach.

This followed from Friedman's inclusion of real and financial assets in the demand for money function, such that when portfolio adjustment occurred it was associated not only with the substitution of one financial asset for another but also with substitution of money balances for real assets like consumer durables, housing and so on. In crude terms, although the demand for money was viewed as being a function of a larger range of variables than envisaged by the simple quantity theory approach, it was nevertheless a *stable* function, ensuring relative stability of V. In the event therefore, that the authorities increase the money supply, stock disequilibrium is created in the money market. Individuals hold excess money balances in their portfolios and, in order to clear this excess supply, expenditure increases. Thus, the link between monetary expansion and expenditure is direct.With respect to the division of a change in M between P and Y, subsequent work by Friedman suggested that in the short run both would be affected, whilst in the long run the full impact of any monetary expansion would be felt on prices. This will shortly be examined more closely. For the moment it might simply be noted that the essence of demand pull inflation is that an outward shift in the AD function raises the price level. The monetarist position is that monetary expansion is both necessary and sufficient to facilitate this process.Whilst not denying that this may be so, the neo-Keynesian position can be interpreted as one consistent with the view that monetary expansion is sufficient but not necessary. The additional pressure of demand could emanate from an autonomous increase in investment expenditure or from an increase in real investment stimulated by monetary expansion. In so far as both must ultimately be accommodated by an increased supply of money balances, both stands can be interpreted as being consistent with Friedman's assertion that 'inflation is always and everywhere a monetary phenomenon' (which as will be seen in chapter 18 is not the same as saying that control of the money supply is both necessary and sufficient to control inflation).

Cost Push Inflation

Whereas demand pull inflation originates in a shift in the AD curve with a given AS curve, cost push inflation originates with an autonomous shift in the AS curve. In figure 13.2 the leftward shift in AS with a given AD raises the supply prices of factors of production such that less is supplied at any given price level. With a given aggregate

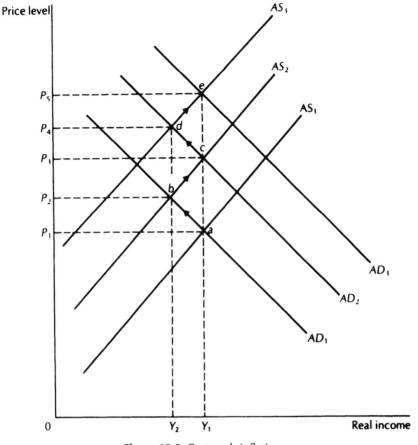

Figure 13.2 Cost push inflation

demand curve of AD_1, aggregate output would fall to Y_2 and the price level would rise to P_2. Thus, the shift in supply has resulted in a price level change which is independent of the level of demand. The resultant inflation is associated with a fall in output (and employment). Such inflationary pressures which originate on the supply side could emanate from any of the following three channels:

(1) increased raw material prices

(2) profit push

(3) wage push.

There are occasions when the prices of raw materials are administered upwards as, for example, in the OPEC price hike of 1973–74 which quadrupled the posted price of crude oil between October 1973 and January 1974. In the event that the commodity concerned has relatively few substitutes, and demand is therefore relatively price inelastic, this feeds straight through into the prices of inputs and finished goods. Given a downward sloping AD schedule, a higher price level reduces the real value of money balances, and real expenditure and income are decreased.

Profit push inflation occurs when product prices are administered upwards in an attempt to increase profit margins. Such a mechanism of course relies on the exploitation of (product) market power, and there have been occasions when commentators have felt that profit push has been an important source of inflationary pressure, for example in the United States during the 1950s. Like imported inflation, however, profit push is only really useful in explaining once and for all changes in the price level, since there are limits to the extent to which prices are raised even if these are only the limits set by profit maximization. The phenomenon is not helpful in explaining the dynamics of an inflationary process once it is under way.

Wage push is the most widely discussed source of cost push inflation. This too relies on the use of market power to attempt to alter the distribution of income. In this case, however, it is factor rather than product market power which is relevant. Here the mechanism which applies is that labour unions push for increases in wages in excess of productivity growth. This is conceded by firms anxious to avoid the costs of a protracted dispute, and passed on in the form of higher prices. Again referring to figure 13.2, the outcome is a leftward shift in *AS*, a rise in the price level and a fall in output and employment. The notion of wage push inflation commands wide popular appeal and, despite the difficulties of finding a proxy for union power, there is some empirical evidence to suggest that the presence of labour unions can induce an inflationary bias in the labour market, especially when they are active in industries where they face employers with some degree of product market power (see Trevethick and Mulvey, 1975, chapter 6). Like the profit push explanation of inflation, wage push is useful for explaining specific inflationary impulses (as in the UK in 1968–69 or 1978–79), but, also in common with profit push, it is fundamentally lacking as an explanation of sustained inflation, and for similar reasons. Since the underlying model is based on market power it is consistent with a once and for all wage push. In the case of a sustained inflation, where does the increased market power come from? Given a downward sloping labour demand curve, increased real wages will be associated with a lower level of employment. As unemployment increases it seems reasonable to suppose that union membership falls, and with it market power.

In a strict sense, then, wage push *per se* is not a *generally applicable* explanation for inflation. This is not, however, to do justice to more sophisticated approaches to wage push inflation which recognize this and which, while continuing to ascribe trade unions a central role in the inflationary process, recognize the importance of monetary accommodation. Thus, in figure 13.2 a wage push shifts AS_1 to AS_2, raises prices from P_1 to P_2 and reduces output from Y_1 to Y_2. The authorities could respond to this by permitting monetary expansion to take place in order to reduce unemployment and re-establish an output level of Y_1. AD_1 therefore shifts to AD_2 and the price level rises from P_2 to P_3. The latter change could provide the stimulus for another wage push, again raising prices (to P_4) and lowering output (to Y_2 again). Monetary accommodation raises prices further and so the process repeats itself with an adjustment pattern of $a \rightarrow b \rightarrow c \rightarrow d \rightarrow e$. This view of inflation would see it as the outcome of a struggle between unions to alter the distribution of income, against the backcloth of a government aiming to hit a particular employment target. It must be noted, however, that even though a central role is given to the activities of labour unions, these activities still have to be 'validated' by monetary accommodation.

This type of mechanism is a far cry from the naïve view that cost push inflation is simply the outcome of the abuse of union power *per se*, and all that is necessary to control inflation is some form of wage control. Indeed this view, although it may claim to be cost push in spirit, is nevertheless consistent with Friedman's assertion that 'inflation is always and everywhere a monetary phenomenon'.

The acceleration of inflation which took place during the 1970s and 80s in most developed market economies stimulated a great deal of research effort directed at establishing whether inflation was principally cost push or demand pull. One thing which has been consistently reported for a great many countries is the close *association between monetary expansion and changes in prices*. This is not to argue that any link between money and prices is mechanistic and straightforward, such that causality is always unambiguous; as has been seen, one could argue the case for money being active or passive. Nor is it to argue that control of the money supply is both necessary and sufficient to control inflation in the short run. Rather it is to argue that, once an inflationary process is under way, the distinction between demand pull and cost push is not very important. The problems of inflationary control will be returned to in chapter 19. For the moment, however, it will be accepted that a long-run relationship between the money supply and inflation exists; attention will be focused on other significant issues from a policy standpoint, such as the precise relationship between inflation and employment, and how this relationship is affected by inflationary expectations. This permits a comment on an issue alluded to earlier in the chapter, namely what, for a given monetary expansion which serves to shift *AD* to the right, determines the distribution of the change in expenditure between prices and real income.

The Phillips Curve Relation

For many years it was felt that a systematic trade-off existed between the rate of inflation and the level of unemployment. The basis of this belief was the publication of a celebrated paper by Phillips (1958) which provided statistical support for the existence of a stable trade-off between the rate of change of money wages and the level of un-

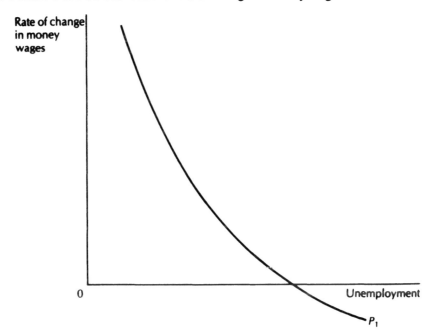

Figure 13.3 Phillips curve

employment. According to Phillips this association held in the UK for long periods during the period 1861–1957. The so-called Phillips curve took the general form outlined in figure 13.3.

The theoretical underpinnings to the Phillips curve were subsequently developed by Lipsey (1961), who focused on the level of excess demand in the labour market at any particular time, and on the implications which this has for the speed of adjustment of money wages. Specifically, Lipsey assumed that

$$\dot{W} = f[(D_L - S_L)/S_L] \tag{13.3}$$

where D_L and S_L refer to the demand for and supply of labour respectively, and $\dot{W}$ refers to the rate of change of money wages.

If a linear functional form is imposed, as by Lipsey, equation 13.3 can be rewritten as

$$\dot{W} = \alpha[(D_L - S_L)/S_L] \tag{13.4}$$

Lipsey therefore takes the relatively uncontroversial proposition, portrayed in panel (a) of figure 13.4, that in the event of excess supply (demand) in the labour market the wage rate will fall (rise), and extends it by arguing that the *speed* at which wage rates rise or fall will be related to the *extent* of excess demand/supply. In the case of an excess demand, therefore, wage rates will rise more quickly from W_2 than W_1 in panel (a).

Speed of adjustment is summarized in panel (b); the origin represents labour market equilibrium, and therefore there is no tendency for money wages to change, and higher levels of excess demand are associated with faster rates of change of wage rates.[1] As excess demand in the labour market cannot be directly observed, a proxy must be used. The most satisfactory proxy according to Lipsey is recorded unemployment. Thus in panel (c) an inverse relationship is observed between recorded unemployment and excess demand. This relationship is non-linear to the left of point z and linear to the right. The former follows because that curve must approach the vertical axis asymptotically since unemployment will never become zero; the latter because increases in excess supply call forth equal increases in unemployment. Point z coincides with the equilibrium wage rate W_e. Although excess demand is zero, recorded unemployment will nevertheless be positive owing to frictional unemployment (with, presumably, the number of frictionally unemployed being equal to the number of vacancies available).

Finally, in quadrant (d) is derived the relationship between the rate of change of money wages and the level of unemployment, that is, the Phillips curve relation. It must be emphasized that what has been done is to derive an individual 'micro' Phillips curve. Although the 'macro' curve will take the same general configuration, it is derived from observations (that is, individual points) on micro curves.

As Laidler (1971b) subsequently remarked, 'The simple theory of the Phillips curve... was absorbed with remarkable speed into the generally accepted corpus of macro-economics.' Furthermore, it must be said that the acceptance was largely uncritical, with most emphasis being placed on testing for the presence of Phillips curves in a variety of countries and circumstances. The reason behind such an open-armed

---

1 The function could be extended to the south-west quadrant to relate wage change and negative excess demand. Presumably, however, an asymmetry would be observed, that is, higher levels of excess supply result in slower reductions in wage rates. This would be explained by reference to institutional arrangements which result in a downward inflexibility of money wages.

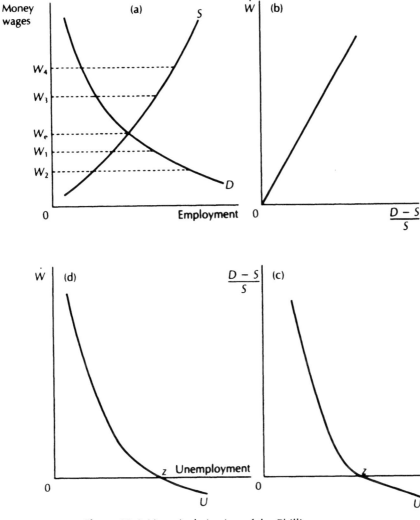

Figure 13.4 Lipsey's derivation of the Phillips curve

welcome is quite simple. The existence of a Phillips-type relation appeared to offer policy makers a straight choice between inflation and unemployment. One could trade off more of one for less of the other. Furthermore, once the curve was identified the rate of unemployment which was consistent with zero inflation could also be identified. Although a good deal of empirical support was identified for the Phillips relation in the mid-1960s, after 1968 the relation was seen to consistently underpredict the rate of inflation. In the UK and other developed market economies, unemployment and inflation were seen to be increasing simultaneously. Initial reactions to this revolved around attempts to resuscitate the relationship. Thus many commentators argued that essentially the Phillips curve had shifted and/or its shape had changed, owing to once and for all changes like an increase in union militancy pursuant on pay restraint and devaluation. Ultimately, however, such explanations were country-specific rationalizations of a shift, and could not explain why the relationship appeared to have broken down in a number of countries, and furthermore it seemed that the breakdown was far from temporary.

Expectations in Macroeconomics

The most convincing explanation of the breakdown of the simple Phillips curve, and the one which has had the most lasting effect on the development of macroeconomic theory in the 1970s and 1980s, was an approach founded on the explicit consideration of the role of expectations in the inflationary process. This was developed independently by Phelps (1968) and Friedman (1968a) and resulted in the refinement of the so-called 'expectations augmented Phillips curve'. We will analyse this in the following section. Prior to that it is useful to outline some simple ideas of the role of expectations in macroeconomics.

Almost all economic decisions deemed to be rational – that is, consistent with utility maximizing behaviour – involve expectations. The purchase of a candy bar or a theatre ticket, for example, is undertaken in the light of a given expectation of the pleasure that consumption of the candy bar or visit to the theatre is going to provide. One expectation may be held with greater certainty than the other; candy bars (at least of the same variety) being more homogeneous than theatre plays or performances, but the principle is the same. The difference, in more formal terms, is simply that in the case of the visit to the theatre the variance around the expected mean value is likely to be greater than that associated with the consumption of the candy bar.

This difference, however, is not without significance. Two goods may possess the same expected mean value of marginal utility but one may have a far greater variance around the mean and therefore may involve – for the risk-averse individual – the prospect of an unacceptable outcome. Without pursuing such complications any further at this point it is sufficient to observe that utility maximization involves individual economic agents forming expectations – if only implicitly or intuitively – both about the expected mean outcome upon the one hand and the degree of variance around the expected outcome upon the other. It is in this sense that virtually all economic decisions involve expectations. Yet expectations have, until comparatively recently, been given scant attention in economic reasoning mainly owing to the difficulties of incorporating them adequately into the main body of economic theory. In recent years two methods of making expectations endogeneous have been defined: namely, adaptive expectations and rational expectations.

Adaptive Expectations

Adaptive expectations are precisely that; they adapt in the light of past experience. We will formally analyse the adaptive mechanism later in the chapter. For the moment the essence of the adjustment process can be summed up with the aid of a simple and rather mechanical equation. Suppose an individual is forecasting the interest rate. Let us write i^e to represent the *expected* rate in any given time period, whilst i refers to the *actual* rate which did in fact prevail. Then we may express the expectation of the interest rate next period in the following way:

$$i^e_{t+1} = i^e_t + \lambda(i_t - i^e_t), \ (0 < \lambda < 1) \tag{13.5}$$

where t denotes the time period and λ is an adjustment coefficient which lies between the values 0 and 1. That is to say our expectation of the rate of interest for the next period is equal to the expectation that we held with respect to the current period plus some fraction of the extent to which our expectation was shown to be incorrect. For purposes of illustration let us assume the adjustment coefficient takes the value 0.5 whilst the market rate of interest is 5 per cent and our expected rate or 'normal' rate is 10 per cent. Then in the next time period, in the light of our expectation being proved incorrect we would have

$$i_{t+1}^e = 10 + 0.5(5 - 10)\% = 7.5\%$$

In the following period, should the market remain stubbornly at 5 per cent we would have

$$i_{t+1}^e = 7.5 + 0.5(5 - 7.5)\% = 6.25\%$$

and subsequently,

$$i_{t+1}^e = 6.25 + 0.5(5 - 6.25)\% = 5.625\%$$

Thus, over time, and confronted by the fact that our expectation has persistently over-estimated the actual rate of interest, we would gradually adjust our expected rate downwards until we attain a coincidence between our expectations and reality.

The speed of adjustment, depends, of course, upon the value of the coefficient lambda. In the limiting case where lambda takes the value 1, the adjustment process is complete within one period. This is a special case of the adaptive expectations thesis which underlies the Cobweb theorem of price determination. In this model, sellers assume that whatever price prevails in the market today, in the current period, will continue to prevail in future periods.

The adaptive expectations thesis was introduced into economics by Cagan (1956) to deal with the formation of inflationary expectations in conditions of hyperinflation and in many respects it has great appeal. It is simple to model, involving only a linear first-order difference equation and econometrically it is not difficult to obtain estimates of the adjustment coefficient. Moreover it has the appealing property that in the case of a once and for all change – say a price increase occasioned by a raising of indirect taxes – then sooner or later economic agents' expectations will come to coincide with reality. None the less, as we shall see later in the chapter, as a means of expectations formation it is not without its drawbacks.

Rational Expectations

An alternative view of the way in which expectations are formed is the rational expectations view. The rational expectations hypothesis possesses immediate appeal to the conventionally trained economist embodying as it does the assumption of utility maximizing behaviour. Specifically, it assumes that individual economic agents do not refer solely to past experience in forming expectations but also take account of current available information should they find it worthwhile. In addition, it is assumed that they process this information in an efficient manner to arrive at an expectation or forecast of the values to be taken by economic variables. So far, so good; few economists would be disposed to deny the foregoing mode of behaviour which conforms very neatly with the predilections of *homo economicus*.

The rational expectations hypothesis, however, comes in weak and strong versions. Loosely speaking, it is the weak version which is epitomized in the preceding paragraph. It implies little more than an assertion that individuals carry out a simple cost-benefit exercise to determine whether it is worthwhile to seek out available information (which oftentimes may be freely available) which they incorporate into their expectations formation process. The strong version of the thesis, however, which derives from Muth's seminal paper (Muth, 1961), is vastly different from the above, is far more stringent in its assumptions, and generates quite remarkable and startling conclusions which carry far-reaching implications for macroeconomics and macroeconomic policy.

The essence of the strict version of the rational expectations thesis can be summarized relatively simply. If economic variables are determined by a relatively easily identifiable process, which recurs, then sooner or later intelligent economic agents will learn to recognize the process and will begin to form their expectations in the light of knowledge of that process. The recognition and identification of the process implies that they possess, implicitly at least, a formal model of the economy. Moreover, ultimately, the model which agents possess will coincide with the *true* model which governs the economy, for if the model which agents use is incorrect they will learn of its falsity – their expectations will be proved wrong and they will modify the model in the light of that proof. Adoption of the correct model analysis to process current information means that the subjective expectations so formed are essentially informed predictions of future events and as such are essentially the same as the predictions of the relevant economic theory. In other words the expected value of an economic variable coincides with the true mathematical expectations to be taken by that variable. A simple example may make this clear.

Consider the tossing of an unbiased six-sided die. The expected value from the toss of the die is simply

$$EV = \frac{1}{6} + \frac{2}{6} + \frac{3}{6} + \frac{4}{6} + \frac{5}{6} + \frac{6}{6} = 3.5$$

Suppose the die were to be tossed a hundred times and an economic agent asked to predict the eventual score. An agent familiar with probability theory (knowing the true model) would opt for 350. Moreover, an agent lacking a knowledge of probability theory would also learn from experience to predict something in the region of 350 if the experiment were to be repeated again and again. In particular, he would soon learn that an expectation of, say, 500 was incorrect and in addition was *systematically* overly high. Sooner or later agents will learn to recognize the process and their expectation will eventually coincide with the true mathematically expected value. Now, of course, the expectation may prove to be incorrect in the sense that the value 350 may never actually occur; none the less this mode of expectations formation is efficient in the sense that over time it will minimize the extent of any error (minimize the variance around the mean value) and moreover the expected value of any forecast error will itself be zero. It is in this sense that rational expectations formation is deemed to be the optimal mode of expectational behaviour.

A number of implications follow. First, any forecast error will be completely uncorrelated with any available information which the economic agent finds worthwhile to analyse since if this were not the case – if any correlation existed – then the rational agent should logically use it in deriving his initial expectation. Secondly, it is implicit in this process that whilst an agent may make forecast errors – his expectation proves incorrect – he will not make systematic expectational errors. Thus forecast errors which remain are essentially random, that is, they possess a mean value of zero and reveal no discernible pattern.

Few people would be inclined to object to the sense of rational expectations in the case of our simple die experiment discussed above. However, the major implications derived from the hypothesis assume similar behaviour upon the part of economic agents with respect to the progress of the macroeconomy as a whole. That is to say, it is assumed that economic agents – and especially agents in labour markets – ultimately learn the true model of the economy and form expectations of interest rate movements, price movements and so on in the light of changes in aggregate demand which influence real wages – and hence their own behaviour. Moreover, in the case of changes in the level of aggregate demand arising from government macroeconomic policy the modification of agents' behaviour in the light of their expectations is such as to negate the impact of government policy. Stabilization policy is rendered impotent. This is what is referred to as the policy ineffectiveness proposition arising out of rational expectations theorizing.

As we shall see below, the assumption of rational expectations, and its implications for macroeconomic policy are not without their critics. For the moment let us explicitly incorporate expectations into our Phillips curve model.

The Role of Inflationary Expectations

At the heart of the *expectations augmented Phillips curve* were three assumptions, one of which was consistent with the original Phillips/Lipsey formulation, two of which questioned fundamental tenets of the Phillips/Lipsey versions. These assumptions were:

(1) At the market clearing wage there will always be a certain amount of recorded unemployment which is voluntary and/or frictional in type. This level of unemployment has come to be known as the *natural rate of unemployment*. Since it is determined by institutional factors such as the presence (or absence) of minimum wage legislation, institutional barriers to factor mobility, social security arrangements and so on, it can be shifted in the longer run by labour market policies.

(2) The Phillips/Lipsey model generally emphasized money wages as being the target variable for agents in the labour market. Friedman/Phelps argued that this was an unreasonable proposition. Workers would bargain in real rather than money terms. To assume that they bargained in money terms is tantamount to arguing that money illusion is a persistent feature of the labour market.

(3) The Phillips/Lipsey formulation had the rate of change of money wages as dependent on the level of unemployment. The Friedman/Phelps approach suggested that the level of unemployment was dependent on the real wage rate rather than vice versa.

The reformulation of the Phillips curve once these criticisms are taken into account can alter the basic relationship fundamentally. If for the moment it is assumed that prices are set as a mark-up on wages and, further, that productivity change is zero, then

$$\dot{P}_t = \dot{W}_t \tag{13.6}$$

The obvious question now is, what determines $\dot{W}_t$? Because workers are assumed to bargain in real terms, they must make some allowance in their bargain for any changes in prices which they expect to occur over the contract period. Thus, if they agree on a wage deal to last for a twelve-month period, some allowance will be made for price changes which are expected to occur during the coming year ($\dot{P}_t^e$) as well as excess demand in the labour market (as proxied by U) that is,

$$\dot{W}_t = f(U_t, \dot{P}_t^e) \tag{13.7}$$

or taking a more formal specification, and substituting $\dot{P}_t$ for $\dot{W}_t$,

$$\dot{P}_t = \alpha \dot{P}_t^e - \beta(U_t - U_{Nt}) \tag{13.8}$$

where $\dot{P}_t$ is the actual rate of change of prices, $\dot{P}_t^e$ the expected rate of change of prices, U_t the actual level of unemployment and U_{Nt} the 'natural' rate of unemployment. If for the moment it is assumed that $\alpha = 1$, and therefore that expected inflation is fully incorporated into actual price (and wage) changes, then the important result which follows is:

$$\dot{P}_t - \dot{P}_t^e = -\beta(U_t - U_{Nt}) \tag{13.9}$$

or

$$U_t - U_{Nt} = -\frac{1}{\beta}(\dot{P}_t - \dot{P}_t^e) \tag{13.10}$$

In other words, *unemployment will only diverge from its natural rate if there exists a discrepancy between actual and anticipated inflation rates.* When actual inflation is equal to expected inflation, unemployment will be steady at its natural rate. When, however, *unanticipated* inflation is present in the system, (i.e. P_t and $\dot{P}_t^e$ differ) unemployment can diverge from its natural rate.

This natural rate hypothesis can be explained more intuitively by reference to figure 13.5. If the movement begins at point *a* with a zero rate of price inflation which is *fully anticipated*, then unemployment would by definition be at its *natural rate* U_N. Suppose now that the authorities decide to expand aggregate demand by inducing a rightward shift in *IS* and/or *LM* which pushes *AD* to the right. The outcome of this will be assumed to be a 5 per cent expansion of the money supply. If the basic quantity theory identity is accepted, then actual prices will rise in proportion to the expansion of the money supply as long as velocity remains constant. What will happen to real output and employment? According to the Phillips/Lipsey analysis, *real* output will rise, unemployment will fall, and movement will take place along the Phillips curve S_0, with equilibrium being established at *b*. For this to be a stable equilibrium, however, money illusion must be present, since what is implied is that labour supply has increased in response to a rise in money wages whilst real wages remain unchanged. In the Friedman model, however, workers bargain in real terms and set money wage demands according to the expected rate of inflation. Thus, assume

$$\dot{P}_t^e = \alpha \dot{P}_{t-1} \tag{13.11}$$

If the assumption is retained that $\alpha = 1$, full adjustment takes place in the period following any inflation. In terms of figure 13.5, wage bargains are struck in $t - 1$ on the basis of an expected inflation rate of zero. Thus, as money wages rise this is initially perceived as an increase in real wages (since it is deflated by $\dot{P}e = 0$) and labour supply increases. Once it becomes obvious, however, that prices are increasing at the same rate as wages, and that the real wage is in fact unchanged, the additional labour is withdrawn and unemployment returns to U_N. If nothing else changes, inflation will remain

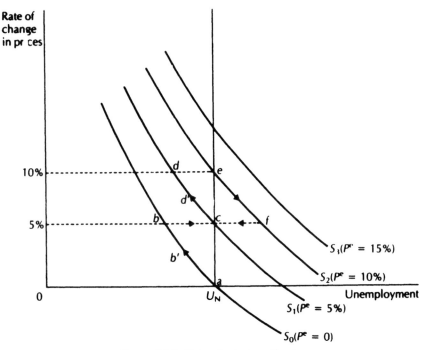

Figure 13.5 Natural rate hypothesis

stable at 5 per cent. If, however, the authorities attempt to raise real output again by monetary expansion the process is repeated with an initial shift from c to d on the short-run Phillips curve S_2, and ultimately a return to point e.

As originally formulated, this natural rate hypothesis suggests the following fundamental conclusions:

(1)   There is no long-run trade-off between inflation and unemployment.

(2)   Any trade-off which exists is entirely transient.

(3)   It follows therefore that demand management policies can have no long-run effect on real output and employment, but instead only influence monetary variables (prices, wage rates and interest rates).

(4)   The natural rate of unemployment can only be changed in the longer run by supply side policies designed to improve the flexibility and efficiency of labour markets.

(5)   Any attempt to use demand management policy to maintain unemployment permanently below (above) the natural rate will simply result in explosive inflation (deflation). This follows from the configuration of the Phillips curves, that is, the asymptotic approach to the vertical axis.

Since the natural rate hypothesis can explain the coincidence of rising inflation and unemployment, and the apparent shifting of the Phillips curve,[2] many commentators

2 As figure 13.5 is constructed, adjustments take place in the manner $a \rightarrow b \rightarrow c \rightarrow d \rightarrow e$. In practice, one is however likely to observe something consistent with $a \rightarrow b' \rightarrow c \rightarrow d' \rightarrow e$ (and vice versa for reductions) such that any combination of inflation and unemployment could be observed.

have accepted the fundamentals of the analysis (although there might be disagreement over what the natural rate of unemployment is for any given economy). Clearly, however, much depends on the role of expectations. The absence of a long-run trade-off rests upon full adjustment being made for any discrepancy between actual and anticipated inflation, and the duration of any disequilibrium is determined by the length of time it takes for expectations to catch up with reality. These are issues which will now be investigated further. First, however, the attention of the reader is drawn to the similarity of this analysis with that revolving around figure 13.1, where it was discussed whether AS would be positively sloped or vertical. One important reason for a positively sloped AS was in a situation where expectations of inflation lagged behind reality. This is the analogue of the Phillips relation discussed here.

Output, Inflation and Adaptive Expectations

In developing the natural rate hypothesis above, it was assumed in equation 13.11 that expectations lagged behind reality by one period; since it was assumed that $\alpha = 1$, any past changes in inflation are fully adjusted for within one period. A more sophisticated formulation would permit agents to make mistakes in forecasting inflation and to learn from those mistakes. If therefore individuals made an error in forecasting the price level in the previous period, they would learn from that error in preparing their current forecast of inflation. This is the simple *error learning process* of expectations formation, which postulates that agents form their expectations *adaptively*. Thus, if the following formula was chosen

$$P_t^e - P_{t-1}^e = \lambda(P_{t-1} - P_{t-1}^e) \tag{13.12}$$

the individual would be allowed to revise his forecast of the price level (P_t^e) by some fraction of the error which he made in forecasting the price level in $t - 1$. The adjustment which he would make is determined by the coefficient λ, where $0 < \lambda < 1$. Equation 13.12 can be arranged to:

$$P_t^e = \lambda P_{t-1} + (1 - \lambda)P_{t-1}^e \tag{13.13}$$

Since, analogously,

$$P_{t-1}^e = \lambda P_{t-2} + (1 - \lambda)P_{t-2}^e \tag{13.14}$$

$$P_{t-n}^e = \lambda P_{t-n-1} + (1 - \lambda)P_{t-n-1}^e \tag{13.15}$$

then backward substitution to eliminate P_{t-1}^e, P_{t-2}^e, P_{t-3}^e, ..., P_{t-n}^e yields

$$\begin{aligned} P_t^e = \lambda P_{t-1} + \lambda(1 - \lambda)P_{t-2} + \lambda(1 - \lambda)^2 P_{t-3} \\ + \ldots + \lambda(1 - \lambda)^n P_{t-n-1}^e \end{aligned} \tag{13.16}$$

Clearly, since $0 < \lambda < 1$, the further one goes back into the past the smaller is $(1 - \lambda)^n$ and the less important is P_{t-n} in determining the forecast of P_t^e; that is, the weights decline geometrically. The general form for this system of expectations formation could be written as:

$$Pt = \lambda \sum_{i=0}^{n} (1 - \lambda)^i P_{t-n-1} \tag{13.17}$$

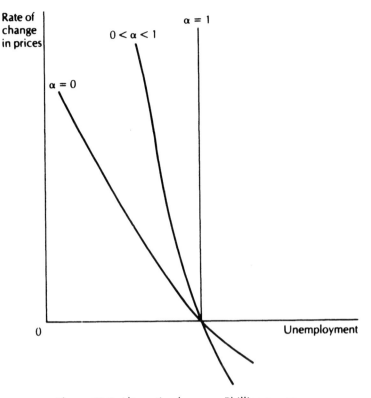

Figure 13.6 Alternative long-run Phillips curves

Substitution of 13.13 and 13.8 yields an adaptive expectations augmented Phillips curve of

$$P_t = \alpha\lambda P_{t-1} + \alpha(1 - \lambda)P^e_{t-1} + \beta(U_t - U_{Nt}) \tag{13.18}$$

If expectations are formed in this fashion they will always lag behind reality and a short-run trade-off between inflation and unemployment will exist. Furthermore, if $\alpha = 1$ full adjustment will take place and the long-run Phillips curve will be vertical. The possibility exists, however, of $0 < \alpha < 1$, in which case the long-run Phillips curve will have a negative slope and a trade-off could exist, even in the long run. If $\alpha = 0$, then the short-run and long-run Phillips curves coincide. These possibilities are outlined in figure 13.6.

The issue of which of these curves is the actual long-run Phillips curve is far from being an academic question, since alternative configurations are consistent with alternative configurations of the aggregate supply curve. It seems quite implausible to contend that $\alpha = 0$ since this means that money illusion persists in the long run, a proposition which would find few adherents. More plausibly one might argue that $0 < \alpha < 1$ such that incomplete adjustment takes place, permitting some degree of long-run trade-off.

What we have provided is a more rigorous formulation of the adaptive expectations mechanism introduced in the previous section. One might, however, enquire as to why expectations of price level changes should lag behind reality. Why should adjustment fail to take place quickly? If expectations lag behind reality does it not imply money illusion? There may in fact be very good reasons why expectations lag behind reality thereby slowing up the process of adjustment to price level changes. As we saw in chapter 7, there may be a variety of institutional arrangements which protract adjustment, for instance the presence of implicit or explicit contracts. Moreover, agents in the labour market may have incomplete/imperfect information about what is actually happening. In a regime of relatively low and slowly changing inflation it may be felt that the costs of acquiring full information are not justified by the benefits of a marginally better inflation forecast. In a high-inflation environment this calculus will of course change since the benefits of better forecasts are higher, making the probability of full adjustment higher.

The adaptive expectations hypothesis therefore provides a view of expectations formation which has a certain plausibility. It argues that agents adapt to past mistakes in making forecasts of price level changes. If individuals do behave in this way then the Phillips curve trade-off between inflation and unemployment is preserved. This, however, is only so in the short run. In the long run expectations catch up with reality and the trade-off disappears.

Output, Inflation and Rational Expectations

Despite its inherent plausibility, the view that expectations are formed adaptively has been subject to a radical and fundamental attack over the last few years. This attack has been based on a number of objections to the concept.

(1)   The most compelling criticism perhaps is that if expectations are formed adaptively, the individual agent in the labour market (or his representative, the trade union) only takes account of past price changes and takes no account of current events. Thus it implies that, for example, a devaluation or an incomes policy will not affect the formation of price expectations. Clearly this is consistent with non-rational behaviour.

(2)   If expectations are formed adaptively, and if the rate of inflation is increasing, then expectations will always lag behind the inflation rate. Thus no allowance is made for the individual agents adjusting fully for past mistakes. Again, it might be objected that it is essentially non-rational behaviour which would lead an agent to *systematically* make errors in his forecasts of inflation.

(3)   No explanation is given of how the value of λ is set, that is, what determines the fraction of past forecast error which influences current forecasts. Fleming (1976) has suggested that this might be directly related to the size of previous errors – large errors leading to a large λ, low errors leading to a low λ. With adaptive expectations the individual uses information in a mechanistic fashion. There is no attempt to use information efficiently.

These criticisms, in particular the assertion that agents will not in general systematically make mistakes since this is inconsistent with optimizing behaviour, led to the refinement of the idea of *rational expectations*. Basically the rational expectations doctrine asserts that agents have an incentive to acquire, and use efficiently, information about the variables which they are forecasting. In the case of a labour union preparing for wage negotiations, account would be taken not only of current price changes but also of the authorities' current posture on fiscal and monetary policy, the probability of an incomes policy being imposed, and so on. Moreover, this information will be used in a very deliberate way since the individual is assumed to have invested resources in learning about the way in which the economy functions. If expectations are formed in this manner, the implications for stabilization policy differ radically from those associated with adaptive expectations. With rational expectations not even a short-run trade-off is possible unless agents are taken by surprise when some policy action results in an unexpected change in prices.

Credit for the refinement of the concept of rational expectations and its implications for economic policy is most usually ascribed to Lucas (1972, 1973, 1975), Sargent and Wallace (1975) and Barro (1976), although the concept (and some of its implications for policy), was originally introduced by Muth (1960, 1961).

Muth (1961) summarized rational expectations as follows:

> Expectations of firms (or more generally the subjective probability distribution of outcomes) tend to be distributed for the same information set, about the prediction of the theory (or the 'objective' probability distributions of outcomes). (p. 316)

In other words, the rational agent will obtain information about the 'objective' probability distributions of outcomes associated with particular policy actions based on the relevant economic theory, and he will use this information to generate expectations about the variables in which he is interested. If the information is used efficiently, the individual's predictions or expectations will turn out to be the same as the relevant theories.

Thus, rather than taking information on past values of a particular variable and using this mechanistically to predict future values (as the adaptive expectations hypothesis implies), the agent uses past information to discern regularities in the pattern of economic activity, such that he can make efficient use of current information. Suppose again that an agent is forecasting inflation. His expectation of the price level can be written as:

$$P_t^e = E(P_t | I_{t-1}) \tag{13.19}$$

that is, the expected price level will be equal to his forecast of the actual price level which is conditional on all relevant information available at the time the forecast is made. Given this formulation, the difference between actual and expected price levels turns out to be:

$$P_t - P_t^e = P_{t-1} - E(P_t | I_{t-1}) = \varepsilon_t \tag{13.20}$$

where ε_t is some random forecast error. The important point to note about ε_t is that it is random. As such it is unpredictable. When making his forecast of the price level, the best guess that the individual can make about ε_t is that it will turn out to be zero.

Thus, if an agent is aware that there exists a systematic relationship between the rate of growth of the money supply in the past and the current price level of the form:

$$P_t = M_{t-1} + \sigma_t \tag{13.21}$$

where σ_t is some random term, he will exploit this knowledge in forming his expectations about price changes such that

$$P_t^e = M_t^e \tag{13.22}$$

If the monetary authorities follow a simple rules approach to monetary policy such that

$$(M_t - M_{t-1}) = \gamma \tag{13.23}$$

then P_t would always be predicted with perfect accuracy except for the influence of any unexpected (and by definition unpredictable) shocks. Therefore,

$$P_t - P_t^e = M_t - M_t^e + \sigma_t \tag{13.24}$$

Substituting this back into the Phillips curve, when M_t^e is set equal to M_t,

$$U_t - U_{Nt} = -\frac{1}{\beta}(\sigma_t) \tag{13.25}$$

In other words, *the only thing which can generate a deviation of unemployment from its natural rate is some unexpected and unpredictable shock to the system.* The staggering implication which this has for demand management policy is that there exists no systematic trade-off between inflation and employment – *even in the short run.* Thus shifts in *AD* only result in movements up and down a vertical *AS* curve. In figure 13.1 a policy-induced shift in *AD* from AD_1 to AD_2 to AD_3 simply means a movement $a \rightarrow c \rightarrow e$. In this schema the only way in which the authorities could alter unemployment and cause it to deviate from its natural rate is to use demand management policy in a wholly unpredictable and capricious manner such that all government action is consistently unexpected.[3] This is the case of the *surprise supply function* which was outlined in chapter 7 and which can usefully be re-examined here. In figure 7.9 *AS** is set by the natural rate of unemployment. The authorities could announce a policy of demand contraction, indicating their intention to shift AD_1 to AD_2. Agents acting rationally on this information revise their expectations of inflation and shift from *a* to *b*. Instead of actually contracting demand however, the authorities could do the opposite and shift AD_1 to AD_3. Employers reacting to actual prices respond to a fall in real wages by increasing their demand for labour. Employees on the other hand acting on the basis of expectations geared to AD_2 interpret any increase in money wages as an increase in real wages and increase labour supply. Consequently, movement takes place from point *b* towards point *c*. Once however it is realized that prices are in fact rising more quickly than wages, labour supply contracts and movement is towards *d*. The locus *b* to *c* would be called a surprise supply function, because it relies on the dissemination of misleading information which agents act upon, and are subsequently surprised by. The point is, however, that since agents act rationally they will sooner or later discover the facts regarding misinformation and act accordingly. Furthermore, such capricious behaviour could not be followed systematically otherwise any 'rules' which were being followed would be discovered, and agents would condition their behaviour accordingly.

The implications of this line of reasoning are striking, to say the least, and the basis of the argument must be made absolutely clear. In general terms it is assumed that individuals are optimizing agents and that they therefore have an incentive to acquire and use information efficiently. Thus in an uncertain world, knowledge about economic regularities will be exploited in such a way that the implications of, for example, changes in government policy are quickly processed and acted upon. As Kantor

---

3 This conclusion follows even if a more sophisticated money supply rule is allowed for.

(1979) puts it, 'rational expectations are profit maximizing expectations'. Individual agents are aware of how the system operates and cannot be systematically fooled.

If this is a reasonable representation of reality, it has devastating consequences for demand management policy and policy evaluation. In the case of the former it means that monetary and fiscal policy cannot influence output, even in the short run. A decision, for example, to increase the rate of growth of the money supply will feed through immediately to inflationary expectations thereby affecting monetary variables but leaving real variables unaffected. The only role ascribed to monetary and fiscal policy is one of reducing uncertainty by providing a stable financial environment. In other words a rules approach to policy should be adopted whereby the rate of growth of the money supply is fixed, and a target is set for public borrowing which is consistent with this growth rate. It also means, as Lucas (1976) pointed out, that the conventional process of policy simulation–evaluation is undermined. One can no longer simulate the effects of various macroeconomic strategies because the exercise in effect assumes fixed expectations. The rational expectations doctrine revolves around the assertion that in fact expectations can be altered quite quickly. One cannot therefore compare simulations without allowing for changes in expectations.

Doubts Regarding the Rational Expectations Hypothesis

From this highly simplified presentation of the rational expectations thesis, the 'revolutionary' nature of its policy implications should be clear. They are quite distinctly neo- classical rather than neo-Keynesian and indeed go rather further in their denial of the role of stabilization policy than many 'orthodox monetarists' might be willing to go. The policy prescriptions associated with the analysis have an attraction of quite compelling simplicity in much the same way as those of the classical model did. Although there are some very obvious kindred features in the two systems (most obviously the real/monetary dichotomy, and the recommendation of non-discretionary intervention), the rational expectations thesis has a rather more sophisticated superstructure than the classical thesis.

As well as the compelling simplicity of its prescriptions, the approach has attractions because it conforms so closely with the predilections of *homo economicus*. It assumes that individuals are rational. It assumes that they have an interest in acquiring information and use that information efficiently in order to avoid making costly mistakes. It assumes that in the event that mistakes are made, they will not be systematic. It assumes that agents will not knowingly leave profitable opportunities unexploited. In sum it argues that agents are self-interested and act accordingly.

The thesis has not, however, been given anything like unqualified support. Criticism of the approach has centred on the following issues.

Ability of Agents to Process Relevant Information

Interpreted literally, the rational expectations (RE) hypothesis asserts that agents have the ability to process information in a manner which permits them to forecast all future paths of the economy. As Arrow (1978) puts it:

> In the rational expectations hypothesis, economic agents are required to be superior statisticians capable of analysing the future general equilibria of the economy. (p. 160)

In other words a literal interpretation would mean that individual agents are sophisticated forecasters themselves rather than enjoying 'limited powers of information
acquisition'.

Begg (1982) counters this criticism by contending that such a strong assumption is
unnecessary. The information would in the main be processed by 'specialist' bodies,
individuals and institutions whose comparative advantage lies in this practice and,
indeed, who can process the changes in policy very quickly. Furthermore, Begg contends that it is not necessary to interpret the RE hypothesis in such a stringent manner.
All that is necessary to obtain the RE results is to assume that individuals do not make
systematic errors in their forecasting.

Costs of Acquisition of Relevant Information

A second criticism of the RE model is that information collection is a costly exercise
and this in itself will limit the access which agents have to relevant information. If
agents acquire information in an optimizing manner, they would presumably obtain
information up to the point where the marginal cost of acquisition is equal to the marginal benefit. Clearly, the higher the marginal cost of acquisition, the less information
will be collected.

This is certainly correct. A defendant of the RE approach might, however, respond
by making two points. First, the marginal cost of information acquisition may be very
low indeed. Economic forecasts are widely publicized and disseminated. Furthermore, the unit of acquisition may be a labour union for which the benefit/cost ratio will
be very much higher than a typical individual agent.

A variant on this argument is the point that agents, or groups of agents, might have
differential access to information. Thus an agent may be much better informed about
what is happening in his own market than what is happening at the macro level. This is
certainly likely to be the case. According to Begg, this need not undermine the RE
approach; all it does is point to the need for models which emphasize differential access
and explore further the implications of such behaviour for expectations formation. It
is ultimately still consistent with agents forming expectations using all relevant information which they have on hand. The other way in which the argument may be cast is
that government may have better access to information than non-government agents,
which may provide them with a basis for responding more quickly and possibly even
allow them a handle for stabilization policy. Governments invariably do have better
access to relevant data since they tend to generate most of it. The lead time, however,
in most cases is very short – probably too short to give them a stabilization handle.

Adjustment Lags and Credibility Problems

Agents may not respond instantaneously to any given change in the 'forcing variables'
of the economic system. This may be true of many markets, and indeed the implications of different markets clearing at different speeds will be considered further. In the
context of stabilization policy in a RE model there may be an adjustment lag associated with the time taken by individuals to realize that the 'rule' governing policy has
changed. Thus, for example, when the incoming Conservative administration of June
1979 announced the medium-term financial strategy, there may have been a time lag
before the precise implications of this change in policy rule were processed. This
time lag might also have been lengthened by a credibility problem; that is, agents may

simply not have believed that a given preannounced monetary and fiscal regime would be maintained. This would occur if for instance it were widely believed that the probability of a policy reversal or 'U-turn' were high or because the probability of changes in some other forcing variable were high, for example a widespread expectation of an incomes policy. In this event, forecast inflation might be largely unaffected by changes in policy variables.

It is widely accepted that credibility can be a problem. The response of proponents of RE however is that this merely strengthens the case for preannouncement of policy intent, and regular statements to reinforce any particular policy stance.

The three previous criticisms relate to the assumption of rational expectations *per se*. To obtain the most devastating results for stabilization policy, one must combine an assumption of rational expectations with an assumption of efficient markets, that is, markets which clear relatively quickly and tend to equilibrium. The combination of these two assumptions is the hallmark of the new classical school. In addition to the criticisms of rational expectations *per se*, one can also object to the assumption of efficient markets and continuous market clearing, as follows.

Differential Flexibility of Prices across Markets

One of the most serious general criticisms of the RE hypothesis is its assumption that markets clear quickly and efficiently. Whilst this may certainly be true of assets markets (an issue explored further in chapter 15), where the product being traded is very homogeneous, transactions costs are relatively low, the market is highly integrated, forward markets are highly developed and variations in the expected inflation rate affect forward prices very quickly, it may not be true in product and labour markets. In practice product and labour markets may be subject to quantity rather than price adjustment, in which case excess supplies could persist for relatively long periods. In the case of product markets this will vary with the nature of the product. Thus where perishables are concerned, price is likely to adjust relatively quickly compared with durables. As was seen in chapter 7, there are a number of well-documented reasons as to why labour markets may be quantity rather than price adjusters such that excess supply may persist for relatively long periods.

Some of the points made in chapter 7 can be repeated. As was noted there, the labour market is segmented by both occupational and geographical classifications. Since there are costs associated with occupational and geographical mobility, adjustment can be slow. One might argue that this is itself the outcome of market imperfections such as externalities (because the social costs of retraining or moving region are lower than private costs) or entry barriers (due perhaps to labour union apprenticeship rules); the solution is to correct the distortions present, by for example subsidizing retraining and/or relocation, relaxing union rules on apprenticeship, and so on. It was also noted in chapter 7 that the existence of contracts could induce wage rigidity. Although from a macroeconomic viewpoint such arrangements could be viewed as being inherently inefficient, from a microeconomic viewpoint there were justifications for their existence.

The Nature of Unemployment

It is implicit in most rational expectations models that unemployment is entirely voluntary. The labour market is assumed therefore to clear continuously, with recorded unemployment being largely those engaged in 'search'. The property does not necessarily follow from an assumption of rational expectations; in fact some RE models permit involuntary unemployment (see Begg, 1982). The presumption is widespread, however, and it is controversial to say the least. It implies that individual agents view labour supply as an intertemporal decision. If the current real wage is 'too low' relative to what can be obtained from state support schemes, agents will engage in search for higher paid employment. If no such employment appears to be available, the agent will consume leisure now when its relative price is low, with a view to working later (for higher real wages) when the relative price of labour is higher. Some of the shortcomings of this view of unemployment have already been examined in chapter 7, and its relevance to current UK unemployment will be considered in chapter 20.

Empirical Evidence on Expectations

By now it should be clear that the manner in which expectations are formed has a crucial bearing on the existence or otherwise of a trade-off between inflation and unemployment, and in turn on the scope for stabilization policy. What light, if any, can empirical evidence shed on the issue?

There are very real problems in testing propositions relating to expectations formation. This is so for several reasons. First, expectations are essentially unobservable. With a few exceptions (such as sealed bids in an auction), it is rarely the case that one can directly observe expectations. Second, even if one can observe expectations, should one directly test the *assumption* of rational expectations, or the *prediction* of a zero trade-off between inflation and unemployment? Third, if one does test the trade-off proposition, one is essentially testing a joint hypothesis of both the natural rate hypothesis *and* the way in which expectations are formed. For instance, suppose one tests the zero trade-off proposition and rejects it. Is the hypothesis being rejected because expectations are not formed rationally, or because the natural rate hypothesis does not hold?

Despite these difficulties quite a number of tests relating to the formation of expectations have now been completed, both direct tests of expectations regimes, and tests of the natural rate hypothesis. Direct tests have focused on the way in which information is used and have attempted to establish whether information is used efficiently. This work does not provide convincing support for the assumption of rational expectations. For example, Aiginger (1980) summarizes a number of studies which compare 'expert' (that is, professional) forecasters with non-professional forecasters. Two points are particularly interesting. First, there appeared to be evidence of inefficiency in the use of information in the inflation forecasts of professionals; second, the professional forecasts appeared to outperform non-professional forecasts. The former finding sits uncomfortably with the proposition that individuals fully exploit all available information, the latter finding sits uncomfortably with the proposition that in a RE world 'we are all experts'. Non-RE proponents take these findings, in particular the latter, as evidence of the fact that different groups of agents have differential access to information, and different abilities to process a given information set. By contrast RE proponents would argue that empirical evidence which relies upon survey information, as these tests do, is inherently unreliable.

Tests of the trade-off between inflation and unemployment have proceeded in two different directions. Early work attempted to estimate the coefficient in equation 13.18;

more recent work has attempted to disentangle anticipated from unanticipated policy, and attempted to test the proposition that only unanticipated policy has any impact on real output levels.

Early studies for both the UK and the USA predicted the value of to be less than unity (see Solow, 1969, and Parkin, 1970). Subsequent work completed in the 1970s for both economies provides a good deal of evidence for a unity coefficient. Gordon (1976) explains this by reference to a threshold effect – once inflation accelerates beyond a given rate of increase, agents pay more attention to ensuring that full compensation is sought for expected price changes. Despite this empirical support, the natural rate hypothesis has not gone unchallenged. In particular the coexistence of rising inflation and rising unemployment over long periods in the 1970s has attracted much attention. In the same way as efforts to maintain unemployment below the natural rate stimulate accelerating inflation, any maintenance of unemployment above the natural rate should stimulate accelerating deflation. This seems to conflict with the evidence. Opponents of the natural rate hypothesis view this as evidence of its fundamental weakness, whilst adherents of the hypothesis argue that in fact the natural rate has been rising over recent years.

Barro (1979) approached the problem in a different way. He distinguished between anticipated and unanticipated monetary policy, the distinction between the two being made by reference to a model of the money supply in the USA. He related both to changes in real output and concluded that only unanticipated policy exerted an impact on real output. However, this data set was also examined by Mishkin (1982), who assumed a different lag structure in the operation of monetary policy and concluded that in fact anticipated policy had a much more dramatic impact on real output than unanticipated policy!

One final point with regard to empirical work might be noted. If the new classical description of the world (that is, RE with efficient markets) is appropriate we ought to observe random deviations of real output, and in unemployment especially in recent years, we find serial correlation, that is, the persistence of relatively high levels of unemployment from one period to the next. This persistence is not easily explained in an RE context.

In summary, there is as yet no conclusive support for the assumption that expectations are formed rationally, although there is some evidence which can be viewed as consistent with the natural rate hypothesis. In chapters 19 and 20 we will consider the applicability of these ideas to recent inflation and unemployment experience in the UK.

Concluding Comments

In chapters 8 to 12 it was seen that there were a number of issues which could be cast in monetarist–Keynesian terms, one such issue being the determinants of inflation. This chapter has considered in more detail the possible initiating forces behind an inflation, and the dynamics of the inflationary process via a detailed analysis of the role of expectations formation. An analysis of the initiating forces is important since this determines to a large degree the policy prescriptions which one makes. As will be seen in chapter 19, a narrow demand pull view might dictate complete reliance on demand management, whilst a cost push view would see incomes policy of some form as being a necessary component of anti-inflation policy.

The reintroduction of expectations facilitated a clearer analysis of the possible limitations of demand management analysis, and it was found that many of the issues which were raised when the labour market was discussed in chapter 7 were again relevant. As was noted in that chapter, the way in which the labour market responds to various stimuli is at the heart of much current macroeconomic controversy. Clearly in this regard the part played by expectations formation is central.

Further Reading

There exists a voluminous literature on the determinants of inflation which has developed over the last thirty years or so. The survey paper by Bronfenbrenner and Holzman (1963) summarizes developments to that date, and analyses a variety of models of cost push and demand pull inflation. The survey paper by Laidler and Parkin (1975) eschews the distinction between demand pull and cost push, and instead emphasizes the anticipated/unanticipated distinction as their starting-point, which permits them to concentrate more fully on the role of expectations. Useful collections of essays are Heathfield (1979) and Laidler (1975) whilst Laidler (1982) provides an authoratative analysis of all aspects of the literature.

Phillips's original (1958) paper has been reprinted in a number of volumes and can be found, along with Lipsey's (1961) paper, in Surrey (1975). Friedman's (1968) paper is also easily accessible. Non-technical introductions to the adaptive/rational expectations literature are given by Mayes (1981), Maddock and Carter (1982) and Shaw (1983a). A survey of the development of thought on rational expectations is provided by Kantor (1979), whilst one of the most authoritative reviews of the literature up to its year of publication is given in Gordon (1976). A number of texts on expectations have now been published, the most easily accessible and digestible being Shaw (1983a), and Minford (1992). More advanced treatments may be found in Maddock and Carter (1985) and Attfield, Demery and Duck (1985). Notable volumes of collected readings are Fischer (1980), Lucas and Sargent (1981) and Lucas (1981). Fischer (1980) is a collection of papers covering theoretical and empirical aspects of expectations and stabilization policy; Lucas and Sargent (1981) concentrates on econometric applications and problems with rational expectations; and Lucas (1981) provides a collection of the author's papers on the subject. A masterful, non-technical overview of the development of thought on expectations in a macroeconomic context is given by Laidler (1986). Finally, a most interesting summary and extensive annotated bibliography is contained within Redman (1992).

14

Internal and External Balance

The closed economy system (whether Keynesian or neo-classical) is undoubtedly a valuable framework for analytical purposes. Clearly, however, it has one very obvious shortcoming, namely that *autarky* (that is, no trade) is as likely to exist as perfect competition. In other words, countries engage in the process of international specialization and exchange – or more accurately, individuals exchange across national frontiers. Once allowance is made for a traded goods sector, a link is provided between the erstwhile closed economy and the rest of the world, a link through which economic impulses may be transmitted.

The extent to which the traded goods sector influences the domestic economy depends of course on the size of that sector relative to total output. For example, exports and imports account for around 30 per cent of GNP in the UK, whereas for the USA the figure is closer to 10 per cent. Other things being equal, therefore, economic activity in the UK would be expected to be more susceptible to external influences than in the USA.[1]

In this and the following chapter the models will be extended to allow for a foreign trade sector, whilst their relevance to UK experience will be evaluated in chapter 21. Initially, some basic principles of exchange rate determination and balance of payments accounting will be reviewed. Following this, the external sector will be integrated into the *IS/LM* framework. The role of domestic expenditure policies on external balance will be examined, and finally demand management policies and exchange rate regimes will be analysed.

The Foreign Exchange Market

In order to participate in international exchange, individuals, corporate bodies and governmental agencies must have access to internationally acceptable media of exchange. This may involve the acquisition of some generally acceptable asset (like gold or the US dollar), or it may involve the acquisition of the currency of the country with which one is trading. Either way a mechanism for the conversion of domestic currency is necessary. This mechanism is of course the *foreign exchange market*.

---

1 Other things are, however, rarely equal. In the present context, although the ratio of traded goods to GNP may be relatively low in the USA, in evaluating 'openness' the special role of the dollar as a key currency in the international monetary system would have to be borne in mind.

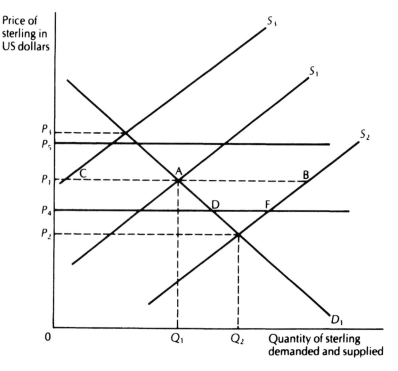

Figure 14.1 Exchange rate determination

In this market, a demand for (supply of) foreign exchange (domestic currency) will be generated by importers, whilst a supply of (demand for) foreign exchange (domestic currency) will be provided by exporters.

Take, for example, the case illustrated in figure 14.1. Here a two-country world is assumed, the trading partners being the UK and USA. 'Foreign exchange' from the UK's standpoint refers therefore to dollars. D_1 and S_1 are the demand for and supply of sterling respectively. Both are expressed as a function of the price of sterling in terms of dollars, or the *nominal exchange rate*.[2]

It is clear from the slope of the curves that the volume of sterling supplied per period is positively related to its dollar price, while sterling demand is inversely related to price. As the dollar price of sterling rises, the home currency price of imports will fall, the ensuing expansion in the demand for imports resulting in an increased supply of sterling. A rise in the dollar price of sterling would however raise the dollar price of exports, stimulate a contraction in the demand for exports, and hence a contraction in the demand for sterling.[3]

---

2 The analysis is conducted entirely by reference to the *nominal exchange rate*, that is, the spot price of a currency in the foreign exchange market. Note, however, that in evaluating exchange rate movements through time much greater emphasis is placed on the *real exchange rate*, and the *effective exchange rate*. The real exchange rate is the nominal exchange rate adjusted for changes in price levels. The effective exchange rate is a trade weighted exchange rate, which is therefore more responsive to movements in the exchange rates of major trading partners compared with relatively minor trading partners. It is also possible to have a *real effective exchange rate*.

3 It is possible for the supply curve to be inversely related to the nominal exchange rate: this occurs when the home demand for imports is price inelastic. Given this condition, as the home currency price of imports rises, demand contracts less than in proportion to the price rise, and the volume of home currency on the market actually increases. For further analysis, see Milner and Greenaway (1979, chapter 6).

Where demand and supply intersect the market clearing exchange rate is established, in this case at P_1. As in any other market, this price will alter with shifts in demand and supply, assuming there is no intervention on the part of the monetary authorities. If, for instance, an increase in real incomes in the UK stimulates an autonomous increase in the demand for imports, S_1 would shift to S_2. At the initial exchange rate, there is clearly excess supply and price falls from P_1 to P_2 to clear the market. The same analysis would apply *mutatis mutandis* if the initial disturbance were a fall in real incomes in the UK.

In principle, therefore, if the exchange rate is permitted to float freely there will be an automatic tendency towards a market clearing price. Adjustment to any autonomous shifts in the underlying import and export functions will be continuous. In reality of course exchange rates are rarely permitted to float freely. Frequently the monetary authorities view a particular value, or range of values, of the exchange rate as a policy target.

At one extreme the exchange rate could be fixed, for example at P_1 in figure 14.1. Under these circumstances no *appreciation* (that is, increase in price) or *depreciation* (decrease in price) would be permitted and the price of P_1 would be defended by official intervention. Thus in the event of a shift in supply from S_1 to S_2, rather than allow the exchange rate to depreciate to P_2 the authorities would soak up the excess supply by entering the foreign exchange market and purchasing AB of sterling, paying for this with holdings of dollars. In the event of a shift in supply to S_3, the opposite action would be taken. Instead of permitting the exchange rate to appreciate to P_3, the authorities would supply AC of sterling and acquire an equivalent volume of dollars, which would be added to their foreign exchange reserves.

Between these extremes of complete fixity and complete floating, there are many shades of flexibility which require varying degrees of management. For instance, the exchange rate may be maintained within present bands, such as P_4P_5. Intervention would then only occur when the rate threatened to fall below P_4 or rise above P_5. Management within pre-defined limits is a feature of many exchange rate systems, the European Monetary System being a good example.

The Balance of Payments

The balance of payments of a country is a systematic record of that country's international transactions. Abstracting from timing complications, it can be stated that the balance of payments will provide a monetary record of activities in the foreign exchange market over a given period.

Accounting conventions vary considerably from country to country (see Veil, 1975). Broadly speaking, however, three groups of transactions can be identified, namely *current transactions, capital transactions* and *balancing transactions*. The items which would typically be included in these accounts are listed in table 14.1. Note that the balance of payments is a systematic record of the value of the various transactions which a given country conducts with the rest of the world over a given period (usually one year). Thus when a balance of payments deficit or surplus is reported it is the nominal value of the imbalance which is reported, and indeed it is this magnitude which is important from a policy standpoint. In this respect the balance of payments is unambiguously a monetary phenomenon.

Whether the balance of payments is in surplus or deficit depends on whether the value of *credit* items in the current and capital accounts exceeds the value of *debit* items. Another way of stating this would be to say that it depends on whether *autonomous credits* exceed or fall short of *autonomous debits*. In stating it thus, it is assumed that all transactions recorded in the current and capital accounts are autonomous. This is not an uncontroversial assumption. As will be seen, there are occasions when monetary

TABLE 14.1
A Schematic Representation of the Balance of Payments

Credit	Debit
Current transactions	
Visible exports	Visible imports
Invisible exports	Invisible imports
Unilateral receipts	Unilateral payments
Capital transactions	
Official long-term inflows	Official long-term outflows
Official short-term inflows	Official short-term outflows
Private long-term inflows	Private long-term outflows
Private short-term inflows	Private short-term outflows
Balancing transactions	
Fall in official reserves	Increase in official reserves
Official foreign currency borrowing	Official foreign currency lending

policy is used deliberately to influence short-term capital flows which are potentially enormous. Frequently, for instance, nominal interest rates are raised to relatively high levels in deficit countries, in order to attract short-term capital flows. Since these transactions are policy induced it becomes difficult to draw the line between autonomous and *accommodating transactions*. For the purposes of this discussion this complication will be ignored (for the present anyway) such that we can classify all transactions in the balancing account as accommodating transactions.

The balancing account is, quite literally, those transactions which make the balance of payments balance. Clearly if a country runs a net deficit on current and capital accounts, this implies indebtedness to its trading partners. This indebtedness would be settled by accommodating payments. In this case foreign exchange reserves would be disbursed. Thus a deficit (surplus) on current and capital accounts will be matched by an equal reserve outflow (inflow) in the balancing account. Thus, although in an accounting sense the balance of payments will always balance, the overall deficit or surplus situation will be reflected in the volume (and sign) of accommodating finance.

In figure 14.1 it can be seen that *in principle* payments imbalance will only arise when there is some degree of exchange rate management. In the example where the exchange rate is held at P_1 following a shift in supply from S_1 to S_2, the distance AB gives an indication of the volume of accommodating finance, and of the magnitude of the balance of payments deficit. If, instead of being fixed, the exchange rate were maintained in the band P_4P_5, it would depreciate to P_4 and the resultant deficit would be DF rather than AB. If the exchange rate were free to float, abstracting from the problem of lags, it would depreciate to P_2 and no deficit would emerge.

From this relatively simple analysis *external balance* can therefore be identified as being a situation where there is a *net balance of zero on current and capital accounts.* In practice of course external balance may be rather more difficult to identify, in part due to difficulties associated with defining a time scale over which the accounts would be expected to balance, and in part because it necessitates some judgement about the relationship of external balance to internal balance. (This issue will be considered in greater detail when the UK balance of payments is analysed in chapter 21.) Using these definitions of the balance of payments and the exchange rate, we will now proceed to evaluate the implications of allowing for an external sector in our income determination models.

The Foreign Trade Sector and the Income Multiplier

Within the context of a simple *IS/LM* income determination model, exports are an injection into the system whilst imports are a withdrawal. The condition for equilibrium in the goods market within such a model is therefore revised to:

$$I + G + X = S + T + Z \tag{14.1}$$

where X and Z refer to *real* exports and *real* imports respectively. In the simplest models, real exports of goods and services would be regarded as exogenous (being determined by disposable income overseas) whilst real imports are positively related to the level of disposable income:

$$X = \bar{X} \tag{14.2}$$

$$Z = z Y_d \tag{14.3}$$

Substitution of equations 14.2 and 14.3 into equation 14.1 gives the equilibrium condition rewritten as:

$$\bar{I} + \bar{G} + X = s(Y_d) + t(Y) + z(Y_d) \tag{14.4}$$

Casual inspection of equation 14.4 reveals the first important implication of including a traded goods sector in a Keynesian *IS/LM* model, namely that the value of the multiplier changes. Specifically, a further leakage from the system has been included. Thus the multiplier of chapter 4 is extended to:

$$= \frac{1}{1 - b + bt + z - zt} \tag{14.5}$$

where b and t are, as before, the marginal propensity to consume and the marginal tax rate, whilst z is the *marginal propensity to import.*

In the same way as the inclusion of a government sector introduced an additional leakage which reduced the value of the multiplier, the inclusion of an overseas sector does likewise. The apparent simplicity of this result should not detract from its importance. Within a Keynesian framework, it has a significant impact on policy prescriptions. Clearly, if one is recommending a strategy founded on demand reflation, the implications of any injection of import demand have to be carefully considered. In an economy like the UK, for example, there have been occasions when the marginal propensity to import has been as high as 0.6 – that is to say, some 60 per cent of increased expenditure 'leaked' overseas. Such a

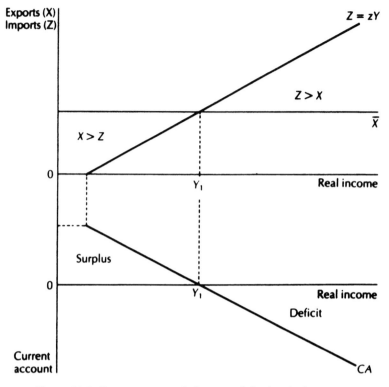

Figure 14.2 Current account balance and the level of income

situation is only sustainable in the short run and ultimately imposes a (balance of payments) constraint on expansion. This interpretation of the relationship between income expansion and the balance of payments has led one influential group to argue for general import controls to prevent additional expenditure from demand reflation in the UK from leaking overseas (see Cambridge Economic Policy Group, 1981). It is also this consideration which leads some commentators to prefer fiscal expansion via increased government expenditure, rather than via cuts in direct taxes.

It should be noted, however, that one important shortcoming of this simple multiplier model (and indeed policy prescriptions which follow from it) is that in a two-country or multicountry system exports of all countries are endogenized. There are therefore *responding effects* which must be considered – increased import demand generates income overseas, and ultimately increased demand for home exports. None the less, it generally remains true that the country initiating an income expansion will experience a worsening of its trade account despite an element of responding from abroad. This must follow when the overseas marginal propensity to import is less than one since under these circumstances only a fraction of the increase in income is respent. (For a formal demonstration of this point see Peacock and Shaw, 1976, pp. 48–9.) For the moment, responding will be ignored; the simplest possible case will be used to explore more fully the relationship between imports, exports and the level of income.

It must be emphasized that the simple income multiplier model deals with *real exports* and *real imports*. For policy purposes, however, it is the *value of exports relative to the value of imports*, measured in a common currency, which is the object of interest. In the event that, for a given level of real income, the value of exports (imports) exceeds the value of imports (exports) a balance of payments surplus (deficit) will be recorded. As will be seen in the next chapter, this apparent dichotomy between real and nominal exports and imports resulted, in the judgement of many neo-classical economists, in neglect of the monetary implications of the balance of payments. For the moment it must be remembered that in discussing balance of payments imbalance the magnitude is nominal.

Another, equally important, feature of this model which also may not be immediately obvious is that it only includes current transactions, that is, imports of goods and services which would be recorded in the current account of table 14.1. As will shortly be seen, this imposes important limitations on the policy conclusions of the model. However, although the simple income multiplier approach is restrictive, a number of interesting insights can be developed from it.

In the upper panel of figure 14.2, equality between the value of exports and the value of imports is associated with a unique level of real income Y_1. Income levels below (above) Y_1 result in an excess of exports (imports) over imports (exports). This information permits the derivation of a current account schedule in the lower panel (CA). The CA schedule is negatively related to the level of income, indicating that other things being equal (in particular the exchange rate), increases (decreases) in the level of real income will result in a tendency towards a deficit (surplus) on the current account. The slope of this schedule is determined by the marginal propensity to import, higher values being associated with steeper CAs.

Figure 14.3 therefore presents diagrammatically the deductions made above with respect to the marginal propensity to import (MPM) and the foreign trade multiplier. The higher the value of the MPM (the steeper the CA schedule), the larger the potential current account deficit associated with a given income expansion. Compare, for example, the deficits associated with CA_1 and CA_2 in figure 14.3 as income increases from Y_1 to Y_2. It can also be noted parenthetically that if income-reducing policies are employed for current account adjustment, the effectiveness of these policies will vary directly with the value of the MPM. Refer again to figure 14.3 and compare the income reduction necessary to remove a payments deficit of B_2. Because of the lower MPM, a greater reduction in real income (from Y_3 to Y_1) is necessary for CA_1 than for CA_2 (from Y_2 to Y_3).

The CA schedule, which for present purposes can be taken as the analogue of the current account in table 14.1, is drawn simply as a function of the level of real income. In this respect it fits well in a Keynesian framework. It is of course constructed on *ceteris paribus* assumptions, and any given schedule could shift for a variety of reasons, in particular as a consequence of changes in the prices of domestic goods and services *relative* to goods and services produced abroad. Thus a general improvement in the competitiveness of domestically produced goods and services would shift CA to the right, facilitating payments balance at a higher income level.

Certain specific policy actions might be designed to change competitiveness, for example exchange rate changes. An exchange rate *devaluation* reduces the number of units of foreign currency which can be obtained with a unit of domestic currency (or looked at from the other side of the transaction, increases the number of units of domestic currency which must exchange for a unit of foreign currency). If

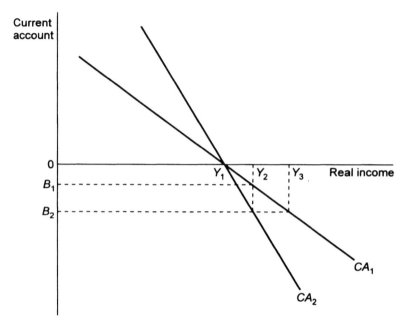

Figure 14.3 Current account imbalance and import propensity

these changes are translated into changes in the final prices of goods and services,[4] the domestic currency price of imports rises relative to import substitutes and the foreign currency price of home produced exports falls relative to competing products. Table 14.2 illustrates the way in which final prices can be affected by the devaluation. Clearly, if the home demand for imports and the overseas demand for exports are price elastic, the *CA* will shift to the right as a consequence of devaluation.[5] The same analysis applies *mutatis mutandis* to revaluation, and it should be obvious that this shifts *CA* to the left.

TABLE 14.2 Effects of Sterling Devaluation on UK Import and Export Prices

Before devaluation	After devaluation
£1 = $2.80	£1 = $2.40
$1 = 35.7p	$1 = 41.7p
$100 of US exports sells in UK at domestic price of £35.7p	$100 of US exports sells in UK at domestic price of £41.70p
£100 of UK exports sells in US at domestic price of $280	£100 of UK exports sells in US at domestic price of $240

4 The changes in prices of goods and services need not fully reflect the devaluation. Exporters could for example increase their profit margins by allowing the overseas price of their goods to fall less than the devaluation. Similarly, importers could allow profit margins to be squeezed by failing to increase the domestic price fully in line with the exchange rate change.

5 For a devaluation (revaluation) to improve (worsen), the current account balance, the well-known Marshall–Lerner condition should hold, namely:

Changes in commercial policy can also shift CA. So far an absence of tariffs and non-tariff barriers (such as quantitative restrictions, voluntary export restraints and export subsidies), has been assumed. There is, however a wide range of such instruments which may be implemented in order to shift X or Z. For instance an import tariff may be imposed to encourage import substitution. This would shift CA to the right (assuming no retaliation). Likewise an export subsidy would shift CA to the right. Other less obvious instruments might be employed with the same objective, such as discriminatory government procurement policies, administrative and technical barriers to trade and so on. Instruments like these became increasingly common with the growth of the new protectionism in the 1970s (see Greenaway, 1983a).

The CA schedule can be combined with the IS and LM curves to consider the interrelationships between external balance (as given by zero imbalance on the current account) and internal balance (as given by the intersection of the IS and LM schedules at the full employment level of income). In defining internal balance in this way, it may at first appear as if a retrograde step is being taken, given the discussion of the IS/LM framework and the analysis of expectations in the previous chapters. These limitations still apply. In the same way as the IS/LM framework proved useful for analytical purposes in the closed economy context, it has its uses here. Its limitations in the open economy context will be considered further in the next chapter.

Internal and External (Current Account) Balance

The IS/LM framework requires only minor modification to accomodate exports and imports. To see this, refer back to figure 10.2 where we derived the IS schedule with a government sector and taxation. Government expenditure was treated as exogenous and was incorporated into the model by way of a horizontal displacement of the ID function in quadrant (a). Since, as we can see from equation 14.2, we treat exports as exogeneous, we can incorporate them into the model in exactly the same way. Other things being equal, a given amount of exports will displace $ID + G$ to the right in quadrant (a), and therefore cause a rightward shift in the IS schedule (without affecting its slope). Because taxes were a function of income, we found in figure 10.2 that the inclusion of taxes into the model caused the savings function to rotate to the left. We now know from equation 14.3 that imports too are a function of income and can be incorporated into the model in the same way as taxes were. Inclusion of imports therefore causes the $S + T$ function of quadrant (c) in figure 10.2 to rotate to the left. Other things being equal, this will result in the IS curve being steeper over the relevant range. In the

$$\sum dx + dm > 1$$

That is, the domestic price elasticity of demand for imports (dm) and the foreign price elasticity of demand for exports (dx) should sum to greater than unity. If they sum to less than unity, because the home demand for imports and the foreign demand for exports are price inelastic over the relevant range, the trade balance actually worsens following devaluation. It is not unusual to find that in the short run the condition does not hold as agents take time to adjust to relative price changes. This can give rise to the so-called 'J-curve' effect of a devaluation. Immediately following the devaluation the current account deficit deteriorates, then as agents react to price changes in the longer run it improves.

remainder of this chapter we will assume that these adjustments are incorporated in the *IS* schedule.

In figure 14.4, simultaneous internal and external balance as defined above, or *twin balance*, could be achieved if the relevant schedules were IS_1 and LM_1. The internal target of full employment (and price stability) is ensured by the intersection of IS_1 and LM_1 at Y_F whilst the external target of a zero trade balance is guaranteed by the intersection of CA_1 with the Y axis at Y_F.

Suppose, however, the relevant trade balance schedule were CA_2 such that at Y_F a trade deficit of $0B_1$ is recorded. There is internal balance but external imbalance, and if it is assumed that financing options have been exercised (that is, the country has run out of foreign exchange reserves and cannot borrow) the deficit has to be eliminated – *adjustment* must take place.

Adjustment action could be taken via *expenditure changing policies* and/or *expenditure switching policies* (Johnson, 1958). In the case of the former, policy would be directed at altering domestic expenditure in order to influence import demand; in the case of the latter, policy would aim to induce domestic residents and overseas residents to switch demand from overseas goods to domestically produced goods. Common expenditure switching policies are exchange rate changes and tariff/non-tariff interventions.

Within the context of figure 14.4, devaluation would raise the home currency price of imports whilst lowering the foreign currency price of exports. The resultant expenditure switches would push CA_2 to the right. It might appear that the required

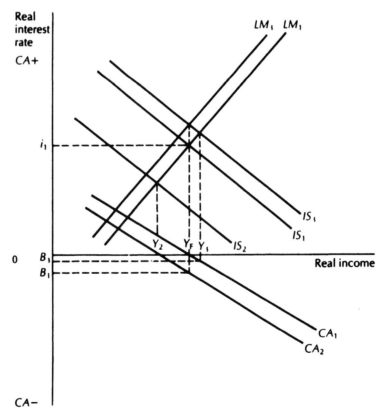

Figure 14.4 Internal and external (current account) balance

devaluation ought to displace CA_2 until it coincides with CA_1. Such a deduction would, however, be erroneous since it ignores the impact which exchange rate adjustments have on the goods market. If devaluation stimulates an increased demand for import substitutes and exports, IS_1 will be pushed to the right, increasing the income level to $Y_3 > Y_F$. Clearly, if twin balance is to be achieved, the devaluation has to be accompanied by policy action directed at reducing domestic expenditure at home, policy which would, for instance, shift LM_1 to LM_3. Ideally this expenditure reduction would *precede* the exchange rate adjustment, thereby creating excess capacity which will accommodate the secondary income effects caused by the devaluation induced shift of *IS*.

The analysis of figure 14.4 is of course a simple piece of comparative statics which abstracts from certain fundamentally important complications, like identification lags and reaction lags. It nevertheless serves to bring out an important principle of policy implementation, namely the *Tinbergen principle*. This asserts that if the relevant objective function embodies a number of targets, the number of independent instruments at the policy-maker's disposal should be at least as great as the number of objectives. Within the present context it can be seen that the application of one instrument (the exchange rate) to meet two targets simultaneously (internal and external balance) results in neither being met. As with any other rule there are exceptions, and it should be obvious from figure 14.4 that there are likely to be circumstances (under full employment and balance of trade deficit) when it may be possible to attain simultaneous internal and external balance via exchange rate adjustment only; these are so-called 'single policy' solutions.

Possible policy conflict can be highlighted within the context of figure 14.4 if it is assumed that the exchange rate is fixed, and international agreements forbid recourse to tariff and non-tariff interventions. CA_2 would therefore be fixed and external balance could only be attained by shifting *IS* and *LM*, that is through expenditure changing policies. For example, fiscal contraction would shift IS_1 to IS_2. With an unchanged *LM* schedule, external balance would be attained, but at the cost of internal balance, since $Y_2 < Y_F$. Because the exchange rate is now viewed as a target rather than an instrument, the system is underdetermined in the sense that there are too few instruments for the given number of targets. As a result, there is policy conflict, with current account balance acting as a constraint on the level of income which can be attained.

This scenario exercised the minds of a number of commentators in the early days of the Bretton Woods regime of pegged exchange rates (1948–71). It appeared that, because the exchange rate was fixed and the use of commercial policy instruments for balance of payments purposes proscribed under the GATT,[6] policy conflict was inevitable.

The simplest analyses of the stop–go cycle in the UK in the 1950s and 1960s can be cast within this type of framework. CA_2 was viewed as being immutably fixed because a sterling dollar exchange rate of £1 =$2.80 was regarded as a constraint on policy (up until devaluation in 1967). Thus, every time the economy appeared to expand towards its full employment level of output a current account deficit appeared. Deflationary policies designed to curb import demand and remove the deficit resulted in the level of income (and employment) falling. There seemed to be a trade-off between internal and external balance of the type depicted in figure 14.4.

---

6 The use of commercial policy for balance of payments reasons is not actually forbidden under GATT. Emergency action to relieve a payments deficit can be taken under Article XII.

Even such a simple Keynesian framework can therefore generate useful insights into policy conflict in an open economy setting. Figure 14.4 is, however, lacking in one very important respect; external balance is equated with a balanced *current account*, with the capital account being disregarded. In practice external balance is equated with zero imbalance on both current and capital account. Thus, for example, the current account deficit at Y_F in figure 14.4 could be 'covered' by a capital account surplus such that adjustment is unnecessary. As will now be seen, inclusion of the capital account alters the analysis quite radically.

Internal and External (Current and Capital Account) Balance

The policy options available for the simultaneous attainment of internal and external balance when the latter is defined to include capital transactions were rigorously analysed in a pair of classic articles by Mundell (1962, 1963). The focus here will be principally on the analysis incorporated in Mundell's 1962 paper.

This model is underpinned by a number of (essentially Keynesian) assumptions:

(1)   Tax revenue and private disposable income vary directly with the level of real income.

(2)   Consumption and investment expenditure vary directly with disposable income, and inversely with the rate of interest.

(3)   The current account varies inversely with domestic expenditure.

(4)   Money wages are constant in domestic money.

(5)   Capital movements are interest sensitive.

(6)   Constant terms of trade, constant productivity, a given commercial policy, and fixed exchange rates.

The targets in the model are internal balance (the equality of aggregate demand and aggregate supply at full employment) and external balance (a situation where the balance on current account equals net capital exports).

In the discussion of figure 14.4, expenditure changing policy was referred to as if it were a single policy instrument; indeed, policy conflict emerged for this very reason. Mundell argued, however, that it is crucially important to distinguish between different expenditure changing instruments – monetary policy and fiscal policy because these instruments may have a differential impact on the two targets.

In figure 14.5, fiscal policy is represented by the government budget surplus[7] on the vertical axis, and monetary policy by the rate of interest on the horizontal. *IB* in panel (a) traces out those combinations of the budget surplus and the rate of interest which are consistent with internal balance. The schedule is downward sloping because any (reflationary) reduction in the budget surplus would have to be accompanied by a (deflationary) increase in the interest rate, otherwise aggregate demand would exceed

---

7 For consistency with the Mundellian analysis the use of budget surplus is retained. In practice, of course, variations in the budget deficit (or the PSBR) would be monitored as indicating the posture of fiscal policy. This is of course not inconsistent with the use of the term 'budget surplus', since a budget deficit is simply a negative budget surplus.

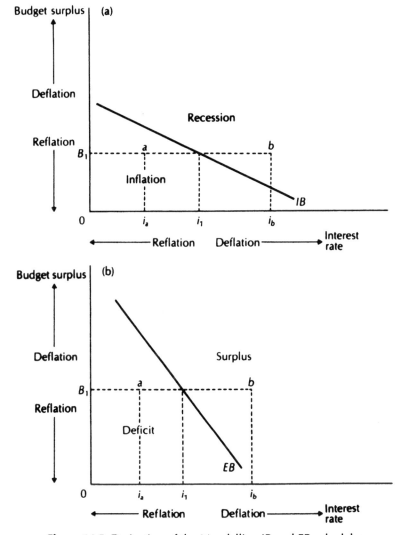

Figure 14.5 Derivation of the Mundellian IB and EB schedules

aggregate supply. Points below *IB* are consistent with an excess of aggregate demand over aggregate supply, and therefore inflationary pressures, whilst points above *IB* are consistent with deficient demand and recessionary pressures.

For example, for a given budget surplus of B_1, an interest rate of i_1 is required to generate internal balance. An interest rate of i_a is 'too low' for internal balance to be attained, that is, monetary policy is too relaxed and inflationary pressures are experienced (at point *a*). Similarly an interest rate of i_b would indicate an unnecessarily restrictive monetary policy, with consequent recessionary pressures at *b*.

Inspection of panel (b) also reveals that the external balance *(EB)* schedule is downward sloping. If the budget surplus were reduced, a fraction of the consequent increase in expenditure would be spent on imports (depending on the marginal propensity to import). Other things being equal, this will push the balance of trade and hence the balance of payments into deficit. If a surplus could be induced on the capital account which exactly matched the current account deficit, then overall the balance of payments would balance. If capital flows are interest sensitive, then a rise in domestic interest rates (relative to those prevailing elsewhere) would accomplish this. Thus points below the *EB* schedule are consistent with overall payments deficit, and points above with overall payments surplus.

Thus, given a budget surplus of B_1, an interest rate of i_a is too low to be consistent with payments balance. Because it is too low it affects the current account by stimulating expenditure on imports, and the capital account by encouraging capital to seek more lucrative returns elsewhere. In contrast an interest rate of i_b would be high relative to one's competitors, thereby encouraging capital imports. Together with the fact that monetary policy is accordingly restrictive, this stimulates a payments surplus. Clearly i_1 is the interest rate which is consistent with payments balance.

Both schedules are therefore downward sloping. Crucially, however, the *EB* schedule has a steeper slope. This follows from the assumption that international capital flows are interest sensitive. If both fiscal and monetary policy affected internal and external balance in precisely the same way, both schedules would have the same slope. By assumption, both policies have qualitatively similar effects on internal balance but a differential impact on external balance. A change in the interest rate affects both the current account *and* the capital account of the balance of payments, whereas a change in the budget surplus only affects the current account.[8] Thus the *EB* schedule is more interest sensitive throughout its entire range than the *IB* schedule.

When the two schedules are combined as in figure 14.6 (if the schedules are linear throughout their range), there is a single unique point where twin balance is attained. If fortuitously the budget surplus and interest rate were set at levels consistent with point *e* then static equilibrium would be guaranteed and policy action unnecessary. If the start were from any other point which represents some combination of internal and/or external imbalance, then some form of policy response would be in order. In a few special cases single-policy solutions are conceivable. Thus, on the lines *ab* and *cd* the budget surplus and the interest rate are always at the 'desired' level, and twin balance is achieved simply by manipulating one of the instruments. The more usual case, however, would commence from a point in one of the segments labelled $f \rightarrow n$, and here manipulation of both policy instruments is necessary.

Mundell argued that from wherever one commences, it is possible to achieve both internal and external balance if one follows the Tinbergen rule, and if one solves the *assignment problem*. The Tinbergen rule has already been introduced. The assignment rule requires that each policy instrument should be assigned to the policy target on which it exerts the greatest impact. In the present model, both instruments have a similar effect on the trade balance (via changes in domestic expenditure). Monetary policy, however, has a relatively greater impact on the capital account because of the interest sensitivity of capital. Overall, therefore, monetary policy has a relatively greater impact on external balance and should be assigned to this target, whilst fiscal policy is assigned to internal balance.

Figure 14.7 illustrates the assignment problem more fully. Suppose the starting-point is *a*, where full employment is associated with a balance of payments deficit. If monetary policy is assigned to external balance, an increase in the interest rate deflates the level of income, reduces import demand and attracts a capital inflow. If the interest rate is raised sufficiently the result is point *b*, where the deficit is completely eliminated. The

---

8 As has been seen, modern monetary analyses emphasize the effects of changes in the budget deficit on interest rates. This indeed is one of the limitations of this analysis which will be considered shortly.

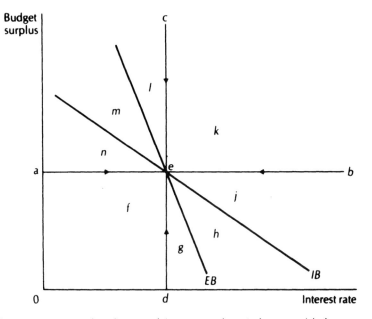

Figure 14.6 Internal and external (current and capital account) balance

deflationary increase in the interest rate has, however, lowered income and employment and there has been a movement away from internal balance. To reattain full employment the budget surplus is reduced and there is movement from point *b* to point *c*. The reflationary fiscal expansion, however, disturbs external balance by attracting additional imports (given a positive marginal propensity to import). Note, however, that the deficit at *c* is smaller than the deficit at *a*. Another increase in the interest rate

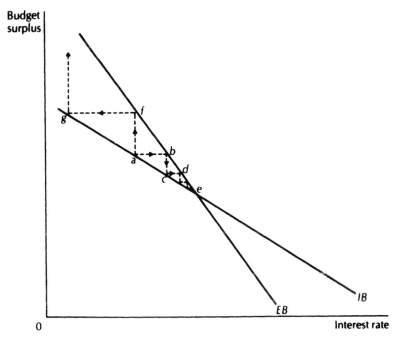

Figure 14.7 Assignment problem

gives movements towards *d*, and further manipulation of monetary and fiscal policy ensures convergence on point *e*. If for some reason the policy instruments are mis-assigned, the result is divergence rather than convergence. Thus, if fiscal policy is initially assigned to external balance there is a shift from *a* towards *f*. When monetary policy is used to remove the resultant unemployment there is movement from *f* towards *g*. Clearly, the movement is away from rather than towards *e*.

The analysis contends that twin balance can be attained from any disequilibrium point by judicious assignment of fiscal and monetary policy. As long as these policies are correctly assigned, even if they are apparently conflicting (with one being reflation-ary and one deflationary), the system will be stable and convergent progress to equili-brium is possible. Table 14.3 summarizes the combinations of fiscal and monetary policy which would be required for disequilibrium points in segments *f* through *n*, mapped out in figure 14.6.

TABLE 14.3
Policy Summary for Disequilibrium Points of Figure 14.6

Segment	Internal balance	External balance	Change in budget surplus	Change in i ·
f	Inflation	Deficit	+	+
g	Inflation	Deficit	+	+
h	Inflation	Surplus	+	−
j	Unemployment	Surplus	−	−
k	Unemployment	Surplus	−	−
l	Unemployment	Surplus	+	−
m	Unemployment	Deficit	−	+
n	Inflation	Deficit	+	+

This rather neat piece of comparative statics can also be conducted within the *IS/LM* framework, as was done when external balance was equated with a balanced current account. To do so, an external balance schedule has to be derived, where *EB* is a func-tion of the rate of interest and the level of real income. This is done in figure 14.8. In quadrant (a) is reproduced the *CA* schedule, which was derived in figure 14.2. Quadrant (b) introduces a capital account schedule (*KA*) which is shown to be a function of the interest rate (or more accurately the domestic interest rate relative to that prevailing overseas). Note that capital account deficits are measured in the upper part of the dia-gram, capital account surpluses in the lower part. In this way the extent of any capital account deficit (surplus) which is required to cover fully a given current account sur-plus (deficit) can immediately be identified.

If, for example, the level of income is Y_1, a current account surplus of CA_1 would emerge. For overall payments balance this requires a capital account deficit of KA_1 which can be obtained with an interest rate of i_1. If the interest rate is taken through a transformation schedule as in quadrant (c) to transfer *i* from the horizontal to the verti-cal axis, it is found that the combination of an interest rate of i_1 and a level of real income of Y_1 generates overall payments balance; this point is a point on the *EB* sched-ule which lies somewhere in interest-rate/income space.

Consider now the higher income level of Y_2. Other things being equal, this would result in a smaller current account surplus of CA_2. To maintain overall payments bal-ance, the capital account deficit would also have to be reduced from KA_1 to KA_2, this

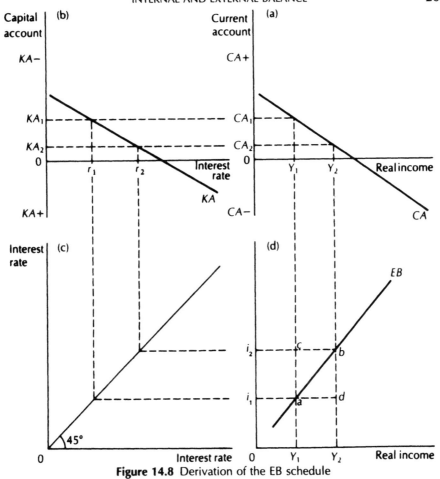

Figure 14.8 Derivation of the EB schedule

being accomplished by an increase in the interest rate from i_1 to i_2. If this is taken through quadrant (c) to quadrant (d), point b is another point on the EB schedule. Further changes in Y and i would result in EB emerging.

In quadrant (d) EB is positively sloped; this indicating that, if overall payments imbalance is to be maintained, increases (decreases) in the level of income which worsen (improve) the current account have to be accompanied by increases (decreases) in interest rates which improve (worsen) the capital account. Points above and to the left of EB are consistent with an overall payments surplus, whilst points below and to the right are consistent with overall payments deficit. If, for example, the level of income were Y_1 and the interest rate i_2, the latter would result in a capital account deficit which is smaller than the current account surplus, the result being overall payments surplus (at point c). Similarly, with an income level of Y_2 and an interest rate of i_1, the capital account deficit exceeds the current account surplus, and the overall balance of payments is in deficit (at point d). The slope of the EB schedule is determined by the slopes of the CA and KA schedules. The former, as has already been seen, is determined by the marginal propensity to import. The latter is determined by the interest elasticity of capital flows. Thus, other things being equal, the higher the MPM the steeper the slope of the CA and EB schedules; the more interest elastic are capital flows, the shallower will the slopes of KA and EB be.

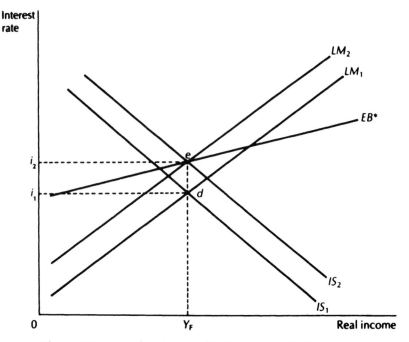

Figure 14.9 Internal and external balance in an IS/LM framework

Having derived *EB* it is a simple matter to consider the adjustment process examined in figure 14.7; this is done in figure 14.9. IS_1 and LM_1 intersect at an interest rate of i_1, with income being at its full employment level Y_F. *EB* is however fixed at *EB**, since the exchange rate is fixed, and the balance of payments is therefore in overall deficit since point *d* lies below *EB**. The Mundellian solution is to assign monetary policy to the attainment of external balance and fiscal policy to the attainment of internal balance. LM_1 is shifted to LM_2, inducing an increase in the rate of interest (and a capital inflow) which reduces the payments deficit. The deflationary impact of the policy results in a fall below the full employment level of income, however; this is countered by fiscal expansion that is, a rightward shift in *IS*. Eventually twin balance is attained at point *e* with income restored to its full employment level, and the interest rate at i_2.

The *IS/LM* framework then provides an alternative medium for outlining the Mundellian approach and can be applied to a variety of disequilibrium situations.

Limitations of the Mundellian IB/EB System

The Mundell model provides a framework within which it proved possible to derive some useful insights into the problem of simultaneously attaining internal and external balance when the exchange rate is fixed, or quasi-fixed, as it was for a very long time in the Bretton Woods system. The methodology has been frequently invoked (as will be seen in chapter 21) to explain UK attempts to achieve twin balance by financing current account deficits with capital account surpluses induced by relatively high interest rates. The approach has certainly had a lasting impact on the development of balance of payments theorizing over the last two decades or so. As a recipe for policy formulation, however, it suffers from a number of drawbacks which must be mentioned.

(1)   The policy mixing prescribed is essentially an exercise in *fine tuning*. As such, it is subject to similar identification and implementation lags as other efforts at fine tuning. One might even use this as a basis for arguing that policy could be destabilizing rather than stabilizing, if circumstances have altered by the time any action has been taken.

(2)   It is implicitly assumed that any level of budget surplus or deficit, and any level of interest rates, is politically feasible. In practice of course political constraints invariably set upper limits on both magnitudes. In the examination of UK experience with monetary control in chapter 6 it was seen that on many occasions there has been an unwillingness to permit interest rates to reach unacceptably high levels. Likewise with the government budget. Budget surpluses generate pressures for increased expenditure; budget deficits, beyond a certain level, may likewise generate pressures for decreased expenditure.

(3)   A related assumption is that monetary and fiscal policies are independent instruments. As has already been seen, they are in fact interdependent; thus the scope for unambiguous assignment may be rather limited. For example in segment *k* of figure 14.6 the prescription would be a decreased budget surplus (or more probably an increased budget deficit) and a lower interest rate. If crowding out is important, execution of the former policy would increase interest rates, thereby frustrating the latter.

(4)   The model implicitly assumes that any current account deficit can be corrected by compensatory capital flows. Even if this is in principle possible, in practice the composition of capital and current account is likely to be an objective policy. In addition, the composition of aggregate demand may be an objective of policy. If the budget surplus is being altered by changes in government expenditure, then the composition of demand will be altered accordingly.

(5)   The most serious criticisms perhaps relate to the fact that the monetary implications of accommodating a current account deficit by attracting short-term capital inflows are largely ignored. Fausten (1981) has argued that it is possible to deduce monetary implications. The issue has, however, been rigorously addressed by recent work on the monetary approach to the balance of payments. It is also the case that the ability to conduct a completely independent monetary policy is assumed. As was indicated in chapter 6, when the exchange rate is fixed monetary policies are interdependent rather than independent.

IS/LM Analysis with a Floating Exchange Rate

So far, the exchange rate has been maintained at a fixed level, the implications of using monetary and fiscal policy to attain internal and external balance have been considered. Most of the models using this methodology concentrated principally on fixed exchange rate regimes (reflecting their period of development more than anything else). A few, however, have considered the problem within a floating exchange rate context (most notably Mundell, 1963) and indeed this is easily done. In fact all that has to be done is to permit the *EB* schedule to shift around in response to any tendencies towards payments imbalance, and allow for the fact that shifts in *EB* will induce shifts in *IS* and *LM*. For example, exchange rate depreciation in response

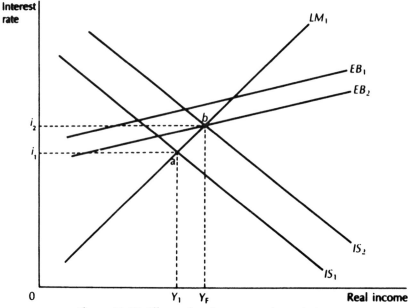

Figure 14.10 Effects of exchange rate depreciation

to a payments deficit generates an increased demand for import substitutes and exports; this in turn will induce a shift in *IS* to the right. Figure 14.10 illustrates the process.

At the initial income level Y_1 and interest rate i_1 there is a balance of payments deficit. When the exchange rate is free to float, it depreciates to clear the excess supply of domestic money on the foreign exchange market. EB_1 therefore shifts towards EB_2. As output and employment increase to meet the increased demand for import substitutes and exports, IS_1 shifts to IS_2 and twin balance is realized at point *b*. Of course the problem has been simplified by commencing from a position of less than full employment, but it should nevertheless be obvious that when the exchange rate is a policy instrument rather than a policy target, the attainment of twin balance is in principle more straightforward than when the exchange rate is fixed, simply because there is one more policy instrument at one's disposal.

Stabilization Policy under Fixed and Flexible Exchange Rates

The final issue in this chapter is the relative effectiveness of fiscal and monetary policy under fixed and flexible exchange rates. Are there grounds for believing that fiscal policy is likely to be more effective at influencing real output than monetary policy when the exchange rate is fixed or flexible? This is an issue which papers by Fleming (1962) and Mundell (1963) addressed and, notwithstanding the earlier analysis of monetary – fiscal interdependence, it is an important facet of this present framework for analysing balance of payments problems.

This question will be considered within the Mundellian/neo-Keynesian framework already developed. Monetary policy will take the form of open market operations, fiscal policy, a change in government expenditure financed by borrowing. The only additional assumption which will be invoked is that foreign exchange reserves are a form

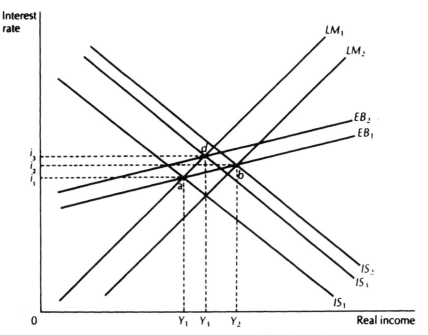

Figure 14.11 Fiscal policy under fixed and flexible exchange rates

of high-powered money, and variations in foreign exchange reserves influence the domestic money stock. This is consistent with the treatment of the determinants of the money supply in chapter 6.

In figure 14.11 the effects of fiscal policy under fixed and flexible exchange rates are compared. Y_1 and i_1 are the initial income and interest rate levels. Initially, it will be assumed that the exchange rate is fixed; therefore EB_1 cannot shift. Expansionary fiscal policy is represented by a rightward shift in IS_1 to IS_2. This takes the form of an increase in government expenditure, which calls forth a multiplied increase in income and in turn an increase in the demand for transactions balances, which (with a fixed money supply) has to be met by a rundown of speculative balances. The resultant upward pressure on interest rates generates a capital inflow, a tendency to payments surplus and an accumulation of foreign exchange. The latter results in a multiplied expansion of credit and LM_1 shifts to LM_2. Ultimately, equilibrium is re-established at point b with the intersection of IS_2, LM_2 and EB_1. Both real income and the interest rate are higher than in the initial situation, at Y_2 and i_2 respectively.

Contrast this with a situation where the exchange rate is flexible. Here the same initial shift in IS_1 to IS_2 and the consequent upward pressure on the interest rate stimulates an exchange rate appreciation (that is, an upward shift in EB_1 towards EB_2). This follows because the increase in the domestic interest rate attracts a capital inflow. The resultant decreased demand for exports and import substitutes shifts IS_2 back towards IS_1. Ultimately, equilibrium is established at the intersection of IS_3, EB_2 and LM_1. Income is higher than in the initial situation (Y_3 compared with Y_1) and the interest rate is higher (i_3 compared with i_1). Compared with the fixed exchange rate case, however, income is lower and the interest rate is higher (compare i_3 Y_3 with i_2 Y_2). This result follows from the fact that when the exchange rate is flexible, no reserve accumulation takes place, expanding the money supply 'by the back door'. Furthermore, because the exchange rate is flexible, exchange rate appreciation causes a reduced demand for

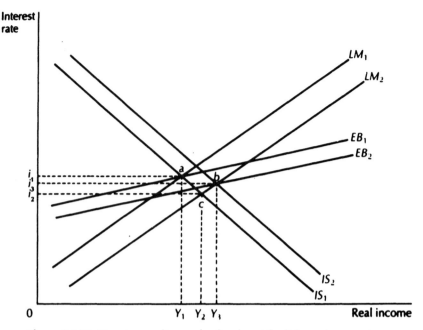

Figure 14.12 Monetary policy under fixed and flexible exchange rates

exports and import substitutes and this chokes off some of the income expansion resulting from increased government expenditure.

Thus it seems that *the effect of fiscal policy on real output (and employment) is stronger when the exchange rate is fixed than when it is flexible.*

Figure 14.12 conducts a similar analysis for monetary policy. Take first the fixed exchange rate case. Open market operations result in an increase in the money supply which shifts LM_1 to LM_2 and pushes income towards Y_2. It should be clear, however, that the downward pressure on interest rates stimulates a capital outflow and creates a balance of payments deficit at c. In turn this causes a drain on the country's foreign exchange reserves and a multiplied contraction of the domestic money supply, pushing LM_2 back towards LM_1. Equilibrium would be re-established at the *initial* combination of income and the interest rate as given by i_1 and Y_1. The level of real income has been unaffected by the monetary expansion. Because of the effect of the increase in the money supply on foreign exchange resources it would seem that monetary policy is impotent in a fixed exchange rate regime.

When the exchange rate is free to float, however, the analysis is rather different. Assume the same initial shift in LM from LM_1 to LM_2, which places the same downward pressure on interest rates. On this occasion the capital outflow stimulates exchange rate depreciation. In turn this stimulates increased demand for domestically produced import substitutes and exports which pushes IS to the right. Eventually equilibrium is restored at point b with the intersection of LM_2, IS_2 and EB_2, the equilibrium interest rate and level of income being i_3 and Y_3.

In contrast to the case of fiscal policy then, it seems that *monetary policy is relatively more effective at changing the level of real income under flexible exchange rates than under fixed exchange rates.* Again this follows from an explicit recognition of the impact which reserve changes may have on the domestic money supply. In a world of fixed exchange rates monetary policies are interdependent and the domestic monetary authority can lose control over the domestic money supply. Permitting the exchange rate to float restores responsibility for monetary control to the central bank. This is a principle which, as will be seen in the next chapter, was formalized and stated more emphatically in the monetary approach to the balance of payments.

The conclusions of this analysis are then that the authorities can still use domestic stabilization policies to influence real output and employment even in an open economy. Its freedom of action may be constrained in so far as different instruments of financial policy may have differing degrees of potency under alternative exchange rate regimes. Nevertheless, judicious selection of policies, with greater emphasis being placed on fiscal policy if the exchange rate is fixed and monetary policy if the exchange rate is flexible, can mean that stabilization policy has real effects even in the open economy.

If this were to be cast in the *AD/AS* framework which has been deployed at various points throughout the text, net exports become a component of aggregate demand, and aggregate supply remains unaffected. In a Keynesian world, then, with a positively sloped (or in the extreme) horizontal *AS* there is scope for stabilization policy which has real effects.

There are clearly certain limitations to the analysis which are analogous to the limitations identified in connection with the closed economy *IS/LM* model; namely that the dynamics of the adjustment process have been set aside, and in particular the implications of such policy manipulations for inflationary and exchange rate expectations. These will be addressed in the next chapter.

Concluding Comments

In this chapter we have extended our closed economy models to allow for the effects of international trade, and to explore the implications which this has for policy. We have seen that the introduction of an external target, external balance, complicates the process of demand management. The existence of an external sector can create the potential for an external constraint on policy. When the exchange rate is fixed this constraint can, in principle, be relieved by a judicious manipulation of fiscal and monetary policy. However, the practical complications of this kind of fine-tuning may mean that it is only a useful guide to policy in the short run. When the exchange rate if flexible policymarkers appear to have an additional degree of freedom. Moreover, once the exchange rate is free to float, the relative efficacy of demand management policies may be different from what applies in a fixed rate context. Specifically, it appears that monetary policy may exert a greater impact on real output when the exchange rate is flexible than when it is fixed; by contrast, fiscal policy appears to exert a greater impact on real output when the exchange rate is fixed than when it is flexible. More recent developments with regard to flexible exchange rate models will be considered in the next chapter, whilst the relevance of these models to UK experience over the post-war period will be evaluated in chapter 21.

Further Reading

Most texts on international economics include chapters dealing with the balance of payments and the problems of simultaneously attaining internal and external balance; see, for example, Milner and Greenaway (1979, chapters 5 and 6) and Winters (1985, chapter 22). A thorough review of open economy macroeconomics is to be found in Rivera-Batiz and Rivera-Batiz (1985). The most rigorous and comprehensive analysis of open economy systems is that provided by Dornbusch (1980). A less rigorous but none the less useful survey of the Keynesian models is provided by Thirlwall (1980).

Mundell (1962) remains the most elegant and concise statement of the targets-instruments approach. This is well supplemented by Fleming (1962). Mundell (1963) extends the analysis to a floating exchange rate model. These and other relevant pages are reprinted in Mundell (1968).

Whitman (1970) offers a critique of the twin balance model whilst Fausten (1978) provides an interesting empirical analysis of the targets–instruments approach in the UK context.

15

Monetary Disturbances, Expectations and Exchange Rate Dynamics

If one were to summarize the view of the balance of payments taken by many Keynesian models, two features would figure prominently. First, the external sector is frequently viewed as being something which is linked to the domestic economy, but which if need be can be considered as separate for analytical purposes. Second, frequently balance of payments problems are viewed as essentially short-run problems which can be corrected by demand manipulation. In contrast much recent neo-classical work has taken a contrary stance by viewing the external sector as fully integrated with, rather than simply linked to, the domestic economy, and has viewed the balance of payments as a long-term policy problem.[1] Methodologically, this has resulted in models of the balance of payments which emphasize these interdependencies to a greater extent and focus in particular on the monetary consequences of payments imbalance.

This chapter will examine in some detail recent work on the monetary approach to balance of payments analysis, as well as the implications of formally allowing for expectations in a floating exchange rate world. Prior to this, however, the *absorption approach* will be examined; as well as being the intellectual precursor to the monetary approach, this provides a bridge between neo-Keynesian and monetary (or neo-classical) analyses.

The Absorption Approach to the Balance of Payments

The absorption approach is the name given to a set of ideas about the balance of payments associated with the work of Meade, Alexander and Mundell, which was given most coherent expression in a classic paper by Johnson (1958). The approach is of interest because, by viewing the balance of payments as an economic aggregate rather than a subsector, it naturally tended towards a general equilibrium analysis of balance of payments imbalance. In addition, many of the ideas inherent in the absorption approach were subsequently refined into the monetary approach to payments imbalance.

---

1 This applies not only to neo-classical/monetary approaches, but also to some approaches which claim to be neo-Keynesian, such as the views associated with the Cambridge Economic Policy Group.

If the familiar national income identity is taken,

$$Y = C + I + G + (X - Z) \tag{15.1}$$

and domestic expenditure $C + I + G$ is relabelled *absorption* A and, $X - Z$ payments balance B, then

$$Y = A + B$$

or

$$B = Y - A \tag{15.2}$$

such that

$$B \gtreqless 0 \quad \text{as } Y \gtreqless A \tag{15.3}$$

In other words, payments imbalance is the outcome of over- or under-absorption. If absorption exceeds income the result will be a balance of payments deficit; if absorption falls short of income then a balance of payments surplus results. The magnitude of absorption relative to income is determined by real factors like the average and marginal propensities to import, save and consume. Other things being equal, a relatively high average propensity to save would tend to result in a tendency towards under-absorption and therefore payments surplus. Likewise, high consumption propensities in general and relatively high propensities to import in particular would generate a tendency to over-absorption and payments deficit. In this respect the approach has a distinctly Keynesian ring to it. As was seen in the last chapter, for example, a relatively high marginal propensity to import means that, commencing from a situation of payments balance, an increase in income generates a payments deficit. Likewise, within a Keynesian framework a loss of competitiveness could be seen as a source of rising import propensities and therefore a source of payments imbalance.

The absorption approach diverges from the standard Keynesian analyses, however, in a number of important respects. First of all it suggests that there are likely to be certain automatic adjustments associated with payments imbalance which, if allowed to operate, will mean that imbalance may be entirely self-correcting rather than necessitating (discretionary) policy action. Thus, the simple Keynesian income multiplier model and the Mundell (fixed exchange rate) *IB/EB* models assume that payments imbalance results from relative prices being out of line, and the imbalance will remain unless some discretionary action is taken to adjust or accommodate the imbalance. The absorption approach suggests that a *cash balance mechanism* may be operative which sets in motion certain automatic adjustment forces. The second distinctive difference is that the absorption approach suggests that even if policy action is taken (such as devaluation) it need not necessarily follow that such policy action will be successful, even when elasticities are appropriate (a possibility which was raised within the Mundellian framework but not fully analysed).

Cash Balance Adjustment in the Absorption Approach

Consider first the central role played by cash balance adjustments. In the event of a balance of payments deficit, for example, absorption exceeds income and therefore individuals and corporate bodies would find that cash balances were being depleted. This follows because cash balances must be leaking overseas via the balance of payments. Johnson (1958) argued that this cannot continue indefinitely if the money supply is fixed. There will come a point when the cash balances of corporate bodies and individuals will reach some minimum desired level. In order to maintain them at that level, expenditure has to decrease – that is, absorption falls as savings increase. If this tendency is permitted to occur, the inequality between A and Y which was the original source of the deficit will ultimately be removed. Of course, if cash balances are continually replenished by the monetary authorities, that is to say if they allow the money supply to increase to accommodate the over-absorption, then any tendency to self-correction is frustrated. In terms of the IS/LM framework the process of adjustment can be illustrated by reference to figure 15.1. With an interest rate of i_1 and a level of real income of Y_1, a balance of payments deficit is being run at point a. Assuming the exchange rate is fixed, and the authorities maintain the nominal value of the domestic money stock constant, expenditure leaks overseas and depletes cash balances. In an attempt to maintain the real value of cash balances speculative balances are run down, putting upward pressure on interest rates. This results in a tendency towards capital account improvement. Simultaneously the loss of high-powered money through foreign exchange decumulation drives LM_1 towards LM_2, with payments balance being achieved at point b. Thus as long as the monetary authorities refrain from replenishing cash balances, adjustment will be automatic.

This cash balance mechanism is an important feature of the monetary approach since it directs attention towards some of the monetary implications of imbalance. This relationship was developed further by the monetary approach, and a final assessment of the mechanism will be deferred until discussion of the monetary approach.

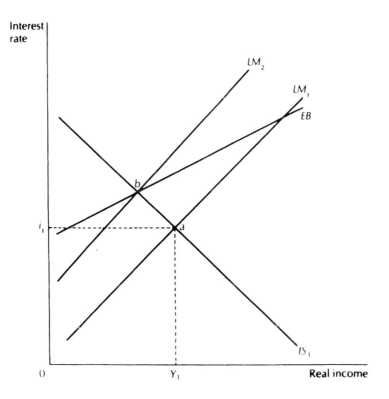

Figure 15.1 Cash balance adjustment in the absorption approach

Exchange Rate Adjustment in the Absorption Approach

Consider now a second contribution made by the absorption approach, namely the possibility that policy action may fail to eliminate payments imbalance. Prior to the absorption approach it had been assumed that, if import and export demand elasticities were appropriate, exchange rate devaluation would successfully eliminate a payments deficit. The absorption approach made it clear that this need not be so. The reasoning behind this is as follows.

Payments deficit results from over-absorption. The aim of a devaluation would be to reduce absorption relative to income. Given that

$$B = Y - A \tag{15.4}$$

taking first differences, a successful devaluation requires

$$\Delta B = \Delta Y - \Delta A \tag{15.5}$$

The increment to absorption is the outcome of two forces, an indirect income-induced increase in absorption and a direct cash balance effect. The former arises because, as was noted in connection with figure 14.4, devaluation has an income increasing effect as idle resources are put to work. It is this which accounts for the post-devaluation shift in the IS curve. But a devaluation can also result in an increase in absorption. As long as the 'marginal propensity to absorb' a out of increased income is positive, increased absorption is generated. (The value of this parameter is dependent on the value of the marginal propensity to consume and the marginal propensity to import.) The cash balance effect g arises because the real value of cash balances will be squeezed following devaluation (as the home currency price of tradeables rises), and some reduction in absorption will take place in an attempt to maintain their real value. Thus,

$$\Delta A = a\Delta Y - g \tag{15.6}$$

Substituting equation 15.6 into equation 15.5,

$$\begin{aligned} \Delta B &= \Delta Y - (a\Delta Y - g) \\ &= (1 - a)\Delta Y + g \end{aligned} \tag{15.7}$$

The change in the balance of payments therefore depends on the magnitude of any income change, the magnitude of the marginal propensity to absorb, and whether the cash balance effect is permitted to operate. The latter is taken first, since this has already been considered at some length. Devaluation raises the prices of tradeable goods in home currency; as long as the nominal money stock remains fixed, there will be a reduction in the real value of cash balances. If their real value is to be maintained, absorption will be reduced. If the monetary authorities permit the money supply to increase following the devaluation, this mechanism is frustrated. This is an important consideration in practice. Other things being equal, a devaluation results in a cut in real incomes. If there is downward wage inflexibility (for any of the reasons discussed in chapters 7 and 13), there may be an unwillingness to accept the cuts associated with devaluation. Money wage demands might therefore increase and (if firms price on a cost plus basis) prices may follow, negating in part the effect of the devaluation. If this does occur then either unemployment results or the monetary authorities accommodate the process by allowing the money supply to increase.

The magnitude of the income change depends on the extent of any 'idle resources' – that is, the amount of spare capacity. Income can only be generated if devaluation

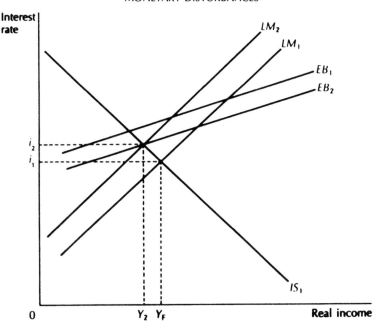

Figure 15.2 Devaluation without an idle resources effect

results in an expansion of the export and import substitute sectors; the latter can only be facilitated by the presence of idle resources. If, for example, a deficit country devalues whilst at full employment there would be little opportunity for the income effect to operate. A possible outcome is described by figure 15.2. Initially, with an income level of Y_F and a rate of interest of i_1 there is a balance of payments deficit. Devaluation shifts EB_1 to EB_2. As a result of the increase in the price of traded goods and the squeeze on cash balances, the real value of the money supply falls and LM shifts to the left from LM_1 to LM_2. Payments balance is ultimately attained at $i_2 Y_2$. The move to payments balance is entirely accomplished by direct disabsorption. Although there is payments balance it occurs at less than the full employment level of income.

Clearly, the absorption approach has certain kindred features with the internal–external balance approach discussed in the previous chapter. After all, the latter approach also pointed to the problems of taking policy action to adjust to payments imbalance at full employment. Furthermore, it also pointed to the impact which reserve accumulation/decumulation could have on the domestic money stock. The innovatory features of the absorption approach are in its emphasis on interdependencies between domestic economic aggregates and payments imbalance, and its more explicit consideration of some of the monetary consequences of payments imbalance, via the cash balance effect. Both themes are picked up and refined in the monetary approach.

The Monetary Approach to the Balance of Payments

The monetary approach can be viewed as the extension of many closed economy monetarist precepts and principles to the open economy; indeed, theorizing along these lines is often described as 'international monetarism'.

The monetary approach is a generic term applied to a collection of models and empirical analyses which have emerged over the last twenty years or so. There is no definitive monetary approach, rather a number of models/theories which share certain kindred features. It is these distinguishing features which will be concentrated on in building up an impression of the monetary approach. Concern is less with the characteristics of particular models than with the contribution which this body of thought has made to the analysis of external balance and the role of stabilization and exchange rate policy.

A Stylized Model of the Monetary Approach

The monetary approach to the balance of payments commences from the tautological statement that all transactions recorded in the balance of payments accounts are essentially reflections of monetary phenomena. Rather than focusing on the transactions themselves or any subgroup thereof (such as the current account or capital account), the monetary approach focuses on the role of adjustments in the money market in generating and sustaining imbalance. Thus the analysis of any change, whether policy-induced or not, commences from an analysis of how this change affects money market equilibrium. Another way of stating this is as follows. The approaches discussed in chapter 14 concentrated on 'above-the-line' transactions' – that is, transactions in goods markets and assets markets which are recorded in the current account and capital account of table 14.1. The monetary approach shifts attention to 'below-the-line settlements', that is, the balancing transactions of table 14.1 which record the monetary implications of payments imbalance.

To illustrate, recall the equation for the money supply which was derived in chapter 6 (equation 6.7a):

$$M_j = \left(\frac{c+1}{c+r}\right) H_j \tag{15.8}$$

where M refers to the money stock, H to the volume of high-powered money, c to the public's currency deposit ratio and r to the commercial banks' reserve ratio. Denoting the money multiplier by m, equation 15.8 can be written as

$$M_j = m_j H_j \tag{15.9}$$

or taking first differences

$$\Delta M_j = m_j H_j \tag{15.10}$$

In other words, the change in the money supply in country j is equal to some multiple of the change in high-powered money. In chapter 6 the change in high-powered money was identified with a domestically determined component, the issue of currency and the sales of securities to the clearing banks, and an externally controlled component, the change in foreign exchange reserves. If the former is referred to as D_j and the latter as R_j, equation 15.9 can be rewritten as

$$M_j = m_j (D_j + R_j) \tag{15.11}$$

(and similarly if changes are taken as in 15.10).

Assume now that, following the monetarist contention as outlined in chapter 5, the demand for money in country j is a stable function of a small number of variables, namely real income, 'the' domestic interest rate relative to 'the' world rate and expected changes in the price level,

$$L_j = f\left(y_j, \frac{r_j}{r_w}, P_j^e\right)$$ (15.12)

Furthermore, assume that the government budget is initially balanced,

$$G_j = T_j$$ (15.13)

and that all markets are efficient and tend to clear quickly and smoothly.

If initially payments are balanced, exports would equal imports and the change in foreign exchange reserves would be zero. In equilibrium the only source of any monetary disturbance would be through variations in D_j. If the rate of growth of the money supply is set in line with the natural rate of growth of real income, then the economy would be in a steady state, with unemployment at its natural rate and with actual inflation equal to expected inflation. More formally,

$$X_j = Z_j$$ (15.14)

$$\therefore \dot{R} = 0$$ (15.15)

$$\dot{M}_j = \dot{Y}_j$$ (15.16)

and

$$\dot{P}_j = \dot{P}_j^e$$

$$\therefore U_j = \bar{U}_j$$ (15.17)

Assume now that the authorities attempt to increase output beyond its natural level through domestic monetary expansion. The immediate impact of this disturbance is felt in the domestic money market in the form of a *stock* disequilibrium. Specifically, *actual* money balances exceed *desired* money balances. As has been claimed time and again, by monetary approaches this disequilibrium will be cleared through the markets for goods, services and securities. Since real output cannot be increased (because in equilibrium the starting-point is the natural rate of unemployment), the rate of change of prices rises in j, and domestic residents expend the excess money balances on goods, services and securities produced abroad. The outcome of this is a balance of payments deficit and, if the exchange rate is fixed, an outflow of foreign exchange reserves. The monetary shock therefore leads directly to a balance of payments deficit.

Implications of the Monetary Approach

The first important implication of the monetary approach is that, given time, adjustment to this imbalance will be automatic. It can be seen from equation 15.11 that foreign exchange reserves are an uncontrollable component of the domestic money supply. The balance of payments deficit causes reserve contraction at home (and simultaneous reserve expansion overseas) in turn this will induce domestic monetary contraction (and the reverse overseas).

Again it is adjustments in the money market which are emphasized. Reserve contraction and the resultant monetary contraction lead to a situation where actual money balances fall short of desired money balances. In other words, there is an excess demand for money in the domestic economy. In order to build up cash balances to their desired level expenditure on goods, services and securities contracts. (In the language of the absorption approach, disabsorption takes place.) This in turn slows down the rate of change of domestic prices and ultimately the deficit is eliminated. The entire process of adjustment to the deficit is therefore automatic.

A second implication of the monetary approach is that any attempt by the government to resist automatic adjustment is futile. For example, suppose during the process of adjustment the domestically controlled component of the money stock is further increased. This simply re-creates stock disequilibrium in the money market and re-creates the need for adjustment. It is argued that attempts by the monetary authorities to sterilize the effects of reserve outflows simply cause further inflation and further reserve outflows thereby maintaining disequilibrium.

It should be clear from this how the monetary approach extends the analysis of the Mundellian and absorption approaches. Considerable stress is laid on the links between the money market and payments imbalance, and the longer-run consequences of imbalance are emphasized. The approach asserts that under a regime of fixed exchange rates, all balance of payments disequilibria are the outcome of differential rates of growth of real income which impact upon the demand for money and differential rates of monetary expansion. The central tenet of the approach is that since the reserve flows associated with imbalance cannot be sterilized in the long run, payments disequilibrium is necessarily a transitory phenomenon. The only circumstances in which an imbalance is persistent occurs where the rate of growth of the domestically controlled component of the money supply is continually in excess of (or below) the world average. Ordinarily this could not be sustained owing to the constraint of reserve loss and exhaustion of credit (in the case of a deficit country). One exception would of course be where the currency concerned was a 'key currency', i.e. is the principal asset for international exchange. Thus, the rest of the world was for some time content to accommodate a persistent US deficit in the early 1960s in order to acquire dollars since the US dollar was the key currency under the Bretton Woods arrangements. It should be noted, however, that even this situation could not continue indefinitely. Persistent US deficits created a sharp deterioration in the USA's ratio of assets (gold and foreign exchange reserves) to liabilities (outstanding dollar claims). Ultimately this created a crisis of confidence in the USA's ability to honour these liabilities which contributed to the breakdown of the Bretton Woods arrangements in the early 1970s.

The final implication we should note of the monetary approach is the impotence of domestic monetary policy in a fixed exchange rate setting. Monetary policy is completely ineffective with regard to real income. As we saw in chapter 14 this is in fact an insight which was generated in the Fleming–Mundell approach to the balance of payments and is reaffirmed here.

The Monetary Approach and Flexible Exchange Rates

When the exchange rate is free to float the monetary approach has to be modified to allow for the fact that reserve flows no longer affect monetary growth. This is determined solely by the growth of the domestic monetary base. In terms of the above analysis, monetary expansion which creates a stock disequilibrium in the money market results not in a payments deficit but in exchange rate movements. This follows because any tendency towards payments deficit is corrected by exchange rate depreciation. This has the effect of restoring autonomy over domestic monetary policy to the domestic authorities in that a rate of growth of nominal income, and a rate of price inflation, which differ from the world average can be 'chosen'. If such a rate is chosen and domestic monetary policy adjusted accordingly, monetary expansion in excess of (below) the world average results in exchange rate depreciation (appreciation). An important implication of this is that domestic inflation is the cause of currency depreciation rather than vice versa as many Keynesian models predict.

Note further, however, that although autonomy over domestic monetary policy is restored to the domestic monetary authorities, the conclusions regarding the *effects* of monetary policy differ from the Keynesian model. In the monetary model, the long-run impact on real output and employment is still zero as in the closed economy model. Given the interdependence between monetary and fiscal policy this applies to fiscal as well as monetary policy. Thus in contrasting the Keynesian and monetary models it can be seen that the 'transmissions mechanism' for payments imbalance is different; Keynesian analyses emphasize expenditure flows whilst monetary models emphasize money market disequilibrium. In addition, as with closed economy systems, Keynesian models perceive a basis for demand management policies which have real effects, whilst monetary models simply reassert the neutrality of demand management policies.

Criticisms of the Monetary Approach

The monetary approach is therefore of interest because it stresses the longer-run interdependence between domestic financial policies and the external accounts. In so doing it delineates the limits of demand management policy in affecting the external situation. It is appropriate, however, to note that the analysis is subject to a number of general criticisms, criticisms which by and large tend to be levelled against monetarist philosophy in general. For example, the mechanisms described above rely on a stable money demand function. As Tsiang (1977) noted, this assumes that the variables to which money demand is related can be identified as well as the nature of the relationship. Although, as was seen in chapter 5, there are some difficulties in empirically analysing money demand, a growing literature does appear to suggest that, in the long run, money demand is stably related to income. There is more controversy with respect to interest rates.

A second area of controversy relates to the adjustment mechanism. This relies on efficiently and smoothly operating markets. In practice, of course, goods and factor markets in particular may clear relatively slowly. The implications of this when accompanied by assets markets which clear relatively quickly will be explored in the next section. Finally, in connection with the analysis of systems, note has been taken of the central question of exogeneity or endogeneity of the money stock. If it is determined by the level of money income (rather than determining it) then clearly the entire approach would be undermined.

Monetary Disturbances, Expectations and the Exchange Rate

Towards the end of the previous section, brief comment was made on the implication of the monetary approach for a regime of flexible exchange rates. Following the *de facto* collapse of the Bretton Woods regime of pegged exchange rates in 1971, a much greater degree of exchange rate flexibility has been evident in the international economy. This has not meant that exchange rate targets have been entirely abandoned; they do appear to have been maintained by most Western authorities, even if only in the form of target ranges. Nevertheless, it is the case that greater exchange rate flexibility has served to relax (and in some cases remove) the constraint of defending a particular exchange rate

in many Western industrialized countries. Inevitably this has encouraged a reorienta-
tion of academic interest away from the relationship between domestic financial policies and the balance of payments towards the relationship between domestic financial
policies and the exchange rate. This relationship has been closely scrutinized in the
UK and USA in particular, where official attitudes towards the exchange rate in the
later 1970s and early 1980s of 'non-intervention' and 'benign neglect' appeared to be
associated with marked fluctuations in those exchange rates.

Our comparative static analysis of demand management policy under floating exchange rates in the Fleming–Mundell setting of chapter 14 implied that adjustment from
one equilibrium exchange rate to another would be relatively smooth. Likewise, the
monetary approach implies that exchange rate movements will be driven by changes in
relative inflation rates between one economy and another and it is implicit in that analysis that exchange rate changes will be stable and continuous. Smooth adjustment has
not been a characteristic of exchange rate movements in the late 1970s and 1980s however. On the contrary, month-to-month, and even day-to-day fluctuations in many of
the major exchange rates have been quite dramatic. In chapter 21 we will examine in
detail the behaviour of the sterling exchange rate in recent years. For the moment we will
evaluate the way in which expectations may influence exchange rate behaviour, as well
as exploring a phenomenon known as exchange rate overshooting.

Purchasing Power Parity and the Exchange Rate

A useful starting point for the evaluation of the role of expectations is the purchasing
power parity concept. This is a simple explanation of exchange rate behaviour which
we have in fact already introduced in our discussion of the monetary approach.

The purchasing power parity (PPP) doctrine asserts that in a world of floating rates,
exchange rate movements serve to equalize the purchasing power of different currencies after making due allowance for complications caused by imperfections such as
transport costs and trade barriers. In a two-country world, for example, a rise in the
rate of inflation in country A reduces the real value of country A's domestic money
stock. The purchasing power of the currency on the home market would be reduced.
In an open trading system, with fixed exchange rates, arbitrage in goods markets would
ensure that a balance of payments deficit emerges. When the exchange rate is free to
float, however, arbitrage results in exchange rate depreciation. Furthermore, this
depreciation would continue until the incentive to purchase goods had been removed,
that is, when the depreciation of the exchange rate is just sufficient to offset the inflation
differential. At this point *purchasing power parity* would be re-established.

Formally, if the current or spot rate of exchange is defined as the number of units of
domestic currency D_c per unit of foreign currency D_f:

$$S_t = \frac{D_c}{D_f} \tag{15.18}$$

such that

$\Delta S_t > 0$ denotes exchange rate depreciation

$\Delta S_t < 0$ denotes exchange rate appreciation

then according to the purchasing power parity theorem,

$$\dot{S}_t = \dot{P}_d - \dot{P}_w \tag{15.19}$$

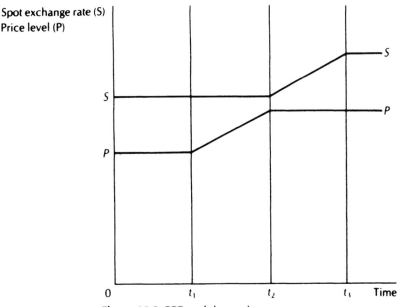

Figure 15.3 PPP and the exchange rate

That is, changes in the spot rate are determined by the domestic rate of inflation ($\dot{P}_d$) relative to the world rate $\dot{P}_w$, other things (such as relative rates growth) being given. This is essentially the monetary approach and summarizes the points which were made at the end of the previous chapter, that relative rates of monetary expansion, and therefore relative rates of inflation, drive exchange rate appreciation and depreciation.

This is the simplest possible statement of the PPP doctrine; it assumes that the spot exchange rate is determined by transactions which take place in the goods market. The speed and path of adjustment of the exchange rate to the change in the inflation rate is determined by how quickly agents in goods markets react to the latter. In terms of figure 15.3, a once and for all increase in the inflation rate between t_1 and t_2 (where t is time) might induce a once and for all depreciation of the spot exchange rate between t_2 and t_3. Alternatively, the adjustment could take place more quickly or more slowly. Ultimately, it depends on how smoothly and efficiently the markets concerned operate – how long it takes for the agents concerned to acquire, process and react to all relevant information about the change in the inflation rate.

Although the PPP doctrine is regarded by some as describing reasonably accurately the way in which exchange rates are determined in the longer run (see for example Friedman, 1980), it is not empirically well supported (see Winters, 1985). In addition, a difficulty with the approach as we have outlined it is that it concentrates entirely on the components of the current account of the balance of payments; it is this which leads to the dominant influence of relative rates of inflation. In a world of relatively mobile capital flows, the effects of capital transactions which take place in response to interest rate differentials can (and do) swamp the effects of current transactions in the short run. With the increasing volume of internationally mobile capital in the world economy, this is an effect which has been given an increasing amount of attention. Moreover, note that it is not only *actual* capital transactions which are important but *potential* capital transactions – the threat of capital inflows or outflows might in many circumstances be sufficient to change the exchange rate.

Since capital movements can clearly exert an important influence on exchange rate movements, we need to understand the forces which influence international portfolio investment decisions. What motivates an investor to hold a sterling-denominated asset rather than a dollar-denominated asset, or to switch from holding a sterling-denominated asset to a yen-denominated asset? Clearly this will be determined by the riskiness of alternative assets as well as the expected returns on those assets. If, to simplify matters, we assume that all assets are equally risky (or riskless) we can focus wholly on relative rates of return. In the Fleming–Mundell model relative rates of return were determined solely by relative interest rates. If the exchange rate is fixed this is a permissible simplification. When, however, the exchange rate is free to float the return on an asset will be influenced not only by the interest rate, but also by changes in the exchange rate. Thus, if an investor is holding a sterling-denominated asset, exchange rate depreciation reduces the capital value of that asset. Thus, when individuals, corporate treasurers, or portfolio managers are making judgements about which assets to invest they look not only at interest rates on alternative assets, but also at how they expect the exchange rate to behave during the period they are holding the asset. The expectations of investors with regard to exchange rate movements has a crucial bearing on capital flows.

Expectations and Exchange Rate Movements

For simplicity, consider a model in which capital is perfectly mobile across frontiers. Information flows are smooth and efficient, and transactions costs are relatively low. Thus differences in expected rates of return will quickly be followed by capital movements which arbitrage these rates of return. The expected rate of return on an asset for which substitutes exist will be influenced by two elements. The first is relative rates of interest; *ceteris paribus*, a higher nominal rate of interest in country *j* will be associated with a higher rate of return. Second, any change in the capital value of the asset which is expected to occur will affect its rate of return. Exchange rate appreciation raises the value of the asset whilst exchange rate depreciation lowers it. The way in which agents in the market form their expectations is crucially important. Let us assume that agents form their expectations rationally. They are therefore well informed and use information efficiently. Although as we saw in chapter 13 there are reasons for doubting the appropriateness of the assumption of rational expectations in the labour market, it may not be an inappropriate assumption where the foreign exchange market is concerned. Agents in this market tend to be specialist transactors who are well informed.

To establish the relationship between capital inflows/outflows, interest rate differentials and expected exchange rate changes, consider first the circumstances for zero capital mobility. At the margin there will be no capital inflows to or outflows from the domestic economy when the expected rates of return on domestic and foreign assets are identical – that is, when

$$i_t^d = i_t^f + (S_t^e - S_t) \tag{15.20}$$

where i_t^d and i_t^f refer to the current domestic and foreign interest rates respectively, S_t refers to the prevailing spot exchange rate and S_t^e refers to the expected spot exchange rate. Thus, when domestic interest is equal to the foreign interest rate, plus the expected rate of depreciation of the domestic currency (over a given time period), rates of return will be equalized. Rearranging 15.20, we can put this slightly differently:

$$i_t^d - i_t^f = S_t^e - S_t \tag{15.21}$$

This states that when the exchange rate is expected to depreciate ($S_t^e > S_t$), the domestic interest rate must exceed the foreign interest rate (and vice versa). The intuition between this equilibrium condition is quite straightforward. It simply states that where investors expect the exchange rate to depreciate, thereby lowering the capital value of a given asset, investors have to be compensated by a higher rate of interest. If they are not so compensated, they will not hold assets in the domestic currency and a capital outflow will result. The contrary condition holds for a currency whose value is expected to appreciate. In this case domestic interest rates need to be less than those prevailing elsewhere to stem capital inflows.

This is a crucially important result which must hold for equilibrium where markets operate efficiently and investors form their expectations rationally. One interesting thing about the result is that, superficially it appears to contradict our findings in the context of the Fleming–Mundell model. There it was argued that an increase in the interest rate would induce a capital inflow whilst a decrease in the interest rate would generate a capital outflow. This seems to conflict with the proposition that a positive interest rate differential will be associated with exchange rate depreciation whilst a negative interest rate differential is associated with exchange rate appreciation.

Dornbusch (1976) argues that the two can be reconciled relatively easily once anticipated and unanticipated variations in exchange rates are allowed for. If agents have full information and therefore form their expectations of how the exchange rate will move rationally, a positive interest rate differential will be expected to be associated with exchange rate depreciation in order to equalize rates of return. It is the *expectation* of a capital loss (via depreciation) which stems the capital inflow otherwise a country with a positive interest rate differential would attract all mobile capital! Assume that some 'steady state' exists with a positive interest rate differential and a degree of exchange rate depreciation; some entirely *unexpected* policy change then raises the domestic interest rate to an *unexpectedly* high level, and makes assets denominated in the domestic currency appear *unexpectedly* attractive. What happens? Since assets denominated in domestic currency are *unexpectedly* attractive there is a capital inflow and exchange rate appreciation.

Thus, the predictions of the efficient markets model and the Fleming–Mundell model can be reconciled. When interest rate differentials are known and fully anticipated a positive interest rate differential will be associated with exchange rate depreciation (and a negative interest rate differential will exchange rate appreciation). This is the prediction of the efficient markets hypothesis. When, however, some unexpected change occurs this relationship alters. If an exogenous shock occurs which makes the domestic currency unexpectedly attractive then a capital inflow results. For instance, if the domestic interest rate unexpectedly rises this results in a capital inflow and the exchange rate appreciates. This prediction is consistent with the Fleming–Mundell model.

This theorem is interesting not just because it introduces relative rates of return into the determination of the exchange rate but because it brings the role of exchange rate expectations into play, and in the same way as unexpected stabilization shocks can affect real output, it is found that they may also affect the exchange rate. As it is outlined above it is incomplete in so far as it has not been specified how relative interest rates are determined. Niehans (1975) and Dornbusch (1976), among others, have developed these ideas within the context of complete macroeconomic models where the interest rate is determined by expected inflation. One very interesting and important idea which has developed from this work is that one may have certain markets which clear quickly (where expectations are formed rationally and institutional arrangements are amenable to price flexibility) – like the foreign exchange market – alongside markets which clear more slowly (where expectations are formed adaptively and institutional arrangements impede price flexibility) – like the labour market. When these conditions coexist it is possible to find a phenomenon termed *exchange rate overshooting* which, as well as being an interesting explanation of exchange rate behaviour, also provides a somewhat unexpected channel by which monetary policy can exert real effects in a rational expectations world.

Exchange Rate Overshooting

As noted above, one feature of exchange rate movements in recent years has been their sudden and erratic changes. One way of explaining recent movements is by reference to the process of exchange rate overshooting. This refers to the phenomenon whereby the exchange rate reacts to a change in economic circumstances not in a smooth transitional fashion, but in a rather abrupt and erratic manner. Specifically, instead of tracking towards its new long-run equilibrium value the exchange rate initially adjusts beyond its long-run value, then gradually converges on equilibrium. For example, if a monetary expansion occurs this leads to exchange rate depreciation. Initially, however, the exchange rate depreciates more than is necessary for full equilibrium – it overshoots its long-run value in other words. Having done so it then gradually appreciates back towards its final equilibrium value. Figure 15.4 illustrates the process. At t_0 the exchange rate is S_0. At this point in time a monetary expansion occurs. The exchange rate reacts by depreciating to S_1 immediately. Between t_0 and t_1 the exchange rate then appreciates until it reaches its final equilibrium value of S_2. If no further changes take place, the exchange rate remains at S_2. If we compare S_2 with S_0 we observe that a depreciation has occurred in response to the monetary expansion. The adjustment path from S_0 to S_1 is rather odd however. The initial fall in the exchange rate is greater than that required for full equilibrium. This is the exchange rate overshoot. Let us con-

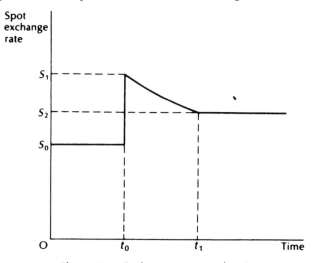

Figure 15.4 Exchange rate overshooting

sider more carefully the circumstances under which this phenomenon may occur and evaluate in more detail what is actually behind the overshoot.

Suppose that agents in assets markets and agents in goods and factor markets react at different speeds to monetary shocks. Specifically assume that agents in assets markets form their expectations rationally. Information flows are efficient, agents are able to process information about changed monetary conditions quickly, and prices are flexible. Agents in goods and factor markets, on the other hand, take more time to process information and react. They form their expectations adaptively, prices are sticky and market clearing occurs more slowly.

Refer again to figure 15.4. Assume that up to t_0 the exchange rate is at its PPP value. At t_0 an unexpected monetary expansion occurs. The immediate effect of this is to cause a fall in domestic interest rates relative to foreign interest rates. In turn this makes the domestic currency unexpectedly unattractive and results in a capital outflow and a fall in the exchange rate. Once all adjustments have taken place, the new equilibrium PPP value of the exchange rate will be S_2. In the short run, however, the exchange rate must depreciate beyond S_2. Remember that we have assumed rapid adjustment in assets markets and sluggish adjustment in goods and factor markets. In the short run therefore the entire burden of adjustment falls on the exchange rate. An initial depreciation to S_2 is insufficient to stem the capital outflow. This follows because there is now both a negative interest rate differential and a depreciating exchange rate. Returns on foreign assets still exceed returns on domestic assets. When will returns on the two assets be equalized? This will occur when the exchange rate has fallen sufficiently to ensure that future expected exchange rate appreciation compensates fully for the lower domestic interest rate. At this point the equilibrium condition of equation 15.21 holds again. In terms of figure 15.4 this is the appreciation which occurs between t_0 and t_1.

This may appear counter-intuitive. It must be remembered, however, that in the short run no adjustments are taking place in goods and factor markets. Agents in these markets take longer to adjust to the monetary shock. After a lag, agents react to the exchange rate depreciation, demand for import substitutes and exports expands whilst demand for imports contracts. It is this which is behind the appreciation which occurs. If there were complete flexibility and rapid adjustment in goods and factor markets as well as in the foreign exchange market, the overshoot would not occur.

'Overshooting' is a phenomenon associated with assets markets in general and not just the foreign exchange market. It is a possibility which has been recognized for some time (for instance, Friedman, 1953b, discusses it). We have described the phenomenon in a highly stylized fashion and it should be noted that the overshooting model is subject to several theoretical objections. For example, instantaneous adjustment in assets markets may not occur. In addition the model ignores the fact that changes in the domestic price level will have wealth effects which will have real effects. Notwithstanding these objections many analysts believe that the basic insight provided by the overshooting model is of value in understanding recent exchange rate behaviour. For instance some commentators feel that the behaviour of sterling over the period 1979–82 is a dramatic example of the process. Here the process was opposite to that just described. An announcement of monetary contraction in the spring of 1979 was associated with a significant appreciation of the sterling exchange rate to a point where many commentators were convinced that it was overvalued. The exchange rate had overshot, and subsequently approached its long-run equilibrium level by depreciating – this being the mechanism whereby the holders of foreign assets were penalized for the positive interest differential in the UK, and the equality of equation 15.21 restored.

A glance forward to the sterling dollar exchange rate charted in figure 21.2 gives some idea of the behaviour of sterling over this period. Prima facie the evidence is not inconsistant with the overshooting hypothesis. It must be noted, however, that some commentators have invoked other explanations, such as the role of North Sea oil in conferring petrocurrency status on the UK. This question will be considered further in chapter 21. It might be noted for the moment, however, that if overshooting is a valid explanation of sterling's behaviour, one finds monetary policy having real effects via the back door – namely via its effect on the exchange rate. Sterling appreciation in 1979 and 1980 was one of the factors which influenced the dramatic deterioration in competitiveness, which in turn squeezed UK industry in general and manufacturing industry in particular.

Concluding Comments

Chapter 14 was concerned primarily with the comparative statics of macroeconomic policy in a neo-Keynesian setting. This chapter has complemented chapter 14 by considering neo-classical models of the balance of payments which stress the monetary implications of payments imbalance. In addition, we have explored the role of expectations in a flexible exchange rate setting in order to evaluate some aspects of exchange rate dynamics. Our analysis in this chapter has provided us with a number of insights which complement those generated in chapter 14. We have seen that it is important to examine fully the monetary implications of payments imbalance. From a policy standpoint two particularly important points emerged from this examination. First, the possibility exists that payments imbalances may be self-correcting. Although this may be true in the long run however, as was pointed out, the period over which adjustment occurs may be so long as to be irrelevant from a policy perspective. Second, the impotence of monetary policy in a fixed exchange rate setting which was alluded to in the Fleming–Mundell model is reconfirmed here. Our analysis also extended to a consideration of exchange rate dynamics in a world where large volumes of internationally mobile capital exist. The possibility of sudden and erratic exchange rate changes being explained by exchange rate overshooting was explored. The most important insight which emerges from this analysis is that expectations play a crucially important role in short-run exchange rate changes.

We will return to many of these ideas in chapter 21. Then we shall look closely at UK balance of payments and exchange rate policies over the post-war period and consider the relevance of the models examined in chapters 14 and 15 to UK experience.

Further Reading

An overview of the absorption and monetary approaches can be found in most texts on international economics; see Milner and Greenaway (1979, chapters 5 and 6) and Winters (1985, chapters 20 and 21). For a much more sophisticated and rigorous analysis, see Dornbusch (1980, part 3) and Rivera-Batiz and Rivera-Batiz (1985, chapters 9, 10 and 11). Johnson (1976) provides a concise non-technical overview of the post-war development of thought on the balance of payments.

The two most influential papers on the absorption approach are Alexander (1952) and Johnson (1958); the latter makes especially worthwhile reading. There are a great many papers on the monetary approach; a representative paper is Johnson (1977). For the interested reader there are a number of symposia dealing with theoretical and empirical aspects of the monetary approach, namely Frenkel and Johnson (1976), IMF (1977) and Putnam and Wilford (1979). Critiques of the monetary approach are provided by Tsiang (1977) and Coppock (1978). A review of exchange rate economics that has developed since the early 1970s is covered in Macdonald and Taylor (1991).

A classic paper on floating exchange rates is Friedman (1953b) and there are a number of useful papers in Corden (1977). The most important papers on expectations and the exchange rate are Black (1973), Niehans (1975) and Dornbusch (1976), whilst extremely useful review type articles are Frenkel and Rodriguez (1982) and Krueger (1983). Chrystal and Dowd (1988) provide an evaluation of the macroeconomic implications of overshooting. Empirical studies of PPP are provided by Frenkel (1981) and Branson (1981). Swoboda (1981) and Blackhurst and Tumlir (1980) provide empirical assessments of some of the macroeconomic implications of floating exchange rates. See also Bailey, Tavlas and Ulan (1986). Finally, the implications of the models reviewed in chapters 14 and 15 for international interdependence and policy co-ordination are evaluated by Frenkel (1986) and Hughes-Hallet (1988).

PART III

Macroeconomic Policy

*The reasonable man adapts himself
to the world; the unreasonable one
persists in trying to adapt the world
to himself. Therefore all progress
depends on the unreasonable man.*
George Bernard Shaw

Part III of this book differs from parts I and II in two very important respects. First, it is concerned with macroeconomic policy and thus with the attempt to intervene and change the functioning of the economy in order to improve upon the existing state of affairs. This involves making a normative judgement as to what constitutes a desired state of affairs and the need to be able to determine priorities amongst policy goals in the event of conflict. Thus these are fundamental questions of what *ought* to be, and nothing encountered in parts I and II of this book will be of assistance in determining these priorities. Second, the focal point of part III is very decidedly with policy and experience in the UK. The previous discussion of macroeconomic sectors and macroeconomic theories had a certain universal applicability, to the extent that this discussion was abstracted from the institutional framework; in the present section the concern is specifically with the success or otherwise of macroeconomic policy within the UK. Particular attention is paid, therefore, to schools of thought which have exercised influence in the UK and also the particular policy problems which have been the most acute for the UK authorities. Without any doubt, these have been and continue to be the problems of unemployment, inflation and, until recently, comparatively poor economic growth performance. In addition, considerable attention is given to balance of payments considerations, since these have acted as a constraint upon policy formulation under past regimes of fixed exchange rates and continue to carry implications for counter-inflation policy under flexible exchange rate regimes.

This part begins, however, with a detailed analysis of the current controversies in macroeconomic policy and with a discussion of possible alternative approaches to macroeconomic policy prescription. Consideration is also given to the importance of the system of expectations formation in governing the impact of macroeconomic policy actions. Some attention is also paid to the problems encountered in the attempt to formulate macroeconomic policy under conditions of uncertainty where, for example, the authorities may be uncertain about the future course of exogenous variables. It is shown that, although uncertainty complicates the policy choice, one can still derive optimal rules of policy intervention.

In dealing with the problem of inflation the micro- and macroeconomic costs of inflation will be examined first since, in the absence of such costs, inflation would be a matter of indifference. Alternative counter-inflation policies are then considered, ranging from conventional demand management policies to wages and price controls. This analysis of the UK experience is concluded by looking at the case for indexation and the logic underlying the medium-term financial strategy. In examining the problem of unemployment in the UK particular attention is devoted to distinguishing between alternative forms of unemployment and the extent to which they might respond to alternative policy measures, which in turn reflect the differing viewpoint of the leading schools of thought. In the analysis of the balance of payments and exchange rate policies of recent UK governments, three distinct exchange rate regimes are distinguished: the regime of fixed exchange rates which prevailed through 1950–67; the post-devaluation period 1967–72; and the period of managed floating exchange rates which has prevailed from 1972 to the present day. The British experience is also analysed in relation to the European Monetary System (EMS) and the Exchange Rate Mechanism (ERM) which the United Kingdom finally joined in November 1990 before being forced to abandon it in September 1992. This event dealt a severe blow to the credibility of the Government's macroeconomic policy as well as to that of the then Chancellor of the Exchequer (Norman Lamont) who had gone on record to claim, 'The ERM is not an optional extra, an add-on to be jettisoned at the first hint of trouble. It is and will remain at the very centre of our macroeconomic strategy.'

Finally, the book concludes by surveying Britain's recent growth performance and some of the policy recommendations designed to raise overall growth rates.

The book as a whole attempts to explain alternative theoretical positions, the implications stemming from those positions and the policy recommendations and conclusions that might justifiably be drawn. It does not attempt to come out with one particular viewpoint, either as to how the economy actually operates or as to what the chosen economic policy should be. That is hardly in keeping with the purposes that a macroeconomic text should serve. Nor would it realistically be possible, since the authors themselves do not share a common ground and one doubts that the present book would have been enhanced had they done so.

16

The Macroeconomic Policy Debate

Prior to the publication of Keynes's *General Theory*, there was virtually no *theoretical* justification for interventionist macroeconomic stabilization policy. True, there were advocates of public works programmes to alleviate unemployment, especially in the United States (Hutchinson, 1978; Bleaney, 1985), but these were largely the counsels of despair and there appeared to be no logical refutation of the Treasury View that public sector investment must necessarily be at the cost of investment in the private sector.

The Keynesian revolution transformed this state of affairs. Suddenly there appeared to be a firm foundation for the belief that the classical macromodel, with its inherent tendency towards full employment equilibria, was fundamentally flawed. Equally, a rationale was provided for macroeconomic intervention; rising incomes would provide the savings for new investment without depleting the resources of the private sector. By controlling demand, government could offset those fluctuations in demand which precipitated instability. Nor was this seen simply as the need to provide for random public works programmes to mop up unemployment in periods of recession which could then be discontinued when they had achieved their purpose. Rather it was conceived as a fundamental change in the responsibilities of the government sector. Keynes was in no doubt of the implication: 'I conceive, therefore, that a somewhat comprehensive socialisation of investment will prove the only means of securing an approximation to full employment' (Keynes 1936, p. 378).

The Keynesian victory was remarkably swift, not only in academic circles but also amongst policy makers. Both in the United Kingdom and the United States, even before the ending of the Second World War, governments had committed themselves to the maintenance of full or high employment levels in the post-war years. In turn this implied a rejection of the doctrine of the annually balanced budget and a willingness to sanction fiscal deficits. And indeed, the immediate post-war experience, of full or near full employment being maintained without serious inflation, seemed to confirm the wisdom and relevance of the Keynesian prescription. A general consensus prevailed that governments could so fine tune the economy that the business cycle was now a relic of the past.

With the passage of time, however, this consensus gradually began to be called into question. In particular, it was argued that the maintenance of high levels of employment in the immediate post-war years stemmed less from the pursuit of Keynesian stabilization policies than from a rather fortuitous and largely autonomous raising of the level of aggregate demand in the world economy. Matthews (1968), for example, pointed to the impressive growth in post-war world trade in excess of the growth of world output as a key factor in maintaining employment. Other authors pointed to the generosity of the Marshall Plan, the reconstruction of Europe, the cost of maintaining the cold war as well as the excessive liquidity built up during the war years as government debt/GNP ratios reached unprecedented heights. More recently, Christian Romer (1986a, 1986b) has argued that the improved stabilization performance of the post-*General Theory* period is more apparent than real and stems primarily from improvements in the reported economic data.

The return of the business cycle undermined the confidence in stabilization policy generally. Already, there had been increasing awareness that conventional Keynesian demand management policies were ill suited to deal with structural unemployment – unemployment associated with the decline of staple industries and accentuated by regional concentration and relative labour immobility. Now, however, there emerged a new phenomenon in the post-war period, namely destabilizing shocks from the supply side.

Prior to the 1970s, there was general agreement that fluctuations and instability stemmed from fluctuations in demand. Disagreements between Keynesians and non-Keynesians focused mainly upon the differing ingredients and causes of the demand change. Now, however, the experience of the 1970s and 1980s was to point to the importance of supply shocks which initiated the era of stagflation (Bruno and Sacks, 1985). Conventional demand management was less confident and less able to deal adequately with these developments and increasingly the spectre of world recession re-emerged.

The Policy Debate

Today, there is no clear consensus over the desirability of macroeconomic stabilization policy. Rather, one can identify two distinct approaches; to quote Fischer (1988),

> One view and school of thought, associated with Keynes, Keynesians and new Keynesians, is that the private economy is subject to co-ordination failures that can produce excessive levels of unemployment and excessive fluctuations in real activity. The other view, attributed to classical economists, and espoused by monetarists and equilibrium business cycle theorists, is that the private economy reaches as good an equilibrium as is possible given government policy. (p. 294)

Fundamentally, the issue of macroeconomic policy turns upon whether one views the economy as being inherently unstable – subject to random shocks generating unemployment, lost output and inflation – or whether one views the economy as being naturally stable and basically efficient. In the former case, economic policy measures, particularly monetary and fiscal, are seen as necessary to counteract undesirable fluctuations, whereas in the latter, mistaken and badly conceived policies are seen as a major cause of large and inefficient departures from the natural rate.

The case for active interventionist policy rests upon the belief that government can effectively counter and mitigate random shocks. But since macroeconomic policy measures operate subject to time lags of one kind or another, this in turn implies that the policy makers can effectively forecast the future path of the economy in the absence of intervention. Economic forecasting is, of course, a highly skilled activity. It involves surveying leading indicators, such as housebuilding, employment trends and so forth on the one hand and policy simulations derived from large scale econometric models on the other. In the latter case, having estimated the parameters governing the model's behaviour, changes in crucial economic variables such as the money supply are then invoked to predict the outcome.

Either method, however, encounters difficulties. Firstly, the data being analysed will seldom be current but will refer to the time when the data was collected – perhaps one, two or three months ago. Secondly, a good deal of national income data is subject to revision with the passage of time, as errors are detected and better sources come to light. Especially when a variable is derived essentially as a residual (as, for example, savings determined by estimating income and consumption expenditures) are subsequent revisions often substantial. Broadly speaking, the record of economic forecasting in the United Kingdom, including that of the Treasury, has been far from impressive, especially in forecasting the length and depth of recession. Moreover, there is quite a marked disparity in the predictions of competing forecasters (Holden, 1989).

Accurate economic forecasts, whilst necessary for effective policy intervention, are not in themselves sufficient. If uncertainty exists over the time lags required for the policies to be enacted and take effect, then it is possible for interventionist policy to be actively destabilizing. The attempt to stimulate the economy in periods of recession, for example, may, because of the time lags involved, exert its effect when the economy has already moved out of recession. In this case, discretionary policy may turn out to be inflationary and inherently destabilizing.

The time lags in macroeconomic policy intervention can be categorized as either inside or outside lags. Inside lags refers to the time needed, first of all, to determine that the economy is in need of some corrective treatment (recognition lag) and, secondly, to plan and implement the necessary policies (administrative lag). Implementation may need sanction and legislative approval which may not be readily forthcoming. In the United States, for example, fiscal policy changes normally require the agreement of both Houses of Congress which may be controlled by parties hostile to the president who is initiating the policy. In contrast, in the United Kingdom fiscal policy changes are fairly easily enacted if the government of the day enjoys a parliamentary majority.

Outside lags refer to the time needed for policies to take effect once they have been enacted. It is generally conceded that in the case of monetary policy the outside lag is relatively long. This is partly because the policy works through interest rate changes which may take time to adjust. Moreover, the response to an interest change, particularly upon the side of investment spending, may be sluggish.

Those economists who tend to emphasize the length and uncertainty of the lags involved in discretionary macroeconomic policy, and who are therefore generally opposed to activist interventionist policies, stress the need for greater reliance upon automatic stabilizers. In effect, automatic stabilizers dispense with the inside lag. There is no need to recognize where the economy is headed or to obtain legislative approval before such stabilizers take effect. Examples of such stabilizers would include personal income taxes which automatically fall, and unemployment benefits which automatically rise as the economy heads into recession. Undoubtedly, the economy could be made more responsive along these lines – by increasing the degree of progressivity, for example. However, it will be appreciated that automatic stabilizers work both ways in that they slow down the movement to recovery.

The forgoing discussion pertains to the distinction between active and passive macroeconomic policy. Another distinction frequently made is between discretionary policy on the one hand and policy following predetermined rules on the other. Many economists advocating rules versus discretion do so essentially because they distrust the motives of the policy makers involved; policy might be distorted to secure short-term political goals as opposed to long-term economic benefits. This concern, controlling the economy for purely electoral benefit, has been dubbed the *political business cycle* – see Nordhaus (1975) and Whynes (1989). Presumably, the scope for exploiting such a cycle would be greater in the United Kingdom, where the electoral timetable permits discretion, as opposed to the situation in the United States where both presidential and congressional elections follow a rigid timetable.

The Expectations Revolution and Macro-policy

The debate upon whether activist macroeconomic policy is desirable or not took on renewed significance in the wake of the expectations revolution in macroeconomics. Previously, Keynesian-oriented economists had been eager to endorse the Phillips curve as providing the missing link – namely, an explanation of prices – to the Keynesian model. Moreover, the original Phillips curve suggested that there existed a menu of policy choice in that increased output and employment could always be bought at the cost of higher inflation.

As will be recalled from chapter 13, however, the adoption of adaptive expectations and their incorporation into the expectations augmented Phillips curve by monetarists economists led to the conclusion any such trade-off would be but short-lived. Ultimately, the natural rate of unemployment would be regained. The question then arises as to whether the short-term benefits of increased output justify the ultimate higher rate of inflation, given that inflation is not without cost. In turn, this depends upon the slope of the aggregate supply curve, on the one hand and the speed of adjustment on the other. The greater the value of the expectations coefficient and the less elastic the aggregate supply curve, the smaller would be the output gains associated with discretionary demand management policy. None the less, such gains were there for the taking. In principle, there is nothing in the concept of the natural rate to deny Keynesian demand management policy.

However, the introduction of the rational expectations hypothesis takes this argument one crucial step further. Again, as we have seen in chapter 13, if economic agents are able to perceive the true model governing the economy, and respond accordingly to policy stimulus without delay, then they may so act as to negate the policy impact in its entirety. This is the famous *policy ineffectiveness proposition* of the New Classical economics which signifies the death knell of conventional demand management strategies.

Now, of course, it may be argued that the assumption that economic agents react without delay to new policy measures is too extreme. However, the rational expectations thesis is even stronger than this. For, essentially, it asserts that if government policy is sensible and systematic in the business cycle context, then sooner or later economic agents will learn to anticipate government policy even before it is announced! Countercyclical stabilization policy is denied. Only policy measures which cannot be anticipated by economic agents – that is, policy measures which are random or arbitrary – can exert real effects. Such unanticipated policy actions are hardly likely to be consistent with stabilization goals; the indictment of conventional Keynesianism would appear complete.

Even if delays or impediments to market clearing were to provide a partial justification for demand management strategies, however, the rational expectations thesis sug-

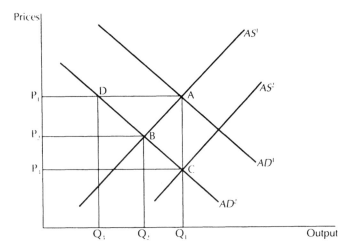

Figure 16.1 The cost of curbing inflation

gests alternative reasons why policy may generate perverse effects. Normally, policy prescriptions are derived from large-scale structural equation models describing the economy, in which the crucial parameters have been estimated from time series data. Alternative policies can then be evaluated by simulation exercises based upon the assumption that the parameters remain constant. However, the rational expectations philosophy would suggest that changes in the policy regime may themselves cause changes in the manner in which individual agents respond – including changed values of the underlying parameters! The imposition of constant values to coefficients which are not invariant to the policy measures calls into question the validity of econometric modelling exercises. More importantly, this so-called Lucas Critique (Lucas, 1976) suggests sound reasons why policy measures can be actively destabilizing.

There is, however, one situation where the rational expectations thesis suggests a greater role for demand management strategies than would more Keynesian-oriented policies. This pertains to the cost of eliminating or curbing inflation – the so-called *sacrifice ratio*. If the authorities wish to reduce the level of inflation by curbing the level of aggregate demand, they will be more successful if rational expectations and market clearing applies rather than alternative monetarist or Keynesian assumptions. We can illustrate this argument with the aid of figure 16.1.

We assume initially the price–output combination $0P_1$, $0Q_1$ determined by the intersection of the aggregate supply and demand schedules AS_1, AD_1. For expositional purposes, let us also assume that this output level corresponds to the natural level of output and employment. Suppose now that the authorities attempt to lower the rate of inflation by reducing the level of aggregate demand. Accordingly, the aggregate demand schedule falls to AD_2. What are the consequences?

Keynesians, emphasizing the comparative rigidity of nominal prices, would tend to argue that the entire adjustment would be thrown upon the side of output changes indicated in the movement A–D with prices remaining at $0P_1$ and output falling to $0P_3$. In contrast, the monetarist employing adaptive expectations would point to a simultaneous fall in both output and prices in the short term, depicted in the movement A–B, implying the price–output combination $0P_2$, $0Q_2$. The fall in prices raises the real wage of those remaining in employment. Over time, however, renegotiation will result in the outward shift of the aggregate supply curve to AS^2, restoring the former real wage at the natural level of employment with the price–output combination $0P_3$, $0Q_1$. The monetarist, therefore, views the eventual adjustment in terms of the movement A–B–C. Ultimately, the natural level of employment is regained at the lower desired price level but a cost is imposed in terms of the lost output during the adjustment period. And, of course, in this view the adjustment period can be long and drawn out. In sharp contrast, the rational expectations viewpoint would argue that economic agents perceiving and anticipating the effects of the policy would move immediately from A to C, minimizing the output loss in principle to zero.

The New Keynesian Response

Rational expectations combined with market clearing as the norm virtually excludes any role for discretionary macroeconomic policy apart from the desire to eliminate or reduce inflation as discussed above. Certainly, it would rule out any role for conventional *expansionary* Keynesian demand management policies. However, this rather optimistic view of the way in which the economy behaves has been challenged by a group of economists, generally dubbed *New Keynesian*, who entertain a more active role for government agencies. It should be emphasized that these economists are broadly sympathetic to the concept of rational expectations formation; indeed, many of them expressly include rational expectations in their models. Moreover, they are also willing to endorse the concept of market equilibrium – in contrast to *post-Keynesians*, who question the relevance of the concept to historical analysis. Also, New Keynesians are willing to concede the need for macroeconomic models which are consistent with the principles of utility maximization derived from microeconomics. None the less, whilst conceding all these points they have sought to suggest reasons why certain markets, particularly the labour market, may fail to clear.

Conventionally trained economists, committed to the belief in utility maximization upon the part of rational and well-informed economic agents, have a natural tendency to endorse the principle of market clearance. Indeed, if markets fail to clear, then we encounter a welfare loss in terms of the consumer and producer surplus foregone. Self-interest *on both sides of the market* should point to the speedy elimination of such a situation. However, New Keynesians, whilst accepting the logic of this argument, maintain that the labour market may fail to clear for considerable periods of time; in so doing they provide yet again a rationale for positive discretionary macroeconomic policy.

Implicit Contract Theory

One element in the New Keynesian case turns upon the idea of contracts, implicit or otherwise, which detail the highly complex agreements reached by workers and management in a two-way bargaining process. Such contracts, aptly termed the 'invisible handshake' by Arthur Okun, are reached by bilateral negotiation, implying a radical methodological departure from the highly decentralized and competitive models assumed in conventional analysis. The rationale for such contracts stem from the fact that both parties perceive positive benefits – the worker in the form of income smoothing, and management in the form of reduced risk and costs. The greater the degree of job specificity – that is, the greater the need for specialized training by management or particular qualifications on the part of labour – the greater will be the potential benefits involved.

In general, it is assumed that labour is risk averse and is willing to accept a certain reduction in its real wage in return for greater certainty. In effect, labour pays a premium to disassociate the real wage from its marginal revenue product which may reveal substantial volatility over the course of the business cycle. In return, apart from the premium involved, the worker grants to the firm greater freedom of action by agreeing *ex ante* to accept certain changes in its conditions of employment in certain specified circumstances. In addition, the firm may see the benefit of such contracts in the reduced risk of strike activity and the time saved in avoiding continual wage negotiations.

Implicit contract theory need not imply real wage rigidity and certainly there is no implication of nominal wage rigidity. Indeed, nominal wages may be wholly or partially index-linked as part and parcel of the contract. None the less, it does suggest reasons why both wages and prices may reveal greater stability than would otherwise be the case and in particular it suggests reasons why the real wage need not equate supply and demand in the labour market for considerable periods of time. This conclusion is perfectly consistent with maximizing behaviour; it stems from the substitution of imperfect competition in the wage-bargaining process for the more conventional perfectly competitive model of New Classical Macroeconomics.

Efficiency Wage Models

Efficiency wage models also attempt to offer a rational explanation of non-market clearing wage levels. Stated simply, these models start from the premise that firms find it profitable to pay more than the market clearing wage since they perceive that labour productivity is positively geared to the wage paid. There are several variants along these lines. One of the most influential has been the so-called *shirking model*. Here it is assumed that labour has some discretion over how well it performs and also that the cost of policing and monitoring work performance is reasonably high. In such circumstances labour has an incentive to diminish its work effort to the detriment of the firm. However, shirking involves a risk, namely the possibility of detection and dismissal, and the potential cost of job loss will be greater the greater the wage paid. Indeed, in a full employment economy with market clearing wages the cost of job loss would be minimal since the unemployed worker could then readily find similar employment elsewhere. By raising wages above market clearing levels, however, firms make it costly for workers to be dismissed and hence they provide an incentive to raise worker productivity. Efficiency wages act essentially as a disciplinary device whilst at the same time permitting firms to decrease their outlays on policing and monitoring activity.

Alternative efficiency wage models stress the importance of turnover costs or selectivity preferences upon the part of the employing firm. In the former case, the payment of wages in excess of the market clearing rate will reduce the incentive of existing workers to quit their employment and hence reduce the costs involved in hiring and training new workers. With regard to selectivity preferences, the payment of wages in excess of the market clearing wage will ensure a wider range of job applications by progressively overcoming reservation wage barriers. The firm is then more able to exercise selectivity

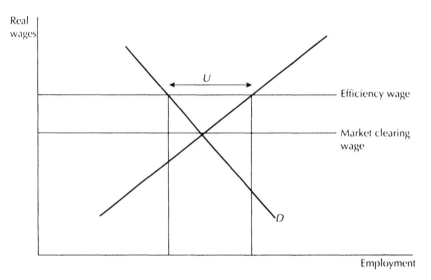

Figure 16.2 Efficiency wages and unemployment

in its hiring policy and choose workers who conform more closely to its perception of superior quality.

It should be emphasized that efficiency wage models are perfectly consistent with the hypothesis of maximizing profits behaviour. Having determined the efficiency wage, the profit maximizing firm will then determine the amount of labour it employs by equating the efficiency wage with labour's marginal revenue product. It will be appreciated that the resulting unemployment is not simply the difference between the amount of labour employed at the efficiency wage and the amount that would be employed at the market clearing wage; it also includes those unemployed who are seeking work at the efficiency wage level but who would be unwilling to work for the market clearing wage. This point is illustrated with the aid of figure 16.2.

Precisely what determines the efficiency wage? This is altogether a more complex issue. There is, of course, no reason to assume that the efficiency wage will be uniform throughout the economy. Presumably, it will be greater for those firms with greater monitoring and turnover costs or selectivity preferences. At the same time, however, one would assume a good deal of interdependence. Efficiency wage levels paid in one firm will not be independent of those paid elsewhere. Moreover, it is perfectly possible that efficiency wages paid in some sectors of the economy will influence wages paid elsewhere, even though no efficiency wage considerations are involved. Again, one would expect the efficiency wage to depend upon the state of the business cycle and equally to be positively correlated with the rate of unemployment benefit.

Efficiency wage models have gone a long way in explaining the phenomenon of the persistence of wages much in excess of market clearing levels combined with substantial unemployment – the situation which has characterized the 1970s and the 1980s. In so doing, they have brought a new credibility to the concept of Keynesian unemployment equilibria. For this reason it is perhaps of interest to note that some of the implications generated are decidedly un-Keynesian. For example, they might suggest that employment levels would be raised either by reducing unemployment benefits or by taxing the firm's wage bill or its annual rate of increase.

Insider–Outsider Analysis

One of the enigmas of the 1970s and 1980s was why the growing volume of unemployment seemed to exercise no restraint upon the rate of wage increases. Indeed, empirical observation suggested increasing unemployment combined with rising real wages for those fortunate to remain employed – a finding carrying grave implications for the relevance of the conventional competitive model as applied to labour markets. One resolution of this puzzle lay in the development of the insider–outsider dichotomy.

Insiders are those fortunate to be employed; outsiders are the unemployed and the thesis is developed to suggest that the latter exercise little or no influence upon actual wage levels. Increasing unemployment, therefore, does not reduce the power of the employed (the insiders) engaged in wage negotiations.

What gives the insiders the ability to ignore the presence of outsiders? Various arguments have been put forward in answer to this question but the majority appear to stress the costs involved in hiring, training and dismissing workers. Hiring and training costs have already been borne with regard to those currently employed. To dismiss these workers and replace them by lower paid outsiders would involve incurring such costs again. In addition, dismissal could involve substantial severance pay. Furthermore, the bargaining position of insiders is reinforced by the fact that they will often enjoy a measure of discretion with regard to the extent that they cooperate with newly employed outsiders. Cooperation amongst insiders is sufficient to account for their far greater productivity and explains the willingness of firms to negotiate with entrenched insiders (often unionized) as opposed to turning to non-unionized outsiders.

The power of insiders may also be reinforced by the perceptions of employers. It is argued, for example, that the long-term unemployed – those unemployed for a year or more – may be looked upon as unemployable by potential employers, owing to the erosion of skills, worker discipline and similar considerations. Consequently, such outsiders can exercise no influence over the bargaining position of insiders.

Insider–outsider models have been influential in suggesting valid reasons to account for the simultaneous growth in both unemployment and real wages. In particular, they would appear to explain why growing unemployment amongst school leavers has exercised virtually no impact upon national labour markets. Essentially, these new additions to the labour force are priced outside the market by the wage bargains struck by insiders. It will be noted, in contrast to efficiency wage models, that insider–outsider models rely upon the bargaining power of the employees and not upon any claims that higher wages imply increased efficiency.

Finally, insider–outsider models would appear to possess relevance for the duration of search unemployment models. Such models attempt to account for some portion of the unemployed in terms of the unemployed worker rejecting offers of employment because the wage proffered falls below expectations. Models of this nature then depend upon some form of adaptive expectations mechanism whereby the unemployed worker revises downward his expectations in the light of experience. Clearly, the duration of search unemployment will depend upon just how quickly the potential worker revises his expectation of the real wage downwards towards the market clearing level. However, if those seeking work perceive similarly qualified insiders enjoying comparatively high wage levels, this adjustment process will be delayed and the length of search unemployment extended accordingly.

The essence of the New Keynesian economics is the assertion that optimizing agents *chose* to create nominal rigidities in wages and prices. Once such rigidities are established, then nominal shocks will produce real effects and in particular can explain persistent departure from full employment equilibria. The macroeconomic costs of such rigidities can thus be measured in terms of the output foregone. One interesting implication of this thesis is that nominal flexibility will probably be greater in economies experiencing greater rates of inflation. Accordingly, it is arguable that the output costs stemming from factors making for rigidities will be less in countries with higher than average rates of inflation. Finally, since inflexible prices and perfect competition are inherently incompatible, it will be appreciated that this New Keynesian perspective relies heavily upon the introduction of imperfect competition in the modelling of labour markets.

Real Business Cycle Theory

As we have seen at various points in this volume, the emergence of New Classical economics carried enormous implications for macroeconomic policy. In particular, combining rational expectations formation with market clearing (as required by the adoption of the Walrasian competitive framework) implied virtually the elimination of involuntary unemployment. Indeed, any departure from the natural level of employment could only be explained in terms of mistaken expectations and perceptions of the price level – leading in turn to mistaken expectations and perceptions of real wages. Thus the Lucas aggregate supply curve posited;

$$Y - Y_n = \alpha(P - P^e)$$

where Y_n is the natural level of output, Y and P the actual level of output and prices respectively and P^e the expected price level. If actual prices exceeded those expected when contracts were negotiated, real wages would fall and employers would have the incentive to expand output. In this scenario, the main reason for mistaken expectations concerning future prices stems from *unanticipated* changes in the money stock.

Such expectational errors, however, were never fully adequate to explain the length and severity of the recession years. Although reasons were advanced to account for *persistence* – why, for example, the effects of any output change could be drawn out over future time periods – it became increasingly difficult to account for the business cycle in these terms, given the ready access to information at relatively low cost. In general, it became impossible to maintain that the business cycle stemmed from monetary shocks along these lines.

Thus, the conditions were appropriate for a transition to a *real*, as opposed to a *monetary*, explanation of the business cycle. Although the importance of the monetary impulse is dispensed with, in all other respects Real Business Cycle theory continues to be fundamentally classical. Thus, economic agents are utility maximizing individuals, forming expectations rationally and co-existing in a world where markets continuously clear.

Paradoxically, Real Business Cycle theory begins as a denial of the very concept of a business cycle as conventionally understood. The conventional view perceives the cycle as a deviation from the long-term growth trend generated by some autonomous shock. The shock, real or monetary, is the *impulse* mechanism which generates the

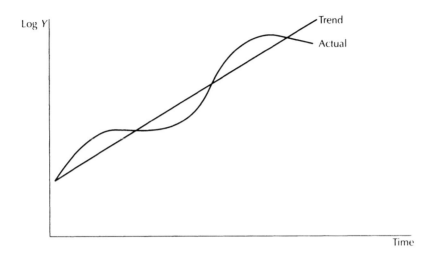

Figure 16.3 Conventional business cycle

departure from trend. The *propagation* mechanism then determines the manner in which the initial shock works itself out over time. This may take the form of acceler-ator–multiplier interaction, full employment ceilings and other factors governing the change in output and employment. Normally, however, the influence of the initial shock wanes over time and, given certain restrictions upon the difference equations involved, the economy will ultimately return to its long-term growth path dictated essentially by autonomous influences such as population growth and long-run tech-nical progress. The cycle then reveals itself in a series of oscillations around the long-term growth path, as indicated in figure 16.3.

In contrast, Real Business Cycle theory perceives technological shocks as changing the *actual* trend rate of growth instead of producing deviations from the trend. Thus, positive technological shocks shift the economy to a new permanent higher trend path whilst negative shocks force the economy to a lower growth trend. There is no cycle as such, merely changes in the long-term trend rate of growth. However, if such shocks are sufficiently frequent and also sufficiently random, they will generate changes in the long-run growth path which resemble closely the concept of a business cycle. Thus, for example, in figure 16.4, we assume positive shocks at time t_1, t_4 and t_5 and negative shocks at time t_2 and t_3. Joining points such as a, b, c, d and e produces a cyclical re-presentation of the path of income which in reality does not exist. Real Business Cycle theory is essentially a theory of economic growth driven by technological change.

What Real Business Cycle theory is attempting to do, however, is to account for the observed fluctuations in output and employment characteristic of the modern eco-nomy – which we normally identify with the business cycle. Moreover, to be consistent with the empirical evidence, it must account for the fact that output and employment move together and also that employment responds positively and significantly to rel-atively small increments in the real wage.

Consider figure 16.5. We assume initially that the economy is at point a upon the pro-duction function Y in the upper portion of the figure with the labour supply L and real wage W/P determined by the labour supply and demand curves S_L and D_L in the lower part of the figure. Now assume that *negative* technological change generates a

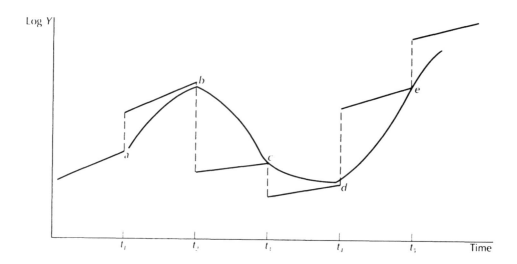

Figure 16.4 Real business cycle

downward shift of the production function to Y^*. If this change lowers the marginal product of labour (if it decreases the slope of a tangent drawn to the relevant production function at any input of labour) then the demand for labour will decrease – say, to D_{L2}. Output falls to b in the upper portion of the figure whilst employment and real wages decline to L^* and W^*/P respectively in the lower part of the figure. Clearly, this result demands that the labour supply is extremely elastic in response to a change in real wages – as indicated in the composite diagram.

The importance of this point is fundamental, for the increase in unemployment is seen to be a *voluntary* response to the decline in the real wage! The Walrasian competitive framework and rational behaviour dictate market clearing solutions. The decrease in output and employment is nothing more that an optimal Pareto response of supply and demand to the change in relative prices. Moreover, in such a world, government intervention to try and stabilize the economy and smooth the cycle would be self-defeating. By interfering with the free choice of rational economic agents, it would be creating a loss in welfare from the indicated Pareto ideal.

In this example, the initial shock to the system – the *impulse* – is the adverse productivity change which disturbs the steady state. What drives the cycle onwards, however – the *propagation* mechanism – causing the deviation from the steady state to persist, is the intertemporal substitution of labour. This refers to the willingness to switch between work and leisure in response to changes in comparative prices particularly wages and interest rates. Real Business Cycle theory depends upon the assumption that the intertemporal substitution of labour is extremely high.

Consider an elementary example adapted from Mankiw (1994). A student has the option of working this summer and taking a holiday next summer or alternatively working next summer and holidaying this summer. Suppose the wage this summer is W_1 and next summer is expected to be W_2. If the interest rate is currently i per cent the relevant comparison is given by the ratio

$W_1(1 + i)/W_2$

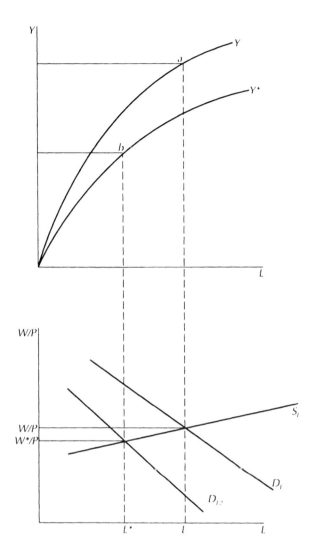

Figure 16.5 Technological shocks, output and employment

If the current wage is relatively high compared to what is anticipated next summer, or if the interest rate is unduly high, working this summer becomes more attractive and vice versa. The Mankiw example is a good one in that such a choice situation often applies to those enjoying a student-like existence. Real Business Cycle theory, however, extends this principle to all workers; rational behaviour demands that they move between work and leisure in response to quite small comparative prices changes regardless of existing or future committments.

The major critique of Real Business Cycle theory has focused upon this crucial point. Fundamentally, the evidence does not support a very high intertemporal substitution of labour, either with respect to change in real wages or in interest rates (Mankiw, 1989). In brief, it is difficult to reconcile recent unemployment levels as being consistent with workers voluntarily choosing leisure. Perhaps the most damning critique along these lines stems from Solow (1990). If this were the case, one would 'expect sales of goods complementary with leisure – like golf clubs, beachwear, skis and Carribean cruises – to be higher in recessions when there is a lot of measured unemployment than in prosperous periods when the unemployment rate falls... there is no sign that anything so amusing is true'.

In addition, the theory relies upon the concept of technological shocks which are not observed as such but merely *inferred* from the movement of the cycle. Many economists are doubtful that such shocks are sufficiently frequent or significant enough to produce such fluctuations especially in cases of technical regress required to account for the downturns.

Conclusion

The present chapter has attempted an introductory survey of the debate surrounding the desirability of macroeconomic policy. We have seen that the early Keynesian optimism concerning the potential of discretionary stabilization policy waned both under theoretical onslaughts on the one hand and in the light of actual experience on the other, to be replaced by a general scepticism concerning the efficacy of interventionist policy.

The danger that discretionary policy could be destabilizing, owing to unpredictable time lags, was superseded by the policy ineffectiveness proposition, which claimed that *systematic* policy would have no real effect. Real Business Cycle theory went one step further by claiming that attempts to curb fluctuations could only be welfare reducing by definition, since fluctuations represented the free choices of welfare maximizing economic agents.

Recently, however, there has been a resurgence of the Keynesian position that well-thought-out and well-executed policy measures can reasonably be expected to improve upon the normal functioning of the market economy. In turn, this conclusion rests upon the premise that there are strong reasons why market clearing behaviour need not apply to labour markets and that the highly decentralized model of perfect competition may be inappropriate to analyse behaviour in such markets.

Further Reading

The literature concerning the pros and cons of discretionary stabilization policy is now extremely extensive. A classic debate remains that of Friedman and Heller (1969) whilst the contributions in Hafer (1986) provide a more recent update. The policy ineffectiveness proposition and the Lucas Critique stem originally from Sargent and Wallace (1975) and Lucas (1976). Ball, Mankiw and Romer (1988) extend the New Keynesian approach which is extensively analysed in the text by Carlin and Soskice (1990). A simpler survey of New Keynesian models is contained in Shaw (1990).

Major contributions to Real Business Cycle theory include Barro (1981), Kydland and Prescott (1982), Nelson and Plosser (1982) and Long and Plosser (1983). Important surveys, some critical, include Mankiw (1989), Plosser (1989), McCallum (1989, 1992), Phelps (1990) and Stadler (1993, 1994).

Finally, both Cross (1991) and Solow (1990) offer insightful comment and a highly readable textbook presentation is that by Snowdon, Vane and Wynarczyk (1994) in a volume which is itself replete with references.

17

Approaches to Macroeconomic Policy

Assuming that it is possible to define adequately the policy objectives and their order of priority in the event of conflict, the next step is to decide upon the approach to macroeconomic policy formulation. Broadly, two general approaches may be distinguished, both of which spring from the theoretical and practical contribution of two Dutch economists. On the one hand there is what has become known as the *optimizing approach*, associated largely with the name of Henri Theil, whilst on the other there is the so-called *fixed targets approach*, intimately linked with the work of Nobel prize winner Jan Tinbergen. In what follows, the essence of these diverse approaches will be sketched briefly before the problems arising from the existence of uncertainty are tackled. To this end it is convenient to reintroduce the short-run Phillips curve. For expository purposes it will be assumed that this summarizes the choice available to the policy-maker, an infinite number of inflation–unemployment combinations are potentially attainable; how does one select from this infinite range?

The Optimizing Approach

The *optimizing approach* to economic policy assumes that it is conceptually possible to specify *the social welfare function*. Once this is determined, and the preference pattern of society with respect to all possible outcomes of inflation and unemployment is known, the task of policy is simply to select whatever attainable combination will maximize welfare. Thus, for example, in figure 17.1 the objective function is summarized in the collective indifference curves in unemployment–inflation space superimposed upon the diagram. In this simple model, with only two policy objectives, the indifference curves indicate successively higher stages of collective well-being *as they approach the origin.*[1] Clearly the optimum position would be at the origin where perfect price stability is reconciled with full employment. However, the Phillips curve imposes a

---

1 The community indifference curves are drawn concave to the origin for precisely the same reason that conventional indifference curves are usually portrayed as convex – namely, that the marginal significance of one good in terms of the other will normally increase the less one has of the one good and the more one has of the other. In the present case, however, the indifference diagram portrays not goods but positive 'bads' – inflation and unemployment. Thus, as successively higher rates of inflation are encountered, the objective of price stability becomes more desirable and further increments in inflation are only acceptable if progressively greater increments in employment are offered. Hence the concavity of the indifference curves.

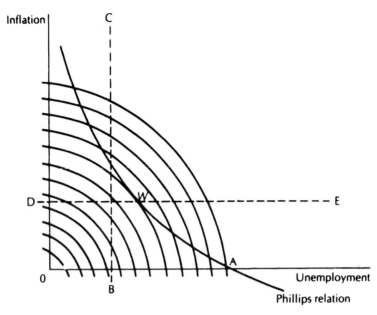

Figure 17.1 Optimizing and fixed targets approaches to macroeconomic policy formulation

constraint by specifying all feasible combinations of employment and inflation. The policy decision-maker must select from this limited choice. If he is successful, he will juggle with alternative policy mixes to obtain a solution at point W, which maximizes the well-being of society given the predetermined indifference map. Implicit in this approach is the assumption that no one policy objective is sacrosanct: objectives, as well as instruments, are flexible. It is the task of the policy-maker to decide, in the light of all the available information, the extent to which any one objective must be compromised to maximize total well-being.

In many ways the optimizing approach is theoretically appealing and being stated in terms of constrained maximization enjoys an affinity with conventional micro-economic techniques. However, its fundamental drawback is that it requires some theory of group decision-making in order to be able to determine with a reasonable degree of confidence the social welfare ordering. There are serious difficulties with this proposition. Modern welfare economics would suggest that transitive choice will not emerge from the simple majority voting principle as practised in the UK.

The Fixed Targets Approach

In many respects it may be contended that the *fixed targets approach* is a more pragmatic way of formulating macroeconomic policy. This approach to policy-making neatly sidesteps the difficulties associated with approximating social welfare functions. Instead, policy goals are stated as constituting fixed targets from which no departure is permitted. In effect, this is tantamount to the decision-making authorities intervening in the role of benevolent dictator in specifying what the social welfare function should be. Once the objectives have been determined, policy-making then reduces to the search for an adequate armoury of instruments to secure their attainment.

Assume, for example, that the decision-making authorities have decreed that the objective of price stability should be interpreted as no more than D per cent inflation per year, whilst the goal of full employment is consistent with B per cent unemployed. In this case, the fixed targets limit the acceptable region of figure 17.1 to the area left of the vertical line BC and below the horizontal line DE. Moreover, given the Phillips curve, these twin objectives are incapable of being achieved simultaneously with the existing conventional tools of macroeconomic policy. The existing policy measures are able to achieve either goal at the sacrifice of the other. The introduction of new policy tools, therefore, is required in order to secure the additional policy objective, by affecting the appropriate inward shift of the Phillips curve. The Tinbergen principle was introduced in chapter 14; this derives from the fixed targets approach and concludes that successful policy execution necessitates having at least as many *independent* policy instruments as one has policy targets.

The Tinbergen approach has exercised considerable influence upon policy discussion and in reality this has been the approach favoured by policy-makers. This has arisen because in practice governments have chosen to accord priority to one objective to which the others have then been subordinated. Thus, for example, in terms of figure 17.1 this approach is akin to promulgating one target as fixed and letting the other be passively determined by the technical relationship underlying the Phillips curve. One difficulty which arises with the Tinbergen approach to macroeconomic policy formation concerns the independence of the policy instruments. Recent theoretical work arising from the monetarist controversy and especially the analysis of the budget constraint has questioned the assumed independence of many of the major instruments. In any case it can be demonstrated that once uncertainty is allowed to enter the analysis the necessary equation between objectives and instruments is no longer sufficient; with uncertainty, optimum policy-making requires that more than one instrument must be directed towards each objective.

If one policy objective is accorded overriding priority, so that other objectives are passively determined as residuals, then the fixed targets approach can be simply illustrated by reference to an elementary national income model. Assuming a closed economy model of the form

$$Y = C + I + G \tag{17.1}$$

where the symbols represent income, consumption, investment and government expenditures respectively, the policy objective can be represented by a target level of income Y^*. Assume that this target income level acts as a proxy for the ultimate policy goal, employment. Let consumption be a function of disposable income so that

$$C = bY_d \tag{17.2}$$

where b is the marginal propensity to consume, and Y_d is disposable income and is equal to

$$Y_d = Y(1 - t) \tag{17.3}$$

where t is a proportional rate of income tax. Let both private sector investment and government expenditure be exogenous so that

$$I = \bar{I} \tag{17.4}$$

and

$$G = \bar{G} \tag{17.5}$$

but with the latter being under government control and hence constituting an available policy instrument. Solving for the equilibrium level of national income,

$$Y = \frac{\bar{I} + \bar{G}}{1 - b + bt} \tag{17.6}$$

Given the model, and assuming that an estimate of the value of the marginal propensity to consume and a forecasted value of the exogenous variable $\bar{I}$ can be obtained, then the task of the policy-maker reduces to selecting values of the policy instruments, G and t, so as to secure the target income level Y^*. It will be appreciated that, in this simple case, one policy instrument is sufficient to secure the one objective. Holding government expenditures constant, t could be varied so as to secure Y^*. Alternatively, holding t constant, the appropriate value of G could be determined so as to give the same result. Equally, however, the two policy instruments could be combined; indeed, it may well be the case that in order to secure the target income level Y^* more than one combination of G and t is available. If this situation prevails, then the actual choice of G and t will be determined by reference to additional criteria – perhaps, for example, by the desire to minimize the budget deficit. Here the Tinbergen principle is seen at work. With just one policy objective, Y^*, either the expenditure tool or the tax tool was sufficient in itself. As soon as secondary objectives are allowed to enter the analysis, as in this case the size of the budget deficit, then the additional policy tool is required to provide the optimal policy mix.

The Problem of Time Inconsistency

Both the optimizing approach and the fixed targets approach assume that the objective of the policy-maker is to secure the maximum welfare of society. The only fundamental difference between the two is that the fixed targets approach bypasses the difficulty of determining the social welfare ordering. None the less, no conflict is assumed to exist between the objectives of government and those of society. The government acts – and indeed exists in this scenario – to serve the well being of society.

This assumption, namely that objective functions of government and society coincide, has been called into question by the problem of time inconsistency, which is yet another important consequence stemming from the assumption of rational expectations formation. The important policy implication which derives from this concept strengthens the case for rules as opposed to discretion by showing that the latter is likely to impart an inflationary bias to equilibrium outcomes.

When expectations are formed rationally, the position of the Phillips curve will depend upon the price expectations held by the private sector. Consider figure 17.2 which is a modified form of the previous figure with the vertical axis now being drawn through the point of the natural level of employment. Consequently, any point on the vertical axis is consistent with equilibrium. Thus, for example, with expectations of zero inflation the Phillips curve P_0^e applies and equilibrium is found at A; with expectation of inflation at 10 per cent, P_{10}^e is the relevant Phillips curve and equilibrium occurs at point B. With expected inflation of 20 per cent we obtain position C and so forth.

Suppose the government (which we assume can control the money supply) announces a target of zero inflation and suppose this announcement is believed by the private sector. Point A thus becomes attainable and will be achieved and we will have

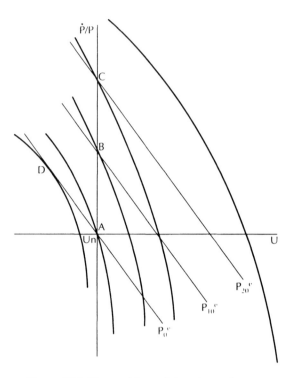

Figure 17.2 The problem of time inconsistency

a Pareto optimal situation combining zero inflation and the natural rate of employment.

In such a situation, however, the government now has an incentive to renege upon its
stated intention and to increase the money supply to generate, say, a 10 per cent rate of
inflation. With the Phillips curve P_0^e real wages fall, employment is increased and we
will observe a movement to point D as unemployment falls below the natural level.

The indifference curves drawn here illustate the preferences of the *policy-maker.*
Point D implies, from his standpoint, a higher level of welfare with output above and
unemployment below their natural levels. Of course, point D is not sustainable; as the
new inflation becomes perceived, the Phillips curve is shifted outwards and the natural
level will ultimately be regained at point B. This outcome, it will be noted, represents a
stable solution. The policy-maker no longer has any incentive to attempt to generate a
surprise inflation.

But whilst B represents a stable outcome, it is clearly inferior to point A. The difference between points A and B is that A is optimal but *time inconsistent* whilst B is a
sub-optimal but *time consistent* outcome. We may now define what is meant by time
inconsistency. If a policy deemed optimal at time t is subsequently altered or re-
optimized at a later date, it is deemed time inconsistent. Alternatively, a policy is
deemed time inconsistent if optimality *ex ante* differs from optimality *ex post.*

The importance of this distinction should now be clear. Assuming rational expectations formation, economic agents will ultimately – by painful experience or otherwise
– perceive the options open to the government. Time inconsistent policies will simply

not be believed. A government announcement of a zero inflation target will simply cease to be credible. Rational agents will anticipate the policy-makers' deception and will expect, in our current example, an inflation rate of 10 per cent. The best the government can now achieve in such a situation is the time consistent position B – a game theoretic outcome in a game played by two players, with the government the dominant partner but with the private sector anticipating government strategy.

Of course the conflict would not arise if the government or the policy-maker did not have discretion. If he were bound by a fixed rule, such as, say, to maintain the money supply in line with a zero inflation rate, then the Pareto optimal outcome A, is perfectly attainable. The time inconsistency thesis is thus yet another argument against discretionary interventionist policy by suggesting that powers of discretion possess an inherent inflationary bias.

Just how important this inherent bias is remains a matter of debate. Governments that are concerned with their reputation or future success may feel constrained not to stray too far from the preferences expressed by society in general. None the less, it does suggest that the traditional approach to macroeconomic policy-making exemplified by Tinbergen and Theil may be an oversimplification which is no longer tenable. The elementary mathematics of time inconsistency is outlined in the appendix to this chapter.

Macroeconomic Policy and Uncertainty

Given the formal model result contained in equation 17.6, it has been seen that macroeconomic policy reduces to selecting that combination(s) of G and t consistent with the attainment of a target Y, Y^*. However, this rather *simpliste* approach tacitly assumes that the forecasted investment figure $\bar{I}$ is considered to be absolutely certain. In actual fact, purely exogenous variables are likely to be viewed with a considerable amount of caution with regard to their ultimate values. If uncertainty exists with reference to the purely exogenous values then equally uncertainty will prevail with regard to the values to be given to the control instruments G and t.[2]

To pursue this line of thought, assume that there are two possible values to be accorded the purely exogenous variable $\bar{I}$, I_A and I_B, where $I_A > I_B$. Assume also there are two possible levels of government expenditure, $G_A > G_B$, and two possible rates of taxation, $t_A > t_B$. For simplicity of exposition, the range of government policies are collapsed into two possible alternatives, an expansionary policy denoted by the combination $G_A t_B$ and a restrictive policy indicated by $G_B t_A$. All possible outcomes can then be illustrated as in the composite table 17.1, which also indicates the preferences of the policy-makers between the competing possibilities. Thus, for example, with the expansionary policy $G_A t_B$, if the event I_B occurs, the target income level Y^* is established and the policy-makers award this a value of 95, whereas should event I_A occur, then the outcome is inflation which earns a value of 85. Similarly, with a restrictive government policy indicated by $G_B t_A$, if the event I_A occurs, the target income Y^* is obtained with a value of 100, whereas should event I_B occur, then the result will be unemployed resources which will be valued at 75. It will be noted that the

---

2 In a world of uncertainty, there is a set of all possible states of nature denoted by the possible values of $\bar{I}$, a set of possible acts denoted by the possible values to be accorded to the instruments G and t, and a set of possible outcomes denoted by the possible values of Y. This terminology and related argument follows Peston (1982).

TABLE 17.1
Outcomes of Two Government Policies

	Outcomes		Values	
	I_A	I_B	I_A	I_B
Expansionary policy				
$G_A t_B$	Inflation	Y^*	85	95
Restrictive policy				
$G_B t_A$	Y^*	Unemployment	100	75

securing of Y^* does not imply equal valuations; that is to say, the policy-maker will not be indifferent to the manner in which it is secured. Thus, in the present example, the policy-maker reveals a preference for securing Y^* *via* the 'restrictive' fiscal policy $G_B t_A$ as opposed to the 'expansionary' policy $G_A t_B$, presumably upon the grounds that the former implies a smaller public sector deficit.

It is now possible to examine alternative policy strategies. The optimal welfare value is secured only with strategy $G_B t_A$, but this is also the strategy with the greatest *potential* welfare loss. Assuming equal chances of I_A or I_B occurring, the mean value of this strategy is given as 87.5. In contrast, strategy $G_A t_B$ never secures the optimal 100 valuation but its mean value is 90. Moreover, this is also the strategy which avoids the worst possible outcome, namely that of unemployment. In these circumstances, it is quite feasible that the policy-maker will always opt for strategy $G_A t_B$. It never secures the maximum welfare but it is quite possible that the outcomes of the strategy are consistent with the retention of public office. In contrast the worst feasible outcome associated with strategy $G_B t_A$ might guarantee certain electoral defeat. It will be noted that if the policy $G_A t_B$ is chosen then *ex post* it will always appear that a preferable alternative did exist. In retrospect, a higher valuation was always attainable had the value to be taken by $\bar{I}$ been known with certainty. It is in this sense that the optimal policy with uncertainty may differ from the optimal policy with certainty. In this manner, the existence of uncertainty acts as a constraint upon the design of optimal policy measures.

Admittedly, the preceding analysis is rather elementary. In particular, it assumes an equal chance of occurrence of outcome I_A and outcome I_B, and furthermore it restricts government policy intervention to one of two extremes. In principle, however, these restrictions can be readily dispensed with without modifying the essential conclusions in any fundamental way (see Peston, 1982).

The Principle of Certainty Equivalence

Largely because of the difficulties of dealing with uncertainty in macroeconomic policy formulation, economists were quick to endorse what appeared to be a generally accepted principle, without arguably taking full account of the reservations which might reduce its applicability. This principle of *certainty equivalence* has exercised considerable influence both in the realm of pragmatic policy-making and in academic circles. In keeping with the previous discussion, it is assumed that the target level of income is Y^* and any departure from this income level will imply a welfare loss. Assume also, *in contrast to the previous example*, that the welfare loss is symmetrical about the target income level. This implies that a 2 per cent overshooting of the target income level generates the same loss of welfare as a 2 per cent undershooting. This situation is summarized with the aid of figure 17.3.[3]

Again, in keeping with the previous example, it is assumed that departures from the target level Y^* arise owing to the existence of uncertainty with respect to investment outlays, which may be either I_A or I_B. How is this difficulty dealt with? In principle, this question reduces to one in constrained minimization. Given estimated probabilities about events I_A and I_B, the task of the policy-maker is to select that combination of instruments, in this case G and t, so as to minimize the welfare loss. Pursuing this strategy may never result in attaining the desired income level Y^*, but it can be shown to be optimal in the sense that over time it will minimize the welfare losses associated with *departures from* Y^*. It may be demonstrated that the optimal policy mix is that combination of instruments which would secure the target level Y^* had the level of investment forthcoming been equal to the mathematically expected level of investment expenditures (see the appendix to this chapter). In the present example, if p is the probability of event I_A occurring then $(1 - p)$ is the probability of the event I_B and the mathematical expectation of investment is simply given by

$$ME = p(I_A) + (1 - p)I_B = \tilde{I} \qquad (17.7)$$

If this value of $\tilde{I}$ is now inserted into the macroeconomic model so that

$$Y = \frac{\tilde{I} + G}{1 - b + bt} \qquad (17.8)$$

where $\tilde{I}$ is now looked upon as a certainty, then the combination of instruments G and t can be chosen consistent with Y^*. That is to say, the values of the instruments are chosen to attain the targeted Y^* upon the assumption that the level of investment forthcoming is certain to be $\tilde{I}$. This is the principle of certainty equivalence. It provides a control guide to the policy-makers concerned with formulating economic policy. It may never succeed in generating the desired income level Y^* but it can be defended upon the ground that over time it will minimize the welfare loss associated with departures from Y^*.

The principle of certainty equivalence appeared to provide a control rule to guide rational decision-making. Moreover, part of its appeal doubtless lay in the fact that it was a proxy for what policy-makers had in fact been doing with their economic models which did not admit of uncertainty. Simply stated, elementary macromodels relied upon the forecasted values of the purely exogenous variables and these forecasts would normally coincide with their mathematically expected value. The principle of certainty equivalence not only provided a control guide to policy formation under certain conditions but it also provided a rationale for the existing code of practice. It is not surprising, therefore, that the principle was quickly endorsed. However, although the principle provided a useful insight into a difficult theoretical terrain, it is important to be aware of its reservations. First of all, its validity depends upon the crucial assumption that the utility function depicted in figure 17.2 is indeed symmetric about the target level Y^*. If this is not the case – if, for example, the welfare losses associated with unemployment exceed those associated with inflation so that the welfare function is

---

3 Figure 17.3 implies that the welfare function is quadratic in that the welfare loss of departure from Y^* increases at an increasing rate. Thus, 4 per cent unemployed resources is more than twice as bad as 2 per cent unemployment.

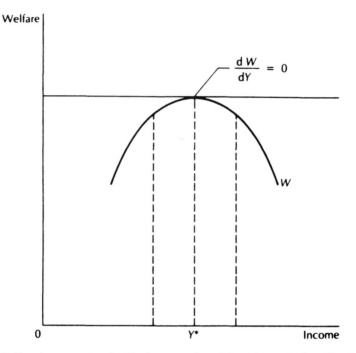

Figure 17.3 Welfare loss associated with departure from Y^* with quadratic utility function

asymmetric – then the analysis becomes decidedly more complex and the fundamental conclusion would no longer apply. Second, it is important to realize that the principle applies only to cases where uncertainty surrounds the purely exogenous variables. It cannot, for example, be extended to cases of uncertainty surrounding the estimated value of the parameter b – the marginal propensity to consume. It may well be the case that the major losses of welfare stem not so much from uncertainty regarding purely exogenous variables but rather from forecasting errors in the structural parameters determining national income multipliers. As we have seen in the previous chapter, this issue takes on major importance if the structural parameters themselves are subject to change *in response* to active policy measures. This prospect, usually referred to as the Lucas Critique, has seriously called into question the validity of large-scale econometric models aimed at simulating the impact of macroeconomic policy.

Concluding Comments

In this chapter we have been examined alternative ways of macroeconomic policy formulation. The optimizing and fixed targets approaches has been contrasted and the difficulties associated with each indicated. The difficulties created by the existence of uncertainty were then examined in greater detail and it was demonstrated that, even if one is unsure of the values taken by exogenous variables, none the less optimal decision rules still exist. This was illustrated by the principle of certainty equivalence, examined more formally in the appendix to this chapter. One consequence of uncertainty is that correctly conceived policies *ex ante* will almost always appear second-best solutions with the wisdom of hindsight. The macroeconomic policy-maker might justifiably conclude that economics is indeed the 'dismal science'.

Appendix: The Principle of Certainty Equivalence

Given the equation for the equilibrium level of income as

$$Y = \frac{\bar{I} + \bar{G}}{1 - b + bt} \tag{17.9}$$

simplify the analysis by assuming the tax rate to be invariant. That is, assume that the government seeks to attain the target level of income Y^* solely by the use of variations in the level of government expenditures. This gives

$$Y = k(\bar{I} + \bar{G}) \tag{17.10}$$

where k is the multiplier and is equal to $1/(1 - b + bt)$. If Y^* is the target income level, variations from Y^* are indicated by

$$Y^* - k(\bar{I} + \bar{G}) \tag{17.11}$$

that is, target income minus actual income levels. Assuming that the welfare function is symmetrical about Y^*, the welfare loss arising from deviations from Y^* can be expressed as

$$WL = [Y^* - k(\bar{I} + \bar{G})]^2 \tag{17.12}$$

The expected welfare loss depends upon the expected values of $\bar{I}$, so that

$$EWL = p[Y^* - k(I_A + \bar{G})]^2 + (1 - p)[Y^* - k(I_B + \bar{G})]^2 \tag{17.13}$$

This is the expression which must be minimized for maximum welfare. The task is to select the value of G consistent with the minimization of this expression. Differentiating with respect to G, and setting the result equal to zero to satisfy first-order conditions, yields

$$kpI_A + (1 - p)I_B + k\bar{G} - Y^* = 0 \tag{17.14}$$

Since $pI_A + (1 - p)I_B$ is the mathematical expectation of I, namely $\tilde{I}$, this reduces to

$$k\tilde{I} + k\bar{G} - Y^* = 0 \tag{17.15}$$

Accordingly,

$$Y^* = k(\bar{G} + \tilde{I}) = \frac{(\bar{G} + \tilde{I})}{1 - b + bt} \tag{17.16}$$

and

$$\frac{Y^*}{k} - \tilde{I} = \bar{G} \tag{17.17}$$

Thus, the value of $\bar{G}$ consistent with the target income level Y^* is obtained by substituting into the equation for equilibrium national income the mathematically expected value of I, $\tilde{I}$ as if this value was assured with certainty. This is the principle of certainty equivalence.

The Problem of Time Inconsistency

Unemployment falls below the natural level whenever inflation exceeds expected inflation, as indicated by the Phillips curve relation:

$$U = U_n - \alpha(P - P^e) \tag{17.18}$$

where, as before, P represents actual and P^e expected inflation. Both inflation and unemployment impose a cost upon the government denoted by the welfare loss function:

$$WL(U, P) = U + \beta P^2 \tag{17.19}$$

That is to say, we assume (for expositional purposes) that the welfare loss is quadratic with respect to inflation and we assume the government's objective is to minimize this welfare loss function.

If the government is bound by fixed rules with no discretion, then clearly expected inflation will equal actual inflation and unemployment will coincide with its natural rate. Thus,

$P^e = P => U = U_n$ and the optimal outcome is simply obtained by setting $P = 0$.

With discretion, the government will seek to minimize $WL(U, P)$ subject to the constraint imposed by the Phillips curve which pertains once the expected rate of inflation is determined. Substituting the Phillips curve into the welfare loss function gives

$$WL(U, P) = U_n - \alpha(P - P^e) + \beta P^2 \tag{17.20}$$

Notice that the welfare loss is greater, the greater the rate of inflation expected by the private sector. To minimize the welfare loss we need

$$dWL/dP = 0 => -\alpha + 2\beta P = 0 \tag{17.21}$$

Thus,

$$P = \alpha/2\beta > 0 \tag{17.22}$$

This is the optimal rate of inflation for the government to choose and it is positive and greater than the zero rate optima in the non-discretion case. But since it is the optima when discretion prevails, it will also be anticipated by rational economic agents. Consequently,

$$P^e = P = \alpha/2\beta \quad \text{and} \quad U = U_n \tag{17.23}$$

Thus, equilibrium employment implies higher inflation with discretion than without. This is the problem of time inconsistency.

Further Reading

Theil (1961) and Tinbergen (1952, 1965) are the seminal contributions on the optimizing and fixed targets approaches to policy formulation respectively. As was noted in the text, one of the principal difficulties with the optimizing approach is in identifying a social welfare function. Recent contributions in the theory of public choice have analysed this issue further. See, for example, the survey paper by Mueller (1976). The targets instruments approach has been applied to a variety of problems. One of the most tractable and interesting applications is the Mundellian internal–external balance model as outlined in Mundell (1962).

Brainard (1967) analyses the role of uncertainty, whilst a straightforward overview of the principle of certainty equivalence can be found in Peacock and Shaw (1976).

The seminal paper on time inconsistency is that of Kydland and Prescott (1977) Other important contributions include Barro and Gordon (1983), Taylor (1985), Barro (1986) and Blackburn (1992).

18

Macroeconomic Policy: Objectives, Instruments and Constraints

The design and formulation of macroeconomic policies presupposes the need for positive intervention and interference with the normal functioning of the macroeconomy. That is to say, it is implicitly assumed that the economy left to its own devices will not ordinarily attain a state consistent with the maximum well-being of its constituent members. This conclusion might be defended upon the Keynesian assumption that the economy possesses no inherent tendency automatically to adjust to a desired state of affairs following some autonomous disturbance; alternatively, invoking the classical view that there is an inherent tendency for the economy to approach 'natural' levels of employment, output, inflation and so forth, this conclusion may still be defended upon the grounds that the adjustment process is too slow and encounters too many artificial rigidities in the modern complex economy where atomistic competition does not always prevail.[1]

Recognition of the fact that it may be possible, at least in principle, to improve the existing macroeconomic performance of the economy is of course only the beginning of macroeconomic policy. It then becomes necessary to specify the *objectives* of policy more precisely and to determine their *order of priority* in the event of possible conflict.

Determining the policy objectives and their priority rankings does not, however, advance the decision-taker very far. He will then be faced with the need to choose between alternative policy recommendations proffered by his economic advisers as a means of achieving stated goals. In some cases there may be genuine alternatives; more commonly, different recommendations will reflect differences in the way in which different economic advisers view the economy. In turn, this may reflect on the one hand fundamental differences in the intellectual attachment to opposing theoretical viewpoints and on the other differing assumptions of how the economy responds. Either form of difference may result in diametrically opposing conclusions as to the effectiveness of any given macro measure.

To summarize, therefore, macroeconomic policy involves three initial steps. The first is the determination of the policy objectives and their respective ranking in the event of conflict. This, it is assumed, is accomplished (doubtless imperfectly) via

---

1 Alternatively, intervention may be justified as a means of reducing uncertainty, as for example in the case of prescribing set rules for financial policies, money supply growth rates and so forth.

the political process. The second is the formulation of policies which are logically consistent with the attainment of the objectives, given a formal theoretical structure and set of assumptions which appear relevant to real world conditions. The third is some elementary cost-benefit calculation of policy effectiveness to ensure that net benefits outweigh the costs involved.

Policy Objectives

Although considerable differences of opinion exist with respect to the way in which policy objectives should be defined, and even greater differences emerge with regard to their relative ranking, there exists a remarkable consensus upon what broadly constitutes the macroeconomic objectives.

Employment

A high level of employment has been included amongst the objectives of government economic policy ever since the message of the Keynesian revolution suggested that employment lay within the domain of government control. The Keynesian view of employment is relatively simple; the involuntary unemployed can be divided into two categories, those who could be effectively employed by macroeconomic policies raising the level of aggregate demand and those who could not.[2] The latter category takes account of those who are seasonally unemployed or in the process of changing jobs, the structurally unemployed and the chronically unemployable. The goal of full employment, therefore, should be defined solely with respect to the former from the viewpoint of macroeconomic policy. The ratio of those unemployed owing to demand deficiency to those unemployed for other reasons has, as will be seen in chapter 20, declined in recent years. One major reason has been the secular decline in traditional industries such as textiles, shipbuilding and steel. Moreover, the difficulties have been compounded by a tendency towards regional concentration within these industries and by housing policies which have rendered labour geographically immobile. If unemployment is more the consequence of major structural decline, then arguably the scope of conventional macroeconomic demand management policies has declined. Indeed, it is partly this reduced employment generating potential that has contributed to the greater degree of scepticism now accorded to Keynesian orthodoxy. An alternative view of the employment objective, associated with the monetarist school, would argue that macroeconomic policy is powerless to influence the long-term or 'natural' level of employment. The natural rate is determined by a host of influences including the level of unemployment benefits (in relation to the post-tax wage), the degree of regional and occupational mobility, and so forth – all factors which are essentially microeconomic. Thus, whilst the natural rate may be amenable to government policy it will not be amenable to macroeconomic policy measures in the long term. In the short run, however, this monetarist argument concedes that the actual level of employment may depart from its natural level – rising above it at the expense of increasing the rate of inflation, and falling below it to achieve a reduction in the rate of inflation.

---

2 This dichotomy derives from Keynes (see, for example, Kahn, 1976).

Price Stability

Inflation is commonly defined to imply a *persistent* tendency for the aggregate price level to rise as measured by some acceptable price index. This immediately raises the question of which price index to use, for different indices may signal different outcomes and indeed may move in opposite directions on occasions. The *wholesale price index*, for example, is greatly influenced by changes in the terms of trade and in the rate of exchange and is perhaps the best index to invoke as a pointer to future changes in the level of industrial costs. In contrast, the *retail price index* indicates changes in the average cost of living for the representative family, and in contrast to the wholesale index is influenced by changes in the level of indirect taxation. A decision to effect a major shift from direct to indirect taxation, for example, would have an immediate impact upon the retail price index whilst leaving the wholesale index unchanged. The retail price index is dominated primarily by the costs of foodstuffs, transportation and housing and is the one most frequently invoked by trade unions in justifying wage increases. It is not, however, typical or representative of all income groups and may be positively misleading for special interest groups such as old age pensioners, students and the like. In recent years, the relevance of the retail price index to wage claims has been questioned upon the ground that it ignores changes in direct taxation which affect welfare whilst leaving price levels unchanged. It has been suggested that the *tax price index*, which takes into account both direct and indirect tax changes, would be a better indicator of the compensation needed to maintain real living standards intact.

Why is inflation such a major source of concern? The answer to this question derives from the belief that inflation imposes major costs upon society whilst conferring few benefits. As will be argued in more detail in chapter 19, many of the costs associated with inflation can be avoided if the rate of inflation is correctly anticipated. Since it is easier to anticipate the rate of inflation the more stable its rate, it could be argued that the policy objective should be to ensure stability in the rate of inflation over time rather than to seek its elimination, especially as the latter may imply strenuous adjustment costs. None the less, even if inflation is fully anticipated certain costs will remain which warrant consideration. First of all, there is the resource cost involved in adjusting to inflation contained in the time and inconvenience of changing prices, adapting to new prices, informing customers and sales staff and forcing changes to advertising projects. This is a real cost which depletes real net income and welfare. Second, as Friedman has frequently emphasized, inflation may be considered a form of taxation imposed upon the holders of money balances. This effectively transfers money from creditors in the private sector to the government as a net debtor in an arbitrary and unjustified manner. Moreover, this is a form of taxation imposed without regard to ability to pay and thus imposed without reference to the standard canons of equity. Third, inflation will carry consequences for those sectors engaged in international trade and in this event one encounters increased uncertainty as to future exchange rates, which in itself may impose transaction costs upon those engaged in trading.

Balance of Payments

The balance of payments objective is identified as the desire for long-run equality between international payments and receipts. It arises from the awareness that there are costs associated with any imbalance between payments and receipts. The nature of the costs involved, however, will depend upon the nature of the exchange rate regime.

In the case of a fixed rate regime the consequences of a payments surplus would be a potentially inflationary inflow of money. Alternatively, in the event of a deficit the domestic money supply would fall as money balances are run down in exchange for foreign currency holdings. It is for this reason that a distinction is sometimes drawn between the change in the money stock after allowing for these transactions and the change which would occur in the absence of such transactions. The latter, referred to as domestic credit expansion (DCE), is often looked upon as being a better indicator of monetary policy; the control of DCE is seen to appear crucial in meeting the balance of payments target.

If there were no limit to the extent to which a payments deficit could be financed by exchanging domestic currency for foreign currency *via* central bank mediation there would be no particular need to concern oneself unduly with the existence of a deficit. However, there will normally be a limit to the extent of foreign exchange reserves held by the central bank. Once these reserves are exhausted then the country becomes bankrupt in an international context and is unable to pay for its excess of imports which would quickly be curtailed. The choking- off of essential goods and imports of raw materials would have a profound and disruptive impact upon the economy; few economies have allowed matters to reach this stage but have preferred to correct the imbalance by resorting to deflationary measures. Such measures, often imposed by international agencies such as the IMF as a condition of aid, do themselves involve costs such as increased unemployment and a slowing down in the rate of economic growth. For these reasons, then, equality in the overall balance of payments is considered a desirable goal.

Nor is this conclusion altered by the adoption of a freely floating exchange rate. Under such a regime the consequences of a balance of payments surplus or deficit would be appreciation or depreciation of the currency with no change in official reserves.[3] Fluctuating exchange rates may generate uncertainty which, as was seen in chapter 15, may be intensified by a tendency for exchange rate movements to 'overshoot' and go beyond a range that would appear to be justified solely by reference to purchasing power parity. Temporarily high exchange rates can create competitive problems for both exporters and domestic producers alike, whilst temporarily low exchange rates raise import prices with discriminatory effects throughout the economy. All things considered, therefore, exchange rate stability is a logical goal of policy.

Economic Growth

The case for economic growth being included within the objectives of macroeconomic policy is clear and compelling. Increased real income per caput[4] permits the increased consumption of all goods including leisure and hence an increase in economic welfare as commonly understood. Second, with natural increases in the labour force combined with a tendency for economic activity to become increasingly capital intensive, economic growth becomes a necessary prerequisite for the maintenance of full

---

3 And in such a situation no distinction exists between the domestic money supply and the extent of domestic credit expansion.

4 This would be a generally acceptable definition of economic growth providing some possible dangers are recognized. For example, the sudden elimination of the retired part of the population would raise per caput incomes but one might hesitate to include this under the heading of economic growth. There are other similar distributional qualifications one might wish to make to the above definition.

employment and for the elimination of the social tensions which accompany unemployment. In addition, economic growth is the only feasible means of terminating poverty. This arises from the compounding nature of the growth process; in contrast, once and for all distributional transfers from rich to poor have but a relatively insignificant effect, and this is equally true of transfers effected by the tax transfer mechanism within an economy as it is of international aid grants between countries.

Although most economists would endorse this general desirability of economic growth, it should be emphasized that a consensus does not exist. There are also costs associated with economic growth including pollution, congestion, the tensions associated with living in a highly complex and urbanized society and the speeding up of structural change which generates displacement effects and regional decline. In addition, many economists have drawn attention to the impact of economic growth upon the depletion of natural resources, many of which are in finite supply, and also have pointed to the environmental and ecological damage inflicted by uncontrolled growth.

Regional Balance

Finally, one may justifiably include amongst the objectives of macroeconomic policy the desire to promote or maintain a relatively uniform spatial allocation of incomes and resources. It is recognized that labour is still relatively immobile and that there are severe costs associated with the secular regional decline of highly specialized industry. This is particularly the case with respect to traditional industries such as shipbuilding and textiles now facing intense Third World competition, and it has led to the formulation of structural economic policies for specified industries, discriminatory fiscal treatment of the regions and interventionist government mediation. It has also witnessed the growth in importance of regional transfers in the EC total budget.

Policy Instruments

Fiscal

Fiscal policy is defined to encompass any change in the level, composition or timing of government expenditures or any change in the burden, structure or frequency of the tax payment. Since fiscal policy normally influences the size of the actual public sector borrowing requirement (PSBR), changes in the latter are commonly looked upon as an indicator of the government's fiscal stance. Such a view, however, is essentially fallacious unless carefully qualified, since the size of the PSBR will vary in response to changing income levels quite independently of policy changes. Thus, for example, an exogenous movement into recession will deplete tax revenues and increase unemployment benefits leading to a widening of the PSBR without any conscious policy change upon the part of the fiscal authorities.

The essence of fiscal policy is that it is the means to influence expenditure *flows* in the economy whether directly through expenditure changes or indirectly through tax and transfer changes; such changes in flow magnitudes are seen to be a principal means of controlling the level of aggregate demand. In earlier Keynesian theorizing, such 'demand management' was looked upon as the principal means of maintaining demand at a sufficiently high level to provide full employment, and also as the primary means of 'fine tuning' the economy so as to smooth if not entirely eliminate the trade cycle. In this view, fiscal policy was the dominant macropolicy instrument and the monetary or budgetary consequences of fiscally induced deficits or surpluses were conveniently ignored. More recently, and partly as a consequence of the monetarist revival, more sophisticated Keynesian treatments, whilst still insisting upon the primacy of fiscal policy, have given an increasingly important role to the monetary and debt implications.

In examining the record of fiscal policy it would appear that the authorities have a marked preference for tax/transfer changes as opposed to expenditure changes as a means of macroeconomic control. There exists a number of reasons for this preference. First, expenditure programmes are the means of providing desired public services and meeting agreed social objectives; attempts to alter the volume of expenditure in line with macroeconomic goals will inevitably interfere with the attainment of these ends. Second, expenditure changes may, for administrative reasons, require time before they can be put into effect and may tend to be regionally concentrated in their impact. In contrast, tax changes can be speedily put into effect and will generally have a relatively uniform influence throughout the economy.

Monetary

The primary tools of monetary policy are the volume of money upon the one hand and the level of interest rates upon the other. These two are highly interdependent in that for a given PSBR the control of one inevitably implies loss of effective control over the other. In turn, both the money supply and the interest rate are intimately linked with fiscal policy. This is because, in the context of a closed economy, the increase in high-powered money is simply equal to the PSBR *minus* non-bank lending to the government by the private sector; for a fuller discussion of this relationship refer to pages 110 to 111. Both non-bank lending to the government by the private sector and bank lending to the private sector will be a function, *ceteris paribus*, of the level of interest rates. Thus, for any given PSBR, there will be an infinite number of money supply/interest rate combinations consistent with financing the deficit. However, once the money supply target is specified, so too will be the interest rate; alternatively, once the interest rate is decided upon, so too will be the money supply, consistent with the given PSBR. If the government wishes to dictate both the money supply and the interest rate, then it must adjust fiscal policy to obtain a PSBR consistent with the desired money supply/interest rate combination. This is precisely the contention of the new classical position – namely, that if inflation is to be controlled without imposing excessively high rates of interest then the public sector deficit must be sharply curtailed. Hence the rationale of the monetarist assertion that fiscal policy should be rendered subordinate to monetary policy.

Faced with the choice between controlling either the money supply or the interest rate for any given PSBR, the authorities in the past have tended to opt for the interest rate target. In part this preference stemmed from the belief that too great a degree of fluctuation in interest rates, implying fluctuating government debt prices, would jeopardize the ability of the authorities to sell future government debt. In addition, high interest rates were considered politically undesirable, especially because of their impact upon mortgage payments. Since 1976, however, this policy has effectively been reversed. Money supply targets were formally introduced for the first time and nominal interest rates were subsequently allowed to rise to record levels.

In addition to changes in the volume of money and the level of interest rates, monetary policy may also encompass selective controls over certain forms of credit – as, for example, hire purchase restrictions. These usually take the form of fixing minimum deposits and specifying the maximum period of repayment and generally exert a fairly immediate impact upon the level of aggregate demand. Although such forms of control were much in vogue in the UK during the 1960s they were virtually abandoned in the wake of the Bank of England's conversion to competition and credit control (1971). Whatever the virtues of competition and credit control in promoting competition, it did not serve as an effective means of controlling the money supply. Intense competition within the banking sector led to a sharp rise in loans to the private sector and hence a dramatic expansion of the M3 money supply. It was in order to regain control over the effective money supply that the experiment was finally abandoned in the attempt to control bank lending. In recent years UK governments have attempted a much firmer control of the effective money supply, reflected in their adoption of supplementary special deposits which commercial banks have to make with the Bank of England (the corset) and in a much greater willingness to accept the interest rate implications of financing by government debt sales to the non-bank private sector.

Price and Income Controls

Keynesians often argue that prices reflect costs, largely wage costs, and that the latter are determined mainly by sociological factors and are relatively immune to general macroeconomic control. Hence the need to impose direct controls over prices and incomes in order to meet the inflation objective. In contrast, monetarists view inflation as being determined almost entirely by monetary influences. Since trade unions cannot directly control the money supply they cannot generate inflation and thus controls over price and wage increases become an irrelevancy. This view was given its sharpest test during the 1973 OPEC-induced oil price rise. Monetarists contended that if the money stock were held constant then with a relatively stable demand for money function (stable velocity) the only consequence would be a rise in the *comparative* prices of oil intensive to non oil intensive products. From a purely long-term viewpoint, with unlimited price and wage flexibility, this may have been correct; however, in the short term, the comparative downward rigidity of non oil intensive product prices implied quantity adjustments with severe deflationary consequences for real income. Unwilling to accept such short-term changes, the monetary authorities attempted to cushion the blow by permitting a degree of monetary expansion and thus, in monetarist eyes, permitted a general rise in the retail price index.

Even if inflation is a purely monetary phenomenon in the long term, it is possible that price and wage controls have a useful role to perform. On the one hand they may condition expectations towards lower increases than might have been expected to emerge from the normal wage bargaining process, and to this extent to make the adjustment to lower inflation rates less painful than anticipated. In addition, it can be argued that the adoption of a monetarist approach, exercising a stringent control over monetary aggregates, requires an incomes policy, if only to ensure that sacrifices are made in a reasonably equitable manner. A rigid monetary squeeze in a completely free market environment would imply arbitrary changes in income distribution, with the expectation that the strong would benefit at the expense of the weak. Against these possible benefits must be offset the possible costs of resource misallocation as comparative prices and incomes are prevented from adjusting to the changing composition of demand. Moreover, it has been contended that income policies may operate in a decidedly perverse manner in that the ceiling rate becomes a minimum rate which arguably would have exceeded that determined by collective bargaining in many instances.

Exchange Rate

Exchange rate policy refers to the decision to adopt fixed or floating exchange rates and also, in the event of the former, to determine the appropriate rate of exchange and whether to alter the existing rate (revaluation or devaluation). Post-war UK experience would suggest that the authorities have placed little reliance upon the exchange rate instrument. Indeed, prior to 1971, under the Bretton Woods arrangements, the authorities identified the exchange rate not as a policy instrument but rather as a policy objective. In this view the confusion between objectives and instruments implied a welfare loss for society as a whole; the attempt to maintain a fixed and overvalued exchange rate for prestige reasons and to preserve an international role for sterling conflicted with the attainment of other policy objectives. In this perspective, the devaluations of 1949 and 1967 were not so much conscious policy decisions as events forced by the severity of balance of payments deficits.

Since 1971, the exchange rate has been allowed to float although not always without central bank intervention to 'manage' the exchange rate adjustments. In consequence, a new awareness as to the possible consequences of exchange rate movements has developed and the appropriate exchange rate policy, instead of being the 'great unmentionable', has become a lively topic of controversy.

In pursuing an active exchange rate policy, it is necessary to distinguish between the *nominal* and the *real* exchange rate. (The real exchange rate reflects the nominal rate adjusted for differential rates of inflation.) Those people convinced of the need to contain inflation are likely to emphasize the need to stabilize or even appreciate the nominal exchange rate to curb import costs. In contrast, concern with employment and growth objectives would point to the need to maintain or possibly even depreciate real exchange rates – the inverse of which may be looked upon as a guide to international competitiveness. Here we encounter an example of the potential conflicts inherent in macroeconomic policy. A country with a higher rate of inflation than that of its immediate competitors is faced with a possible dilemma in that stabilization of the nominal exchange rate will imply a decline in international competitiveness, whereas depreciation of the currency to maintain competitiveness will trigger inflation.

When two countries agree upon fixing a nominal rate of exchange, it follows that the country with the higher rate of inflation will suffer a decline in its real rate and will become increasingly uncompetitive. In this situation it may be thought that the required adjustment to the real rate can be obtained by depreciating the nominal rate. Wouldn't a given percentage change in nominal exchange rates imply an equivalent change in the real rate? Superficially, this may be correct but the equivalence may be short-lived, especially in an economy characterized by real wage resistance. Depreciation of the currency, implying higher import costs, for example, would translate into higher wholesale prices. In turn, this would feed through to higher consumer prices and higher wage costs until the former real wage and real exchange rate is regained together with a lower nominal exchange rate. The conflict between real and nominal exchange rates can accordingly be very significant – a fact which has only recently received full recognition in macroeconomic policy debates.

Exchange Rate or Money Supply Targets?

One issue which has come to the fore in recent years turns upon the question whether it is preferable to pursue an exchange rate target or a money supply target – given the fact that normally the pursuit of either one will imply that the other becomes endogenously determined as a residual. The simultaneous pursuit of independent monetary and exchange rate targets becomes inherently inconsistent.

Recent UK experience is illustrative in this regard. In 1979, the incoming Thatcher administration clearly adopted a money supply target – embodied in the Medium Term Financial Strategy (MTFS) – which relegated the exchange rate to being passively determined. The outcome – especially in the period to mid-1981 – was a dramatic rise in the real exchange rate, forcing many export-oriented companies into bankruptcy despite the fact that the money supply targets were substantially exceeded. Thereafter, explicit consideration was given to exchange rates. Initially, money supply targets were reiterated but were now conditional upon some exchange rate band. Later, the conditions were tightened and ultimately as the MTFS was substantially modified (scrapped in the eyes of some observers when sterling M3 ceased to be a targeted variable) the exchange rate was elevated to the status of an explicit target in itself. The exchange rate policy which ultimately emerged was that of pegging the pound closely to the Deutschmark (a low-inflation currency) with the intention of maintaining an exchange rate close to 3DM = £1.

The idea of linking the pound sterling to a low-inflation currency such as the Deutschmark is basically sound if the intention is to curb inflation. However, it implies, at least in the short term, a possible deterioration in the real exchange rate. Such a deterioration would be intensified if the pound rose above the 3DM ceiling; in the attempt to prevent this outcome monetary control was lost and later inflationary pressures were generated. Once again we encounter a conflict in macroeconomic policy formation.

In an attempt to contain demand, interest rates were forced up; the pressure upon interest rates, however, further exaggerated the appreciation of the pound. Eventually, after little more than a year, the exchange rate policy was abandoned – only to be resurrected in a new guise in the decision to join the exchange rate mechanism (ERM) of the European Monetary System (EMS) in 1990. Many commentators believed that the decision to join the ERM had been taken at too high a rate of exchange which could only have deflationary consequences for the UK economy and would in any case entail severe balance of payments problems. Ultimately this view was proved correct and the UK was forced to abandon the ERM in September 1992 – an ignominious failure which has probably contributed to the scepticism now prevailing within the UK concerning a common or single European currency.

If control of the money supply and control of the exchange rate are seen as possible alternatives in the attempt to constrain inflation, is there any reason to prefer one method over the other? One advantage of the exchange rate policy, emphasized by Artis and Lewis (1991), is that exchange rate movements are recorded daily, whereas money supply figures become available only with a substantial lag; accordingly, greater precision of control on a day-to-day basis is attainable by targeting the exchange rate. By the same token, the policy is more visible, and if adhered to, more credible to the private sector with possible implications for expectations formation.

The Public Sector Borrowing Requirement – An Intermediate Policy Target

The incoming Conservative government of 1979 made the control of inflation its primary macroeconomic target. This was not merely a reflection of its views on the desirability of competing goals and a subjective preference for inflation *vis à vis* employment objectives; rather, it was founded upon the objective belief that the control of inflation was an essential prerequisite for the attainment of alternative goals, especially employment and economic growth.

If control of inflation was the primary objective of policy, control of the money supply was looked upon as the primary instrument by which to achieve it. It was believed that there was a strong and decisive relationship between the size of the PSBR and the money supply; the PSBR had become the intermediate policy target.

Does control of the PSBR imply effective control of the money supply? Needless to say, the empirical evidence is far from conclusive. None the less, the issues themselves are relatively clear. Conceptually, any projected positive PSBR can be financed simply by the expedient of the government issuing IOUs to the central bank and receiving cash in return, which is then put into circulation in the process of government expenditure. Alternatively, the government could sell bonds to the commercial banks and receive in turn an augmentation of its deposits with the banking system against which it can write cheques. Normally, this exchange will also imply an increase in the money supply. Equally, the government could offer its securities to the overseas sector and receive payment denominated in foreign currency, which it may then translate into £s sterling via the exchange equalization account in order to meet its domestic obligations. In order to conduct this transaction the exchange equalization account will be obliged to sell Treasury bills, implying that more Treasury bills have to be sold elsewhere. This additional sale will offset the sale of debt to the overseas sector, but the money supply is still increased by the event of the subsequent government expenditure. In each of these cases, therefore, there is a direct and immediate relationship between the financing of the projected PSBR and the money stock as conventionally defined.

However, there remains a fourth form of finance, namely bond sales to the non-bank private sector, upon which Keynesians have implicitly relied and which in their view leaves the total money supply unchanged. Here cash is transferred from private sector deposits to the government in exchange for increased bondholding by the non-bank private sector. The increased willingness to hold more government bonds upon the part of the non-bank private sector is explained in terms of enhanced yields on government debt. It is this increase in interest rates or the change in relative yields on financial assets which induces the non-bank private sector to adjust its portfolio and substitute bonds for cash.

The foregoing argument is now widely accepted in Keynesian circles, and implies that the relationship between the PSBR and the money supply is at best tenuous and uncertain; indeed the logic of the argument would lead to the conclusion that the authorities can minimize the monetary implications of the PSBR provided that they are willing to accommodate the required change in the level of interest rates. There may, of course, be all sorts of political difficulties and objections to accepting the interest rate cost, but in principle the choice remains.

Moreover, even if the entire PSBR translates into a money supply increase with no sale of government debt to the private non-bank sector, it does not follow that the increase is significant in terms of the increase in the total money supply. The latter includes bank lending to the private sector, and in recent years it has been the increase in lending to the private sector which has accounted for the vast bulk (on occasions some 90 per cent) of the increase in recorded M3. How then does one account for this monetarist emphasis upon the importance of the PSBR for the overall money supply?

The answer lies in the belief that there exists a reasonably stable relationship between the amount of public sector debt and the amount of bank lending to the private sector. Thus private sector borrowing from the banks is itself seen as a consequence of an enlarged PSBR. The rationale for this belief rests upon the proposition that the private sector seeks to maintain a given portfolio of financial assets related to its income and wealth, and that within this portfolio it wishes to maintain a given balance between cash and alternative financial assets, including government bonds.

More specifically, it is asserted that over the medium or long term there is a relatively constant relationship between the nominal public sector debt held by the private sector and national income. If this relationship reveals a short run-decline, say owing to the impact of inflation, it will establish the basis for further sales of debt as the private sector seeks to adjust its portfolio. Second, it is claimed that there is a relationship between bank lending to the private sector and national income. Although this relationship reveals short-run cyclical fluctuation and is distorted by interest rate changes and so forth, it is claimed that it is reasonably stable over the medium or long term.

Hence the claim that there is a strong and important relationship between the PSBR as a percentage of GDP and the total change in the money supply. It is for this reason that monetary targets have often been approximated in terms of establishing a target PSBR figure as a percentage of GDP. The implications for fiscal policy intervention are clear and unyielding. If inflation is the number one priority and if it is to be controlled by containing the PSBR then fiscal policy *per se* ceases to be an independent policy instrument. Expenditure and taxation are to be set so as to be consistent with the required *ex post* PSBR figure compatible with the pre-announced money supply target. In brief, fiscal policy becomes entirely subordinated to monetary considerations. Nothing could be more indicative of the incoming government's dismissal of Keynesian orthodoxy.

This was the essence of the Medium Term Financial Strategy – the subordination of fiscal policy to meet purely nominal monetary targets. In contrast to the conventional Keynesian wisdom, fiscal policy was no longer to be directed towards the control of *real* variables! Thus, 'It is the conquest of inflation, and not the pursuit of growth and employment, which is or should be the objective of macroeconomic policy'.[5]

Another aspect of the new policy also displayed its anti-Keynesian or arguably pre-Keynesian stance. Keynesian-oriented fiscal policy had stressed not only the importance of the *size* of the budget deficit but also its *composition*. Expenditure changes were held to be more high powered than equivalent tax changes (shades of the balanced budget multiplier theorem) whilst indirect taxes were held to be more powerful in their macroeconomic impact when compared pound for pound. Indeed, such considerations were commonplace in studies concerned with determining the demand impact of budgetary policy – see, for example, Hansen (1969). In such a framework, it is perfectly possible for an increase in the size of the budget deficit to exert contractionary impulses and *vice versa*.

---

5 Nigel Lawson, Mais Lecture, June 1984.

Now, however, such sophistications were pushed firmly into the background. All that mattered was the size of the PSBR. Its composition was judged irrelevant. This ideological position arguably carried unfortunate consequences in that the first budget of the new administration saw a substantial switch of direct to indirect taxation (3 pence off the standard rate of income tax being compensated by a virtual doubling of the rate of VAT from 8 to 15 per cent). As the economy was already moving towards recession, such a change – in conventional Keynesian thinking – would only serve to intensify and lengthen the downturn.

In the event, the new policy was quickly discredited. First and foremost, the PSBR displayed enormous endogeneity, with the outturn figures widely exceeding intentions. Consequently, money supply targets were substantially overshot. More seriously, however, the underlying rationale was called into question. We have already mentioned the unprecedented increase in the real exchange rate which led to the policy being modified to define money supply targets with respect to exchange rate conditions. In addition, however, disagreement emerged with regard to the appropriate monetary aggregate to target. Initially, control of the money supply had been taken to mean the control of sterling M3 upon the grounds that this was probably the most relevant variable in relation to ultimate spending and the control of inflation. Unfortunately, however, the behaviour of sterling M3 did not correspond to its predicted path; it appeared that demand (i.e. velocity) demonstrated greater instability than expected.

As time went by and sterling M3 became increasingly difficult to target, other monetary aggregate came into prominence. In the budget statement for 1985, equal prominence was now accorded to sterling M0 – a much narrower definition of the money supply. In 1987, there was no attempt to target M3 upon the grounds that it 'remains difficult to interpret'. In the following year the budget statement again gave no role to sterling M3 but argued that M0 had proved to be a reliable indicator of monetary conditions. The same budget statement is of interest in defining the PSBR objective as being zero over the medium term.

The tendency to dispense with a monetary aggregate and replace it by an alternative when it no longer performed adequately invited criticism of the underlying policy. Moreover, the replacement of M3 by M0 meant that there was now no targeted broad monetary aggregate. In any event, the decision to shadow the Deutschmark, if only for a limited period, effectively signalled the end of the policy. In the 1992 budget, at the end of the third consecutive term of Conservative rule and with the economy deep into a long and drawn-out recession, the *planned* PSBR figure was raised to a substantial £28 billion. Although never claimed as such, to many observers this represented at least a partial return to Keynesian demand management strategies – long eschewed during the Thatcher years.

Money supply targets had effectively been imposed upon the previous Labour administration as a condition of aid from the IMF. What was new about the policy of the Conservative administration was the belief that the adoption of a PSBR figure as a percentage of GNP was the best way of securing the targeted money supply figure. The evidence of a direct and robust relationship between the size of the PSBR and *any* definition of the money supply was and remains far from conclusive. If the relationship proves to be weak then the unavoidable conclusion must be that the government has chosen the wrong indicator by which to control the all-important variable (in its eyes) of the money supply.

Of course, even if one disagrees with the monetarist contention of a strong and dominant relationship between the money supply and the PSBR, one can still argue along Keynesian lines the need to reduce or constrain the rise in the latter. The greater the public sector deficit, the greater, *ceteris paribus*, will be the pressure upon interest rates. Not only will this tend to crowd out a certain portion of private sector expenditures but also will it put upward pressure upon the exchange rate to the general detriment of the competitive position of British industry.

Constraints on Macroeconomic Policy

Both the objectives and the instruments of macroeconomic policy have been outlined, and the following is a consideration of the major constraints which might inhibit policy formulation.

International Agreements

One major constraint faced by all economies is the force of international commitments and agreements entered into with such bodies as the IMF, GATT and EC. Such agreements will circumscribe the ability to alter tariffs, quotas, tax rates and structure and may also imply a commitment to money supply targets. The force of these constraints is not lessened by the fact that they were initially entered into by a government other than the one presently enjoying office.[6]

Non-macroeconomic Objectives

Other objectives of policy may conflict with the attainment of macroeconomic goals. For example, belief in the desirability of a *laissez-faire* economy and the maintenance of a non-interventionist stance may inhibit the adoption of macroeconomic measures or render macroeconomic policy more difficult to effect. A good example in the United Kingdom experience was the abolition of exchange controls, which arguably renders it more difficult to control the money supply, interest rates and the volume of domestic investment. Similar considerations apply to the adoption of certain competition policies, which may constrain the monopoly power of government, industry and the nationalized sector.

An extremely powerful non-macroeconomic objective which may constrain macroeconomic policy is the principle of equity. The need to establish an income distribution and a tax/transfer system which is accepted as 'fair' may significantly blunt incentives and impair the objective of economic growth. Lower growth today, to satisfy equity considerations, may imply lower overall incomes in the future, especially for the lower paid. Thus, a tax structure deemed progressive in the static sense may be regressive when viewed dynamically and vice versa.

Legislative Sanction

Virtually any macroeconomic policy with a sizeable impact will require legislative approval. The force of this constraint, and the extent to which it influences the

---

6 One might argue that such constraints' do no more than recognize the extent of international interdependence by placing 'limits to sovereignty'. Given free rider problems there have to be obligations as well as rights in any such international agreements.

modification of policy proposals, is determined by the relevant political institutions and systems of government. It is of considerable importance in the United States, where presidential policies may need the sanction of a Congress dominated by the alternative political party and where, in any case, political affiliation does not prevent opposition to the official party line. It is of decidedly less significance in the UK where the government of the day can, if it has an effective majority, virtually ensure the adoption of a given policy by invoking a three-line whip. None the less, opposition can mean delay, and whilst the overall strategy may remain intact, piecemeal amendments can be made at the committee stage.

Uncertainty

Perhaps the single most important constraint stems from the existence of imperfect information and hence uncertainty as to the outcome of any given policy measure; the importance of this point is that it may dissuade the policy-maker from adopting the policy which *ex post* would have been optimal, and persuade him to adopt a policy which *ex ante* minimizes the risk of an unacceptable outcome. To illustrate this point, consider two alternative macroeconomic policy measures, A and B. Policy A has a mean expected value which coincides with the target income level Y^*, but also possesses a standard deviation which implies that an unacceptable outcome remains a distinct if distant possibility. In contrast, policy B has a mean falling substantially below the target income level but its smaller standard deviation renders it a less risky policy. *Ex ante* the policy-maker who, electorally, will normally be risk averse will opt for policy B, although its chances of hitting the income level are comparatively remote. Such behaviour is, of course, perfectly rational; all that is emphasized here is that the existence of uncertainty renders the optimal policy *ex ante* different from the optimal policy *ex post* in the majority of outcomes. One consequence of such rational risk-averse behaviour is that in the majority of cases the chosen policy will appear in retrospect to have been wrongly conceived. That is to say, looking back, it will appear that a preferable alternative existed.

Concluding Comments

In this chapter the case for macroeconomic policy has been assumed – at least in principle – and the problems facing the individual or individuals charged with the decision-making process have been examined. The policy objectives and the instruments that can be employed for their attainment have also been surveyed. Whilst a broad consensus emerges with respect to the policy objectives – although not necessarily with regard to their ranking – considerable differences emerge with respect to the potency of policy instruments. Such differences reflect differences in opinion concerning the structure and functioning of the macroeconomy. Thus Keynesians and monetarists, for example, differ substantially with respect to the relative efficacy of monetary and fiscal policy and with regard to the relevance of prices and incomes policies, since they possess a different model analysis of the way in which the economy actually works. Finally, some of the constraints imposed upon macroeconomic policy formulation were examined, and it was indicated that perhaps by far the most important was the uncertainty of living in an uncertain world.

Further Reading

Since chapters 19 to 22 are concerned with the principal macroeconomic objectives, there is no need to provide detailed references on objectives at this stage. The further reading suggested at the end of those chapters provides an adequate number of references.

With regard to the policy instruments, Peacock and Shaw (1976) provide a thorough analysis of most aspects of fiscal policy, whilst Shaw (1977) offers a more concise review of the principal issues associated with the design and implementation of fiscal policy. Accounts of the principal instruments of monetary policy are provided in most specialist texts on monetary economics. Sound recent reviews which concentrate on UK experience are provided by Gowland (1982) and Artis and Lewis (1981). Prices and incomes policy is covered by Jones (1976) whilst a concise introduction to balance of payments policy can be found in Cohen (1971). A more specifically UK oriented balance of payments text is Thirlwall (1980).

The most valuable insights into the constraints on policy formulation are provided in accounts of experiences of policy formulation and implemented as for example in Peacock (1979) and Pliatzky (1982). On monetary and exchange rate policies generally and on the Thatcher years in particular, both Artis and Lewis (1991) and Johnson (1991) are invaluable.

19

Inflation and Counter-inflation Policy in the UK

Inflation as an object of policy interest has shifted to centre stage in the last quarter of a century, not only in the UK but also in many other developed market economies. The most obvious reason for this is the significant fluctuation in inflation which has been recorded in the UK over that period (see table 19.1) and in other OECD countries (see table 19.2). The weighting given to control of inflation relative to employment and growth in the policy-maker's objective function has certainly increased in the UK.

The first question which will be addressed in this chapter is why recent governments have placed such a high priority on inflationary control. Their 'enthusiasm' presumably reflects a belief that inflation imposes real costs on society and a belief that the costs of 'squeezing inflation out of the system' are less than the benefits which will flow as a consequence. Following the review of the kind of costs which inflation *may* impose, a review will then be given of the policy instruments which can be deployed in order to reduce and/or stabilize the rate of inflation, with particular reference to UK experience with these policies over the post-war period.

TABLE 19.1
Inflation in the UK, 1970–95

Year	Change in RPI (%)	Year	Change in RPI (%)	Year	Change in RPI (%)
1970	6.4	1980	18.4	1990	7.7
1971	9.4	1981	13.0	1991	9.0
1972	7.1	1982	12.0	1992	4.1
1973	9.2	1983	4.9	1993	1.7
1974	16.1	1984	5.1	1994	2.5
1975	19.9	1985	5.0	1995	3.3
1976	23.4	1986	5.5		
1977	16.6	1987	3.9		
1978	9.9	1988	3.3		
1979	9.3	1989	7.5		

Source: *Economic Trends* (various issues).

TABLE 19.2
Rates of inflation for selected industrial countries, 1970–94

	Year						
	1970	1974	1978	1982	1986	1990	1994
Canada	4.7	13.8	6.4	10.4	3.2	4.8	0.2
United States	5.5	10.3	7.3	6.5	2.2	5.4	2.6
Japan	6.7	20.9	3.4	1.9	1.3	2.8	0.7
France	5.5	9.6	9.7	2.5	3.5	3.4	1.7
West Germany	7.1	6.6	3.9	4.4	5.0	–	–
Germany	–	–	–	–	–	2.7	3.0
Italy	6.6	16.3	14.0	17.8	7.1	6.5	4.0

Source: IMF Annual Reports (various issues).

Why Should Governments Control Inflation?

Macroeconomic Costs of Inflation

From various statements made by government officials it is quite clear that the government since 1979 has seen the principal cost of inflation as being a macroeconomic one, namely that it generates unemployment. Take, for example, the following statement from Leon Brittan, a former government minister:

> We have put at the forefront the goal of reducing inflation... because by doing that we are tackling the problem which has been at the heart of our trouble. It is not a question of choosing to tackle inflation rather than unemployment. It is rather a recognition that past inflation has been the *cause* of present unemployment. (Authors' emphasis)

In effect this is tantamount to arguing that in so far as a Phillips relation exists, it is *positively* sloped rather than negative or even vertical. This is a possibility which has in fact been posited by Friedman (1977) and merits further exploration.

One possible link between higher inflation and higher unemployment may be via disincentive effects on investment. This may occur as a result of greater uncertainty being associated with higher levels of inflation, especially in a regime of floating exchange rates. In taking a decision about whether or not to commit resources to investment one would have to make a judgement about how product prices will change relative to factor prices, and how the exchange rate will respond in consequence. If, as some have suggested, *higher levels* of inflation are associated with *greater variability* of inflation rates, then a greater element of uncertainty can be expected. Investment might also be affected if, as part of the inflationary process, income is redistributed away from profit and towards wage income. This link is rather more tenuous, however. There certainly have been specific examples of such redistributions, but as with the uncertainty argument it is difficult to ascribe specific values to the effects involved. A third and more convincing connection between inflation and investment is via the effect which the former has on long-term nominal interest rates and short-term real interest rates. As a consequence of periods of rising inflation, long-term interest rates have risen as well. However, when inflation rates have fallen, such as in the early 1980s and 1990s, interest rates have been slow to respond. This implies that real interest rates remain high although nominal interest rates may fall. Given the wide variation in inflation rates which has occurred, investors have to be persuaded that any fall in inflation is permanent. As a consequence, short-term interest rates also remain high despite falling inflation, and relatively high real rates are recorded. High real rates are unequivocally a disincentive to investment. One might argue that this phenomenon is associated with variability in inflation rather than the actual level of inflation. Thus in the event that one had a relatively high *fully anticipated and stable* rate of inflation, relative interest rates would more accurately reflect society's rate of time preference. In this respect the cost (of output forgone) is a cost due to unanticipated and variable inflation, rather than inflation *per se*.

Another way in which inflation may adversely affect output and employment is through its effect on the demand for tradeables in an open economy. A relatively high rate of inflation at home would result in increased demand for import substitutes and a lower demand for exports. Unless the inflation differential is eliminated, unemployment results. Note again, however, that the variable of concern here is the *relative* rate of inflation rather than inflation *per se*. The most graphic illustration of this point can be seen if an examination is made of UK inflation rates in the 1960s, which were low in absolute terms but high relative to the UK's competitors such that balance of payments crises were frequent. One might contend that even this potential cost can be avoided by operating with a floating exchange rate. In a smoothly operating system the exchange rate will adjust in line with inflation differentials to maintain purchasing power parity and competitiveness. The effect which capital flows (and in the UK case) resource windfalls can have on the exchange rate are sufficient to call into question whether the link can be broken in this way. For example, despite a relatively high inflation rate in 1979–80, the sterling effective exchange rate *appreciated* rather than depreciated; despite a relatively low inflation rate in 1984–85, the sterling effective exchange rate *depreciated* rather than appreciated.

Microeconomic Costs of Inflation

It is traditional to comment on the (sometimes pernicious) income redistribution effects which inflation can have. Thus in the event that one agent borrows from another agent at a fixed *nominal* rate of interest and there follows an unexpected increase in inflation, there is a redistribution from creditor to debtor. Likewise, individuals on fixed income contracts find that real incomes are squeezed; students and pensioners are frequently singled out as cases in point. Such redistributions can and do take place. Note, however, that they result because fixed price contracts are agreed, and the inflation that is referred to is unanticipated. If inflation were fully and correctly anticipated contracts could be agreed which made allowance for inflation and thereby avoided redistributive effects. Furthermore there are administrative arrangements, such as *index linking*, which can be introduced to protect those on fixed incomes. Thus this cost is one which is associated with unanticipated inflation rather than inflation *per se*.

Another argument advanced in this connection is that as inflation increases it becomes more difficult for agents to distinguish between *absolute changes* in the price level and changes in the *structure of relative prices*. As well as generating uncertainty this may lead individuals to make mistakes, giving rise to resource misallocation. In referring to this argument, however, it must again be noted that the cost in question is not just of inflation *per se* but is rather associated with variable and essentially unanticipated inflation. The point is important because, as will be seen shortly, one might argue as a result of this and the previous point that the policy-maker's objective should be one of stabilizing inflation rather than seeking a reduction in the level *per se*.

Even when inflation is fully anticipated, however, there are likely to be other costs generated by the inflationary process, such as an increase in transactions costs. In an inflationary situation, nominal values have to be changed more frequently (wages, prices, taxes and income transfers). These transactions costs may be lower for one type of variable than another (for instance, compare the costs of a wage change for a large supplier of homogeneous labour with the costs of a supermarket chain altering prices). One thing is certain, however – these costs are positive. They are extremely difficult to quantify, although the paper by Minford and Hilliard (1978) does make an attempt to do so. The most surprising result of this study is that the costs turn out to be relatively low and somewhat insensitive to the level of inflation. Thus Minford and Hilliard estimate transactions costs as 0.06 per cent of GNP for a 2 per cent inflation and 0.11 per cent for a 30 per cent inflation. Even if these figures are accurate, 0.11 per cent of GNP is not an insubstantial amount. They are, however, almost certainly an underestimate since the proxy for the cost of price changes is the cost of new price lists, and that for the cost of wage changes is days lost in wage negotiations. As Gordon (1981, 1982a) shows, there are many more costs associated with price and wage changes respectively.

A specific type of transactions cost which may be associated with anticipated inflation and which has received considerable attention in the academic literature is the effect of inflation on holdings of money balances. Refer to figure 19.1. The demand curve refers to an individual's demand for real balances. As expected inflation rises, nominal interest rates increase from r_1 to r_2 and the demand for *real balances* contracts

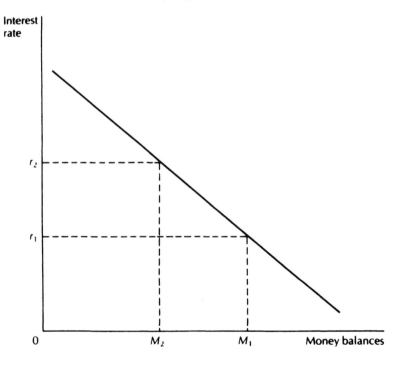

Figure 19.1 Inflation and the demand for real balances

from M_1 to M_2 as individuals economize on money holdings and switch assets to interest-bearing near monies (perhaps switching from current accounts to deposit accounts). This involves the agent in costs; for example, he has to make more visits to the bank than formerly. Attempts have been made to estimate this cost and it turns out to be higher than the transactions costs which were listed earlier (again, see Minford and Hilliard, 1978), although given the increasing practice of interest being paid on current accounts it is not clear how important this really is. Tobin (1972), for example, regards it as trivial.

It is possible then to identify a number of costs which might be incurred by a society as the result of an inflationary process, although it is far from easy to be precise about the order of magnitude of such costs. From public statements it would seem that policy-makers are more concerned with what has been referred to as the macroeconomic costs, that is, the output and employment effects of inflation and its effect on the balance of payments, and it would seem to be these considerations which are most important in stimulating anti-inflation policy. One point which has emerged from the foregoing discussion, however, is that the objective of policy might be to lower not inflation *per se* but rather the rate of inflation *relative* to one's international competitors and/or to *stabilize* the level cf inflation such that it is more likely to be anticipated than unanticipated.

Instruments of Anti-inflation Policy

As with any other macroeconomic target, diagnosis should precede prescription. In other words, prior to a particular combination of policies being assigned to a given objective, the underlying causes of the problem concerned should first be identified. As we saw in chapter 14, this is far from straightforward in the case of inflation. For some years a good deal of controversy has surrounded discussion of its driving forces. Thus if one takes the view that all inflation is the manifestation of monetary mismanagement, then counter-inflation policy is 'simply' a case of keeping the rate of growth of monetary expansion within certain predetermined limits. Alternatively, one might take the view that although inflation is generally demand determined, control of the rate of growth of the money supply is necessary but not sufficient for inflationary control. Monetary policy would have to be supported by a consistent fiscal policy. Another view might be that inflation is the outcome of some kind of 'social struggle' over the distribution of the national product and is basically therefore cost push. In this case the key to inflationary control is some form of incomes policy. Finally, instead of, or in combination with, all of these instruments one may attempt to minimize the damage done by inflation through the introduction of some form of indexation of wage contracts and transfer payments. Which combination of these policies is used, and the vigour with which they are applied, depends on the policy-maker's perception of the underlying causes, and the weight given to inflation in his objective function. All of these instruments have been deployed in the UK over the post-war period.

Inflationary Control in the UK, 1950–1979

The combination of policies chosen by any policy-maker depends in part on the prevailing economic orthodoxy and in part on his own particular philosophical inclinations. The complexion of the latter tends to change as governments change, whilst the former changes rather more slowly. One can trace particular switches in inflation policy to changes of government, and indeed if necessary one could compare the anti-inflation policies of alternating governments over this period. This, however, would be to ignore the thread of continuity which has run through policy for fairly long periods of time. Thus, despite the fact that different emphases may have been ascribed to different instruments at various times, it remains true that the prevailing orthodoxy from 1950 through to the mid-1970s was in the Keynesian tradition of emphasizing demand management manipulation as the basis to inflationary control, occasionally with the backing of direct controls. Since 1975 at least, a 'sea change' in orthodoxy has occurred (which is not incidentally confined to the UK) where monetary policy is seen as being the central instrument. In reviewing UK experience the discussion will therefore be structured around demand management manipulation, which dominated the post-war experience; the intermittent recourse to wage and price controls; and the recent primary reliance on monetary management, with particular reference to the Medium Term Financial Strategy.

Demand Management and Inflationary Control

In discussing the use of demand management policies for inflationary control, two points must be borne in mind. First, that for most of this period the inflation objective was intertwined with the employment, balance of payments and growth objectives. Furthermore, with the discovery of the Phillips curve in 1958 it was widely accepted that a functional relationship between inflation and unemployment held. Employment policy will be considered specifically in the next chapter, but in discussing inflation it must be kept in mind that the two are related. Second, in covering such a lengthy period a great deal of detail will have to be omitted in order to focus on general issues.

The roots of the 'prevailing orthodoxy' on inflationary control in the 1950s and 1960s can be traced to three related pieces of policy analysis. First, there was the direct contribution of Keynes. The work of Keynes and others in the 1930s, and in particular the *General Theory*, had a profound effect on the way in which economic policy was formulated and executed in the UK. In the context of inflationary control, the Keynesian analysis of the inflationary gap is especially relevant. At its simplest, this idea is expressed in figure 19.2. In the upper panel aggregate expenditure of E_1 results in an inflationary gap of AB. The resultant level of income Y_1 is in excess of the full employment level of income, and demand pull inflation ensues as increased expenditure is translated into increased prices rather than increased output. The prescription for removing such inflation is to restrict the level of aggregate demand – precisely opposite to the case of the deflationary gap where the policy stance recommended was one of reflating aggregate demand. This could be accomplished by engineering a shift in *IS* and/or *LM* such that they intersected at the full employment level of income rather than at point *a*. Since the authorities can shift *LM* by changing the money supply, and can shift *IS* by changing government expenditure and/or taxes, this is within their power.

The second strand which fed into the policy stance was the discovery of the Phillips curve and the belief that a trade-off existed between inflation and unemployment. This served to reinforce the inflationary gap type analysis by suggesting that reductions in inflation could only be attained by increasing the level of unemployment, i.e. by manipulation of demand management.

This still leaves a missing link. Even if one believes that manipulations of *IS* and *LM* are the key to inflationary control a question is begged; namely, is there any basis for

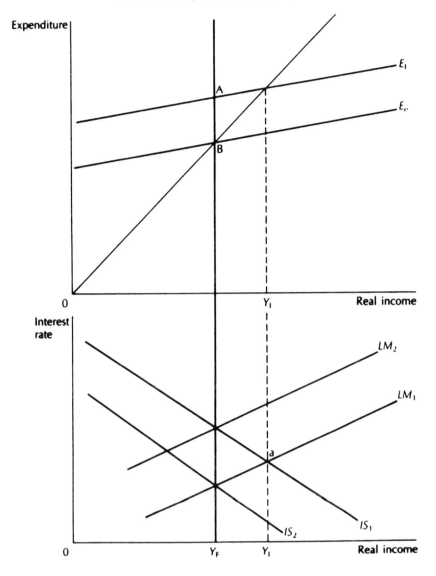

Figure 19.2 Keynesian inflationary gap

relying on one policy option to a greater extent than another? It is widely believed that Keynes firmly favoured reliance on fiscal policy rather than monetary policy. Keynes himself, however, was in no doubt as to the potency of monetary policy *especially* when it came to inflationary control. The relative downgrading of monetary policy had more to do with the inordinate amount of attention paid to his special cases (of the liquidity trap and interest inelastic investment), and possibly the third strand, that is, the publication of the highly influential *Radcliffe Report* on the monetary system in 1959. The main thrust of this report was to reinforce the view that monetary policy was likely to be of little help in short-term demand management. Furthermore, by emphasizing the broad supply of liquidity in the economy rather than any monetary aggregate, it lent further support to the view that monetary manipulation affected final expenditure principally through its effect on investment demand rather than directly impacting on consumer expenditure.

The essence of UK economic policy after World War II until the 1970s was one of demand management, with the main reliance on fiscal policy. This consisted of changes in both government revenue and expenditure, causing periods of both deflation and reflation. Monetary policy was largely confined to changes in the bank rate to affect capital flows to assist with balance of payments disequilibria. In addition, the Bank of England periodically issued directives towards the financial sector, principally retail banks, to influence credit availability. The performance of the UK economy over this period is best summarized by the phrase 'as one of stop–go'.

A number of comments can be made on the experience of using demand management policies in this way as the central plank in anti-inflation policy. First of all, policy has been largely of a 'fine tuning' type; that is to say, once inflation has been reduced both fiscal and monetary policy have taken on a counter-cyclical posture. Note that the objective of policy over the period has principally been one of actually reducing inflation rather than necessarily stabilizing it around a particular level. Apart from one or two occasions when inflation was relatively high for particular reasons (like the Korean War boom of 1951–52), the level of inflation was in fact relatively stable through until the late 1960s. Further, it can be stated that the principal objective of policy was to reduce inflation relative to the rates prevailing in the UK's main trading partners. By the end of the period, however, it is quite clear that this approach to policy had failed to reverse the recurrent tendency of UK inflation to outstrip that of her main competitors. There are a number of reasons which have been advanced for this. On the one hand, it has been argued that fine tuning was bound to fail because it did not control wage inflation – thus attempts to control inflation via incomes policy (which will be reviewed shortly) were made. On the other hand, it could be argued that fine tuning was bound to fail because it created greater uncertainty and was itself responsible for a deteriorating competitive performance. The alternative which would emerge from this line of reasoning is a rules rather than discretionary approach to demand management. Yet another line of reasoning is that the policies were bound to fail because they did not strike at the roots of the problem, that is, excessive monetary expansion – the policy implication of this being that monetary control be uppermost.

Wage and Price Controls

A number of post-war governments have taken the view that the chronic tendency for UK inflation to exceed that of her competitors is essentially due to a tendency for wages per unit of output to rise faster in the UK than abroad. At source, inflation is perceived as being fundamentally cost push in origin. To 'correct' this, there has been intermittent recourse to wage and price controls – that is, limits on the rate of growth of money wages and/or prices. Wage control was used as an anti-inflation instrument as far back as 1948 but it was especially 'popular' in the 1960s and 1970s. Controls can take a variety of forms. They may be statutory or voluntary; if voluntary they may or may not be backed with sanctions; they may impose a complete freeze on the rate of growth of money wages (and prices) or they may permit some increase; if the latter a percentage rate of increase might be permitted, or some lump sum amount; the 'norm' may or may not be related to productivity growth. Most of these options have been tried in the UK in various permutations.

The central objective behind wage and price controls is to run the economy at a higher level of employment and lower level of inflation than would be possible in their absence. However, there is a good deal of evidence to suggest that wage and price con trols generate distortions by disturbing the pattern of relative prices and incomes, and by encouraging the deployment of resources into avoidance activities (in the same way as was found with credit controls in chapter 6). Furthermore, such controls can be extremely costly to operate, given the bureaucracy which has to accompany their implementation. One could argue that, nevertheless, wage and price controls could still be associated with net benefits if inflation falls as a result, and employment is higher than it otherwise would be. This brings us to the final point – how successful have wage and price controls been as an instrument of counter-inflation policy?

Evaluating the effect of such controls is not straightforward, largely because it can never be known exactly what would have occurred in their absence. It is, however, possible to use a wage equation to predict what may have happened in the absence of controls and then compare this to what actually occurred. A number of studies have attempted to do just this and there is a good deal of agreement on at least two points. First, there is evidence to suggest that temporary freezes do help to slow down the rate of change of money wages. There is a good deal of evidence to suggest that once controls are relaxed a little – for example, some provision is made for productivity gains – 'wage drift' becomes important (as a result of job reclassifications, bogus productivity awards and so on) and ensures that the actual out-turn on wages exceeds the 'norm'. There is a good deal of evidence to indicate that, once controls are removed, there is a catch-up period as labour unions attempt to regain some of the ground lost during the period of restraint. There are many such examples of this occurring in the UK. Many commentators, for example, would ascribe the wage explosions of 1969–70, 1974–75 and 1979–80 to a reaction to wage restraint in the years immediately preceding the explosion. Thus it would seem from UK experience that, although controls *may* have had beneficial short-term effects, any gains have been quickly eroded and the subsequent situation has been at least as bad as the precontrols period.

Policy since 1979

The recurrent failure to control inflation (with or without an incomes policy) led to a disillusionment with the ability of the government to fine tune the economy as it desired in the short run. Instead, policy became much more focused on the medium term. The principles which underlie the medium-term strategy are a radical departure from previous practice in at least two important respects – first, the stress laid on monetary control as being both necessary and sufficient for the control of inflation, and second, the way in which monetary control has been administered, the practice of *preannouncement* of target ranges of growth. The former reflects the rise of monetarism in a general sense to the prevailing orthodoxy; the latter embodies a particular assumption about the manner in which expectations are formed, and is associated with the New Classical Macroeconomics school.

The most graphic indication that orthodox monetarism had been accepted as the prevailing orthodoxy is given in a speech by the then leader of the Labour party in September 1976, when he said:

We used to think that you could just spend your way out of a recession by cutting taxes and boosting government spending. I tell you in all candour that that option no longer exists, and that in so far as it ever did exist, it worked by injecting inflation into the economy. And each time that happened the average level of

unemployment has risen. Higher inflation, followed by higher unemployment.
That is the history of the last 20 years.

In other words, it was accepted that a relationship existed between government
budgetary policies and inflation, and that the *natural rate hypothesis* held. Although
Mr Callaghan did not spell out any relationship between budgetary policies and inflation, it is clear from subsequent statements and actions that the intermediate link
was via the money supply – monetarism had arrived! Note, however, that although the
Labour administration accepted this link, it nevertheless still saw a role for wage and
price controls. In other words, although it regarded monetary control as being necessary for the control of inflation, it was not viewed as being sufficient. This can certainly
not be said of the Conservative administration from 1979 to the mid-1980s which pursued an altogether different brand of monetarism whereby, in the early stages at least,
monetary control was viewed as being both necessary and sufficient for the control of
inflation. It was felt, however, that in order to make monetary targets realistic, targets
had to be set for the government borrowing requirement. Furthermore, there was an
implicit premise that agents form their expectations about inflation rationally, and
therefore the pre-announcement of policy intent would allow them to revise their
inflationary expectations quickly and more accurately.

The fullest statement of the Medium Term Financial Strategy (MTFS) was provided
in the March 1980 Budget White Paper. It is quite clearly stated here that the central
objective of government economic policy was the progressive reduction in the rate of
inflation between 1980 and 1984 to provide the basis for a sustainable (non-inflationary)
growth in output. The mechanism by which inflation was to be reduced was a progressive reduction in the growth of the money supply, and targets for public borrowing were
set which were consistent with the money supply objective. The target indicator
selected for monetary control was initially sterling M3 (notes and coin in circulation,
demand deposits and sterling time deposits held by UK residents). The targets set for
the growth of M3 are set out in table 19.3. As can be seen, target ranges were set in
recognition of the difficulties of hitting a specific figure, and the idea was that there
would be a staged reduction in the range. Table 19.4 details the government budget cal-
culations which were forecast as being consistent with these target ranges. The target
which was viewed as being important in this case was the *public sector borrowing
requirement* (PSBR). Again the point to note in this table is that the PSBR was forecast
to fall progressively, both in absolute terms and as a proportion of GDP. As well as
facilitating attainment of the monetary objectives (by reducing the amount of money
which is created to fund the borrowing requirement), it was envisaged that it would also
facilitate a reduction in nominal interest rates (by reducing the amount which the government actually has to borrow). If these targets were met it was felt that inflation could
be reduced to around 16 per cent by the end of 1980, with the possibility of single-figure
inflation being attained by the end of 1981, and a progressive reduction thereafter.

This is really just an outline of the details of the 'mark I' version of the strategy, but a
number of distinctive features should be noted. First, the entire strategy centred on two
target variables, sterling M3 and the PSBR. Second, the fact that targets were set for
both provided an explicit acceptance of the interdependence of monetary and fiscal
policy and of a government budget constraint. Third, the strategy actually provided a
statement of intent for up to four years ahead. Fourth, the inflation objective was
divorced entirely from any employment objectives – labour markets were to be left
entirely to themselves (in principle, anyway).

TABLE 19.3

Target Ranges for the Rate of Growth of the
Money Stock 1980–1984

Year	% change in £M3 during year
1980–1	7–11
1981–2	6–10
1982–3	5–9
1983–4	4–8

TABLE 19.4

Forecast 'Targets' for the Public Sector Borrowing Requirement (PSBR)
1978–1984

Year	Government expenditure £bn	Tax revenue £bn	CGBR £bn	PSBR £bn	PSBR/GDP %
1978–9	74.0	65.0	9.0	9.3	5.5
1979–80	74.5	66.0	8.5	8.0	4.75
1980–1	74.5	67.5	7.5	6.5	3.75
1981–2	73.0	67.5	5.5	5.0	3.0
1982–3	71.0	69.5	4.0	3.5	2.25
1983–4	70.5	71.0	3.0	2.5	1.5

Source: Economic Progress Report, April 1980.

The targets reported in tables 19.3 and 19.4 are those which were stated in the original MTFS. As we can see from the first two rows of table 19.5, these targets were overshot for sterling M3, the PSBR and inflation. We will comment on the reasons for this overshoot below. One point which can be noted here is that revisions to the targets took place as a consequence of these overshoots. This can be clearly seen by comparing, for example, the targets for sterling M3 for 1982–83 and 1983–84 (these being the original targets), with those for the same years in table 19.5 (these being the revised targets of 1982). As we shall see below, these and other revisions to the MTFS have led some commentators to argue that the 'strategy' was to all intents and purposes abandoned at an early stage and replaced by a much more pragmatic approach to monetary control which relied principally on interest rate manipulation.

The first two rows of table 19.5 compare forecast and actual out-turns for 1980–81 and 1981–82. As can be seen, the targets for sterling M3 and the (nominal) PSBR overshot the objectives laid down in the 1980 White Paper quite substantially. In no case did the growth of sterling M3 lie within its target range, and the nominal value of the PSBR has exceeded its target in all cases, although it must be pointed out that as a fraction of GDP it has been a little closer to its target. The obvious question begged is, therefore, why the targets were missed and what are the economic implications (in particular the effect on inflation). The easy answer is that aggregates like the nominal PSBR and sterling M3 are simply uncontrollable, the former because it is subject to cyclical and political pressures, the latter because the banking system can always find ways around controls. Although these aggregates are certainly difficult to control, it is unduly simplistic to argue that they cannot therefore be controlled. In the UK case there appear

TABLE 19.5
Forecast and Actual Out-turns on £M3, PSBR and Inflation

	£M3		PSBR		Inflation	
	Forecast %	Actual %	Forecast %	Actual %	Forecast %	Actual %
1980–1	7–11	16.7	6.5	13.2	16	18
1981–2	6–10	15.2	5.0	10.5	9	12
1982–3	8–12	8.9	9.5	8.9	7.5	8.6
1983–4	7–12	10.3	8.5	9.8	4.5	4.6
1984–5	6–10	9.6	6.5	10.2	3.5	5.0

to have been a number of factors which have contributed to the initial targets being exceeded.

Take first of all the PSBR. It will be recalled from chapter 6 that this is essentially the difference between government expenditure and revenue which has to be funded. This being so, the out-turn on the PSBR is crucially dependent on unanticipated variations in expenditure and taxation. Thus, when the original targets were set for the PSBR insufficient allowance was made for the payment of comparability awards in the public sector, an election commitment inherited from the previous government and honoured within six months or so of taking office. Even more important, inadequate allowance was made for the impact of *automatic stabilizers*. As recessionary pressures intensified, government revenues automatically decreased (as a consequence of fewer people paying income tax, and decreased expenditure on taxable commodities), whilst expenditure automatically rose (as increased social security payments were made to the unemployed). Thus when the original targets were set for the PSBR, the forecast fall in output between 1979–80 and 1980–81 was 2 per cent; the actual fall in output turned out to be 4 per cent. The effect this had on expenditures and revenues accounted for a large portion of the PSBR overshoot.

It is tempting to go directly from an overshoot on the PSBR to the overshoot of sterling M3. After all, the economic theory on which the medium-term strategy is founded suggests that a stable and predictable relationship between the PSBR and the money supply exists. This, however, is an issue of some controversy; many, whilst accepting the existence of a longer-run relationship between monetary growth and price change, would deny the existence of any mechanistic link between the PSBR and monetary growth, emphasizing not only that this depends on the way in which the PSBR is funded but also the particular assumptions which underlie a mechanistic link (see Peacock and Shaw, 1981). As well as any contribution made by the PSBR to the growth of sterling M3, there are other reasons why it overshot its target, reasons which provide an interesting insight into the way in which fixing on one particular target can create problems.

In the first instance, although monetary control was the objective of policy, this was not administered by attempting to contract the monetary base but rather by interest rate manipulation. In other words, the authorities were attempting to slow the rate of growth of sterling M3, essentially through controlling the demand for credit. Given that one is effectively therefore guessing at the appropriate level of interest rates required to hit a given target, the technique is fundamentally imprecise. This has already been discussed in chapter 6, when it was noted that the use of interest rate manipulation as a basis for monetary control necessitates having the political will to permit nominal interest rates to rise to extremely high levels. The Bank of England's minimum lending rate did reach historically high levels (17 per cent in 1979–80), but this was nevertheless consistent with low real interest rates due to high inflation. Furthermore, overdraft facilities were widely used to finance current expenditure as profit margins were squeezed and, given high nominal interest rates, frequently had to be extended just to service the initial borrowing. As was also seen in chapter 6, there were a number of *ad hoc* and distorting influences. Reliance on the supplementary special deposits scheme (the corset) had encouraged the growth of fringe methods of credit creation, like the issuing of acceptance credits. When the scheme was abandoned in 1981 these credits were converted, and as a result sterling M3 was increased by about 6 per cent. The increasing amount of mortgage business conducted by the banking system also resulted in sterling M3 growing faster than desired.

The response of the government to these targets being broached has taken several forms. The first and most obvious response was the rebasing of the monetary targets. Thus rather than sticking to the original targets and attempting to 'claw back' the overshoot, the overshoot was in effect written off and the targets rebased. In the circumstances this was probably quite sensible. The monetary targets have now been revised on several occasions. A second response has been to redefine the monetary targets. Initially targets were set by reference to sterling M3 only. In 1982 this practice was altered with target ranges being set for M1 and PSL2 as well as sterling M3. The justification for this was that in order to gain a comprehensive view of monetary conditions, one had to have an eye to narrow and broad definitions of money. Critics of the MTFS argued that this particular change provided evidence of the failure of the policy. The authorities had failed to control sterling M3; in order to disguise this failure they included targets for other variables. Since, as we saw in chapter 6, these different measures of monetary control frequently provide different impressions of current monetary conditions, the authorities can select their monetary aggregate depending upon the story which it tells. There is something to be said for both views. On the one hand, given the complexities of monetary control, one should perhaps inspect information on both broad and narrow money. On the other hand, however, the proliferation of monetary targets is apt to cause confusion. Given the rationale behind the MTFS this is a fundamental criticism. After all, the whole point of targeting and pre-announcement is to clarify government intentions and provide a stable environment for private sector activity.

There is evidence to suggest that a third response occurred, namely the downgrading of explicit monetary targets to be subservient to an exchange rate target. In other words the laxity or tightness of monetary conditions is, at least in part, being judged by reference to the exchange rate. Other things being equal, exchange rate depreciation provides evidence of a 'market view' that monetary conditions are too lax and a tightening of conditions, via a change in the interest rate is in order (and vice versa for exchange rate appreciations). Even when sterling approached parity with the dollar in January 1985, the monetary authorities steadfastly denied the existence of an exchange rate target. Their actions suggest otherwise, however.

This experience over the past few years had led many commentators to assert that the medium-term strategy has failed, and that this in turn is an indication of a wider disproof of monetarist beliefs. Although one cannot make any final judgement about the experience since we do not know what would have happened in the absence of the policy, a number of concluding remarks can be made. First, the medium-term strategy is not 'monetarist' in an orthodox sense, although it contains elements of monetarism (if that is taken to mean a belief in the natural rate hypothesis, and a belief in a systematic relationship between changes in the money stock and changes in inflation). Despite this a central role would not be given to the PSBR by many scholars who would ordinarily be dubbed 'monetarist' (such as Friedman and Laidler). Second, the experience has highlighted the technical difficulties of monetary control when this is administered via interest rate manipulation rather than monetary base control (whereby interest rates are then endogenous). Third, the experience cannot be used naïvely to assert that monetarism has been shown to be a failure. If one were to argue this on such frail grounds, then one could equally use the growth rate of M1 over the last few years to demonstrate that monetary restraint has been successfully administered. Fourth, judged by reference to the narrow criterion of inflationary control, the strategy had some measure of success, with the inflation rate having fallen significantly during the 1980s. Moreover, the inflation rate has stabilized at around this level. Fifth, as we shall see in the next chapter, the dramatic fall in inflation has coincided with an even more dramatic rise in unemployment. There are a variety of reasons behind this increase which we will discuss in chapter 20. Here it might be noted that monetary contraction has probably contributed to the increase. This being so, the assumption of a zero trade-off between inflation and unemployment which was implicit in the original MTFS has been invalidated.

The change in intermediate targets for assisting with the control of inflation alluded to earlier can be said to date from November 1985 when it was announced that sterling M3 was to be downgraded from a targeted variable to one that was monitored. From 1987 onward the only monetary aggregate to which attention was paid was M0. While the Prime Minister, Margaret Thatcher, and her economic adviser, Alan Walters, continued to believe that the money supply was a major determinant of domestic economic conditions, the Chancellor, Nigel Lawson, argued that greater emphasis should be placed on the exchange rate. As will be seen in chapter 21, the UK exchange rate has been highly volatile in a world of floating exchange rates. This is partly explained by the pound becoming a petrocurrency following the exploitation of North Sea oil. It was felt that this volatility was one alternative or even compounding factor in explaining domestic economic performance. Volatility itself created uncertainty that was detrimental for producers.

An appreciating currency was harmful to exporters and led to balance of payments difficulties; while a depreciating currency would assist with the balance of payments, it made the price of imports higher and therefore created imported inflation. Attention therefore was focused away from using the interest rate as an instrument for affecting the money supply to one of stabilizing the exchange rate. It was further felt that if sterling anchored itself to the currency of a stable, low-inflation country, then the UK's own inflation rate would have to be low in order for the exchange rate to be maintained without the UK economy becoming significantly uncompetitive. This philosophy of convergence lies behind the ERM which will be considered in chapter 21.

For the latter half of the 1980s, the pound shadowed the Deutschmark at an unofficial rate of £1 = DM 3.00. If the pound appeared to be depreciating, then domestic interest rates would be raised, and if appreciating, rates would be lowered unless countervailing action was taken by the Bundesbank. In order to maintain the unofficial rate during the period 1985–88, interest rates were lowered, leading to an expansion of domestic demand. This was added to by further relaxation of monetary policy following the stock market crash in October 1987 and a tax-cutting budget in March 1988. A consequence was that M0 rose above its target values and inflation started rising. Attention was now focused more directly on domestic matters, and interest rates rose from 7.5 per cent in May 1988 to 15 per cent by October 1990, a level at which they were to remain for over twelve months.

In October 1990 the UK finally decided to officially join the ERM and chose a rate of £1 = DM 2.95 ± 6%. The adoption of a quasi-fixed exchange meant that the government's main instrument of macroeconomic policy, namely that of interest rates, had to be directed toward this main target and that other targets became subordinated.

Soon after joining the ERM it became clear the UK economy was moving into recession as the deflationary policies of the late 1980s were beginning to take effect. As unemployment began to rise, there was a strong case for a faster reduction in interest rates than actually occurred but this was ruled out by the need to keep the pound at what many now considered too high a level. However, the Chancellor, Norman Lamont, argued that unemployment was a 'price worth paying' if the consequence was a fall in inflation that was beginning to occur.

By 1992 there was the feeling that the pound was valued too highly and some realignment would be necessary. Despite repeated assurances by ministers that this could not occur, speculation against sterling continued escalating and it was evident that the central parity of DM2.95 was increasingly untenable. On 16 September 1992, the UK suspended its membership of the ERM.

Since the UK's exit from the ERM, economic policy has again been directed once more at domestic-oriented policies. The pound has depreciated significantly against the Deutschmark and other currencies and this has lead to an export-led recovery. Interest rates were consistently reduced during 1993–94, although this failed to lead to a consumer-induced recovery. This was generally attributed to a lack of confidence mainly induced by a collapse of the property market and the creation of negative equity, as well as lack of job security for many as the UK economy had become more dynamic.

The period since 1979 can be characterized as one when there was a desire for economic stability but in reality one of great volatility. Many believe this has been enhanced rather than reduced by the switching of economic policy toward different intermediate targets and that this lack of consistency has had a detrimental effect on the ultimate goal, that of inflation. Indeed, one might even say that the 1980s and 90s has been as much 'stop–go' as that of earlier decades.

Concluding Comments

It has been seen that there are costs associated with inflation, although these costs are largely related to unanticipated inflation or relative inflation rather than necessarily to inflation *per se*. Nevertheless, they provide a rationale for inflationary control, although it is a matter for debate whether the objective of policy should be the elimination of inflation, the stabilization of its level, or its reduction to a level below that of one's competitors. For most of the post-war period it would seem that the latter objective has been uppermost, although the high and variable rates experienced in the 1970s have meant that this objective has become intertwined with one of stabilizing the level of inflation.

Policy in the UK has been a mixture of Keynesian fine tuning and/or wage and price controls for most of the period, and more latterly the setting of monetary targets with or without wage and price controls. The evidence appears to indicate that fine tuning failed to eliminate the phenomenon but rather helped it become an integral part of the stop-go cycle. Although there have been occasions when wage and price controls have been associated with reductions in inflation, overall they appear to have created more problems than they have solved. Monetary targets have been set for most of the last twenty years or so. There have been very real practical problems associated with monetary control although it is reasonable to assume that it contributed to the reduction of inflation in 1978, and between 1981 and 1986. Monetary contraction over this period has probably contributed to the dramatic increase in unemployment which has occurred. This will be examined in more detail in the next chapter.

Further Reading

An extremely useful volume on all aspects of demand management policy in the UK is Posner (1978). Here alternative (monetarist–Keynesian) assessments of UK economic performance are outlined, and their implications for particular targets assessed. Reviews of counter-inflation policy in the UK are also presented in Prest and Coppock (1982, chapter 1), Morris (1978, chapter 7) and Cross (1982a). An altogether more rigorous assessment of the determinants of UK inflation is given by the collection of papers in Parkin and Sumner (1978).

Dawkins (1980) provides a review of experience with incomes policy in the UK, whilst a more rigorous appraisal of the economic effects of incomes policy can be found in the papers edited by Parkin and Sumner (1972) and in Fallick and Elliott (1981).

A great deal of bank review space and rather less journal space was devoted to the Medium Term Financial Strategy. The strategy is originally set out in the Budget White Paper of March 1980. Important alternative views on its efficacy are to be found in the evidence to the Treasury and Civil Service Committee (1981). Artis and Lewis (1991) cover many of the recent changes in the financial system and monetary policy as well as analysis of the European Exchange Rate Mechanism as well as Britain's entry into it. Britain's exit and its aftermath are discussed in European Economic Perspectives No. 1 (1993) as well as various issues of the Bank of England *Inflation Report*.

20

Unemployment in the UK

In the 1980s and early 1990s, developed market economies in general, and the UK in particular, have experienced a dramatic increase in recorded unemployment (see figure 20.1). In the UK case, recorded unemployment has reached levels (both in absolute numbers and as a proportion of the labour force) which have not been experienced since the inter-war period. For many years it has been widely accepted that there are grounds for positive intervention in the labour market to reduce unemployment on both social and economic grounds. What has characterized recent debate, however, is a marked paucity of policy prescription with respect to what can or should be done. As with most (if not all) other economic problems, there are a variety of diagnoses/ prescriptions on offer which fill the spectrum from extreme rational expectations to Cambridge 'alternative strategy' proposals.

In this chapter the principal features of unemployment in the UK in the late 1980s and early 1990s will be examined in an attempt to build up some kind of picture of

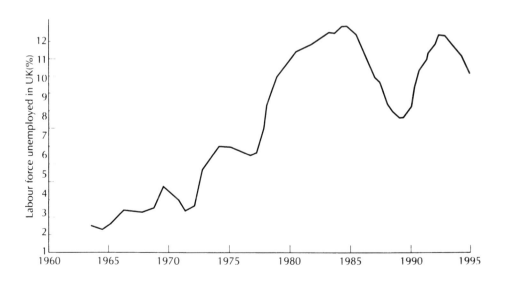

Figure 20.1 Unemployment in the UK 1964–1995

unemployment. This will then provide a basis for identifying possible 'causes' of the recent dramatic increase. Following this, alternative views will be considered on what the instruments of employment policy can or should be, with particular reference to policies which have been applied in post-war Britain.

Types of Unemployment

Chapter 7 distinguished between voluntary and involuntary unemployment. The former was found to be a feature of classical and neo-classical analyses of the labour market, whilst the latter tended to figure more prominently in Keynesian/neo-Keynesian analyses. In essence, classical and neo-classical approaches emphasized the role of the rational optimizing agent who takes a deliberate decision to withdraw from the labour market and substitute leisure for work when real wages are regarded as being too low. Given the self-equilibrating nature of the system, all unemployment is therefore voluntary. Keynesian and neo-Keynesian analyses, on the other hand, stress the possibility of involuntary unemployment appearing as a consequence of money wage rigidity, the latter being an outcome of institutional features of the labour market such as labour unions or contracts.

This distinction is useful for policy purposes, as has already been seen in chapters 7 and 13. Thus, given the neo-classical emphasis on the equilibrium nature of the labour market and the stress placed on voluntary unemployment, the role for government policy would essentially be one of removing constraints to flexibility. This would permit the real wage to fall and allow the market to clear. There would be no role whatsoever for demand management policies. By contrast a neo-Keynesian prescription would take the source of the rigidity as a constraint on the grounds that there are good socio-economic justifications for the existence of labour unions (or minimum wages) and/or there are sound microeconomic reasons for contracts. Policy prescription might then be a case of using monetary and fiscal policies to shift labour demand and absorb the involuntary unemployment. This is the world of the upward sloping AS curve.

This distinction between voluntary and involuntary unemployment can be usefully supplemented by a further distinction made by reference to the apparent source of unemployment (although arguably this only applies to involuntary unemployment), namely:

1 frictional unemployment
2 seasonal unemployment
3 cyclical unemployment
4 structural unemployment.

Frictional unemployment arises simply as a result of timing differences which occur when a worker quits one job in order to take up alternative employment. It is conceivable that frictional unemployment is zero if the transition from one job to another is perfectly synchronized, that is one quits one job and starts another the following day. This may in fact be the norm for certain occupations, for example academic posts where it is usual to resign only when one has arranged alternative employment. In many unskilled and semi-skilled occupations, however, the norm is frequently one of quitting and registering as unemployed whilst one searches for alternative employment. In this case the worker is recorded as unemployed for the duration of his search.

Even in the most smoothly operating of labour markets a certain amount of frictional unemployment is bound to be recorded.

Seasonal unemployment arises because the demand for certain goods and services is seasonal. Note that this is only a necessary condition for seasonal unemployment to emerge. Take the case of coal, for example; demand is certainly seasonal, but the relative ease with which the commodity can be stored ensures that the demand for labour in the coal industry is not seasonal. The same cannot be said of ice-cream vendors or cricket players. Of course ice-cream vendors or cricketers could obtain winter employment which is seasonal, such as shop work; or the seasonal increase in demand could be met by temporary additions to the labour force from students, for example. Despite such offsetting tendencies, however, one invariably finds a certain amount of recorded seasonal unemployment.

Cyclical unemployment arises during the downswing of the business cycle as a result of deviations in output from its 'full employment' level. As the economy runs through recession into depression, output falls and unemployment rises. The pattern of such unemployment would depend on which activities were cyclically prone. For example, construction services are often one of the first activities to 'suffer' in a downswing. Service industries where demand is income elastic find themselves in an exposed position. The point about cyclical unemployment is that once economic activity recovers and economic growth picks up, cyclical unemployment falls.

Structural unemployment: whereas cyclical unemployment is associated with the rundown and expansion of essentially similar activities, structural unemployment tends to be associated with the rundown of certain activities and their replacement by different activities which have essentially different labour requirements and/or are sited in different geographical locations. To take an extreme example, a shift in comparative advantage might result in the decline in shipbuilding on Clydeside and the emergence of computer manufacture in south-east England. There may as a result be an excess supply of labour in central Scotland and an excess demand for labour in south-east England. The two could coexist owing to a mismatch of skills and a mismatch of geographical requirements. The unemployment which is recorded would be referred to as structural unemployment.

Although it is far from easy to identify different types of unemployment from the data, the distinction between these alternative forms of unemployment is important from a policy standpoint. If one felt that there was a conclusive case for intervention the kinds of policy instrument applied would vary according to the type of unemployment one wished to alleviate. In the case of frictional unemployment, for example, policy would be directed at improving the efficiency of the labour market by way of providing Job Centres to make search activity easier; or it perhaps could take the form of subsidies designed to reduce the cost of search activity (like reimbursement of expenses incurred in attending interviews). In the case of seasonal unemployment, it might be felt that policy could be directed at encouraging activities to areas which are heavily dependent on commodities/services for which demand is seasonal, for example those areas heavily dependent on tourist-related services. One might feel that if cyclical unemployment is essentially transient then there is no need for policy intervention. This really depends, however, on the length of the cycle. In the event that recession is prolonged for years rather than months, one might feel that positive action is required to shorten the cycle and/or avoid some of the longer-term effects of prolonged cyclical unemployment – so-called *hysteresis* effects where cyclical unemployment essentially becomes structural. Structural unemployment emerges, as has been noted, essentially because certain factor-specific skills become redundant. One might argue that change is of the essence in a dynamic market-based economy, and if skills become redundant then workers will retrain for more productive employment. One might even argue that since the social cost of redundant skills is zero (on the principle that bygones are bygones), there is no case for any kind of policy. There are, however, a range of barriers to occupational and geographical mobility which may serve to frustrate the reallocation of labour from one activity to another. Furthermore these may be bound up with the fact that the private costs of retraining diverge from the social costs (as they undoubtedly do). The point is that, if policy is pursued, the kind of instruments with which one is dealing are the subsidization of retraining, subsidization of relocation and so on. In the event that structural unemployment is region specific one might feel that policies designed to stimulate investment in the regions concerned is the appropriate instrument to deploy.

These various instruments, and the extent to which they have been deployed in the UK, will be returned to in due course. For the moment the pattern of unemployment in the UK over the post-war period will be examined in greater detail in order to establish whether the relative importance of different types of unemployment has altered in recent years.

Patterns of Unemployment in the UK

Figure 20.1 traces the trend in unemployment rate for the period 1964–95.
Although there are known to be a number of well-known defects associated with both unemployment and vacancy data,[1] which are acknowledged, the data will continue to be used here to identify trends. The first feature of these figures which may be noted is the cyclical pattern of unemployment. This is quite evident throughout the post-war period. In crude terms, one could take the difference between the actual level of unemployment and the trough level (which would coincide with an output peak) as an indication of cyclical unemployment. Since the figures are seasonally adjusted, seasonal influences have already been ironed out. However, the data would include recorded frictional unemployment. Despite this one thing is clear, namely that the recorded swings in unemployment have been very much greater in the 1970s, 1980s and 1990s than in the 1950s or 1960s – deviations from trend have been of a greater magnitude in the 1970s, 1980s and 1990s. A second feature of figure 20.1 is that the levels of unemployment associated with both peaks and troughs in the cycle have been rising since the late 1960s. With each successive recovery since 1965, unemployment has bottomed at a higher rate than in the previous cycle; whilst with each successive downswing unemployment has peaked at a higher level than before. This can be seen most emphatically

---

1 Basically, there are a number of distortions which tend to result in recorded unemployment and recorded vacancies understating actual unemployment and actual vacancies. In the case of umemployment it appears that certain groups simply do not bother to register as unemployed (for example, married women, casual labour). In the case of vacancies many firms have their own channels of dissemination which they rely on rather than report them to Job Centres.

by reference to 1985–86. Unemployment appears to have peaked and levelled off. It has done so, however, with in excess of 3 million people unemployed. This is taken by many commentators to be evidence of an increase in the natural rate of unemployment in the UK. The 1993 peak was just under 3 million but it should be noted that changes in the definition of unemployed may make intertemporal comparisons difficult. In terms of the classification introduced above, we could take it as indicative of an increase in structural unemployment. A variety of explanations have been advanced for this.

Neo-Keynesian explanations revolve around the part played by exogenous forces and emphasize the involuntary nature of such unemployment (for example, world recession, the shift in comparative advantage in standardized manufactures, the crowding out effect of North Sea oil on manufacturing employment); whilst neo-classical commentators argue that the increase is endogenously determined, by a combination of real wages which are 'too high' and which have contracted the demand for labour, and real benefits which are 'too high' and have consequently contracted the supply of labour. The essential feature of this line of argument is that unemployment is basically voluntary – agents leave the labour market of their own free will.

The incidence of unemployment has not been evenly spread throughout the country, and there have been distinct regional disparities. The South East, East Anglia and the East Midlands have all had rates of unemployment consistently below the national average. On the other hand, the North, Wales, Scotland and Northern Ireland have recorded rates persistently in excess of the national average. Although all of the regions have been subject to cyclical pressures, these disparities have been evident throughout the post-war period. Most commentators would agree that this phenomenon is bound up at least in part with structural change, namely the decline of the 'staple' industries (iron and steel, shipbuilding, cotton textiles and coal, until recently), which were predominantly located in the regions, and the growth of light engineering and services located closer to the main markets, in the South East and the Midlands.

TABLE 20.1
Mean Duration of Claimant unemployment in Great Britain ending July 1995

Age (years)	Duration (weeks)
16–17	10
18–19	19
20–4	29
25–29	36
30–4	39
35–9	39
40–4	37
45–9	36
50–4	37
55–9	62
60+	65
All ages	35

Source: Employment Gazette, 103 (10), table 2.21.

Another feature of unemployment has been the dramatic increase in the number of long-term unemployed. At the end of July 1995, the mean duration of unemployment was 38 weeks. The duration of unemployment increases with age and only those workers under 25 years can expect to be unemployed for a shorter time than the average, as is shown in table 20.1. This trend is viewed by most as the single most disturbing feature of current UK unemployment, not only because many of the debilitating effects of unemployment appear to be associated with long-term unemployment, but also because the probability of re- employment falls with length of unemployment. This is a consequence of so-called hysteresis effects – that is, lack of recent work experience and a depreciation of the human capital stock.

A final feature is the occupational structure of unemployment. It is most heavily concentrated in unskilled occupational groupings, with over half of total unemployment being accounted for by 'general labourers' and 'other manual'. The most obvious explanation of this phenomenon is that such workers lack much in the way of human capital, and in a recessionary period it is easier for firms to lay off such workers rather than skilled workers. One might also argue that the 'replacement ratio' is highest for unskilled workers and therefore voluntary unemployment is higher. As will be seen, however, the support for this proposition is limited.

Employment Policy in the UK

One of the most forceful and unambiguous commitments to any target of economic policy was enshrined in the 1944 White Paper on Employment Policy. Following the traumatic experience of the inter-war period, when unemployment averaged 14.2 per cent between 1921 and 1938 (reaching a zenith of 22 per cent in 1932 and a nadir of 9.5 per cent in 1927), an undertaking was given by the government to 'accept as one of their primary aims and responsibilities the maintenance of a high and stable level of employment'. This commitment was adhered to by both Conservative and Labour administrations right up until the middle of the 1970s when, as was seen in the previous chapter, inflation took over as the 'primary' objective of government policy.

Over this quarter of a century from the later 1940s through to the early 1970s various threads of employment policy can be identified. On the one hand, governments were quite willing to tackle what they viewed as cyclical unemployment by manipulation of monetary and fiscal policies. Whenever UK unemployment pushed much above 2 per cent of the total workforce (or, in absolute terms, around 0.5 million unemployed), an expansionary posture was invariably assumed on fiscal and monetary (or, more accurately, credit) policies. Deviations from the employment target, as with the inflation, growth and balance of payments objectives, were integrally bound up with the stop-go cycle of activity. The commitment to 'full employment' undoubtedly ensured that the authorities were willing to comply with (or acquiesce in) a stop-go pattern of activity and, for whatever reason, aggregate unemployment remained relatively low. One could argue that this was a measure of the success of fine tuning policy. Alternatively, one could point to the unprecedented expansion of trade which occurred over this period, and the increasing openness of the UK economy (in 1950 imports/exports accounted for around 12 per cent; by 1980 this had risen to 30 per cent). Both influences are relevant. Certainly, it appears to be the case that a short-run trade-off between inflation and unemployment did hold for at least part of this period, allowing the authorities some kind of handle for employment policy. As was seen in our discussions of expectations, acceptance of a Phillips relation means acceptance of a possible role for money illusion in the labour market or it relies on some other imperfection. Although money illusion is unreasonable as a long-run postulate, it may not have been inappropriate over periods such as the 1950s and early 1960s, for the simple reason that the average inflation rate was low in absolute terms and deviations around that average were also small. With inflation at such a low level, and deviations around the inflation rate being so small, it seems reasonable to suppose that individuals formed their expectations adaptively, and in many instances it is likely that expectations lagged behind reality facilitating a short-run trade-off. Even if it is accepted that the era is testimony to the efficacy of demand management manipulations, one might argue, as Bacon and Eltis (1978) have done, that the maintenance of a relatively high level of employment was achieved at a cost, namely a slowdown in the underlying rate of productivity growth. Bacon and Eltis argue that a high level of employment was maintained by expanding the share of public sector employment. In other words, as unemployment rose, fiscal expansion through increased government expenditure reduced unemployment by increasing employment in public services. Given that most such services are non- marketable, an increasing share of national product is therefore accounted for by non-market activity where productivity change is slow. The Bacon and Eltis thesis has been questioned (see Hadjimatheou and Skouras, 1979) but nevertheless provides an interesting view of the role which demand management may have played in employment policy.

A low average rate of unemployment continued to mask quite wide regional variations. It seems as if the 'depressed' regions were more susceptible to cyclical pressures than the 'prosperous' regions, as one can observe from the marked procyclical pattern of deviations from the average. Since, however, rates of unemployment were *persistently* higher for these areas it does suggest that a certain amount of structural unemployment was being experienced, unemployment bound up with the erstwhile dependence of these areas on heavy industry and subsumed under the euphemism of the 'regional problem'. Although this is not the place to explore this aspect of policy, it is nevertheless relevant to the discussion since one can view much of UK post-war regional policy as an extension of employment policy. Certain instruments were designed to take 'workers to the work', for example the availability of relocation grants. In the main, however, policy has been directed to try and encourage 'work to the workers', that is, a great many incentives have been made available to encourage investment in the peripheral regions. At times these have taken the form of tax incentives. Recently, however, greater use has been made of cash grants on plant and equipment. In the main, subsidies have been given to capital, although there have been occasions when subsidies to labour have been offered (such as the regional employment premium).

All of these instruments can be viewed as attempts to alleviate structural rather than cyclical unemployment. There is some debate over the extent to which they have been successful (see Brown and Burrows, 1978). In evaluating such policy, one faces the classic counter-factual problem; that is, it is simply not known what the situation would have been in the absence of intervention. Furthermore, extricating the effects of one policy from others is especially problematic in this case. Some evidence exists to suggest that regional policy type instruments have served to preserve *and* create employment in the peripheral regions. For example, Moore and Rhodes (1973) contend that some 220,000 jobs were created between 1963 and 1970. Against this, however, it has been argued that regional policies have served to compound regional disparities and done little to alleviate structural unemployment, in part because they have encouraged relatively capital intensive activities, and, related to this, in part because they have discriminated against services activity. This line contends that since the UK economy (like many other developed market economies) is undergoing a process of tertiarization, service employment will expand relative to manufacturing employment. The explicit bias in UK regional policy towards manufacturing activity has served to prevent the peripheral regions from taking full advantage of the growth of the service sector (see McEnery, 1981). According to this line of analysis, regional policy has served to encourage rather than reduce structural unemployment.

By way of summarizing policy over this period, two observations can be made. First, since the employment target was consistently hit up until the latter part of the 1960s, the overall level of unemployment was not really viewed as a pressing policy problem. If unemployment reached a critical level of around 0.5 million, demand manipulation was seen as the obvious and appropriate response. Second, in terms of long-term policy problems, the *distribution* of unemployment was seen as a more pressing issue and a variety of instruments were deployed to this end.[2]

Unemployment since the 1970s

There are two immediately striking features of unemployment in the UK. The first is the dramatic increase which has been recorded, and the second is the equanimity with which it has been viewed by both Labour and Conservative governments. This does not mean they have been unconcerned by the increase. Rather, it is simply a comment on their resistance to the temptation of demand management as a means of reducing unemployment. In this section will be considered more fully alternative diagnoses of the underlying causes of this staggering increase in unemployment, and the policy prescriptions associated with each. To emphasize the poles in the debate, these will be examined first; the 'middle ground', which is occupied by many neo-Keynesians and monetarists, will then be discussed in rather more general terms.

New Classical View

At various points in part II the central features of the New Classical Macroeconomics were outlined. It will be recalled that the foundations of this model are threefold. The first is that agents form their expectations rationally rather than adaptively. The second is that markets are efficient. The third is that the rate of change in prices is solely determined by the rate of change in the money supply and, given rational expectations, variations in the latter feed through to variations in the former with a very short lag and with minimal output/employment effects. If these assumptions hold, and if this is taken as a reasonably accurate description of the way the world works, there are a number of important implications for the explanation of current unemployment. In the more extreme models, for example, all unemployment would be viewed as voluntary or search unemployment. In terms of the classification introduced earlier, this view of the world would see cyclical unemployment as relatively unimportant and frictional/structural unemployment as more important – the former because agents spend more time in job search, the latter because they simply perceive the costs of relocation/retraining as being too high. Thus the increase in unemployment in the UK would be explained by the interaction of a number of factors. One would be random cyclical

2 This should not be read to imply that there was continuity in UK regional policy. In fact, one of the problems with UK policy has been that Conservative and Labour administrations have favoured different instruments, and consequently one might argue that policy has been characterized by a distinct lack of continuity.

pressures, like the 'second oil shock' of 1979. Another would be an increase in the natural rate of unemployment. This has occurred as a result of lack of incentive to work because the real value of welfare benefits are so high, and as a result of factor market distortions raising real wages and pricing people out of jobs. In an open economy this would be viewed as especially important.

The policy implications of this analysis are first of all that the natural rate of unemployment cannot be reduced by demand reflation – 'real' targets require 'real' policies. Thus to achieve a longer-run reduction in the level of unemployment, policy should be directed at the following. First, incentives to work should be improved. This could be achieved by reducing marginal rates of income taxation and reducing the real value of welfare benefits. Second, the operation of the markets allocative function should be improved by the removal of distortions, basically to encourage greater competition in product and factor markets. In product markets this would involve a more vigorous competition policy, whilst in factor markets it would involve proscribing the market power of labour unions. The role of government therefore is constrained to providing an environment within which markets can function efficiently (see Minford and Peel, 1981).

New Cambridge View

At the opposite extreme in the spectrum is the new Cambridge view. This view denies the validity of the rational expectations assumption and views inflation as essentially cost push in origin. In explaining unemployment it focuses on demand deficiency, and views unemployment as essentially involuntary rather than voluntary. In terms of the classification introduced earlier, unemployment would be viewed as largely cyclical and structural, the cyclical element being due to a combination of deficient domestic demand and deficient overseas demand; the former is seen as the outcome of contractionary fiscal and monetary policies, the latter as a consequence of world recession. Structural unemployment would be viewed as largely a result of competition from 'relatively successful' industrial countries, in practice other Western European countries and Japan. The policy implications of this analysis are, first, that active demand expansion is a necessary condition for a reduction in unemployment. In order, however, to ensure that increased expenditure does not leak abroad, fiscal expansion should be accompanied by general import controls. In this particular scenario, therefore, there is an extremely active role for government to play.

It should be noted that this description of the new Cambridge position is based on the strategy proposed up until April 1982, a fuller statement on which can be found in Cripps and Godley (1978), for example. It seems, however, judging from the April 1982 *Cambridge Policy Review*, as if the group have shifted ground and now argue that demand management policies can have no lasting effect on the level of unemployment. From the analysis in part II of this book, the reader might be struck by the similarity of this stance with the natural rate hypothesis.

Both these extreme analyses have shortcomings in explaining recent unemployment in the UK. The new classical analysis, for example, would have some difficulty in explaining the regional pattern of unemployment in the UK as well as the huge increase in the long-term unemployed which has occurred. Furthermore, some of their arguments regarding incentives simply do not square up with the facts. Empirical analysis of the effects of unemployment and related benefits on recorded unemployment in the UK seem to indicate that as a causal factor this has a limited role to play. For example, Nickell (1979) estimates that some 14 per cent of the actual increase in unemployment between 1964–65 and 1973 can be attributed to the increase in unemployment benefits relative to average after-tax income (the replacement ratio). Thus although there is evidence to indicate that this has made a contribution, it is not a pervasive explanation. This sits oddly alongside the increase in the long-term unemployed.

The most serious limitations of the new Cambridge view are the dissociation between demand reflation and inflation (prior to April 1982, anyway) and the limited role played by market forces or supply constraints. The latter are clearly viewed as important given the crucial role ascribed to import controls. Despite their shortcomings an examination of the extremes is useful if only to emphasize differing views on supply- and demand-based explanations. Most 'intermediate' views of unemployment emphasize these to different degrees.

Demand Deficiency

It is certain that demand deficiency has a part to play in the explanation of recent UK unemployment. On the one hand there are external pressures generated by the adjustment to the 1979 oil shock. The most obvious evidence of this is relatively high unemployment in other developed market economies (DMEs). On the other hand, as was seen in the previous chapter, the medium-term economic strategy of 1979–83 was explicitly directed at demand deflation an experience repeated following the reversal of economic policy after 1988. In a rational expectations world with a vertical aggregate supply curve a minimal effect on output and employment could have been anticipated. This does not seem characteristic of the UK economy and it seems as if fiscal and monetary contraction did contribute to the increase in unemployment. In other words, there has been movement some way along a positively sloped aggregate supply curve. How much of a contribution these two forces have made to present unemployment is difficult to say; it really depends which model of the economy is accepted as being most representative. Suffice it to say that those strategies explicitly founded on reflation forecast, at their most optimistic, a reduction in unemployment of around one million as a result of this kind of policy package. If these forecasts are accurate it indicates that more fundamental forces are at work than simply demand deficiency. This is implied by the picture of the long-run trend in unemployment conveyed in figure 20.1 where, as has already been noted, the unemployment rates associated with successive peaks and troughs of cycles in the post-1965 period has been increasing with each successive cycle, which implies that demand deficiency cannot in itself offer a comprehensive explanation for rising unemployment.

Supply Constraints

It has been suggested (Layard, Nickell and Jackman, 1994) that the increase in the replacement ratio and trade union influence appeared to contribute to the increase in unemployment between 1964 and 1973. Since then, the replacement ratio has generally tended to decline, and trade union influence certainly has, since 1979. Yet unemployment has continued to increase. It would seem then that this is a less important causal factor, although some recent commentators have downgraded the importance of the replacement ratio *per se* and focused more on the role of high marginal tax rates and the poverty trap. At the very least this may have encouraged the growth of the black economy with the result that *recorded* unemployment is higher than *actual* unemployment.

Of more significance are developments in the labour market. Here employment protection legislation which makes it more difficult to vary employment demand in response to cyclical pressures has probably served to raise the natural rate. Finally, at the 'micro' level there is some evidence to suggest that housing market imperfections have exerted an impact through their effect on labour mobility. In particular the presence of a large local authority housing stock, where allocation is administered via queueing rather than price, makes it difficult for local authority residents to move from one area to another. In this connection it is worth noting that Nickell (1980) finds that the unemployment rate for local authority residents in 1972 was higher than for non-local authority residents. Of course it has to be conceded that local authority tenancy might simply be a proxy for other relevant influences like socioeconomic group, skill endowment or family circumstances. Nickell does, however, calculate that even on *ceteris paribus* assumptions the unemployment rate for local authority residents is still 60 per cent higher than for the 'standard man' of the study, a finding which can be interpreted as lending some weight to the mobility argument.

Although the micro- macro distinction is somewhat arbitrary, several developments can be identified which can reasonably be labelled macro. First of all there is the build-up in production of North Sea oil. It seems that this could have had a 'crowding out' effect on manufacturing through its effect on the external account – basically, since the balance of payments must balance with reduced oil imports, there are reduced exports of manufactures (see Forsyth and Kay, 1980). In so far as the presence of North Sea oil contributed to sterling appreciation it also helped reduce the competitiveness of UK manufacturing activity. Also on the macro side a structural change has been taking place in the world economy with a shift in comparative advantage in many standardized manufactures away from DMEs like the UK towards the so-called newly industrializing countries (NICs), namely Korea, Taiwan, Singapore, Hong Kong, Brazil, Mexico and so on.

Co-ordination Problems

Finally, alongside these demand and supply forces might also be identified what could be described as co-ordination problems. These are the kinds of geographical and occupational mismatches of labour demand and supply that can result in structural unemployment. The influence of this factor has already been considered under the heading of labour market segmentation in chapter 7. There, it will be recalled, the emphasis was on the way in which segmentation can induce rigidities into the market and frustrate market clearing.

A mismatch of labour across sectors is especially likely during a period of high unemployment, given that depreciation of the human capital stock occurs. In other words, with over forty per cent of the total number unemployed suffering long-term unemployment, a large fraction of the excess labour supply has little in the way of recent 'on the job' experience which can help make them re-employable. Comment has already been made at length on the geographical mismatch of labour demand/supply which is such an integral feature of the regional problem in the UK.

Policy Implications of Present Unemployment

This stylized outline of the kind of forces which have interacted to generate such a high level of unemployment in the UK serves to emphasize one very important point, namely that there is no single factor which is unequivocally responsible, and therefore there is no single policy which can be unambiguously recommended to produce instant and/or lasting results. It is certainly the case that demand reflation *per se* would not be efficacious in the UK.

Layard, Nickell and Jackman (1994) suggest a combination of policies broadly directed at the workers and wages. With regard to policies for the unemployed, they advocate a reform of the benefit system combined with a more active manpower policy such as that adopted by Sweden which appeared to work well throughout the 1980s, although has been called into doubt more recently (see Robinson, 1995). Finally, they suggest much more pin-point targeting of policy towards specific groups, such as the long- term unemployed, specific aims, such as reducing skills mismatch, and towards specific regions. Such interventionist policies could take the form of employment sub-sidies and training programmes.

Reforms to the wage bargaining process and the reintroduction of incomes policies is an even more contentious suggestion. Although different countries have different systems for wage determination generally, these have evolved rather than been imposed. To suggest that one could transport such systems across borders with their perceived benefits seems a spurious argument. As noted in the previous chapter, while such policies may be short-term palliatives, the evidence suggests that the distortions they introduce mean they are not long-term solutions.

Actual government policy towards unemployment tends to be multi-faceted. Since 1975 over twenty separate employment and training schemes have operated at one time or another. Most of these have a specific target such as youth unemployment, the long-term unemployed or the creation of local training through the creations of eighty-two Training and Enterprise Councils in England and Wales, together with twenty-two Local Enterprise Companies in Scotland.

One other aspect of policy which ought to be mentioned is the encouragement given to small businesses. Most budgets since 1981 have provided a range of incentives to encourage the setting up of small firms in line with a government belief in the role which such (labour intensive) enterprises could play in any recovery.

These are the main strands of what might be termed employment policy. If they do have a common thread it is that they are essentially supply side oriented rather than demand side.

Concluding Comments

It is clear from the foregoing that unemployment in the UK increased dramatically between 1979 and 1981 and has remained stubbornly high since then. Some analysts argue that this is due largely to the deflationary impact of counter-inflation policies; others contend that it has more to do with market imperfections on the supply side of the economy. Both arguments have some relevance. It seems plausible that various supply side influences have combined to help raise the natural rate of unemployment. Estimates of what this rate may be vary. For instance, Metcalf (1984) puts the range at 4–9 per cent. Even accepting the upper bound of these estimates suggests that the cur-rent unemployment level is beyond the natural rate by a significant degree. Quite what scope this offers for expansionary demand management policies is a matter of contro-versy. Many commentators feel that some non-marginal impact on the level of unem-ployment could be affected via increased public expenditure. The real concern here, however, is the implication of expansionary demand management policies for inflation. Layard (1986) argues that potential inflationary pressures can be defused by targeting assistance at the long-term unemployed where the pressures for wage inflation are likely to be at a minimum, and by introducing a tax-based incomes policy to contain any pressures which do result.

The present Conservative administration shows no inclination towards greater reliance on demand side policies, preferring to trust the (longer-term) supply side changes which have been so far effected. Whether such policies will ultimately be successful remains to be seen.

Further Reading

Data on unemployment in the UK are provided monthly by *Economic Trends*. This is a readily accessible source of information for aggregate and regional unemployment. A much more valuable source is the Department of Employment's monthly publication *Employment Gazette*. This provides detailed breakdowns by employment group, region, locality, duration of unemployment and so on, as well as regular special features on unemployment. More rigorous analyses of unemployment are provided by Nickell (1980) and the readings in Creedy (1981). The paper by Atkinson in the latter volume examines evidence on the disincentive effects of unemployment benefits, as does Nickell's (1979) paper.

A concise review of the new classical view of current UK unemployment can be found in Minford and Peel (1981). Brown and Burrows (1978) provide an overview of regional problems and their role in generating structural employment, as well as comparing UK regional unemployment problems with experience in other developed market economies. The Cambridge demand deficiency payments constraint analysis is outlined in most *Cambridge Economic Policy Reviews*. For a comparative empirical study of the role of labour market institutions on output and employment, see Gordon (1982a).

Effects of unemployment on the economy are dealt with comprehensively by Layard, Nickell and Jackman (1991); however, their subsequent text (1994) is more accessible to the non-specialist. Benoît-Guilbot and Gallie (1994) consider the effects of long-term unemployment and the creation of an underclass, although they approach the subject from more of a European perspective. A highly readable if contentious view of the causes of unemployment and a variety of other ills is offered by Hutton (1995).

21

Balance of Payments and Exchange Rate Policies in the UK

The balance of payments has occupied a central position in post-war UK macroeconomic debates. Recurrent sterling crises have been a feature of this period, which spans an era of both pegged exchange rates and managed exchange rates. In chapters 14 and 15 the interrelationships between internal and external balance, and the technical difficulties of simultaneously aiming to attain both, were considered. In this chapter the rather more specific issue of balance of payments and exchange rate policy in the UK will be considered.

As was seen in chapter 14 there are direct links between domestic expenditure policies and the balance of payments. Once a particular monetary/fiscal policy posture is adopted, there will be a given balance of payments outcome associated with it. This will be taken as given and, rather than examine further the links between domestic expenditure policies and the balance of payments which were extensively explored in chapters 14 and 15, the discussion will focus more sharply on those instruments which have been deployed to alter a specific balance of payments situation. Moreover, the discussion will take place against the backcloth of British experience over the post-war period.

The Meaning of External Balance

In chapter 14 external balance was equated with a situation where the sum of any surplus (or deficit) on the current account and any deficit (or surplus) on capital account is equal to zero. This would also be consistent with an absence of 'below the line' settlements. Such a definition was extremely convenient for analytical purposes as it permitted the tracing out of a locus of combinations of the interest rate and the level of income which were consistent with the sum of current and capital transactions netting out to zero. The *EB* schedule derived as a result was then used to explore the implications of various combinations of internal and external imbalance. When an attempt is made to transform this theoretical concept of external balance into a meaningful policy target, however, a number of difficulties are faced, in particular the time scale over which payments balance is expected to occur, the 'composition' of payments balance, and the relationship of external to internal balance.

Take first of all the question of time scale. Since the concern in chapters 14 and 15 was principally with comparative statics, this is a question which was largely ignored. Unless it is assumed that there are efficient markets throughout the system and freely floating exchange rates such that any tendency towards payments imbalance immediately alters the market clearing exchange rate, it is an issue which cannot be ignored. Even when exchange rates are relatively free, adjustment towards the market clearing rate invariably takes place in discrete steps. When, as is usually the case, some degree of exchange rate management is practised one has to be clear on the period over which one expects the accounts to balance. It would, for example, be quite absurd to aim at a target of daily, weekly or even monthly balance if only because of the complications caused by seasonal variations in demand for exports and imports. If, on the other hand, one were to view the relevant period as, say, a decade, then it could take an extremely long time to confirm any evidence of fundamental disequilibrium. In a famous tract, Nurkse (1945) argued that a period of five to ten years would be appropriate for the identification of external balance. The reasoning behind this suggestion is that it would probably take this long for any cyclical influences to even themselves out and, according to Nurkse, cyclical influences should be treated in the same way as seasonal influences, that is, as self-equilibrating. This too is probably an excessive period and most commentators would accept that any surplus or deficit which persisted beyond a couple of years was evidence of payments imbalance and a candidate for policy action. There is in fact a good deal of qualitative evidence to suggest that the policy-maker's time horizon may be even shorter than this.

Even when one has identified the period over which the balance of payments should balance, the composition of the overall balance of payments may itself be viewed as an intermediate policy target. In other words there may be a preference for a surplus on current account matched by a deficit on capital account (or vice versa). It is of course likely that such a division will be primarily dictated by a country's relative resource endowments. Thus, in the UK it is usual to find a deficit on the trade account and a surplus on services, reflecting the fact that the UK is a resource scarce (notwithstanding the advent of North Sea oil) and capital abundant economy. This may not, however, prevent policy-makers from offering inducements to encourage the export of manufactures rather than services or capital. It may also mean that there may be an (implicit) limit on the volume of short-term capital which a country is willing to attract to generate a capital account surplus and overall payments balance.

This leads to a third important issue, namely the mix of domestic financial policies which is seen as being consistent with external balance. For example, a current account deficit could be matched, if necessary, by a capital account surplus if the authorities were willing to maintain the necessary short-term interest rate differential. This is familiar from the Mundellian *IB/EB* model. What was also noted in connection with that model, however, is that there may be political constraints on the use of interest rates which impose an upper limit on the extent to which the domestic interest rate can rise. Thus although payments' balance may in principle be attainable, in practice it may prove to be unattainable owing to an inability or unwillingness to mix the appropriate combination of policies.

For these reasons payments balance is rather more difficult to identify than, say, price stability or even full employment. For present purposes it will be taken to mean a tendency towards the current and capital accounts summing to zero over a period of a couple of years. As will be seen in the review of UK policy over the post-war period, this appears to be the kind of time scale within which most (vote maximizing) policy-makers operate.

An Overview of UK Balance of Payments

Figure 21.1 describes the salient trends in the UK balance of payments over the period 1950–94. It traces the behaviour of the current account balance (that is, the sum of the visible and invisible balances) which follows a distinctly cyclical pattern, and certainly up until 1967 the cyclical pattern on the current account was integrally related to the stop-go pattern of economic activity which was such a prominent feature of UK experience. As was noted in chapter 14, monetary and fiscal policies are perforce related to one's payments situation. What is evident from experience over the 1950–67 period in particular is that full employment and a balanced current account were incompatible.

The order of magnitude of recorded deficits and surpluses has increased dramatically since 1970, compared with the period before then. This is in part due to the acceleration of inflation over this period and the effect which this has had on nominal values. However, both the deficits and surpluses that have occurred since then have, when expressed as a proportion of GDP, been high by historical standards. There are, however, specific developments that can explain certain cases and these will be explored further shortly.

In explaining these developments and trends it is helpful to break the period down into sub-periods 1950–67, 1967–72 and 1972–94.

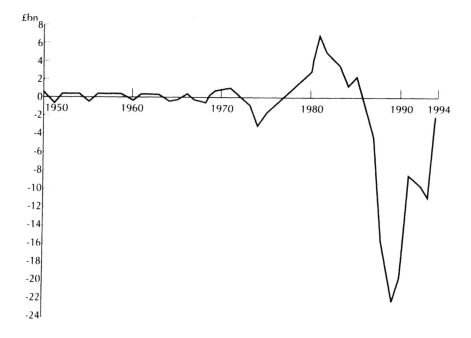

Figure 21.1 Balance of payments current account surplus/deficit, 1950–94

1950–1967: Pegged Exchange Rates and the Stop–Go Cycle

In 1948 the Bretton Woods arrangement regarding exchange rate movements was signed; it formed one of the bases of post-war international economic relations.[1] As a direct result of the Bretton Woods agreement a gold exchange rate system was introduced. Each country which participated in the system fixed a *par value* for its currency against gold and this in turn bore a fixed relationship to the dollar (initially this was set at $35/oz). Thus the dollar was the *numeraire* in the system and all exchange rates were pegged against it. Only minor variations were permitted on a day-to-day basis, which amounted to a fluctuation around the par value (or central rate) of ±1.25 per cent. If the exchange rate threatened to fluctuate outside this band, support buying or selling was obligatory. In certain circumstances, the par value could be changed by devaluation or revaluation – this was permitted in the event of *fundamental disequilibrium*. In practice, exchange rate changes under the Bretton Woods regime were infrequent; to all intents and purposes there was a quasi-fixed exchange rate.

This is really background information but it is central to an understanding of the crucially important role played by the balance of payments in post-war UK policy, and proved instrumental in generating the ubiquitous stop–go cycle to which reference has frequently been made.[2] It will be recalled that the combination of low productivity growth and relatively high inflation together resulted in absorption exceeding income whenever the economy expanded at a relatively healthy rate. Given the overhang of sterling balances, balance of payments crises were relatively common, and this period is characterized by the following factors:

(1) The balance of payments acted as a constraint on the rate of growth of domestic output.

(2) Since the exchange rate was viewed as being *de facto* fixed, balance of payments policy was largely a matter of expenditure reduction.

(3) As the years passed, crises occurred more frequently and were of greater severity This is partly a consequence of the increasing openness of the UK economy, but also a result of the cumulative effects of relatively poor productivity growth.

(4) Related to the last point, the UK steadily lost ground in markets for manufactures and semi-manufactures.

In terms of the models discussed in chapters 14 and 15 the experience of this period can be thought of in the framework of the internal–external balance setting of figures 14.4 and 14.9. Since the exchange rate was pegged the CA schedule of figure 14.4 was fixed. Attempts to reflate the economy resulted in a current account deficit which was remedied by deflationary shifts of *IS* and *LM*. In terms of the Mundell–Fleming model of figure 14.9 the domestic interest rate was manipulated on occasions in an attempt to secure external balance. The persistence of current account imbalance through time, however, illustrates one of the points made in criticizing that framework, namely that such fine-tuning is merely a palliative and as such cannot substitute for adjustment.

---

1 The others being the GATT and the World Bank group. The former provided a framework of rates for the conduct of international commerce, whilst the latter was introduced specifically as a development agency.

2 The stop–go cycle of growth is further analysed in chapter 22.

1967–1972: Breaking the Mould of Pegged Exchange Rates

Given current attitudes to exchange rate movements, it may appear absurd that devaluation was resisted for so long in the UK. Without doubt political considerations were paramount, with devaluation being viewed as a symptom of national failure both at home and abroad. There were, however, some genuine doubts about whether devaluation could result in a permanent change in the UK's competitiveness – doubts about the way in which money wages would react to devaluation, and reservations about whether resources were sufficiently mobile to permit expansion of the import substitute and export sectors. Notwithstanding these considerations, the domestic political palatability of a devaluation, given that it would have been the first since 1949 (which was also initiated by a Labour administration), and anxieties over the effect on overseas holders of sterling balances, appear to have been the principal forces behind resistance to devaluation (see Crossman, 1976). It is now a matter of historical record that a decision to devalue sterling by 14.3 per cent was finally taken on 18 November 1967. This reduced sterling's dollar value from $2.80 to $2.40.

Devaluation was followed by a turn-around from current account deficit in 1967–68 to current account surplus in 1969, 1970 and 1971. Two points should be noted here. First, the effect of the devaluation was recorded after a lag. This is the so-called J-curve effect of devaluation which follows from the lags involved in adjustment – agents take time to respond to the higher domestic price of imports and the lower foreign price of exports, and as a result the trade balance initially deteriorates. Following the reaction lag the trade balance improved strongly which, in terms of the analysis in chapter 14, implies that the Marshall–Lerner condition was satisfied; that is, the sum of import demand and export demand elasticities exceeded unity. The second point to be noted is that the turnaround on the current account was not only the result of devaluation. It will be recalled from chapter 14 that the absorption approach stressed the crucial role of idle resources; namely, even where elasticities are appropriate a devaluation may be unsuccessful if insufficient idle resources are available to accommodate increased demand for import substitutes and exports. In this particular episode the expenditure switching policy of devaluation was accompanied by an expenditure reducing package (of tax increases and public expenditure cuts). As well as helping to create the conditions in which devaluation might be effective, this undoubtedly had a direct effect on reducing import demand.

A number of econometric analyses of the effects of the 1967 devaluation have been completed (see NIESR 1972; Ball, Burns and Miller, 1972; and Artus, 1975). The general conclusion which can be drawn from these studies was that devaluation was a 'success' in transforming a current account deficit into a current account surplus. NIESR (1972) estimated that by 1976, devaluation had resulted in a 16.5 per cent increase in the value of imports but a 19 per cent increase in the value of exports; Ball, Burns and Miller (1972) estimated figures of 10 and 16.5 per cent, whilst Artus arrived at estimates of 7 and 18.7 per cent. All three studies suggest a change in export value of a similar order of magnitude, but differ on imports largely as a result of differing import demand elasticities employed.

It is also clear from figure 21.1 that the devaluation did not result in a permanent reversal of UK balance of payments difficulties. By 1971 the current account surplus was already declining, in 1972 it moved into deficit and remained in deficit for five years. This is in part related to specific events, in part due to an inherent difficulty of a policy of devaluation. To be effective it is necessary that the relative price effects of a

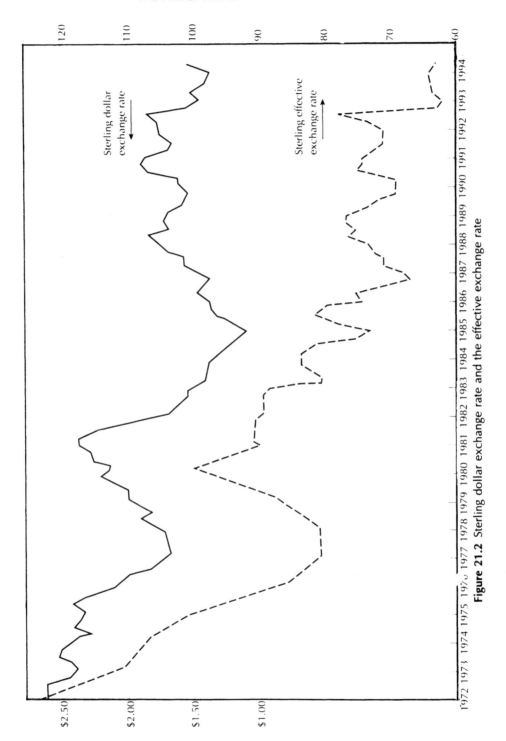

Figure 21.2 Sterling dollar exchange rate and the effective exchange rate

devaluation are not quickly eroded by an increase in the rate of change of money wages. Devaluation raises the domestic price of imports and exportables. If labour unions suffer from money illusion then the change in relative prices can result in a permanent gain in competitiveness. If, however, attempts are made to maintain real wages by seeking compensatory increases in money wages, the competitive edge conferred by devaluation is transient. In the UK an attempt was made to hold the line on money wages with the introduction of an incomes policy in April 1968. With hindsight this could be said to have been completely ineffective in part because the upper limit (of 3.5 per cent!) was relatively generous, in part because of the scope for 'productivity' related increases. The ensuing wage inflation of 1969–71 contributed significantly to the erosion of the benefits of devaluation.

In addition, there are a number of specific developments which were important. First, there was the Smithsonian realignment of exchange rates in December 1971 which was effectively the death-knell of the Bretton Woods gold exchange standard. As a result of the exchange rate realignments which actually took place sterling was *re-valued* by 8.6 per cent, with its dollar value rising from $2.40 to $2.60. Second, the incoming Conservative administration in 1970 engaged in an expansionary demand management programme in an attempt to reduce unemployment. All of these factors combined to help the current account back into deficit by 1972 and in June of that year a decision was taken to float sterling. This decision was as momentous in its own right as the decision to devalue; the former could not have been taken, however, without the latter. Devaluation in 1967 and the Smithsonian realignments of December 1971 broke the pegged rate psychology and opened the way to greater exchange rate flexibility. What followed is the longest period of exchange rate flexibility recorded in the UK, and it is to this experience that we now turn.

1972–1994: The Managed Floating Experience

Figure 21.2 outlines the movements which have taken place in the sterling dollar exchange rate and the sterling effective exchange rate[3] over the period 1972–94. In very general terms it can be seen that between June 1972 when sterling was floated and late 1976/early 1977, sterling's dollar value depreciated from $2.60 to around $1.60 (the actual nadir being $1.56 in November 1976). Between early 1977 and early 1981 an equally dramatic appreciation took place with the dollar value rising from around $1.60 to almost $2.40. Between 1981 and 1985 a further dramatic turnround occurred with the rate falling from $2.38 to $1.05 in January 1985. Since then the rate has fluctuated around $1.60, although there have been peaks of over $1.90 in the early 1990s. The sterling/dollar rate is of course only one bilateral exchange rate and a clearer indication of sterling's relative strengths and weaknesses is given by the effective exchange rate. Although this shows the same pattern of depreciation between 1972 and 1976, it is greater than that implied by the nominal exchange rate, whilst the effective appreciation from 1977 to 1981 is less. In other words sterling depreciated relative to other currencies in addition to the dollar in the earlier period, but appreciated relative to fewer in the later period. When one examines the effective exchange rate after 1981 one sees evidence of further sustained depreciation. The extent of the change again implies depreciation relative to other currencies as well as the US dollar.

---

3 The effective exchange rate is a weighted average index of exchange rates between sterling and the UK's principal trading partners.

By historical standards these are extremely wide fluctuations. The simple theory of floating exchange rates might lead one to expect that they were associated with a continuous tendency towards payments balance. In fact, as perusal of figure 21.1 makes clear, no such tendency can be observed. Indeed the absolute magnitude of payments imbalance increased. How then can these fluctuations be explained.

From chapter 15 it will be recalled that one view of exchange rate determination is the purchasing power parity (PPP) doctrine. This asserts that exchange rate movements will be determined by relative rates of price inflation. More specifically it argues that the rate of change of the exchange rate will be proportionately equal to the difference between domestic price inflation and the 'overseas' price inflation – the latter being a (trade) weighted average of the inflation rates of one's competitors. It is certainly true that over most the period under discussion the UK's rate of inflation exceeded that of her major trading partners.

While PPP explains in part movements in sterling over the past twenty years, there are also other forces at work which have to be acknowledged.

EEC Accession   In January 1973 the UK became a full member of the European Community. With regard to the UK's external situation and the value of sterling this had two interrelated effects. First, there followed a significant shift in the direction of trade away from the United States and Commonwealth partners towards members of the EEC. Thus in 1975 UK imports from and exports to the EEC accounted for 36 per cent of total imports and exports respectively. By the 1990s these shares had accounted for over 50 per cent of both imports and exports. Second, prior to accession UK tariffs were on average higher than the EEC common external tariff – they were therefore lowered to a greater extent during the adjustment period. These together with the budgetary implications of the common agricultural policy have resulted in the overall balance of payments effects of entry being negative. There is some debate over the precise balance of payments effects of EEC entry (see for example, Morgan, 1980, and Winters, 1986). Here it may merely be noted that it accounts for some of the depreciation in excess of that predicted by PPP.

Oil Shocks   Between October 1973 and January 1974 the posted price of crude oil quadrupled, whilst in the summer months of 1979 it again doubled. Given the suddenness and magnitude of the first oil shock, and given that it was an experience shared with other developed market and developing market economies, the induced deficit was largely accommodated. Given the highly inelastic demand for oil, exchange rate depreciation to eliminate the deficit would have been quite inconceivable. In the event the oil-induced recession which followed served to deflate import demand and helped turn around the deficit. None the less, this episode undoubtedly contributed to the exchange rate depreciation in excess of PPP which followed.

North Sea Oil   The second oil shock of 1979 did not have the same impact on the current account as the first oil shock, largely due to the cushion of North Sea oil. (It is also possible to argue that the expectation of North Sea oil coming 'on tap' eased adjustment to the first oil shock by providing collateral for foreign borrowing to accommodate the deficit.) The move towards self-sufficiency in oil and the contribution which this has made to payments surplus in the early 1980s are likely to have had an important effect on the effective appreciation of sterling which occurred in 1979–82. As with the effect of EEC entry on the exchange rate, the precise impact of North Sea oil is a matter of some debate, although the direction of its impact is uncontroversial, as the current account surpluses of the early 1980s indicate. However, the stabilization of North Sea oil production after the mid-1980s and the fall in the price of oil indicate that the bonanza predicted by many in the early 1980s became rather muted.

Expectations and Capital Flows   In chapter 15 was stressed the role which expectations of exchange rate changes play in driving currency inflows and outflows. In this connection was discussed the concept of exchange rate *overshooting* which was associated with changes in macroeconomic policy – the idea that anticipated changes in PPP are quickly taken into account and exert an influence on the spot rate of exchange. All that was necessary for this to occur is an efficient foreign exchange market, where differences in rates of return in assets which are close substitutes for each other are quickly arbitraged. Given the magnitude of potentially mobile international capital in an economy like the UK, which has a well-developed capital market and for historical reasons is an attractive centre for short-term 'investors', this is undoubtedly a contributory factor. Between 1974 and 1976 the rundown of sterling balances (by OPEC holders in particular) was instrumental in driving the depreciation which occurred. Similarly, the accumulation of sterling balances in 1979–80 (in anticipation of a falling rate of inflation, and because of sterling's petrocurrency status) played a significant part in driving exchange rate appreciation. Furthermore, the very dramatic depreciation of sterling in late 1984/early 1985 was stimulated by a substantial capital outflow.

The Exchange Rate Mechanism   Although the UK did not formally join the ERM until October 1990, for a number of years it had followed an informal policy of shadowing the Deutschmark at a rate of around DM3. When the UK formally joined the ERM, the official rate was set at DM2.95. This was despite the fact that the UK had a huge balance of payments current account deficit and inflation was on a dangerously rising trend. As has already been noted, interest rates were used as the main weapon in an attempt to keep sterling at a rate many felt was unsustainable. The UK left the ERM in September 1992, after which there was an immediate and significant depreciation in the effective exchange rate. There have thus been a number of influences as well as relative rates of inflation which have influenced exchange rate movements over the 1972–95 period.

Balance of Payments Policy, 1950–1995

In chapters 14 and 15 the distinction between balance of payments accommodation and adjustment was emphasized. The former, it will be recalled, referred to the practice of financing a payments deficit by foreign exchange decumulation, foreign borrowing or attracting short-term capital inflows by engineering relatively high interest rates (the analogues in the case of a surplus are foreign exchange accumulation, foreign lending or encouraging short-term capital outflows by maintaining relatively low interest rates). Balance of payments adjustment by contrast refers to the use of policies to remove the source of the payments imbalance. Thus to use the terminology of the absorption approach, adjustment to a payments deficit requires that domestic absorption be reduced relative to income. This in turn necessitates reliance on expenditure reducing policies and/or expenditure switching policies.

This distinction between accommodation and adjustment is crucially important in any evaluation of balance of payments policy. In principle the distinction between the two is quite clear. In practice, however, it can be somewhat opaque. The extent of any reserve decumulation (accumulation) or foreign borrowing (lending) can be adduced from the balance of payments accounts, but reliance on short-term capital inflows cannot since the latter is not broken down into autonomous and induced components. One thing is clear, however; accommodation is a short-term palliative which can only be expected to remove what Johnson (1958) referred to as *stock imbalances*. Since most payments imbalances are flows, accommodation can only be used to buy time (although the length of time which can be bought is invariably longer for a surplus than a deficit). This follows because reserves are finite, creditworthiness has its limits and there are political constraints on the limits which nominal interest rates can reach.

Over the last thirty years there have been many occasions when the UK has attempted to rely on accommodation rather than adjustment, in both the period of pegged rates and during the managed float. In the earlier period interest rates (as indicated by bank rate) were frequently raised when the balance of payments was in deficit and the sale of sterling balances was placing sterling under pressure (for example, 1951–52, 1955–56, 1960, 1964). In addition, the authorities were willing to borrow on an extensive scale to finance payments deficits. A particularly good example of this in the era of pegged rates is the agreements reached between 1964 and 1967. Thus, in December 1964 $1 billion was drawn from the IMF. This was supplemented by a drawing of $1.4 billion in May 1965. In addition, bilateral borrowing arrangements were made with other central banks (most notably the Federal Reserve Bank), in part to repay the IMF drawings but also to support sterling. In the end of course the parity was changed.

After 1972 one also observes the use of interest rate manipulation as a means of payments accommodation. Despite the fact that sterling has been floating, the authorities have been unwilling to permit it to fluctuate outside certain (unannounced) limits. For example the possibility that the sterling dollar rate might move significantly below $1.80 in the second half of 1981 was instrumental in stimulating a rise in interest rates. Likewise when sterling approached parity with the US dollar in January 1985, interest rates were increased dramatically to arrest the decline. One can also find occasions when accommodation via borrowing/reserve use has been important over the managed float period. The clearest example is during the period of the post-OPEC deficit 1974–77. The oil-induced deficit of 1974 and 1975 would have required an unacceptable reduction in absorption and/or an unacceptable effective depreciation to remove them (always assuming that such interventions would have been successful). The deficits were accommodated in part by borrowings from the IMF, in part by borrowings from the Euro-currency markets (through encouraging UK public corporations to borrow in non-sterling currencies), and in part by the 'recycling' of OPEC surpluses. The latter was especially popular with many Western governments given the size of the OPEC surplus and their inability to absorb much of it on current consumption. In the UK case one finds that OPEC holdings of sterling balances rose from $1 billion in 1973 to $3.2 billion in 1974. Although this proved to be an essential expedient, the subsequent rundown of these balances in 1975 and 1976 placed sterling under considerable pressure.

Invariably this aspect of policy has tended to be a holding operation; adjustment action has had to be taken sooner or later. Over the period 1950–67 this took the form principally of expenditure changing policies, with only peripheral use of explicit expenditure switching policies (such as the travel allowance introduced in 1966, the export rebate of 1964–68, the import surcharge of 1964–66, the import deposit scheme of 1968–70 and efforts to reduce government overseas expenditure). Demand deflation through the use of restrictive fiscal and monetary policies (the latter via credit restrictions) was the principal instrument of payments adjustment. It has already been noted that this tended to be effective in removing the deficit but not the balance of payments constraint to growth – whenever the economy recovered and moved on to a growth path the deficit invariably returned. With the recognition that the UK was in fundamental disequilibrium and that an exchange rate of $2.80 could not be defended indefinitely, a greater willingness to use the exchange rate as an instrument rather than viewing it simply as a target has been evident.

It has already been noted that the devaluation of 1967 served to transform a payments deficit into a surplus, but its effects were relatively short lived. Between June 1972 and the end of 1976 a sustained depreciation occurred, with the effective rate for sterling being more than one-third lower at the end of the period compared with the beginning. Trade competitiveness did improve over this period but there is no more evidence of any permanent change in competitiveness than there was as a consequence of expenditure reducing policies. Furthermore, any gains were reversed in the late 1970s/early 1980s. A dramatic deterioration in competitiveness followed as a consequence of accelerating domestic inflation, against the backcloth of an appreciating exchange rate. Subsequent exchange rate depreciation combined with a depreciating exchange rate have seen some improvement in competitiveness (relative to the 1979–81 period).

Evaluation of the floating experience in the UK (and indeed in other developed market economies) is far from being an easy task. One is not, as with the 1967 devaluation, dealing with a discrete event, where one is likely to have a clearer idea of what might have been. A number of concluding remarks can however be made about the period. First, a greater degree of exchange rate flexibility did undoubtedly ease adjustment to the first oil shock. It is difficult to see how a fixed or pegged rate system could have survived such an experience – especially given the high and divergent inflation rates which accompanied it. One might argue that the latter were facilitated by the movement to a (managed) floating arrangement. One of the arguments for a floating system consistently advanced by sympathizers is the fact that it confers on governments autonomy over domestic monetary policy. The corollary to this argument is that it may thereby provide a basis for irresponsible use of this instrument, this in turn leading to inflationary pressures. This may, for instance, have been the case with the infamous 'Barber boom' of the early 1970s. One might argue that the money supply could only expand by more than 20 per cent in two successive years because the exchange rate was left to depreciate. A second point which may be made is that there is some evidence to indicate that speculative movements of funds have been more important in causing exchange rate fluctuations than would have been forecast by the adherents of flexible exchange rates. Note that this is not the same as saying that speculation has been destabilizing. No conclusive evidence is available on this point. What it does mean, however, is that the *real* effects of exchange rate movements, especially sudden appreciations, have been greater than many would have forecast. This certainly seems to have been the case with recent UK experience.

A third point to note is that support exists for a proposition which was an integral part of the absorption approach, namely that exchange rate movements of themselves are not sufficient to generate adjustments to payments imbalance – they have to be backed up with appropriate fiscal and monetary policies. Thus, for example, the depreciation of 1975–76, which it was initially hoped would lead to some permanent improvement in the payments position, was not brought under control until an appropriate package of monetary and fiscal measures designed to reduce inflation restored confidence in the currency.

A fourth point is that although the relative price effects of devaluation and depreciation are theoretically identical in practical terms there is an important difference which hangs on the role of the expectations of traders. In a pegged rate system with relatively low inflation rates, one can be reasonably confident that discrete changes in par values will hold for a reasonable length of time. In a floating system, however, with high and divergent rates of inflation and where speculative flows are influential, the variance associated with exchange rate changes may be quite high. Thus traders may take rather longer to commit themselves to a particular investment decision.

As we noted earlier, it is extremely difficult to evaluate the managed floating experience, given the structural changes which have occurred during the period in question. It is certainly true that exchange rate fluctuations have been more dramatic than most commentators would have anticipated. To some this constitutes grounds for a movement towards greater official intervention to stabilize the exchange rate. Others argue that the sheer volume of potentially mobile international capital makes any hope of intervention futile. One thing is reasonably clear however. A more flexible exchange rate does not seem to have been the panacea which some expected. The evidence since 1970 suggests that the external constraint has not been removed.

Monetary Union

The origins of the original European Monetary System (EMS) lay in the 1970 Werner Report which first proposed the idea of full monetary union within the EC and set 1980 as the date for its achievement. Whilst this timetable was swiftly abandoned, the EMS itself began in 1979.

The EMS is a regional system of pegged rates introduced as part of a long-term move towards monetary union in Western Europe. It was envisaged that participation in the scheme would help insulate Western European economies from dollar instability and would provide a means of generating a convergence of inflation rates. Furthermore, it was hoped that the stabilization of exchange rates would serve to stimulate trade expansion. In the event, all member countries agreed to participate in a system (albeit on different terms) apart from the UK. Although participation in the scheme has been raised from time to time since then, the UK resisted joining.

British objections revolved around a number of issues. It was felt, for example, that (as under the Bretton Woods system) there would be asymmetries in the incentives to adjust in the event of payments imbalance – with greater pressures being applied to deficit than surplus countries. The UK argued for a specific type of arrangement (a weighted basket of currencies as the *numeraire*) to avoid this, which in the event was not accepted. Another aspect of this which caused concern was the effective removal of monetary policy as an independent policy instrument. In a system like the EMS, the rate of monetary expansion would effectively be dictated by Germany, given its absolute importance in Community trade and its relatively low inflation rate. The feeling of UK negotiators was that once the devaluation option was removed a deflationary bias would be imposed on the system. In the event that this was the case the question of resource transfers became paramount, especially given UK sensitivity to her position as the largest net contributor to the Community budget. The final issue over which the

UK was anxious was the position of sterling balances given the probability that, as under the Bretton Woods regime, one-way option speculation would again become a source of pressure.

None the less, sterling joined the EMS in October 1990 at a central rate against the mark of £1 = DM2.95. The UK had delayed joining earlier, arguing that conditions were not suitable due to the pressure on sterling, given its petrocurrency status. However, political momentum began to move towards economic and monetary integration within the EC as a whole after the Delors Committee report in April 1989. This movement was given extra weight by the December 1991 Maastricht agreement among EU heads of state, which laid down a further timetable for the establishment of a common currency within Europe.

Despite the UK's suspension from the ERM in September 1992 and its further fragmentation in subsequent months, Parliament finally ratified the treaty in the summer of 1993. The main component of the treaty is that member states would seek to converge their economies in order for monetary and economic union to take place. The five criteria to be met by countries joining monetary union were set as follows.

- Inflation: to be no more than 1.5 per cent above the average of the three EC countries with the lowest inflation

- Interest rates: long-term rates to be no more than 2 per cent above the average of the three countries with the lowest rates

- Budget deficit: should be no more than 3 per cent of GDP

- National debt: should be no more than 60 per cent of GDP

- Exchange rates: should not have been realigned in the previous two years and remained within the 2.25 per cent intervention band.

Countries satisfying the above criteria would embark upon monetary union by 1 January 1999, with others joining later when they met the criteria. The fact that only a minority of member states currently satisfy the convergence criteria suggests that if the original timetable is to be adhered to, initial monetary union will only be undertaken by a few. Alternatively, the timetable could be changed and/or the criteria reviewed. Such a decision would have a significant political as well as economic dimension.

Import Controls

The one instrument which has not so far been mentioned, and which can be used to influence the balance of payments, is trade policy. The General Agreement on Tariffs and Trade (GATT), of which the UK is a contracting party, does permit the use of *temporary* trade controls for balance of payments purposes under article XII. Trade interventions can take a variety of forms. They may be fiscal instruments (like import tariffs or export subsidies) or direct quantitative restrictions; they may be overt (like tariffs) or covert (like voluntary export restraints). Within the framework outlined in the absorption approach, such instruments are expenditure switching; that is, they are intended to encourage domestic consumers to switch consumption from imports to import substitutes, and/or overseas consumers to switch purchasing from other countries exports to 'home' produced exports. In principle, therefore, commercial policy instruments can be used for payments adjustment.

GATT proscribes the use of commercial policy instruments for this purpose largely because they are inefficient relative to the alternatives (exchange rate adjustment or demand deflation). There is a well-founded body of theory, dating back to the work of James Meade (1955), which underpins this belief. In the main, recourse to article XII by developed market economies has been infrequent; indeed, the occasions when trade instruments have been temporarily deployed for balance of payments reasons are conspicuous by their presence – the Wilson import surcharge of 1964 and the Nixon import surcharge of 1971, for example.

Despite the presence of a well-developed body of theory (and a good deal of empirical evidence to back it up) which suggests that trade policy is an inefficient instrument for balance of payments adjustment because of the distortions introduced by their use, one school of thought has recently proposed that the most efficacious means of relieving the UK balance of payments constraint would be via general import controls. This has been a central feature of the analysis of the Cambridge Economic Policy Group. Although the proposal has been consistently propounded, as yet it has failed to persuade a governing party that it would be a superior instrument to relative price adjustment via exchange rate change or demand deflation.

It may be noted in closing that although the temptation of general import controls has been resisted there has been a proliferation of selective import controls in the UK (as well as in other developed market economies), often in the guise of voluntary export restraints (a euphemism for import quotas). Most of these have been applied in response to pressure for employment protection in specific sectors (see Greenaway, 1983a, and Greenaway and Hindley, 1985).

Concluding Comments

Balance of payments policy is much less easy to identify than inflation or growth policy simply because the balance of payments is integrally linked to domestic demand management policies. Nevertheless, governments do engage in balance of payments policy if only on a 'reactive' basis – that is, because they have a balance of payments problem.

During the period 1949–67 such policies were primarily expenditure changing policies in the UK. Following devaluation, in 1967, and, more especially the floating of the exchange rate in 1972, exchange rate changes have played a much more important role than previously. It is probable that this greater degree of exchange rate flexibility facilitated easier adjustment to several major shocks, in particular the oil price rises of 1973–74 and 1978–79, and the discovery and exploitation of North Sea oil. Having said that, it is clear that exchange rate fluctuations have been more marked than many expected, so much so that some commentators believe that a return to a greater degree of exchange rate management is appropriate. Whether this takes the form of a revised exchange rate mechanism or full monetary union remains to be seen.

Further Reading

There are a number of treatises on UK balance of payments experience over the post-war period. Milner and Greenaway (1979) provide an overview of the difficulties of identifying payments 'policy' and a review of the institutional background to the 1950–67 period. Metcalfe and Green (1986) outline post-war UK experience as a whole, as does Sinclair (1978). Tew (1978) concentrates on the pre-1967 period, whilst Milner (1980) focuses on the post-1967 period. The two Brookings studies of the UK balance of payments are excellent analyses, Cooper (1968) covering the experience of the 1950s and 1960s and Dornbusch and Fischer (1980) covering the experience of the 1970s. The latter in particular is an exemplary piece of applied economics. A worthwhile international comparison of the experience with floating exchange rates is given by Swoboda (1981). Emerson (1979) concentrates on Britain and the European Monetary System.

A number of analyses of the effects of North Sea oil are available. The theoretical framework for evaluating 'Dutch Disease' effects is developed in Corden and Neary (1982). Forsyth and Kay (1981) provide estimates of the exchange rate effects of North Sea oil which are supported by Chrystal (1984). An alternative view which argues that monetary contraction was largely responsible for appreciation is provided by Buiter and Miller (1983).

A full statement of the argument for general import controls can be found in Cripps and Godley (1978) or Nield (1979), whilst critiques of this strategy are given in Scott, Corden and Little (1980) and Greenaway and Milner (1979). Greenaway (1983a) documents the recent proliferation of non-tariff interventions as well as providing an economic analysis of their effects.

More recent analysis of the UK balance of payments and exchange rate policies are addressed by Curwen (1994) and Griffiths and Wall (1995). The economics of the European Exchange Rate Mechanism and its effects on the UK's economic performance and policy are covered by Artis and Lee (1994) and El-Agraa (1994).

A comprehensive analysis of the problems and benefits of monetary integration is contained within De Grauwe (1992) and Emerson et al. (1992).

22

Policies for Economic Growth
in the UK

Thus far, the policy issues we have examined with respect to the UK economy have been essentially short-term in nature. Now, however, we turn our attention to the long-term issue of economic growth – that is, with the question of what determines the trend growth of *potential* output over time. The recognition of factors influencing the trend of long-run potential output is the first step in the devising of policies which may be invoked in raising the long-run future growth path of the economy. Whilst policy measures may have comparatively little effect when compared to more fundamental determinants which may be realistically viewed as autonomous, they should certainly not be ignored. Such is the compounding nature of the growth process that even *minor* changes in the underlying growth rate can make for a profound difference to standards of consumption and welfare over a relatively short time span.[1]

The Sources of Economic Growth

Let us consider then, possible sources of economic growth. Assuming, for expositional simplicity, that full employment of both labour and the capital stock prevails, growth depends either upon an augmentation of factor inputs, or alternatively an increase in their productivity, or some combination of the two. To illustrate, let us invoke the concept of the aggregate production function of the form

$$Q = A(L, K) \tag{22.1}$$

---

1 To illustrate this point, invoking a rule-of-thumb procedure, consider two individuals born on the same day with the same per capita income and facing identical life spans of 70 years. Assume one can look forward to a constant increase in per capita income of 2 per cent per year whilst the other enjoys 3 per cent. At the time of his death the former will be enjoying an income approximately four times that he was endowed with but the latter would be more than twice as well off, enjoying an income equal to eight times his initial endowment. Small differences in the rate of economic growth, therefore, are crucial in changing *comparative* living standards over the space of one or two generations. Moreover, it is this critical compounding nature of the growth process which render it the only possible solution to the elimination of poverty and destitution whether in advanced or Third World economies. In contrast, policies of income redistribution, whether internally or intra-country, and whilst arguably desirable upon grounds of equity, can exert little real beneficial effect when compared to the overriding importance of promoting a raising of the growth rate.

where Q is real output expressed as a function of labour and capital inputs, L and K respectively, and of a residual influence A. Output may be increased in consequence of either increasing labour and capital inputs, or alternatively by increasing the value of the coefficient A – which may be viewed as encompassing a host of non-factor influences, such as innovation and technical change, educational and cultural factors, fiscal influences and so forth. This dichotomy is useful in highlighting one of the controversies surrounding the current growth debate. On the one hand, there are those economists who point to the need for increased productive inputs, particularly capital inputs, as the driving force in economic expansion, whilst upon the other there are those who, emphasizing diminishing returns, are sceptical of factor augmentation and point to alternative 'environmental' influences.

In order to bring out some of the implications of this general approach let us simplify the argument by assuming that the production function is Cobb-Douglas and exhibits constant returns to scale. Such a production function implies that a doubling of the factor inputs, *ceteris paribus*, will lead to a doubling of the output, or alternatively a halving of the factor inputs will imply a halving of the final product. We may write such a production function in the following manner:

$$Q = AL^{\alpha}K^{(1-\alpha)} \tag{22.2}$$

The exponents α and $(1 - \alpha)$ indicate the respective productivity of the two factor inputs. Constant returns production functions are commonly invoked in economic analysis primarily because of their great convenience and mathematical simplicity. However, it is perhaps necessary to note that they are also relatively biased against factor augmentation *per se* because they exhibit diminishing returns to any one factor input.[2]

The comparative impact of augmenting labour *vis-à-vis* the capital input depends therefore upon the exponents α and $(1 - \alpha)$. The effect of factor augmentation upon output is given by the increment in the factor multiplied by its marginal productivity. Thus, for example, increased output arising from the augmentation of the labour input is given by

$$\Delta Q = \Delta L.MP_L = \Delta L\alpha AL^{\alpha-1}K^{(1-\alpha)} \tag{22.3}$$

---

2 To see this consider the marginal product of labour and capital respectively.

$$\frac{\partial Q}{\partial L} = \alpha AL^{\alpha-1}K^{1-\alpha}$$

gives the marginal product of labour and

$$\frac{\partial^2 Q}{\partial L^2} = (\alpha - 1)\alpha AL^{\alpha-2}K^{1-\alpha} < 0$$

implying that the marginal product declines with increasing augmentation of the factor input. Likewise,

$$\frac{\partial Q}{\partial K} = (1 - \alpha)AL^{\alpha}K^{-\alpha}$$

shows the marginal product of capital and

$$\frac{\partial^2 Q}{\partial K^2} = -\alpha(1 - \alpha)AL^{\alpha}K^{-\alpha-1} < 0$$

whilst the corresponding increase arising from augmentation of the capital input is simply

$$\Delta Q = \Delta K.MP_K = \Delta K(1 - \alpha)AL^\alpha K^{-\alpha} \qquad (22.4)$$

An α value of 0.5 would mean that it was a matter of indifference whether one increased the input of labour or the input of capital upon total output. However, if α were to be approximately 0.75, implying a value of the capital exponent of 0.25, then a 10 per cent increase in the input of labour alone would lead to a raising of the level of output by 7.5 per cent, whilst 10 per cent increase in the capital input alone would lead to a raising of the level of output by 2.5 per cent. A 10 per cent increase in the input of both factor inputs would, of course, raise output by 10 per cent. The values of the exponents 0.75 and 0.25 are not randomly picked out of the air; there are indeed very close to values suggested by the empirical evidence which accordingly questions the wisdom of policies concentrating solely upon the need for increased capital formation.

Some Growth Theory

This general scepticism concerning the efficacy of capital formation as a means to increased economic growth is reinforced by the general conclusions of what is probably the best-known theoretical growth model, the so-called neo-classical growth model. The general conclusion stemming from the elementary version of this model is that the ultimate determinant of the economic growth process is the rate of growth of population which to all intents and purposes is exogenously determined. Thus although there are policies which may be successful in promoting the pace of capital formation and thereby increasing the amount of capital per capita, they are relatively ineffective as a means of promoting a higher rate of growth of potential output. As always, elementary statements of complex theoretical positions are necessarily deficient and subject to considerable qualification and reservation. None the less, it is perhaps instructive to present this elementary proposition first. As a means of proceeding we borrow a diagrammatic analysis first proposed by Johnson (1966) in an influential paper which introduced monetary issues into growth models.

In figure 22.1 the vertical axis displays income per capita and savings per capita, the latter being assumed a constant proportion of the former. On the horizontal axis we illustrate the amount of capital per capita. The autonomous rate of population growth is shown by the slope of the ray On; an increase in the slope of On implies a raising of the pace of population expansion and vice versa. Given this framework the only possible long-term equilibrium solution is indicated at point T, implying a capital/output ratio of OK/OY. At T, the amount of saving per capita is just equal to the rate of population expansion. Accordingly, the rate of capital formation is just offset by the rate of population growth leaving the aggregate capital per capita ratio unchanged.[3] To illustrate further, consider the consequences of a decline in the rate of population expansion as indicated by the ray n'. This would imply that at the initial equilibrium T, the rate of capital formation now exceeds the rate of population growth. The amount of capital per capita would accordingly increase and the increase must continue until

---

3 It will be appreciated that savings here are to be understood as net i.e. after allowing for depreciation. For a fuller and more elaborate discussion on this point, see Mankiw (1994, pp. 81–8).

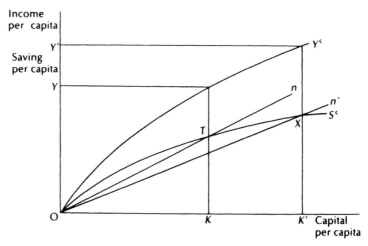

Figure 22.1 The neo-classical model

position X is obtained when once again the rates of capital formation and population expansion are equated. Whatever the rates of population expansion or whatever the savings ratio there is always an indicated solution implied by the appropriate adjustment in the capital/output ratio. In the movement from T to X, for example, the capital/output ratio rises from OK/OY to OK'/OY' as the labour supply declines.

Once the equilibrium is attained it follows that the capital/output ratio is rendered a constant, the capital/labour ratio remains constant and moreover the level of income per capita is also invariant through time. Thus the economy expands at the predetermined rate of population growth n, but with no change in the level of income per capita. This 'golden age' solution implies constant real income being maintained over time – a vision of an eternally moving stationary state.

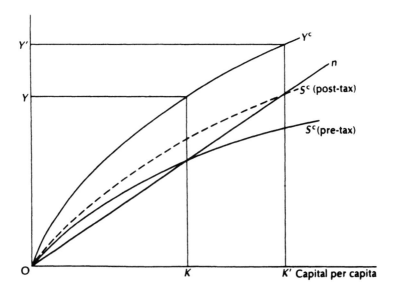

Figure 22.2 The effect of fiscal policy on the growth rate

The policy implication of this result is well known: namely, that if the growth rate is autonomously determined by population expansion then it remains immutable to policy intervention. In particular, fiscal policy which by generating forced savings can influence the overall savings ratio, is powerless to influence the overall rate of growth. To see this consider figure 22.2. Restrictive fiscal policy is able to generate an increase in the aggregate savings ratio revealed as an upward shift of the savings per capita curve as indicated by the hatched line. The result is an increase in the amount of capital per capita, a changed capital/output ratio and an increase in the level of income per capita. But once the adjustment is complete the economy continues to grow at rate n. Thus fiscal policy is able to alter income per capita levels but not the actual growth rate of the economy.

One should note an immediate implication: whilst population expansion ultimately determines the growth rate in the neo-classical model it does not follow that the maximization of population growth is the desired objective even if it is assumed that population may respond to policy stimulus. *Ceteris paribus*, the higher the rate of population growth the lower the level of income per capita and vice versa. Nor should the objective be unquestioningly to maximize the level of income per capita. Rather the welfare maximizing condition resides in the maximization of consumption per capita – that is, the difference between the level of income per capita and savings per capita. This reduces to an elementary problem in constrained maximization. We wish to maximize the difference between Y^c and S^c subject to the constraint that the ultimate outcome must also imply an equality between S^c and the autonomously determined population growth rate n. Accordingly, we need to maximise the gap between Y^c and n and adjust savings so as to equate n at this point. In figure 22.3., the difference between Y^c and n will be maximized when a tangent to the production function has the same slope as the population ray. This occurs at K^*. Fiscal policy is then invoked to either raise or lower the savings schedule to bring about the equation between S^c and n at this point as illustrated in the figure.

The situation which maximizes consumption per capita, as depicted in figure 22.3, is usually referred to as the *Golden Rule of Capital Accumulation*. It is perhaps instructive to consider what is implied. The tangent to the production function indicates, of course, the marginal product of capital. It shows the increment in income per capital with respect to some small change in capital per capita and is estimated by the tangent slope – namely, CB/AB. Now, if we assume that capital is paid a return equal to its marginal product, then the total payment to capital will be this marginal product multiplied by the amount of capital employed, OK^*. Alternatively, we can express the payment to capital as

$$(CB/AB) \times AB = CB = AY \tag{22.5}$$

Thus, when the amount of consumption per capita is maximized at the optimum capital per capita level, K^*, the share of income accuring to capital is AY. What remains is the share paid in the form of wage labour income OA. Now, by construction, OA equals DC. Accordingly, AY must equal K^*D. In other words, consumption per capita will be maximized when the savings ratio K^*D is precisely equal to the share of income accuring to the owners of capital AY. This is what is referred to as the Golden Rule of Capital Accumulation.

This brief excursion into growth theory has suggested that the long-run steady-state growth path is relatively immune from policy influence. Indeed, in conventional neo-classical growth models with autonomous population growth and exogenous technical

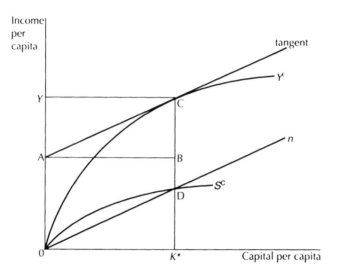

Figure 22.3 The Golden Rule of Capital Accumulation

change, there was virtually no role for government to play. It can hardly be surprising that there was little attempt to apply modern growth theory to the problems of the Third World; development economics had to emerge as a distinct discipline.

However, this essentially unsatisfactory and pessimistic position is transformed once it is realized that technical progress may be the key element in the growth equation and that, *in addition*, technical progress may be susceptible to policy intervention – that is, that technical progress may be endogenous upon other acts of government policy. Before turning specifically to the growth problems of the UK economy, therefore, it is perhaps instructive to examine this issue in somewhat more detail.

The Solow Growth Formula

In a pioneering paper, Robert Solow (1957) devised a framework for distinguishing the contributions of labour, capital and technical change to the growth record. Starting with a production function along the lines of 22.1, Solow derived the following general growth formula as being applicable to the United States economy:[4]

$$\Delta Y / Y = \Delta A / A + 0.7 \Delta L / L + 0.3 \Delta K / K \tag{23.6}$$

What this implies is that a 1 per cent increase in output growth can be achieved either by a 1 per cent increase in productivity growth, or a 1.4 per cent increase in the employ-

---

4 Thus the growth rate of income $\Delta Y / Y$ has three component parts: the contribution of overall factor productivity $\Delta A / A$ (technical progress), the contribution of labour input given by the increase in labour input multiplied by its marginal productivity, and the contribution of capital input given by the increase in capital multiplied by the marginal productivity of capital. The marginal productivities assumed reflect labour and capitals share in national income and assumes factors are indeed paid their marginal product. It should be emphasized that $\Delta A / A$ is not observed; it is the change in output not accounted for by the change in factor inputs and is therefore obtained as an unobserved residual. For a simple derivation of the Solow growth formula see, for example, Hall and Taylor (1993, pp. 119–20).

ment of the labour input, or a 3.3 per cent increase in the employment of capital. Solow further concluded, from time series data over the period 1909–49, that the vast bulk of US growth had stemmed from increased productivity as opposed to the augmentation of factor inputs.

Although the Solow growth formula did not go uncriticized, it none the less focused attention firmly upon the importance of technical progress. If only the sources of technical progress could be identified then the implications for government policy could be far-reaching. Recent research agendas have directed themselves to this fundamental issue. At the present time, it would perhaps be fair to conclude that no single unique source of overall economic growth has been identified with any great precision; at the same time, however, there is no doubt that attention is very firmly directed towards the importance of human capital and investment in human capital. In particular, Learning by Doing models (Arrow, 1962), which emphasize the beneficial spillover effects of increased knowledge and the importance of knowledge as a factor in the production function, and research and development models (Romer, 1990), which stress the role played by key sectors specializing in the production of new ideas, have come to the fore.

If these models do succeed in identifying the main determinants of economic growth more precisely, then the policy implications are immense. In particular, they would highlight the possible role of education and training and also the importance of multinational enterprise as a vehicle for the transmission of technical progress to the developing economies. Finally, a note of caution. Although the Solow growth formula had indicated a comparatively minor role to the capital input, it may be that productivity growth is not independent of the rate of investment. That is to say, technical progress may be embodied in the very act of investment. The need to distinguish between disembodied technical progress, which is able to be exploited by the existing stock of capital, and embodied technical progress, which does not benefit existing machinery, remains a crucial element in the debate.

Recent Policy and Experience in the UK

The idea that economic growth may be relatively immune to policy action takes on greater credibility when one examines the historical record of the UK. At first glance, over the period 1950–89, the average growth rate approximates some 2.58 per cent with no discernible trend emerging other than the fact that the latter portion of the period revealed greater variation and even recorded years of negative growth rates. This is remarkable in the light of the fact that differing administrations have adopted widely different policy stances, ranging from nationalization and price and income controls, through to privatization and supply side economics. Perhaps more disconcerting is the fact that Britain's growth performance over this period has been comparatively poor by international comparison. Having already indicated the crucial importance of even small differences in growth rates, there can be little doubt that continuation of the post-war growth trends would render the UK one of the poorest nations in Europe. It is for this reason that the remarkable improvement in economic growth achieved in the 1983–87 period which allowed the proud election boast that Britain now topped the European growth league takes on renewed significance. Is this to be a permanent relative improvement or merely a reflection of unusual and exceptional circumstances? Time alone will judge. The salient features are summarized up with the aid of tables 22.1a and 22.1b.

TABLE 22.1a
UK Economic Growth, 1950–89

1950–54	2.9
1955–59	2.1
1960–64	3.9
1965–69	2.8
1970–74	2.5
1975–79	2.0
1980–84	0.8
1985–89	3.7
*Average	2.58

* Average % change in GDP at factor cost
Source: Matthews, Feinstein and Odling-Smee
(1982) and Johnson (1991)

TABLE 22.1b
International Economic Growth

Period	Growth					
	UK	France	Germany	Italy	Japan	USA
1980–84	0.8	1.5	1.1	1.9	3.9	1.9
1985–89	3.7	2.8	2.7	3.1	4.5	3.4

* Average Annual % Change in Real GDP
Source: Johnson (1991), Feinstein (1990) and Economic Trends

As we have already indicated, the incoming Thatcher administration in 1979 was less sanguine about the ability of demand management and macroeconomic intervention to influence growth rates within the economy. Rather, the reduced scope for macroeconomic policy lay in the elimination of inflation and hence in creating the climate and conditions conducive to enterprise, innovation and growth. Effectively, the incoming administration broke with tradition; economic growth was to be pursued through *micro*economic intervention and in particular by supply side strategies.

Supply side policies view the growth strategy in terms of raising *natural* levels of output and employment by providing incentives to greater work effort, risk taking and investment upon the one hand, and by removing impediments to increased efficiency by improving market forces upon the other.

The fundamental point underlying supply side strategies is that long-run aggregate supply is completely unresponsive to aggregate demand conditions. Demand changes may, and indeed will, carry implications for the price level, but they will leave the 'natural' level of output and employment unaffected. This situation is depicted with the aid of figure 22.4, where the aggregate supply curve is shown to be completely inelastic with respect to price. However, the *position* of the aggregate supply curve will depend on a host of microeconomic influences which are amenable to policy choice and which can be manipulated to produce a favourable outward shift of the supply schedule – see figure 22.5. The major microeconomic factors that might produce such a shift can be briefly indicated as follows.

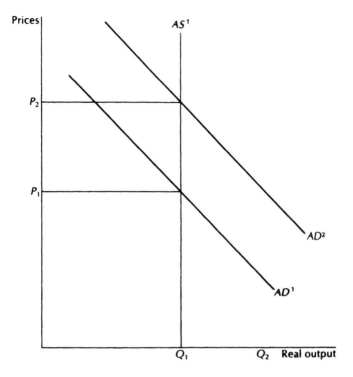

Figure 22.4 Non-response of supply to aggregate demand change

Increased Privatization

The private sector is regarded as being naturally more efficient than the public sector. Curtailment of public sector spending and a gradual return of assets to private owner-ship are seen as one means of increasing aggregate output. This thesis, that productive private sector undertakings are 'crowded out' by the public sector, is of course closely linked to the belief in the overriding importance of the market sector to economic growth.

Reduced Taxation

Decreases in the marginal rate of income taxation, combined with a shift in the mix of taxes from direct to indirect, is looked upon as a principal means of encouraging sav-ing, risk-taking and work effort. This issue is closely linked to the need to reform the system of unemployment and welfare benefits which are held to be disincentives to work effort, especially in often cited cases of the poverty trap where marginal implicit tax rates may approach 100 per cent.

Increased Competition and Deregulation

Under this general heading may be grouped a number of diverse elements. The trade union movement, with its insistence upon restrictive practices and its ability to gener-ate wages over and above what would prevail in a non-union situation, is looked upon as a cause of both inefficiency and unemployment. In addition, employment

Figure 22.5 Altering natural output levels by supply side strategies

legislation, especially measures such as the Employment Protection Act of 1975, raise the cost of employing labour and therefore contribute to raising the natural level of unemployment. Other controls, such as rent controls, impede mobility as do certain private sector retirement pension provisions, all of which contribute to inefficiency and higher unemployment.

Measures such as the ones mentioned here by no means exhaust the arsenal of supply side economic strategies. They do, however, serve to indicate the flavour of the policy, and stress the important need to condition attitudes and expectations towards a more dynamic competitive climate. In short, supply side strategies may be considered a resurrection of Say's Law, in that they affirm the adage 'let competition prevail and demand will take care of itself'. By the very nature of the policies involved, many of these recommendations are essentially qualitative and do not lend themselves readily to empirical verification. Consequently, their espousal frequently requires an act of faith on the part of their advocates who usually, and not surprisingly, are to be found in the monetarist camp.

The Conservative government was not slow in claiming success for its new growth policy. The period 1983–88 was hailed as unique in having attained an average growth rate of some 3.7 per cent – well in excess of the post-war average and, indeed, second only to Japan – see table 22.1b. However, this claim must be judged doubtful on at least two grounds. Firstly, the recession of 1980–82 had been especially severe – partly in consequence of the restrictive monetary policy – with the result that there was substantial excess capacity in existence. It was accordingly comparatively easy to generate an initially high rate of growth coming out of the recession. Secondly, and more importantly, estimates of the underlying growth rate are best obtained by comparing GNP data over the course of the business cycle from peak to peak. However, the period in

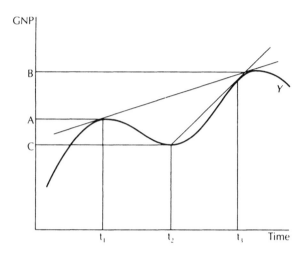

Figure 22.6 Measuring economic growth

question corresponded more closely to that of *trough* to peak. Such a procedure will inevitably overstate the sustainable rate of growth. This is a simple and obvious point but none the less important. It is brought out with the aid of figure 22.6. The peak-to-peak figures give an income gain of AB over the two time periods, t_1 to t_3. In contrast, the trough-to-peak estimate shows a larger gain, CB, over half the time, t_2 to t_3. Accordingly, the latter exercise would more than double the reported average growth rate.

If we move closer to a peak-to-peak approach and consider the decade 1980–89, then the average growth rate falls to 2.2 per cent, precisely equal to that of the previous decade, 1970–79. Indeed, the average growth under the Thatcher administration, at 2.2 per cent, fell below that of both the six-year Wilson government, 1965–70 (2.7 per cent) and the four years of the Heath government, 1971–74 (2.6 per cent) (see Johnson, 1991). At first glance, therefore, it would be difficult to conclude that the supply side strategy has been an unqualified success.

It is true that the era of the Thatcher administration witnessed an improvement upon the performance of the period 1973–79–a period of exceptionally slow growth worldwide under the impact of supply shocks and OPEC-induced stagflation. It is also true that over the same period there was a marked increase in productivity per worker, especially in manufacturing industry.[5] However, closer examination of the post-war record suggests that the period 1951–73 was far and away the most successful in terms of sustained higher growth. The period 1951–64 witnessed annual average growth rates in GDP and manufacturing at 2.7 per cent and 3.2 per cent respectively. For 1964–73 the

5 However, in part, the improvement in labour productivity is a consequence of the decline in manufacturing employment. The period 1979–88 witnessed a fall in manufacturing employment of approximately 25 per cent. We would expect that those becoming unemployed would be amongst the least productive and located in the least productive industries – thus creating an apparent increase in the average productivity of those remaining in employment.

corresponding figures are 3.0 per cent and 3.0 per cent (Matthews, Feinstein and Odling-Smee, 1982). These figures are significant in that they reflect an improvement upon Britain's own long-term historical record – an improvement which we are no longer matching – and yet they were not sufficient to prevent Britain's relative decline in the international growth stakes.

Explaining Britain's Relative Growth Performance

As indicated, Britain's comparatively poor growth performance in the post-war period implies a progressive decline in relative income standards. Is it possible to identify any one dominant factor or overriding constraint responsible for this state of affairs? If so, then policies may be designed to weaken or overcome the constraint.

Labour Constrained Growth of Manufacturing Output

One of the most fashionable explanations for Britain's inadequate growth performance has rested upon the proposition that the manufacturing sector – characterized by increasing returns – has been held back by the shortage of labour. The initial version of this thesis was linked to the name of Kaldor (1966), who argued that traditionally, the progressive contraction of the agricultural sector was the source of the labour supply into manufacturing. In the case of the UK, the first nation to industrialize, this source was now exhausted. Moreover, this exhaustion had occurred long before it had been eliminated in competing nations and before productivity per head had achieved high levels. Britain's poor growth performance was thus accounted for in terms of her being the first country to achieve economic maturity.

An alternative version of this thesis, associated with the names of Bacon and Eltis (1978), contends that it is the growth of public sector employment which has constrained the supply of labour into manufacturing activity – as well as raising overall tax burdens on the market economy. Neither thesis would appear applicable to the decade of the 1980s, however, when there existed a substantial pool of unemployed and when the female participation rate increased dramatically.

Capital Constrained Growth of Manufacturing Output

An alternative thesis points to the capital input. Two issues are involved: firstly, whether the overall investment/GNP ratio is too low and, secondly, whether capital is being misallocated into sectors with extravagant capital–output ratios. The first may be a consequence of punitive taxation and reduced profit prospects; the latter the consequence of tax-induced distortions of capital towards land and property and away from industrial plant and equipment.

The Over-valuation of Sterling

The desire to maintain a role for sterling as an international currency in world financial markets has led – so it is argued – to a persistent tendency to overvalue the currency. In turn, this generates a reluctance to transfer venture capital into the export sector which accordingly becomes even less competitive, exacerbating the initial overvaluation. Britain's decision to join the Exchange Rate Mechanism (ERM) of the

European Monetary System (EMS) in 1990 at the exchange rate of £1 = DM 2.95 was – in the eyes of many observers – but a further example of this mistaken strategy. Such an exchange rate was held to be palpably unrealistic given the combination of heavy unemployment *and* substantial payments deficit. Any recovery from recession could only intensify the pressures on the external account.

This thesis is linked with another popular explanation for Britain's poor growth performance, namely that it is handicapped by 'stop–go economics'. According to this view, any attempt to promote economic growth will sooner or later encounter the balance of payments constraint. Given a decidedly high marginal propensity to import, characteristic of the UK economy, the implication is that it will be sooner rather than later. In the attempt to protect the pound, interest rates are raised, contractionary policies are imposed and the growth process reversed. Clearly, the greater the overvaluation of sterling, the more will 'stops' predominate over 'goes'.

Slow Productivity Growth

One feature of British growth performance which has been singled out by many commentators is the relatively poor rate of growth of output per head, especially in manufacturing. Here there are many competing and appealing explanations but little in the way of hard evidence. Thus, for example, one school identifies the resistance to change in the conservative and generally non-professional nature of British management. Equally, others have pointed to the restrictive practices of British trade unions and the practice of decentralized bargaining which characterizes British industrial relations (see Kilpatrick and Lawson, 1980). Worldwide, there has been a productivity slowdown commencing in 1973 and associated with the OPEC oil price crisis and the consequent deflationary impacts (Bruno and Sachs, 1985). Indeed, it was the claim of the Thatcher administration that the decade of the 1980s and the commitment to enterprise, free markets and deregulation had reversed and overcome this trend allowing Britain to approach a new growth plateau. There is no doubt that productivity in manufacturing did improve markedly to record levels in the period 1979–88. However, this was accompanied by a relatively slow growth in manufacturing output as manufacturing industry shed labour. Whether the productivity gain is a once and for all improvement arising from the increased unemployment or whether it is the beginning of a period of continuous gains stemming from deep-seated changes in the economy is too soon to judge. The answer to this question, however, will in large measure determine the ultimate judgement on the Thatcher experiment.

What emerges from this brief excursion into growth experience and policy in the UK are many diagnoses, many prescriptions, but very little agreement, apart from the general consensus that growth is complex and no simple solution exists. In particular, it now seems reasonably clear that mere membership of the European Community has not been the palliative for Britain's growth rate that many supporting membership believed it to be.

Concluding Comments

The survey of the major policy problems confronting the British economy has been completed by examining the case of economic growth – or rather the comparative lack of it. It is clear that no broad consensus prevails as to the ultimate reasons for Britain's comparatively poor post-war growth performance. Rather, a host of factors and influences appear to interact and combine. This conclusion is, frankly, disturbing, for if there is no simple single cause of Britain's poor growth, then the obvious corollary is that there is no simple single cure. And whilst the current emphasis upon supply side economics may, if proved successful, generate a welcome once and for all increase in productivity, it may not, of itself, generate an increase in the *rate* of growth. Neither the advent of North Sea oil nor membership of the European Community appears to have disturbed the historically observed trend, although it has to be conceded that since 1982 productivity growth in the UK has been relatively high compared with during most of the post-war period.

Further Reading

One of the most influential empirical studies of comparative growth performance is Denison (1967). Denison (1968) concentrates specifically on UK growth performance over the period 1950–62. The finding from this (and other studies) has been, as noted in the chapter, that the UK's rate of growth has been relatively poor. The question of why it has been relatively poor has generated much controversy. Kaldor (1966) argues the case via slow employment growth in manufacturing, a view which is challenged by Beckerman (1965). The role of the balance of payments constraint is outlined in Thirlwall (1980), whilst Bacon and Eltis (1978) discuss the role played by the growth of the non-market sector. Shaw (1980) provides a concise appraisal of all of these competing explanations. More comprehensive reviews of alternative views are to be found in Peaker (1974) and Stafford (1981) (although the former is still quite terse). Giersch (1981) provides a compendium of papers directed at re-evaluating the determinants of growth.

  Mishan (1967, 1977) and Beckerman (1974) are the most readily accessible sources on the debate about the net benefits of economic growth. See also Meadows (1967) and Hirsch (1977) for further insights into the controversy. Matthews (1986) examines the possible role of institutional change as a positive (or negative) contribution to the growth process. On UK economic growth in an historical context see Matthews, Feinstein and Odling-Smee (1982), updated by Feinstein (1990). On growth theory, Hahn and Matthews (1964) remains a classic reference. More recent contributions include Scott (1989), Stern (1991) and Shaw (1992). See also the excellent symposia in *Economic Perspectives,* Wonter 1994.

Bibliography

Abel, A. B. (1985) 'A Stochastic Model of Investment, Marginal q and the Market Value of the Firm' *International Economic Review* **26**.

Ackley, G. (1961) *Macroeconomic Theory* New York, Macmillan.

Ackley, G. (1978) *Macroeconomics: Theory and Policy* New York, Macmillan.

Aiginger, K. (1980) Empirical Evidence on the Rational Expectations Hypothesis Using Reported Expectations. Paper presented to the World Conference of the Econometric Society, Aix en Provence.

Akerlof, G. A. (1979) 'The Case against Conservative Macroeconomics' *Econometrica* **46**.

Akerlof, G. A. (1984) 'Gift Exchange and Efficiency Wage Theory: Four Views' *American Economic Review* **74**, Papers and Proceedings.

Akerlof, G. A. and Yellen, J. L. (1985) 'A Near Rational Model of the Business Cycle, with Wage and Price Inertia' *Quarterly Journal of Economics* **C.**, Supplement.

Akerlof, G. A. and Yellen, J. L. (1985) 'Can Small Deviations from Rationality Make Significant Differences to Economic Equilibria?' *American Economic Review* **75**.

Akerlof, G. A. and Yellen, J. L. (eds) (1986) *Efficiency Wage Models of the Labour Market* Cambridge, Cambridge University Press.

Akerlof, G. A. and Yellen, J. L. (1987) 'Rational Models of Irrational Behaviour' *American Economic Review* **77**, Papers and Proceedings.

Alchian, A. (1955) 'The Rate of Interest, Fisher's Rate of Return over Cost and Keynes's Internal Rate of Return' *American Economic Review* **45**.

Alexander, S. S. (1952) 'Effects of a Devaluation on a Trade Balance' *IMF Staff Papers* **2**.

Alpine, R. L. W. (1985) A Pedagogical Note on Bond Financing of Government Expenditure. *Journal of Economic Studies* **12**.

Amadeo, E. J. (1989) *Keynes's Principle of Effective Demand* Aldershot, Edward Elgar.

Andersen, L. C. and Jordan, J. L. (1968) 'Monetary and Fiscal Actions: A Test of Their Relative Importance in Economic Stabilization' *Federal Reserve Bank of St. Louis Review* **50**.

Ando, A. and Modigliani, F. (1963) 'The Life Cycle Hypothesis of Saving' *American Economic Review* **53**.

Ando, A. and Modigliani, F. (1965) 'The Relative Stability of Monetary Velocity and the Investment Multiplier' *American Economic Review* September.

Arestis, P. (1992) *The Post-Keynesian Approach to Economics: An Alternative Analysis of Economic Theory and Policy* Aldershot, Edward Elgar.

Arrow, K. J. (1962) 'The Economic Implications of Learning by Doing' *Review of Economic Studies* **29**.

Arrow, K. (1978) 'The Future and the Present in Economic Life' *Economic Inquiry* **16**.

Artis, M. (1979) 'Recent Developments in the Theory of Fiscal Policy: A Survey' in Cook, S. T. and Jackson, P. M. (eds) *Current Issues in Fiscal Policy* Oxford, Martin Robertson.

Artis, M. J. and Lee, N. (eds) (1994) *The Economics of the European Union* Oxford, Oxford University Press.

Artis, M. and Lewis, M. K. (1981) *Monetary Control in the UK* Oxford, Philip Allan.

Artis, M. and Lewis, M. (1991) *Money in Britain: Monetary Policy, Innovation and Europe* Hemel Hempstead, Philip Allan.

Artus, J. (1975) 'The 1967 Devaluation of the Pound Sterling' *IMF Staff Papers* **22**.

Aschauer, D. A. (1985) 'Fiscal Policy and Aggregate Demand' *American Economic Review* **75**.

Attfield, C., Demery, D. and Duck, N. (1985) *Rational Expectations in Macroeconomics* Oxford, Basil Blackwell.

Azariadis, C. (1975) 'Implicit Contracts and Underemployment Equilibria' *Journal of Political Economy* **83**.

Bacon, R. and Eltis, W. (1978) *Britain's Economic Problem: Too Few Producers* (2nd edn) London, Macmillan.

Bailey, M. J. (1962) *National Income and the Price Level* New York, McGraw-Hill.

Bailey, M. J., Tavlas, G. S. and Ulan, M. (1986) 'Exchange Rate Variability and Trade Performance' *Weltwirtschaftliches Archiv* **122**.

Bain, A. D. (1976) *The Control of the Money Supply* (2nd edn) Harmonsworth, Penguin.

Ball, R. J., Burns, T. and Miller, G. (1972) 'Preliminary Simulations of the London Business School Model' mimeo.

Ball, R. J. and Drake, P. S. (1963) 'The Impact of Credit Control on Consumer Durable Spending in the UK, 1957–61' *Review of Economic Studies* **30**.

Ball, L., Mankiw, N. G. and Romer, D. (1988), 'The New Keynesian Economics and the Output–Inflation Trade-Off' *Brookings Papers on Economic Activity* **1**.

Barro, R. (1976) 'Rational Expectations and the Role of Monetary Policy' *Journal of Monetary Economics* **2**.

Barro, R. (1977) 'Long Term Contracting, Sticky Prices and Monetary Policy' *Journal of Monetary Economics* **3**.

Barro, R. J. (1979) 'Unanticipated Money Growth and Unemployment in the United States: Reply' *American Economic Review* **69**.

Barro, R. J. (1981) 'Output Effects of Government Purchases' *Journal of Political Economy* **89**.

Barro, R. J. (1986) 'Recent Developments in the Theory of Rules versus Discretion' *Economic Journal* **96**, Supplement.

Barro, R. J. (1989) 'The Ricardian Approach to Budget Deficits' *Journal of Economic Perspectives* **3**.

Barro, R. J. (ed.) (1989) *Modern Business Cycle Theory* Oxford, Basil Blackwell.

Barro, R. J. (1990) *Macroeconomic Policy* Cambridge, Mass., Harvard University Press.

Barro, R. J. and Gordon, D. (1983) 'A Positive Theory of Monetary Policy in a Natural Rate Model' *Journal of Political Economy* **91**.

Batchelor, R., Batchelor, A., Bendle, E. and Griffiths, B. (1980) 'Inflation, Unemployment and Reform', in Blackaby, F.T. (ed.) *The Future of Pay Bargaining* London, Heinemann.

Baumol, W. (1952) 'The Transactions Demand for Cash: An Inventory Theoretic Approach' *Quarterly Journal of Economics* **66**.

Bean, R. (1978) 'The Determinants of Consumers' Expenditure in the UK' *Government Economic Service Working Paper no.4*.

Becker, G. S. and Baumol, W. J. (1952) 'The Classical Monetary Theory: The Outcome of the Discussion' *Economica* **19**.

Beckerman, W. (1965) *The British Economy in 1975* Cambridge, National Institute of Economic and Social Research and Cambridge University Press.

Beckerman, W. (1974) *In Defence of Economic Growth* London, Jonathan Cape.

Beckerman, W. and Jenkinson, T. (1986) 'What Stopped the Inflation? Unemployment or Commodity Prices' *Economic Journal* **96**.

Begg, D. K. H. (1982) *The Rational Expectations Revolution in Macroeconomics* Oxford, Philip Allan.

Benoît-Guilbot, O. and Gallie, D. (eds) (1994) *Long-Term Unemployment* London, Pinter.

Bernheim, D. (1987) 'Ricardian Equivalence: An Evaluation of Theory and Evidence' *Macroeconomics Annual*, National Bureau of Economic Research, Washington, pp. 263–303.

Bickerdike, C. F. (1914) 'A Non-Monetary Cause of Fluctuations in Employment' *Economic Journal* **24**.

Black, J. (1985) *The Economics of Modern Britain: An Introduction to Macroeconomics* Oxford, Martin Robertson.

Black, S. (1973) *International Money Markets and Flexible Exchange Rates* Princeton Studies in International Finance no. 32, Princeton, Princeton University Press.

Blackburn, K. (1992) 'Credibility and Time – Consistency in Monetary Policy' in Dowd, K. and Lewis, M. K. (eds) *Current Issues in Financial and Monetary Economics* Basingstoke, Macmillan.

Blackhurst, R. and Tumlir, J. (1980) *Flexible Exchange Rates and International Trade* GATT Studies in International Trade no. 7, GATT, Geneva.

Blanchard, O. and Fischer, S. (1989) *Lectures on Macroeconomics* Cambridge, Mass., M.I.T. Press.

Blaug, M. (1981) *The Methodology of Economics* Cambridge, Cambridge University Press.

Bleaney, M. (1985) *The Rise and Fall of Keynesian Economics* London, Macmillan.

Blinder, A. S. (1981) 'Temporary Taxes and Consumer Spending' *Journal of Political Economy* **89**.

Blinder, A. S. (1983) 'Can Income Tax Increases Be Inflationary?' *National Tax Journal* **26**.

Blinder, A. S. (1989) *Macroeconomics under Debate* Hemel Hempstead, Harvester Wheatsheaf.

Blinder, A. S. (1991) 'Why Are Prices Sticky? Preliminary Results from an Interview Study' *American Economic Review* **81**, Papers and Proceedings.

Blinder, A. S. and Solow, R. M. (1973) 'Does Fiscal Policy Matter?' *Journal of Public Economics* **3**.

Brainard, W. (1967) 'Uncertainty and Effectiveness of Policy' *American Economic Review* **57**.

Branson, W. H. (1981) 'Comment' *European Economic Review* **16**.

Branson, W. H. and Klevorick, A. K. (1969) 'Monetary Illusion and the Aggregate Consumption Function' *American Economic Review* **59**.

Breit, W. and Hochman H. M. (eds) (1968) *Readings in Microeconomics* New York, Holt Rinehart and Winston.

Bronfenbrenner, M. and Holzman, F. (1963) 'A Survey of Inflation Theory' *American Economic Review* **53**.

Brothwell, J. F. (1975) 'A Simple Keynesian's Response to Leijonhufvud' *Bulletin of Economic Research* **27**.

Brown, A. J. and Burrows, E. M. (1978) *Regional Economic Problems* London, George Allen and Unwin.

Brown, E. C. (1950) 'Analysis of Consumption Taxes in Terms of the Theory of Income Determination' *American Economic Review* **40**.

Brunner, K. (1981) 'The Case against Monetary Activism' *Lloyds Bank Review* no. 139.

Brunner, K. and Meltzer, A. (1973) 'Mr Hicks and the Monetarists' *Economica* **40**.

Bruno, M. and Sachs, J. D. (1985) *The Economics of Worldwide Stagflation* Cambridge, Mass., Harvard University Press.

Buiter, W. E. (1977) 'Crowding out and the Effectiveness of Fiscal Policy' *Journal of Public Economics* **8**.

Buiter, W. and Miller, M. (1983) 'Changing the Rules: Economic Consequences of the Thatcher Regime' *Brookings Papers on Economic Activity* **8**.

Burrows, P. (1974) 'The Upward Sloping IS curve and the Control of Income and the Balance of Payments' *Journal of Finance* March.

Burrows, P. (1979) 'The Government Budget Constraint and the Monetarist–Keynesian Debate' in Cook, S. T. and Jackson, P. M. (eds) *Current Issues on Fiscal Policy* Oxford, Martin Robertson.

Burton, J. (1986) *Keynes's General Theory: Fifty Years On: Its Relevance and Irrelevance to Modern Times* Hobart Paper 24, London, Institute of Economic Affairs.

Cagan, P. (1956) 'The Monetary Dynamics of Hyperinflation' in Friedman, M. (ed.) *Studies in the Quantity Theory of Money* Chicago, University of Chicago Press.

Cagan, P. (1987) 'Monetarism' in Eatwell, J. Milgate, M. and Newman, P. (eds) *The New Palgrave Dictionary of Economics* London, Macmillan.

Caldwell, B. J. (1991) 'The Methodology of Scientific Research Programmes in Economics: Criticisms and Conjectures' in Shaw, G. K. (ed.) *Economics, Culture and Education: Essays in Honour of Mark Blaug* Hants., Edward Elgar.

Cambridge Economic Policy Group (1981) *Economic Policy Review* Cambridge, Cambridge University Press.

Carlin, W. and Soskice, D. (1990) *Macroeconomics and the Wage Bargain: A Modern Approach to Employment, Inflation and the Exchange Rate* Oxford, Oxford University Press.

Caves, R. E. (1968) *Britain's Economic Prospects* London, Allen and Unwin.

Chick, V. (1977) *The Theory of Monetary Policy* (2nd edn) Oxford, Parkgate Publishers.

Chick, V. (1983) *Macroeconomics after Keynes* Oxford, Philip Allan.

Chick, V. (1995) 'Is there a Case for Post-Keynesian Economics?' *Scottish Journal of Political Economy* **42**.

Chrystal, A. K. (1984) 'Dutch Disease or Monetarist Medicine? The British Economy under Mrs. Thatcher' *Federal Reserve Bank of St. Louis Review* **66**.

Chrystal, A. K. and Dowd, D. (1988) 'Exchange Rate Overshooting and Macroeconomic Policy' in Greenaway, D. (ed.) *Current Issues in Macroeconomics* London, Macmillan.

Clark, J. M. (1917) 'Business Accumulation and the Level of Demand: A Technical Factor on Economic Cycles' *Journal of Political Economy* **25**.

Clark, P. K. (1979) 'Investment in the 1970s: Theory, Performance and Prediction' *Brookings Papers on Economic Activity* **1**.

Clower, W. (1965) 'The Keynesian Counter-Revolution: A Theoretical Appraisal' in Hahn, F. H. and Brechling, F. (eds) *The Theory of Interest Rates*, reprinted in Shaw, G. K. (ed.) (1991) *Economics, Culture and Education: Essays in Honour of Mark Blaug* Hants., Edward Elgar.

Clower, R. (1975) 'Reflections on the Keynesian Perplex' *Zeitschrift fur Nationalökonomie* **35**.

Clower, R. and Johnson, M. B. (1968) 'Income, Wealth and the Theory of Consumption' in Wolfe, N. (ed.) *Value, Capital and Growth* Edinburgh, Edinburgh University Press.

Clower, R. and Leijonhufvud, A. (1975) 'The Coordination of Economic Activities: A Keynesian Perspective' *American Economic Review* **65**.

Cochrane, J. L. (1970) *Macroeconomics before Keynes* Glenview, Ill., Scott, Foresman.

Coddington, A. (1976) 'Keynesian Economics: The Search for First Principles' *Journal of Economic Literature* **14**.

Coddington, A. (1983) *Keynesian Economics: The Search for First Principles* London, George Allen and Unwin.

Coghlan, R. T. (1973) 'Special Deposits and Bank Advances' *Bankers Magazine* 216.

Coghlan, R. (1980) *The Theory of Money and Finance* London, Macmillan.

Cohen, B. J. (1971) *Balance of Payments Policy* Harmondsworth, Penguin.

Cook, S. T. and Jackson, P. M. (eds) (1979) *Current Issues in Fiscal Policy* Oxford, Martin Robertson.

Cooper, R. N. (1968) 'The Balance of Payments' in Caves, R. (ed.) *Britain's Economic Prospects*, London, George Allen and Unwin.

Coppock, D. J. (1978) 'Some Thoughts on the Monetary Approach to Balance of Payments Theory' *Manchester School* **46**.

Corden, W. M. (1977) *Inflation, Exchange Rates and the World Economy* Oxford, Oxford University Press.

Corden, W. M. and Neary, J. P. (1982) 'Booming Sector and De- Industrialization in a Small Open Economy' *Economic Journal* **92**.

Corry, B. A. (1962) *Money, Saving and Investment in English Economics, 1800–1850* London, Macmillan.

Creedy, J. (ed.) (1981) *The Economics of Unemployment in Britain* London, Butterworths.

Cripps, F. and Godley, W. (1978) 'Control of Imports as a Means to Full Employment and the Expansion of World Trade: The UK's Case' *Cambridge Journal of Economics* **2**.

Cross, R. (1982a) *Economic Theory and Policy in the UK* Oxford, Martin Robertson.

Cross, R. (1982b) 'The Duhem–Quine Thesis, Lakatos and the Appraisal of Theories in Macroeconomics' *Economic Journal* **92**.

Cross, R. (1991) 'Macroeconomics into the 1990's' *Scottish Journal of Political Economy* **38**.

Crossman, R. (1976) *The Crossman Diaries* London, Jonathan Cape.

Crouch, R. L. (1970) 'Special Deposits and the British Monetary Mechanism' *Economic Studies* 5.

Currie, D. A. (1978) 'Macroeconomic Policy and Government Financing: A Survey of Recent Developments' in Artis, M. J. and Nobay, A. R. (eds) *Studies in Contemporary Economic Analysis: vol. I* London, Croom Helm.

Currie, D. A. (1981) 'Monetary and Fiscal Policy and the Crowding-out Issue' in Artis, M. J. and Millar, M. M. (eds) *Essays on Fiscal and Monetary Policy* Oxford, Oxford University Press.

Currie, D. (1984) 'Monetary Overshooting and the Exchange Rate' *Manchester School* 52.

Currie, D. (1985) 'Macroeconomic Policy Design and Control Theory: A Failed Partnership?' *Economic Journal* 95.

Curwen, P. (ed) (1994) *Understanding the UK Economy* (3rd edn) London, Macmillan.

Cuthbertson, K. C. (1985) *The Demand and Supply of Money* Oxford, Basil Blackwell.

Darby, M. R. (1974) 'The Permanent Income Theory of Consumption: A Restatement' *Quarterly Journal of Economics* 88.

Davidson, J., Hendry, D. F., Srba, F. and Yeo, S. (1978) 'Econometric Modelling of the Aggregate Time Series Relationship between Consumers' Expenditure and Income in the UK' *Economic Journal* 88.

Davidson, P. (1994) *Post-Keynesian Macroeconomic Theory: A Foundation for Successful Economic Policies for the Twenty-first Century* Aldershot, Edward Elgar.

Dawkins, P. J. (1980) 'Incomes Policy' in Maunder, W. P. (ed.) *The British Economy in the 1970s* London, Heinemann.

Deaton, A. (1978) 'Involuntary Saving through Unanticipated Inflation' *American Economic Review* 68.

De Grauwe, P. (1992) *The Economics of Monetary Integration* Oxford, Oxford University Press.

Denison, E. F. (1967) *Why Growth Rates Differ: Postwar Experience in Nine Western Countries* Washington, D.C., Brookings Institution.

Denison, E. F. (1968) 'Economic Growth' in Caves, R. (ed.) *Britain's Economic Prospects* London, George Allen and Unwin.

Dennis, G. E. J. (1980) 'Money Supply and Its Control' in Maunder, W. P. (ed.) *The British Economy in the 1970s* London, Heinemann.

Dennis, G. E. J. (1981) *Monetary Economics* London, Longman.

Deprano, M. and Mayer, T. (1965) 'Tests of the Relative Importance of Autonomous Expenditure and Money' *American Economic Review* September.

Desai, M. (1987) 'Endogenous and Exogenous Money' in Eatwell, J., Milgate, M. and Newman, P. (eds) *The Palgrave Dictionary of Economics* London, Macmillan. Reprinted in Eatwell, J., Milgate, M. and Newman, P. (eds) (1989) *Money* London, Macmillan.

Dillard, D. (1948) *The Economics of John Maynard Keynes: The Theory of a Monetary Economy* Englewood Cliffs, NJ, Prentice-Hall.

Dornbusch, R. (1976) 'Expectations and Exchange Rate Dynamics' *Journal of Political Economy* 84.

Dornbusch, R. (1980) *Open Economy Macroeconomics* New York, Basic Books.

Dornbusch, R. and Fischer, S. (1980) 'Sterling and the External Balance' in Caves, R. E. and Krause, L. B. (eds) *Britain's Economic Performance* Washington, D.C. Brookings Institution.

Dornbusch, R. and Fischer, S. (1994) *Macroeconomics* (6th edn) New York, McGraw-Hill.

Dow, J. C. R. and Saville, I. D. (1990) *A Critique of Monetary Policy*, Oxford, Clarendon Press.

Duesenberry, J. (1952) *Income, Saving and the Theory of Consumer Behavior* Harvard, Harvard University Press.

Eatwell, J., Milgate, M. and Newman, P. (eds) (1987) *The New Palgrave Dictionary of Economics* London, Macmillan.

Eatwell, J., Milgate, M. and Newman, P. (eds) (1989) *Money* London, Macmillan.

Eckaus, R. S. (1953) 'The Acceleration Principle Reconsidered' *Quarterly Journal of Economics* 67.

Eichenbaum, M. S., Hansen, L. P. and Singleton, K. J. (1984) 'A Time Series Analysis of Representative Agents' Models of Consumption and Leisure Choice under Uncertainty' mimeo, Carnegie Mellon University.

El-Agraa, A. M. (ed.) (1994) *Economics of the European Community* (4th ed.) Hemel Hempstead, Harvester Wheatsheaf.

Emerson, M. (1979) 'The United Kingdom and the European Monetary System' in Major, R. (ed.) *Britain's Trade and Exchange Rate Policy* London, Heinemann.

Emerson, M., Gros, D., Italianer, A., Pisany-Ferry, J. and Reihchenbach, H. (1992) *One Money, One Market* Oxford, Oxford University Press.

European Economic Perspectives No. 1 (1993) *Anchors Away*, London, CEPR.

Fallick, J. and Elliott, R. F. (eds) (1981) *Incomes Policy, Inflation and Relative Pay* London, Allen and Unwin.

Farrell, M. (1959) 'The New Theories of the Consumption Function' *Economic Journal* 69.

Fausten, D. K. (1978) *The Consistency of British Balance of Payments Policies* London, Macmillan.

Fausten, D. (1981) 'A Partial Rehabilitation of the Policy Mix Approach' *Kyklos* 34.

Feinstein, C. (1990). 'British Economic Growth: International and Historical Perspectives' *The Economic Review* May.

Feldstein, M. (1982) 'Government Deficits and Aggregate Demand' *Journal of Monetary Economics* 9.

Feldstein, M. (1986) 'Supply Side Economics: Old Truths and New Claims' *American Economic Review* Papers and Proceedings, 76.

Fender, J. (1981) *Understanding Keynes: An Analysis of 'The General Theory'* Brighton, Wheatsheaf Books.

Ferber, R. (1973) 'Consumer Economics: A Survey' *Journal of Economic Literature* 11.

Fischer, S. (ed.) (1980) *Rational Expectations and Economic Policy* Chicago, University of Chicago Press.

Fischer, S. (1987) 'New Classical Macroeconomics' in J. Eatwell, J., Milgate, M. and Newman, P. (eds) *The New Palgrave Dictionary of Economics* London, Macmillan.

Fischer, S. (1988) 'Recent Developments in Macroeconomics' *Economic Journal* 98.

Fischer, I. (1963) *The Purchasing Power of Money* New York, Augustus M. Kelly.

Fleming, J. M. (1962) 'Domestic Financial Policies under Fixed and Floating Exchange Rates' *IMF Staff Papers* 9.

Fleming, J. S. (1973) 'The Consumption Function when Capital Markets Are Imperfect: The Permanent Income Hypothesis Reconsidered' *Oxford Economic Papers* 25.

Fleming, J. S. (1976) *Inflation* Oxford, Oxford University Press.

Forster, B. A. and Shaw, G. K. (1976) 'The Tax Mix and Aggregate Demand: A Respecification' *Public Finance* 31.

Forsyth, P. and Kay, J. (1980) *The Economic Implications of North Sea Oil* London, Institute of Fiscal Studies.

Forsyth, P. J. and Kay, J. A. (1981) 'Oil Revenues and Manufacturing Output' *Fiscal Studies* 2.

Frenkel, J. A. (1981) 'The Collapse of Purchasing Power Parties during the 1970s' *European Economic Review* 16.

Frenkel, J. A. (1986) 'International Interdependence and the Constraints on Macroeconomic Policies' *Weltwirtschaftliches Archiv* 122.

Frenkel, J. and Johnson, H. G. (eds) (1976) *The Monetary Approach to the Balance of Payments* London, Allen and Unwin.

Frenkel, J. and Rodriguez, C. (1982) 'Exchange Rate Dynamics and the Overshooting Hypothesis' *IMF Staff Papers* 29.

Friedman, B. M. (1988) 'Lessons on Monetary Policy from the 1980's' *Journal of Economic Perspectives* 2.

Friedman, M. (1953a) 'The Methodology of Positive Economics' in *Essays in Positive Economics* Chicago, University of Chicago Press.

Friedman, M. (1953b) 'The Case for Flexible Exchange Rates' in *Essays in Positive Economics* Chicago, University of Chicago Press.

Friedman, M. (1956a) 'The Quantity Theory of Money: A Restatement' in Friedman, M. (ed.) *Studies in the Quantity Theory of Money* Chicago, University of Chicago Press.

Friedman, M. (ed.) (1956b) *Studies in the Quantity Theory of Money* Chicago, University of Chicago Press.

Friedman, M. (1957) *A Theory of the Consumption Function* Princeton, N.J., National Bureau of Economic Research.

Friedman, M. (1958) 'The Supply of Money and Changes in Prices and Output' in *The Relationship of Prices to Economic Stability and Growth*, 85th Congress, 2nd session, Joint Economic Committee Print, US Government Printing Office, Washington, D.C. Reprinted in Friedman, M. (1969) *The Optimum Quantity of Money and Other Essays* London, Macmillan.

Friedman, M. (1968a) 'The Role of Monetary Policy' *American Economic Review* **58.**

Friedman, M. (1968b) 'Money: Quantity Theory' *The International Encyclopaedia of the Social Sciences* **10.**

Friedman, M. (1969) *The Optimum Quantity of Money* London, Macmillan.

Friedman, M. (1977) 'Inflation and Unemployment' *Journal of Political Economy* **85.**

Friedman, M. (1980) 'Prices, of Money and Goods across Frontiers: the £ and $ over a Century' *The World Economy* **2.**

Friedman, M. and Heller, W. W. (1969) *Monetary versus Fiscal Policy: A Dialogue* New York, Norton and Co.

Friedman, M. and Meiselman, D. (1963) 'The Relative Stability of Monetary Velocity and the Investment Multiplier in the United States, 1897–1958' in *Commission on Money and Credit: Stabilization Policies* Englewood Cliffs, N.J., Prentice-Hall.

Friedman, M. and Schwartz, A. (1963) *A Monetary History of the United States, 1867–1960* Princeton, Princeton University Press.

Friedman, M. and Schwartz, A. (1982) *Monetary Trends in the US and the UK* Chicago, University of Chicago Press.

Gibson, N. J. (1971) 'Competition and Innovation' *Bankers Magazine* **212.**

Giersch, H. (ed.) (1981) *Macroeconomic Policies for Growth and Stability* Tubingen, J. C. B. Mohr.

Goldfield, S. (1973) 'The Demand for Money Revisited' *Brookings Papers on Economic Activity* Washington, D.C.

Goldfield, S. M. (1987) 'Demand for Money: Empirical Studies' in Eatwell, J., Murray, M. and Newman, P. (eds) *The New Palgrave Dictionary of Economics* London, Macmillan. Reprinted in Eatwell, J., Murray, M. and Newman, P. (eds) (1989) *Money* London, Macmillan.

Goodhart, C. (1973) 'Analysis of the Determinants of the Stock of Money' in Parkin, J. M. and Nobay, A. R. (eds) *Essays in Modern Economics* London, Longman.

Goodhart, C. (1975) *Money, Information and Uncertainty* London, Macmillan.

Goodhart, C. (1989) 'The Conduct of Monetary Policy' *Economic Journal* **99.**

Goodhart, C. and Crockett, A. D. (1970) 'The Importance of Money' *Bank of England Quarterly Bulletin* **10.**

Gordon, R. J. (1976) 'Recent Developments in the Theory of Inflation and Unemployment' *Journal of Monetary Economics* **2.**

Gordon, R. J. (1981) 'Output Price Fluctuations and Gradual Price Adjustment' *Journal of Economic Literature* **19.**

Gordon, R. J. (1982a) 'Price Inertia and Policy, Ineffectiveness in the United States, 1890–1980' *Journal of Political Economy* **90.**

Gordon, R. J. (1982b) 'Why US Wage and Employment Behaviour Differs from that in Britain and Japan' *Economic Journal* **92.**

Gordon, R. J. (1990) *Macroeconomics* (5th edn) Glenview, Ill., Scott, Foresman/Little, Brown Higher Education.

Gowland, D. (1982) *Controlling the Money Supply* London, Croom Helm.

Gowland, D. (1990) *Understanding Macroeconomics* Aldershot, Edward Elgar.

Greenaway, D. (1982) 'Identifying the Gains from Pure Intra Industry Trade' *Journal of Economic Studies* 9.

Greenaway, D. (1983a) *International Trade Policy: From Tariffs to the New Protectionism* London, Macmillan.

Greenaway, D. (1983b) 'Patterns of Intra-Industry Trade in the UK' in Tharakan, P. K. M. (ed.) *Intra Industry Trade* Amsterdam, North Holland.

Greenaway, D. (ed.) (1988) *Current Issues in Macroeconomics* London, Macmillan.

Greenaway, D. and Hindley, B.V. (1985) *What Britain Pays for Voluntary Export Restraints* Thames Essay 43, London, Trade Policy Research Centre.

Greenaway, D. and Milner, C. R. (1979) *Protectionism Again... ?* Hobart Paper 84, London, Institute of Economic Affairs.

Greenaway, D. and Milner, C. R. (1983) 'On the Measurement of Intra Industry Trade' *Economic Journal* 93.

Greenaway, D. and Milner, C. R. (1986) *The Economics of Intra Industry Trade* Oxford, Basil Blackwell.

Greenaway, D. and Shaw, G. K. (eds) (1985) *Public Choice, Public Finance and Public Policy: Essays in Honour of Alan Peacock* Oxford, Basil Blackwell.

Griffiths, A. and Wall, S. (eds) (1995) *Applied Economics* Harlow, Longman.

Grossman, H. I. (1972) 'Was Keynes a "Keynesian"?' *Journal of Economic Literature* **10**.

Grubel, H. G. and Lloyd, P. J. (1975) *Intra-Industry Trade* London, Macmillan.

Hacche, G. (1974) 'The Demand for Money in the UK: Experience since 1971' *Bank of England Quarterly Bulletin* **14**.

Hadjimatheou, G. and Skouras, A. (1979) 'Britain's Economic Problem: The Growth of the Non Market Sector' *Economic Journal* **89**.

Hafer, R. W. (ed.) (1986) *The Monetary and Fiscal Policy Debate: Lessons from Two Decades* Totowa, N.J., Allanheld.

Hagen, E. (1966) 'The Classical Theory of the Level of Output and Employment' in Mueller, M. G. (ed.) *Readings in Macroeconomics* New York, Holt, Rinehart, Winston.

Hahn, F. (1980) 'Monetarism and Economic Theory' *Economica* **47**.

Hahn, F. H. and Matthews, R. C. O. (1964) 'The Theory of Economic Growth: A Survey' *Economic Journal* December. Reprinted in A. E. A. and R. E. S. (1965) *Surveys of Economic Theory* Vol. 2, London, Macmillan.

Haley, J. (1990) 'Theoretical Foundations for Sticky Wages' *Journal of Economic Surveys* **4**.

Hall, R. E. (1978) 'Stochastic Implications of the Life Cycle–Permanent Income Hypothesis: Theory and Evidence' *Journal of Political Economy* **86**.

Hall, R. E. (1980) 'Employment Fluctuations and Wage Rigidity' *Brookings Papers on Economic Activity* no. 1, Washington, D.C.

Hall, R. E. (1978) 'Stochastic Implications of the Life-Cycle–Permanent Income Hypothesis: Theory and Evidence' *Journal of Political Economy* **86**.

Hall, R. E. and Jorgenson, D. W. (1967) 'Tax Policy and Investment Behaviour' *American Economic Review* **57**.

Hall, R. E. and Taylor, J. B. (1993) *Macroeconomics* (4th edn) New York, W. W. Norton and Company.

Hands, D. W. (1991) 'Popper, the Rationality Principle and Economic Explanation' in Shaw, G. K. (ed.) *Economics, Culture and Education: Essays in Honour of Mark Blaug* Aldershot, Edward Elgar.

Hansen, B. (1969) *Fiscal Policy in Seven Countries, 1955–65* Paris, OECD.

Hansen, B. (1973) 'On the Effects of Fiscal and Monetary Policy: A Taxonomic Discussion' *American Economic Review* **63**.

Harcourt, G. C. (ed.) (1977) *The Microeconomic Foundations of Macroeconomics* London, Macmillan.

Hargreaves Heap, S. (1992) *The New Keynesian Macroeconomics: Time Belief and Social Interdependence.* Aldershot, Edward Elgar.

Hayashi, F. (1982) 'Tobin's Average and Marginal q: A Neoclassical Interpretation' *Econometrica* **50.**

Heathfield, D. (ed.) (1979) *Perspectives on Inflation* London, Longman.

Helliwell, J. F. (ed.) (1976) *Aggregate Investment* London, Penguin.

Hendry, D. F., (1980) 'Econometrics: Alchemy or Science?' *Economica* **47.**

Henry, S. G. B. and Karakitsos, E. (1987) 'Inflation, Unemployment and Indirect Taxation' *Bulletin of Economic Research* **39.**

von Heusinger, R. (1995) 'What Is Left of New Classical Macroeconomics' Wincott Discussion Papers, School of Business, University of Buckingham.

Hicks, J. R. (1937) 'Mr Keynes and the Classics: A Suggested Interpretation' *Econometrica* **5.**

Hicks, J. R. (1967) *Critical Essays in Monetary Theory* London, Oxford University Press.

Hicks, J. R. (1973) 'Recollections and Documents' *Economica* **40.**

Hicks, J. R. (1974) *The Crisis in Keynesian Economics* Oxford, Basil Blackwell.

Hicks, J. R. (1980) 'ISLM: An Explanation' *Journal of Post-Keynesian Economics* November.

Hicks, J. R. (1981) 'Are There Economic Cycles?' The Robbins Lecture, University of Sterling.

Hillier, B. (1977) 'Does Fiscal Policy Matter? The View from the Government Budget Restraint' *Public Finance* **32.**

Hillier, B. (1991) *The Macroeconomic Debate: Models of the Closed and Open Economy* Oxford, Basil Blackwell.

Hines, A. G. (1971) *On the Reappraisal of Keynesian Economics* London, Martin Robertson.

Hirsch, F. (1977) *Social Limits to Growth* London, Routledge and Kegan Paul.

HMSO (1991a) *National Income and Expenditure* London, CSO.

HMSO (1991b) *The National Accounts: A Short Guide* London, CSO.

Holden, K. (1989) 'Macroeconomic Forecasting' in Greenaway, D. (ed.) *Current Issues in Macroeconomics* London, Macmillan.

Holmes, J. M. and Smyth, D. J. (1972) 'The Specification of the Demand for Money and the Tax Multiplier' *Journal of Political Economy* **80.**

Hudson, W. D. (ed.) (1979) *The IS/OUGHT Question* London, Macmillan.

Hughes-Hallett, A. J. (1988) 'Macroeconomic Interdependence and Policy Coordination' in Greenaway, D. (ed.) *Current Issues in Macroeconomics* London, Macmillan.

Hutchinson, T. W. (1978) *On Revolution and Progress in Economic Knowledge* Cambridge, Cambridge University Press.

Hutton, W. (1986) *The Revolution that Never Was* Longman, London.

Hutton, W. (1995) *The State We're In* London, Cape.

IMF (1977) *The Monetary Approach to the Balance of Payments* Washington, D.C., International Monetary Fund.

Jackman, R. (1974) 'Keynes and Leijonhufvud' *Oxford Economic Papers* **26.**

Jackman, R. and Sutton, J. (1982) 'Imperfect Capital Markets and the Monetarist Black Box: Liquidity Constraints, Inflation and the Asymmetric Effects of Interest Rate Policy' *Economic Journal* **92.**

Johnson, B. M. (1971) *Household Behaviour* Harmondsworth, Penguin.

Johnson, C. (1991) *The Economy under Mrs Thatcher, 1979–1990* Harmondsworth, Penguin.

Johnson, H. G. (1958) 'Towards a General Theory of the Balance of Payments' in Caves, R. and Johnson, H. G. (eds) *Readings in International Economics* London, Allen and Unwin.

Johnson, H. G. (1966) 'The Neo-Classical One-sector Growth Model: A Geometric Exposition and Extension to a Monetary Economy *Economica* **33.**

Johnson, H. G. (1970) 'Keynes and the Keynesians' *Encounter* January.

Johnson, H. G. (1976) 'Money and the Balance of Payments' *Banca Nazionale del Lavoro Quarterly Review* March.

Johnson, H. G. (1977) 'The Monetary Approach to Balance of Payments Theory and Policy: Explanations and Policy Implications' *Economica* **44**

Jones, A. (1973) *The New Inflation: The Politics of Prices and Incomes* Harmondsworth, Penguin.

Jorgenson, D. (1963) 'Capital Theory and Investment Behaviour' *American Economic Review* **53.**

Jorgenson, D. W. (1967) 'The Theory of Investment Behaviour' in Ferber, R. (ed.) *Determinants of Investment Behaviour* New York, National Bureau of Economic Research.

Jorgenson, D. W. (1971) 'Econometric Studies of Investment Behaviour' *Journal of Economic Literature* 9.

Jorgenson, D. W. and Siebert, C. D. (1968) 'A Comparison of Alternative Theories of Corporate Investment' *American Economic Review* 58.

Junankar, P. N. (1972) *Investment Theories and Evidence* London, Macmillan.

Kahn, R. F. (1976) 'Unemployment as Seen by Keynesians' in Worswick, G. D. N. (ed.) *The Concept and Measurement of Involuntary Unemployment* London, George Allen and Unwin.

Kaldor, N. (1966) *Causes of the Slow Rate of Growth of the United Kingdom: An Inaugural Lecture* Cambridge, Cambridge University Press.

Kaldor, N. (1975) 'Economic Growth and the Verdoorn Law' *Economic Journal* 85.

Kaldor, N. (1977) 'Capitalism and Industrial Development: Lessons from British Experience' *Cambridge Journal of Economics* 1.

Kaldor, N. and Trevithick, J. (1981) 'A Keynesian Perspective on Money' *Lloyds Bank Review* no. 139.

Kantor, B. (1979) 'Rational Expectations and Economic Thought: A Survey' *Journal of Economic Literature* 17.

Kay, J., Mayer, C. and Thompson, D. (1986) *Privatisation and Regulation: The UK Experience* Oxford, Clarendon Press.

Kareken, J. and Solow, R. M. (1963) 'Monetary Policy: Lags versus Simultaneity' in *Commission on Money and Credit: Stabilization Policies* Englewood Cliffs, N.J. Prentice-Hall.

Kern, D. (1978) 'An International Comparison of Major Economic Trends' *National Westminster Quarterly Review* May.

Keynes, J. M. (1923) *Tract on Monetary Reform* London, Macmillan.

Keynes, J. M. (1983) *A Treatise on Money* London, Macmillan.

Keynes, J. M. (1936) *The General Theory of Employment Interest and Money* London, Macmillan.

Keynes, J. M. (1937a) 'The General Theory of Employment' *Quarterly Journal of Economics* 51.

Keynes, J. M. (1937b) 'Professor Pigou on Money Wages in Relation to Unemployment' *Economic Journal* 47.

Kilpatrick, A. and Lawson, T. (1980) 'On the Nature of Industrial Decline in the UK' *Cambridge Journal of Economics* 4.

King, M. (1995) 'Creditability and Monetary Policy: Theory and Evidence' *Scottish Journal of Political Economy* 42.

King, R. G. and Plosser, C. I. (1984) 'Money, Credit and Prices in a Real Business Cycle' *American Economic Review* 74.

Knox, A. D. (1952) 'The Acceleration Principle and the Theory of Investment: A Survey' *Economica* 19.

Kohn, M. (1986) 'Monetary Analysis, the Equilibrium Method and Keynes's "General Theory"' *Journal of Political Economy* 94.

Korilas, P. J. and Thorn, R. S. (1979) *Modern Macroeconomics* New York, Harper and Row.

Kreinin, M. (1961) 'Windfall Income and Consumption: Additional Evidence' *American Economic Review* 51.

Krueger, A. O. (1983) *Exchange Rate Determination* Cambridge, Cambridge University Press.

Kuznets, S. (1946) *National Product since 1869* New York, National Bureau of Economic Research.

Kydland, F. E. and Prescott, E. C. (1977) 'Rules Rather Than Discretion: The Inconsistency of Optimal Plans' *Journal of Political Economy* 85.

Kydland, F. E. and Prescott, E. C. (1982) 'Time to Build and Aggregate Fluctuations' *Econometrica* 50.

Laidler, D. W. (1971a) 'The Influence of Money on Economic Activity; A Survey of some Current Problems' in Clayton, G., Gilbert, J. C. and Sedgwick, R. (eds) *Monetary Theory and Policy in the 1970s* Oxford, Oxford University Press.

Laidler, D. W. (1971b) 'The Phillips Curve, Expectations and Incomes Policy' in Johnson, H. G. and Nobay, A. P. (eds) *The Current Inflation* London, Macmillan.

Laidler, D. W. (1975) *Essays on Money and Inflation* Manchester, Manchester University Press.

Laidler, D. W. (1977) *The Demand for Money* New York, Crowell.

Laidler, D. W. (1982) *Monetarist Perspectives* Oxford, Philip Allan.

Laidler, D. (1986) 'The New Classical Contribution to Macroeconomics' *Banca Nazionale Del Lavoro Quarterly Review* March.

Laidler, D. (1990) *Taking Money Seriously and Other Essays* Hert, Philip Allan.

Laidler, D. (1991) *The Golden Age of the Quantity Theory: The Development of Neoclassical Monetary Economics, 1870–1914*. London, Harvester Wheatsheaf.

Laidler, D. (1993) *The Demand for Money: Theories, Evidence, and Problems* (4th edn) New York, Harper Collins.

Laidler, D. W. and Parkin, M. (1975) 'Inflation: A Survey' *Economic Journal* **85**.

Lane, T. D. (1985) 'The Rationale for Money-Supply Targets: A Survey' *Manchester School* **53**.

Lavoie, M. (1992) *Foundations of Post-Keynesian Economic Analysis* Aldershot, Edward Elgar.

Lawson, N. (1984) Mais Lecture, London.

Lawson, N. (1988) *The State of the Market* London, Institute of Economic Affairs.

Layard, R. (1986) *How to Beat Unemployment* Oxford, Basil Blackwell.

Layard, R., Nickell, S. and Jackman, R. (1990) *Unemployment* Oxford, Oxford University Press.

Layard, R., Nickell, S. and Jackman, R. (1991) *Unemployment: Macroeconomic Performance and the Labour Market*, Oxford, Oxford University Press.

Layard, R., Nickell, S. and Jackman, R. (1994) *The Unemployment Crisis* Oxford, Oxford University Press.

Leighton Thomas, R. (1984) 'The Consumption Function' in Demery, D., Duck, N.W., Sumner, M. T., Leighton Thomas, R. and Neil Thompson, W. (eds) *Macroeconomics* London, Longman.

Leamer, E. E. (1983) 'Lets Take the Con out of Econometrics' *American Economic Review* **73**.

Leijonhufvud, A. (1968) *On Keynesian Economics and the Economics of Keynes: A Study in Monetary Theory* London, Oxford University Press.

Leijonhufvud, A. (1969) *Keynes and the Classics* Occasional Paper no. 30 London, Institute of Economic Affairs.

Leijonhufvud, A. (1981) 'Say's Principle, What It Means and Doesn't Mean' in *Information and Coordination* Oxford, Oxford University Press.

Lerner, A. P. (1944) *The Economics of Control* New York, Macmillan.

Levitt, M. and Joyce, M. (1987) *The Growth and Efficiency of Public Spending* London, NIESR.

Lindauer, J. (1968) *Macroeconomic Readings* New York, The Free Press.

Lindbeck, A. and Snower, D. J. (1988) *The Insider–Outsider Theory of Employment and Unemployment* Cambridge, Mass., MIT Press.

Lipsey, R. G. (1961) 'The Relation between Unemployment and the Rate of Change of Money Wage Rates in the United Kingdom, 1862–1957: A Further Analysis' *Economica* **27**.

Loasby, B. (1976) *Choice, Complexity and Ignorance* Cambridge, Cambridge University Press.

Long, J. Jr. and Plosser, C. I. (1983) 'Real Business Cycles' *Journal of Political Economy* **91**.

Lucas, R. E. (1972) 'Expectations and the Neutrality of Money' *Journal of Economic Theory* **4**.

Lucas, R. E. (1973) 'Some International Evidence on Output Inflation Trade Offs' *American Economic Review* **63**.

Lucas, R. E. (1975) 'An Equilibrium Model of the Business Cycle' *Journal of Political Economy* **83**.

Lucas, R. E. (1976) 'Econometric Policy Evaluation: A Critique' *Journal of Monetary Economics* **1**.

Lucas, R. E. (1981) *Studies in Business Cycle Theory* Oxford, Basil Blackwell.

Lucas, R. E. and Sargent, T. (1981) *Rational Expectations and Econometric Practice* London, George Allen and Unwin.

Lucas, R. E., Jr. (1994) 'Review of Milton Friedman and Anna Schwartz's *A Monetary History of the United States, 1867–1960*' *Journal of Monetary Economics* **34**.

Lund, P. J. (1971) *Investment: The Study of an Economic Aggregate* Edinburgh, Oliver and Boyd.

Macdonald, R. and Taylor, M. P. (1991) 'Exchange Rate Economics' in Green, C. J. and Llewellyn, D. T. (eds) *Surveys in Monetary Economics: Vol. 1* Oxford, Blackwell.

Maddock, R. and Carter, M. (1982) 'A Child's Guide to Rational Expectations' *Journal of Economic Literature* **20**.

Maddock, R. and Carter, M. (1985) *Rational Expectations* London, Macmillan.

Mankiw, N. (1989) 'Real Business Cycles: A New Keynesian Perspective' *Journal of Economic Perspectives* **3**.

Mankiw, N. (1990) 'A Quick Refresher Course in Macroeconomics' *Journal of Economic Literature* **28**.

Mankiw, N. (1992) 'The Reincarnation of Keynesian Economics' *European Economic Review* 36.

Mankiw, N. (1994) *Macroeconomics* (2nd edn) New York, Worth Publishers.

Mankiw, N. G. and Romer, D. (eds) (1991) *New Keynesian Economics: Vol. 1, Imperfect Competition and Sticky Prices; Vol. 2, Coordination Failiures and Real Rigidities.* Cambridge, Mass., MIT Press.

Marshall, A. (1920) *Principles of Economics: An Introduction Volume* (8th edn) London, Macmillan.

Matthews, R. C. O. (1968) 'Why has Britain had Full Employment Since the War?' *Economic Journal* **78**.

Matthews, R. C. O. (1986) 'The Economics of Institutions and the Sources of Growth' *Economic Journal* **96**.

Matthews, R. C. O., Feinstein, C. H. and Odling-Smee, J. C. (1982) *British Economic Growth, 1856–1973.* Oxford, Clarendon Press.

Mayer, T. (1959) 'The Empirical Significance of the Real Balance Effect' *Quarterly Journal of Economics* **73**.

Mayer, T. (1972) *Permanent Income, Wealth and Consumption: A Critique of the Permanent Income Theory, the Life Cycle Hypothesis and Related Theories* Berkeley, Calif., University of Los Angeles Press.

Mayes, D. (1981) 'The Controversy over Rational Expectations' *National Institute Economic Review* **96**.

Maynard, G. (1982) 'Microeconomic Deficiencies in UK Macroeconomic Policy' *Lloyds Bank Review* no. 145.

McCallum, J. (1986) 'Unemployment in OECD Countries in the 1980s' *Economic Journal* **96**.

McCallum, B. T. (1989) 'Real Business Cycle Models' Barro, R. J. (ed.), in *Modern Business Cycle Theory* Oxford, Basil Blackwell.

McCallum, B. T., (1992) 'Real Business Cycle Theories' in Vercelli, A. and Dimitri, N. (eds) *Macroeconomics: A Survey of Research Strategies* Oxford, Basil Blackwell.

McCallum, B. T. and Goodfriend, M. S. (1987) 'Demand for Money: Theoretical Studies' in Eatwell, J., Milgate, M. and Newman, P. (eds) *The New Palgrave Dictionary of Economics* London, Macmillan. Reprinted in Eatwell, J., Milgate, M. and Newman, P. (eds) (1989) *Money* London, Macmillan.

McCombie, J. S. L. (1981) 'What Still Remains of Kaldor's Laws?' *Economic Journal* **91**.

McEnery, P. (1981) *Manufacturing Two Nations* Research Monograph 36, London, Institute of Economic Affairs.

McLean, A. A. (1978) 'The Direct/Indirect Tax Ratio and Effective Demand: A Comment' *Public Finance* **33**.

Meade, J. E. (1955) *Theory of International Economic Policy: vol. 2, Trade and Welfare* Oxford, Oxford University Press.

Meade, J. E. (1982) *Stagflation: vol. 1, Wage Fixing* London, Allen and Unwin.

Meade, J. E. (1985) *Wage Fixing Revisited* Occasional Paper 72, London, Institute of Economic Affairs.

Meadows, K. (1967) *The Limits to Growth* London, Earth Island.

Metcalf, D. (1984) 'On the Measurement of Employment and Unemployment' *National Institute Economic Review* no. 109.

Metcalfe, J. S. (1980) 'Foreign Trade and the Balance of Payments' in Prest, A. R. and Coppock, D. J. (eds) *The UK Economy: A Manual of Applied Economics* London, Weidenfeld and Nicholson.

Metcalfe, J. S. and Green, C. (1986) 'Foreign Trade and the Balance of Payments' in Artis, M. (ed.) *The UK Economy: A Manual of Applied Economics* London, Weidenfeld and Nicholson.

Middleton, R. (1982) 'The Treasury in the 1930's: Political and Administrative Constraints to Acceptance of the "New" Economics' *Oxford Economic Papers* **34**.

Mill, J. S. (1844) *Essays on Some Unsettled Questions of Political Economy* London, John W. Parker.

Mill, J. (1966) *Selected Economic Writings* Edinburgh, Oliver and Boyd.

Milner, C. R. (1980) 'Payments and Exchange Rate Problems' in Maunder, W. P. (ed.) *The British Economy in the 1970s* London, Heinemann.

Milner, C. R. and Greenaway, D. (1979) *An Introduction to International Economics* London, Longman.

Minford, P. (1992) *Rational Expectations Macroeconomics*, Oxford, Blackwell.

Minford, A. P. and Hilliard, G. (1978) 'The Costs of Variable Inflation' in Artis, M. J. and Nobay, A. R. (eds) *Contemporary Economic Analysis* London, Croom Helm.

Minford, A. P. and Peel, D. (1981) 'Is the Government's Economic Strategy on Course?' *Lloyds Bank Review* April.

Miron, J. A. (1986) 'Seasonal Fluctuations and the Life-Cycle–Permanent Income Model of Consumption' *Journal of Political Economy* **94**.

Mishan, E. J. (1967) *The Costs of Economic Growth* London, Staples Press.

Mishan, E. J. (1977) *The Economic Growth Debate: An Assessment* London, George Allen and Unwin.

Mishkin, F. S. (1982) 'Does Anticipated Monetary Policy Matter?' *Journal of Political Economy* **90**.

Modigliani, F. (1944) 'Liquidity Preference and the Theory of Interest and Money' *Econometrica* **12**.

Modigliani, F. (1986) 'Life Cycle, Individual Thrift and the Wealth of Nations' *American Economic Review* **76**.

Modigliani, F. and Brumberg, R. (1954) 'Utility Analysis and the Consumption Function; Interpretation of Cross Section Data' in Kurihara, K. (ed.) *Post Keynesian Economics* New Brunswick

Modigliani, F. and Steindel, C. (1977) 'Is a Tax Rebate an Effective Tool for Stabilization Policy? *Brookings Papers on Economic Activity* **2**.

Moggridge, D. (ed.) (1973) *The Collected Writings of John Maynard Keynes: Vols XIII and XIV, The General Theory and After* London, Macmillan.

Moore, B. and Rhodes, J. (1973) 'Evaluating the Effects of British Regional Policy' *Economic Journal* **83**.

Morgan, A. D. (1980) 'The Balance of Payments and British Membership of the European Community' in Wallace, W. (ed.) *Britain in Europe* London, Heinemann.

Morgan, B. and Shackleton, J. R. (1990) 'The Ups and Downs of Business Cycle Theory' in Shackleton, J. R. (ed) *New Thinking in Economics* Aldershot, Edward Elgar.

Morris, D. (ed.) (1978) *The Economic System in the UK* (2nd edn) Oxford, Oxford University Press.

Morris, D. and Sinclair, P. (1985) 'The Assessment: The Unemployment Problem in the 1980s' *Oxford Review of Economic Policy* Summer.

Mueller, D. (1976) 'Public Choice: A Survey' *Journal of Economic Literature* **14**.

Mueller, M. G. (ed.) (1966) *Readings in Macroeconomics* New York, Holt, Rinehart and Winston.

Mundell, R. A. (1962) 'The Appropriate Use of Monetary and Fiscal Policy for Internal and External balance' *IMF Staff Papers* **9**.

Mundell, R. A. (1963) 'Capital Mobility and Stabilisation Policy Under Fixed and Flexible Exchange Rates' *Canadian Journal of Economics and Political Science* **23**.

Mundell, R. A. (1968) *International Economics* New York, Macmillan.

Musgrave, R. A. (1959) *The Theory of Public Finance: A Study in Public Economy* New York, McGraw-Hill.

Muth, J. F. (1960) 'Optimal Properties of Exponentially Weighted Forecasts' *Journal of the American Statistical Association* 55.

Muth, J. F. (1961) 'Rational Expectations and the Theory of Price Movements' *Econometrica* 29.

Nagel, E. (1963) 'Assumptions in Economic Theory' *American Economic Review* 53.

Nelson, C. R. and Plosser, C. I. (1982) 'Trends and Random Walks in Macroeconomic Time Series: Some Evidence and Implications' *Journal of Monetary Economics*, September.

Nickell, S. J. (1979) 'The Effect of Unemployment and Related Benefits on the Duration of Unemployment' *Economic Journal* 89.

Nickell, S. J. (1980) 'A Picture of Male Unemployment in Britain' *Economic Journal* 90.

Nickell, S., Vianiomanski, J. and Wadhani, S. (1992) 'Wages, Unions, Insiders and Product Market Power' Discussion Paper 77, London School of Economics Centre for Economic Performance.

Niehans, J. (1975) 'Some Doubts about the Efficacy of Monetary Policy under Flexible Exchange Rates' *Journal of International Economics* 5.

Nield, R. (1979) *Managed Trade Between Industrial Countries* in Major, R. (ed.) *Britain's Trade and Exchange Rate Policy* London, Heinemann.

NIESR (1972) 'The Effects of the 1967 Devaluation on the Current Balance of Payments' *Economic Journal* 82.

Nordhaus, W. (1975) 'The Political Business Cycle' *Review of Economic Studies* 42.

Nurkse, R. (1945) *Conditions of International Monetary Equilibrium*, Essays in International Finance no. 4, Princeton, Princeton University Press.

O'Brien, D. P. (1975) *The Classical Economists* Oxford, Clarendon Press.

Okun, A. (1981) *Prices and Quantities: A Macroeconomic Analysis* Oxford, Basil Blackwell.

Parkin, M. (1970) 'Incomes Policy: Some Further Results on the Determination of the Rate of Change of Money Wages' *Economica* 37.

Parkin, M. and Bade, R. (1982) *Modern Macroeconomics* Oxford, Philip Allan.

Parkin, M. and Sumner, M. T. (eds) (1972) *Incomes Policy and Inflation* Manchester, Manchester University Press.

Parkin, M. and Sumner, M. T. (eds) (1978) *Inflation in the United Kingdom* Manchester, Manchester University Press.

Patinkin, D. (1948) 'Price Flexibility and Unemployment' *American Economic Review* 38.

Patinkin, D. (1951) 'Price Flexibility and Full Employment' in Lutz, F. A. and Mints, L. W. (eds) *Readings in Monetary Theory* New York, Blakiston Press.

Patinkin, D. (1955) *Money Interest and Prices* New York, Harper and Row.

Patinkin, D. (1959) 'Keynesian Economic Rehabilitated: A Rejoinder to Professor Hicks' *Economic Journal* 69.

Patinkin, D. (1965) *Money, Interest, and Prices* (2nd edn) New York, Harper and Row.

Patinkin, D. (1969) 'The Chicago Tradition, the Quantity Theory and Friedman' *Journal of Money, Credit and Banking* 1.

Patinkin, D. (1987) 'Keynes, John Maynard' in Eatwell, J., Milgate, M. and Newman, P. (Eds) *The New Palgrave Dictionary of Economics* London, Macmillan.

Patinkin, D. (1991) 'On the General Theory' in Shaw, G. K. (ed.) *Economics, Culture and Education: Essays in Honour of Mark Blaug*. Aldershot, Edward Elgar.

Peacock, A. T. (1972) 'The Multiplier and the Valuation of Government Expenditures' *Finanzarchiv* 30.

Peacock, A. T. (1979) 'Giving Economic Advice in Difficult Times' in Peacock, A. T. (ed.) *The Economic Analysis of Government* Oxford, Martin Robertson.

Peacock, A. T. and Shaw, G. K. (1976) *The Economic Theory and Fiscal Policy* (2nd edn) London, George Allen and Unwin.

Peacock, A. T. and Shaw, G. K. (1978) 'Is Fiscal Policy Dead?' *Banca Nazionale Del Lavoro Quarterly Review* June.

Peacock, A. T. and Shaw, G. K. (1981) *The Public Sector Borrowing Requirement* Occasional Papers in Economics no. 1, University of Buckingham.

Peacock, A. T. and Williamson, J. (1967) 'Consumption Taxes and Compensatory Finance' *Economic Journal* 77.

Peaker, A. (1974) *Economic Growth in Modern Britain* London, Macmillan.

Peston, M. H. (1971) 'The Tax Mix and Effective Demand' *Public Finance* 26.

Peston, M. H. (1981) *Theory of Macroeconomics Policy* (2nd edn) Oxford, Philip Allan.

Peston, M. H. (1982) *The British Economy* Oxford, Philip Allan.

Peston, M. H. (1985) 'The Efficacy of Macroeconomic Policy' in Greenaway, D. and Shaw, G. K. (eds) *Public Choice, Public Finance and Public Policy: Essays in Honour of Alan Peacock* Oxford, Basil Blackwell.

Peston, M. H. (1986) 'The Elementary Macroeconomic Consequences of Differing Public and Private Sector Wages' *Public Finance* 41.

Phelps, E. S. (1968) 'Money Wage Dynamics and Labour Market Equilibrium' *Journal of Political Economy* 76.

Phelps, E. S. (1990) *Seven Schools of Macroeconomic Thought* The Arne Ryde Memorial Lectures, Oxford, Clarendon Press.

Phelps, E. S., Alchian, A. A., Holt, C. C., et al. (1970) *Microeconomic Foundations of Employment and Inflation Theory* New York, Norton.

Phillips, A. W. (1958) 'The Relationship between Unemployment and the Rate of Change of Money Wage Rates in the United Kingdom, 1862–1957' *Economica* 25.

Pigou, A. C. (1933) *The Theory of Unemployment* London, Macmillan.

Pigou, A. C. (1937) 'Real and Money Wages in Relation to Unemployment' *Economic Journal* 47.

Pigou, A. C. (1941) *Employment and Equilibrium* London, Macmillan.

Pigou, A. C. (1944) *Lapses from Full Employment* London, Macmillan.

Pigou, A. C. (1952) *Keynes's General Theory: A Retrospective View* London, Macmillan.

Pissarides, C. A. (1978) 'Liquidity Considerations in the Theory of Consumption' *Quarterly Journal of Economics* 92.

Pissarides, C. (1985) 'Job Search and the Functioning of Labour Markets' in Pissarides, C. et al. *Labour Economics* London, Longman.

Pliatzky, L. (1982) *Getting and Spending: Public Expenditure, Employment and Inflation* Oxford, Basil Blackwell.

Plosser, C. (1989) 'Understanding Real Business Cycles' *Journal of Economic Perspectives* 3.

Poole, W. (1970) 'Optimal Choice of Monetary Policy Instruments in a Simple Stochastic Macro-Model' *Quarterly Journal of Economics* 84.

Poole, W. (1988) 'Monetary Policy Lessons of Recent Inflation and Disinflation' *Journal of Economic Perspectives* 2.

Posner, M.V. (ed.) (1978) *Demand Management* London, Heinemann.

Presley, J. (1979) *Robertsonian Economics* New York, Holmes and Meier.

Prest, A. R. and Coppock, D. J. (eds) (1982) *The UK Economy* (9th edn) London, Weidenfeld and Nicholson.

Prescott, E. (1986) 'Theory Ahead of Business Cycle Measurement' *Quarterly Review of the Federal Reserve Bank of Minneapolis* Fall.

Price, R. (1978) 'Budgetary Policy' in Blackaby, F. T. (ed.) *British Economy Policy, 1960–74* Cambridge, Cambridge University Press.

Putnam, B. and Wilford, D. S. (eds) (1979) *The Monetary Approach to International Adjustment* New York, Praeger.

Redman, A. (1992) *A Reader's Guide to Rational Expectations*, Aldershot, Edward Elgar.

Redman, D. A. (1994) 'Karl Popper's Theory of Science and Econometrics: The Rise and Decline of Social Engineering' *Journal of Economic Issues* 28.

Ricardo, D. (1951–55) *Works and Correspondence of David Ricardo* (P. Sraffa, ed. with M. M. Dobb) Cambridge, Cambridge University Press.

Rivera-Batiz, F. and Rivera-Batiz, L. (1985) *International Finance and Open Economy Macro-economics* New York, Macmillan.

Robinson, J. (1969) 'Review of "On Keynesian Economics and the Economics of Keynes" by A. Leijonhufvud' *Economic Journal* 79.

Robinson, J. (1973) 'What has Become of the Keynesian Revolution?' in Robinson, J. (ed.) *After Keynes* Oxford, Basil Blackwell.

Robinson, P. (1995) 'The Decline of the Swedish Model and the Limits to Active Labour Market Policy' Discussion Paper 259, London School of Economics Centre for Economic Performance.

Romer, C. D. (1986a) 'Is the Stabilization of the Postwar Economy a Figment of the Data?' *American Economic Review* 76.

Romer, C. D. (1986b) 'Spurious Volatility in Historical Unemployment Data' *Journal of Political Economy* 94.

Romer, P. M. (1990) 'Endogenous Technical Change' *Journal of Political Economy* 98.

Rostow, W. W. (1960) *The Stages of Economic Growth* Cambridge, Cambridge University Press.

Robbins, L. (1952) *The Theory of Economic Policy in English Classical Political Economy* London, Macmillan.

Rowthorn, R. E. (1975) 'What Remains of Kaldor's Law?' *Economic Journal* 85.

Salant, W. (1957) 'Taxes, Income Determination and the balanced Budget Multiplier' *Review of Economics and Statistics* 39.

Samuels, W. (1966) *The Classical Theory of Economic Policy* Ohio, Cleveland.

Sapsford, D. R. (1981) *Labour Market Economics* London, Allen and Unwin.

Sapsford, D. and Tzannatos, Z. (eds) (1990) *Current Issues in Labour Economics* London, Macmillan.

Sapsford, D. and Tzannatos, Z. (1993) *The Economics of the Labour Market* London, Macmillan.

Sardoni, C. (1987) *Marx and Keynes on Economic Recession*, Brighton, Wheatsheaf.

Sargent, T. J. (1978) 'Rational Expectations, Econometric Exogeneity and Consumption' *Journal of Political Economy* 86.

Sargent, T. J. and Wallace, N. (1975) 'Rational Expectations, the Optimal Monetary Instrument and the Optimal Money Supply Rule' *Journal of Political Economy* 83.

Say, J. B. (1964) *Traite d'economie politique*, (trans. Prinsep, C. R., 4th edn) New York, Augustus Kelly.

Scarth, W. M. (1975) 'Fiscal Policy and the Government Budget Restraint under Alternative Exchange Rate Systems' *Oxford Economic Papers* 27.

Schumpeter, J. (1961) *History of Economic Analysis* (4th edn) Oxford, Oxford University Press.

Scott, M. (1989) *A New View of Economic Growth* Oxford, Oxford University Press.

Scott, M., Corden, W. M. and Little, I. M. D. (1980) *The Case against General Import Restrictions* Thames Essay 24, London, Trade Policy Research Centre.

Schwartz, A. J. (1992) *Monetarism and Monetary Policy* Occasional Paper no. 86, London, Institute of Economic Affairs.

Shapiro, M. D. (1987) 'Supply Shocks in Macroeconomics' in Eatwell, J., Milgate, M. and Newman, P. (eds) *The New Palgrave Dictionary of Economics* London, Macmillan.

Shaw, G. K. (1967) 'Monetary-Fiscal Policy for Economic Growth and the Balance of Payments Constraint' *Economica* 34.

Shaw, G. K. (1972) *Fiscal Policy* London, Macmillan.

Shaw, G. K. (1976) 'A Simple View of a Simple Keynesian: Comment on Brothwell's Strictures on Leijonhufvud' *Bulletin of Economic Research* 28.

Shaw, G. K. (1977) *An Introduction to the Theory of Macro-Economic Policy* (3rd edn) Oxford, Martin Robertson.

Shaw, G. K. (1980) 'Economic Growth: Causes, Consequences and Constraints' in Grant, R. M. and Shaw, G. K. (eds) *Current Issues in Economic Policy* Oxford, Philip Allan.

Shaw, G. K. (1981) 'Leading Issues of Tax Policy in Developing Countries: The Economic Problems' in Peacock, A. T. and Forte, F. (eds) *The Political Economy of Taxation* Oxford, Basil Blackwell.

Shaw, G. K. (1983a) *Rational Expectations: An Elementary Exposition* Brighton,Wheatsheaf.

Shaw, G. K. (1983b) 'Fiscal Policy under the First Thatcher Administration, 1979–1983' *Finanzarchiv* **41**.

Shaw, G. K. (1987a) 'Fiscal Policy under the Second Thatcher Administration, 1983–1987' *Finanzarchiv* **45**.

Shaw, G. K. (1987b) 'Rational Expectations' *Bulletin of Economic Research* **39**.

Shaw, G. K. (1987c) 'Macroeconomic Implications of Fiscal Deficits: An Expository Note' *Scottish Journal of Political Economy* **34**.

Shaw, G. K. (1988a) 'Expectations in Macroeconomics' in Greenaway, D. (ed.) *Current Issues in Macroeconomics* London, Macmillan.

Shaw, G. K. (1988b) *Keynesian Economics: The Permanent Revolution* Aldershot, Edward Elgar.

Shaw, G. K. (1988c) *The Keynesian Heritage: Vols 1 and 2*, Aldershot, Edward Elgar.

Shaw, G. K. (1990) 'Neo-Keynesian Theories of Unemployment' in Shackleton, J. R. (ed.) *New Thinking in Economics* Aldershot, Edward Elgar.

Shaw, G. K. (ed.) (1991) *Economics, Culture and Education: Essays in Honour of Mark Blaug* Aldershot, Edward Elgar.

Shaw, G. K. (1992) 'Policy Implications of Endogenous Growth Theory' *Economic Journal* **102**.

Shaw, G. K. (1994) 'Fiscal Policy: The Third Thatcher Administration, 1987–1990, and the Thatcher Legacy, 1990–1993' *Finanzarchiv* **51**.

Shoup, C. S. (1960) *Ricardo on Taxation* New York, Columbia University Press.

Signer, A. (1978) 'The Direct/Indirect Tax Ratio and Effective Demand: An Extension and A Comment on a Respecification' *Public Finance* **33**.

Silber, W. L. (1970) 'Fiscal Policy in IS-LM Analysis: A Correction' *Journal of Money, Credit and Banking* **2**.

Sinclair, P. (1978) 'International Economics' in Morris, D. (ed.) *The Economic System in the UK* Oxford, Oxford University Press.

Smith, A. (1904) *An Enquiry Into the Nature and Causes of the Wealth of Nations* (2 vols) (E. Cannan, ed.) London, Methuen.

Snowdon, B., Vane, H. and Wynarczyk, P. (1994) *A Modern Guide to Macroeconomics: An Introduction to Competing Schools of Thought* Aldershot, Edward Elgar.

Solow, R. M. (1957) 'Technical Change and the Aggregate Production Function' *Review of Economics and Statistics* **39**.

Solow, R. (1969) *Price Expectations and the Behaviour of the Price Level* Manchester, Manchester University Press.

Solow, R. M. (1980) 'On Theories of Unemployment' *American Economic Review* **70**.

Solow, R. M. (1985) 'Insiders and Outsiders in Wage Determination' *Scandinavian Journal of Economics* **87**.

Solow, R. M. (1990) *The Labour Market as a Social Institution*. Oxford, Basil Blackwell.

Sowell, T. (1972) *Say's Law: An Historical Analysis* Princeton, N.J., Princeton University Press.

Sowell, T. (1994) *Classical Economics Reconsidered* Princeton, N.J., Princeton University Press.

Sowell, T. (1987) 'Say's Law' in Eatwell, J., Milgate, M. and Newman, P. (eds) *The New Palgrave Dictionary of Economics* London, Macmillan.

Spiro, A. (1962) 'Wealth and the Consumption Function' *Journal of Political Economy* **70**.

Stadler, G. W. (1994) 'Real Business Cycles' *Journal of Economic Literature* **32**.

Stafford, G. B. (1981) *The End of Economic Growth: Growth and Decline in the UK since 1955* Oxford, Martin Robertson.

Stein, H. (1949) 'Price Flexibility and Full Employment: Comment' *American Economic Review* **39**.

Stern, N. (1991) 'The Determinants of Economic Growth' *Economic Journal* **101**.

Summers, L. H. (1981) 'Taxation and Corporate Investment: A q-Theory Approach' *Brookings Papers on Economic Activity* 1.

Surrey, M. J. (ed.) (1975) *Macroeconomic Themes* Oxford, Oxford University Press.

Surrey, M. J. C. (1989) 'Aggregate Consumption and Saving' in Greenaway, D. (ed.) *Current Issues in Macroeconomics*, London, Macmillan.

Swoboda, A. K. (1981) 'Exchange Rate Flexibility in Practice: A Selective Survey of Experience from 1973 to 1979' in Giersch, H. (ed.) *Macroeconomic Policies for Growth and Stability* Tubingen, J. C. B. Mohr.

Taylor, C. T. (1979) 'Crowding Out: Its Meaning and Significance' in Cook, S. T. and Jackson, P. M. (eds) *Current Issues in Fiscal Policy* Oxford, Martin Robertson.

Taylor, J. B. (1982) 'The Swedish Investment System as a Stabilization Policy Rule' *Brookings Papers on Economic Activity* 1.

Taylor, H. (1985) 'Time Inconsistency: A Potential Problem for Policymakers' *Federal Reserve Bank of Philadelphia Business Review* March/April.

Tew, T. H. B. (1978) 'Policies Aimed at Improving the Balance of Payments' in Blackaby, F. T. (ed.) *British Economy Policy, 1960–74* Cambridge, Cambridge University Press.

Thatcher, A. R. (1979) 'Labour Supply and Employment Trends' in Blackaby, F. T. (ed.) *De-industrialisation* London, Heinemann.

Theil, H. (1961) *Economic Forecasts and Policy* Amsterdam, North-Holland.

Theil, H. (1964) *Optimal Decision Rules for Government and Industry* Amsterdam, North-Holland.

Theil, H. (1965) 'Linear Decision Rules for Macro-Dynamic Policy' in Hickman, B. (ed.) *Quantitative Planning of Economic Policy* Washington, D.C. Brookings Institution.

Thirlwall, A. P. (1980) *Balance of Payments Theory and the United Kingdom Experience* London, Macmillan.

Tinbergen, J. (1952) *On the Theory of Economic Policy* Amsterdam, North-Holland.

Tinbergen, J. (1965) *Central Planning* New Haven, Yale University Press.

Tobin, J. (1947) 'Money Wage Rates and Employment' in Harris, S. E. (ed.) *The New Economics* New York, Alfred A. Knopf.

Tobin, J. (1956) 'The Interest Elasticity of the Transactions Demand for Cash' *Review of Economics and Statistics* 38.

Tobin, J. (1958) 'Liquidity Preference as Behaviour towards Risk' *Review of Economic Studies* 25.

Tobin, J. (1963) 'Commercial Banks as Creators of Money' in Carson, D. (ed.) *Banking and Monetary Studies* Homewood, Ill., Irwin.

Tobin, J. (1969) 'A General Equilibrium Approach to Monetary Theory' *Journal of Money, Credit and Banking* 1.

Tobin, J. (1970) 'Money and Income: Post hoc ergo propter hoc?' *Quarterly Journal of Economics* 82.

Tobin, J. (1972) 'Friedman's Theoretical Framework' *Journal of Political Economy* 80

Tobin, J. (1986) 'The Monetary–Fiscal Mix: Long-Run Implications' *American Economic Review*, Papers and Proceedings, May.

Tobin, J. and Brainard, W. (1977) 'Assets Markets and the Cost of Capital' in Balassa, B. and Nelson, R. (eds) *Economic Progress, Private Values and Public Policy: Essays in Honor of William Fellner* New York, North Holland.

Townend, J. C. (1976) 'The Personal Savings Ratio' *Bank of England Quarterly Bulletin* 16.

Treasury and Civil Service Committee on Monetary Policy (1981) *Third Report*, House of Commons, 27 February.

Trevethick, J. A. and Mulvey, C. (1975) *The Economics of Inflation* Oxford, Martin Robertson.

Tsiang, S. C. (1977) 'The Monetary Theoretic Foundations of the Modern Monetary Approach to the Balance of Payments' *Oxford Economic Papers* 29.

Turnovsky, S. T. (1977) *Macroeconomic Analysis and Stabilisation Policy* Cambridge, Cambridge University Press.

Vane, H. R. and Thompson, J. L. (1992) *Current Controversies in Macroeconomics: An Intermediate Text* Aldershot, Edward Elgar.

Veil, E. (1975) *Surpluses and Deficits in the Balance of Payments: Definition and Significance of Alternative Concepts* Paris, OECD.

Verdoorn, P. J. (1949) 'Fattori che regolano lo sviluppo delia produttivita del Pavoro' *L'Industria*.

Vines, D. (1986) 'Macroeconomic Policy after Monetarism' *The Royal Bank of Scotland Review* no. 152, December.

Weiss, A. (1991) *Efficiency Wages: Models of Unemployment, Layoffs, and Wage Dispersion* Oxford, Clarendon Press.

Whalen, E. H. (1966) 'A Rationalisation of the Precautionary Demand for Cash' *Quarterly Journal of Economics* **80**.

White, W. H. (1956) 'Interest Inelasticity of Investment Demand: The Case from Business Attitude Surveys Re-examined' *American Economic Review* **26**.

Whiting, A. (1976) 'An International Comparison of the Instability of Economic Growth' *Three Banks Review* **109**.

Whitman, M. V. N. (1970) *Policies for Internal and External Balance* Special Papers in International Economics no. 9, Princeton, N.J.

Whynes, D. K. (1989) 'The Political Business Cycle' in Greenaway, D. (ed.) *Current Issues in Macroeconomics* London, Macmillan.

Wicksell, K. (1934) *Lectures in Political Economy: Vols 1 and 2.* (trans L. Robbins) New York, Routledge.

Wilson Committee (1977) *Progress Report on the Financing of Industry and Trade* Committee to Review the Functioning of Financial Institutions, National Research Development Corporation, London, HMSO.

Wilson, T. and Andrews, P. W. S. (eds) (1951) *Oxford Studies in the Price Mechanism* London, Oxford University Press.

Winters, L. A. (1985) *International Economics* London, George Allen and Unwin.

Winters, L. A. (1986) 'Britain in Europe: A Survey of Quantitative Trade Studies' Discussion Paper no. 110, London, Centre for Economic Policy Research.

Wright, C. (1969) 'Estimating Permanent Income: A Note' *Journal of Political Economy* **77**.

Yellen, J. (1984) 'Efficiency Wage Models of Unemployment' *American Economic Review* **74**. Papers and Proceedings.

Index

Lightning Source UK Ltd.
Milton Keynes UK
08 May 2010

153912UK00001B/8/P